Economics of Evidence, Procedure and Litigation
Volume II

Economic Approaches to Law

Series Editors: Richard A. Posner
Judge, United States Court of Appeals for the Seventh Circuit and Senior Lecturer, University of Chicago Law School, USA
Francesco Parisi
Professor of Law, University of Minnesota Law School, USA and Professor of Economics, University of Bologna, Italy

A full list of published and future titles in this series is printed at the end of this volume.

Wherever possible, the articles in these volumes have been reproduced as originally published using facsimile reproduction, inclusive of footnotes and pagination to facilitate ease of reference.

For a list of all Edward Elgar published titles visit our site on the World Wide Web at www.e-elgar.com

Economics of Evidence, Procedure and Litigation Volume II

Edited by

Chris William Sanchirico

Professor of Law, Business and Public Policy,
University of Pennsylvania Law School
and The Wharton School, USA

ECONOMIC APPROACHES TO LAW

An Elgar Reference Collection
Cheltenham, UK • Northampton, MA, USA

Published by
Edward Elgar Publishing Limited
Glensanda House
Montpellier Parade
Cheltenham
Glos GL50 1UA
UK

Edward Elgar Publishing, Inc.
William Pratt House
9 Dewey Court
Northampton
Massachusetts 01060
USA

A catalogue record for this book is available from the British Library

Library of Congress Control Number: 2007927951

ISBN 978 1 84542 939 3 (2 volume set)

Printed and bound in Great Britain by MPG Books Ltd, Bodmin, Cornwall.

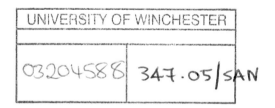

Contents

Acknowledgements

The editor and publishers wish to thank the authors and the following publishers who have kindly given permission for the use of copyright material.

Ronald J. Allen and *Boston University Law Review* for article: Ronald J. Allen (1986), 'A Reconceptualization of Civil Trials', *Boston University Law Review*, **66**, 401–37.

Blackwell Publishing Ltd for article: David Kaye (1982), 'The Limits of the Preponderance of the Evidence Standard: Justifiably Naked Statistical Evidence and Multiple Causation', *American Bar Foundation Research Journal*, **7** (2), Spring, 487–516.

California Law Review, Inc. and University of California for article: Stephen McG. Bundy and Einer Richard Elhauge (1991), excerpts from 'Do Lawyers Improve the Adversary System? A General Theory of Litigation Advice and Its Regulation', *California Law Review*, **79**, Parts I, II and VB, 313–20, 335–61, 401–20.

Columbia Law Review Association, Inc. via Copyright Clearance Center for article: Chris William Sanchirico (2001), excerpts from 'Character Evidence and the Object of Trial', *Columbia Law Review*, **101** (6), October, Introduction, Parts II, III and IV, 1227–39, 1259–81.

Duke University School of Law for articles: Chris William Sanchirico (2004), excerpts from 'Evidence Tampering', *Duke Law Journal*, **53** (4), February, Introduction, Part III and Appendix, 1215–29, 1286–303, 1318–36; Chris William Sanchirico (2004), excerpt from 'Evidence Tampering', *Duke Law Journal*, **53**, Part IV, 1303–17.

Elsevier for articles: Steven Shavell (1989), 'Optimal Sanctions and the Incentive to Provide Evidence to Legal Tribunals', *International Review of Law and Economics*, **9**, 3–11; Chris William Sanchirico (1997), 'The Burden of Proof in Civil Litigation: A Simple Model of Mechanism Design', *International Review of Law and Economics*, **17**, 431–47; Luke M. Froeb and Bruce H. Kobayashi (2001), 'Evidence Production in Adversarial vs. Inquisitorial Regimes', *Economics Letters*, **70**, 267–72; Francesco Parisi (2002), 'Rent-seeking through Litigation: Adversarial and Inquisitorial Systems Compared', *International Review of Law and Economics*, **22**, 193–216.

Richard O. Lempert for his own article: (1977), 'Modeling Relevance', *Michigan Law Review*, **75** (5–6), April–May, 1021–57.

Minnesota Law Review for article: Richard D. Friedman (1992), excerpts from 'Toward a Partial Economic, Game-Theoretic Analysis of Hearsay', *Minnesota Law Review*, **76**, Parts I–II and Part V, 723–9, 750–91.

Oxford University Press for articles: Kathryn E. Spier (1994), 'Settlement Bargaining and the Design of Damage Awards', *Journal of Law, Economics, and Organization*, **10** (1), April, 84–95; Luke M. Froeb and Bruce H. Kobayashi (1996), 'Naive, Biased, yet Bayesian; Can Juries Interpret Selectively Produced Evidence?', *Journal of Law, Economics, and Organization*, **12** (1), April, 257–76; Chris William Sanchirico (2000), 'Games, Information, and Evidence Production: With Application to English Legal History', *American Law and Economics Review*, **2** (2), Fall, 342–80; Andrew F. Daughety and Jennifer F. Reinganum (2000), 'On the Economics of Trials: Adversarial Process, Evidence, and Equilibrium Bias', *Journal of Law, Economics, and Organization*, **16** (2), October, 365–94; Chris William Sanchirico (2001), 'Relying on the Information of Interested – and Potentially Dishonest – Parties', *American Law and Economics Review*, **3** (2), May, 320–57.

RAND Corporation for articles: Paul Milgrom and John Roberts (1986), 'Relying on the Information of Interested Parties', *RAND Journal of Economics*, **17** (1), Spring, 18–32; Hyun Song Shin (1998), 'Adversarial and Inquisitorial Procedures in Arbitration', *RAND Journal of Economics*, **29** (2), Summer, 378–405.

University of Chicago and *Journal of Law and Economics* for article: Louis Kaplow and Steven Shavell (1996), 'Accuracy in the Assessment of Damages', *Journal of Law and Economics*, **XXXIX** (1), April, 191–210.

University of Chicago and *Journal of Legal Studies* for articles: Richard A. Posner (1973), excerpts from 'An Economic Approach to Legal Procedure and Judicial Administration', *Journal of Legal Studies*, **II** (2), June, Introduction and Parts I, II and III, 399–417; Bruce L. Hay and Kathryn E. Spier (1997), 'Burdens of Proof in Civil Litigation: An Economic Perspective', *Journal of Legal Studies*, **XXVI** (2), June, 413–31.

Every effort has been made to trace all the copyright holders but if any have been inadvertently overlooked the publishers will be pleased to make the necessary arrangement at the first opportunity.

In addition the publishers wish to thank the Marshall Library at the University of Cambridge, UK, and the Library at Indiana University at Bloomington, USA, for their assistance in obtaining these articles.

Introduction to Volume II

Chris William Sanchirico

This volume is the second of two on the economic analysis of evidence, procedure and litigation. The articles collected in Volume I focus on parties' incentives to initiate lawsuits and to settle them out of court. The articles in Volume II take a complementary approach, eschewing a detailed analysis of filing and settlement in favor of a more in-depth account of what it is that filing leads towards and settlement avoids. The focus is specifically on judicial fact finding, the process by which courts sort out parties' accounts of disputed events, the chief business of courts of original jurisdiction.[1]

Several sub-fields of economics seem particularly well suited to the study of legal fact finding, including game theory, information economics and mechanism design. These (overlapping) fields, which have been fruitfully applied in such diverse areas as taxation, regulated industries and auction design, concern themselves with problems that arise from the combination of hidden information and conflicting interests. As we shall see, however, the potential for applying and extending these fields to encompass legal fact finding has hardly been exhausted.

The first set of papers in Volume II provides several alternative accounts of what judicial fact finding is and ought to be. The second set considers the objectives of fact finding and, in particular, the relationship between accurate fact finding and the cost-effective regulation of out of court behavior. The third set of papers concerns the advantages and disadvantages of an adversarial system of fact finding, one that (in caricature) passively relies upon party competition to provide evidence for determining facts. Several of these papers specifically compare adversarial process to an alternative 'inquisitorial' system whereby the judge, as fact finder, takes a more active role in generating and testing evidence. The last set of papers analyzes several specific rules of procedure and evidence: the burden of proof, character evidence, hearsay evidence, attorney client privilege and sanctions for evidentiary misconduct.

The remainder of this Introduction attempts to connect and contextualize the articles included in the volume. Reference is made to the larger scholarly literatures in which these articles reside, as well as to the real legal phenomena that they strive to address. Like the volume itself, the Introduction is crafted for a dual audience: economists interested in legal issues and legal scholars interested in the economic approach. Each may wish to make allowances for attempts to reach the other.

Part I: The Production and Interpretation of Legal Evidence: Four Approaches

How does, and should, the fact finder – be that judge or jury – make deductions from the joint performance staged before her by the parties? The articles in this part identify several approaches to this fundamental question.

A. Pure Probabilistic Deduction

Lempert (1977; Chapter 1) clearly and comprehensively lays out the first approach, the purely probabilistic. Charged with deciding, say, whether to hold the defendant guilty of the crime charged, the fact finder has two tasks. The first is to determine the likelihood of guilt. On seeing a given piece of evidence, the fact finder 'updates' her 'prior belief' regarding guilt into a 'posterior belief' – just as one might change one's beliefs regarding the speediness of a horse on seeing it win a race. Beliefs, prior and posterior, are represented as probabilities and are thus subject to the mathematical properties thereof. One of those properties, Bayes rule, provides a formula for updating beliefs. The key to Bayes rule is the likelihood ratio: the probability of seeing the evidence were the defendant truly guilty divided by the probability of seeing the evidence were the defendant truly innocent. Having updated her beliefs on all the evidence, the fact finder's second task is to decide on a verdict. In doing so, she considers not just her posterior assessment of guilt, but also her view of the relative harm of wrongful conviction versus wrongful acquittal.

This description of fact findings is an application of the conventional approach to decision-making under uncertainty followed by probabilists, statisticians, and economists.[2] Even in these originating fields, however, the approach is not without detractors. Paradoxes such as those identified by Allais and Ellsberg, for instance, call into question the conventional approach's descriptive power as well as its normative validity.[3]

As a description of legal fact finding, in particular, the conventional approach to decision-making under uncertainty has been subject to a number of specific objections. Two of these are clearly laid out in Allen (1986; Chapter 2). The first is the 'conjunction problem', which itself is the result of a conjunction of legal features. First, guilt or liability often turns on two or more findings of fact – as when a verdict requires findings regarding how the defendant acted, what harm she thereby caused and whether she intended the consequences of her actions. Second, the law requires that each element of the charge, claim or defense be found to have obtained with a threshold probability, a 'standard of proof' (commonly thought to be 50% in civil actions and something more, perhaps 90%, in criminal actions). The requirement that each element must individually be subject to a 50% threshold, say, implies a weaker requirement, possibly much weaker, for the probability of the *conjunction* of elements, which is to say of the charge, claim, or defense itself. In the extreme case in which the elements are statistically independent, the fact that each is more likely than not implies only that their conjunction is more likely than $.5^n < .5$, where n is the number of components. Particularly troubling is the fact that the implied threshold probability for a charge, claim or defense decreases (quite rapidly) in the number of elements it contains, a factor with uncertain relevance. With four independent elements, it is not 50%, but 6¼%.[4]

Allen also describes the 'gatecrasher paradox'. Suppose that the defendant was in attendance with 1000 others at an event at which it is known that 499 attendees purchased tickets and 501 crashed the gate. Assuming no other evidence is available, could (should) a fact finder conclude that the defendant more likely than not failed to pay for his seat, and could (should) the law hold the individual liable for the ticket price? While probabilistic analysis appears to imply that the defendant should be held liable, some see this finding as strongly contrary to intuition. Allen (1986) comments on Kaye's (1979)[5] effort to defend conventional probabilistic analysis from this troubling hypothetical.

Allen's article was prepared for a watershed symposium held at Boston University on the benefits and drawbacks of applying probabilistic deduction to evidence law. Many of the other papers in the corresponding issue of the *Boston University Law Review* are also well worth examining.[6] Taken as a whole, the symposium issue provides a comprehensive picture of evidence scholarship at the time regarding the utility of applying formal theories of probability, conventional and unconventional, to the problem of legal evidence.

Yet, the symposium and contemporaneous evidence scholarship largely ignore an arguably more serious drawback of the pure probabilistic approach.[7] The approach gives short shrift to a fundamental and distinctive fact about legal evidence. Unlike experimental evidence generated in a chemist's laboratory or field evidence gathered in a macroeconomist's survey of inventories, legal evidence is provided by conscious, animate individuals with strong interests in what the fact finder decides and a strong possibility of influencing that decision.[8] It is one thing to prescribe, as does the pure probabilistic approach, that the fact finder interpret evidence according to the relative likelihood of its production under alternative truths. It is another thing to explain how these relative likelihoods ought to account for the interests of the parties responsible for the production. And it is another thing altogether to ask how fact finding should be structured to account for the necessity of this accounting. If the defendant in a criminal case produces for us her oath-bound testimony that she is innocent, how do we evaluate the relative likelihood of observing such a performance if she really were innocent versus if she were in fact guilty? Wouldn't she claim innocence either way? If so, what constitutes convincing evidence of innocence?

B. Omission Models

Where, then, should we turn for a better understanding of how deductions from evidence are and ought to be made in light of the parties' interests? Within the discipline of economics, game theory – including the sub-fields of information economics and mechanism design – seems like the natural candidate. Much of game theory, after all, concerns the situation in which one individual or entity would like to make use of information in the possession of another whose interests differ from her own.[9] The theory of optimal auction design, for example, is founded on the tension between the seller's desire, on the one hand, to learn – and charge – the maximum price that a bidder would be willing to pay, and the seller's realization, on the other hand, that the bidder, anticipating this plan, would not readily reveal this value. The theory of optimal taxation is similarly based on taxpayers' reluctance to truthfully reveal their immutable endowments and preferences – upon which the government would ideally base its tax system – if doing so would aversely affect their tax bill.

Oddly, though, on the relatively limited number of occasions that economists have turned their attention to legal evidence, they have taken a more limited approach. That approach is typified by Milgrom and Roberts (1986; Chapter 3). Although these authors do account for litigants' incentive to manipulate the information reaching the fact finder, their account is substantially incomplete. Parties in their model may refrain from reporting to the fact finder all that they know. But parties may not falsify, fabricate or forge.

From this stark assumption flow stark results. Milgrom and Roberts show how the fact finder may costlessly determine the true state of affairs from a nonetheless interested party who is known to be in the know with regard to that state of affairs. The fact finder need only announce that, if the party supplies her with ambiguous information, she will assume the worst for the party within the bounds of that ambiguity.[10] It follows that the worst deduction for the party consistent with the information that she provides will in fact be the truth. This is because the party would always have an incentive to clear up any ambiguity between the truth and any less favorable deduction.

A toy example will clarify. Suppose that the truth is a number between 1 and 10. The fact finder does not know the truth. The party does, and the fact finder knows that the party knows. The fact finder would like to learn the true number. The party would like the fact finder to think the number is as high as possible, and the fact finder knows the party's preference. The party chooses what to report about the true number to the fact finder. The fact finder makes a deduction about the true number based on this report. The rules of the game are that the party may not lie, but she may omit to say all that she knows. She may decline to report the exact number, providing instead a subset of numbers in which the true number lies. She might, for example, reveal that the number is odd (if in fact it is), or that the number lies between 3 and 7 (if in fact it does). The fact finder can be assured of learning the true number by announcing that upon hearing the party report a subset of numbers, she will assume that the number is the lowest in that subset. The party would therefore never find it in her interest to report a subset containing a number lower than the truth. She can always do better removing any number from her report that is lower than the truth. Therefore, the lowest number in the report, the number in fact chosen by the fact finder must be the truth.

This assume-the-worst-of-omission rule is akin to an adverse inference from 'spoliation',[11] an ancient component of evidence doctrine. Less formal analysis of the idea crops up in evidence scholarship preceding Milgrom and Roberts's paper. Indeed, the idea appears in attempts to resolve the gatecrasher paradox, as discussed above. The plaintiff's failure to present any information beyond the naked statistical evidence of ticket sales and attendance is taken to indicate that the rest of the evidence which is likely to be available to him would hurt his case.[12]

Milgrom and Roberts also put forward a related dual-party model. In this model, the fact finder again learns the truth, but here a sophisticated rule of inference is unnecessary. If the parties have strictly opposing interests and each knows the truth, the fact finder will always end up learning the truth so long as she restricts her decision to the intersection of the parties' reports. The reason is that whatever the fact finder's decision within that intersection, if it is not truth, one party will prefer the truth and so will have an incentive to refine her report.

Thus, in the numerical example just presented, imagine that two parties know the truth and each reports a subset containing it. Suppose that one party wants the fact finder to think the number is as high as possible and the other as low as possible. And suppose that the fact finder unthinkingly takes the average of the numbers in the intersection of the reports. Then, if the average of the points in the intersection of reports is not the truth, one party or the other will prefer the truth to this average and thus have an incentive to report the truth as a singleton. If, for example, the truth is 4, one party says '3 or greater' and the other '7 or less', then the intersection of reports is 3 through 7, the average is 5 and the party that prefers lower numbers to high has an incentive to refine her report to '4'. Again, this result assumes that parties may not lie, but only omit. Its logic also resonates with earlier less formal discussions within evidence scholarship, here regarding the benefits of adversarial procedure as discussed in Part III.

Twenty years after Milgrom and Roberts's article, the approach taken in that seminal paper continues to dominate the economic literature on legal evidence.[13] Yet it must be recognized that the results in that paper and in the literature it has spawned are quite precariously balanced on the assumption that agents cannot and will not fabricate evidence. If we remove this restriction from the single-agent example above, for instance, the fact finder's assume-the-worst-of-omission rule merely induces the single agent to report '10'. In the two-agent example, one agent will respond to the fact finder's intersection rule by reporting '1', and the other '10', and there will not even be an intersection of reports.

Papers in this literature sometimes attempt to justify the no-lying assumption by pointing out that lying in court is illegal by virtue of statutes criminalizing perjury.[14] This is a problematic defense in several respects. Firstly, much behavior that these papers would probably characterize as 'omission' is also illegal – by virtue of subpoena enforcement, compelled discovery, obstruction of justice and contempt.[15] What is not illegal might be made so. If illegality does (or can) rule out behavior, then it does (or can) rule out a fair portion of the problem that omission models set out to solve. Secondly, despite the fact that lying in court is illegal, what limited data exist suggest that it is a regular occurrence.[16] Results that proceed from the assumption that what parties say is at least true, if not complete, would thus seem to be of limited practical applicability. Thirdly, if the no lying assumption is legitimate in the context of judicial process, one must question why is it so rarely deployed by economists in other more frequently studied settings in which the government is also the principal. There is no corresponding no-fabrication assumption in the literatures on optimal regulation or optimal taxation, for example. Such an assumption would dramatically change the classic results in those fields. Yet perjury and related crimes, like lying to investigators and tax fraud, often apply in these settings as well.

Fourthly, and perhaps most importantly, by assuming that agents cannot lie, the economic literature on evidence effectively assumes away both a fundamental challenge and an important source of potential utility. Studying legal evidence assuming that agents tell the truth, if not the whole truth, is like studying aeronautics assuming lift, if not control. Crucial and interesting questions central to the practical design of evidentiary procedure are avoided. How precisely, for instance, do perjury laws function? What if individuals perjure themselves at hearings held to determine whether perjury was committed in the first instance? To what end do we sanction perjury? At what cost? More generally, what is the best way to structure litigation if we do not take as already solved the problem that parties have an incentive to falsify their testimony and forge their tangible evidence?[17]

C. Endogenous Cost Evidence

Sanchirico (2001; Chapter 4) analyzes the production and interpretation of legal evidence in a world in which parties can and will attempt to mislead the fact finder whenever it is in their interest to do so, and in whatever manner furthers those interests. This allowance necessitates viewing evidence production – to the extent that it is at all effective – as a form of differential cost signaling, as described below. More than this, to the extent that legal evidence production is effective at the specific task of setting ex-ante incentives in the 'primary activity' – incentive to, for instance, refrain from physical violence, take adequate precaution, adopt safe product designs, comply with environmental regulations, disclose material adverse information or fulfill contractual promises – the signaling costs of legal evidence must be endogenous to parties' primary activity decisions.

The more basic idea of *exogenous* cost signaling is often attributed to Spence (1973), who models educational attainment as a signal of natural ability. Suppose an employer would be willing to pay higher wages to individuals of higher ability if only she knew who these individuals were. Merely asking job candidates whether they are of high ability won't do: given the prospect of a higher wage, many candidates would answer 'yes', whatever the truth. A candidate's possession of a college degree might, however, act as a more reliable signal. Even though individuals of all abilities could conceivably raise their wage by earning a degree, this step might be cost justified only for individuals of high ability, for whom earning the degree is less arduous.

Whatever the merits of this account of education, Spence's (1973) general point regarding credible information transmission has resonance: an individual's action reliably 'signals' that she is of a particular 'type' – i.e. has particular characteristics or knows particular information – when it would not have been in her interest to take that action were she some other type. In other words, talk is cheap and actions speak louder than words.

In the case of legal evidence, parties' 'types' are what they know about the event or condition in question, or how they acted in the primary activity. The relevant actions/signals are parties' 'performances' before the fact finder. Such 'performances' include whether they present documents and things that are difficult to forge, as well as whether the witnesses they offer give consistent, detailed, robust and coordinated testimony. These 'performances' are more costly for some 'types' than for others. A real-seeming document is generally cheaper to produce when it is in fact real. Consistent and detailed testimony robust to cross examination is generally cheaper to produce when truthful.[18]

Another toy example will help to explicate the role of these cost differences. Suppose that some piece of evidence costs $10 to produce when it is real and $100 when it is fake. If it is understood that production of this piece of evidence increases the party's payoffs at litigation by some amount strictly between $10 and $100, then the evidence would be worth producing only when it is real. That is, the fact finder may reliably deduce that the evidence is real from the fact that it is produced, because it would not have been in the party's interest to produce it otherwise. Sanchirico (2001; Chapter 4) argues that something like the dynamic in this (albeit stark) example must be at work if evidence production is to have any value in a world of interested parties and hidden information.

Sanchirico ties the idea of evidence as a costly signal directly to the creation of primary activity incentives by positing that parties' evidence costs are not exogenous, but rather *endogenous*, to their behavior in the primary activity. Adding this feature alters the model in several ways. Most importantly, it drives a wedge between truth finding and incentive setting, as discussed in Part II.[19]

D. Correlated Private Information

Sanchirico (2000; Chapter 5) combines the idea of endogenous cost evidence, just discussed, with another potential device for obtaining information from interested parties. This is the idea of 'cross-wiring' the information presented by different individuals – i.e. using Peter's reports to determine Paul's payoffs and vice versa.[20] Because each individual's report does not directly affect their own payoffs, use of this device significantly reduces each individual's incentives to mislead. Sanchirico (2000) examines the constraints on employing this device and the tradeoffs that determine its optimal mix with the mechanics of endogenous cost evidence described above.

Part II: Truth Finding versus Primary Activity Incentive Setting

Another foundational question about judicial fact finding is just this: why bother? The answer may seem obvious. We want to know what actually happened in the dispute between these parties. We want to know whether the defendant really did fail to take adequate precaution in this apparent accident, whether the defendant really did break a contractual promise, whether the victim's death really was caused by the defendant's intentional actions. But this answer begs the question of *why* we want to know these things in the first place? Could knowing for its own sake really be the goal? If not, what precisely is it that we hope to do with the information we gather? And shouldn't this affect the way we do the gathering?

One might imagine that the economist's typical reply to these questions would rest on primary activity incentive setting. The reason to find facts, that is, is that doing so enables us to effectively regulate individual behavior outside of court, in the marketplace, in the home and on the road. This is after all the predominant approach of lawyer economists to substantive law fields like torts, contracts and criminal law, as is evident from other volumes in this series. And it is, in fact, the approach taken in many of the reduced form models of litigation included in Volume I.

It is not, however, the most common approach taken in economic models of fact finding. Most such models posit as the ultimate objective of fact finding the minimization of trial error or, equivalently, the maximization of trial accuracy. In the simplest case of a binary decision, the analysis is quite similar to the weighted loss minimization described in Lempert (1977; Chapter 1): given her posterior belief about guilt, say, the fact finder chooses the verdict that minimizes the expected loss from wrongful conviction plus the expected loss from wrongful acquittal.

Certainly there are important positive linkages between accuracy and incentive setting. False exoneration typically dampens incentives: were murderers never caught, prosecuted and convicted, the incentive to refrain from murder would be severely compromised; were tortfeasors rarely called to task for their carelessness, precaution would be in short supply. False liability may have the same dampening effect, as when a manufacturer believes it will be exposed to substantial liability whether or not it incurs the cost to make its products safer. On the other hand, false liability may produce excessive deterrence, as when potential injurers who are nonetheless non-negligent see the opportunity to further reduce their legal exposure by taking excessive care. These basic connections between accuracy and incentive setting are explored in the included excerpt from Posner (1973; Chapter 6).[21]

Kaplow and Shavell (1996; Chapter 7), however, suggest that the connection between accuracy and incentives is less obvious than it may seem. They provide an example in which greater accuracy has no effect whatsoever on primary activity incentives. In their model, there is no positive incentive effect to determining the precise amount of harm caused by the defendant in any particular accident, as compared to simply charging the defendant the ex-ante expected damages that she might have caused. The (risk neutral) defendant's incentives depend entirely on how her actions alter the *expected* penalty that she will have to pay.

As Spier (1994; Chapter 8) points out, however, Kaplow and Shavell's argument relies on the assumption, built into their model, that the size of actual harm is no indication of other hidden and valuable pieces of information. In particular, one might well expect that the level of actual harm would be negatively correlated with the defendant's hidden level of precaution – that greater precaution would mean not only fewer accidents, but also less severe harms when accidents occur. In this case, discerning the actual level of harm might be part of an efficient mechanism for setting incentives for precaution. This source of informational value for actual harm is removed from Kaplow and Shavell's model by the assumption that the defendant's level of precaution is already perfectly observed by the court, the level of harm being the only issue for fact finding.[22]

Other articles included elsewhere in this volume propose other important differences between truth finding and incentive setting. Sanchirico emphasizes these differences in analyzing the often seen prohibition on using evidence of an individual's character, possibly as revealed in other acts, to prove that the individual acted in conformity with that character on a particular occasion. Sanchirico argues that the general prohibition, which makes little sense from a truth finding perspective, is easier to understand in terms of primary activity incentive setting. He emphasizes the differing status of 'predictive evidence' in service of truth finding versus incentive setting. Predictive evidence, which includes evidence of someone's disposition or past behavior, is evidence that indicates that the conditions were ripe for an event to occur. Such evidence is informative of whether the event occurred and so of clear value from a truth finding perspective. Its incentive effects, however, are less certain. A defendant who anticipates that he will be punished on the basis of predictive evidence that he committed the wrongful act may well view himself as damned if he does and damned if he doesn't. Conversely, a defendant who anticipates that he would be exonerated on the basis of predictive evidence indicating that he is *not* the kind of person who would commit the act may regard himself as partially immune. Creating the incentive for an agent to act in a particular way requires tying changes in his actions to changes in his penalty or reward. This requirement, in turn, necessitates keying penalties and rewards to evidence that *changes* depending on how the agent actually acts. Evidence that exists either way is at best secondary to this enterprise.

Sanchirico (2001; Chapter 4), discussed earlier, identifies a second fissure between truth finding and primary activity incentive setting. Litigation expenses are as much a punishment as unfavorable verdicts. Thus, even a system in which all defendants win may set primary activity incentives if exoneration is cheaper to secure for the truly innocent. Refer again to the numerical example in which exonerating evidence costs \$100 for defendants who are truly liable and \$10 for defendants who are not. If the stakes of the case were greater than \$100, all defendants, liable or not, would produce the evidence and win the case. Verdicts would be quite inaccurate. But the system would be providing incentives because the cost of exoneration would be \$90 greater for liable defendants. A similar point is explored in Sanchirico (2004) in the context of sanctioning evidentiary misconduct.[23]

Part III: Adversarial Process versus Inquisitorial Process

The Anglo-American system of fact finding relies for evidence on the adversarial efforts of the parties. The continental European system, by contrast, assigns the judge a more active role in investigating the case and questioning witnesses.[24] What are the relative advantages and disadvantages of the two systems? The papers in this part consider that question. Papers in Section B make explicit comparison between the two systems. Papers in Section A set the focus on the effects of adversarial competition in isolation.

A. Balance or Bias in Adversarial Competition

Folk wisdom has it that the competitive evidence production of adversaries leads to accurate fact finding. But is this really so? Economics seems like a good place to turn for an analysis of competition. And a number of important papers in the economic analysis of legal disputes have made substantial headway on the question.

Milgrom and Roberts (1986; Chapter 3), discussed earlier, contains an argument for evidentiary competition. Recall that in their dual-party model the fact finder makes the correct decision in a dispute between two parties with opposing interests even though the fact finder is naïve, and even though the parties are free to withhold information (though they cannot lie). It is always in the interest of one party to supply any missing evidence.

Froeb and Kobayashi (1996; Chapter 9) show that this result extends to the case in which evidence is costly to produce and the decision-maker may be biased. Evidence production is modeled as ‘strategic search’. Each party pays a fixed cost for each sample she draws from an exogenous distribution of evidence (which is the same for each party). She then reports to the court only the portion of her accumulated sample that favors her case. (The parties may not fabricate sampled evidence.) The fact that evidence is costly to acquire does not prevent a correct decision in Froeb and Kobayashi’s model because, all else the same, the party in the right, being favored by the distribution of evidence from which parties draw, ends up presenting more favorable evidence to the fact finder. Moreover, the system automatically compensates for decision-maker bias because the party favored by the bias reacts by slacking off on evidentiary effort.

Daughety and Reinganum (2000; Chapter 10) are less sanguine about the benefits of adversarial competition. They highlight the dependence of Froeb and Kobayashi’s results on symmetries in sampling costs and sampling distributions. And they suggest that, all told, the adversarial system favors defendants.

B. Explicit Comparisons

The economic literature that explicitly compares adversarial and inquisitorial process has generally cast the comparison as a tradeoff between the number of sources of information and the purity of each. Adversarial process offers two (or more) sources of evidence to the inquisitor’s one. But inquisitorially gathered evidence is not as subject to party manipulation.

Shin (1998; Chapter 11) argues that inquisitorial process generates less information than adversarial even when the inquisitor’s investigative ability is as good as that of each adversary (taken individually). Shin’s model is an omission model in the mold of Milgrom and Roberts

(1986; Chapter 3): parties can suppress evidence but not fabricate it. Shin shows, in essence, that the downside of adversarial process – the fact that evidence may be manipulated – can be significantly alleviated by the kind of assume-the-worst-of-omission deductions studied in Milgrom and Roberts. With this downside mitigated, the upside of adversarial process – the fact that it offers multiple sources of evidence – becomes decisive in comparing systems.

Froeb and Kobayashi (2001; Chapter 12) take a more direct and arguably more informative approach. They employ a model of evidentiary sampling similar to that in Froeb and Kobayashi (1996; Chapter 9). Under adversarial process, each party decides first how many times to draw from a given distribution of evidence, and second what of her sample to present in court. (Again, parties cannot fabricate any portion of their sample.) The fact finder 'averages' the evidence placed before her. This induces each party to present only the single piece of evidence in her sample that most favors her case. Under inquisitorial process, on the other hand, the inquisitor herself samples from the distribution and averages *all* the data. Which system does better? If the parties face the same sampling costs, both systems leave the fact finder with the same assessment on average, namely the true mean of the distribution. In other words, whether one takes the average of extreme draws in each case or the average of all draws in each case, one's average assessment over all cases will equal the true mean of the sampled distribution: both estimating procedures are 'unbiased'. However, the two estimators differ in their variance – a proxy for their degree of error.[25] Which system has less error is indeterminate. The outcome depends on the shape of the underlying distribution and the cost of sampling.

Parisi (2002; Chapter 13) adds to the comparison of alternative systems variations in the level of endogenous litigation spending.[26] In his model, parties have less of an incentive to amass private evidence when judges engage to a greater extent in their own investigations of cases and when judges more closely scrutinize the parties' privately produced evidence. Parisi embeds this private costs story in an account of the optimal level of inquisitorial control. Among his several findings are that the judge's role should be reduced in cases that have greater visibility and social relevance. Because evidence is more valuable in such cases, there is reason to increase the total amount of evidentiary expenditure across all parties and the judge. The parties increase evidentiary spending in response to less inquisitorial control. The judge reacts in the opposite manner. Nevertheless, if the judge's opposite reaction is roughly equal in size to the reaction of *each* of the parties, evidentiary expenditure will increase on net for the fact that the parties outnumber the judge.[27]

Part IV: Specific Rules of Evidence and Procedure

The final part of Volume II collects a number of articles that go directly to specific rules of evidence and procedure.

A. Proof Burdens

The presentation of evidence is organized according to the assignment across parties of a number of 'burdens of proof'. One such burden is the burden of persuasion. In a civil (as opposed to criminal) context, the plaintiff typically bears this burden with respect to the claims in her complaint. Applied to the issue of liability, this burden means roughly that she will recover the full extent of the harm she suffered if and only if she convinces the fact finder with a preponderance of the evidence that the defendant is liable for such harm. A 'preponderance of the evidence' for liability is often interpreted in scholarship and case law as that which leaves the fact finder thinking that the defendant is more likely than not to be liable. Kaye (1982; Chapter 14) provides the classic justification for this all-or-nothing 50% rule. He shows that such a rule minimizes trial error if the two possible errors, wrongful liability and wrongful exoneration, are equally weighted.

Sanchirico (1997; Chapter 15) suggests that the persuasion burden plays a role in filtering out cases with inconclusive evidence. In such cases, the court's final ruling, although potentially the best that it could make based on the limited evidence available, is likely to be not much less erroneous than the status quo. The cost of hearing the case, therefore, will have been pointlessly incurred. Unfortunately, the court only finds out that the evidence is inconclusive after expending the resources necessary to hear the case. To help resolve this difficulty, the law stipulates that in order to recover at all, plaintiffs must not only prove that they deserve recovery in expected value, but they must also inspire in the fact finder a minimum degree of certainty regarding the level of their deserved recovery. Cognizant of this requirement, plaintiffs with cases that would leave the fact finder with dispersed beliefs regarding proper recovery refrain from filing even if they would deserve recovery in an expected value sense. Unlike a simple 50% rule, this rule gives some content to the statement that the plaintiff has a burden to bear relative to the defendant. It also offers an alternative explanation for ruling against the plaintiff in the gatecrasher paradox described above.

Hay and Spier (1997; Chapter 16) focus mostly on the 'burden of production' rather than the burden of persuasion. The burden of production in their model determines who will win if neither party comes forward with evidence.[28] They argue that the burden should rest on the party least likely to have a valid claim in the class of cases under consideration. When the righteous party bears the burden, she must expend resources to come forward with evidence in order to win. When the party in the wrong bears the burden, she simply declines to go forward and no resources are consumed. Correct outcomes are thus more cheaply procured when the burden rests with the party who tends to be in the wrong.

B. Character, Hearsay, Privilege and Evidentiary Misconduct

Sanchirico (2001; Chapter 17) provides a primary activity incentive analysis of restrictions on the admissibility of character and past act evidence, emphasizing the important distinction in this context between 'trace' and 'predictive' evidence. Friedman (1992; Chapter 18) provides a game theoretic analysis of restrictions on 'hearsay evidence' – as when a party attempts to convince the fact finder that an event occurred by offering a witness to testify that she *heard* someone else *say* that he witnessed the event occur. Friedman takes account of the effect of prohibiting or allowing hearsay evidence on both parties' incentives to produce as a witness, at the hearing, the declarant whose out of court statement is at issue. Bundy and Elhauge (1991; Chapter 19) emphasize the positive informational benefits of legal advice and thus the propriety of privileging attorney–client communications.[29] Shavell (1989; Chapter 20) and Sanchirico (2004; Chapter 21) study the primary activity effects of sanctioning evidentiary foul play. The second excerpt from Sanchirico (2004; Chapter 22) examines the law's tendency to punish evidentiary foul play to a greater degree, the farther downstream it occurs in litigation.

Notes

1. Courts of original jurisdiction try cases in the first instance rendering a verdict that is often then appealable to a court of appellate jurisdiction. In the US Federal Judiciary, for example, the District Courts are the courts of original jurisdiction.
2. See Savage (1954).
3. See Allais (1953) and Ellsberg (1961).
4. Recent discussion of the conjunction problem appear in Levmore (2001), Stein (2001) and Allen and Jehl (2003).
5. See Kaye (1979).
6. See Boston University Symposium on Probability, Inference and Evidence in the Law (1986).
7. Indeed, the problem is one that spans both the application of conventional probabilistic analysis, as described in Lempert (1977; Chapter 1), as well as many alternative systems for representing and manipulating the phenomenon of likelihood, such as that laid out in L. Jonathan Cohen, *The Probable and the Provable* (1977), which is often cited in evidence scholarship.
8. One can see evidence scholarship starting to bump up against this fact in analyzing the Gatecrasher paradox. Kaye, in particular, suggests that the plaintiff's inability to provide anything other than the 'naked statistical evidence' of seats filled versus seats purchased should itself be taken as evidence; see Kaye (1979).
9. See Kreps (1990).
10. Within economics scholarship, this result is referred to as 'unraveling' and is usually jointly attributed to Grossman (1981) and Milgrom (1981). An early critical analysis appears in Farrell (1986).
    The separate pedigree of this idea within evidence law and scholarship is discussed within.
11. 'Spoliation' is a general term referring to evidentiary misconduct. But it is perhaps most often used to describe a party's failure to produce evidence when so required – either because the evidence has been destroyed or is being withheld.
12. See e.g. Kaye (1979), cited above.
13. The following papers employ a similar model: Sobel (1985), Shavell (1989), Okuno-Fujiwara *et al.* (1990), Lipman and Seppi (1995), Froeb and Kobayashi (1996), Hay and Spier (1997), Shin (1998), Daughety and Reinganum (2000), Bull and Watson (2004) and Demougin and Fluet (2005).
14. It is interesting to note that economists make no such lying assumption when studying auctions or optimal taxation, though this would greatly simplify the analysis. Yet the latter is regulated.
15. See Sanchirico (2004; Chapter 21, 1247–86) for a description of the laws governing evidentiary misconduct in US federal civil cases.
16. See Sanchirico (2004a), surveying in Part I the empirical evidence on evidentiary misconduct.
17. On this question see Chris Sanchirico (2005), *Detection Avoidance* (manuscript available from the author).
18. For a more detailed exposition of the ideas in this paragraph, see Sanchirico (2004b).
19. For an application of endogenous cost evidence to legal presumptions, see Bernardo *et al.* (2000). For an application to contract design see Sanchirico and Triantis (2004). For an application to the burden of proof and optimal strategic complementarities in litigation, see Sanchirico (2005).
20. For antecedents in economics, see e.g. Crémer and McLean (1985, 1988).
21. A portion of this article's appendix that is relevant to the current discussion (pp. 452–5) is reproduced in Volume I. For ease of publication it was necessary to reproduce the appendix intact, and it was believed that the appendix was more important to the portion of Volume I where it currently appears.
    Other relevant articles include Craswell and Calfee (1986), Polinsky and Shavell (1989) and Kaplow and Shavell (1994).

22. The authors consider incentives for precaution separately in a companion paper; see Kaplow and Shavell (1994).
23. Other implications of this point are analyzed in Sanchirico and Triantis (2004). For an application to the burden of proof and optimal strategic complementarities in litigation, see Sanchirico (2005).
24. There are many other dimensions along which these systems differ. The economic literature has focused on this one. For a more general discussion of differences see Langbein (1985, 1988), Allen *et al.* (1988) and Allen (1988).
25. The variance of each system depends on the size of each sample. The authors compare the same amount of sampling: the inquisitor samples as many times as the two adversaries combined.
26. See Volume I, Part I, for more on endogenous litigation expenditure.
27. Dewatripont and Tirole (1999) is often cited in the economic literature comparing adversarial and inquisitorial process. However, the relevance of its very special model to judicial fact finding is uncertain.
28. In fact, Hay and Spier model an amalgam of both burdens. When both parties come forward in their model, the burdened party loses, which seems more like the operation of the persuasion burden than the production burden.
29. For an analysis of the privilege against self-incrimination, see Seidman and Stein (2000).

References

Allais, M. (1953), 'Le Comportement de l'Homme Rationnel devant le Risque: Critique des Postulats et Axiomes de l'Ecole Américaine', *Econometrica*, **21**, 503–46.

Allen, Ronald (1988), 'Idealization and Caricature in Comparative Law Scholarship', *Northwestern University Law Review*, **82**, 785.

Allen, Ronald and Sarah A. Jehl (2003), 'Burdens of Persuasion in Civil Cases: Algorithms v. Explanations', *Michigan State Law Review*, 893.

Allen, Ronald J. *et al.* (1988), 'The German Advantage in Civil Procedure: A Plea for More Details and Fewer Generalities in Comparative Scholarship', *Northwestern University Law Review*, **82**, 705.

Bernardo, A.E., E. Talley and I. Welch (2000), 'A Theory of Legal Presumptions', *Journal of Law, Economics and Organization*, **16**, 1–49.

Boston University Symposium on Probability, Inference and Evidence in the Law, *Boston University Law Review*, April 1986.

Bull, Jesse and Joel Watson (2004), 'Evidence Disclosure and Verifiability', *Journal of Economic Theory*, **118**, 1–31.

Craswell, Richard and John Calfee (1986), 'Deterrence and Uncertain Legal Standards', *Journal of Law, Economics and Organization*, **2**, 279–303.

Crémer, J. and R.P. McLean (1985), 'Optimal Selling Strategies under Uncertainty for a Discriminating Monopolist', *Econometrica*, **53**, 345–61.

Crémer, J. and R. McLean (1988), 'Full Extraction of the Surplus in Bayesian and Dominant Strategy Auctions', *Econometrica*, **56**, 1247–58.

Daughety, A.F. and J.F. Reinganum (2000), 'On the Economics of Trials: Adversarial Process, Evidence, and Equilibrium Bias', *Journal of Law, Economics, and Organization*, **16**, 365–94.

Demougin, Dominique and Claude Fluet (2005), 'Deterrence versus Judicial Error: A Comparative View of Standards of Proof', *Journal of Institutional and Theoretical Economics*, **161** (2), June, 193–206.

Dewatripont, Mathias and Jean Tirole (1999), 'Advocates', *Journal of Political Economy*, **107**, 1–39.

Ellsberg, D. (1961), 'Risk, Ambiguity, and the Savage Axioms', *Quarterly Journal of Economics*, **75**, 643–69.

Farrell, J. (1986), 'Voluntary Disclosure: Robustness of the Unraveling Result, and comments on its importance', in R.E. Grieson (ed.), *Antitrust and Regulation*. Boston, MA: Lexington Books, 91–103.

Froeb, Luke M. and Bruce H. Kobayashi (1996), 'Naive, Biased, Yet Bayesian: Can Juries Interpret

Selectively Produced Evidence?', *Journal of Law, Economics, and Organization*, **12**, 257–76.
Grossman, S.J. (1981), 'The Informational Role of Warranties and Private Disclosure about Product Quality', *Journal of Law and Economics*, **24** (3), 461–89.
Hay, Bruce L. and Kathryn E. Spier (1997), 'Burdens of Production in Civil Litigation: An Economic Perspective', *Journal of Legal Studies*, **26**, 413–32.
Kaplow, Louis and Steven Shavell (1994), 'Accuracy in the Assessment of Liability', *Journal of Law and Economics*, **37**, 1–16.
Kaye, David (1979), 'The Paradox of the Gatecrasher and Other Stories', *Arizona State Law Journal*, 101.
Kreps, David M. (1990), *A Course in Microeconomic Theory*. Princeton, NJ: Princeton University Press (Part IV: Topics in Information Economics).
Langbein, John (1985), 'The German Advantage in Civil Procedure', *University of Chicago Law Review*, **52**, 823.
Langbein, John H. (1988), 'Trashing the German Advantage', *Northwestern University Law Review*, **82**, 763.
Levmore, Saul (2001), 'Conjunction and Aggregation', *Michigan Law Review*, **99**, 723.
Lipman, Bart and Duane Seppi (1995), 'Robust Inference in Communication Games with Partial Provability', *Journal of Economic Theory*, **66**, 370–405.
Milgrom, P.R. (1981), 'Good News and Bad News: Representation Theorems and Applications', *Bell Journal of Economics*, **12** (2), 380–91.
Okuno-Fujiwara, Masahiro, Andrew Postlewaite and Kotaro Suzumura (1990), 'Strategic Information Revelation', *Review of Economic Studies*, **57**, 25–47.
Polinsky, A.M. and S. Shavell (1989), 'Legal Error, Litigation, and the Incentive to Obey the Law', *Journal of Law, Economics and Organization*, **5**, 99–108.
Sanchirico, Chris (2004a), 'Evidence Tampering', *Duke Law Journal*, **53**, 1215.
Sanchirico, Chris (2004b), 'Evidence, Procedure, and the Upside of Cognitive Error', *Stanford Law Review*, **57**, 291.
Sanchirico, Chris (2005), *Harnessing Adversarial Process: Proof Burdens, Affirmative Defenses, and The Complementarity Principle* (U. Pa., Inst. L. & Econ. Res. Paper Series No. 05-01, January).
Sanchirico, Chris and George Triantis (2004), *Evidentiary Arbitrage: The Fabrication of Evidence and the Verifiability of Contract Performance* (U. Pa., Inst. L. & Econ. Res. Paper Series No. 04-10).
Savage, L.J. (1954), *The Foundations of Statistics*. New York: Wiley; 2nd edn, 1972, Dover.
Seidmann, Daniel J. and Alex Stein (2000), 'The Right to Silence Helps the Innocent: A Game-Theoretic Analysis of the Fifth Amendment Privilege', *Harvard Law Review*, **114**, 430.
Shavell, Steven (1989), 'Optimal Sanctions and the Incentive to Provide Evidence to Legal Tribunals', *International Review of Law and Economics*, **9**, 3–11.
Shin, Hyun Song (1998), 'Adversarial and Inquisitorial Procedures in Arbitration', *Rand Journal of Economics*, **29**, 378–405.
Sobel, Joel (1985), 'Disclosure of Evidence and Resolution of Disputes', in Alvin Roth (ed.), *Game-Theoretic Models of Bargaining*. Cambridge: Cambridge University Press.
Spence, M. (1973), 'Job Market Signalling', *Quarterly Journal of Economics*, **87**, 355–74.
Stein, Alex (2001), 'Of Two Wrongs that Make a Right: Two Paradoxes of the Evidence Law and their Combined Economic Justification', *Texas Law Review*, **79**, 1199.

Part I
The Production and Interpretation of Legal Evidence: Four Approaches

A
Pure Probabilistic Deduction

[1]

MODELING RELEVANCE

*Richard O. Lempert**†

During the past decade, particularly during the years immediately following the California Supreme Court's decision in *People v. Collins*,[1] a number of articles have appeared suggesting ways in which jurors might use certain mathematical techniques of decision theory as aids in the rational evaluation of circumstantial evidence.[2] Professor Tribe, in an important response to the post-*Collins* articles, argues against introducing these techniques into the factfinding process. Problems that Tribe foresees include the necessary imprecision of the probabilistic estimates that these techniques require, the dwarfing of soft variables by those that are more readily quantified, and the potential dehumanization of the trial in the name of rational factfinding.[3]

I find Tribe's arguments convincing: with certain narrow exceptions "the costs of attempting to integrate mathematics into the factfinding process of a legal trial outweigh the benefits."[4] This judgment is apparently shared by others, for the spate of articles following *Collins* diminished substantially after Tribe's published response.[5] However, mathematics relates to trial processes in a way that Tribe's article does not address: mathematical models may serve as heuristic devices.[6] As a language, mathematics can help

* Professor of Law, The University of Michigan. A.B. 1964, Oberlin College; J.D. 1968, Ph.D. 1971, The University of Michigan.—Ed.

† I would like to thank Don Regan, Mel Guyer, and Judith Lachman for their careful reading of this paper and their many helpful suggestions. Work on this article was supported in part by the Cook Funds of The University of Michigan Law School.

1. 68 Cal. 2d 319, 438 P.2d 33, 66 Cal. Rptr. 497 (1968).

2. *See, e.g.*, the articles cited in Tribe, *Trial by Mathematics: Precision and Ritual in the Legal Process*, 84 HARV. L. REV. 1329, 1332 n.5 (1971). For those interested, the Tribe article contains a description of the *Collins* case. *Id.* at 1334-37.

3. *Id.* at 1393.

4. *Id.* at 1377.

5. Some who have continued writing have become more sensitive to the problems involved in offering mathematical arguments as an aid to jury decision making and more cautious in what they advocate. *See, e.g.*, Fairley, *Probabilistic Analysis of Identification Evidence*, 2 J. LEGAL STUD. 493 (1973).

6. Tribe recognizes this possibility and reserves the right to object to it. *See* Tribe, *supra* note 2, at 1331 & n.4.

clarify those legal rules that involve weighing evidence in an essentially probabilistic fashion.[7]

In this article I try to show the utility of two simple models, Bayes' Theorem and regret matrices, for thinking about the meaning of relevance and for analyzing those evidentiary rules, which I call the "relevance rules," generally associated with this topic.[8] The discussion assumes that the factfinder is a jury and, unless otherwise noted, that the issue to be resolved is a defendant's guilt. However, the analysis may be readily generalized to the situation where the factfinder is a judge and/or a question other than guilt is at issue. The first section of this article applies the two models to a simplified situation where the factfinder must evaluate only one item of indisputably accurate testimony.[9] The second section explores complexities that can arise when a case involves two or more items of possibly unreliable evidence.

I. Mathematical Models and the Relevance Rules

A. *Bayes' Theorem*

First we must attend to Bayes' Theorem. This theorem follows directly from two elementary formulas of probability theory: if A and B are any two propositions, then:

$$P(A\&B) = P(A|B) \cdot P(B)^{10} \qquad (1)$$

$$P(A) = P(A\,\&\,B) + P(A\,\&\,\text{not-}B)^{11} \qquad (2)$$

7. Daniel Kornstein, for example, has used Bayes' Theorem as an aid in analyzing the problem of harmless error. Kornstein, *A Bayesian Model of Harmless Error*, 5 J. Legal Stud. 121 (1976). A second model used in this article, the regret matrix, a form of utility matrix, is also helpful in thinking about the problem of harmless error. *See also* Ball, *The Moment of Truth: Probability Theory and Standards of Truth*, 14 Vand. L. Rev. 807 (1961); Kaplan, *Decision Theory and the Factfinding Process*, 20 Stan. L. Rev. 1065 (1968).

8. *See* R. Lempert & S. Saltzburg, A Modern Approach to Evidence 148-53 (1977). Portions of this article reproduce arguments made there. By "relevance rules" I mean rules like those codified under Article IV of the Federal Rules of Evidence. They relate to evidence of character, habit, subsequent remedial measures, compromises and offers to compromise, payment of medical expenses, pleas and offers to plea, and liability insurance.

9. In the first section of this paper I shall generally ignore problems that exist because evidence is always received in a context that includes other evidence. The discussion shall proceed as if the evidence in question were the last piece of evidence received in a trial and as if the probability of receiving that evidence were conditionally independent of all the evidence previously received. In addition, I shall assume that the evidence discussed presents no problems of veracity or authenticity. These assumptions simplify the discussion in the text.

10. These symbols mean that the probability that events A and B will both occur is equal to the probability that A will occur if B has occurred times the probability that B will occur. For example, if A = a warm day and B = a sunny day, the probability that it will be both warm and sunny equals the probability that it will be warm if it is in fact sunny times the probability that it will be sunny.

11. These symbols mean that the probability that an event A will occur equals

From these rather basic equations the following formula may be derived:

$$O(G|E) = \frac{P(E|G)}{P(E|\text{not-}G)} \cdot O(G)^{12} \qquad (3)$$

This formula describes the way knowledge of a new item of evidence (E) would influence a completely rational decision maker's evaluation of the odds that a defendant is guilty (G).[13] Since the law assumes that a factfinder *should* be rational, this is a normative model; that is, the Bayesian equation describes the way the law's ideal juror evaluates new items of evidence.[14] What this equation says is that the odds (O) that a defendant is guilty, given the introduction of a new item of evidence, is equal to (1) the probability that the evidence would be presented to the jury if the defendant is in fact guilty, (2) divided by the probability that that evidence would be presented

---

the probability that event A will occur with event B plus the probability that event A will occur with any event that is not B. If A = a warm day and B = a sunny day, the probability that it will be a warm day equals the probability that it will be warm and sunny plus the probability that it will be warm and not sunny.

12. Bayes' Theorem follows directly from the equations given in the text at notes 10 & 11 *supra*. Expressing these in terms changed from A's and B's to G's (guilt) and E's (new evidence) to fit the paradigm case, a criminal trial in which the issue is the defendant's guilt:

(1) $P(G \& E) = P(G|E) \cdot P(E)$

(2) $P(G) = P(G \& E) + P(G \& \text{not-}E)$

it can be shown that

(3) $P(G|E) = \frac{P(E|G)}{P(E)} \cdot P(G)$

and

(4) $P(E) = P(E|G) \cdot P(G) + P(E|\text{not-}G) \cdot P(\text{not-}G)$.

Using (4) to calculate P(E) in (3), we obtain

(5) $P(G|E) = \frac{P(E|G)}{P(E|G) \cdot P(G) + P(E|\text{not-}G) \cdot P(\text{not-}G)} \cdot P(G)$.

Equation (5) is one form of Bayes' Theorem. If O(G) represents the "odds of G," defined as P(G)/P(not-G), then (5) can be rewritten as

(6) $O(G|E) = \frac{P(E|G)}{P(E|\text{not-}G)} \cdot O(G)$,

the form of the theorem that appears in the text.

13. The symbol G could as easily be L for liable, N for negligent, or M for any matter in issue.

14. One might define two normative models of jury behavior. From the standpoint of the law of evidence the normative model implicit in most discussions of jury factfinding is the model of the "rational juror" described in the text. From the standpoint of the legal system one might argue that we employ jurors in large part because we want to inject values other than rationality into the factfinding process. *See generally* H. KALVEN & H. ZEISEL, THE AMERICAN JURY (1966).

to the jury if the defendant is in fact not guilty,[15] (3) times the prior odds[16] on the defendant's guilt. The prior odds are the odds that would have been given of the defendant's guilt before receipt of the item of evidence in question.

For example, suppose at some point in a criminal trial the factfinder believes that the odds are fifty-fifty, or 1:1, that the defendant is guilty. A more familiar way of stating this is that the factfinder believes that the probability of the defendant's guilt is .50.[17] The evidence next received proves the following: that the perpetrator's blood, shed at the scene of the crime, was type A; that the defendant's blood is type A; and that fifty per cent of the suspect population[18] has type A blood. Thus, if the defendant were the perpetrator the probability that the blood found at the scene would be type A is 1.0.[19] The probability that the blood would be type A if someone else committed the crime is .50, or ½, since half of the other possible suspects have type A blood. Plugging these figures into the formula indicates that after receiving the evidence on the blood a rational decision maker would evaluate the odds of guilt as:

$$O(G|E) = \frac{1}{.5} \cdot \frac{1}{1} = \frac{1}{.5} = 2:1.$$

15. In this section it is assumed implicitly that the probability that evidence would be presented to the jury is the same as the probability that the evidence exists.

16. The figure for these odds is not important to the following analysis, though it might be very important in analyzing other problems such as harmless error. It seems unlikely that jurors consciously think in terms of the odds of guilt after each item of evidence is received. Yet it may well be that, without stopping to quantify, they are influenced to make incremental changes in their perception of the parties' chances after hearing items of evidence in much the way Bayes' Theorem suggests, and, if asked, they may be able to express these odds in mathematical terms. *See, e.g.*, Weld & Roff, *A Study in the Formation of Opinion Based upon Legal Evidence*, 51 AM. J. PSYCH. 609 (1938). *Cf.* J. THIBAUT & L. WALKER, PROCEDURAL JUSTICE chs. 6 & 7 (1975).

17. Many find Bayes' Theorem more intuitively understandable when expressed in terms of probabilities, as in equation (5) in note 12 *supra*, than when it is expressed in terms of odds.

18. The suspect populations could be people in the United States, people in a particular locality, males in a locality, black people, white people, etc., based upon what already has been proved about the characteristics of the perpetrator. The textual example assumes that the suspect population is relatively large.

19. At this point some might object that it can never be completely clear that the blood found was the perpetrator's. The point is well taken and is a reason why (1) I don't advocate using this model as an aid to jury factfinding, and (2) I have stipulated that the matter has been proved. The fact that absolute certainty may never exist with respect to an item of evidence does not affect the basic argument of this section. Certain implications of this fact will be discussed in the following section when I introduce the idea of conditional independence and talk about cases involving several items of evidence.

The new evidence has raised the odds in favor of the defendant's guilt to 2:1. Another way of stating this result is that the factfinder's best estimate of the probability that the defendant is guilty is now .67. Evidence that changes an estimated probability of guilt in this fashion is clearly relevant in a criminal trial.

Consider another case. Assume that the range of possible suspects has been limited to voters in a community so conservative that only one out of ten voters supports the liberal candidate. While a group of conservative jurors drawn from this community might be angered by evidence that the defendant supports the liberal candidate, such a showing would not influence the judgment of an ideal juror. Absent some reason to believe that liberals are more prone to commit the crime in question, the probability that the defendant could have been shown to be a liberal were he guilty is .1, the same as the probability that he could have been shown to be a liberal were he not guilty. Solving the Bayesian equation we find:

$$O(G|E) = \frac{.1}{.1} O(G) = O(G)$$

The odds on the defendant's guilt remains O(G); the same as they were before the jury learned of the defendant's political affiliation. In these circumstances evidence of the defendant's political affiliation is not relevant.

1. *Logical Relevance*

In both examples the effect of the evidence on the decision maker's final judgment as to guilt turns entirely on the ratio $\frac{P(E|G)}{P(E|\text{not-}G)}$, conventionally called the *likelihood ratio.* In the first example P(E|G) was twice P(E|not-G), and the factfinder doubled his prior odds of the defendant's guilt. In the second example P(E|G) and P(E|not-G) were the same, so the likelihood ratio was one and the factfinder's prior estimate of the defendant's guilt remained unchanged. In terms of the Bayesian model, it will always be the case that the impact of new evidence on prior odds on guilt, or on any other disputed hypothesis, will be solely a function of the likelihood ratio for that evidence. Where the likelihood ratio for an item of evidence differs from one, that evidence is *logically relevant.* This is the mathematical equivalent of the statement in *Federal Rules of Evidence* (FRE) 401 that "relevant evidence" is "evidence having *any* tendency to make the existence of any fact that is of consequence to the determination of the action more probable or less probable than it would be without the evidence."[20] Hence, evidence is logically relevant only when the probability of finding that evidence given the truth of some hypothesis at issue in the case differs from the probability of finding the same evidence given the falsity of the hypothesis at issue. In a criminal trial, if a particular item of evidence is as likely to be found if the defendant is guilty as it is if he is innocent, the evidence is logically irrelevant on the issue of the defendant's guilt.

As a practical matter courts may be justified in rejecting evidence as logically irrelevant when the likelihood ratio is only *slightly* different from one, since such evidence will have little effect on the odds that the disputed hypothesis is true.[21] A slight difference in this context must be very small indeed, since a likelihood ratio of 1.5 would lead a factfinder to increase by fifty per cent the estimate of the odds in question and a likelihood ratio of 2.0 would result in a doubling of the prior odds.[22]

It is clear from the model that the likelihood ratio depends entirely on the relative magnitudes of $P(E|G)$ and $P(E|\text{not-}G)$ and not on the absolute magnitude of either. Thus evidence that is very unlikely to be associated with a guilty defendant will nevertheless be probative of guilt so long as the evidence is more (or less) likely to be associated with an individual who is not guilty. Suppose, for example, that in an assault case it can be shown both that the defendant is a heroin addict and that one out of 500 criminal assailants are heroin addicts. The latter information means that it is very unlikely that any given criminal assailant is a heroin addict. However, if it can also be shown that of the people who never engage in criminal

20. FED. R. EVID. 401 (emphasis added).

21. A court will often be unable to specify the precise likelihood ratio that is appropriate given the evidence and the issue in question. What a judge may be able to sense is that, although the likelihood ratio may take on any of a range of values, the most probable value of the ratio is one and that it would be unreasonable for a jury to find the likelihood ratio to be more than slightly different from one. When this is the case, the court is justified in excluding the evidence on the ground of logical irrelevance. When a reasonable jury could find the appropriate likelihood ratio to be more than slightly different from one, the jury's responsibility for weighing evidence precludes the court from excluding the evidence as logically irrelevant even if the court believes that the most probable likelihood ratio is one or very close to it.

22. Since we are assuming the evidence is the last evidence received, the argument clearly holds except where the prior odds on guilt are at the very threshold of being sufficient to convict. If additional evidence was still to be offered it is possible that a number of items of evidence that were individually of low relevance would, when taken together, be of considerable relevance.

assault only one in 1000 are heroin addicts, knowledge that the defendant is an addict should result in a doubling of the prior odds that the defendant was the assailant. Conversely, if it could be proved that for every 250 nonassailants there is one heroin addict, evidence of the defendant's addiction and the rate of criminal assault among addicts should lead to a halving of the prior odds that the defendant is guilty of assault. In either of these supposed cases there may be good reason to keep evidence of the defendant's addiction from the jury, but the reason is not that the information standing alone is logically irrelevant.[23]

2. *Estimation Problems*

Courts declare evidence irrelevant for several reasons. Sometimes they are concerned that the likelihood ratio may be one or very close to it. This problem, examined above, is properly called the problem of "logical relevance." On other occasions courts are concerned with the possibility that the factfinder will misestimate the probabilities that make up the likelihood ratio; *i.e.*, $P(E|G)$ and/or $P(E|\text{not-}G)$. Overestimating the numerator or underestimating the denominator makes the conclusion sought by the proponent of the evidence appear more probable than it actually is; underestimating the numerator or overestimating the denominator has the opposite result. In the assault hypothetical presented above, if the factfinder thought that the probability that a nonassailant would be a heroin addict was one in 10,000 rather than one in 1,000, this misestimation would lead to a twentyfold increase in the odds that the defendant was the assailant rather than the twofold increase that was in fact justified. I call such problems "estimation problems."

Estimation problems take several forms. The most obvious is that evidence may be given more weight than it deserves. The jurors may exaggerate the probative value of the evidence because they believe that the association between evidence and hypothesis is more powerful than it in fact is or because they are not estimating probative worth in the context that is proper given the facts of the case. The heroin example of the preceding paragraph is a situation in which the jurors misestimate the strength of a crucial association, throwing the denominator of the likelihood ratio off by a factor of ten. FRE 404, the general rule excluding character evidence, is a relevance rule that can be justified, in part, on this ground. When

23. The evidence is likely to be prejudicial. Also, in the context of other evidence it may be irrelevant for reasons discussed in section II of this article.

courts reject evidence because of this type of estimation problem, they often categorize the problem as one of prejudice, a term I prefer to reserve for another situation,[24] or they may speak of the danger of confusing or misleading the jury.

Courts rarely recognize explicitly the danger that jurors will misestimate the probative value of evidence by failing to appreciate the context in which the evidence should be evaluated.[25] However, several of the relevance rules may be justified, in part, because the evidence they exclude appears likely to raise such problems.[26] For example, rules like FRE 410, excluding evidence of withdrawn guilty pleas, are often justified on the ground that the excluded evidence *is too probative*: to admit evidence of a guilty plea after allowing the plea to be withdrawn would effectively cancel the benefits of the right to withdraw.[27] The presumed probative value of the plea is used to justify decisions admitting this evidence where withdrawal does not depend upon a showing that the plea was coerced or otherwise improperly elicited and is an argument against the federal rule of general exclusion. Attention to estimation problems suggests, however, that the federal approach has much to commend it. Jurors might well perceive the numerator of the likelihood ratio for this evidence as the probability that a guilty person would plead guilty and the denominator as the probability that an innocent person would plead guilty. The first, given known rates of guilty pleas, might be reasonably estimated by jurors to be anywhere between .1 and .9. The second would probably be given a very low value, .001, for example. Dividing numerator by denominator suggests that the evidence is quite probative. But these hypothetical jurors would in fact be estimating the likelihood ratio for only part of the evidence before them. In the context of the case, the probabilities that the jurors should be evaluating are the probability that a plea of guilty would

---

24. *See* text at notes 36-53 *infra*.

25. This judicial attitude is often defensible, for ordinarily it is the task of the opposing counsel to put a party's evidence into context. However, when the jurors' intuitions are likely to be grossly inaccurate, setting evidence in context may require substantial attention to collateral matters. In these circumstances the decision to exclude evidence rather than open up collateral issues may be justified.

26. Elsewhere I argue that a feature characterizing most of the relevance rules is that they can be justified on several different grounds. Thus the likelihood of estimation problems differs for each of the relevance rules, and no rule is justified *solely* on the ground that the evidence it excludes is likely to pose estimation problems. For a further exposition of these views, see R. LEMPERT & S. SALTZBURG, *supra* note 8, ch. 4.

27. *Cf.* MCCORMICK'S HANDBOOK OF THE LAW OF EVIDENCE 635 (2d ed. E. Cleary 1972) [hereinafter cited as MCCORMICK].

be made *and later withdrawn* if the defendant were in fact guilty and the probability of the same event if the defendant were in fact innocent. The first probability is likely to be *substantially* less than the probability that a guilty person would plead guilty. The second probability, while necessarily less than the probability that an innocent person would plead guilty, would not be as substantially decreased.[28] Jurors who fail to appreciate the information conveyed by the fact that a plea of guilty is withdrawn will give withdrawn guilty pleas considerably more weight than they deserve.[29] I believe the likelihood that jurors will estimate the wrong set of probabilities is sufficiently great as to be one justification for rules like FRE 410.[30]

An estimation problem also exists when there is so little information about the relationship of certain evidence to the hypothesis in question that the implications of the evidence are unclear. In these circumstances courts often exclude evidence as irrelevant rather than let the jurors speculate on its import. Since such evidence might well relate to the probability of guilt or innocence if its true implications were known, a more precise justification for exclusion is "relevance unknown." If the textual example that posited a relationship between heroin addiction and assault did not ring true, it is probably because we lack the base rate information needed to evaluate the relationship between heroin addiction and the likelihood of engaging in an assault. Although the image of the "dope fiend"

28. This probability is necessarily less because it is a probability of two events: (A) a plea of guilty would be made, and (B) the plea would be later withdrawn. P(A & B) can never be greater than P(B). What is crucial, however, is the *ratio* between the probability that a plea would be entered and later withdrawn if the defendant were guilty and the probability of the same event if the defendant were innocent. If the empirical assumptions that underlie the textual argument are correct, this ratio will be much closer to 1:1 than the ratio of the probability that the defendant would plead guilty if he were guilty to the probability that the defendant would plead guilty if he were innocent.

29. The argument in the text conceptualizes the two aspects of the evidence, that the plea was made and that it was later withdrawn, as if they are aspects of one item of evidence. This appears reasonable because the jurors are likely to receive the information as if it were a single fact and, I believe, are likely to treat it as such. However, one could also conceptualize this as a situation involving two discrete items of evidence, one being that a plea was made and the other that it was later withdrawn. When the evidence is conceptualized in this way, the approach taken in section II applies.

30. For those who accept my analysis of the probabilities involved but believe that I underestimate the perceptiveness of jurors, let me point out that a number of intelligent commentators have apparently made the mistake I expect of jurors. McCormick, for example, writes, "[I]t may be argued, a plea of guilty if freely and understandingly made is so likely to be true that to withhold it from the jury seems to ask them to do justice without knowledge of one of the most significant of the relevant facts." McCormick, *supra* note 27, at 635.

is that of a violent personality, effects associated with addiction suggest that addicts are less likely than nonaddicts to engage in physical violence for its own sake.[31] With no good evidence of appropriate base rates and conflicting images of the violent propensities of heroin addicts, it makes sense to keep evidence of heroin addiction from a jury in assault cases because its relevance is unknown.[32]

Under FRE 403 and at common law, courts have discretion to exclude logically relevant evidence likely to pose estimation problems if the probative value of the evidence is substantially outweighed by the danger that it will mislead the jury. The Bayesian model suggests that in exercising this discretion the more the court's estimate of the proper likelihood ratio for an item of evidence deviates from 1:1 the less willing the court should be to exclude that evidence. If the likelihood ratio for an item of evidence is 2:1 and the factfinder perceives it as 20:1 the misevaluation might well be of critical importance. However, if the likelihood ratio for the evidence is 100:1 and the factfinder misperceives it as 1000:1, the error is less likely to be critical because the evidence whether properly weighed or overweighed usually leads to the same conclusion: that the favored hypothesis is established by the appropriate standard of proof.[33] Furthermore, excluding evidence where the likelihood ratio deviates substantially from 1:1 deprives the factfinder of information that might aid considerably in the rational resolution of disputed factual claims and may prevent a party from making what is, on a *fair* reading of all the evidence, a powerful case. This analysis supports the judicial practice of rarely, if ever, excluding evidence of substantial probative value simply because the jury appears likely to give the evidence even more weight than it deserves or because the precise weight to be given is unclear.[34] The preferred solution is to provide the jury with the information needed to assess accurately the probative value of the offered evidence.

A similar analysis applies where a court is called on to weigh the probative value of evidence against such factors as confusion of

31. Since there is good reason to believe that addicts often find it necessary to resort to crime in order to support their habits, if the assault were with an intent to rob the probative value of the evidence of addiction would, no doubt, be higher and the likely direction of the relationship would be clearer.

32. Other good reasons for this exclusion may also exist. *See, e.g.*, the discussion of prejudice in the text at notes 36-53 *infra*.

33. One can, of course, think of situations where the prior odds will be such that this argument does not hold. However, as a general matter trials are likely to be close enough that the analysis in the text applies.

34. There are other values that may justify the exclusion of highly probative evidence, *e.g.*, the rules of privilege and the rules regarding illegally seized evidence.

the issues, delay, and waste of time. Where the likelihood ratio for the evidence is far from 1:1, exclusion on these grounds is almost never justified except in the special case where, after considering all other admissible evidence, the court is convinced that the prior odds in favor of the disputed hypothesis are so high or so low that even highly probative evidence is unlikely to change the jury's judgment. This means that courts should be more reluctant in close cases than in clear ones to exclude probative evidence on such grounds as threatened delay, confusion, or waste of time. Appellate courts are certainly influenced by the closeness of cases in reviewing claims that the exclusion of evidence on such grounds was erroneous.

Each of those exclusionary rules that I call the relevance rules bars evidence of a particular type, but in most cases the bar is not complete. Exclusion is mandated only with respect to certain issues; on other issues the evidence remains admissible. Elsewhere I have argued that a general characteristic of the relevance rules is that the excluded evidence is rarely very probative of the issues on which it is inadmissible.[35] If this argument is correct, these rules of exclusion seldom force courts to contravene the policies advocated in the two preceding paragraphs. Instead they codify for recurring situations the decision rule that will usually be correct.

The Bayesian model that has been presented thus far aids in understanding the following aspects of the law relating to relevance: (1) the meaning of logical relevance, (2) the principle that only logically relevant evidence is admissible, (3) the discretion that courts have to exclude relevant evidence when the jury is likely to give it undue weight, (4) the reluctance of courts to exclude highly probative evidence although the jury is likely to give it undue weight, (5) the ways in which rules excluding certain evidence on specific issues relate to considerations of relevance, and (6) some of the justifications for those exclusionary rules that are generally seen as relating to relevance.

35. *See* R. Lempert & S. Saltzburg, *supra* note 8, ch. 4. In some situations the excluded evidence will appear to have probative value. Where this is so it will almost always be the case that, if the hypothesis that the evidence is offered to support is true, there will be other available evidence that supports the desired inference even more strongly. In these circumstances, the other evidence will usually be sufficient to demonstrate by the appropriate standard of proof the truth of the hypothesis favored by the proponent of the evidence. The absence of such other evidence usually is an indication that on the facts of the particular case the inadmissible evidence has less than its usual tendency to prove the fact in dispute and suggests that the case presents one of those rare situations in which the inadmissible evidence is present although the hypothesis with which it is usually associated is not true. For an example of this, see the discussion of subsequent repairs in the text at notes 66-67 *infra*.

The Bayesian model does not, however, indicate why in some cases it might be desirable to exclude probative evidence not likely to raise estimation problems nor why it should be reversible error for a court to admit logically irrelevant evidence. However, another model drawn from decision theory helps clarify these aspects of the law of relevance. This model, called a *regret matrix*, aids in thinking about prejudice.

B. *Prejudice and the Regret Matrix*

A regret matrix[36] is not a normative model since it is not clear that the law expects the ideal decision maker to act in a manner consistent with it. It may, however, be a good descriptive model of the way decision makers, be they jurors or judges, acutally behave, and values may be inserted into the model that are, arguably, normative. The model assumes that individuals wish to minimize the expected regret felt in the long run as a result of their decisions. In law, for example, a decision maker might wish to find for plaintiffs only when defendants were negligent. In terms of this model, the decision maker would have no regret in finding for plaintiffs when defendants were negligent and no regret in finding for defendants when they were not negligent.[37] Since in the uncertain world of litigation the decision maker can never be absolutely sure that a particular defendant was or was not negligent, the decision maker can never be absolutely sure of avoiding outcomes that would be regretted if the truth were known.

Although absolute certainty is impossible, the decision maker might be able to estimate a probability that the defendant was negligent, *e.g.*, .6 or .7. If this can be done and if the decision maker can articulate the *relative* regret associated with different possible outcomes, a regret matrix can be constructed that indicates which decision—given the probabilities—leads to the least total regret in the long run. Consider the situation portrayed in Figure One.

36. What I shall refer to as a "regret" matrix is generally called a "utility" matrix in the decision theory literature. Since, as the matrix is used in this article, some disutility or regret is assigned to each of its various cells, I have followed the suggestion of Kaplan and call the matrix a "regret" matrix. *See* Kaplan, *supra* note 7, at 1078-82.

This use of the term "regret" should not be confused with the "risk" or "regret" payoffs associated with Professor L. Savage's minimax risk criteria of decision making that is applicable to decision problems in which the probabilities associated with various true states are unknown to the decision maker. *See* R. LUCE & H. RAIFFA, GAMES AND DECISIONS 280-82 (1957).

37. The example assumes that defenses such as contributory negligence are unavailable in this case, so liability turns solely on the issue of the defendant's negligence.

FIGURE 1

VERDICT	DECISION MAKER'S REGRET MATRIX TRUE STATE OF AFFAIRS		DECISION MAKER'S ESTIMATED PROBABILITY THAT D WAS:		DECISION MAKER'S EXPECTED REGRET IF VERDICT IS FOR:	
	D Negligent	D Not Negligent				
For P	0	1	Negligent	.6	P	.4
For D	1	0	Not Negligent	.4	D	.6

In this matrix no regret is associated with a decision for P when D was negligent or with a decision for D when D was not negligent. One unit of regret is associated with each mistake, that of finding for P when D was not negligent and that of finding for D when D was negligent. How should a decision maker with these values decide? That depends on his estimate of the probability that D was negligent. In the above example this probability is estimated at .6, making the estimated probability that D was not negligent (1 - .6) or .4. Knowing these probabilities, the expected regret for each verdict can be calculated by multiplying the regret associated with the verdict given the defendant's actual negligence or non-negligence times the probability that the defendant actually was negligent or not negligent. The sum of these products for a given verdict equals the total regret to be expected (in the long run) if that verdict were reached in all cases having the same regret matrix and probability of negligence. In the example, there is a .6 probability that D was negligent. Hence there is a .6 probability the decision maker who decides for P will feel no regret [.6 x 0 = 0]. Conversely, there is a .4 probability that D was not negligent and that a decision for P will result in one unit of regret [.4 x 1 = .4]. Thus, the regret expected from deciding for P given these probabilities of D's negligence will, in the long run, average .4 of whatever unit regret is measured in [0 + .4 = .4]. The situation is reversed when the decision is for D. There is a .6 probability that the decision maker will feel one unit of regret and a .4 probability that the decision maker will feel no regret. Consequently, the average expected regret from deciding for D is .6 units in the long run. An individual concerned with minimizing expected regret will decide for P in these circumstances.

The regret matrix used in this example is normative for most civil cases. A judge or juror *should* feel the same regret in reaching a mistaken decision for P that is felt in reaching a mistaken decision for D. If this is in fact the case (*i.e.*, if this particular regret matrix actually models the decision maker's values), one can show algebraically that regret is minimized by deciding for P whenever the probability of negligence is greater than .5 and deciding for D whenever the probability of negligence is less than .5.[38]

There are many civil cases in which a factfinder might feel uncomfortable with a norm that ascribes equal regret to the two kinds of mistakes. If this norm is rejected and if the factfinder seeks to minimize regret, he may strain to reach decisions that run counter to the weight of the evidence. For example, a juror whose insurance company connections make him sympathetic to tort defendants and hostile to injured plaintiffs might regret mistakenly deciding for P when D was not negligent twice as much as the opposite mistake. (This may be portrayed by changing the value in the upper right-hand cell of the matrix in Figure One to 2 while leaving the value in the lower left-hand cell at 1.) With this relative regret and the same probability that D is negligent as in the earlier example, .6 units of regret would be associated with a decision for D (the same as before) and .8 units of regret [0 x .6 + 2 x .4] with a decision for P. Hence a decision for D could be expected, although the decision maker's estimated probability of D's negligence is sixty per cent.[39]

At law the burden of proof needed to sustain a conviction is the same for all defendants: good or evil, young or old, attractive or unattractive, dangerous or nonthreatening. Yet it is likely that jurors regret the mistake of convicting basically good people more than the mistake of convicting the basically evil. These feelings are reversed if the mistake is acquitting. The situation is undoubtedly similar with respect to other characteristics that affect people's attitudes toward their fellow human beings. If most jurors cannot avoid being influenced by such preferences in reaching their verdicts, the burden of proof is effectively changed by any information that affects these preferences. Consider, for example, the following regret matrices: one hypothesizes relative regret when a defendant is perceived as evil and the other relative regret when the defendant is perceived as good.

38. This is what is meant by a burden of proof by the preponderance of the evidence. Regret is equal when the probability of negligence is exactly .5. Here the law has decided that the defendant should prevail.

39. This assumes that a factfinder with the hypothesized regret schedule would be unwilling to accept the court's instruction that P should prevail if he establishes his case by a preponderance of the evidence.

FIGURE 2

		Regret Matrix for Evil Defendant		Regret Matrix for Good Defendant	
		True State of Affairs		True State of Affairs	
		D Truly Guilty	D Truly Innocent	D Truly Guilty	D Truly Innocent
Verdict	Guilty	0	5	0	10
	Innocent	1	0	1	0

In the case of the evil defendant, the juror seeking to minimize regret would vote to convict whenever his estimated probability of the defendant's guilt exceeded .83. In the case of the good defendant the decision maker would require a probability of .91 before convicting.[40]

The law's ideal juror estimates only the probabilities pertaining to the defendant's guilt and does not independently judge the regret associated with possible mistakes. This information is provided, in theory, by the court's instructions on the burden of proof. The requirement that guilt be proved beyond a reasonable doubt may mean that an accused should not be convicted unless the probability of guilt is judged to be at least .91, which is equivalent to saying that the law regards a wrongful conviction as being ten times more regrettable than a wrongful acquittal,[41] or it may mean that conviction should

40. These probabilities are those which exist when the expected regret from the two possible verdicts (guilt and innocence) are equal. For the case where the regret associated with wrongful conviction is 5 times that associated with wrongful acquittal the appropriate equation is $0(X) + 5(1\text{-}X) = X + 0(1\text{-}X)$, which leads to $6X = 5$, or, after rounding, $X = .83$ where X is the probability the defendant is guilty. When the regret associated with wrongful conviction is 10 times that associated with wrongful acquittal the equation to be solved is $0(X) + 10(1\text{-}X) = X + 0(1\text{-}X)$, which leads to $11x = 10$, or, after rounding, $X = .91$.

41. This assumes that the two cells of the matrix which form what is called the "principal diagonal" are zero, *i.e.*, that no regret is associated with convicting a guilty person or acquitting someone who is innocent. It is possible that at least one of these two cells is not zero. For example, suppose that the decision maker believes that convicting a guilty person has regret or disutility associated with it because placing a person in the penal system is ultimately damaging to both the defendant and society. Preserving the perception that a wrongful conviction is ten times as regrettable as a wrongful acquittal, the following matrix might represent the relative regrets:

		True State of Affairs	
		Guilty	Innocent
Verdict	Guilty	1	50
	Innocent	5	0

In this case, even though the relation between the regret associated with wrongful conviction and that associated with wrongful acquittal remains the same, the probability of guilt which one interested in minimizing expected regret would find necessary to convict is increased from .91 to .926. [$1(X) + 50(1\text{-}X) = 5(x) + 0(1\text{-}X)$, $50 = 54X$, $X = .926$]

It is likely that the regret matrices that would best model the behavior of actual not follow unless some other minimum probability of guilt is obtained; but whatever the degree of certainty associated with proof beyond a reasonable doubt, the law does not contemplate that the standard of proof will vary with the defendant's personal characteristics or with the sordid details of the defendant's criminal activity.[42]

In practice, the ideal of an unvarying standard is not achieved. Instructions on burden of proof, particularly in criminal cases, are so ambiguous that jurors necessarily exercise discretion in determining the degree of certainty needed to support a particular verdict. Furthermore, there is considerable evidence that jury verdicts are influenced by the personal characteristics of victims and defendants and by aspects of criminal activity that do not logically relate to the issue of guilt or innocence.[43] Where this occurs one may properly speak of prejudice, *for prejudicial evidence is any evidence that influences jury verdicts without relating logically to the issue of guilt or innocence.* Evidence that does relate logically to a disputed issue may also have a prejudicial effect, since the probative value of evidence may not fully determine its impact in the case. In terms of the regret model, one can conceptualize the prejudicial *potential* of evidence as the degree to which it affects the regret matrix of a juror viewing the case. The prejudicial *impact* of evidence depends upon prejudicial potential discounted by the juror's ability to ignore personal preferences in interpreting and applying the court's charge on burden of proof. Often the law fictively assumes that this ability is complete so long as the juror is instructed not to use evidence inappropriately. For simplicity's sake, this discussion shall

jurors would often contain nonzero values in the two cells of the principal diagonal. In this paper these values are set at zero because the ideal juror should feel no regret at reaching correct decisions. Indeed, evidence designed to make the factfinder regret correct decisions is typically considered irrelevant or prejudicial. A defendant, for example, could not introduce evidence of the conditions at the state prison to which he would be sent as part of his substantive case. Similarly it would be improper for a prosecutor to argue that the jury should hesitate to acquit an innocent person because an acquittal would give the impression that the jurisdiction was "soft on crime."

42. One might argue that the standard of proof should vary with certain characteristics of the defendant and that more doubt should be required to acquit the obviously evil or dangerous than to acquit the obviously good or nonthreatening. The argument, however persuasive it might be on the issue of how juries should behave given the interests of the larger society, is not relevant at this point in the analysis where I am treating law on its own terms, as an ideal system, in order to elucidate certain aspects of the law of relevance.

43. *See, e.g.*, H. KALVEN & H. ZEISEL, *supra* note 14, at 301-47, 395-410. Relationships between verdicts and fact situations as reported in the Kalven and Zeisel study are consistent with the claim that jurors act, at least in part, to minimize personal regret.

proceed on the opposite and equally fictive assumption that prejudicial impact equals prejudicial potential.

The Bayesian model as it is used in this paper differs from the regret matrix used to model prejudice in an important respect. The discussion focusing on the Bayesian model assumes that the fact-finder assigns values rationally to the Bayesian equation. Either the values are assumed to be correct, as in the discussion of logical relevance, or errors are defined and attributed to a lack of information, as in the discussion of estimation problems. The regret matrix, as used here, admits of deviation from normative values but not of error and makes no assumptions about the rationality of the process that assigns values to the matrix. This process may be more or less logical, as when information of a defendant's felony record results in lowering the regret associated with the mistake of convicting because certain of the disabilities of conviction, most notably the stigma of a criminal record, already attach to the defendant. On the other hand, the process may be entirely devoid of logic, as where a change in regret results from evidence that is emotionally arousing, such as a gruesome photograph or an impassioned speech.[44]

Much of the law relating to relevance reflects an awareness of the way in which prejudicial information can influence jury decision making. The danger of prejudice justifies the exclusion of some logically relevant evidence that does not pose estimation problems, and the same danger explains why the admission of logically irrelevant evidence may be reversible error. More specifically, a number of the relevance rules are justified in part because the evidence they exclude is fraught with prejudicial potential. I shall look at two of these rules by way of example.

---

44. It might be argued that with actual jurors the impact of emotion generally affects judgments that are analogous to those modeled by the Bayesian equation rather than by the regret matrix. For example, emotion may lead a juror to misestimate the probabilities in the likelihood ratio, or it may prevent a juror from "thinking straight" and thus lead to mistakes in calculation that make evidence appear more probative than it in fact is. If one could examine the psychological processes that underlie such mistakes, I would expect to find that they are most often made by jurors who wish to avoid confronting the fact that their relative regret is such that they are willing to convict on very flimsy evidence. In any case, the analytic value of the two-stage model proposed in this essay does not depend on the degree to which the two stages mimic the actual thought processes of jurors. Given the assumption that jurors seek to minimize personal regret, any mistake in a Bayesian calculation that would affect a juror's verdict can be portrayed as a change in the juror's regret matrix. This is analytically desirable regardless of actual decision processes, for it allows a clear separation between problems involving the probative value of evidence and problems that may arise because evidence can have an impact apart from its probative worth.

Consider first the rule that precludes introducing evidence of liability insurance to show negligence. The possession of liability insurance appears so unrelated to carefulness that a jury is not likely to treat the fact that a defendant was insured as tending to prove the defendant's negligence. Thinking solely in terms of Bayes' Theorem, evidence of the defendant's insurance coverage might be objectionable on the ground that its introduction wastes the court's time, but there is no reason to believe that such evidence will hurt either party. However, the regret matrix suggests a more substantial reason for excluding evidence of insurance. Knowledge that the defendant was insured may inappropriately affect the verdict whenever the factfinder's relative regret at mistakenly finding for or against an insured defendant will differ from the regret that would be felt if the factfinder thought the defendant would pay personally for the damages. Such a difference appears likely. Interestingly enough, some have argued that jurors should be informed of the existence of insurance because today's jurors assume insurance exists in all cases and construct their regret matrices accordingly. Insurance companies are not worse off when their interest in the case is revealed, so the argument goes, but uninsured defendants are harmed if jurors are not aware of their status.

The regret matrix also illustrates the sense behind rules like FRE 404(b) that forbid introducing evidence of other crimes, wrongs, or acts with the purpose of proving that a person acted in conformity with the character suggested by these delicts. While evidence that an accused committed some crime in the past may have probative value in that the probability of a history of crime may be higher for guilty defendants than for innocent ones, the probative value is likely to be outweighed by the effect that this knowledge will have on the jury's standard of proof.

If any regret matrix is normative for criminal cases it is probably the following:

FIGURE 3

		True State of Affairs	
		D Truly Guilty	D Truly Innocent
Verdict	Guilty	0	10+
	Innocent	1	0

This matrix is a mathematical portrayal of the oft-quoted statement that it is better that ten guilty men go free than that one innocent man be convicted. A substantial proportion of jurors may, in fact, subscribe to approximately this norm.[45] Any evidence that leads a juror to change this initial regret matrix by diminishing his regret at convicting the innocent, raising his regret at acquitting the guilty, or associating regret with acquitting the innocent will prejudice the defendant in contravention of this arguably normative standard of proof. Evidence of other crimes is likely to do just this.

I have already alluded to one reason why such a change in the regret matrix might be expected from the revelation of a defendant's prior felonies: the stigma of being a felon attaches with the first conviction; subsequent convictions may also be stigmatizing, but they are not seen as having the same implications for a person's later life chances or his definition of self.[46] The other side of this is that the unblemished record, lost with the first conviction, has value in itself. Furthermore, some may regard a convicted felon as essentially criminal and believe that if he did not commit the crime charged he probably has committed or will commit other crimes. For these reasons the mistaken conviction of those with criminal records is likely to be perceived as less regrettable than the mistaken conviction of individuals thought never to have been in trouble with the law.

The danger of prejudice is likely to be even greater when it is shown that the defendant has engaged in illegal acts that have not resulted in criminal convictions. Here regret associated with a mistaken conviction is likely to be diminished because it is felt that the defendant deserves to be punished for his prior criminal activity whether or not he has committed the crime charged. For the same reason, regret, in contravention of the normative ideal, may be associated with the correct acquittal of such a defendant.[47] In addition to these difficulties, the attempt to prove guilt through evidence of bad character is fraught with estimation problems.[48]

45. *See* Simon & Mahan, *Quantifying Burdens of Proof*, 5 LAW & SOC'Y. REV. 319, 324 (1971).

46. *See generally* D. MATZA, BECOMING DEVIANT (1969); E. SCHUR, LABELING DEVIANT BEHAVIOR: ITS SOCIOLOGICAL IMPLICATIONS (1971).

47. The matrix that follows is an example of the kind of deviation from the normative that could be expected when a juror learns of the defendant's prior unpunished criminal activity.

		TRUE STATE OF AFFAIRS	
		Guilty	Innocent
VERDICT	Guilty	0	5
	Innocent	1	.5

In the arguably normative matrix, figure 3 in text *supra*, the probability of guilt necessary to convict is .909. The effect of halving the regret associated with a mistaken guilty verdict is to decrease the requisite probability to .83. Associating regret in the magnitude shown with a correct verdict of innocent further reduces this probability to .818.

48. There is the "simple" problem of deciding exactly how character relates to

Of course these same problems exist when evidence of prior illegal or bad acts is admissible for permitted purposes, such as showing identity, opportunity, intent, motive, guilty knowledge, a criminal plan, or absence of mistake. Allowing the admissibility of other-crimes evidence to turn on the purpose for which the evidence is offered may be justified if such evidence has greater probative value and is less likely to raise estimation problems when it is offered for a permissible rather than an impermissible end. One can imagine situations where such evidence satisfies these criteria,[49] but whether this is the case generally is an empirical question that has not yet been answered. It does not, however, appear that even a colorable case can be made on relevance grounds for the common-law rule that allows evidence of *any* felony conviction to be admitted on the issue of a defendant's credibility.[50] The impeachment of non-party witnesses through evidence of other crimes is less objectionable because the evidence is not likely to affect substantially the relevant regret matrices. Moreover, if the evidence suggests that the witness is peculiarly susceptible to pressure from the state or the accused, as where a prosecution witness has been convicted but not yet sentenced, the evidence may be quite important in assessing the witness' credibility.

I have suggested that when a court weighs the probative value of evidence against such factors as delay, confusion, or waste of time, it should, in a close case, be reluctant to exclude the evidence if the

action and a more complex problem which exists because the defendant's record may have played a part in the decision to arrest and prosecute him. This latter problem will be discussed when I treat certain issues raised by the fact that evidence introduced at a trial is often not independent of other evidence introduced or of those factors that led the accused to be brought to trial in the first place. *See* text at notes 68-70 *infra*.

49. For example, in the famous "brides of the bath" case evidence of other drownings appeared highly probative on the issue of whether the drowning for which the defendant was tried was accidental. *See* NOTABLE BRITISH TRIALS, TRIAL OF GEORGE JOSEPH SMITH (E. Watson ed. 1922).

50. This rule might be explained as an historical anomaly or attributed to the tradition of not distinguishing for evidentiary purposes between defendants and other witnesses. A possible contemporary justification is that there may be a high probability that the truth will be distorted by anyone testifying in his own defense in a criminal case. This probability may justify putting a price on the decision to take the stand. But if the price—admission of evidence of previous criminal convictions—has no independent relevance on the issue of credibility, it does not seem fair that it be exacted only from those who have prior criminal records. If defendants without prior records are less likely to lie from the stand, but only because they are less likely to have committed the offense charged and so less likely to need to lie, the evidence is really relevant only for its bearing on character and the relationship of character to criminal activity, a purpose for which evidence of other crimes is generally not admitted.

likelihood ratio is much different from 1:1.[51] One can easily imagine cases where evidence with a likelihood ratio of 2:1 or even lower would properly tip the balance.[52] A court should be more willing to exclude probative evidence when it poses the danger of prejudice. It is easy to imagine evidence that might change a juror's regret matrix from the one that is arguably normative in criminal cases, *i.e.*, where mistakenly convicting generates ten times as much regret as mistakenly acquitting, to one in which the regret associated with these two mistakes is approximately the same.[53] In a close case, a change in juror regret of this magnitude could be devastating. Thus, a court is justified in excluding highly prejudicial evidence even if its probative value is substantial. However, it appears from the appellate cases that trial courts often refuse to exclude probative but prejudicial evidence. So long as the probative value of the admitted evidence is clear, appellate courts usually affirm such trial court decisions without attempting to weigh prejudicial effect against probative value.

II. Relaxing the Simplifying Assumptions in the Application of Bayes' Theorem

A. *Cumulative and Redundant Evidence*

Two simplifying assumptions are implicit in the portion of the preceding discussion that relies on Bayes' Theorem: (1) that the probative value of a given item of evidence may be determined with-

51. *See* text at note 34 *supra*.

52. If, for example, the prior odds in favor of the defendant's negligence were 3:5, a juror after receiving evidence supporting the defendant's negligence with a likelihood ratio of 2:1 would conclude that the odds were 6:5 that the defendant was negligent. Odds of 3:5 require a verdict for the defendant, while odds of 6:5 require a verdict for the plaintiff.

53. At this point, the analytic utility of the model does depend on the degree to which it represents, at least schematically, the actual behavior of jurors. It is possible that jurors can hear evidence that affects the regret they associate with possible verdicts yet neither distort the burden of proof as presented in the court's instructions nor make compensating distortions in their evaluation of the weight of the evidence. A juror's statement, "I would have preferred to convict the defendant, but given the evidence and the judge's charge I felt obligated to vote for acquittal" is not logically inconsistent, nor is it necessarily hypocritical. I believe that some jurors some of the time can separate their judgments about the desirability of convicting an accused from their obligation to render a fair verdict in accordance with the law and that many jurors most of the time can discount to some degree their own preferences in deciding a case. The discounting will not, however, be complete and in some cases may not occur at all. If these empirical hunches are correct, the situation depicted in the text may be rarer than one might intuitively guess, but it will occur, although frequently at levels of prejudice not as great as that suggested by the example.

out considering the other evidence in the case, and (2) that the reliability of evidence is not open to dispute. Relaxing these assumptions brings the Bayesian model into closer accord with the actualities of litigation and increases its utility as a heuristic device. The hypothetical trial that was the focus of the earlier Bayesian analysis consisted of only one item of evidence. Jurors receiving this evidence were expected to revise their odds on the defendant's guilt in light of the likelihood ratio, $\frac{P(E|G)}{P(E|\text{not-}G)}$. The likelihood ratio was used to explain the meaning of logical relevance and to explicate some of the concerns that courts have when dealing with problems of relevance.

Extending this model to trials involving two or more items of evidence would be straightforward if the revised odds of guilt after considering one item of evidence could be taken as the prior odds when considering the next item of evidence.[54] The extension is not this simple. Let us call the first item of evidence E_1, the second item E_2. Using $O(G|E_1)$, the odds on guilt arrived at after evaluating E_1, as the odds on guilt existing before receipt of E_2 generally yields incorrect results except in the special case where E_2 is conditionally independent of E_1 with respect to the hypothesis of interest—*i.e.*, except where $P(E_1 \& E_2|G) = P(E_1|G) \cdot P(E_2|G)$ and $P(E_1 \& E_2|\text{not-}G) = P(E_1|\text{not-}G) \cdot P(E_2|\text{not-}G)$.[55] These equations will not both be satisfied where part of the information conveyed by the presence of E_1 is taken into account when the implications of E_2 are evaluated.

54. The equations suggested by this straightforward extension, which in the general case is *not* correct, are

$$O(G|E_1) = \frac{P(E_1|G)}{P(E_1|\text{not-}G)} \cdot O(G)$$

$$O(G|E_2) = \frac{P(E_2|G)}{P(E_2|\text{not-}G)} \cdot O(G|E_1)$$

$$\vdots$$

$$O(G|E_n) = \frac{P(E_n|G)}{P(E_n|\text{not-}G)} \cdot O(G|E_{n-1})$$

where the first item of evidence is E_1, the second item is E_2, and the last item is E_n.

55. There are special cases where the chaining procedure illustrated in note 54 *supra* will yield correct results in the absence of conditional independence; *e.g.*, where $P(E_1|G)>0$ and $P(E_2|G) = 0$.

An extreme example of redundant evidence should provide a clear illustration of why the straightforward extension of the Bayesian model is improper. Suppose in a murder case the factfinder at some point estimates the odds on the defendant's guilt as 1:100. The evidence that follows proves that the defendant's thumb print was found on the gun the killer used. The print of an innocent man might be found on a murder weapon because he handled the gun before or after the murder or because the print was planted there with the intention of framing him. Nevertheless, evidence of the print is surely more consistent with the hypothesis that the defendant is guilty than with its opposite. For the sake of this example assume that the factfinder believes that the presence of this evidence is 500 times more likely if the defendant is guilty than if he is not guilty.[56] Multiplying the prior odds of 1:100 by this likelihood ratio of 500 gives new odds on guilt of 5:1. Now suppose the prosecution wished to introduce evidence proving that a print matching the defendant's index finger was found on the murder weapon. If this were the only fingerprint evidence in the case, it would lead the factfinder to increase his estimated odds on the defendant's guilt to the same degree that proof of the thumb print did. Yet, it is intuitively obvious that another five hundredfold increase is not justified when evidence of the thumb print has already been admitted. This intuition is justified because having found the defendant's thumb print on the weapon, the probability of finding a print of the defendant's index finger if the defendant is guilty is not very different from the probability of finding this evidence if the defendant is not guilty. Thus, given the evidence of the thumb print, the likelihood ratio for the second fingerprint is approximately one.[57]

56. A mathematically inclined juror might, for example, believe that there is a .2 probability that the print would be found if the defendant were guilty (the probability is considerably less than one because guilty people often have taken the trouble to wipe their prints from weapons and, even if they had not, not all prints are identifiable) and a .0004 probability that the evidence would be found if the defendant were not guilty. Note that later evidence, suggesting a plausible reason why the defendant, although innocent, might have left his prints on the gun, could substantially increase this probability, thus leading the juror to reduce substantially the probative weight accorded this evidence.

57. The presence of the second print depends largely on the way the defendant held the gun when he left the thumb print. Unless murderers hold guns differently than nonmurderers or are more likely to wipe off some but not all their fingerprints, the finding of the second print is no more consistent with the hypothesis that the defendant is guilty than with its opposite. Indeed, because a murderer is more likely to attempt to wipe off fingerprints from a gun than one with no apprehension of being linked to a murder and since an attempt to wipe off fingerprints might be only partially successful, there is a plausible argument that the presence of the second print should lead jurors to be somewhat less confident that the defendant is the murderer than they would be if only one of the defendant's fingerprints were found.

Where items of evidence are not independent, the simplest way to apply the variant of Bayes' Theorem that we have been using is to treat the interdependent evidence as a single event when calculating the likelihood ratio. Thus for any two items of interdependent evidence the likelihood ratio equals:

$$\frac{P(E_1 \& E_2|G)}{P(E_1 \& E_2|\text{not-}G)}$$ [58]

This procedure, conceptualizing two items of evidence as a single item, may be generalized to account for interdependence among any number of items of evidence, generating a likelihood ratio of the form:

$$\frac{P(E_1 \& E_2 \& \ldots \& E_n|G)}{P(E_1 \& E_2 \& \ldots \& E_n|\text{not-}G)}$$

Since the analysis for more than two items of evidence is basically the same as for two items, this article will focus on the two-item case to simplify the discussion.

Extending the model in this way makes it a useful device for exploring ways in which evidence may be cumulative. An item of evidence, E_2, introduced after some other item, E_1, is properly considered cumulative and may be excludable for that reason when the ratio $\frac{P(E_1|G)}{P(E_1|\text{not-}G)}$ is identical with or very close to the ratio

$$\frac{P(E_1 \& E_2|G)}{P(E_1 \& E_2|\text{not-}G)}.$$

Where this condition is met, consideration of the second item of evidence, E_2, adds little or nothing to what may be learned from the proper consideration of the first item, E_1.

Another variant of Bayes' Theorem, expressing the chance of guilt in terms of probabilities rather than odds, is helpful in specifying when the likelihood ratio for E_1 will be close to or identical with the likelihood ratio for E_1 and E_2 taken together. For the case where there are two pieces of evidence, Bayes' Theorem may be expressed as:

58. This likelihood ratio is correct for any two items of evidence, whether or not they are interdependent. However, where the items are conditionally independent, this ratio will be equal to the product

$$\frac{P(E_1|G)}{P(E_1|\text{not-}G)} \cdot \frac{P(E_2|G)}{P(E_2|\text{not-}G)}$$

This result follows immediately from the equations in the text at note 55 *supra*. When the items are conditionally independent, the extension of the Bayesian model suggested in note 54 *supra* is appropriate.

$$P(G|E_1 \& E_2) = \frac{P(E_2|G \& E_1)}{P(E_2|E_1)} \cdot P(G|E_1)^{59} \qquad (4)$$

When the ratio $\frac{P(E_2|G \& E_1)}{P(E_2|E_1)}$ equals or is close to one the likelihood ratios for E_1 and for E_1 and E_2 taken together are identical or virtually so.[60] This situation exists when E_2 adds little if any information concerning the probability of the defendant's guilt to that which was provided by E_1. In these circumstances the likelihood of finding the second item of evidence, E_2, depends upon the relationship between E_2 and E_1 rather than on whether the defendant is guilty. In the example of the fingerprints, once it is known that the defendant's thumb print was left on the gun the estimated probability of finding another of the defendant's fingerprints there will not change with knowledge of the defendant's guilt. The reason for this is that finding the thumb print related to the defendant's guilt only insofar as it proved that the defendant handled the gun, and finding another fingerprint relates to the defendant's guilt in exactly the same way. Since the second print proves a fact already established it is redundant.

A second situation in which $\frac{P(E_2|G \& E_1)}{P(E_2|E_1)}$ equals one is when E_1 is sufficient to establish G, since where this is true, knowing E_1

---

59. This variant of the Theorem is derived through successive applications of equations (1) and (3) of note 12 *supra*:

$$P(G|E_1\&E_2) = \frac{P(G)\cdot P(E_1\&E_2|G)}{P(E_1\&E_2)} = \frac{P(G\&E_1\&E_2)}{P(E_1\&E_2)} = \frac{P(G\&E_1)\cdot P(E_2|G\&E_1)}{P(E_1\&E_2)} = \frac{P(E_1)\cdot P(G|E_1)\cdot P(E_2|G\&E_1)}{P(E_1)\cdot P(E_2|E_1)} = \frac{P(E_2|G\&E_1)\cdot P(G|E_1)}{P(E_2|E_1)}$$

60. Where $\frac{P(E_2|G \& E_1)}{P(E_2|E_1)} = 1$, the formula in the text at note 59 *supra* indicates that $P(G|E_1 \& E_2) = P(G|E_1)$. Application of equation (3) in note 12 *supra* results in

$$\frac{P(E_1 \& E_2|G)\cdot P(G)}{P(E_1 \& E_2)} = \frac{P(E_1|G)\cdot P(G)}{P(E_1)}$$

which can be shown to imply

$$\frac{P(E_1 \& E_2|G)}{P(E_1 \& E_2|\text{not-}G)} = \frac{P(E_1|G)}{P(E_1|\text{not-}G)}$$

i.e., the likelihood ratios are identical when

$$\frac{P(E_2|G \& E_1)}{P(E_2|E_1)} = 1.$$

means that one also knows G.[61] Thus, the numerator and denominator of the ratio are identical.

The Bayesian analysis demonstrates that where the likelihood ratios for E_1 and for E_1 and E_2 taken together are identical or virtually so, consideration of the second item of evidence adds little or nothing to what may be learned from a proper evaluation of the first item. Nevertheless, there are situations in which a court should admit evidence that is analytically cumulative in this sense. The first such situation is where it is possible that the jury does not appreciate fully the information conveyed by the first item of evidence. For example, suppose that a gynecologist was accused of participating in a criminal abortion. Evidence that cervical dilators, instruments used with any of the standard techniques of early abortion, were found in the gynecologist's office would be cumulative once the defendant's profession was shown, for the ordinary practice of gynecology requires a physician to have these instruments available. However, the jury might not realize that all gynecologists have access to cervical dilators, so the prosecution should be allowed to introduce evidence showing access in the particular case. In Bayesian terms, $P(E_2|G \ \& \ E_1)$, the probability of finding E_2 (evidence of the dilators), would be perceived as one if the defendant were guilty and a gynecologist (E_1), but $P(E_2|E_1)$, the probability of finding the dilators knowing only that the defendant was a gynecologist, would be misperceived as less than one. Thus, a juror would attach different values to the ratios $\frac{P(E_1|G)}{P(E_1|\text{not-}G)}$ and $\frac{P(E_1 \ \& \ E_2|G)}{P(E_1 \ \& \ E_2|\text{not-}G)}$ so the evidence of the dilators would not be perceived as cumulative in the context of the case.

There is, however, the danger that admitting evidence of the cervical dilators would raise another estimation problem. Jurors who know little about gynecology might not find evidence of the defendant's profession very probative of guilt, but they might find the defendant's possession of the cervical dilators highly so. In this situation, the defense counsel must attempt to put the evidence in context by showing the uses of these instruments in the ordinary practice of gynecology. If both the prosecution and the defense counsel do

61. As a practical matter one may point to a third situation where courts may be justified in rejecting evidence as cumulative even though this ratio does not equal one. This is where E_1, although not sufficient to establish G to a certainty, is sufficient to increase the probability of G far beyond what is required for conviction beyond a reasonable doubt. The discussion of the second situation described in the text applies generally to this third situation, also.

their jobs properly, the jurors should be able to estimate the true probative value of the evidence that the defendant is a gynecologist, and they should realize that once this fact is taken into account the defendant's possession of cervical dilators adds nothing.

A second situation in which cumulative evidence should be admitted is where the jury expects that the evidence will be produced if it exists. The absence of evidence conveys information to the jury, and it is possible for the proven availability of evidence to be cumulative while its proven unavailability has considerable probative value. In these circumstances cumulative evidence should be admissible, despite slight probative value, in order to dispel the implication that it is unavailable. An example should make this clear. Consider a murder trial in which the following facts have been established and weighed by the jurors in setting their odds on guilt: (1) the victim was killed by a shotgun, and (2) the killer is a resident of a particular community, 99% of whose residents have access to shotguns. Once E_1, that the defendant is a resident of the suspect community, has been established, the further evidence E_2, that the defendant has access to a shotgun, does little to increase the estimated probability of the defendant's guilt. Since it is certain that the defendant will have access to a shotgun if he is both the killer and a resident of the suspect community, and there is a .99 probability that he will have access to a shotgun if he is a resident of the community, the Bayesian equation is[62]

$$P(G|E_1 \& E_2) = \frac{1.0}{.99} \cdot P(G|E_1).$$

Thus, specific evidence that a shotgun was available to the defendant raises the previously estimated probability of the defendant's guilt by only about one per cent. Yet failure to introduce evidence of ownership might harm the prosecution's case, since the jury might treat the absence of such evidence as a fact having probative value. Indeed, for a juror who was certain that the prosecution would introduce evidence of the defendant's access to a shotgun if the defendant had access, the lack of evidence would be reason to acquit, for E_2 would be "evidence of no access" and the appropriate equation would be

$$P(G|E_1 \& E_2) = \frac{0}{.01} \cdot P(G|E_1).$$

62. Equation (4), the variant of Bayes' Theorem developed in the text at note 59 *supra*, is used here.

Thus, whatever the prior odds of guilt, the failure to produce evidence of access is exonerative. A juror with this perspective would be confused, for the prosecution's failure to show that the defendant is a shotgun owner is not equivalent to proof by the defendant that he is not. Nevertheless, some jurors might be confused in this way. Furthermore, failure to prove ownership is more consistent with the hypothesis that the defendant is not guilty than with its opposite, so even a juror who was not confused would be justified in lowering his odds on the defendant's guilt if the defendant's ownership of a shotgun were not shown. The lesson of this example is that there are times when a party may properly insist on the admission of cumulative evidence in order to dispel unwarranted inferences about its unavailability.

Ordinarily the admission of cumulative evidence will not be reversible error, since cumulative evidence by definition does not affect the rational factfinder's judgment of the odds on the defendant's guilt. Indeed, if the costs of presenting cumulative evidence are not great, the decision to allow cumulative evidence is often wise. Modes of proving the same fact differ in the degree to which they command attention and in the likelihood that they will be understood. Thus a juror might appreciate the implications of certain evidence without realizing that the information conveyed by that evidence was implicit in earlier proof. Of course, when a fact is being proved for a fifth or sixth time the benefits of redundancy are likely to be low.

The admission of cumulative evidence may be reversible error where the evidence is prejudicial. Since cumulative evidence ordinarily is not needed to establish a point, its probative value will be outweighed by even a slight possibility of prejudice.[63] However, the problem a trial judge faces is not as simple as this analysis might suggest, for evidence that appears cumulative when offered may not appear cumulative after the opposing side has cross-examined a witness or presented its case. One solution is to require the opposing party to stipulate to the proposition that the evidence tends to establish before excluding it as cumulative. Another solution is temporarily to exclude the evidence, subject to an opportunity to reoffer it if later evidence suggests that it is not, in fact, cumulative. Where

63. If the evidence is cumulative (in the sense that it is further proof of something that has been indisputably established) on the ultimate issue in the case (*e.g.*, guilt) rather than on some constituent fact, a mistaken decision to admit prejudicial evidence should be harmless error, since even without the evidence a reasonable jury would not have reached a different conclusion.

the potential for prejudice is substantial rather than slight, outright exclusion is often justified.

Special problems exist where several items of evidence persuasively prove the same fact and nothing more. In this situation courts are well advised to allow proof only by the least prejudicial evidence even though the evidence first offered to prove a fact cannot be considered cumulative. Many courts, however, are reluctant to interfere with a party's chosen mode of proof. Thus, in homicide cases prosecutors have been allowed to prove the fact of the victim's death by gory photographs despite the availability of less emotive testimony or, even, a stipulation.[64] This reluctance to interfere with a party's preferred form of proof exists even when the preferred proof follows the admission of less prejudicial evidence and so is clearly cumulative. Evidence of other crimes, for example, has been received for its bearing on issues not actually in dispute or on facts provable by the overwhelming weight of other evidence.[65]

Several of the relevance rules may be justified, in part, because the evidence they exclude is likely to be either cumulative or of low probative value. Evidence of subsequent repairs, for example, is by rule inadmissible on the issue of negligence.[66] Even if this evidence generally has some tendency to prove negligence, the rule of exclusion is unlikely to harm deserving plaintiffs. Where the defendant was, in fact, negligent, other more probative evidence is likely to be available. Thus, in a typical well-founded negligence action, evidence of subsequent repairs is likely to be cumulative on the central issue. On the other hand, where the only evidence of negligence is a subsequent repair, it is unlikely that the plaintiff had a valid claim to begin with since the probability of finding this evidence and no other is probably less in the case of negligent defendants than in the case of nonnegligent defendants.[67]

---

64. Courts differ in this respect. Some cases do hold that it is an abuse of discretion to admit potentially prejudicial evidence when a party has offered to stipulate to everything that evidence might legitimately be admitted to prove. *See, e.g.*, Note, *Inflammatory Photographs: How Sensitive Are Texas Courts to Unfair Prejudice?*, 29 BAYLOR L. REV. 154 (1977).

65. *See, e.g.*, State v. Goldberg, 261 N.C. 181, 134 S.E.2d 334, *cert. denied*, 377 U.S. 978 (1964).

66. FED. R. EVID. 407.

67. Even if this is the case, one might ask why evidence of subsequent repairs should be excluded, since this type of evidence is not likely to prove prejudicial. My answer is that this rule, like most of the relevance rules, has multiple justifications. I believe the likelihood of low relevance is crucial because it frees courts to look at other considerations. In the case of the rule regarding subsequent repairs, the classic other justification is that the decision to admit such evidence would be

When evidence is excludable as cumulative, the factfinder has considered all of its relevant informational content in his weighing of other evidence. It is also possible for evidence to be in some degree redundant without being so redundant as to be cumulative. Evidence of this sort is admissible subject to the court's ordinary discretion to weigh probative value against such factors as prejudice, confusion, and waste of time. The major danger in admitting partially redundant evidence is the possibility of an estimation problem: the jurors may not appreciate the redundancy; thus they might give the evidence more weight than it deserves.

Recall that the Bayesian model presumes that the factfinder approaches new items of evidence with some estimate of the prior odds that the defendant is guilty. These odds change as relevant evidence is received, and each subsequent item of evidence is evaluated with respect to the most recent estimate of the prior odds. When evidence is cumulative or redundant, part or all of the informational content of the evidence has been considered in setting the odds that exist prior to the receipt of that evidence. In this situation, it is the task of counsel to put the evidence in its proper context, one that suggests the evidence is not as persuasive as it might otherwise appear. Otherwise there is the likelihood that certain aspects of the evidence will be counted twice.

When separate items of evidence are introduced the possibility of redundancy is generally clear. What may not be obvious is that information conveyed by an item of evidence may be redundant even though previous evidence conveying that information has not been received. If the Bayesian model approximates the process by which people evaluate evidence, a factfinder must begin with the belief that there is some chance that the defendant is guilty because once the estimated prior odds on guilt are zero no amount of subsequent evidence, however persuasive, will change the rational factfinder's evaluation of those odds. One might argue that the presumption of innocence means that at the commencement of a case the factfinder's estimated odds on guilt should be one to whatever figure represents

---

harmful because it would discourage the making of repairs after accidents. Elsewhere I suggest that this justification is vulnerable to criticism because of the assumption it makes about knowledge of the rule. There I suggest another possible justification: recognition that a defendant who has repaired a hazardous condition has taken a socially responsible action and should not be made to suffer, or even to appear to suffer, for this. Evidence of subsequent repairs is admissible on issues other than negligence because as its relevance becomes greater such delicate considerations as this one must give way to the need to get at the truth. *See* R. LEMPERT & S. SALTZBURG, *supra* note 8, at 186-89.

the size of the relevant population from which the defendant came.[68] However, the little empirical evidence that exists suggests that jurors begin with much higher estimated odds on guilt, sometimes as high as 1:1.[69] In part, this is because jurors quite rationally assume that the defendant would not be before them if there were not special reasons to suspect him of the crime. Where this assumption has played a part in setting the initial odds, some part of the evidence that was crucial to the police's decision to arrest and the prosecution's decision to proceed to trial has been implicitly counted against the defendant before its presentation to the jury. Since it is not clear how much double counting has occurred or which evidence is most likely to be redundant, controlling for this possibility is difficult, if not impossible.[70]

One class of evidence poses special dangers of double counting. This category consists of evidence that relates more strongly to the probability that the defendant would be arrested than to the probability that he committed the crime in question. Most likely to fall into this category is evidence relating to the defendant's prior record. When the perpetrator of a crime is unknown, police commonly focus their attention on individuals known to have committed similar crimes in the past. Furthermore, when a photographic identifica-

---

68. John Kaplan has suggested that from a normative perspective the prior odds on a defendant's guilt should be one to about 200,000,000, since that is the approximate population of this country. Kaplan, *supra* note 7, at 1085-86. If a juror began with these prior odds, he would be justified in revising them drastically downward upon receipt of evidence proving such facts as the defendant's age, if it were such as to indicate that the defendant was capable of committing the crime; the defendant's place of residence, if it placed him in a locale convenient to the commission of the crime; the defendant's race, if the criminal had been identified by race and the defendant was of the criminal's race; etc. More realistic prior odds would probably take these kinds of factors as implicit in the defendant's arrest and thus be set at one to whatever figure represents the number of people possessing those gross characteristics that were virtually certain to characterize anyone arrested for the crime.

69. *See, e.g.*, Weld & Roff, *supra* note 16, at 617.

70. It is unclear how great a danger exists, since the extent of the danger depends upon the way jurors in fact behave. Even though jurors will report a prior probability of guilt to researchers after hearing an indictment read, *see id.* at 617, this may be a very tentatively held prior probability, subject to revision after some evidence has been presented. Also, jurors may treat a failure to produce evidence as itself evidence, *see* text following note 62 *supra*, particularly where an assumption about the availability of that evidence entered into the initial estimation of the prior odds. Finally, certain evidence that entered into the estimation of the initial prior probability may be received by the jury during the course of the trial without resulting in double counting. For example, a juror may say that he did not increase his estimate of the defendant's guilt upon learning that the defendant's race, sex, or hair color matched those of the criminal because he assumed that the police would not have arrested anyone unless these characteristics were consistent with the known characteristics of the criminal.

tion is sought, photos may be available only for persons with criminal records. These considerations suggest further support for the rule excluding evidence of past crimes where the evidence is relevant only insofar as it suggests the defendant has a propensity toward crime. Such evidence is likely to be redundant because it probably has influenced the decisions to arrest and prosecute and so has figured in the jurors' initial estimation of the odds on the defendant's guilt. Even if jurors could be made aware of the way in which this type of evidence enters into their initial estimation of the odds on guilt, the task of separating the redundant portion of such evidence from the nonredundant poses an insoluble estimation problem. Thus, there is sense in the prevailing view that evidence of other crimes should be dealt with by a rule of exclusion rather than on an ad hoc basis.

B. *Reliability of Evidence*

In determining whether evidence is redundant to the point of being cumulative, attention must be paid to the source of the evidence as well as to its substantive content. Thus far the discussion has taken the reliability of evidence as given and has assumed that the rational factfinder's only task is to compare the probability that certain facts could be proved if the defendant were guilty with the probability that the same facts could be proved if the defendant were innocent. The oversimplification is obvious. The jury does not typically hear proof of facts; rather, it hears testimony tending to prove certain facts or receives evidence that arguably bears on the case but is not indisputably linked to it. Upon hearing testimony, jurors must compare the probability that the testimony *would be given* if the defendant were guilty with the probability that the testimony *would be given* if the defendant were innocent. This comparison involves an estimate of the reliability of the testimony as well as an estimate of the probative worth of the facts that the evidence tends to prove.

Because the jury is faced with this twofold task, impeachment evidence serves an important function. The likelihood ratio based on the facts that the testimony tends to prove sets the upper bound on the probative value of that testimony. Any evidence suggesting that the testimony may be inaccurate will lead a factfinder to decrease his estimated likelihood ratio.[71] Cross-examination holds its

71. Rarely will impeachment evidence be such that the likelihood ratio for the impeached testimony dips below 1:1 on the hypothesis that the facts that the testimony tends to prove are true. Thus, the general rule that a party may not rely solely on the jury's disbelief of an opposing witness to prove an element in his case is a sound one. It should also be noted that an argument analogous to that in the text applies where the authenticity of real evidence is in dispute.

exalted place in the Anglo-American system of trial procedure because it is thought to be an effective means for exploring the possible inaccuracies of testimony and, hence, a valuable aid to rational factfinding.

Since human error is always possible when witnesses report events, it is rarely if ever proper for a court to exclude the testimony of one witness as cumulative simply because another witness has testified to the same fact. At some point, however, similar testimony by additional witnesses will be cumulative. That point will depend upon the degree to which the testimony of earlier witnesses has been challenged and the way in which different testimony is vulnerable. If the testimony of several witnesses has not been challenged, little reason exists for allowing other witnesses to testify to the same point.[72] Where the testimony of earlier witnesses has been challenged, the testimony of later witnesses is unlikely to be cumulative unless open to identical challenge.

As an illustration, consider the likelihood ratio:

$$\frac{P(T_1 \& T_2 \& \ldots \& T_n|G)}{P(T_1 \& T_2 \& \ldots \& T_n|\text{not-}G)}$$

where T_1, T_2, . . . , T_n is testimony from a series of witnesses, W_1, W_2, . . . , W_n. Let us suppose this testimony identifies the defendant as a car thief. If W_1 knew the defendant well but was embroiled in a family feud with him, the factfinder might, after hearing vigorous cross-examination, believe that the likelihood ratio for T_1 taken alone was close to one. W_1 would surely accuse the defendant of theft if he knew the defendant was guilty, but, because of his family's feud with the defendant, he might be almost as likely

72. A potential problem exists because a party might, without overtly challenging opposing testimony, introduce his own witnesses to contradict that testimony. As a practical matter, however, it is unlikely that a party who wished to dispute the story of opposing witnesses would entirely forgo cross-examination.

The desire to avoid cumulative testimony does suggest one justification for the rule forbidding certain types of impeachment by extrinsic evidence unless a foundation has been laid on cross-examination. The knowledge that a party intends to impeach particular witnesses aids a court in determining whether further testimony along certain lines is likely to be cumulative. I do not suggest that this justification, either alone or in combination with other justifications, is sufficient to override the case that can be made for dispensing with a foundation in some of the situations where the common law now requires one. For example, the rule requiring that a witness be confronted with his earlier inconsistent statements before the statements may be proved extrinsically certainly undercuts some of the dramatic force of impeachment. Whether the jury gets a better picture of the witness' trustworthiness from seeing the witness react to an inconsistent statement before it is proved extrinsically or whether they form a more accurate judgment by hearing the statement subject to the witness' later opportunity to explain or deny it is an empirical question. I feel less confident that I know the answer to this question than many who have written on this subject.

to accuse the defendant if the defendant was innocent. If W_2, W_3, and W_4 were members of W_1's family who claimed to have witnessed the same theft, their testimony would be vulnerable in the same way as W_1's testimony and thus add little to the prosecution's case. This additional testimony would not be completely irrelevant because the fear of prosecution for perjury and the innate honesty of the four witnesses might differ, even though they all shared the same interest in seeing the defendant convicted. However, at some point the court would be justified in heeding the defendant's argument that there was little more to be learned from further identification by other members of W_1's family. The jury is likely to have reached a judgment about the probability that everyone in W_1's family would accuse the defendant of theft if he was guilty and about the probability that there would be a similar unanimity of accusation if the defendant was innocent. Further accusations from other family members are unlikely to change this judgment.

On the other hand, the testimony of a second witness who had no quarrel with the defendant but was nearsighted, of a third who caught only a fleeting glimpse of the defendant, and of a fourth who had seen the defendant for about a minute but had a poor memory for faces would not be cumulative, or even redundant, except in its tendency to prove the identity of the car thief. Even if the testimony of each of these witnesses, taken alone, has little probative value because of its peculiar weaknesses, the testimony of all four witnesses has substantial probative value since the probability of the same mistake being made by four witnesses with such different reasons to err appears small.[73] To generalize, where the testimony of two or more witnesses tends to prove the same fact, the relevance of the later testimony will be greater (1) the less the apparent reliability of the earlier testimony and (2) the greater the variability in the reasons for doubting the stories of the different witnesses.[74]

---

73. It is also the case that in balancing relevance against the potential for prejudice, confusion, or waste of time, a court should weigh the evidence in the context of other evidence in the case rather than as a discrete item. Sometimes the evidence will be less relevant when taken in context while on other occasions it will be more so.

74. This argument applies as well when only real evidence is involved or when a combination of real evidence and testimony is presented. For example, where a series of crimes has occurred that is so distinctive that the same individual almost certainly committed all of them, the relevance of the other-crimes evidence will depend upon the strength of the evidence linking the defendant to each crime and the independence of this evidence for each crime. If, for example, it was proved that all the crimes were committed with the same gun and the defendant was arrested

This analysis suggests strategies for seeking and presenting evidence. In attempting to prove a disputable point, an attorney should seek items of evidence that do not share the same sources of possible unreliability. In attempting to destroy an opponent's case, counsel should strive to show that the evidence of the opponent is infected from a common source. In the hypothetical case of the car thief presented above, the prosecutor should, after finding several members of W_1's family willing to testify against the defendant, expend his limited resources searching out witnesses who are not members of W_1's family rather than looking for more witnesses who are parties to this feud. A defense counsel faced with a varied array of identification witnesses should try to show that their identifications share a possible source of error, as would be the case if before identifying the defendant each witness had been shown the defendant's picture and told that the police thought he was the thief. In an attempt to establish a common source of error, counsel offers an explanation for the testimonial coincidence other than the fact that the witneses are all responding to the same initial stimulus.

III. Conclusion

I assert in the introduction that mathematics, as a language, can help clarify those legal rules that involve the weighing of evidence in an essentially probabilistic fashion. This article proceeds on the assumption that the rules relating to relevance are such rules. I believe this to be the case, but I also believe that there are aspects of, and justifications for, the relevance rules that have nothing to do with the rational evaluation of evidence. As with almost any other area of law, values that defy quantification must be attended to in

with that gun in his possession but charged only with the last of the series of crimes, evidence of the earlier crimes would be irrelevant on the issue of whether the defendant committed the crime charged. Whatever excuse the defendant could give concerning his possession of the gun (*e.g.*, he had recently bought it from a friend) would, if accepted, destroy the link between the defendant and each of the other crimes. The evidence of other crimes would, however, be prejudicial, since the jury might regret the mistake of acquitting one who, if guilty of any crime, is guilty of several, more than they would regret the mistake of acquitting one thought to have committed at most one crime. If, on the other hand, the defendant was linked to the other crimes by the identification testimony of different victims, the evidence of the other crimes would be relevant. Even if the defendant could show weaknesses in the testimony of one of these witnesses, it is unlikely that he could show that the testimony of all the witnesses was incredible or was vulnerable to the same objection. Prejudice would still exist here, but there would be substantial probative value since, by hypothesis, it is reasonably certain that the same person is responsible for all of the crimes. Thus the prejudicial impact of this evidence might be outweighed by its probative value, and a court might be justified in admitting it.

analyzing relevance. Any mathematical treatment is necessarily limited.

The mathematical models used in this article do not by themselves answer fundamental policy questions. Their purpose is to stimulate insight and to aid in the clear and concise explication of what is perceived. Although I do not think that jurors in actual cases should be urged to use Bayesian calculations in evaluating evidence, nevertheless, I believe the approach taken here is of more than strictly academic interest. Whatever enables lawyers to think more clearly is of practical importance. When faced with difficult problems of relevance or harmless error, attorneys may find that the models presented aid in thinking about the implications of admitting certain evidence. Using the models requires specification of the probabilities that make up the likelihood ratio for the evidence and a determination of possible prejudicial impact. It may also require attorneys to estimate the jury's likely evaluation of the evidence and the probative value of the other evidence in the case. Typically it will be impossible to obtain general agreement on the specific values to be incorporated into the mathematical analysis, but it may be possible to gain agreement on upper or lower bounds for these measures. If either model suggests that an argument is valid when the values incorporated into the model are at the extreme least favorable to the claim advanced, the argument is almost certain to be valid for the evidence in the case. Where this is so, an attorney has a precise and powerful means of arguing to any judge who can be persuaded to think in terms of these models.

Much of the analysis in this article does not depend upon the extent to which the models used portray the ways in which jurors actually respond to evidence. The Bayesian model is normative—it specifies the way in which jurors are expected to evaluate evidence—and values may be inserted into the regret matrix that are arguably normative. Since these models describe the behavior of the ideal legal factfinder, they allow us to evaluate aspects of legal factfinding in terms of the ideal as well as to speculate on how actual factfinding deviates from the ideal. At some points, however, the argument does depend on the degree to which these models portray actual juror behavior. This was typically the case where I went beyond explanation and drew on these models to suggest how courts *should* respond to certain kinds of evidence. We do not know the extent to which jurors process evidence in a Bayesian fashion, nor do we know precisely how jurors are influenced by the regret that they are likely to associate with alternative verdicts. These are important areas for further research.[75] If empirical research should reveal that jurors act, more or less, as the two models suggest, the utility of approaches like the one taken in this article will be substantially enhanced.

75. For a recent review of some of the literature on people as decision makers, see Slovic, Fischhoff, & Lichtenstein, *Behavioral Decision Theory*, 28 ANN. REV. PSYCH. 1 (1977).

[2]

A RECONCEPTUALIZATION OF CIVIL TRIALS†

RONALD J. ALLEN*

The last two decades have seen an explosion of creative effort directed a the twin tasks of explicating the nature of the reasoning process employed by factfinders at trials and relating that process of reasoning to the rules governing the trial of disputes. Working primarily from the assumption that some form of conventional probability theory[1] must at least roughly describe the nature of the relevant reasoning process, theorists have created models of rationality for factfinders that rely heavily on ideas of conventional probability. This process commenced in earnestness among legal scholars approximately twenty years ago with Professor John Kaplan's demonstration that a decisionmaker could accommodate the ambiguity that permeates the normal trial of a civil dispute by employing the approach to evidentiary matters that is integral to Bayes's Theorem.[2] In addition, he demonstrated through the application of simple decision theory models how rules of decision could be derived that incorporate preferences and perceptions of utility of either the decisionmaker or of the larger society of which the decisionmaker is part.[3]

In the last two decades, a substantial literature has investigated the implications of conventional probability for the trial of civil disputes. For example, the implications of Bayesian theory have been explored in detail by

---

* Professor of Law, Northwestern University. I am greatly indebted to Professors Peter Tillers, of the New England School of Law, David Schum, of George Mason University, David Kaye, of the Arizona State University College of Law, Reid Hastie, of Northwestern University, and Michael Green and Serena Stier of the University of Iowa College of Law, for having read and commented on an earlier draft of this article. In addition, I had the pleasure of, and learned a considerable amount from, delivering this paper at Faculty Workshops at Northwestern University School of Law and Cornell Law School. In both instances, I received valuable suggestions from too many individuals to name.

1 I refer to any form of axiomatic probability theory, such as Pascalian or classical probability, as "conventional." The points I intend to make here are applicable no matter which axiomatic theory is viewed as analytically superior or as better capturing what occurs in litigation. *See* L. COHEN, THE PROBABLE AND THE PROVABLE 116 (1977) ("The paradoxes . . . are common to all normal formulations of the Pascalian calculus.").

2 *See* Kaplan, *Decision Theory and the Factfinding Process*, 20 STAN. L. REV. 1065 (1968).

3 *Id.* at 1065-83.

scholars sophisticated in the relevant methodologies,[4] and a general although not unanimous consensus appears to have emerged that a careful use of Bayesian methodologies—one that is sensitive to its requirements and limitations—should prove useful in reducing errors resulting from trials.[5] Similarly, recent work has extended and deepened considerably the legal system's understanding of the relationship between soft, unquantifiable data and "naked statistical" evidence.[6] Perhaps most importantly, and certainly most impressively, researchers have recently turned their attention to substantive rules with quite interesting results. In particular, the consequences of differing types of remedial rules have been examined, disclosing a wealth of unanticipated consequences.[7] Indeed, even the courts may some day heed the message of this new knowledge, if *Sindell v. Abbott Laboratories*[8] is any indication.

Notwithstanding these impressive achievements, limits on the ability to reconcile conventional views of probability with conventional views of trials are being discovered. It is becoming increasingly obvious, for example, that Bayesian approaches can best be used heuristically as guides to rational thought and not as specific blueprints for forensic decisionmaking.[9] Similarly, there is apparently little disagreement that verdicts based solely on overtly probabilistic evidence[10] should be rare, indeed disfavored, occurrences due to the lack of context in such cases by which the overtly probabilistic evidence may be measured.[11] Moreover, in all but the area of

---

[4] *See generally* 1A J. WIGMORE, EVIDENCE, § 37 (P. Tillers rev. ed. 1983).

[5] *See, e.g.*, Lempert, *Modeling Relevance*, 75 MICH. L. REV. 1021 (1977).

[6] *See, e.g.*, Kaye, *The Limits of the Preponderance of the Evidence Standard: Justifiably Naked Statistical Evidence and Multiple Causation*, 1982 AM. B. FOUND. RES. J. 487; Nesson, *Reasonable Doubt and Permissive Inferences: The Value of Complexity*, 92 HARV. L. REV. 1187 (1979).

[7] *See generally* Kaye, *supra* note 6; Orloff & Stedinger, *A Framework for Evaluating the Preponderance of the Evidence Standard*, 131 U. PA. L. REV. 1159 (1983).

[8] 26 Cal. 3d 588, 607 P.2d 924, 163 Cal. Rptr. 132 (articulating the market share liability theory and allocating the risk of loss to each of several manufacturers when precise manufacturer can not be identified), *cert. denied*, 449 U.S. 912 (1980).

[9] *See* Callen, *Notes on a Grand Illusion: Some Limits on the Use of the Bayesian Theory in Evidence Law*, 57 IND. L.J. 1 (1982).

[10] By "overtly probabilistic" I mean evidence that is largely the presentation of statistical analyses. I have some difficulty with the proposition that there is an important qualitative difference between "statistical" evidence and other kinds of evidence, for it seems to me that all evidence is "probabilistic" in a nontrivial sense. The primary variable in comparing evidentiary proffers is quality of the evidence. The ambiguity in some evidence is quite obvious and quantifiable; the ambiguity in other evidence is itself much more ambiguous. *See infra* notes 41-45 and accompanying text.

[11] As I elaborate in Part III, I am unpersuaded by this general view and think that generally it should be up to the parties to decide what type of evidence they will rely on. *See infra* Part IIIB.

remedial rules there have been no significant creative breakthroughs of late. Indeed, much of the present work seems either fixed at the level of already well-debated issues or focused on relatively insignificant issues that lend themselves to a probabilistic analysis.

There is, in short, a sense of a bit of malaise. Advancement has not proceeded rapidly, and for good reason if Professor Jonathan Cohen is correct. Professor Cohen has recently mounted a frontal assault on the theory that conventional probability is the proper paradigm for the trial of disputes.[12] He argues in great detail that conventional probability simply does not work very well to describe or guide the trial of disputes. What is needed, he argues, is a different conceptualization, one that traces its roots to Bacon and Mill rather than Pascal, and he proceeds to develop in even greater detail a rigorous Baconian theory of inductive probability.[13] According to Professor Cohen, this form of probability theory much better describes the actual operation of trials and thus ought to be a preferred conceptualization. He is unclear, however, as to whether any prescriptions can be drawn from his conceptualization.

As impressive as Professor Cohen's achievements are, and they are quite impressive, his work will not determine the final conceptualization of the trial of disputes. When Professor Cohen's work is interpreted for application to the trial of disputes, it possesses highly analogous attributes to the theory it was designed to replace. Upon reflection, this does not strike me as counter-intuitive. Both conventional and inductive probability theorists are attempting to bring rational thought to bear on identical phenomena. Unless one or the other contrasting camps has widely missed the mark in their perceptions of reality, or unless we exist at a widely irrational plane in the universe, the efforts of rational individuals to describe and explain similar observations should tend to converge.

Counter-intuitive or not, the convergence of these theories leaves a large problem: the theoretical framework for the trial of disputes appears seriously inadequate. Perhaps this is because our level of understanding is not yet sufficient to allow us adequately to explain the relevant phenomena. Perhaps, but I think not. Rather, I think that both conventional and inductive theorists have uncovered inadequacies in the manner in which we conduct trials. Thus, effort should not be directed toward reducing the range of dispute between various ways to conceive of the idea of probability, nor should it be directed toward efforts to create still another formal probability theory in the hopes that it will avoid the limitations of the two models to which I have been referring.[14] My suspicion is that any other theory in the

---

[12] *See* L. COHEN, THE PROBABLE AND THE PROVABLE (1977).

[13] *See, e.g.*, L. COHEN, THE IMPLICATIONS OF INDUCTION (1970).

[14] *But see* G. SHAFER, A MATHEMATICAL THEORY OF EVIDENCE (1976); Comment, *Mathematics, Fuzzy Negligence, and the Logic of Res Ipsa Loquitur*, 75 NW. U.L. REV. 147 (1980).

end will describe the same phenomena in a manner highly analogous to our present conceptualizations. Indeed, a contrary belief seems almost a negation of the implications of rational thought. It is, in short, not our conceptualizations of probability that are in need of serious revision. It is instead our conceptualization of trials.

I intend to propose here a new manner of conceptualizing trials. I will begin first by briefly reviewing the limits of the conventional model of probability as it applies to the trial of civil disputes, and I will add a few new wrinkles to that worn garment. I will then demonstrate that similar limitations are inherent in Professor Cohen's model. My purpose in doing this is only to demonstrate that conventional views of probability and Cohen's views are highly analogous, and not radically different, when interpreted for application to the trial of civil disputes. It is from this similarity that I draw the conclusion that we observe two quite rigorous descriptions of identical phenomena. I will then proceed to sketch out a reconceptualization of civil trials that is designed to ameliorate many of the limitations inherent in our current conceptualization of trials and that is independent of any theory of probability that could be employed by it. The reconceptualization, in other words, works just as well no matter what theory of probability is employed to analyze the relevant factual inquiries at trial.

I. The Limits of Conventional Models of Probability Briefly Reviewed and Extended

Two types of difficulties are posed by the effort to reconcile conventional views of probability with conventional views of trials.[15] There are, first, what might somewhat loosely be called formal problems, in particular the problems of conjunction and negation. In addition, there is a disturbingly strained and unrealistic quality to much of the work of conventional probability theorists that engenders the suspicion that there is a serious problem lurking somewhere. This suspicion is intensified rather than assuaged by the efforts of these theorists to respond to their critics.

---

[15] My concern is with the use of probability theory to explicate the trial process. There are other issues posed by probability theory, however. One example is the dispute over whether jurors should be encouraged to employ mathematical modes of decisionmaking. *Compare* Finkelstein & Fairley, *A Bayesian Approach to Identification Evidence*, 83 Harv. L. Rev. 489 (1970) (advocating explicit use of Bayes's Theorem to aid jury in assessing significance of identification evidence) *with* Tribe, *Trial By Mathematics: Precision and Ritual in the Legal Process*, 84 Harv. L. Rev. 1329 (1971) (costs of attempting to integrate mathematical techniques into factfinding process at trial exceeds benefits). Another is the question whether individuals think in conventional probabilistic fashions. *See* D. Kahneman, P. Slovic, & A. Tversky, Judgment Under Uncertainty: Heuristics and Biases (1982) [hereinafter Kahneman].

A. *Formal Limits of Pascalian Probability*

Conventional probability theory entails rules of negation and conjunction that are difficult to reconcile with the Anglo-American system of civil trials. The implications of negation are completely discussed in the literature and need only be briefly reiterated here.[16] An axiom of conventional probability is that the probability of any fact plus the probability of its negation must equal 1.0. Thus, if the probability of the plaintiff's case being factually true is .500001, the probability of the defendant's case being true, which is the negation of the plaintiff's, must equal .499999. In such a case, the normal burden of persuasion rule mandates a verdict for the plaintiff, yet this seems unfair to some commentators in light of the high probability that the defendant is not factually liable.[17] I will return to this problem below in analyzing Professor Kaye's response to it.

The second problem of conventional probability theory results from the rules of conjunction that specify that the probability of two independent events occurring is the product of their separate probabilities.[18] If the probability of getting a head is ½ on the flip of a coin, the probability of getting two in a row—or of getting two heads from two identical coins—is ½ × ½, or ¼. This is a serious problem for an account of civil trials in conventional probability terms. Jurors are generally instructed in civil cases that they must find each element to the level required by the relevant standard of proof.[19] That standard is normally a preponderance of the evidence, which is usually defined as "more probable than not" or as "50%+."[20]

Nonetheless, presumably a plaintiff deserves to win a civil trial only if all of the elements of his cause of action are true. We would say that an error was made if a plaintiff recovered for an intentional tort where the defendant caused the injury but did not intend it, or intended it but did not cause it. This understanding, however, is not consistent with the conjunction rule.

Suppose a jury found the probability of intentionality to be .6 and that of causation to be .6 as well. Assuming that these elements are independent, the probability of their conjunction is .36. Thus, the probability of at least one of them not being true—which should result in a defendant's verdict—is 1 − .36, or .64.[21]

---

[16] *See, e.g.*, L. COHEN, *supra* note 1, at 74-81; R. EGGLESTON, EVIDENCE, PROOF, AND PROBABILITY 40-43 (2d ed. 1983); Williams, *The Mathematics of Proof*, 1979 CRIM. L. REV. 297.

[17] *See* L. COHEN, *supra* note 1.

[18] For the purposes of this article, I will generally assume that factual issues are independent, even though this is hardly ever the case. I make this assumption simply for purposes of simplification. In the event of dependence, the phenomena that I describe will still generally occur, but to a lesser degree.

[19] *See, e.g.*, 11 E. DEVITT & C. BLACKMAR, FEDERAL JURY PRACTICE AND INSTRUCTIONS § 71.14 (3d ed. 1977 & Supp. 1986).

[20] MCCORMICK ON EVIDENCE § 339 (E. Cleary 3d ed. 1984).

[21] I wish to make another assumption explicit at this point. The primary goal

The significance of this phenomenon is that there is a divergence between how we instruct juries and how we wish trials to come out. If these numbers were to be at all accurate assessments of the class of cases into which this individual case fell—that is to say that over the long run in about two-thirds of such cases at least one of the necessary elements of recovery is not true—then the system will be biased against defendants, and more errors favoring plaintiffs than defendants will be made.

These are well known problems and I will not belabor them here. I do wish to add to them certain new wrinkles that give further grounds for skepticism concerning either how consistent conventional theories of probability are with conventional theories of civil trials or the wisdom of one or the other of those theories. These wrinkles are generally derivative of the conjunction phenomenon and demonstrate a certain arbitrariness in decisionmaking.

One implication of the conjunction principle is that it injects a certain inequality of treatment into the trial of disputes that is a function of the number of elements of a cause of action. Compare two causes of action. Assume that the first has two elements and that the second has three. To see the inequality of treatment, assume that in both causes of action each element is established to a probability of .75, which more than satisfies the requirement of a preponderance of the evidence. But note the consequences of the conjunction principle. In the first case, the probability of both elements being true, again assuming independence, is .75 × .75, or .56. In that case, a verdict for the plaintiff is obviously justifiable notwithstanding the effect of conjunction. Now consider the result in the second case where the probability that all three elements are true is .75 × .75 × .75, or .42. Here we have an example where errors will favor plaintiffs over defendants if the jury is given the normal instruction to return a verdict for the plaintiff if it finds each element to be true by a preponderance of the evidence. In addition, we have another problem that emerges from comparing the results in the two cases. Defendants as a class are considerably worse off in the second case than in the first even if the jury finds each individual element in both cases by a preponderance of the evidence.

served by burden of persuasion rules is to allocate errors over plaintiffs and defendants. I will proceed for the moment on that assumption and will qualify it at points in this paper even though the economists would argue that this assumption may be unconvincing generally. I should point out that even if that assumption is rejected and some other value than, for example, equalizing errors over plaintiffs and defendants is substituted, the question remains of how to attempt to allocate factual error in light of the substituted policy. For example, recent tort scholarship under the influence of economic theory has argued that verdicts are returned for plaintiffs under various rules that achieve certain conceptions of efficiency. *See, e.g.*, Grady, *A New Positive Economic Theory of Negligence*, 92 YALE L.J. 799 (1983). Even if this is so, the determination of the factual setting of any particular litigated event will contain the same risk of factual error that is present in trials under more conventional views of dispute resolution. Thus, the question will arise how to allocate those risks of error given the desired social values to be maximized.

To generalize, a verdict may be returned for a plaintiff if there are two issues whenever there is a slightly lower probability than $1 - (.5 \times .5)$, or .75, that a defendant should not be liable. When there are three issues, a verdict for a plaintiff may be returned whenever there is a slightly lower probability than $1 - (.5 \times .5 \times .5)$, or .875, that a defendant should not be liable. Moreover, inequality cannot be eliminated by requiring the product of the individual elements to exceed .5. The effect of doing that merely shifts the differential treatment from defendants to plaintiffs. Since each additional element will generally lower the probability of the conjunction, the more elements there are the higher is the probability to which, on average, each will have to be established in order to reach a specified level, regardless of whether it is .5 or something else. Thus, according to conventional probability theory as it would apply in this modified situation, plaintiffs' tasks will become more difficult as each new independent element is added. As a result, plaintiffs will be treated differentially based upon the fortuity[22] of the number of elements in a cause of action, whereas under our present rules defendants are treated differentially based on the number of elements. If conventional probability theory is applicable to the trial of disputes, one or the other disparity must exist, given our present conceptualization of trials.

There is yet another curiosity emanating from the interaction of the conjunction principle of conventional probability and the conventional view of trials. Compare two cases, each containing three elements. Assume that in the first case each element is established to a probability of .6, thus resulting in a verdict for the plaintiff. Assume that in the second case two elements are established to a probability of .9 and the third element is established to a probability of .4. Since a probability of .4 would not meet the preponderance of the evidence standard, the second case would result in a verdict for the defendant. However, if the three elements are independent, there is a $1 - (.6 \times .6 \times .6)$ or .78, probability that at least one of the elements is not true in the first case, and a $1 - (.9 \times .9 \times .4)$, or .68, probability that at least one element is not true in the second case. In other words, the probability is higher in the first case than in the second that the defendant is *not* factually liable, yet under the conventional view of trials a verdict will be returned for a plaintiff in the first case and the defendant in the second.

There are other formal problems implicit in, although not derived from, the conventional conceptualization of trials. I present them here because they are analogous to those just discussed, and their solution, developed in Part III, is the same. Consider from a somewhat different perspective the

---

[22] "Fortuity" may not seem the right choice of word, but from the point of view of the analysis in the text, the number of elements in a cause of action undoubtedly is fortuitous. I doubt that legislators or common law courts gave any thought to the points made here in fashioning the elements of offenses (or affirmative defenses, for that matter).

nature of erroneous judgments that will result if jurors are instructed to find for plaintiffs only if each necessary element is established to a specified probability. Assume that a cause of action has two elements, X and Y. There are four subsets that can be created of all such cases: 1) X and Y are both factually true; 2) X and Y are both factually false; 3) X is true and Y is false; and 4) X is false and Y is true. In subset 1, there are three types of errors that can be made: an error can be made on either element separately or on both of them. In each case, however, the result will favor defendants. Plaintiffs are entitled to a verdict in subset 1, and any error will result in a verdict for the defendant.

Now consider subset 2. Here, two out of the three possible types of errors will not result in an erroneous judgment. Only if the factfinder makes an error with respect to both issues will an erroneous judgment for plaintiffs result. Thus, defendants again seem to be relatively advantaged by this phenomenon, although the precise effect is a function of the actual distribution of errors that occurs.

Combining the analysis of these two subsets, one in which plaintiffs deserve a verdict and one in which defendants deserve a verdict, demonstrates that erroneous verdicts for defendants will be reached as a result of three types of errors whereas erroneous verdicts for plaintiffs will be reached as a result of only one type of error. If the objective at trials is in part to equalize errors among defendants and plaintiffs, this phenomenon should be troublesome.

A consideration of subsets 3 and 4 is not as startling, but it is of some interest. In both cases, defendants deserve verdicts. Thus, the only erroneous verdict that can result is a verdict for plaintiffs. Of the six kinds of errors that can be made, only two of them will result in erroneous verdicts for plaintiffs: erroneous verdicts for plaintiffs will result where an error is made with respect to the factually false issue in each subset. All other errors will still result in verdicts for defendants.

To some extent these consequences may be rationalized away by asserting that sometimes defendants are favored and sometimes plaintiffs are favored. That, however, is a weak explanation for what appears to be a crazy-quilt process. Although it is true that of the twelve kinds of errors that can be made, three result in erroneous verdicts for plaintiffs, three result in erroneous verdicts for defendants, while six leave the ultimate verdict unchanged, they are nonetheless distributed by an apparently nonsensical rule: when both elements are true or both false, defendants are favored; when one is true and one false, plaintiffs are favored.

The distribution of erroneous judgments, coupled with the implications of the conjunction principle, do not paint a picture of a perfectly rational system. Something is amiss. That something, as I elaborate in Part III, is the conventional view of trials. Before doing so, however, I will address the efforts of certain scholars to explain some anomalies that the conventional view of probability gives rise to in the trial of civil disputes. Curiously, these efforts tend to reinforce the conclusion that something is awry somewhere.

B. *The Reconciliation of Conventional Probability and the Conventional Conception of Civil Trials*

The efforts to elaborate the implications of conventional probability theory, as well as to respond to its critics, accentuate rather than ameliorate the concern that there is a poor fit between probability theory and the conventional view of civil trials. This is particularly evident in what is the best of this genre: the examinations of recovery rules by Professor David Kaye[23] and Professors Orloff and Stedinger.[24]

In his very interesting article, Professor Kaye hypothesizes a case where the litigated issue is causation. He then demonstrates that applying to that issue a burden of persuasion rule of a preponderance of the evidence conceptualized as a probability measure of greater than .5 will minimize the sum of defendants who are wrongfully required to compensate plaintiffs and plaintiffs who are wrongfully denied recovery. In addition, it will result in minimizing the total amount of money wrongfully paid by factually liable defendants and not obtained by factually deserving plaintiffs.[25] Professors Orloff and Stedinger extended Kaye's analysis to show that a different burden of persuasion rule is optimal if the policy is to reduce the incidence of large errors. If that is the policy, an expected value rule should be employed that provides for a plaintiff to recover an amount equal to the magnitude of the damages multiplied by the probability that the defendant is liable.[26]

Both of these efforts are impressive and are filled with insights. Furthermore, they seem superficially plausible in the sense that they engender the impression that they could in fact be discussing, and their prescriptions could be easily applied to, the trial of civil disputes. The problem is that this superficial plausibility melts away upon further examination. Both of these efforts make a simplifying assumption that in each case there is only a single litigated issue. Without that simplifying assumption, the prescriptions of these works begin to diverge radically from the present system of trials.

This is most evident in Kaye's work. By assuming that there is only a single issue, Kaye has assumed away the problem of conjunction. He assumes that all relevant issues other than the one under consideration are proven to a probability of one. If that assumption is relaxed, then his argument requires that the probability of the conjunction of all elements of the relevant cause of action be greater than .5. In other words, while he purports to be discussing the system of civil trials, his discussion entails a radical change in the system from one where jurors are instructed to apply the relevant burden of persuasion to each element to a system where they would be instructed to apply the burden of persuasion to the conjunction of all elements.

---

23 Kaye, *supra* note 6.

24 Orloff & Stedlinger, *supra* note 7.

25 Kaye, *supra* note 6, at 494-503.

26 Orloff & Stedlinger, *supra* note 7, at 1166.

In fact, Professor Kaye's discussion entails an even more radical approach. When he expands the analysis to include the possibility that there is more than one person who could be liable, he concludes that liability should attach to that person, including the plaintiff, for whom the probability of liability is greatest, and without regard to whether the probability of the most probable culprit exceeds .5 or anything else for that matter.[27] Thus, upon generalization, Kaye is defending the normal preponderance rule only in a very narrowly constricted context. His analysis, rather than showing the consanguinity of conventional probability theory and the normal rules of civil trials, argues instead for a radical modification of civil trials.[28]

The work of Orloff and Stedinger has an analogous attribute. The example that they employ assumes that the probability of causation is the only litigated issue.[29] When that assumption is relaxed, liability becomes a function of the conjunction of all legally relevant elements, as it does in Kaye's work. Moreover, Orloff and Stedinger do not consider the possibility of multiple defendants. Had they done so, presumably their analysis would have led them to the conclusion that, if reduction of large errors is the goal, a plaintiff should be allowed to recover the "expected value" from all possible defendants.[30]

That may not seem so shocking when the number of possible defendants is limited and easily definable, as in *Sindell*, but it leads to breathtaking possibilities when that is not the case. The implication of their quite persuasive argument is that all persons potentially in the causal chain, or more precisely the legal chain, of a legal injury who can not show to a certainty that they should not be held liable, should be held liable, and thus become, in essence, insurers against social harm. That might be a very good result to reach, but it is quite a distance from our present system of civil dispute resolution.

While some of the works elaborating the implications of probability theory do not appear upon examination to be defending or explicating the present system of civil trials, other efforts that more directly attempt to demonstrate that there is no "fundamental dissonance between mathematical probability theory and forensic proof,"[31] somewhat paradoxically tend to demonstrate

[27] Kaye, *supra* note 6, at 503-08.

[28] This entire genre, going all the way back to Kaplan, *supra* notes 2-3, assumes that the set of plaintiffs going to trial and the set of defendants going to trial will be approximately the same size. Absent knowledge to the contrary, that is a reasonable assumption to make. Nonetheless, the effect of any burden of persuasion rule will be in large measure a function of the size of those sets. Allen, *The Restoration of* In re Winship: *A Comment on Burdens of Persuasion in Criminal Cases after* Patterson v. New York, 76 MICH. L. REV. 30, 47 n.65 (1977). In criminal cases, this is a highly unrealistic assumption, since presumably the screening devices of the pretrial process remove most innocent people from the system.

[29] Orloff & Stedlinger, *supra* note 7, at 1162.

[30] *Id.* at 1160 n.6 (citing *Sindell* with apparent approval).

[31] Kaye, *Paradoxes, Gedanken Experiments and the Burden of Proof: A Response to Dr. Cohen's Reply*, 1981 ARIZ. ST. L.J. 635, 645.

precisely that there is just such a dissonance. I will use as my example the best of this type of work, which is the dispute between Professors Kaye and Cohen over the now famous Paradox of the Gatecrasher.

To understand how odd the debate over the Gatecrasher hypothetical seems, one must bear in mind that the disputants on virtually all sides of the probability debates appear to have the reduction of errors at trial as an important value. Indeed, it appears to be the primary value of Professor Kaye.[32] In light of that, consider his response to that part of Professor Cohen's challenge to conventional probability implicit in his Gatecrasher hypothetical. Professor Kaye, essentially quoting from Cohen, presents the hypothetical thusly:

> Consider a case in which it is common ground that 499 people paid for admission to a rodeo, and that 1,000 are counted on the seats, of whom A is one. Suppose no tickets were issued and there can be no testimony as to whether A paid for admission or climbed over the fence. So there is a .501 probability, on the admitted facts, that he did not pay. The conventionally accepted theory of probability would apparently imply that in such circumstances the rodeo organizers are entitled to judgment against A for the admission money, since the balance of the probability would lie in their favor. But it seems manifestly unjust that A should lose when there is an agreed probability of as high as .499 that he in fact paid for admission.
>
> Indeed, if the organizers were really entitled to judgment against A, they would be entitled to judgment against each person in the same position as A. So they might conceivably be entitled to recover 1,000 admission prices, when it was admitted that 499 had actually paid. The absurd injustice of this suffices to show that there is something wrong somewhere. But where?[33]

Professor Kaye defends against these troubling implications of conventional probability theory for the trial of civil disputes in two ways. First, he asserts that although the "objective probability" of plaintiff's story being accurate is .501, "it may be appropriate to treat the subjective probability as

[32] Kaye, *The Laws of Probability and the Law of the Land*, 47 U. Chi. L. Rev. 35-36, 38 (1979). Cohen's views are less clear. He may simply be trying to describe in a more articulate fashion what he thinks is going on in the trial of disputes. His book, The Probable and the Provable, contains no suggestion that errors will be reduced by embracing his analysis. Nor does it offer any suggestions for changing any currently employed procedure at or before trial. In his contribution to this symposium, he asserts that his thesis is "essentially a normative one, concerned with answering the question 'What is the legally correct way to judge proofs?,' not a factual one, concerned with answering the question 'What is the way proofs are actually judged?' " Cohen, *The Role of Evidential Weight in Criminal Proof*, 66 B.U.L. Rev. 635, 635 (1986). Cohen must be referring here to analysts of the trial process, not to judges or juries, for once again no suggestions for change are offered.

[33] Kaye, *The Paradox of the Gatecrasher and Other Stories*, 1979 Ariz. St. L.J. 101.

less than one-half, and therefore insufficient to support a verdict for plaintiff, simply to create an incentive for plaintiffs to do more than establish the background statistics."[34] There are two problems with this explanation, however. First, it is obviously an attempt to explain away the troublesome aspects of the hypothetical by implicitly rejecting them. The only sensible way to understand the hypothetical is that it presents the question of what should be done when this is all the evidence there is. The answer Professor Kaye gives is to get more evidence. That may be a good idea, but it does not respond to this problem. In the context of this problem, not some other problem that Professor Kaye may prefer to talk about, the answer is that the plaintiff loses—even though Professor Kaye, in the same article, recognizes that the proper conclusion from the point of view of conventional probability is that the plaintiff should win.[35]

A second problem emerges if Professor Kaye's modification of the hypothetical is accepted. If the plaintiff can produce more evidence, then so can the defendant. If this statistical data is all that is presented, it is because that is all both parties wish to present. If one assumes that the classes of plaintiffs and defendants should be treated as equivalently as possible, then one class ought not to bear the costs of the defaults of both classes. Moreover, as I develop in greater detail in Part III, is it not clear to me why a court, or a court system, as a general rule should concern itself with the nature of the evidence produced by participants in a private dispute. If the parties are willing to let the dispute be resolved on this basis, as a general rule they should be allowed to make that choice. Professor Kaye's argument conflates appropriate rules of decision with appropriate discovery sanctions. The only time a court should follow Professor Kaye's advice in this context is if it believes a party (either party) is refusing to disclose relevant information in the discovery process.[36]

At any rate, Professor Kaye's first response sounds very much like an ad hoc rationalization rather than a convincing argument that there is not as much of a conflict as Professor Cohen asserts between the present system of civil litigation and conventional conceptualizations of probability. His second response is in the same vein. Relying on Bayes's Theorem, he argues:

> The very fact that the paradoxical plaintiffs, at the conclusion of their case, have failed to supply any particularized evidence about defendant is itself an important datum. Suppose a juror accepts the statistic about the number of paying customers at face value. For him, the subjective probability, P(X), that defendant did not pay is .501. But, if he stops to

[34] *Id.* at 106.

[35] *Id.* at 103.

[36] What I hope is undue caution militates in favor of pointing out that I am assuming that a mature discovery process is in place. If that assumption is wrong, then there is room for other forms of incentives to produce evidence. Again, however, they should apply to both plaintiffs and defendants.

reflect on the fact that this is all there is to the case, he should revise this probability in light of this new item of "evidence." Under the preponderance of the evidence standard, he should find for defendant if the revised subjective probability, P(X|E), is one-half or less. This will be the case only if the fraction f [in a Bayesian calculation] is more than P(X)/[1 − P(X)], or 1.004. Hence, if it is even slightly more likely that the rodeo organizers would have been able to come forward with more evidence about how the defendant A came onto the premises without paying if he had actually done so, then f could be taken to exceed this figure. Consequently, at the conclusion of plaintiff's case, this rational juror, following the dictates of the probability theory as it is conventionally understood, will think the probability that A is liable is one-half or less and find for A.[37]

As nice as this sounds, again it is not the problem. The problem is what should happen if the hypothesized evidence is all there is at the end of the entire case rather than the plaintiff's case-in-chief. At the end of the entire case, both the plaintiff and the defendant would have had the chance to produce more evidence, and both would have failed to do so. The result, one would think, would be that the inference Kaye discusses would arise on both sides and cancel each other out. Indeed, this rather sensible conclusion can be avoided only by another series of ad hoc moves, such as asserting that plaintiff's default gives rise to a stronger inference than defendant's (or vice versa).

Another curious aspect of Professor Kaye's argument is that it results in defeating the objective of minimizing error. If one understands Professor Cohen's hypothetical to include the fact that the statistical data is all that can be offered in each case, Professor Kaye would apparently deny recovery in each case. That would result in 499 correct decisions and 501 incorrect ones. If recovery were allowed in each case, by contrast, fewer mistakes would be made (499 instead of 501) and less money would be wrongfully paid (whatever the cost of the ticket is times the number of mistakes). This would result in a windfall to the plaintiff, but denying recovery results in a larger windfall, overall, to defendants. Professor Kaye recognizes this,[38] which makes his rationalization even more puzzling.[39]

---

[37] Kaye, *supra* note 33, at 107-08.

[38] *Id.* at 101.

[39] There may be other reasons to dislike this result, but none of those reasons are relevant to the present discussion. One might conclude, for example, that rodeo operators can and should build better fences so that this type of situation will not develop. In that case, denying recovery will encourage them to take such actions. Alternatively, one might conclude that it is not asking too much of patrons to keep their ticket stubs, just as any other receipt would normally be kept, and that failure to do so may result in having to pay once more for the privilege of attending the show. These economic considerations are independent of the error minimization concerns on which I am presently concentrating. Again, though, should a court or legislature

The most distressing aspect of arguments similar to Kaye's response to the gatecrasher hypothetical is that they are ill-defined and appear to be internally inconsistent. Although neither point may directly further the argument that analyses of civil trials in terms of conventional probability do not work terribly well, both tend to corroborate the ad hoc nature of much of that genre.

Implicit in much of the literature on the implications of conventional probability theory for the trial of civil disputes is a dichotomy of evidence into that which is quantified and that which is not. This distinction often is articulated in terms of "statistical evidence" or some derivative thereof on the one hand, and evidence which "personalizes" the case on the other.[40] The former is usually categorical and definite ("501 out of a thousand did not buy tickets") and the latter is specific to an individual and complex ("I saw X take money out of his wallet and exchange it for what appeared to be tickets to the rodeo"). These categories do not exist as mutually exclusive sets, however, although they may reflect points on a spectrum with respect to certain variables.

Although the probabilists do not typically address in detail their epistemological views, they appear generally to hold the view that certainty about prior events is unobtainable.[41] If that is the case, then what distinguishes the quantified from the unquanitified is the clarity of the ambiguity of the evidence. Thus, testimony that 501 out of a thousand people in attendance did not pay for admission is not to make a cold and unassailable statement of a universal truth. It is instead to assert an inference drawn from a set of observations, or to assert the observations (or a summary thereof) themselves, any of which may contain error. Moreover, to make such assertions is to "personalize" data with respect to any person in the audience. Such a person has been culled out from all the rest of humanity and placed in a group of individuals with respect to whom there is some reason to believe that they have committed an actionable wrong. Such evidence may not be very personal, but the point remains that it is "personal" to some degree. What is omitted in the writings about statistical evidence and probability theory is any effort to specify why any particular degree of "personalness" should be treated differently from some other, where and why the line is to be drawn.

---

decide to implement a recovery scheme based upon one of the ideas suggested in this note, the question of how to allocate the risk of factual error will still exist. What if, for example, a patron presents a badly faded ticket stub that may or may not be a stub from a ticket for this rodeo? What if an operator claims every reasonable precaution has been taken, but the defendant disputes the matter? A method of allocating the risk of error on such factual issues will have to be provided, so we will end up once more talking about errors.

[40] *See, e.g.*, Nesson, *supra* note 6; Tribe, *supra* note 15 at 1340-43.

[41] *See, e.g.*, Tribe, *supra* note 15 at 1330 n.2; Kaye, *supra* note 32 at 45 n.41.

Look at the matter from the flip side of the coin. Suppose in the gatecrasher hypothetical that the operator of the rodeo testified that a particular defendant did not buy a ticket. He knows this, he asserts, because the defendant looks unusual to the operator, the operator sold all the tickets himself, and he would have remembered such an unusual character. This evidence would appear to meet the standards of admission to the set of unquantified data.[42] Now consider how a factfinder will analyze that data. If the factfinder will analyze it by reference to his own experience, and I see no other way for him to act apart from reliance on inspiration or intuition, he will have to compare that data, consciously or unconsciously, to his own perceptions of his own experiences and the inferences he drew from those experiences. Regardless whether that is done in a deductive, inductive or analogical manner, eventually a generalization will be formed (again, even if unconsciously) and the "evidence" compared to it.[43] A factfinder, in short, will convert "personalized" data into categorical data to analyze them. Thus, the distinction between quantified and unquantified evidence is again exposed as one of degree in its most crucial variable.

This perspective also demonstrates the curious inconsistency that meanders through arguments about quantified evidence. Viewed from the perspective developed here, the resistance to statistical evidence paradoxically amounts to favoring evidence whose limits are ambiguous over that whose limits are clearer, and indeed creates a bias against increased sophistication in the evidentiary process. As knowledge increases about some matter so that more and more confident statements can be made about it, greater skepticism is engendered about its admissibility as evidence and whether verdicts may rest upon it. The implications of probability theory are directly to the contrary, of course. Probability theory teaches that as ambiguity increases, reliance on the data should decrease.[44] Again there seems to be a dissonance, for which there is no good explanation, between the theory of civil trials and that of conventional probability.

II. The Inductivist Alternative to Conventional Probability

The lesson that at least one distinguished scholar has drawn from the uncomfortable fit between conventional probability and the trial of civil disputes is that trials should be conceptualized from a different perspective than that of conventional probability. According to Professor Cohen, a theory of inductive probability that permits ordinal statements to be made

---

[42] *See* Nesson, *supra* note 6.

[43] These are the "heuristics" that the psychologists, in particular, are fond of discussing. *See* Kahneman, *supra* note 15.

[44] *See* D. Barnes, Statistics as Proof: Fundamentals of Quantitative Evidence 143-230 (1983).

about the relative likelihood of events better captures the essence of civil trials than does conventional probability, which is a cardinal system that requires that the likelihood of an event be associated with a number between zero and one.[45]

Professor Cohen has developed his theory of inductive probability in quite a rigorous fashion.[46] To my knowledge, no aspect of his mathematics has been invalidated by a demonstration of contradictions. The primary criticisms directed toward his efforts have been less technical, focusing rather on important ambiguities contained in his interpretation of how his theory applies in the context of trials.[47] I intend to demonstrate here that not only are there ambiguities in his interpretation, but that even a generous interpretation demonstrates "paradoxes" closely analogous to those he attributes to conventional probability as it applies in the trial setting. Before discussing these paradoxes, a brief description of Professor Cohen's theory is in order. Dr. David A. Schum has provided just such a description that also places Professor Cohen's work into historical context:

> John Stuart Mill proposed a collection of specific methods for induction in his treatise *System of Logic*. Most present-day students of experimental design in various areas of behavioral, biological, and physical sciences study extensions of Mill's method without being aware of it. Mill is frequently not given appropriate credit for systematizing the design of empirical research. A variety of procedures exist for introducing various experimental "controls" so that one can isolate valid causes by removing the confounding effects of other possible alternative causes. Cohen tells us that the process of grading inductive support that one proposition can give another has a close affinity to three of Mill's methods for induction. The *method of agreement* establishes the co-presence of a cause and effect; the *method of difference* establishes the co-absence of a cause and effect; and the *method of concomitant variation* establishes the covariation of cause and effect.
>
> Suppose a situation in which we entertain a particular hypothesis Hj which explains a characteristic of some phenomenon of interest; how do we obtain inductive support for Hj? There may, of course, be other plausible hypotheses or explanations. Imagine now a series of tests which can discriminate among alternative hypotheses. Each test involves some relevant variable which can be manipulated independently of all others. The complexity of the test sequence increases as we proceed because at each stage a new relevant variable is added to those already present. As the test sequence proceeds, some hypotheses are falsified by test results and are eliminated from consideration. Suppose Hj survives the process of elimination. The degree or grade of support

---

45 *See* T. FINE, THEORIES OF PROBABILITY: AN EXAMINATION OF FOUNDATIONS 65 (1973).

46 *See, e.g.*, L. COHEN, *supra* note 13.

47 Wagner, Book Review, 1979 DUKE L.J. 1071, 1077-81.

given by the test sequence to Hj depends upon the complexity level of the test that Hj attains. At some point we run out of relevant variables to manipulate or we run out of time or money and so we stop testing; the surviving hypothesis or hypotheses win the day in this process of eliminative induction. Mill's methods for induction provide the essential logic for the design of the test sequence.

Formally, Cohen identifies a *support function*, s(H,E), which is read "The support for H, given test result E." Suppose there are n test levels 1, 2, 3, . . . , i, . . . n which represent increasingly complex tests. If H resists falsification or elimination up to test level i we can say that the grade of inductive support for H, given test result E, is s(H,E) = i/n. Test result E gives the ith grade of support where n is the highest grade possible. The support function value s(H,E) = i/n says that H has support up to level i and no higher; i.e., H was falsified at level i + 1. Suppose the test sequence is replicable. If you object to the test result the person performing the test sequence says, "do it yourself." If you do and achieve the same result, replicability has provided a measure of confidence in the test result. A test sequence replicated enough times becomes, as the author says, a "solid evidential fact." Thus, if s(H,E) ≥ i/n, on the basis of replicable or "solid" evidence we are entitled to conclude that s(H) ≥ i/n; i.e., we can talk about the support for H without having to qualify it with a particular test result. Suppose s(Hj,E) = 0; Hj is falsified by the simplest test. Hypothesis H_k, however, passes test i but is falsified by test i + 1; s(H_k,E) remains at level i/n and does not drop to zero because H_k obviously has more support than Hj which had none at all.

It is always possible, and the author cites examples of when it has happened, that a theory or proposition H may be true but fails to explain certain effects. Anomalies do occur and any theory of induction must be able to handle them. It would seem foolish to suppose that no theory could remain acceptable when confronted with counterevidence. Perhaps, with some slight modification, theory H can be rescued and resist being falsified at some level; one can buy support for H by revising it.

So far we have an inductive support function s(H,E) which maps ordered pairs of propositions H, E into n + 1 fractions from 0 to n/n, where s(H,E) = 0 means that H is falsified by the simplest possible test and s(H,E) = n/n means that H is not falsified or eliminated throughout the entire test sequence and has the highest level of support. The value of n may not be specifiable in any practical application. Technically, this presents no problem since it is apparent that the support function assigns values with only ordinal properties since there is no apparent equal unit of "test level difficulty" specifiable. Thus s(H,E) only *ranks* evidential support; the numbers thus obtained are not additive nor can they be used to form ratios.[48]

As even this brief summary makes clear, Cohen has created a probability

[48] Schum, *A Review of a Case Against Blaise Pascal and His Heirs*, 77 MICH. L. REV. 446, 458-60 (1979).

theory that differs greatly from conventional probability. Nevertheless, when it is interpreted for application to the trial of civil disputes, it has many implications that are quite similar to those of conventional probability.

A. *The Problems of Conjunction, Negation, and Ad Hoc Rationalization*

Unlike conventional probabilities, inductivist probabilities cannot be added or multiplied. Conjunction can occur, of course, but it occurs in a different manner, according to Professor Cohen:

> The inductivist analysis, however, has no difficulty in dealing with complex civil cases. Either the probabilities of the component elements are incommensurable, in which case no probability-value can plausibly be assigned to their conjunction and separate assignments to each must suffice. Or the conjunction principle for inductive probability gives a quite satisfactory and paradox-free result. The conjunction of two or more propositions about the same category of subject-matter . . . has the same inductive probability on given evidence as each conjunct, if the conjuncts are equally probable on that evidence, or as the least probable of them, if they are not.[49]

Professor Cohen asserts that conventional conjunction problems are avoided by emphasizing the second of the two possibilities referred to in the quoted material—the conjunction of two or more propositions about the same category of subject matter. However, the conjunction problems emerge most clearly when independent events are assumed, and presumably independent events would be "incommensurable" under Cohen's analysis.[50] Accordingly, it is the first, not the second, of the two possibilities that can most usefully be considered. When that is done, a striking similarity is evidenced between inductivist and conventional approaches.

According to the inductivist approach to the trial of disputes, probability statements about the conjunction of incommensurable events cannot be made, and a plaintiff can win only by establishing each of the legally relevant and contested facts. To "establish" a fact means only that it is more probable than it is contradictory, not that it is certain. Therefore, mistakes

---

[49] L. COHEN, *supra* note 13, at 266.

[50] If that is wrong, I am at a loss to understand commensurability. The phenomenon that I am about to describe in the text is also present with "commensurable" events for which, according to Professor Cohen, the lowest probability is the crucial one for forensic purposes. That means that if the plaintiff fails to prove any issue, whether commensurable with some other issue or not, then the plaintiff loses. Accordingly, here again errors will aggregate as errors on those discrete issues, whether commensurable with other issues or not. If, however, "commensurable" means that proof of one issue entails proof of the other, then one is simply talking of issues that are in a one to one relationship (if X is true, Y must be true). In that case, nothing useful emerges from Cohen's analysis that I can see. It collapses to the proposition that the plaintiff must prove by a preponderance the one issue in the case.

will be made. Assume that in a certain set of cases there are two incommensurable, legally relevant elements to be established and that each is established in each case by a "balance of probability." In which of these cases—all verdicts for the plaintiff—should there have been a verdict for the defendant? The answer is obvious—in any case where an error on any element was made since in those cases at least one of the elements of the plaintiff's cause of action will not be true. Thus, under inductivist probability, errors will aggregate as a function of errors on discrete issues. In cases where plaintiffs should win there will be some wrongful defendants' verdicts because of an error on issue one, and others because of an error on issue two. In cases where the defendants should win, there will be erroneous plaintiffs' verdicts whenever an error is made on the element, or elements, that should have been resolved in favor of the defendant.

Compare these implications to those of the conjunction principle of conventional probability. To express the probability of the conjunction of two independent events as the product of their separate probabilities is simply to give a mathematical representation to the rate at which errors will aggregate as a function of errors on the separate issues, at least that is the meaning of the principle so far as it is of any relevance to the legal system.[51] To give a simple example, suppose two evenly balanced coins were to be flipped and a prediction was to be made as to their outcomes. If one predicted that two heads would result, the probability of that prediction being accurate would be ½ × ½, or ¼. What that means as applied to a series of similar events is that the prediction would be wrong approximately 75% of the time because either one coin or the other, or both, will "probably" come up tails about three of every four tosses of the two coins. Errors in the conjunct prediction will aggregate, in short, as a result of errors on discrete issues just as they would under an inductivist approach.

Thus, both inductivist and conventional theories have remarkably similar implications on the conjunction issue when the theories are interpreted for application to the trial of civil disputes. Indeed, each of the points made previously about conjunction will apply equally well to inductivist conjunction, including the curious inequality phenomena resulting from the number of elements in a cause of action. Accordingly, from the point of view of error allocation, the implications of inductivist theory, when interpreted for application to the trial of civil disputes, are highly analogous to and not radically different from those of conventional theory.

Even Professor Cohen's criticism of the negation principle is equally applicable to inductive probability. His primary criticism is that the negation principle operates to require a verdict for a plaintiff even if there is a

---

[51] Moreover, this is true even if one emphasizes a subjective theory of probability. The speculation about subjective theories and degrees of belief is not unrelated to an effort to reduce errors at trial. At least I hope it is not.

significant chance (just barely under .5) that a defendant is not factually liable. He gives as an example of this problem the Gatecrasher hypothetical discussed earlier.[52] Again, though, when inductivist theory is applied to the trial of civil disputes, the same problem is present. In addition, Professor Cohen's discussion of the Gatecrasher hypothetical to show that the problem of negation is not present demonstrates yet another parallel between conventional and inductivist theory—the proponents of both engage in ad hoc rationalization in efforts to minimize the distance between the implications of their preferred theories and the conventional conception of trials.

The desired effect, and indeed the only relevant meaning, of applying the principle of negation to the trial of civil disputes so that a verdict is returned for plaintiffs whenever the relevant probability exceeds .5 is simply to decide the case in such a way as to hopefully reduce erroneous outcomes over time. It may be that in the set of all the cases in which the relevant probability for the plaintiff is .51, there will be a ratio of correct to incorrect results of 51/49. That is better than its inverse, however, and the only implication of the negation principle is to effectuate this desired outcome.

Now, take that same set of cases and analyze it from the point of view of inductive probability. Can it be that a set of plaintiffs do not prove their cases "on a balance of probability," when, over the long run, there will be fewer errors if plaintiff's verdicts are returned than if not? If that is so, I no longer know what the words mean that are being employed.

Professor Cohen asserts that it is so, however, and he argues that the proper result in the Gatecrasher hypothetical from the inductivist point of view is a verdict for the defendant. I think the real point of his argument, although obviously unintended, is to demonstrate that he—like his protagonists—is forced to engage in ad hoc rationalization to deflect the undesirable implications of his own theory. His argument runs thusly:

> Indeed on an inductivist interpretation there can be no case against the man at the rodeo in the circumstances described. If there is no evidence specifically against him, he cannot be brought under any inductively supported generalization from which it could be inferred that he did not pay for admission. Hence in order to elucidate why there can be no case against him we do not need to resort to some ad hoc stratagem. We do not need to postulate a legal rule ordaining some specific inadmissibility of evidence, such as the inadmissibility of statistical evidence in relation to voluntary acts. The heart of the matter is that there just is no inductive evidence against that particular man. So, if inductive probabilities are at issue, we can say quite simply that there is no evidence against him.[53]

Professor Cohen may wish to "say . . . that there is no evidence against" the defendant, but of course that assertion is false. In order to avoid the

[52] L. COHEN, *supra* note 12, at 74-76.
[53] *Id.* at 271.

obvious implication that "on the balance of probability" the plaintiff in Professor Cohen's hypothetical has proven his case on the evidence hypothesized, Professor Cohen ironically relies on the unsupportable distinction between "naked statistical evidence" and evidence that is personalized, just as do conventional probability theorists. That distinction is no more plausible in Professor Cohen's hands than elsewhere. Moreover, there is nothing in Professor Cohen's mathematics—at least that I can detect—that makes the distinction upon which Professor Cohen relies. Thus, he is quite clearly engaging in ad hoc strategems, his protestations to the contrary notwithstanding.

There are additional interesting comparisons between inductivist and conventional theory, some of which suggest that an inductivist conceptualization of trials is not just analogous to a conventional one but is in fact inferior in certain respects. For example, the most insightful work to date of conventional probability theorists has been the efforts to explicate the nature of damages rules. Such efforts, by contrast, are impossible in certain circumstances under an inductivist interpretation and in others possess, once again, analogous features to those of conventional explications of civil trials.

The relative inferiority of inductivist theory is most clear with respect to the case of multiple possible tort-feasors. Because of the meaning ascribed to statements about the probability of responsibility for an outcome, it is coherent and perhaps sensible to allocate damages among the possible tort-feasors proportionate to their likely responsibility for the event in question.[54] This possibility is not obtainable through an inductivist approach, however, for as Professor Cohen says, "inductive probabilities about matters of fact are only rankable."[55] A fact may be said to be more likely than its contradictory or than some other fact, but one cannot allocate damages on that basis.

This points out an interesting "paradox" of inductivist theory. Suppose facts along the lines of *Sindell*, where it is clear that one of eight defendants wrongfully harmed the plaintiff. Assume further that the eight defendants are independent actors, but there is no evidence to distinguish among them so far as their respective relationship to the plaintiff is concerned. Applying inductivist theory to the case, it is quite clear that the plaintiff cannot recover from any of the eight since it is obvious that "the balance of probability" will never favor the plaintiff over any single defendant, for any single defendant will always be able to show a great likelihood that someone else is liable—one of the other seven.

Perhaps the response to this would be to hold all eight liable, but that response is not derivable from the theory Professor Cohen has developed. It

---

[54] King, *Causation, Valuation, and Chance in Personal Injury Torts Involving Preexisting Conditions and Future Consequences*, 90 YALE L.J. 1353, 1396-97 (1981); *see supra* note 8.

[55] L. COHEN, *supra* note 13, at 226.

would instead amount to a change in the trial system to improve its compatibility with inductivist theory. Further, it would be a change that leads to the same radical revision of our existing tort system as does the conventional probability analysis. If the plaintiff can recover here from all eight defendants because one of them is liable, any plaintiff in any case where it is clear that someone should be liable to him should be able to recover from every one possibly in the legal chain leading to the injury for just the same reason. That would be acceptable only if there is a way to make comparisons between defendants that will determine the likelihood of their individual liability. It is just that comparison that inductivist theory cannot make. Moreover, the inability to make that comparison has other secondary consequences, such as making comparative negligence impossible.

Inductivist theory may be able to provide an analogue for Professor Kaye's suggestion that the single most probable cause of an event be determined and liability ascribed to it. However, the manner in which that would be done leads to interesting pragmatic problems very similar to those afflicting the proposals to employ Bayesian analysis at trial.[56]

Suppose again a case with eight defendants. Although the matter is not entirely free from doubt due to Professor Cohen's ambiguous use of terms such as "incommensurable" and "same category of subject-matter," presumably inductivist theory would allow a statement of which defendant is the one who most probably caused a particular event. This would be done by having the factfinder compare the probability of each defendant to that of every other defendant. Only one of the eight should emerge as more likely than each of the others, for otherwise a contradiction would develop.

However, to make such a comparison would require a factfinder to engage in an analytical process as complicated as that which underlies the application of Bayes's Theorem to eight dependent elements, since each defendant's case would have to be compared to every other defendant's case. In addition, it should be noted that the present system does not operate in that fashion, which is not to say that it should not, of course. Still, this incongruence between the implications of inductivist theory and the actual operation of the trial system obviously undercuts Professor Cohen's assertion that inductivist approaches more accurately capture what in fact occurs at trial.

There is one other aspect of inductive probability that demonstrates both a theoretical and a practical problem in the use of an inductivist approach. The formal difficulty leads to the pragmatic one, and so I shall begin there.

Professor Cohen asserts that inductivist theory can explain burdens of persuasion other than the standard of preponderance of the evidence.[57] Unfortunately, this assertion is not explained. Presumably what Professor Cohen has in mind is that a higher level of inductive support emerges each time a hypothesis survives another attempt at falsification. In short, as the

---

[56] *See* Callen, *supra* note 9, at 10-15.

[57] L. COHEN, *supra* note 13, at 225.

number of successful experiments approaches the limit n, the greater is the support for the hypothesis.

The difficulty with this conception is that it provides no consistency among cases and leads to ad hoc results. First of all, n will vary from case to case. Moreover, what it means to resist falsification at level 1, or 2, or whatever, will vary from case to case just because statements that are not about the same category of subject matter are not comparable. Thus, even if it were meaningful (a matter I have doubts about) to say that clear and convincing evidence means validation to a certain number of tests or a certain percentage of possible tests, the result would be to impose quite different evidentiary standards in each case. Secondly, even these suggestions cannot be followed, for n may be unspecifiable.[58] Obviously, if n is not specifiable, portions of n are not specifiable, at least not in a manner of any relevance to trials.

To be sure, the fact that n is not specifiable in a case does not mean that it is never specifiable. Thus, it might prove insightful to look to the process that underlies the specification of n to see what lessons one can learn. Remarkably, that process leads to the conclusion that Professor Cohen's efforts provide an alternative method of analyzing relative frequencies (and vice versa). Thus, it is not at all surprising that many of the implications of conventional probability are reflected in inductivist theory.

These implications are most evident in Professor Cohen's discussion of testing procedures that conform to an inductivist approach. He describes Karl von Frisch's investigation of the behavior of bees as such a case.[59] Von Frisch investigated how communication occurs among bees and whether they could discriminate between colors, odors, tastes, and shapes. He proceeded by constructing tests that permitted variables to be manipulated and the results observed. When a particular manipulation correlated with a behavioral change, and was replicated in subsequent tests, an inference of causality was drawn. In short, the relative frequency of the observed data led to speculations about causality.

Two points deserve to be made here. First, the von Frisch experiments may be an excellent paradigm for Professor Cohen's work, but they are not terribly useful paradigms for the trial of civil disputes. Trials do not proceed by the process of manipulating variables, observing the outcome and then replicating the experiment, although to be sure the beliefs of individual factfinders may emerge over their lifetime from some type of analogous process. Still, the crucial point is that Professor Cohen is conflating a careful and controlled process of experimentation containing planned manipulation of variables with employing much less carefully constructed beliefs to analyze evidence that is not subject to any sort of similar manipulation. Thus, the assertion that the von Frisch experiments capture the essence of

---

[58] *See* Schum, *supra* note 48, at 460.

[59] L. COHEN, *supra* note 13, at 129-33.

the inductivist approach does not advance the proposition that the inductivist approach captures what occurs at trial.

Perhaps Professor Cohen's point is that although the von Frisch experiments do not capture precisely what does go on, nonetheless what does occur approximates von Frisch's approach. To some extent such claims would be true. Presumably factfinders do analyze the evidence before them from the perspective of their own beliefs about the nature of the relevant universe. Moreover, many of those beliefs undoubtedly come from the observation of variables interacting in various ways. For example, it is probably commonly observed that intoxicated people are more careless and less aware of their surroundings. Thus, a demonstration that an intoxicated person driving a car was involved in an accident will raise the probability that he or she caused it through inattention. Now, this can be conceptualized, as Professor Cohen would have it, as an example of inductivist probability where the prior observation of manipulated variables leads to certain conclusions. It can also be conceptualized as the application of a relative frequency approach. Prior observation leads to the conclusion that a certain set of events is usually divided up into certain subsets of a certain size. The size of these subsets indicates the likelihood that the event under investigation at trial falls into one or another subset, given the evidence.

I see very little difference between these conceptualizations so far as they are relevant to the trial of civil disputes, a conclusion that I do not find counter-intuitive at all. Both conventional and inductivist theorists are bringing rational thought to bear upon the same phenomenon. Although it is true that there are a multitude, perhaps an infinite number, of ways to describe any particular phenomenon, any rational approach will perforce have the capacity to overlap that of any other rational approach. When these opposing theories are applied to the trial of civil disputes, quite similar implications must result, for those implications will be generated primarily by the phenomenon under investigation. Take the conjunction principle, for example. If more than a single decision about a matter has to be made, and if mistakes will be made as those decisions are made, how could the total number of errors made not aggregate as a function of errors made in each category of decisions?

This is not to say, of course, that there are no differences between varying rational approaches to any particular question, nor is it to say that differing approaches do not or will not yield insights. It is simply to say that there will be broadly similar implications that result from bringing to bear differing conceptions of rational thought on any particular phenomenon. Thus, that there are certain differences in the implications of inductivist and conventional theory is not surprising, but neither is the fact that they demonstrate many similar implications.

Still, there is at least one major problem. A number of the implications of both theories are troublesome. There are formal limits, pragmatic difficulties and the literature is filled with ad hoc rationalizations of troublesome implications of various theories of probability. These do not, however, reflect problems with our theories of reasoning. Instead, they reflect problems with our theory of trials. What is being demonstrated is not that we need a new conceptualization of probability to apply to trials; rather, we need a new conceptualization of trials that responds to the difficulties posed by our understanding of the meaning of probability.

III. A Reconceptualization of Civil Trials

The unsettling implications of both conventional and inductivist analyses of civil trials are a function primarily of the fact that the conventional conception of civil trials requires comparing the probability of the plaintiff's elements to that of their negation.[60] It is just this conception that produces the problem of negation that is troubling to both Cohen and Kaye.[61] If the probability of the defendant's factual assertion being true is one minus the probability of the plaintiff's factual assertion being true, then whenever the probability of the plaintiff's assertion exceeds .5, a verdict should be returned for the plaintiff.[62] Moreover, the conclusion is the same if, as Cohen conceptualizes it, the plaintiff's burden is to establish the relevant facts as more probable than their negation. It is also this comparative process applied to more than a single factual issue that results in the "paradoxes"[63] of conjunction that Cohen finds in conventional theory, and that I find in his. If one determines the probability of the plaintiff's elements being true by reference to a conventionally conceived burden of persuasion rule, and then allows a verdict for the plaintiff when each element is established, rather than when the conjunction of them is established, the paradoxes do occur. These are not problems in either conception of probability, however. Rather, these are problems in our conceptualization of trials. Many of the unsettling implications of our understanding of probability can be eliminated or ameliorated by conceptualizing trials in a new way. I intend to propose and examine just such a conceptualization here.

My proposal has two parts to it. The first step is to conceive of trials as comparing the probability of the fully specified case of the plaintiff to the probability of the equally well specified case of the defendant. The second step is to structure trials in such a way that will permit the parties to determine how far they will push the particularity or singularity of the relevant facts.[64] These two propositions will be discussed in turn.

---

[60] I am ignoring affirmative defenses because they do not seem to affect the analysis.

[61] *See supra* notes 33-49, 52-53 and accompanying text.

[62] The real paradox here is why we hold the plaintiff to the conventionally conceived preponderance of the evidence standard, not why we only require that. *See infra* Part III.

[63] *See* L. Cohen, *supra* note 13, at 58-67.

[64] I also see a value in encouraging the parties to reduce the scope of factual

A. *Comparing Equally Well-Specified Cases*

Perhaps the single most troublesome implication of probability theory stems from the fact that erroneous judgements in cases will aggregate as a function of errors on discrete issues, as is represented by the conjunction and negation principles. The set of problems associated with or derived from the conjunction principle exists in the trial of disputes because trials are presently conceived of as a comparison between the probability of the plaintiff's assertions and their negations, and in conventional probability the probability of that negation is the probability associated with the plaintiff's elements subtracted from one (a concept formally absent but functionally present in inductivist theory). There is another way to conceptualize trials, however. Just as plaintiffs presently are required to specify with particularity at some point the nature of their claims and factual assertions,[65] defendants could also be required to respond with equally specific and affirmative allegations rather than with simple denials. The trier of fact could then compare its view of the likelihood of the plaintiff's case to that of the defendant's.

Such a conceptualization has numerous advantages over the present conceptualization of trials. First, it moves toward greater equality of treatment of the sets of plaintiffs and defendants. Second, the problem of conjunction is obviated in large measure because the probability of two series of allegations would be compared rather than a series of allegations with their negations. Third, this view requires a greater concentration on specific factual allegations on the part of the defendant, which may lead to a sharper focus on disputed factual matters. This in turn may lead to a commensurate reduction in the amount of extraneous material dealt with at trials, not only saving time and money but simplifying the fact-finding process as well.

Perhaps most importantly, this conceptualization may lead to fewer errors being made at trial. This can be demonstrated by freeing Professor Kaye's treatment of multiple possible sources of liability for an actionable wrong from its present artificial limitation of assuming only a single litigated issue. If one replaces in his efforts the probabilities of single elements with probabilities of the conjunction of all elements, one obtains a more general theory that liability should attach to the most likely sequence of events that explains the litigated event. The proposed conceptualization of trials would operationalize this more general theory by requiring the parties to assert what they

---

disagreements. Accordingly, there are times that supplemental practices, such as allowing the jury to infer from its resolution of previous factual issues that subsequent factual issues should be resolved in favor of the same party, appear attractive to me. The point would be to discourage the propounding of highly dubious factual propositions that may serve only to "muddy the waters." I am not yet ready to say more about such matters, however.

[65] This is done through such devices as pleading, discovery, pre-trial conferences, and the like.

believe are the most likely sequences of events leading to the event in question and then instructing the jury to choose between them. To be sure, this would allow a plaintiff to recover from a defendant when the jury concludes that the probability of the plaintiff's case is low, but that of the defendant's is lower. This would be inconsistent with minimizing errors only when there is yet another possible sequence of events leading to the event in question, such as some other person who is more probably liable than the defendant. In that case, however, the defendant would be allowed to implead that third party.

This proposal also can accommodate the Orloff and Stedinger view of allocation rules after it, too, is freed of the artificial constraint of assuming a single litigated issue. Orloff and Stedinger's work may be generalized in precisely the same manner as Kaye's. The question that would then remain is simply the political one of which allocation scheme is preferred.

A number of implications of this proposal deserve elaboration. The first is that it involves a dramatically different role for single elements than the current system of trials possesses. If a plaintiff and a defendant assert quite different factual allegations, with only a few common points, a factfinder could determine that the probability of a common element favors the defendant but that, taking each case as a whole, the probabilities favor the plaintiff. Nonetheless, the work of Kaye, Orloff and Stedinger shows upon generalization that to return a verdict for the defendant in this circumstance would lead to increased errors. Thus, the real lesson here is the counterproductive consequences of the present focus at trial on the individual elements of the plaintiff's case. If, however, there is a dispute over only one fact that has mutually exclusive possibilities (for example, was the light green or red when the car entered the intersection), then the probability of the respective cases will be determined by the appraisal of that single fact. In that case, the proposal would operate as the system does presently.

This conception of trials also eliminates the formal problems resulting from instructing the jury to find each, rather than all, elements to a specified level of probability. The jury will be comparing two fully specified versions of reality, rather than comparing discrete issues to their negations. As a result, the problems of conjunction do not create paradoxes where verdicts will be returned for plaintiffs even though there is an enormously high probability that at least one of the plaintiff's necessary elements is not true. Rather, the conjunction effect will be contained within *both* parties' evidentiary proffers. Similarly, the bizarre effect of distributing errors differentially over the parties based upon whether all or some of the elements are in fact true will not occur. Errors will occur, of course, but they will effect both parties in the same manner.

There is one obvious objection to this proposal. The proposal rests upon the distinction between a simple denial of the plaintiff's case and an affirmative allegation of the defendant's case. I am quite sure that no bright line separates these two concepts and that they are points on a spectrum.

Nonetheless, the proposal made here is coherent so long as the parties are required to be fairly specific, although I cannot say what "fairly" means with any specificity.

B. *Exploring the Particularity of the Case*

Another indirect implication of treating plaintiffs and defendants in as equivalent a manner as possible is that the parties, not the state, should decide to what extent they wish to explore the particularities of the case. The primary concern of the state should be to provide the mechanisms by which the parties can explore the singularity of the relevant events to the extent that they choose to do so. This certainly means providing and enforcing liberal discovery rules. It may in addition mean permitting assistance to be given to the trier of fact to help it analyze the data provided by the parties.

Civil disputes in our culture are primarily disputes between parties that, so far as the law is concerned, are entitled to equal respect. The primary obligation of the state is to provide a disinterested forum that will assist in the rational resolution of the dispute. It is the parties' dispute, however. Thus, as a general matter the state has no serious ground to concern itself with the level of particularity of the evidence that the parties wish to provide the factfinder. While there may be a social interest in minimizing mistakes and I am willing to assume that mistakes are reduced as the level of specificity of the evidence increases, that does not seem to me adequate to impose upon the parties a case structure that they do not prefer. Rules governing the propriety of allowing verdicts to rest on quantitative evidence, or on the admissibility of such evidence, are in essence rules of relevancy. The only justification for such rules is that the evidence can not be understood, which includes evidence being put to an inappropriate purpose such as unfairly prejudicing a party. The state interest in minimizing errors is satisfied by creating the conditions whereby the parties are able to probe the uniqueness of the litigated event to the extent they choose to do so based on coherent evidentiary proffers. If they choose not to pursue particularity very extensively, and to rely instead on relatively crude statistical data, for example, then they should be competent to make that choice.[66]

[66] I am not yet ready to provide a complete catalog of the exceptions to this view. The outlines of justifiable exceptions are obvious enough, however. Case structure should not be left to the choice of the parties when there is some public interest at stake that would suffer otherwise. In addition, there may be sets of cases in which following the proscription in the text will lead to increasing rather than decreasing erroneous results due to the inability of defendants to generate evidence demonstrating their lack of liability. I must say, it is difficult to conceive of such cases. The blue bus hypotheticals certainly are not examples. If all you know is that a blue bus ran over the plaintiff, and company A runs 80% of the blue buses in town, and company B runs 20%, disallowing a verdict for plaintiffs in such cases is probably going to lead to more rather than fewer errors. Moreover, unless there is reason to

The primary method that facilitates the parties in probing the uniqueness of the relevant events is the discovery process. Thus, broad and liberal discovery rules should be implemented and enforced. In fact, those cases where courts have not allowed verdicts based upon statistical evidence make much more sense if viewed as involving a sanction for discovery violations or an inference drawn from the failure to produce available evidence.[67]

---

believe that the discovery process is not functioning properly, not allowing verdicts in such a case makes plaintiffs bear the entire cost of the lack of evidence in both parties' possession. To be sure, allowing a verdict for plaintiffs in this context will make company A bear more than its share of the cost. The answer to that is to embrace a proportional damages rule rather than make plaintiffs bear all the cost of the lack of more particularized evidence. It is important to note, however, that this is true regardless of the nature of the evidence—whether it is in quantitative form or not.

The textual discussion raises a number of related issues. For example, to what extent is the state justified in imposing on the parties rules concerning such issues as cross-examination or impeachment? Similarly, what is the justification for order of proof rules such as the Best Evidence Rule? These matters deserve fuller treatment. In brief, I would point out that there is a justification for creating a usable form of dispute resolution, since that seems to be an important component of contemporary life. What I object to is the state going beyond that minimum in civil cases, as it does when it forbids private parties to rely on perfectly good evidence. Although there is a justification for a state-created case structure that is neutral in regards to how particular evidentiary proffers must be, parties to litigation by agreement should be permitted to alter that structure. If parties accept an alteration, I see no reason for the rest of us to forbid that choice. What I hope is undue caution again counsels that I point out that other collective values may at some point intrude to forbid parties from resolving their disputes in certain ways, such as fights to the death, for example.

[67] Support for the proposition that courts are reluctant to allow cases to be decided on the basis of "statistical evidence" is greatly exaggerated in the literature. For example, Nesson, *The Evidence or the Event? On Judicial Proof and the Acceptability of Verdicts*, 98 HARV. L. REV. 1357, 1380 (1985), asserts that "[p]laintiffs in such cases would almost certainly lose by directed verdict; the evidence would never reach the jury." The support for that proposition is Guenther v. Armstrong Rubber Co., 406 F.2d 1315 (3d Cir. 1969), where, in reversing a directed verdict *for the defendant* and remanding for a new trial, the court in passing referred to one "probabilistic" argument raised by the plaintiff with disapproval. That, however, was dictum and it was in the context of sending the case back for a new trial. Nesson also cites Smith v. Rapid Transit, Inc., 317 Mass. 469, 58 N.E.2d 754 (1945), in which a verdict for the defendant was sustained. *Smith* is difficult to view as a "statistical evidence" case, however. The plaintiff did not rely on any such evidence. She merely asserted that she was forced off the road by a bus and in addition proved that Rapid Transit, Inc. was the only bus company operating regularly on the road where the accident occurred. In appraising the strength of the evidence, the court concluded that it was a matter of "conjecture" who owned the bus and that "[t]he most that can be said of the evidence in the instant case is that perhaps the mathematical chances somewhat favor the proposition that a bus of the defendant caused the

Suppose, for example, a case where a pedestrian is injured by a blue bus, and the plaintiff shows that 100 out of 102 blue buses are owned by the defendant. If both parties are willing to let the factfinder decide the case on that basis alone, I see no reason for the state to intervene to forbid that choice. Furthermore, if the state does wish to forbid it, there is no reason why that policy should redound solely to the detriment of plaintiffs, as it generally does.[68] However, it would be a different matter if a court is convinced that one party has evidence that it has not adduced or turned over to the opponent in discovery, thus forbidding the opponent to particularize the evidence to a greater degree.

There are other consequences that may result from this conceptualization. For example, the pursuit of rationality by the parties ought not to be stymied by the potential lack of understanding by the jury; and as cases become more complex, the difficulty of a rational analysis of the evidence most likely tends to increase. Accordingly, the parties should be allowed the creative use of experts to educate the factfinder on the problems presented by efforts to rationally evaluate the evidence. Although this point may appear to be indifferent to the level of particularity of evidence employed at trial, it nevertheless should result in encouraging issues to be joined at trial at the level of the most particularized evidence available. Presumably, the more particularized the evidence, the more persuasive in general it will tend to be if understood by the factfinder. Thus, greater latitude to explain complex matters encourages the parties to rely on more particularized evidence and to respond in kind to such proffers by opponents.

Another conceivable by-product of my general scheme may be an increase in the use of various types of experts. Expert testimony that would improve the factfinder's ability to rationally deliberate on the evidence would be

---

accident. This was not enough." *Smith*, 317 Mass. at 470, 58 N.E.2d at 755. That is the language of a traditional sufficiency of the evidence decision. Nesson does not mention here the case that *Smith* relied on, Sargent v. Massachusetts Accident Co., 307 Mass. 246, 29 N.E.2d 825 (1940). The *Sargent* court did make the assertion that evidence is insufficient when "mathematically the chances somewhat favor a proposition to be proved . . . ." *Id.* at 250, 29 N.E.2d at 827. However, the decision of the court reversed a directed verdict for the defendant and entered a directed verdict for the plaintiff in a factual context that is easily as probabilistic as that in *Smith*.

An example of a court employing a directed verdict as a sanction for the evidentiary practices of the plaintiff may be Galbraith v. Busch, 267 N.Y. 230, 196 N.E. 36 (1935), where the court reversed a jury verdict for the plaintiff and remanded for a new trial where the plaintiff had failed to call the defendant, who could have considerably dispelled the ambiguity about the nature of the litigated events. *See* Rubinfeld, *Econometrics in the Court Room*, 85 COLUM. L. REV. 1048, 1048 (1985) ("The use of statistical methods for resolving disputes has found increasing acceptance within the adversary system.").

[68] I know of no cases forbidding "statistical" defenses, for example. *See* Lilley v. Dow Chemical Company, 611 F. Supp. 1267 (D.C.N.Y. 1985), resting a summary judgement for defendant in part on statistical evidence.

encouraged. This, in turn, may disadvantage parties who are at a relative financial disadvantage. Accordingly, it may be necessary to institutionalize means to offset that advantage. If there is a general consensus that the state should provide a forum for the rational resolution of disputes, then a justification for providing the means by which that can be accomplished obviously exists.[69]

---

[69] In a recent article, Professor Nesson has constructed a justification for the status quo based upon his assertions that "[a] primary objective of the judicial process . . . is to project to society the legal rules that underlie judicial verdicts," Nesson, *supra* note 67, at 1357, and that the conventional proof rules "will produce the single most probable story." *Id.* at 1390. He demonstrates this latter assertion by arguing that if a cause of action has two elements, requiring the plaintiff to prove both of them by a preponderance will result in the probability of the conjunction of the two being more probable than the conjunction of any other combination of each element or its negation with the other element or its negation. *Id.* Although this argument has certain similarities to mine, I think it is problematic in its present form.

In the first place, the primary thesis confuses the effect of verdicts, which is to resolve disputes, with the effect of the underlying law relevant to any particular dispute. It is the law that projects substantive standards, not the verdicts in light of that law. The primary "affirming" that goes on at trials is that rules will be enforced if their violation is established, not what the rules are. Moreover, I know of no serious support for the proposition that anyone except the parties to litigation pays much attention to what goes on in the overwhelming proportion of courtrooms in this country. Yet, Professor Nesson asserts that a trial "is a drama that the public attends and from which it assimilates behavioral messages." His support for that proposition is a reference to speculation about the effect of court procedures in eighteenth-century England. *Id.* at 1360 n.14. My difficulties with Professor Nesson's central thesis are elaborated in greater detail in Allen, *Rationality, Mythology, and the "Acceptability of Verdicts" Thesis,* 66 B.U.L. REV. 541 (1986).

In addition to the main thesis being somewhat questionable, the discussion of proof rules is problematic. Professor Nesson asserts that negations are incoherent, implying that if A and B are the plaintiff's factual issues, not-A and not-B as an explanation of reality is not coherent. Nesson, *supra* note 67, at 1389. He proceeds to argue that if A and B are each proven to more than .5, the probability of the conjunction of A and B will be more probable than any other possibility, such as A and not-B, not-A and B, or not-A and not-B. But if these latter possibilities are "coherent" (and if they are not, why are they being compared to something that is?), that implies that their components are. That, of course, simply contradicts the earlier assertions about the incoherency of negations. It also causes another problem. If not-A and not-B is coherent, so is not-A *or* not-B, and not-A or not-B is more likely, given Professor Nesson's hypothetical, than A and B. Professor Nesson does not address why it is that only conjunctions matter. In part, this may be because his consideration of probability theory is inadequate. At one point, Professor Nesson asserts that conjunction problems do not arise with dependent elements. *Id.* at 1387. That is false, of course. The conjunction effect is reduced by the extent of the dependency, but it still occurs unless the two elements are completely dependent one on the other.

IV. A Final Paradox

I wish to address one last difficulty that may appear to beset the theory I have developed here. One of the implications of the theory is that if a party wished to do so, he should be permitted to advance alternative explanations of the relevant factual inquiry that are consistent with a verdict for that party, and that the factfinder should return a verdict for the party who has advanced the single most likely version of the facts.[70] An alternative, however, is that the decisionmaker should return a verdict in favor of the party whose factual propositions *collectively* are the most likely. For example, assume each party advances two competing versions of reality. Assume further that the jury would assess the likelihood of plaintiff's version one to be .05 and that of version two to be .3, while it would assess the likelihood of the defendant's version one to be .2 and that of version two to be .2. Assume further the radically unlikely but helpfully simplifying proposition that these four versions of reality are completely independent of each other.

Under my earlier argument, the jury should return a verdict for the plaintiff in this situation because the single most likely course of events is plaintiff's version two. Still, the probability is greater that one of the defendant's versions is correct than that one of the plaintiff's versions is correct. Thus, if the objective is to reduce errors, a verdict should be returned for the defendant rather than for the plaintiff. In short, a generalization of my theory is that a verdict should be returned for that party for whom it is most likely true that one of the party's factual versions is correct.

This creates a mild paradox, or at least a bit of irony. I have been developing my proposal as though it were somewhat radical, but this point, which I believe accurate, may appear to make my argument a rather convo-

---

In any event, Professor Nesson's discussion of the proof rules is difficult to reconcile with his main thesis. If the concern of trials is to project the reasons for verdicts, it is certainly coherent to project a rule that defendants are not liable if the plaintiff fails to prove all (not "each") of the elements to a specified level of certainty. Again, this possibility is not considered. Thus, it is unclear why we should not be troubled by critiques such as Cohen's even if we accept Nesson's view.

There are other problems with Professor Nesson's argument, as well. For example, he purports to be defending the present proof rules, but his argument would work just as well so long as the plaintiff proved one element to more than .5 and all others to .5. That is not our system, of course.

In one respect, Professor Nesson's argument is similar to mine in its emphasis on stories. His error, in my view, is the attempt to emphasize stories in the context of the conventional conception of trials. His discussion of the persuasiveness of historical accounts is instructive in this regard. *Id.* at 1389. In deciding which historian has provided the most persuasive account, one would not compare an historian's account with its negation. Rather, one would compare one historian's account with that of another. That, of course, is the model I am advancing in this article.

[70] *See supra* text accompanying notes 61-67.

luted justification for the status quo. The reason for this is that the plaintiff's burden will be to establish some version of the facts consistent with what the law requires for a verdict. Accordingly, the plaintiff will attempt to prove factual propositions that, if believed, will result in an inference of the necessary elements of his cause of action. The defendant, on the other hand, will attempt to prove factual assertions that will result in the inference that at least one of the necessary elements in the plaintiff's cause of action is not true. Thus, the final form of the inferential process under my theory may appear to be identical to that which occurs now. If the probability of the plaintiff's factual assertions concerning any single element is less than .5, the defendant can admit all other elements and defend solely with respect to this particular element. If the plaintiff can only establish an element to some probability less than .5, then the defendant has established that this element did not occur to more than .5, and the single most likely sequence or sequences of events favors the defendant.

I think all of this is right except the last point. A jury in evaluating evidence should conclude that the probability of the defendant's versions of reality is the probability of the plaintiff's versions subtracted from one only if it feels that it has before it all relevant versions of reality. Although it is an empirical matter, I doubt that this is often the case.

Take another oversimplified example that makes this point. Assume there is a cause of action that in the jury's view entails ten equally likely factual explanations.[71] Assume further that the plaintiff asserts four of them to be true and supports those assertions with credible evidence. In addition, assume that the defendant asserts three of the ten possibilities as true, and supports those assertions with credible evidence. Lastly, assume that the versions asserted by each party justify a verdict for that party.

In this hypothetical, under the conventional view of trials, presumably the defendant should win. Of the ten possibilities that the jury thinks may explain the relevant state of affairs, the plaintiff has provided evidence that

[71] The point about the jury thinking that there are ten possible explanations, although a crude over-simplification of reality, nonetheless presents an interesting problem. Much of the probability debate, indeed just about all of it, proceeds as though the concept of "evidence" were clear and coherent. I suggest it is neither. What counts as "evidence" is what sways a factfinder. That will be in part what is contained in the formal proffers at trial. In much larger part, I suggest it will be how what is proffered interacts with the intellectual tools that the decisionmaker brings to bear on the problem. These tools will include the decisionmaker's understanding, knowledge, judgement and experience. It is the failure to make this distinction that allows Professor Cohen to criticize conventional probability theory in his contribution to this symposium. Cohen, *supra* note 32. He proceeds as though the only "evidence" a factfinder has is what is presented at trial, whereas a much more accurate perspective is that the evidence emerges from the process of judgement brought to bear on what is presented. Obviously, there are subtleties here that deserve extended exploration.

only four of those may be true. If there are ten possible explanations of an event, four of which favor the plaintiff and thus six of which do not, certainly the plaintiff has not proven his case to a preponderance of the evidence. Indeed, this is true regardless of whether the defendant produces any evidence with respect to its three factual assertions.

The difficulty with this explanation, which highlights for me the single most troublesome aspect of our present conceptualization of trials, is that it results in resolving all ambiguity against the plaintiff. The "thus" in the penultimate sentence of the preceding paragraph is inaccurate, in other words. Presumably the jury does not know how to evaluate the three possibilities for which no evidence has been produced. In that case, a verdict for the defendant results in all possible inferences for which neither party has produced evidence being drawn against the plaintiff. A better view, I would suggest, is that the ambiguity in a case should be distributed over the parties. That is what my theory would do, and why on the facts of this hypothetical a verdict should be returned for the plaintiff.

V. The Continuing Process of Reconceptualization

The efforts to establish the superiority of conventional or inductivist approaches to the trial of civil disputes have not achieved their objective. Upon being interpreted for application to the process of civil trials, both generate quite similar implications, and it would be astonishing were this not so. The trial of civil disputes is a phenomenon with observable characteristics. Any rational thought process brought to bear upon it must reflect those characteristics, whether that process is inductivist or conventional in its nature, or one of the other conceptualizations of rationality and probability that have been developed recently, such as fuzzy set theory[72] or Shafer's idea of belief functions.[73] This is not to say that much has not been learned by these various efforts, or that they do not differ in many important respects. It is to say, however, that to the extent that these varying conceptions are employed to explain the phenomena of trials, there will be broad areas of similar implications. Moreover, many of those implications are troublesome. These implications are not to be avoided by changing the explanation of them; rather, they can be avoided only by changing the nature of the observed phenomenon.

I have sketched out one suggestion for just such a change. It is just a sketch, though, and it is obviously incomplete. The basic conception presented here will have to be tested by further work, and undoubtedly unanticipated implications will emerge. In addition, the implications of this approach for a whole range of trial-related issues must be examined. For example, what would be meant under my approach to impose a burden of

---

[72] Comment, *supra* note 14.

[73] G. Shafer, *supra* note 14.

production? Can burdens of persuasion other than by a preponderance be brought within the analysis? What would the standards be for preclusive motions such as directed verdicts and summary judgments? What happens to the idea of insufficiency of the evidence? What would be the role of inferences, presumptions and comments on the evidence? Will this conceptualization stimulate the filing of civil suits? These and other issues await development.[74]

Although an appraisal of the wisdom of my proposed conceptualization of trials will have to await its further explorations, I take some comfort in the fact that it has the curious feature of combining the wisdom of the common law with the essence of modern practice, thus being more theoretically than pragmatically radical. The common law system of pleading had as its objective the narrowing and clarifying of the range of factual dispute.[75] That, in essence, captures the crux of my proposal. Moreover, it is my understanding that the dominant view of contemporary litigation is that to convince a jury requires the presentation of an affirmative story, regardless of one's formal posture in the case.[76] Again, that is quite consistent with the theoretical approach presented here.[77]

---

[74] Perhaps of overriding significance is the determination of the purposes served by various branches of the law. Whether, for example, the primary concern in tort law is accuracy in verdicts, and justice to the parties conceived of as some version of equal treatment, or whether tort law should pursue other values. Again, though, no matter how such issues are worked out, there will be the need for rules of decision to inform the jury how to decide when faced with uncertainty as to the historical facts.

[75] *See* Epstein, *Pleadings and Presumptions,* 40 U. CHI. L. REV. 556 (1973).

[76] D. BINDER & P. BERGMAN, FACT INVESTIGATION: FROM HYPOTHESIS TO PROOF 16 (1984).

[77] The intuitive sense of litigators that they must provide jurors with coherent presentations is beginning to receive support from the work of cognitive psychologists. Bennett and Feldman have provided an account of criminal trials as involving the construction of stories. W. BENNETT & M. FELDMAN, RECONSTRUCTING REALITY IN THE COURTROOM (1981). As they correctly point out, "[l]egal judgments must emerge from the juror's everyday cognitive repertoire." *Id.* at 64. These authors create a convincing argument that "[w]hether the concern is with how jurors apply legal statutes or how they process large bodies of information, stories provide the most obvious link between everyday analytical and communicational skills and the requirements of formal adjudication procedures." *Id.* at 10. Empirical support for analogous propositions is provided by Pennington & Hastie, *Evidence Evaluation in Complex Decision Making*, 51 J. PERSONALITY & SOC. PSYCHOLOGY 242 (1986), which found that trial evidence was represented in story form.

Both of these efforts involve criminal trials, however, and that is unfortunate, for the work is more easily applicable to civil trials. The problem is that neither can explain reasonable doubt. Pennington and Hastie do not even try, and Bennett and Feldman can only assert that the measure of doubt is "whether an inference is based on a set of connections that are internally consistent and that yield no other interpretations." W. BENNETT & M. FELDMAN, *supra*, at 64. That is not terribly helpful.

There is one last implication of my proposal that deserves mention that is both troublesome and liberating. The approach suggested here could not be applied to criminal trials without a drastic reordering of the present procedures employed in the criminal process—so drastic as to be implausible. Perhaps that may weigh against my proposal by demonstrating a limited capacity for generalization. I think there is a more cogent proposition lurking here, though, and that is that the objectives and purposes of criminal trials may be so far different from those of civil trials as to make them alien to each other. Unlike civil trials, the purpose of criminal trials is not to provide a forum where parties essentially equal before the law can resolve their private disputes. Rather, a criminal trial involves unequal parties upon whom reciprocal burdens are not placed. The objective of a criminal trial is not to choose among stories of the parties. Rather, it is to determine whether or not the only plausible explanation of the event in question is that the defendant is guilty as charged. Moreover, as a check upon a potentially abusive government, the defendant is permitted to sit passively and to require the government to establish just that proposition. To do so requires that the government not only establish its own case but to negate any reasonable explanations of the relevant affairs consistent with innocence.[78]

Internal consistency should be a variable in all types of verdicts, and "yielding no other interpretations" either lacks a measure by which that conclusion is reached or simply refers to certainty, which is obviously somewhat problematic. The accounts of both pairs of authors, however, work well within the structure offered in this article.

[78] I believe that what I am suggesting here is similar to what Professor Cohen has discussed in his contribution to this symposium. Cohen, *supra* note 32. Unless I misunderstand his argument, one way to understand my argument is that evidential weight of the evidence in criminal cases is of the utmost importance, and it must weigh heavily in favor of guilt. By contrast, in civil cases the decisionmaker's task is merely to compare the evidential weight provided by the parties for their respective factual assertions.

Although I am quite in agreement with what Professor Cohen has written on evidential weight, I must say that Professor Cohen's inability to say how heavy evidential weight must be in a criminal case to justify a conviction injects into his analysis a difficulty similar to that which he sees in the difficulty of going from a conditional to an unconditional probability assessment under conventional probability notions. In essence, his argument is that other evidence not before the decisionmaker may substantially qualify its willingness to rely on its assessment of the evidence before it. That, however, is also true if one conceives of the evidentiary process in Baconian terms. In either case, what is occurring is that a disinterested third party is analyzing the evidence in light of his or her own experience. If the decisionmaker believes that there is other evidence that should have been presented, its assessment of what has been presented will be influenced by that belief. Thus, if a statistic is provided to a criminal jury that, if true, shows a high probability of guilt, but the jury believes there is good reason to doubt its accuracy, the Pascalian probability it would assign to the evidence before it would be based on both the statistic and the reason it is of doubtful accuracy. *See supra* notes 41-45 and accom-

If these assertions are true, it should not be surprising at all that a conceptualization of civil trials will not encompass criminal trials. Different tasks will call for different procedures. The mere fact that there are superficial similarities between entities does not guarantee fundamental similarity. Civil trials are designed to resolve disputes in an amicable fashion among parties who are indistinguishable before the law. Criminal trials pit an individual against the virtually inexorable power of the state. As a result, the concept of certainty assumes much greater importance in criminal than in civil trials. The implications of that difference deserve careful evaluation, but that is a task for another day.

---

panying text concerning the meaning of "evidence." It is only by denying this possibility that Professor Cohen's demonstration of the inaptness of Pascalian accounts of criminal trials is made cogent, and there is no satisfactory reason for denying it.

Perhaps I should also point out an apparent tension in what I have argued here and my discussion of Professor Kaye's work, *see supra* notes 35-39 and accompanying text, where I argued against his suggestion that the failure of the plaintiff to produce evidence could count against him. I was there not denying that phenomenon but rather pointing out that it was a two-way street running against both plaintiffs and defendants.

B
Omission Models

[3]

Rand Journal of Economics
Vol. 17, No. 1, Spring 1986

Relying on the information of interested parties

Paul Milgrom*

and

John Roberts**

We investigate the conventional wisdom that competition among interested parties attempting to influence a decisionmaker by providing verifiable information elicits all relevant information. We find that, if the decisionmaker is strategically sophisticated and well informed about the relevant variables and about the preferences of the interested party or parties, competition may be unnecessary to achieve this result. If the decisionmaker is unsophisticated or not well informed, competition is not generally sufficient. If the interested parties' interests are sufficiently opposed, however, or if the decisionmaker is seeking to advance the parties' welfare, then competition can reduce or even eliminate the decisionmaker's need for prior knowledge about the relevant variables and for strategic sophistication. In other settings only the combination of competition among information providers and a sophisticated skepticism is sufficient to allow effective decisionmaking.

". . . [T]he only way in which a human can make some approach to knowing the whole of a subject is by hearing what can be said about it by persons of every variety of opinion, and studying all modes in which it can be looked at by every character of mind."

—John Stuart Mill, *On Liberty*

"So long as dissent is not suppressed, there will always be some who will query the ideas ruling their contemporaries and put new ideas to the test of argument and propaganda."

—Friedrich A. Hayek, *The Road to Serfdom*

"What we usually call 'scientific knowledge' is, as a rule . . . information regarding the various competing hypotheses and the way they have stood to various tests."

—Karl R. Popper, *The Open Society and Its Enemies*

---

* Yale University.

** Stanford University.

This research was supported by National Science Foundation Grants IST-8411595 and IST-8420606 to Yale University and SES-8308723 to Stanford University. Part of this work was completed while Milgrom was a Fellow of the Institute for Advanced Studies at the Hebrew University of Jerusalem.

We thank the participants at the Stanford Summer Accounting Workshop, the Northwestern University Summer Workshop on Strategic Behavior and Competition, the Cowles Foundation Seminar, the Theory Seminar at Princeton, the Stanford University Conference on Adaptive Institutions, and the Conference on Games and the Theory of Firm Behavior at the University of Western Ontario for their suggestions and comments. Bernard Desgagne provided diligent and able research assistance. Stan Besen and the anonymous referees helped us to clarify the exposition.

1. Introduction

■ A common problem faced by decisionmakers is the need to rely on suggestions and information provided by individuals who are affected by their decisions. Although interested parties may try to manipulate the decisionmaker's choice by concealing or distorting information, their efforts do not always succeed. An archetypical example of an institution that is designed to prevent concealment and distortion is the adversary system used to resolve legal disputes. The chief perceived virtue of an adversary system is that, since any relevant piece of information favors one disputant or the other, one can rely on the disputants themselves to report all relevant information. More generally, it has been argued that "free and open discussion" or "competition in the marketplace of ideas" will result in the truth's becoming known and appropriate decisions' being made in a variety of political, scientific, legal, regulatory, and market contexts.

In this article we examine the validity and scope of this argument by studying the problem of a decisionmaker who must rely on one or more interested parties to provide information about possible decisions and their consequences. We identify conditions under which a decisionmaker can reach a good decision despite possibly severe limitations both on the decisionmaker's prior information and ability to draw sophisticated inferences and on the capacity of the interested parties to communicate what they know.

There are two general kinds of strategies that may be available to a decisionmaker to overcome some of these limitations. First, although lacking information about the specific situation, a decisionmaker may nevertheless be sophisticated about interpreting any information reported to him by recognizing that self-interest tinges the reports. We shall find that a sophisticated *skepticism* can be an important weapon in the decisionmaker's arsenal. Second, a decisionmaker—even one who is too unsophisticated to implement an effective skeptical strategy—may still be able to extract useful information by inducing well-informed parties with competing interests to compete in providing information. Sometimes, a combination of these two techniques is required for optimal decisionmaking.

For our formal study of the decisionmaker's problem, we introduce a class of "persuasion games." In these games the decisionmaker and the interested party or parties interact only once, so that issues of reputations do not arise.[1] We assume that the interested parties can withhold information, but that the decisionmaker can freely verify anything that is reported to him. For example, a seller might verifiably report that his product meets or exceeds a standard that is out-of-date or just barely met, but at the same time he might simply fail to mention a more relevant or stringent standard that the product does not meet.

The assumption that reported information can be freely verified is important for our analysis, although one could substitute the assumption that there are penalties for perjury, false advertising, or warranty violations that are sufficiently sure and heavy that false reporting never pays. When information is not verifiable, the reliability of any report depends in part on the degree of consonance between the objectives of the decisionmaker and those of the interested party or parties. The case with one interested party is equivalent to a problem of delegation, and has been studied by Holmström (1977) and Crawford and Sobel (1982), among others.

We begin our formal analysis in Section 2 by studying the problem of a decisionmaker who relies on a single interested party to report information. Initially we investigate how a sophisticated decisionmaker can use skepticism as a weapon to extract maximum information. Our first results here extend ones previously reported by Milgrom (1981) and Grossman (1981): If the interested party has known monotone preferences over the decisionmaker's choice set (e.g., a seller wants to sell as much as possible, an electric utility company prefers

[1] See Sobel (1985) for an analysis of reputation building in information provision.

less restrictive emissions standards) and has information that bears on the decisionmaker's preferences, and if the decisionmaker knows what information to seek, then (i) the decisionmaker's unique equilibrium strategy is to *assume the worst,* that is, to make the inference that, consistent with his information, leads to the least favorable decision for the interested party and (ii) the equilibrium decision is the *full-information decision*—the decision that would have been reached if the decisionmaker had perfect access to the interested party's information.

Often an interested party will be uncertain about whether the decisionmaker is *sophisticated,* that is, capable of game-theoretic reasoning. There are many kinds of unsophisticated behavior. For example, an unsophisticated buyer may be naively credulous, that is, he may interpret any information reported to him as if it were the complete report of some disinterested observer[2] and act accordingly. When the interested party is unsure whether the decisionmaker is sophisticated or naively credulous, his equilibrium reporting strategy is the strategy that elicits the most favorable decision from a credulous decisionmaker.[3] For example, a rational salesman will treat every buyer as if he were naively credulous. This treatment, however, does not harm the sophisticated decisionmaker: at equilibrium, he uses the skeptical "assume-the-worst" strategy, interprets the salesman's report correctly, and reaches the full-information decision. Similarly, the presence in the market of sophisticated buyers does not benefit an unsophisticated buyer; he hears the same report and makes the same decision as he would if the seller knew him to be naively credulous.

It is interesting to contrast these results with the results of search-theoretic models in which consumers search for the lowest price. There, the presence of knowledgeable consumers, or ones with low search costs, benefits less knowledgeable consumers by shifting downward the distribution of prices (Wilde, 1977). Similarly, consumers with high search costs harm other consumers by shifting the distribution of prices upwards. In our model there is no such effect, because the seller finds that the same strategy is effective against both sophisticated and credulous consumers.

The assumptions needed to justify the conclusions of Section 2 are many. First, one needs to assume that the interested party's preferences are known. For example, this assumption would be satisfied if the interested party is a seller who is offering a single product and wants to sell as much as possible, or if he is offering one unit of any of several products and wants to sell the most expensive one. On the other hand, if mark-ups vary across several products in a manner unknown to the buyer, then the result does not apply—the seller may benefit by withholding information. Similarly, if the decision involves, say, setting product safety standards, the interested parties' preferences are likely to be unknown and complex, and the result again does not apply.

Second, the decisionmaker must know the factors about which the interested party has information to detect situations in which information is being withheld. For example, if a used car salesman has information about recent repairs to a car but does not report it, the buyer may not know that information has been withheld.

Third, the decisionmaker must be sophisticated enough to draw the appropriate inference when information is withheld. When any of these first three conditions fails, the decisionmaker will be unable to implement the strategy of extreme skepticism, and will suffer a loss of utility as a result.

Finally, for the full information decision to be an appropriate welfare standard, the decisionmaker must be able to draw the proper inferences and reach the right decision when all relevant information has been made available to him.

---

[2] The way a naively credulous decisionmaker forms his beliefs is made precise in Section 2.

[3] A similar result is shown to hold for a wide class of unsophisticated behaviors, provided that the decisionmaker responds positively to "favorable information." The result that the interested party treats a decisionmaker as if he were unsophisticated also holds for more complex environments, in which various kinds of unsophisticated behavior are possible.

In Section 3 we begin to study how competition among interested parties in providing information may substitute for the many restrictions listed above, so that an unsophisticated decisionmaker, with little or no idea of the set of available options, of the issues bearing on the decision, or of the preferences of the interested parties, might overcome all these handicaps to reach a good decision. Our central result is that if the full-information decision is Pareto-undominated among the interested parties—more precisely, if in every situation and for every proposed decision there is an interested party who is well informed, who has an opportunity to report, and who prefers the full-information decision to the proposed decision—then only the full information decision can be reached at equilibrium. For if any other decision were proposed, some interested party would find it advantageous to propose the full-information decision and provide enough information to support it.

Two sorts of applications emerge from this simple proposition. The first arises in situations where the decisionmaker seeks to maximize a Bergson-Samuelson social welfare function that is an increasing function of the interested parties' utilities. Some regulatory or legislative situations might be appropriately viewed in this light. The second concerns situations where the preferences of the interested parties are generally opposed, as they would be in many purchasing decisions or legal contests. In these applications competition among informed interested parties allows even an unsophisticated decisionmaker who fails to recognize the strategic incentives of the interested parties to reach the full-information decision.

The strategy to be employed by the decisionmaker in Section 3 does not make great demands on his rationality. It does not require the decisionmaker to know the possible states of information, the space of available decisions, or the preferences of the interested parties—or even to have beliefs about these things. Nor does the decisionmaker have to make any sophisticated inferences to unravel possible strategic dissembling by interested parties. The demands placed on the abilities of the interested parties to convey information and on the decisionmaker to process the information he receives are relatively severe, however.

In Section 4 we explore a class of problems in which the interested parties are unable to transmit all of their information; they are constrained to suggesting a limited range of alternatives, to suggesting dimensions to be considered in ranking the alternatives, and to reporting how the alternatives rank on these dimensions. We assume that the decisionmaker faces severe handicaps in dealing with the interested parties: He does not know their preferences, the set of alternatives, the particular attributes of any alternatives that may be suggested, or even the relevant dimensions on which alternatives might be ranked. We do assume, however, that the decisionmaker is sophisticated and that the interested parties are all equally well informed. We retain the assumption of Section 3 that the full-information decision is Pareto-undominated among the interested parties. Then, at the equilibrium of the persuasion game, competition among the interested parties leads them to reveal the dimensions or issues that are relevant to the decision, and the decisionmaker's skepticism extracts enough additional information to ensure that the full-information decision is reached.

The condition that there does not exist another decision that is unanimously weakly preferred to the full-information decision is quite useful for understanding when the full-information decision might not be reached. For example, the condition fails in a selling situation where the buyer can choose only one product to buy and can also buy nothing, thereby avoiding the whole product class. Then, as Posner (1977, pp. 136–137) has noted, if product safety is an issue, "the manufacturer who advertises that his product is safer than his competitors' product [*sic*] runs the risk of planting fears where none existed. This . . . may reduce the advertiser's sales by more than his claim of relative safety increases them."

It is interesting to contrast the main conclusion of Section 2, which requires that the decisionmaker know the interested party's preferences, with that of Section 4, which has no such requirement. To understand this fully, one must understand something of the nature of skeptical strategies. For general persuasion games, we say that a strategy exhibits *skepticism* if it calls for holding pessimistic expectations about alternatives that are (or are thought to be) favored by some well-informed interested party and about which little has been reported. When there is but a single interested party, skepticism involves forming expectations that downgrade his *most favored* alternatives—a strategy that requires information about his preferences. With several competing interested parties who do not unanimously prefer any alternative to the full-information decision, skepticism consists of forming pessimistic expectations about *every* alternative. This is effective because *somebody* favors the full-information decision over any other alternative; that party can be relied upon to suggest it and provide the information needed to justify it.

Our theory is a close cousin to the extensively developed theory of mechanism design. We review some similarities and differences between the theories in Section 5, and present our conclusion in Section 6.

2. One seller and a sophisticated buyer

■ We consider here a game with two players: for concreteness, we take them to be a seller and a buyer, although the model fits other situations as well. The single seller provides verifiable information about product quality to the buyer, who then decides how much to purchase. The seller wants to maximize sales; the buyer's objective is to maximize the expected utility of his consumption, which depends upon the quality of the product being offered.

The extensive form of this persuasion game is as follows. First, Nature selects a point x, representing the seller's information, from a finite set X. The buyer believes that the probability that any particular x has been chosen is $P(x) > 0$.[4] The seller observes x and makes an assertion A to the buyer; A is a subset of X. We restrict the seller to make true assertions, that is, we require that $x \in A$. The buyer observes A and then selects a quantity $q \in \mathbb{R}_+$. The payoffs are $u(x, q)$ to the buyer and $v(x, q)$ to the seller, where v is a function increasing in q. In particular, the monotonicity of v in q implies that the buyer knows the seller's ordinal preferences. Finally, we assume that for each x there is a unique $q^*(x)$ that maximizes the buyer's utility.

The normal form of the game can be derived from the extensive form in the usual way. A *reporting strategy* for the seller is a function r from X to the subsets of X such that $x \in r(x)$; r specifies what assertion the seller will make as a function of his information x. A *buying strategy* b for the purchaser is function b mapping subsets of X to purchase decisions in $\mathbb{R}_+$. When Nature chooses x and the strategies are r and b, the seller's payoff is $v(x, b(r(x)))$ and the purchaser's is $u(x, b(r(x)))$.

To solve the game we use the concept of sequential equilibrium introduced by Kreps and Wilson (1982). For this game, a sequential equilibrium is described by a triple (r, b, p), where r and b are the reporting and buying strategies, respectively, and p specifies what the buyer believes when the seller makes a report. Thus, $p(x|A)$ is the probability that the buyer assigns to the information state x when the seller reports A. The triple is a sequential equilibrium in pure strategies if it satisfies the following four conditions:

(i) *Seller maximization.* r is the seller's best response to b, that is, $r(x)$ is the assertion A that maximizes $v(x, b(A))$ subject to $x \in A$.
(ii) *Buyer maximization.* For all A, $b(A)$ is the best purchase for the buyer, given his beliefs, that is, it is the quantity q that maximizes $\sum_x u(x, q)p(x|A)$.
(iii) *Rational buyer expectations.* If $A = r(z)$ for some z, then $p(x|A)$ is $P(x)/P(r^{-1}(A))$ for x in $r^{-1}(A)$ and is zero otherwise.

[4] The seller may or may not know P or he may have imperfect information about it; that part of the specification of the game does not affect the solution.

(iv) *Consistent beliefs.* $p(x|A) = 0$ for all x not in A.

For the same game, a Nash equilibrium can be described as a triple satisfying conditions (i), (iii), (iv), and a weakened form of (ii) as follows:[5]

(iia) *Nash buyer maximization.* For all A in the range of r, $b(A)$ is the best purchase for the buyer, given his beliefs, that is, it is the quantity q that maximizes $\sum_x u(x, q)p(x|A)$.

The difference between the Nash and sequential equilibrium concepts lies in their notions of what rational behavior is. Sequential equilibrium requires what Kreps and Wilson call "sequential rationality"—the buyer always maximizes when it is his turn, no matter what has previously happened. Nash equilibrium requires the buyer to maximize only if there have been no "surprises."

This game has many Nash equilibria, some of which are quite implausible. For example, one Nash equilibrium (r, b) consists of the pair of strategies $r(x) = X$ for all x and $b(A) = q^*$ for all A, where q^* is the quantity that maximizes $\sum_x P(x)u(x, q)$. At this Nash equilibrium, the buyer is stubbornly determined (contrary to his own interests) to ignore any information offered by the seller, and the seller, believing that what he says is irrelevant, offers no information. But if there is any x such that the buyer's best choice, given x, is to buy more than q^*, one should expect that the seller will try to communicate that information and that a rational buyer will pay heed. Henceforth, we shall focus primarily on the sequential equilibrium solution concept; we use the unmodified term "equilibrium" to refer to it.

How will a sophisticated buyer behave in this persuasion game? Let us call a pair (b, p) satisfying (ii) and (iv) a "posture" for the buyer. A *naively credulous* posture is one in which the buyer takes the seller's report at face value and simply puts $p(x|A) = P(x)/P(A)$ for $x \in A$. A *skeptical* posture $(\bar{b}, \bar{p})$ is one such that, for *every* report A, $(\bar{b}(A), \bar{p})$ solves:

$$\text{Minimize}_{Q,p}\ Q$$

subject to

$$Q \text{ maximizes } \sum_x u(x, q)p(x|A)$$

$$p(\cdot|\cdot) \text{ a conditional probability}$$

$$p(x|A) = 0 \qquad \text{for all} \qquad x \notin A.$$

Every posture requires that the buyer form beliefs consistent with his information and maximize accordingly. A *skeptical* posture minimizes (over all postures) the quantity the buyer will purchase. In the game we have described, there is always an equilibrium in which the buyer adopts a skeptical posture and the seller reports everything he knows. Indeed, somewhat more is true.

Proposition 1. If the buyer's posture (b, p) is a skeptical posture and the full-information decision is always reached, i.e., $b(r(x)) = q^*(x)$ for all x, then (r, b, p) is an equilibrium.

It is straightforward to verify that any triple (r, b, p) satisfying the conditions of Proposition 1 is in fact an equilibrium. In particular, if (b, p) is a skeptical posture and $r(x) = \{x\}$, the hypotheses of the proposition are satisfied, so an equilibrium does exist.

With the assumptions made so far, there may be other equilibria in which the buyer

[5] The condition (iv) is actually irrelevant in the definition of a Nash equilibrium, since it is implied by (iii) for sets A in the range of r (Milgrom and Roberts, 1982). The present description emphasizes that the major difference between the equilibrium concepts lies in the fact that Nash equilibrium does not require maximizing behavior at every node in the game tree.

does not adopt a skeptical posture. For example, if the buyer's preferences would lead him to purchase more than any full-information quantity when he has no information, there is an equilibrium in which the seller is always silent ($r(x) \equiv X$). But the set of equilibria shrinks to just those described in Proposition 1 when the buyer's utility function u is strictly concave and continuously differentiable in q. The argument goes as follows.

At a pure strategy equilibrium, for each state x the buyer will never buy less than the full-information, utility-maximizing quantity $q^*(x)$. Otherwise, the seller could not be optimizing; he could do better by telling the *whole truth* (reporting $r(x) = \{x\}$). The concavity of the buyer's utility function and the uniqueness of the optimum, $q^*(x)$, ensure that if the buyer always buys at least the full-information quantity $q^*(x)$ (as he must at any pure-strategy equilibrium) and sometimes buys an excessive amount, then he could do better by reducing his purchases slightly. Hence, at any pure-strategy equilibrium of the game we have described, the buyer always buys precisely the full-information quantity. (A formal proof, which allows for mixed-strategy equilibria as well, appears in the Appendix.)

Proposition 2. If the buyer's utility function is strictly concave and continuously differentiable in q, then at every equilibrium the buyer adopts a skeptical posture (b, p) and always purchases the full-information quantity: $b(r(x)) = q^*(x)$ for all x.

Notice that the seller's equilibrium strategy is not unique, even though the buyer's response to it is. All that can be said about the seller's strategy is that when his information is x, he reports some A whose elements y are all (at least) *as favorable as* x, in the sense that $q^*(y) \geq q^*(x)$. Notice, too, that the equilibrium strategies of both players are independent of the prior distribution P, so the demands of Bayesian rationality and common knowledge priors are less extreme in our model than in most Bayesian game models.

An interesting variation of the game arises when the seller suspects that the buyer may be too unsophisticated to adopt a skeptical posture. Suppose that the seller believes that with some probability π ($0 < \pi \leq 1$), the buyer will adopt some other posture, such as the naively credulous posture. We restrict attention to postures for which the buyer's purchases increase as the seller's report becomes more favorable. More precisely, a posture is *responsive to favorable information* if whenever $q^*(x) \leq q^*(y)$ for all $y \in A$, and $A \setminus \{x\}$ is nonempty, $b(A \setminus \{x\}) \geq b(A)$.

As before, we describe an equilibrium by a triple (r, b, p), where r is the seller's reporting strategy and (b, p) is the posture of the sophisticated buyer. The strategy of the unsophisticated buyer is not specified as part of the equilibrium, since it is given exogenously.

Proposition 3. In the variant game suppose u is strictly concave and continuously differentiable in q and the unsophisticated buyer's posture is responsive to favorable information. Then the triple (r, b, p) is an equilibrium if and only if (b, p) is a skeptical posture for the buyer and r is a strategy that maximizes sales to the unsophisticated buyer. At equilibrium, the sophisticated buyer purchases the full-information quantity: $b(r(x)) = q^*(x)$.

Propositions 2 and 3 are proved in the Appendix.

Thus, at equilibrium, the seller acts as if the buyer were certain to be unsophisticated, and makes a larger sale if the buyer is, in fact, unsophisticated. Given our assumption that even an unsophisticated buyer is responsive to favorable information, the sales-maximizing report rules out all information states that are "less favorable" than the truth. At equilibrium, a sophisticated buyer adopts a skeptical posture and correctly infers that the actual information state x is the least favorable one consistent with the seller's report.

3. Competition among interested parties

■ In this section we relax substantially our assumptions about the sophistication and the prior information of the decisionmaker, but we introduce multiple interested parties who compete in providing any information upon which the decision will be based. The question at issue is under what circumstances competition among providers of information can help to protect unsophisticated and ill-informed decisionmakers from the self-interested dissembling of information providers.

As examples, when does competition among sellers reveal actual product qualities? When does lobbying by interest groups help regulators and legislators reach better decisions? Does competition between divisions for corporate resources generally assist in making correct investment and capital budgeting decisions? As we shall see, competition may help both the credulous and the sophisticated decisionmaker by reducing the amount of prior information that they need about their sets of options, the relevant aspects of each option, and the interested parties' preferences, and by reducing the strategic sophistication that they need to interpret the messages they receive and to reach the full-information decision.

This persuasion game is structured as follows. First, Nature chooses a point x from the finite set X according to the distribution P. Then, each of N interested parties observes x.[6] Simultaneously, each suggests a set D_i of possible decisions d, chosen from a finite set Δ, and asserts a true proposition (that is, a set A such that $x \in A$). Let $D = \cup D_i$ be the set of decisions suggested.

We model the decisionmaker as a naive automaton—not as a player in the game. The automaton takes the conjunction (intersection) I of the assertions and selects a mixed decision (that is, a probability distribution over D) to maximize the objective function $E[u(x, d)|I]$.[7] The probabilities used by the automaton for the expected utility calculation are such that $P(x|I)$ is zero for information states x not in I. For simplicity, we assume that the maximizing decision is unique for each I and D so that the chosen mixed decision will, in fact, be simply one of the suggested decisions $d \in D$. Recalling the notation of the last section, we call this decision $b(I, D)$. Let $f(x) = b(\{x\}, \Delta)$ designate the full-information decision.[8]

The payoffs to the interested parties are denoted $v_i(x, b(I, D))$. Since these payoffs depend on x, they need not be known *a priori* to the decisionmaker, but they must in effect be verifiably reportable to him.

Proposition 4. Suppose that for every x and every decision d in $\Delta \setminus \{f(x)\}$ there is some interested party who prefers the full-information decision $f(x)$ to d. Then at every pure-strategy Nash equilibrium, the full-information decision is taken. Moreover, if there is no mixed decision with support in $\Delta \setminus \{f(x)\}$ that is weakly preferred to $f(x)$ by every interested party, then at every Nash equilibrium the decision $f(x)$ is taken.

This proposition is supported by a simple argument. If there were an equilibrium with any decision other than $f(x)$ being taken, then some interested party would prefer the full-information decision to the equilibrium outcome. That party could therefore do better by suggesting the full-information decision and reporting $\{x\}$, thereby contradicting the assumption of equilibrium. A similar argument establishes the second part of the proposition.

For ease of reference, we shall sometimes refer to the condition of Proposition 4 as the

---

[6] This assumption is similar to, but is stronger than, the assumption of the conventional argument that each party has access to all the information that favors its side. We could formalize the conventional argument by restricting the model so that each piece of information favors one side or the other, regardless of whatever other information may be reported, and then by allowing each party to know at least all the information that favors its side. We believe, however, that it is significant for some applications (for example, where the interested parties are competing sellers) that such restrictive assumptions about the nature of information are not needed to generate strong conclusions about the effects of competition.

[7] The restriction to truthful reporting ensures that the various reports are consistent in that I contains at least the true state x.

[8] This assumption implies that at any pure-strategy equilibrium of the persuasion game, some particular pure decision will result. Then, pure-strategy equilibria can be analyzed by using only the ordinal preferences of the interested parties.

assumption that the full-information decision is Pareto-optimal. Actually, however, the assumption is a bit stronger than that, since it requires that no other decision be even Pareto-indifferent to it, that is, that no other decision can be so good in the eyes of every interested party.

Proposition 4 has three easy and useful corollaries. First, consider the case of a decision made by a regulatory body that seeks to advance the welfare of the various constituencies affected by the decision. Suppose that each constituency has interests that are aggregated and represented (honestly) by a lobbyist, and that each lobbyist knows all the relevant information, x. Then the regulator's payoff is $u(v_1, \ldots, v_n)$, where u is an increasing function and v_i is the utility of constituency i corresponding to the decision taken. We assume, as above, that there is always a unique maximizing decision for the decisionmaker. Plainly, any full-information decision is a Pareto-optimal one.

Corollary 1. At every pure-strategy Nash equilibrium of this "persuade the regulator" game the equilibrium decision is the full-information decision.

Notice that, in particular, the regulator can rely on the lobbyist to suggest the full-information decision.

A second variation arises when the interests of the parties are *strongly opposed,* that is, for every x and every pair of (possibly mixed) decisions d and d' there are interested parties i and j such that $v_i(x, d) > v_i(x, d')$ and $v_j(x, d') > v_j(x, d)$. For example, the decisionmaker may be deciding how to allocate a given volume of purchases at predetermined prices among a group of suppliers. The archetypal example of competition in information provision—the adversary system in legal disputes—also would often involve strongly opposed interests in this sense.

Corollary 2. At every pure-strategy Nash equilibrium of the persuasion game with strongly opposed interests, the equilibrium decision is the full-information decision.

A third variation, which perhaps better models the selling game, arises when the sellers not only provide information, but also quote prices for their goods. More precisely, suppose each seller has a product to offer whose cost of production is $c_i(x)$. If a sale is concluded at price p, the seller's payoff is $p - c_i(x)$. The buyer's utility from purchasing product i at price p is $u(x, i) - p$. Moving simultaneously, sellers name prices p_i for their products and make reports $r_i(x)$. The buyer then selects one of the products to purchase. Finally, all players receive their payoffs from this "persuasion and pricing" game.

Since all moves are simultaneous, nothing is lost if we choose to think of the sellers as first all setting prices and then, without knowledge of the prices set by others, all making reports. Now, at any *pure-strategy* Nash equilibrium of this game the sellers at the second stage will all act as if they knew the prices that their competitors had set, and Corollary 2 applies. Consequently, given the prices, the buyer will make the full-information decision. Anticipating that result, the sellers will set prices at the first stage as if playing a price-setting oligopoly game with a single fully informed buyer. Thus, we have the following result.

Corollary 3. At every pure-strategy Nash equilibrium of the persuasion and pricing game, the equilibrium choice and price are the same as in the corresponding full-information price-setting game.

Remarks.

(1) Corollaries 2 and 3 would change if we allowed the buyer to purchase nothing and to obtain some utility $u^*(x)$. In that case the arguments made above lead to the conclusion that at every pure-strategy Nash equilibrium, in any state x where the outcome of the full-information price-setting game involves buying from some seller, the equilibrium choice and price are as in the full-information game. An unsophisticated buyer, however, may

sometimes be fooled into making a purchase when he should not. For example, competition among cigarette producers will not lead them to reveal that cigarette smoking may shorten the smoker's life.

(2) It is fair to say that the decisionmaker in this model may have "no idea" what the range of alternatives is, and may have little idea about the possible states of the world. The prior probability distribution P on information states X plays no role at all, since the game is formally one of complete information. All the *players*—the interested parties—know the state x precisely.

(3) Proposition 4 and its corollaries are stated for Nash equilibria, rather than for sequential equilibria as used in the last section. The difference arises because we have specified in the structure of the game how the decisionmaker uses the information provided to him, whereas, in the previous section, the information use assumption was introduced through the equilibrium concept. Here, the Nash and sequential equilibria coincide.

4. Competition and sophistication

■ The results of the last section show that, when the interested parties are all fully informed and able to report all they know and when the full information decision is Pareto optimal for them, competition in suggesting alternatives and providing information can obviate the need for the decisionmaker to be well informed and sophisticated. In this section we relax the assumption that all interested parties can report all they know, but we reintroduce sophistication on the part of the decisionmaker in drawing inferences. We also spell out the dimensions of uncertainty by adding a special structure to the information-state space.

Our model is designed to represent a situation in which not only is the decisionmaker ignorant of the set of possible alternatives, the facts necessary to evaluate the alternatives, and the preferences of the interested parties, but also he does not know the relevant dimensions on which each alternative should be evaluated. For example, the consumer who buys a new forced-air furnace may remember to ask about prices, maintenance costs, and standard fuel-efficiency ratings, but may forget to ask about how quietly it operates or how well it will function with the existing ductwork. Similarly (to recall a historical example), a Department of Defense analyst reviewing an Air Force proposal for a Rapid Deployment Force may not ask whether the huge, newly proposed troop and equipment carrying plane (the C5-A Galaxy Transport) will be wide enough to accommodate the *next* planned generation of tanks (Weintraub, 1980). We do assume, however, that, given a set of alternatives to evaluate and a set of relevant attributes, the decisionmaker can assess the information available about the attributes and can anticipate the strategic dissembling of the information providers.

We also assume that there is too much "relevant" information for any interested party to report it all and that the interested parties cannot verifiably report their own preferences. Accordingly, we limit each interested party to suggesting one or more alternatives, naming some set of relevant attributes or dimensions, and providing information about the standing of his suggested alternatives on each indicated dimension.[9] The parties may not report information about one another's preferences, although the decisionmaker might be able to infer something about them from the suggested alternatives.

The extensive form of this persuasion game is described as follows. First, Nature determines the set of relevant attributes Z, which is some finite subset of the set of possibly relevant attributes $\mathbf{Z}$. Nature also determines grades x_{dm} of each possible decision $d \in \Delta$ on each relevant attribute $m \in Z$ and a parameter y which may affect the interested parties' preferences (but not those of the decisionmaker). The number and the identities of the

[9] This rules out the use of comparative advertising by a seller. When the buyer is too unsophisticated to make his own comparisons, this arrangement can lead to a reduction in his welfare.

elements in Z are random, so that the decisionmaker must rely on the interested parties to identify the relevant attributes. Each grade x_{dm} is selected from some finite set X. In sum, Nature chooses a triple $\omega = (Z, x, y)$ according to some probability distribution P.

Each interested party observes ω. The parties then simultaneously make assertions to the decisionmaker. Interested party i suggests a set of alternatives D_i from some feasible set of suggestions $\boldsymbol{D}$ with the property that for each $d \in \Delta$ there is some $D \in \boldsymbol{D}$ such that $d \in D$. Thus, any alternative can be suggested, but not necessarily in isolation. Some alternatives, once suggested, may necessarily call to mind a whole set of variants. Interested party i also reports a subset A_i of Z, interpretable as the relevant attributes that he chooses to identify, and, for each suggested alternative $d_{ij} \in D_i$, sets A_{ijm} which represent verifiable assertions about the grade of alternative d_{ij} on each attribute $m \in A_i$.

The decisionmaker collects the suggested alternatives and hears all the reports. We represent the information contained in the reports by the letter I. He then selects a decision d from the set of suggested alternatives D. The decisionmaker's payoff is $u(Z, x_d, d)$, where x_d is the list of actual attributes for the decision d actually taken. The ith interested party's payoff is $v_i(\omega, d)$.

A sequential equilibrium is now defined very much as in Section 2. Noting that for any fixed strategy of the decisionmaker there is an induced game among the interested parties, we may describe a sequential equilibrium of the overall game as an $(n + 2)$-tuple $(r_1, \ldots, r_N, b, p)$ such that: (i) given the decisionmaker's strategy b, the reporting strategies r_i of the interested parties form a Nash equilibrium of the induced game; (ii) the decision strategy b is optimal, given the decisionmaker's beliefs; (iii) these beliefs satisfy a rational expectations condition; and (iv) the beliefs are consistent with the decisionmaker's information.

Observe that the analysis of Section 3 does not apply directly to this setting. The reason is that an interested party cannot report fully about all the alternatives to convince the decisionmaker that a particular alternative is best. The decisionmaker must do some of the work on his own and discard alternatives whose advocates do not justify them adequately.

On the basis of the analysis in Section 2, one might think that to adopt an effective skeptical posture the decisionmaker needs to know the interested parties' preferences (that is, the value of y). In the presence of sufficiently intense competition among the interested parties, however, a skeptical posture entails skepticism towards *the alternatives themselves;* the decisionmaker need not consider exactly how the interested parties' preferences color their reports. More precisely, a skeptical posture entails the decisionmaker's believing that Z is the union of the A_i's and adopting beliefs about the attribute ranks of each suggested decision d that, while consistent with Z's being the union of the A_i's and with the information provided, result in the lowest possible expected utility for alternative d. With this posture each interested party is required to prove the merits of his suggestion: any attribute of any suggested alternative not proved to rank high will be regarded as if it were proved to rank low. With such beliefs and the corresponding optimizing choices by the decisionmaker, if the full-information decision is Pareto-undominated (as previously defined), then it will be in someone's interests to suggest it and to provide supporting information.

Proposition 5. Suppose that for no ω and no $d \in \Delta$ is it true that d is preferred or indifferent to the full-information decision at ω by all interested parties. Then there exists a sequential equilibrium at which the decisionmaker adopts the skeptical strategy described above. At every such equilibrium, the decision reached is the full-information decision.

The existence claim is supported by having each interested party suggest the full-information decision, report the full-attribute set, and provide accurate information about the suggested decision. The characterization of all equilibria involving the skeptical strategy follows by noting that once the skeptical posture is adopted, the argument associated with Proposition 4 applies.

In this game there may exist other equilibria as well at which the decisionmaker does not behave skeptically and the full-information decision is not reached. These other equilibria would, of course, be destroyed if we modified the game to allow the opposing parties to rebut each other's alternatives. In a situation like this with multiple equilibria, it is to the decisionmaker's advantage to select (if he can) the one that favors him, for example by announcing his intention to play the skeptical strategy. That equilibrium seems to be a focal point, since there are many specifications of the information-state space for which it is the only equilibrium.[10] Thus, it is reasonable for us to focus on skeptical behavior as a descriptive account of the behavior of rational decisionmakers facing the kind of uncertainties considered here.

5. Comparison with mechanism design

■ The questions we have studied in this article are related to ones that have been studied in the burgeoning economic literature on "mechanism design."[11] In its standard formulation the mechanism designer's problem is to select rules for an institution that advances his objectives by exploiting the private information of one or more individuals or by motivating the individuals to take prescribed actions, or both. Despite the similarity of the problems studied, there are several major differences between the models we have used here and the kinds used in the mechanism design literature.

First, we have focused our attention on general purpose institutions, ones that can be used in a variety of different decision environments and can even be implemented by a decisionmaker with little idea of what the environment is. In mechanism design theory the recommended mechanism is often a function of such fine details of the environment as the exact form of the various agents' prior beliefs.[12] Finely tuned mechanisms may be of limited use to a decisionmaker who knows little about what the relevant environment is, and, indeed, the institutions we actually observe do not typically use the detailed information that is assumed to be common knowledge in theories of mechanism design. Here we have shown that, when reported information can be verified, a decisionmaker can sometimes do quite well with a general purpose mechanism. Moreover, in the games we have studied, the behavior on the part of the interested parties called for by the equilibrium is quite straightforward, so that the assumption of equilibrium does not seem strained. In contrast, equilibrium behavior in theories of mechanism design is often very complicated. Note, too, that it should generally be easier to test theories of general purpose mechanisms, since their predictions do not depend on the unobservable beliefs of the mechanism designer.[13]

Second, we have assumed that the decisionmaker has no power to restrict the kinds of reports that the interested parties can give (other than to ensure that they are consistent with the true state), and that the decisionmaker neither ignores information nor takes any

---

[10] For one example, suppose that each interested party is a potential supplier of a homogeneous product, which not all the sellers have available. The decisionmaker must decide from whom to buy, and how much. The only relevant attributes are who carries the product, at what prices, and the quality of the product. Then the logic of Proposition 2 implies that the skeptical strategy is the only equilibrium strategy for the buyer.

[11] The subject of optimally designing economic institutions or "mechanisms" was introduced by Hurwicz (1960, 1972). Among the many applications of Bayesian mechanism theory are ones to the design of income tax schemes (Mirrlees, 1971), incentive contracts (Harris and Raviv, 1979), and regulatory procedures (Baron and Myerson, 1982), to name just a few.

[12] The sensitivity of optimal schemes to fine details of the environment is particularly evident in the optimal auction work of Matthews (1983), Maskin and Riley (1984), and especially Cremer and McLean (1985).

[13] Assuming that the decisionmaker is sophisticated, our theory generates several testable hypotheses. These include: (i) that the decisionmaker adopts a skeptical strategy; (ii) that a salesman will not differentiate his treatment of customers who are probably sophisticated and those who are probably not and, since that information is valueless to him, will not seek it; and (iii) that with sufficiently opposed interests or in appropriate regulatory settings, efficient decisions will be reached.

decision that is not optimal, given his beliefs. Mechanism design approaches normally assume that the decisionmaker can set the rules of the game to restrict the options of interested parties and to commit himself to making decisions that will not be in his interests *ex post*. For most of the cited applications, it is difficult to justify such an asymmetric treatment of the decisionmaker and the interested parties: Why are not all the parties equally able to commit? It is by no means certain that commitment can often be achieved in the situations we wish to study. One can sometimes break commitments by asserting that the underlying conditions on which the commitment was premised have not been met. When enforcement costs are high, one can simply renege on a so-called commitment. As a result, the commitments required in the mechanism design approach may not be credible. We have shown that the decisionmaker can sometimes do as well without the use either of commitments or of restrictions on the interested parties as he could do with these devices. Consequently, our theory applies even in those situations where the ability of the decisionmaker to control the rules and to achieve commitment is limited or uncertain.

Third, we allow the decisionmaker a far greater range of uncertainty than is common in the mechanism design literature. Our decisionmaker may not know the alternatives that are available or even those that might possibly be available, and may be forced to rely on interested parties for suggestions. Such uncertainties make it impossible to formulate prior beliefs about the set of alternatives, and so rule out the use of Bayesian decision theory. Uncertainty of this kind is an important aspect of reality, and it is a significant finding that competition among interested parties sometimes alleviates this uncertainty. Identifying mechanisms that work well in the face of such thoroughgoing uncertainty lies wholly outside the realm of the traditional approach to mechanism design, since that theory requires Bayesian priors on everything to define an objective function for the optimizing process.

Finally, the models used in this article deal with verifiable information, in the same spirit as earlier work by Milgrom (1981) and Grossman (1981). Research in mechanism design has often dealt with information about variables, like personal taste, for which direct verification may be impossible. In such cases the decisionmaker must provide incentives to the interested parties for reporting their information truthfully. Both perfect verifiability and perfect privacy are highly limited as models of reality, yet both shed some light on the important intermediate cases in which some, but not all, information can be verified.

6. Conclusion

■ We have used game theory to examine the logic of the argument that when all interested parties have access to complete and verifiable information, competition among them in attempting to influence a decision leads to the emergence of "truth" or, more precisely, of all relevant decision alternatives and information. Some parts of our analysis apply to the case of a buyer's being courted by many sellers; other parts apply to governmental proceedings in which all interested parties are represented. Our analysis has obvious relevance for persuasive situations within firms, as well as for legal contests, legislative battles, regulatory hearings, etc. It indicates that, at least in some situations, skepticism on the part of the decisionmaker and/or competition among interested parties can result in the emergence of all the relevant information and the selection of an optimal decision.

The scope of the conclusion that competition leads to the revelation of truth is in some respects wider and in others narrower than would appear to be commonly thought. It is not always true in competitive situations that each piece of information favors one of the interested parties. Interested parties then may not know which piece favors them, and so they may unwittingly withhold even favorable information. On the other hand, even if the parties do not have access to all information, or if they cannot report all that they know, rational skepticism by a decisionmaker can lead to a full-information decision by inducing one party to reveal information that is damaging to its interests. The party reveals this information for fear that withholding it will lead to an *even more unfavorable supposition* by the skeptical decisionmaker.

One of the most striking results of our analysis has been the prominent role played by skeptical strategies. Evidently, sophisticated decisionmakers must often adopt skeptical strategies.

Informally, skepticism means that one assumes the interested parties' reports are tinged by self-interest. Within the models we have studied, sophisticatedly skeptical behavior consists of the decisionmaker's systematically downgrading the alternatives that he suspects may be favored by a well-informed interested party. When the parties' preferences are known, a skeptical strategy is relatively easy to describe and implement. When they are unknown, but the interested parties' interests are strongly enough in conflict, the decisionmaker can safely assume that every relevant decision is preferred by someone. Then, skepticism consists of downgrading *every* suggested alternative. We expect subsequent research to show that sophisticated decisionmakers in more general settings use a strategy of "calibrated skepticism" by downgrading most those alternatives that are expected to find articulate, well-informed advocates and by relying on the advocates to provide the information to justify their favored decisions.

Appendix

■ The proofs of Propositions 2 and 3 follow.

Proof of Proposition 2. Since the buyer's utility function is strictly concave in q, so is his expected utility, given any information. Thus, it will never be optimal for the buyer to adopt a mixed strategy. To accommodate mixed strategies on the part of the seller, we allow that $r(x)$ may be a random variable. Then, for an equilibrium the seller-maximization condition (i) must hold with probability one. In particular, this implies that at equilibrium $b(r(x))$ is a constant, even though $r(x)$ may be a random variable.

In view of Proposition 1, it is only necessary to check that every equilibrium triple (r, b, p) has the specified form.

The seller-maximization condition of equilibrium requires that for every x, the seller must weakly prefer reporting $r(x)$ to reporting $\{x\}$, that is, $b(r(x)) \geq b(\{x\})$ for all x. If this inequality is strict for some x', then the concavity of u implies that

$$E[\partial u(x, b(r(x')) + q)/\partial q | p(\cdot | r(x'))] < 0, \tag{A1}$$

and the buyer could do better by reducing his purchases in response to the report $r(x')$. This contradicts the buyer-maximization condition of equilibrium. Hence, $b(r(x)) = b(\{x\})$ for all x. It remains to show that the buyer adopts a skeptical posture (b, p), that is, for any report A, $b(A) = \min \{b(\{x\}) | x \in A\}$.

The results that $b(r(x)) = b(\{x\})$, together with the seller-maximization equilibrium condition, imply that for all A and all $x \in A$, $b(\{x\}) \geq b(A)$ (otherwise the seller does better to report A when the state is x). Therefore,

$$b(A) \leq \min \{b(\{x\}) | x \in A\}.$$

Suppose that there is some A for which this inequality is strict. Then, using the consistent-beliefs equilibrium condition and the strict pseudo concavity of the buyer's preferences, one obtains

$$E[\partial u(x, b(A) + q)/\partial q | p(\cdot | A)] > 0, \tag{A2}$$

which contradicts the buyer-maximization condition. *Q.E.D.*

Proof of Proposition 3. Let (r, b, p) be a purported equilibrium and let r^* be a strategy that maximizes sales to a naively credulous buyer.

First, we observe that, since the unsophisticated buyer is "responsive" (as defined in the body of the article), r^* must have the property that for all $x' \in r^*(x)$, $b(\{x\}) \leq b(\{x'\})$. (Otherwise, reporting $r^*(x) \setminus \{x'\}$ would result in more sales to the unsophisticated buyer, thereby contradicting the definition of r^*.)

Using the just-proved property, the strict concavity of buyer preferences, and the consistent-beliefs condition, we find that for all $Q < b(\{x\})$,

$$E[\partial u(x, Q + q)/\partial q | p(\cdot | r^*(x))] > 0. \tag{A3}$$

Hence, $b(r^*(x)) \geq b(\{x\})$ for all x. Now, once we show that $b(r(x)) = b(\{x\})$ for all x for any equilibrium strategy r, we shall have established that r sells no more to sophisticated buyers than r^*. Therefore, r cannot be a best response unless, like r^*, it also maximizes sales to unsophisticated buyers, and it will follow that any equilibrium r must maximize sales to unsophisticated buyers.

If for all x, $b(r(x)) \geq b(\{x\})$ and there is strict inequality for some x', then by the consistent-beliefs condition and the strict concavity of buyer preferences, (A1) holds and thus violates the buyer-maximization condition. This leaves two possibilities: either $b(r(x)) < b(\{x\})$ for some information state x, or $b(r(x)) = b(\{x\})$ for all x. Suppose first that $b(r(x)) < b(\{x\})$ for some information state x. For that x, reporting $r^*(x)$ increases sales to sophisticated buyers compared with $r(x)$ and maximizes sales to naive buyers. This contradicts the seller-maximization equilibrium condition. Hence, this case cannot arise at equilibrium, and we conclude that $b(r(x)) = b(\{x\})$, which completes the proof. *Q.E.D.*

References

BARON, D. AND MYERSON, R. "Regulating a Monopolist with Unknown Costs." *Econometrica,* Vol. 50 (1982), pp. 911–930.

CRAWFORD, V. AND SOBEL, J. "Strategic Information Transmission." *Econometrica,* Vol. 50 (1982), pp. 1431–1451.

CREMER, J. AND MCLEAN, R. "Full Extraction of Surplus in Bayesian and Dominant Strategy Auctions." University of Pennsylvania, CARESS Working Paper #85-17, 1985.

GROSSMAN, S. "The Informational Role of Warranties and Private Disclosure about Product Quality." *Journal of Law and Economics,* Vol. 24 (1981), pp. 461–483.

HARRIS, M. AND RAVIV, A. "Optimal Incentive Contracts with Imperfect Information." *Journal of Economic Theory,* Vol. 20 (1979), pp. 231–259.

HAYEK, F. A. *The Road to Serfdom.* Chicago: University of Chicago Press, 1972.

HOLMSTRÖM, B. "On Incentives and Control in Organizations." Ph.D. Dissertation, Stanford University, 1977.

HURWICZ, L. "Optimality and Informational Efficiency in Resource Allocation Processes" in K.J. Arrow, S. Karlin, and P. Suppes, eds., *Mathematical Methods in the Social Sciences,* Stanford: Stanford University Press, pp. 27–46.

———. "On Informationally Decentralized Systems" in C.B. McGuire and R. Radner, eds., *Decision and Organization,* New York: American Elsevier Publishing Company, 1972.

KREPS, D. AND WILSON, R., "Sequential Equilibria." *Econometrica,* Vol. 50 (1982), pp. 863–894.

MASKIN, E. AND RILEY, J. "Optimal Auctions with Risk-Averse Buyers." *Econometrica,* Vol. 52 (1984), pp. 1473–1518.

MATTHEWS, S. "Selling to Risk-Averse Buyers with Unobservable Tastes." *Journal of Economic Theory,* Vol. 30 (1983), pp. 370–400.

MILGROM, P. "Good News and Bad News: Representation Theorems and Applications." *Bell Journal of Economics,* Vol. 12 (1981), pp. 380–391.

——— AND ROBERTS, J. "Limit Pricing and Entry under Incomplete Information: An Equilibrium Analysis." *Econometrica,* Vol. 50 (1982), pp. 443–459.

MILL, J.S. *On Liberty.* Indianapolis: Bobbs-Merrill, 1977.

MIRRLEES, J. "An Exploration in the Theory of Optimum Income Taxation." *Review of Economic Studies,* Vol. 38 (1971), pp. 175–208.

POPPER, K.R. *The Open Society and Its Enemies, Vol. 1.* Princeton: Princeton University Press, 1966.

POSNER, R. *Economic Analysis of Law,* 2nd ed. Boston: Little, Brown and Company, 1977.

SOBEL, J. "A Theory of Credibility." *Review of Economic Studies,* Vol. 52 (1985), pp. 557–574.

WEINTRAUB, B. "Warning Crucial to Air and Sea Transport Abilities." *New York Times* (September 26, 1980).

WILDE, L. "Labor Market Equilibrium under Nonsequential Search." *Journal of Economic Theory,* Vol. 16 (1977), pp. 373–393.

C
Endogenous Cost Evidence

[4]

Relying on the Information of Interested—and Potentially Dishonest—Parties

Chris William Sanchirico, *University of Virginia School of Law*

This article investigates the role of evidence production in the regulation of private behavior via judicial and administrative process. It proposes a model in which the law makes the agent's "fine" depend on the presentation of evidence whose production cost, in turn, depends on how the agent has behaved in the regulated activity. This view of evidence production has several notable implications, including that truth finding has no direct role in deterrence, that nonfalsifiable evidence, even when available, is unlikely to be the best choice for the system, and that "overdeterrence" may well be cost-effective.

This paper was first circulated as the first half of Sanchirico (1995). I thank seminar participants at Stanford Law School (spring 1995), the American Law and Economics Association's Annual Meetings (spring 1995), George Mason School of Law (winter 1995), Columbia University Economics Department (spring 1996), Columbia Law School (spring 1996), the University of Southern California Law School (spring 1997), the California Institute of Technology (spring 1997), and the Stanford Institute for Theoretical Economics (summer 1997). I have benefited from many helpful conversations, including those with Anne Alstott, Jennifer Arlen, Kenneth Leonard, Richard Merrill, Ronald Miller, Andrew Newman, Alexander Pfaff, Mitchell Polinsky, Michael Riordan, Susan Rose-Ackerman, Kathy Spier, Eric Talley, Rip Verkerke, and Rakesh Vohra. I acknowledge financial support from Yale Law School's Career Options Assistance Program and the Olin-sponsored Law and Economics Programs at the University of California, Berkeley, Stanford, Columbia, and the University of Southern California. Special thanks to Rachel Brewster for her outstanding research assistance.

Send correspondence to: Chris William Sanchirico, University of Virginia School of Law, 580 Massie Rd., Charlottesville, VA 22903-1789; Fax: (804) 924-7536; E-mail: csanchirico@virginia.edu.

The incentive-based regulation of private behavior—whether enforced through civil, criminal, or administrative process—requires that "punishments" and "rewards" be appropriately conditioned on how individual agents behave in the regulated activity. In many areas of the law, the state obtains at least some of this information from the agents themselves. Instead of, or in addition to, its own active inspection and investigation, the state invites the party in interest to come forward to prove compliance, desert, or innocence.

Thus, the manufacturer of a new drug must present the FDA with "substantial evidence" that the drug is effective for its intended use, in compliance with 21 U.S.C. 355(d). Similarly, the inventor may provide affidavits, declarations, and other outside evidence in filing her appeal of a rejected patent application, as provided in 37 C.F.R. 1.192-6 (1994). The industrial firm, likewise, must often sample and report to the EPA on emissions content in compliance with the Clean Air Act, 42 U.S.C. 7414(a), and the Clean Water Act, 33 U.S.C. 1318. In civil process, the tort defendant may offer testimony of her reasonable care in order to avoid liability. In criminal process, the accused may try to corroborate an alibi.

But how is it possible for the state to effectively regulate the agent—in particular, to induce her to do something that otherwise is not in her interest—if the state relies, in whole or in part, on the agent's own account of whether she has actually behaved as it desires? Certainly, it cannot be enough that the manufacturer *says* the drug is effective, or that the accused *says* she is innocent. This fundamental, but often ignored, question is the focus of the present article. The proposed answer is a new perspective on evidence production that has advantages, in terms of both coherence and realism, over how evidence production has been treated in the literature to date.

Conceptually, the model goes beyond existing approaches in two respects. First, it captures the full *double* incentive problem, integrating incentives for behavior in both the "primary activity" and the subsequent hearing.[1] Second, it allows for the possibility that agents will lie when it is in their interest to do so. The central idea of this article is to view evidence production as costly signaling, à la Spence (1974), but

1. The primary activity is the activity giving rise to prosecution, suit, or administrative review (e.g., crime, care taking, or pollution control).

to augment that model by supposing that the agent's evidence (signal) production costs are potentially affected by her choice of action in the primary activity.

This view of evidence has a number of counterintuitive implications that make it operationally, as well as conceptually, distinct from existing approaches. First, no amount of truth finding is necessary for achieving deterrence in this model. Deterrence may be possible even though the court or review board learns nothing about what actually happened in the primary activity. Second, despite the conventional assumption that additional accuracy is always more socially expensive, learning more about the primary activity often costs *less*, not more. Third, "overdeterrence" in the primary activity is likely to be optimal. When the system costs of incentive setting are accounted for, it tends to be optimal to require more of individuals than is warranted by the classic balancing of social costs and benefits in the primary activity. This creates the apparent contradiction that the state will typically want to "buy" *more* precaution or clean air, when it accounts for the "price" of these items in terms of enforcement effort.

The research strategy underlying this article is to focus on one component of the regulatory information problem: use of information about an agent's behavior as *supplied by the agent herself.* While this component is important and essential in proceedings as various as administrative review and multiparty litigation, it is rarely the only mechanic at work in the complexity of actual process. Criminal procedure, for example, includes active investigation by the state in the guise of detectives, police, and prosecutors. Both civil and criminal procedures involve intricate adversarial dynamics. In civil procedure, the filing of suit is itself a signal of plaintiff's information. Even ex parte administrative procedures often rely not just on the party's own evidence but also on information independently gathered by the regulator. Thus, the aim here is not to convince the reader that own-party evidence is the only enforcement dynamic worth studying. Rather, the object is to distill and then analyze one element that, although common and fundamental to many settings of interest, is often ignored in the law and economics of litigation and enforcement. Hopefully, once this element is fully understood in isolation, its interaction with other sources of regulatory information can be more fruitfully examined.[2]

1. Discussion

1.1. Existing Formalisms

Before explaining the model and its implications, it is important to be clear about the conceptual differences between the view of evidence production proposed here and views that already appear in the formal literature on evidence. That literature sorts roughly into three approaches. While each approach represents an important step forward in understanding the logic of enforcement and information, none accounts for the full strategic nature of the problem to which evidence production is the apparent solution.

The first and oldest formal approach to legal evidence, the (pure) *Bayesian* approach, supposes that the fact finder considers evidence the way a physical scientist considers inanimate data: by making deductions that combine prior beliefs with an understanding of how observations tend to be associated with underlying truths—that is, according to Bayes' Rule.[3] Many have criticized the Bayesian approach for its false precision (see, e.g., Tribe, 1970). But perhaps more problematic is its failure to account for the strategic nature of evidentiary presentation. The molecules under the scientist's microscope have no particular interest in what the scientist concludes, nor any ability to influence her conclusion. Neither can be said of the agent who supplies evidence of her own behavior, evidence that she understands will be used to set her own punishments and rewards.

Equally serious is the failure of the Bayesian approach to account for how legal rules influence behavior in the primary activity. Indeed, influencing behavior in the primary activity is arguably the main purpose of

2. Understanding such interaction is the aim of a companion paper (Sanchirico, 2000), which considers both own-party information and information supplied by others, and also examines the signaling role of the act of filing suit.

3. See, for example, *People v. Collins* and the law review literature surrounding it, including, for example, Finkelstein and Fairly (1970). See also Symposium (1986). I use fact finder as a generic term for judge, jury, auditor, and administrator: the arm of the state that receives evidence and metes out punishments and rewards accordingly.

legal fact finding. Under this view, a hearing is not a laboratory experiment. Its chief purpose is not to advance our knowledge of the world, but to affect how agents behave outside the hearing, in the workplace, and on the road. Any knowledge obtained in the process has only this instrumental value. (For an example of how focusing on primary activities changes the analysis of particular evidentiary rules, see the treatment of character evidence in Sanchirico [2001].)

The (classic) *Moral Hazard* approach to evidence production solves the second problem of the Bayesian approach, regarding incentives in the primary activity, but not the first problem, regarding incentives at the hearing.[4] The implicit analogy here is to the employer (rather than the scientist) who induces her employee to work hard by conditioning wages on an inanimate, noisy signal of work effort, usually understood to be firm output. The output signal is "noisy" in the sense that hard work occasionally leads to low output and laziness occasionally leads to high output. But in general, the signal is accurate enough to render feasible an output-contingent pay scale that makes it in the interest of the employee to work hard.[5]

The Moral Hazard approach is essentially a generalization of the enforcement approach devised by Becker (1968). In this model, detection is an imperfect signal of the underlying criminal act—both convictions and acquittals may be erroneous—and rewards and punishments are cast in terms of fines and incarceration. The Becker enforcement approach, and by implication the Moral Hazard approach, has become the most popular model of trial in the large literature on the Law and Economics of Procedure.[6] In the typical civil litigation model, for instance, individuals

4. Recent examples of this approach include Davis (1994), Hermalin and Katz (1991), and Schrag and Scotchmer (1994).

5. Typically, the mechanism is also constrained by the requirement that participation be individually rational for the employee.

6. This literature focuses on incentives to file and settle, modeling the trial end game in "reduced form" as a sort of random detection mechanism. Typically in these models, evidence production is packed into a single probability that the court will find the defending agent liable. And when the primary activity is also accounted for in such models, this probability is made to depend on agents' behavior in the primary activity. Thus, trial outcome acts as an exogenous signal of primary activity, just as output is an exogenous signal of the employee's effort. Also in the same category are models that focus on the determinants and effects of error on the random detection mechanism that represents trial. Such models differ fundamentally from the approach taken in this

decide whether or not to exercise care, understanding that less care is more likely to lead to liability.

As a model of procedure, the Moral Hazard approach has proven extremely useful. But as a model of evidence, which by definition must be explicit about how fact finders actually obtain the information on which to base rewards and punishments, it is incomplete. Whereas the employer's signal from our example is exogenously generated (conditional on the employee's choice of effort), the evidentiary signal received by the court is chosen by the agent—a choice separate from her decision of how to behave in the primary activity. Thus, the Moral Hazard approach still fails to take into account the agent's incentive, after she has chosen her action in the primary activity, to manipulate the signals upon which the fact finder conditions rewards and punishments.

The third approach to evidence production consists of the (pure) *Omission* model as typified by Milgrom and Roberts' (1986) well-known and often-cited article, "Relying on the Information of Interested Parties."[7] This approach does account for incentives at the hearing stage, but in a limited way, since it rests on the assumption that agents do not lie even when it is in their interest to do so.[8] The focus of this approach is on agents' incentives to withhold information that is against their interest. The "fundamental theorem" in the literature asserts that the fact finder can learn the full story from an agent who is truth-telling but not nec-

---

article because they posit an exogenous relationship between the accuracy of the trial detection mechanism and either the level of public spending (see, e.g., Kaplow and Shavell, 1994, 1996), the primary activity behavior of the agents (see, e.g., Calfee and Craswell, 1984; and Craswell and Calfee, 1986, which are discussed in more detail in note 30) or the trial preparation effort of the parties (see, e.g., Katz, 1988; and Rubinfeld and Sappington, 1988, which is discussed in more detail in note 10).

7. See also Lipman and Seppi (1995), Okuno-Fujiwara, Postlewaite, and Suzumura (1990), Shavell (1989), and Sobel (1985). Recent advances in the law and economics of evidence that model evidence production in terms of "strategic search" also fall into this category. See, for example, Froeb and Kobayashi (1996) and Daughety and Reinganum (2000). In this literature, parties to a suit sample from a distribution for pieces of evidence, deciding both when to stop sampling and what of their sample to show the court. Parties may decline to report what they observe. But they may not fabricate observations. For a lengthier discussion of the literature modeling evidence as strategic search, see Sanchirico (2000, n. 4).

8. Some papers attempt to justify the no-lying assumption by mentioning that perjury is a crime. This just avoids the problem, however, for perjury itself requires evidentiary proof. Perjury is considered in more detail below.

essarily forthcoming by announcing beforehand that she will assume the worst for the agent on whatever points the agent leaves ambiguous or unmentioned. But the so-called "unraveling" argument that supports this conclusion itself unravels if the agent is capable of actually lying, for then the agent simply responds to the fact finder's rule with precise lies.[9]

1.2. Legal Evidence as Endogenous Cost Signaling: The Framework

In contrast to these three existing approaches to evidence production, this article analyzes the full double incentive problem, integrating incentives in both the primary activity and the subsequent hearing, in a model in which agents can and will lie when it is in their interest to do so. The idea is to view evidence production as costly signaling, á la Spence (1974). Unlike the typical signaling model, however, signaling costs here are not exogenous. Rather, it is crucial to the functioning of the model that the agent's hearing "type" (i.e., evidence production costs) is potentially affected by her choice of action in the primary activity.[10]

9. The following example illustrates the points just made: The "truth," is a number between one and ten. The agent knows that the true number is three but wants the fact finder to think the number is as large as possible. The agent can omit to tell the principal all he knows, by reporting that the number is in some range (e.g., between two and five). But he cannot lie: the reported range must contain the number three. Reporting "between five and eight," for example, is not allowed. Suppose the principal then announces that she will act as if the truth is the lowest number in the range reported by the agent. Then it will be in the agent's interest to report a range whose lowest number is as high as possible. Since the reported range must contain three, the agent will always report an interval whose lowest number is three. Knowing all this, the principal learns the true number—and without cost. Of course, if the agent could lie, the principal's rule would just inspire the agent to report that the number is exactly ten.

10. This formulation resonates with several important papers: First, Rubinfeld and Sappington (1987) is the first paper to suggest that trial is under analyzed in the law-and-economics literature and, further, could and should be seen in terms of "signaling" by the parties. The present paper owes much to Rubinfeld and Sappington but differs in several important respects. (1) While Rubinfeld and Sappington suggest the idea of seeing trial as a signaling session (p. 308)—and even point toward evidence production cost differences as an important mechanism (p. 310)—such signaling is not actually modeled in their paper. Rather, defendant's unobserved trial effort is assumed to affect trial outcome according to a fixed function mapping defendant's trial effort (and the court's "prior belief" in defendant's guilt) onto the court's "posterior" assessment of guilt. How the defendant translates effort into evidence, and how the court translates

Thus, the analysis differs from the Bayesian and Moral Hazard approaches in that it shifts the focus from the correlation between evidence and underlying truths to differences in evidence production costs tied to differences in primary activity behavior. The model differs from the Omission approach because it allows that agents can and will lie whenever it is in their interest to do so, which in turn is what necessitates reliance on costly signaling as opposed to "cheap talk" disclosure.[11]

1.2.1. The basic mechanic. The gist of the model is apparent in the following simple example. A regulator wishes to induce firms to comply with a particular regulation, despite the fact that compliance costs firms an additional $100,000. The regulator requires that at the end of the period each firm appear before a review board to "present evidence" of its compliance. *Based solely on this evidence,* the review board then decides whether and

evidence into an assessment of guilt are not actually modeled. In particular, there is no sense in which the court evaluates the defendant's signal transmission choice in a strategically sophisticated manner—as, for instance, the employer evaluates the applicant's educational degree in Spence's (1974) model of signaling. (2) Rubinfeld and Sappington do not consider how prospective trial rules and outcomes affect incentives in the primary activity (which in their model is the commission of crimes). Their model picks up the story at trial, after the defendant has either committed or not committed the crime. (On this second distinction, note that Rubinfeld and Sappington's focus on trial error is not isomorphic to an explicit treatment of the primary activity. See, for example, Schrag and Scotchmer's [1994] Proposition 1.) Correspondingly, Rubinfeld and Sappington neither suggest nor explore the idea of *endogenous* type signaling.

Second, an application of endogenous type signaling appears in Daughety and Reinganum (1995). In the Daughety and Reinganum model: research and development expenditure is the hidden action; product safety is the type; and, depending on the product liability regime in place, price may act as a signal of safety to consumers.

Third, endogenous type models of evidence can also be recast as a Holmstrom and Milgrom (1991) multitask principal agent problem with two tasks of varying observability (primary activity actions being completely *un*observed, evidence choice being completely observed). (I thank Andrew Newman for this suggestion.) It must be noted, however, that previous work on the multitask problem considers the danger of *substitution* into the observed and rewarded action at the expense of the unobserved action (e.g., the teaching of test-taking skills rather than creativity). In contrast, the model in this article operates by means of *complementarities* between the observable action (evidence production) and the unobservable action (in the primary activity).

11. Below I refine this distinction by reinterpreting the no-lying assumption in terms of extreme evidence cost differences.

how much to fine the firm.[12] One of the major points of this article is that in order for the regulator to induce compliance in this setting, it is both necessary and sufficient that the regulator identify some form of presentation or performance before the review board, some "evidence," whose production costs for the firm vary appropriately with the firm's compliance activity.

To illustrate that the appropriate production cost differences can be sufficient, suppose that compliance happens to lower the firm's cost of a particular presentation from $140,000 to $20,000. Let the regulator announce before the firm's compliance decision that it will fine the firm $130,000 unless it presents this evidence before the review board. How does the firm react? First, consider its choice of what to present to the review board contingent on whether it has complied. If it *has* complied, the presentation will cost $20,000, but saves $130,000 in fines; hence, the firm's "best case" would be to present the $20,000 evidence and avoid the fine. If it has *not* complied, the presentation will cost $140,000 to produce, which is more than it would save in fines; its "best case" now would be simply to show up and pay the fine. Therefore, the firm's prospective payoffs at the review board hearing will be −$20,000 if it complies, and −$130,000 otherwise. Consequently, compliance increases the firm's prospective hearing payoff by $110,000. Stepping back to the firm's choice in the primary activity, we see that this $110,000 benefit outweighs the $100,000 direct cost of compliance. Thus, the firm chooses to comply.

To illustrate that production cost differences are *necessary* for incentive setting, suppose the regulator made avoiding the $130,000 fine dependent

12. It should be clarified that I am folding into the "regulator" and its "review board" many conceptually distinct roles including: (1) the setting of the evidence/reward structure and (2) the implementation of this evidence/reward structure on a case-by-case basis. In many settings, of course, these roles are divided among different actors and institutions. A partial list of the actors that have a hand in the operation of federal criminal law, for instance, would include Congress, the United States Sentencing Commission, the Supreme Court (in the obvious role and as proposer of the Federal Rules of Evidence), the prosecutor, the district judge and, of course, the jury. An analysis of intragovernmental interaction, which this article is not, would focus on the interaction of the various actors that set the ultimate correspondence between evidence and liability/punishment. Much interesting work has been done on precisely this question. See, for example, Schrag and Scotchmer (1994). But since such issues are not my concern here, I adopt a "statist" perspective, viewing the collection of state actors as a single actor who determines all of the components that constitute the ultimate mapping from evidence to outcomes.

on a form of evidence whose presentation cost was always $50 *regardless of the firm's compliance behavior.* Then the firm would always present the evidence at the hearing, regardless of its compliance choice, and its prospective payoffs at the hearing would always be −$50. The hearing would then be irrelevant to the firm's compliance choice, and so it would make this choice solely according to the $100,000 direct cost of compliance. Therefore, it would choose *not* to comply.

The same problem crops up if the designated evidence always costs the firm $1,000,000. In this case, the firm would never present the evidence and would always lose $130,000 at the hearing, regardless of its compliance activities; the hearing would again be irrelevant to its compliance decision. What is important is not that the evidence is costly to present, but that presentation costs tend to be lower following compliance.[13]

1.2.2. Evidence cost differences in practice. The costly signaling framework sheds light on several common forms of evidence. Consider parties' sponsorship of eyewitness testimony subject to cross-examination. True witnesses of the firm's compliance are chosen by fate and the laws of physics help to insure that their stories are mutually consistent even under unanticipated cross-examination. False witnesses need intensive coaching and may demand compensation for time and risk. Even when false witnesses would be worth paying for, their additional cost helps to counteract the direct costs of compliance and this in turn helps to induce the firm to comply. Similarly, expert testimony is a useful regulatory tool when the cost of gathering experts to support one's case increases along with the extent to which the expert must be induced to contradict her professional knowledge and judgment. The firm complies if compliance is less onerous than the extra expense of finding experts who are willing to attest to compliance when, in fact, there has been none.[14]

13. I am making the usual assumption that the regulator can precommit to carry out the costly hearing and collect the determined punishment, even though the agent will have already chosen her action in the primary behavior by the time the hearing is held. In my view, allowing for precommitment is more realistic than requiring "subgame perfection" when the relevant reward structures are set in large part by statute and precedent. In accordance with this notion, many state enforcement models, from Becker (1968) on, also assume that the state has the ability to precommit to the process it has prescribed.

14. See Sanchirico (2000, section 1.1.2.) for more on the practical manifestations of endogenous cost evidence.

1.2.3. What about perjury? Does the threat of perjury more simply explain how the state obtains the information necessary for effective regulation? Individuals tell the truth, this explanation would run, when the (increase in the) probability of being indicted for perjury if one lies, times the punishment for perjury, exceeds the benefits of lying. End of story.

Certainly this explanation would be simpler. But this is only because it avoids the difficult question. More precisely, it just slides the fundamental puzzle of evidence production back one proceeding. We still have to answer the question of how the state ascertains that the agent has perjured herself. If the answer is "based on evidence production at a collateral proceeding," then we have simply replaced the black box of evidentiary process with the black box of *collateral* evidentiary process.

Furthermore, the simple perjury explanation would probably not be more empirically accurate. What data there is suggests that prosecutors are reluctant to bring perjury charges, especially in civil cases. As a result, perjury is by many accounts commonplace—arguably more commonplace than could be reasonably balanced off against the severity of its punishment. It appears, rather, that the real work of sorting out which evidence is and is not reliable is done within the confines of the hearing itself, without much resort to the threat of ancillary process.[15]

15. In partial accordance with this paragraph, Posner (1999, p. 147) writes:

> Even judges have a certain ambivalence about perjury in civil litigation. It is not unusual for one judge to say to another that he or she has just presided at a trial at which several of the witnesses were obviously lying, or that the witnesses seem to have coordinated their stories or to have been "well coached" by the lawyers. I have heard expert witnesses referred to as "paid liars." These comments are generally not made in a tone of indignation, and they very rarely lead to a referral to the Department of Justice to inquire into the possibility of an obstruction of justice. Part of this reaction is due to the difficulty of proving perjury in most cases, and part to the fact that judges like other professionals grow moral calluses. But part is due to a sense that *the court system has been designed, or at least has evolved, to be robust in the face of the known inefficacy of the oath and of the threat oj prosecution for perjury and other obstructions of justice and as result, the frequency of these crimes.* It would be nice if they were less frequent, but fortunately they are less costly to society, less feared and less dangerous than many other felonies. (emphasis added)

Harris (1996) uncovers similar phenomena in her interviews with prosecutors. She reports one prosecutor's statement that "if perjury were water, the people in civil court would be drowning." She explains further: "Prosecutors do not believe that [perjury] is a serious problem that they need to be concerned with. They point out that it is the jury's

This is not to say that the threat of a collateral proceeding could not under a different system play an important role in setting agents' incentives to produce evidence at the "primary hearing." Indeed, the collateral proceeding and the evidence there produced would operate on incentives in the primary hearing just as evidence production in the primary hearing operates on incentives in the primary activity.[16] Certain evidentiary presentations in the primary hearing (e.g., outright lies) would be discouraged to the extent that they made other forms of evidence (those establishing, for example, the defense of truth) more expensive at a later proceeding. It would then be an interesting question whether use of collateral proceedings—as opposed to reliance on dynamics internal to the primary hearing—were a cost-effective method of incentive setting.

I do not explicitly model the possibility of relying on collateral proceedings to create the requisite differences in evidence presentation costs at the primary hearing. Instead, I have chosen to include the incentives provided by such proceedings as one, albeit implicit, component of evidence costs at the primary hearing.[17] This choice is perhaps justified by the obvious complication that would result from adding yet a third stage to the model.

1.3. Implications of the Costly Signaling Framework

The costly signaling approach to evidence production proposed here has several implications that make it operationally (as well as conceptually) distinct from existing approaches.

---

job as the factfinder to assess the credibility of witnesses and evidence and ascertain the truth. By the end of the trial, unreliable testimony and evidence have been rejected, truthful testimony and evidence considered, and an outcome determined" (p. 1771).

16. Indeed, there would in theory be an infinite regress, here, with "second order" collateral processes enforcing "first order" collateral process and so on.

17. See note 35 for the manner in which this manifests in the formal model. With respect to the first numerical example discussed in section 1.2.1, I implicitly account for perjury by leaving open the possibility that part of the noncompliant firm's relatively high presentation cost ($140,000 as opposed to $20,000) is due to the negative effect that such presentation would have on the firm's highest attainable payoff (which may itself be negative) at a collateral evidentiary proceeding that delved deeper into the details and circumstances averred in the primary presentation.

332 American Law and Economics Review V3 N2 2001 (320–357)

1.3.1. Truth's false ally. The first implication of this alternative view of evidence concerns the role of "truth" in litigation and enforcement. Evidence scholars have long recognized the presence of "truth's rivals"—reasons that the law declines to take the route most likely to lead to discovery of what actually happened outside the hearing room.[18] Among the most commonly cited rivals are the sanctity of certain socially beneficial relationships (consider the attorney-client privilege and the spousal privileges), fairness to and the dignity of litigants (consider Federal Rule of Evidence 404, which generally prohibits the use of character evidence to show behavior in conformity therewith on a particular occasion), and the alternative use of resources exhausted by the process of fact finding (cited in Federal Rule of Evidence 403 as a balance against probative value).

But it is conventional wisdom both in law and in law-and-economics that the truth does have at least one ally in the goal of deterrence. After all, if the fact finder never learns anything about what actually happened in the primary activity, how can the law possibly set rewards and punishments so as to encourage the desired behavior? Without some inkling of how the parties are likely to have actually behaved—however indirect and imperfect such information may be—the court might as well determine whether to punish or reward by flip of a coin. Or so it would seem.

Yet, in the model of evidence production proposed here, deterrence offers little assistance to truth in its battle against rival forces. In this model, deterrence does not require that the state learn anything at all about what actually happened in the primary activity. Thus, the hearing performance that would be staged by the negligent and the nonnegligent might be identical, thus providing the court with no means of distinguishing between them and therefore resulting in identical rewards and punishments—in terms of liability and damages. Yet negligence may still be deterred—so long as the hearing performance required for exoneration is sufficiently more expensive for the negligent than taking care in the first place.

In other words, the deterrent effect of litigation and enforcement proceedings is keyed to *overall* hearing payoffs, and these consist not just of the liability, recovery, and fine that are ultimately set by the fact finder on

18. See, for example, the recent Symposium (1997–98), entitled "Truth & Its Rivals: Evidence Reform and the Goals of Evidence Law."

the basis of what she learns from the evidence, but also on the evidence production costs of the parties, which the fact finder does not directly observe.

To make this more concrete, consider the numerical example from above. In that example, the evidence cost either $140,000 or $20,000, depending on whether the firm had been compliant, and the regulator announced that it would fine the firm $130,000 unless it presented the highlighted evidence. With this reward structure, only the compliant firm would present the evidence—so that the regulator would in fact learn whether the firm had been compliant. But the fact that the regulator learned the truth from the evidence was purely collateral. What mattered was the fact that the *hearing payoffs* were sufficiently higher for the compliant firm than for the noncompliant firm. And since evidence production costs differ, this does not require that compliant and noncompliant firms present different evidence.

Suppose, for example, that the regulator announced that the firm would be fined $150,000 if it did not present the evidence. Then *both* compliant and noncompliant firms would find it worthwhile to present the evidence, and the regulator would never learn whether a given firm had been compliant or not. On the other hand, the hearing payoffs for both firms would now consist solely of presentation costs, and the difference in these costs (between $140,000 and $20,000) would still be enough to induce compliance in the primary activity.[19]

19. Note that even though noncompliant firms would present the same evidence as compliant firms were they to come before the regulator, the regulator has set the evidence/reward structure so that in fact no noncompliant firms ever actually come before it. In this sense, then, the regulator does know the "truth" about compliance-not by virtue of the evidence it sees at the hearing, but by virtue of the manner in which it has associated evidence and rewards ex ante. This phenomenon does not, however, detract from my claim in this section that the incentive setting role of evidence production is logically distinct from its role in "revealing truth." In the first place, information gleaned by *conformity* of primary activity action in response to the ex ante evidence schedule is quite a different phenomenon from truths revealed by *differences* in evidence actually produced ex post. Only the latter describes the sense in which evidence production is conventionally thought to reveal truth. Second, such conformity of primary activity action is, in any event, an artifact of my simplifying assumption that all firms are identical. Suppose, for example, that there are two types of firms but that the difference between them is indistinguishable from the regulator's point of view: one liability per evidence schedule would have to be used for both. Imagine, further, that for one type of firm the cost of compliance is $100,000, whereas for the

One way to describe this phenomenon is to say that in the costly signaling model of evidence presented here, "pooling" can do the job just as well as "separation." This is one important way in which the costly signaling model of *evidence* differs from the classic costly signaling model. In the classic model, the principal's object in making use of costly signals is indeed to learn the private information currently in the possession of the agent. Thus, the employer would like to learn whether the employment candidate is of high or low ability—to reference Spence's (1974) seminal application of costly signaling—because she would like to hire only high-ability workers, or is willing to pay high wages only to high-ability workers. On the other hand, the *payoffs* of the workers in the signaling-choice problem solved by the employee are of no direct importance to the employer.[20]

In the evidence-as-signaling setting, however, the hearing payoffs of the agents that come before the review board or court are *all* that matter. Deterrence is effected if doing the wrong thing in the primary activity means that you do not (or are not as likely to) fare as well at the subsequent proceeding. What the court actually learns of how the agent behaved in the primary activity is of subsidiary importance, so long as—by whatever means, whether preparation costs or fines—misbehaving tends to reduce total hearing payoffs.

---

other type it is $125,000. Quite plausibly, the state may wish to induce compliance from only the firm with low compliance costs. The same evidence as in the example in the text (with compliance-dependent costs of $140,000 and $20,000 for both types of firms), coupled with a liability schedule that charged $150,000 to all firms that failed to present this evidence, would induce compliance by only low-cost firms. To see why, note that all firms, compliant or not, would choose to present the evidence. Thus, compliance would save all firms $140,000 –$20,000 = $120,000 in evidence costs, which makes compliance worthwhile for only low-cost firms. As a result, some of the firms coming before the regulator would be compliant, others would not. The regulator would be doing its job of inducing the right firms to comply, though it would be learning nothing about which of the firms before it were actually compliant.

20. Pooling is a common phenomenon in "equilibrium settings," where both principal and agent are imagined to move simultaneously, or where the principal's behavior is shaped by outside forces. Consider, for example, the pooling equilibria that attain in Spence's (1974) own model, which, notwithstanding my simplified description of it here, imposes a market equilibrium condition on wages. But in settings such as in the current paper, where the principal moves first in Stackelberg fashion without any form of feedback equilibration, pooling is a much less common modeling outcome.

This feature of the costly signaling approach to evidence also distinguishes it from the Moral Hazard approach to enforcement, especially as manifest in the well-known and often-applied Becker (1968) model. Incentive setting in that model rests on the assumption that the state's glimpse of the truth will be clear enough that fines can be set so as to have a differential effect on the agent that is sufficiently correlated to the agent's actual behavior. The Becker model certainly allows for errors—errors of both false exoneration/acquittal and false liability/guilt—but deterrence cannot be effected if errors exceed some threshold whose magnitude depends, in the simplest setting, on the relative sizes of the maximal fine and the private benefits of misbehaving.[21] Compare this to the numerical example of the costly signaling model, as just described. There, the chance that the court would learn anything was zero. From the court's perspective (though not the system's perspective), bad and good behavior are completely indistinguishable.

This is all to say that truth finding is not *necessary* for deterrence. However, the most efficient method of deterring will generally entail some amount of separation in evidence production. Importantly, the separation will typically not be total. And to the extent that some separation is optimal, this will not be because of the additional information that such separation gives the principal about what actually happened, but rather because of the cost savings that separation will in some instances make possible. Indeed, since no amount of separation is necessary for deterrence and yet some amount will be system cost minimizing, it must be that learning more is cheaper for the principal. Moreover, it must be that reducing costs is the only purpose of learning more. The relationship between truth finding and system costs in this model is thus almost backwards from that in the Moral Hazard/Becker model. In that model, more truth finding (a less imperfect signal) imposes higher costs on the system but may be necessary

21. Thus, if the benefit of the crime is \$10,000, fines cannot exceed \$100,000, the probability of false acquittal is p, and the probability of false conviction is q, then the expected fine if the crime is committed is $(1-p)$ \$100,000, and the expected fine if the crime is not committed is q \$100,000. The crime is deterred only if the amount by which good behavior reduces the expected fine, $(1-p)$ \$100,000 $-q$ \$100,000 $=$ \$100,000$(1-p-q)$ exceeds the benefit of the crime \$10,000. Accordingly, the sum of the errors $p+q$ cannot exceed 90%. In other words, there has to be at least a 10% chance that the fact finder correctly distinguishes the guilty from the innocent.

336 American Law and Economics Review V3 N2 2001 (320–357)

for implementation. Here, truth finding is unnecessary for implementation and occurs only when, and only because, it *saves* on system costs.[22]

1.3.2. Perfect isn't good enough. As already noted, the Omission approach to evidence production does not—at least on its face—account for agents' incentive to lie. But there is an ingenious way to reinterpret the Omission approach in terms of the costly signaling perspective proposed here, and this reinterpretation does, technically speaking, explicitly account for lying.[23] One simply posits the existence of "perfect evidence": some package of evidence whose presentation is of infinite cost in states of the world other than that which such evidence is meant to indicate. Then lying—i.e., presenting the perfect evidence in other states of the world—is theoretically conceivable but practically impossible.

But the assumption that perfect evidence exists—let alone that it is an important enough factor in evidence production to warrant independent

---

22. While incentive setting by evidence production does not require "truth finding," it does require *information*. In particular, properly setting incentives both in this model and in the world requires that the state possess information about the private and social costs of primary activity actions, as well as the tendencies of primary activity actions to make certain types of performances before the court more or less costly to effect. Yet it is crucial to distinguish this later type of information from the sort of information that would be discovered through the fact-finding process and is typically associated with the evidentiary notion of "truth finding." In particular, the information relevant to the system I have described may be divided into two types: (1) *statistical knowledge* of key functional relationships, such as that between primary activity actions and evidence costs; and (2) *particular knowledge* of the level of relevant variables for a given firm, such as a given firm's compliance behavior. The sort of information that the regulator does or does not discover at each hearing is particular knowledge; the sort of information that it would need to set the system up in the first place is statistical. The focus in this paper is on problems due to lack of particular knowledge. This focus has substantial precedent in the literature. (Consider, for example, optimal taxation and the canonical principal-agent problem). One reason for the focus here and in the literature is that statistical knowledge is more easily obtained than particular. The exercise of gathering statistical knowledge is generally not prey to the serious strategic-revelation problems that are inherent in obtaining particular knowledge. If we ask a particular firm whether it has complied, and the firm knows that we will use this information to set its punishment or reward, then the firm has a compelling incentive to lie. On the other hand, if we ask each firm in an industry about the functional relationship between the primary activity and the cost of various forms of evidence, each individual firm realizes that its answer is just one of many data points for use in the design of a system that it may never encounter.

23. I thank Kathy Spier for suggesting this reinterpretation.

study—is arguably no more plausible than the assumption that agents cannot lie. The advisory committee's notes to the Federal Rules of Evidence boldly assert that "no class of evidence is free of the possibility of fabrication." (Rule 801(a), advisory committee's note). And even if this is overstatement, in practice most available evidence consists of oral testimony, documents, media, and the occasional physical article—all of which are forgeable, at a price.[24]

Even if one could plausibly argue that (near) perfect evidence were readily available for use by the system, it is another matter to support the claim that it should actually be employed. Indeed, the model presented in this paper—which as we have seen can accommodate the *possibility* of employing perfect evidence—tends to eschew its use in actual practice. In particular, the model's emphasis on minimizing evidence production costs—a factor absent from both the Omission approach and its reinterpretation—brings to the fore the fact that setting incentives by own-party evidence production is socially expensive. This then leads one to evaluate evidence not just by whether it can "do the job" but also by how much using it to do the job will cost society.

Seen in this light, perfect evidence is unlikely to be the best available. "Less perfect" evidence that is just sufficiently more costly for disobedient actions is likely to be cheaper all around and thus a more efficient means of setting incentives in the primary activity. Thus, in the numerical example discussed above, both $20,000/$140,000 evidence and $20,001/$140,000,000,000,000 evidence can be used to set incentives (with liability set at $210,002 in the latter case). But the former, "less perfect," evidence does the job at lower cost.[25]

24. Is not the fact that the plaintiff is missing a leg essentially perfect evidence, given that the cost of cutting off one's leg is near infinite? Yes, but the question is: perfect evidence of what? Plaintiff's presentation of severe injuries to the fact finder is perfect evidence only of the bare fact that the plaintiff appears before the fact finder with the injury. The existence of these injuries says nothing about how they were caused-e.g., whether the injury was caused by the defendant's lack of care. Information on how phenomena were *caused*, not just what they are, is crucial to the task of regulating behavior.

25. Note that what is being said here goes beyond the statement that there is a tradeoff between accuracy and cost. Even though $20,001/$140,000,000,000,000 evidence is more difficult to falsify, any cost difference over and above $110,000 (the difference in primary action costs) is superfluous. Thus, there is, over this range, *no* tradeoff between accuracy and evidence cost; higher-cost evidence buys nothing of value.

Why would less perfect evidence tend to be less expensive all around? Certainly, no such relationship falls out of the bare logic of costly signaling: in the example above the perfect evidence might have had cost structure $2/$140,000,000,000,000. Nonetheless, the relationship is inherent in the manner in which "pieces" of evidence are typically "stacked" to produce the overall evidentiary performances upon which rewards and punishments are based. Despite my shorthand usage of the term, "evidence" is of course rarely a single performance or presentation, but rather a conglomeration of many different component performances.[26] A firm's evidence will typically consist of multiple witnesses or documents, or both. Each component performance has a cost for noncompliant firms and, if it is of any use in setting primary incentives, a lesser cost—though still a cost—for compliant firms. Increasing the relevant presentation cost *difference* is typically accomplished by increasing the number of "pieces" of component evidence required for full or partial exoneration. And this produces, as well, greater costs all around. Thus, two "pieces" of evidence, each with cost structure $10,000/$100,000, and so cost differences of $90,000, may be combined to produce an evidentiary performance with cost structure $20,000/$200,000.[27] This combination performance generates a larger cost difference of $180,000, but at a larger cost to the compliant of $20,000.

The direct relationship between perfection and cost is often evident in practice. Before issuing a new license, for example, Departments of Motor Vehicles typically require only a passport and an expired license to prove identity. Requiring additional forms of identification, several witnesses, and DNA test results would increase the cost of forgery, but also the costs of truthful presentation.

Such cost considerations, central to the model in this article, are essentially ignored under the Omission approach to evidence: even if presentation costs are used to justify the Omission model's key no-lying assumption, they still have no role in how that model is solved.

1.3.3. Getting more for less. Another distinguishing implication of the model in this article concerns the optimal choice of which action to target

26. See note 34 for the manifestation of this point in the formal model.

27. I have assumed perfect additivity here. But, any additional cost for producing the two rather than either individually suffices for the point.

in the primary activity. Naturally this choice is informed by the marginal cost of implementing each potential action. If the marginal cost of inducing more intensive compliance activities is positive, for instance, it will be optimal to demand less of agents (relative to what would be demanded of them were implementation costless, for example). This is indeed the result that is obtained in the classic Moral Hazard/Becker model of enforcement, in which the wealth-constrained agent's disobedience is detected with some probability that is a function of either the state's expenditures on detection (in, e.g., a criminal setting) or the opponent's trial preparation effort (in a civil setting).[28] The optimality of underdeterrence in the Moral Hazard/Becker model continues to be important in current research on litigation and enforcement.[29]

In the model offered here, however, the underdeterrence result is turned on its head. Somewhat surprisingly, the marginal cost of implementation will tend to be negative (in the relevant range), implying that requiring *additional* compliance activities would be optimal.

The reason that implementation costs tend to decline in the private cost of the behavior implemented in the primary activity relates to the basic mechanic of costly evidence production. The agent is induced to take more care, for instance, because the evidence used by the court or review board to sort out liability or recovery tends to be less expensive to present the more care she takes. This means that (abstracting from changes in the evidence employed in setting different incentives) higher levels of care are associated with lower evidence costs for the agent, and this dynamic is

28. To understand why implementation costs increase in the standard model, suppose the state is currently implementing middling care at least cost. This means that it must be setting fines at their maximal level so that the probability of detection, which is directly tied to enforcement costs, is as low as possible. It also requires that the increase in expected fines that results from being careless outweighs the cost savings from reducing care effort to zero. Now imagine that the state wishes to increase the enforced level of care. This requires creating an even bigger increase in expected fines for careless behavior since the cost of the target care level is greater for the agent. But since fines are already maximal, this increased difference must come from increasing the probability of detection, and this means that enforcing the higher level of care will impose greater social costs.

29. For example, Polinsky and Shavell (1998) employ an interesting dynamic variant of the Moral Hazard/Becker model to show that imposing higher sanctions on repeat offenders may increase deterrence relative to a world in which sanctions are independent of offense history. As they make clear, increasing deterrence improves social welfare because underdeterrence is optimal with uniform sanctions.

what produces the tendency of implementation costs, inclusive of evidence production costs, to decrease.

In somewhat more detail, implementation costs "tend" to decrease in the same way that demand "tends" to decrease in price. In particular, the slope of the implementation cost schedule can be decomposed into two effects: the "change in presenter effect" (just described) and "the change in case effect" (the fact that different evidence may be used to induce higher levels of care). Similar to the substitution effect on demand, the change in presenter effect is always strictly negative for all parameter values and functional forms. On the other hand, the change in case effect is, like the income effect, patently ambiguous.

This result may have implications for the ongoing debate over tort reform. One of the most rhetorically powerful claims marshaled against current systems is that they "overdeter," causing agents to take too much care.[30] Yet the model proposed here suggests that claims of overdeterrence should be viewed with skepticism. To the extent that evidence production is an important element in the current system of litigation, "too much" care may be just the right amount.[31]

The remainder of the paper is organized as follows: section 2 presents the formal model. It then introduces three questions: (1) When is an action implementable with evidence production? (2) Given that an action is implementable, how is it implemented at least cost? (3) Given the least-cost implementation of all actions, which action should be implemented?

30. Kessler and McClellan (1996), for instance, lend careful empirical support to the claim that the threat of suit causes doctors to practice "defensive medicine." They seem to define overdeterrence relative to optimal deterrence without accounting for implementation costs. Their argument still applies, however, under the classic model of enforcement, where optimal deterrence when implementation costs are taken into account is even less than it is when implementation costs are ignored.

Calfee and Craswell (1984) and Craswell and Calfee (1986) find that agents may overcomply (relative to the first best standard) when the probability of liability is a function of the level of compliance and damages are set equal to harm caused. They further establish that the problem is only exacerbated, if, as is traditionally advocated, damages are adjusted upward to compensate for the probability that offenders are not caught.

31. Hadfield (1994) studies the implications of varying levels of judicial competence arguing that overcompliance may be optimal when the alternative is the undercompliance brought on by the absence of judicial enforcement. The present paper shows that overcompliance tends to be optimal along the full continuum of judicial involvement.

Section 2 presents results on each of the three questions. The results are chosen to highlight the differences, in concept and implication, between existing approaches to evidence and the perspective proposed here. All formal proofs appear in the Appendix.

2. Formal Results

2.1. The model

A risk-neutral agent and a risk-neutral principal interact in a model with three phases.[32] To fix ideas, we will think of the principal as a *regulator* and the agent as a *firm* engaged in an activity that is potentially hazardous to local residents. In the first *promulgation phase*, the regulator announces a *liability (per evidence) schedule* $l(e)$. The schedule tells the firm how much it must pay in fines based on the *case or evidence* $e \in E$ it presents at the *hearing*, the third phase, described below. I impose no mathematical structure on the set E. In the primary activity, the firm chooses an action i (e.g., a care level). The firm's *private cost* for action i is a_i, where $a_1 < a_2 < \cdots < a_I$. The *social cost* (excluding the firm's private costs) is h_i. Only the firm observes its actual choice of action; the regulator receives no exogenous signal of the firm's choice of i.

Some time after its choice of action, the firm appears before the regulator's review board at a hearing.[33] There the firm chooses what case e

32. See Sanchirico (1998) for more detail on the mathematical structure of the model. Sanchirico (1998) also contains three illustrative functional form examples of the framework.

33. The structure described herein is similar to reporting requirements under the Clean Air Act, section 7414(a):

> The EPA Administrator may require any person who owns or operates any emission source... on a one-time, periodic or continuous basis to (A) establish and maintain such records; (B) make such reports; (C) install, use, and maintain such monitoring equipment, and use such audit procedures, or methods; (D) sample such emissions (in accordance with such procedures or methods, at such locations, at such intervals, during such periods and in such manner as the Administrator shall prescribe); (E) keep records on control equipment parameters, production variables or other indirect data when direct monitoring of emissions is impractical; (F) submit compliance certifications... and (G) provide such other information as the Administrator may reasonably require.

to present, balancing the resulting liability under $l(e)$ against the costs, if any, of presentation. The set E contains all possible "performances" that the firm could stage before the court.[34] This includes, for example, the case that consists solely of the cheap talk statement, "We were careful." Importantly, I also allow the possibility that some cases are costly and that—more to the point—the level of these costs is (probabilistically) affected by the firm's choice of action in the primary activity.[35] The *evidence cost schedule* for the firm is thus $c_{is}(e)$, where i is the firm's action and s is the *state*. The state s is drawn from the set of possible states S according to probabilities $(p_1, \ldots, p_S) > 0$, $\sum_s p_s = 1$.[36] I will refer to pairs (i, s) as *circumstances*. Importantly, the dependence of evidence costs on actions is not imposed, only allowed: the model encompasses the situation where for every case e, $c_{is}(e)$ is constant across i. The firm learns the actual value of s after choosing its action i, but before choosing its evidence e. The regulator receives no exogenous signal about the actual value of s. All functional relationships are common knowledge.

Thus, the firm chooses what precautionary procedures to follow in its production process with an understanding of how this choice tends to affect what actually comes to pass at the factory and in the neighboring town—for example, whether an industrial accident occurs, and if so, what part of it is observed by workers and neighbors, what pieces are left on the ground, what documents attest to the cause, and so on. Uncertainty in the causal relationship between care and incident is modeled by including the random component s. This component represents all relevant aspects of the environment known to the firm, but not affected by the firm's choice of care level—for example, unavoidable human or machine error, or whether someone happens to be watching the factory from a nearby window. The firm's choice of i and nature's choice of s together determine what actually happens at the plant and in the town. The model allows for the possibility

34. In accordance with the discussion in section 1.3.2, the set of such performances should be taken to include composite "performances" in which a number of evidentiary presentations are "stacked" to form a whole. This is why I refer to elements of this set of performances as "cases" rather than "evidence."

35. As discussed in section 1.2.3, the cost of a presentation may include expected payoff differences from a collateral perjury hearing.

36. Even though p is fixed across actions, the model does in fact allow for the case in which each action produces a different distribution over evidence cost schedules. See Sanchirico (1998).

that what actually happens at the plant and in the town affects in turn the costs of staging various performances before the review board, taking into account both casting (witnesses) and props (real and documentary evidence).

A primary activity action i and an *evidence plan* $(e_1, \ldots, e_S)$ are *incentive compatible*, given liability schedule $l(e)$, if they minimize the firm's costs $a_i + \sum_{s=1}^{S} p_s(l(e_s) + c_{is}(e_s))$. This requires a fortiori that the evidence e_s to be presented in each state minimizes liability and production costs, given the chosen action. The regulator's *overall problem* is to choose the liability schedule $l(e)$ to minimize *system costs*, $a_i + h_i + \sum_{s=1}^{S} p_s c_{is}(e_s)$, where i and $(e_1, \ldots, e_S)$ are the action and evidence plan that are incentive compatible with $l(e)$.[37] When i and $l(e)$ satisfy the incentive-compatibility constraint with some evidence plan, we will say that $l(e)$ *implements* i, meaning that rewarding evidence in this manner induces the firm to take action i. Action i is said to be *implementable* if we can find some $l(e)$ implementing it.

The regulator's subproblem of implementing a fixed action i at least cost is to choose a liability schedule $l(e)$ under which action i is incentive-compatible, so as to minimize *hearing costs*, $\sum_{s=1}^{S} p_s c_{is}(e_s)$, where $(e_1, \ldots, e_s)$ is the evidence plan that is incentive compatible with $l(e)$.[38] Solving this subproblem, given action i, yields the *(minimal) cost of implementing* i, which we denote as C_i. (Set $C_i = \infty$, if i is not implementable.) Action i is said to "solve" the overall problem if, and only if, it minimizes $a_i + h_i + C_i$.[39]

37. For ease of exposition the problem is here stated in a manner that is not technically complete. The statement neglects the possibility that there will be more than one action/evidence plan pair that is incentive-compatible for a given liability schedule. As is standard, I implicitly allow the regulator to choose which incentive-compatible action and evidence plan the agent will follow. See Sanchirico (1998) for the complete statement of the problem. Also note that more than one liability schedule may be optimal.

38. See Sanchirico (1998) for the technically complete statement of the subproblem.

39. I impose no budget-balance constraint on liability payments (which may be negative). However, translating the liability schedule up or down by a fixed constant has no effect on the constraints or the objective. Thus, the principal can always obtain *expected* budget balance, given the implemented action i, by translating $l(e)$ so that expected net liability payments are zero. Given a large population of agents, the principal can achieve almost sure budget balance if the state s is drawn in a manner that allows application of a law of large numbers.

2.2. Roadmap for Formal Results

The regulator's problem poses three issues, all of which relate to important differences between existing approaches to evidence and the model here proposed.

Implementability. When is it possible for the regulator to induce the firm (agent) to take a given action in the primary activity solely by observing the evidence that the firm presents at the hearing? That is, when can we find some liability schedule implementing a given action i? The main point to be made here is that cost differences are necessary (Proposition 1) but truth finding is not (Proposition 2).

Minimal-cost implementation. Given that an action can be implemented by some liability schedule, what is the cheapest way to do so in terms of evidence costs actually incurred? This is the regulator's (principal's) subproblem. Here it is shown that "perfect evidence," as formally defined within, is never part of the minimal-cost implementation (Proposition 3), and that minimal-cost implementation typically entails limited separation (truth finding) (Proposition 4).

Which action to implement. Given the cheapest way to implement each implementable action, which action should the regulator choose? The main point here is that the best course is likely to be implementing an action whose private costs exceed those of the action that would be chosen if hearing costs were not accounted for (Proposition 5).

2.3. Implementability

2.3.1. The necessity of cost differences. The following result establishes the central role of production cost differences.

Proposition 1. No action in the primary activity, except the action of lowest cost to the agent, is implementable if evidence costs do not vary in action; that is, if for all states $s = 1, \ldots, S$, all pairs of actions $i, i' = 1, \ldots, I$, and all evidence e, $c_{is}(e) = c_{i's}(e)$.[40]

The basic idea behind the result has two logical steps. Consider first the firm's choice of evidence at the hearing. The firm balances two considerations: the cost of presentation (if any) and the extent to which the

40. A more general result is proven in the Appendix.

presentation will change the fact finder's ruling in its favor. Hypothetically, two firms with the same evidence costs who face the same liability schedule will end up with the same payoffs from the hearing. Their optimization problems are the same. Therefore, their best possible payoffs are also the same.

Now, step back in time to the firm's choice of action in the primary activity. In choosing whether to comply, the firm balances its private costs against its forecast of how taking care will improve the best it can do at the hearing. The fact finder induces compliance only when the firm believes that compliance increases how well it can do at the hearing by more than the direct cost of complying. But by the reasoning in the previous paragraph, complying improves the firm's hearing payoffs only if it changes, to the firm's benefit, the optimization problem that the firm faces at the hearing. Since the liability schedule $l(e)$ is fixed with respect to actual compliance, any favorable change must come via a favorable shift in evidence costs. Conversely, if the firm's evidence costs are fixed with respect to compliance, then so are the firm's best possible hearing payoffs. All "evidence" is therefore "cheap talk" and has no effect on compliance incentives. In this case, the direct cost of compliance is the only consideration in choosing whether to comply, and thus the firm is always noncompliant.

2.3.2. The sufficiency of ignorance. The following result establishes that truth-finding (i.e., "separation" as opposed to "pooling") is logically superfluous to the issue of implementability. (The role of truth-telling in *minimal* cost implementation is considered in the sequel.)

Proposition 2. If the set E of available evidence is sufficiently rich, that is if the function $(c_{11}(e), \ldots, c_{IS}(e))$ is onto[41] $\mathbb{R}^{I \times S}$, then every action i can be implemented with a liability schedule under which the firm (agent) presents the same evidence in all circumstances, implying that the regulator (principal) never receives any information about the true circumstance.[42]

41. Technically, this means that for every $I \times S$ dimensional vector x there exists an e such that $(c_{11}(e), \ldots, c_{IS}(e)) = x$. This condition is actually much stronger than necessary, but weaker conditions are more cumbersome to state.

42. A more general result is proven in the Appendix.

2.4. Minimal-Cost Implementation

2.4.1. When perfect isn't good enough. In this section, I show that "perfect evidence" is never used in any cost-minimizing implementation. In particular, I demonstrate that the cost of "forgery" is bounded. For this result I assume only that evidence is "divisible" and that the set of possible evidence includes the presentation of no evidence. Evidence is *divisible* in circumstance (i, s) if, arbitrarily close to any evidence with strictly positive cost in circumstance (i, s), there exists evidence with strictly lower costs.[43] And evidence is *divisible* generally if it is divisible in all circumstances (i, s). Thus evidence is divisible if it is possible to restructure any presentation to shave off production costs. Evidence is often divisible along a time dimension: one can always coach a sponsored witness one minute less, or search one minute less for corroborating documents. *Do-nothing evidence* $0 \in E$ is evidence that is of minimal cost in all circumstances and has the same cost across all circumstances.[44] Showing up and remaining silent is prototypical do-nothing evidence. I allow the uniform cost of do-nothing evidence to be positive to account for the possibility of fixed costs.

Proposition 3. Suppose that liability schedule $l(e)$ implements action i at minimal cost and that e_{is} is the evidence the firm presents in state s after taking action i. In at least one other circumstance (i', s'), the cost of presenting evidence e_{is} will be no more than $(a_i - a_1)/p_s$ greater than the cost of presenting evidence e_{is} in circumstance (i, s).

2.4.2. When learning more costs less. It was previously shown that truth finding is not necessary for implementation. However, truth finding—i.e., separation—will often play a role in the minimal-cost implementation of a given primary activity action. Importantly, this is not because of the additional information that such separation gives the principal, but because of the cost savings that separation makes possible.

To understand how truth finding can save on system costs, imagine that we start with a situation like those examined in Proposition 2, in

43. Formally, $\forall e \in E$ such that $c_{is}(e) > 0$, $\forall$ open neighborhoods $U(e)$ of e, $\exists e' \in U(e)$ such that $c_{is}(e') < c_{is}(e)$. Openness is defined with respect to the coarsest topology under which c_{is} is continuous.

44. Formally, $\forall(i', s')$, $c_{i's'}(0) = \min_e c_{i's'}(e) = F \geq 0$.

which we are implementing a given action i with the firm presenting the same evidence e in all circumstances. The liability schedule inducing uniform presentation of e must be such that failure to present e results in an increase Δl in the firm's liability that exceeds its presentation costs for e—and this must be true in every circumstance.

Now, consider the circumstance(s) in which this evidence e is most expensive for the firm. Instead of having the firm present e in this circumstance, we can instead induce it to present no evidence by reducing the increase in liability Δl so that it is slightly less than the firm's presentation cost. The firm will then present no evidence in this highest-cost circumstance, but its hearing payoffs in this circumstance will be essentially the same. Further, the firm will continue to present e in all other circumstances: we will not have reduced Δl below the cost of presenting e in circumstances besides that in which e is of highest cost. Thus, hearing payoffs in all these other circumstances also will remain unchanged. Since hearing payoffs are essentially the same, the firm will still choose action i in the primary activity. The fact that the firm will not be presenting e in the circumstance in which it is of highest cost has two implications. First, since this circumstance has at least some chance of occurring, system costs will be lower. Moreover, now the principal will learn whether the highest cost circumstance has or has not obtained—rather coarse information, given the full range of circumstances, but more than the principal was receiving at the start. The result: learning more has lowered system costs.

What is the optimal amount of separation in evidence production? Fully general results are difficult to obtain. But for *multiplicatively separable evidence costs,* evidence costs of the form $c_{is}(e) = \zeta_{is}c(e)$ for some function $c(e)$, the results are stark and illustrative. The proof for the following result is lengthy and appears in Sanchirico (1998).

Proposition 4. Suppose that evidence costs are multiplicatively separable. Then in any minimal-cost implementation of any action $i > 1$ no more than I different pieces of evidence will be used, even though there are $I \times S$ different circumstances.

In interpreting this result, note that there is no sense in which individual actions will be associated with individual pieces of evidence: only the total numbers of each are associated. In particular, there will generally be no one-to-one correspondence between the I evidentiary presentations and the I actions: for instance, a given action may be the most probable after several different presentations.

2.5. Which Action to Implement: When Deterring More Costs Less

This section explicates the tendency for the optimally implemented action to exceed the action that minimizes social costs $a_i + h_i$ in the primary activity. To aid in the exposition, I will assume throughout that all actions are implementable.[45] Let us say that action i is *first best* if it minimizes $a_i + h_i$ and *second best* if it minimizes $a_i + h_i + C_i$. The first step is to establish the relationship between the slope of C_i and the relative size of first and second best actions.

Lemma 1. Suppose that implementation costs are decreasing across all actions greater than $i = 1$: that is, given i and $2 \leq i' < i$, $C_{i'} > C_i$. Then if $i^{SB} \geq 2$ is second best and i^{FB} is first best, it must be that $i^{SB} \geq i^{FB}$.

I now decompose the slope of the minimal-cost-of-implementation schedule into two effects. Suppose that liability schedule $l(e)$ implements action $i \geq 2$ at minimal cost whereas $l'(e)$ implements some lower action $i' < i$ at minimal cost. Let $(e_{11}, \ldots, e_{IS})$ and $(e'_{11}, \ldots, e'_{IS})$ represent the respective incentive compatible evidence plans. Then by simply adding and subtracting the term $\sum_{s=1}^{S} p_s c_{i's}(e_{is})$, the net increase in implementation costs caused by increasing the implemented action from i' to i, namely $C_i - C_{i'} = \sum_{s=1}^{S} p_s c_{is}(e_{is}) - \sum_{s=1}^{S} p_s c_{i's}(e'_{i's})$, can be additively decomposed into (1) the *change-in-presenter effect*, $\sum_{s=1}^{S} p_s(c_{is}(e_{is}) - c_{i's}(e_{is}))$, and (2) the *change-in-case effect*, $\sum_{s=1}^{S} p_s(c_{i's}(e_{is}) - c_{i's}(e'_{is}))$. This decomposition says that two things happen when we raise the level of care that we are implementing from i' to i. First, fixing the evidence plan actually employed, we raise the action that is actually presenting the evidence. This corresponds to the change-in-presenter effect. Secondly, we shift the evidence per liability schedule from one that minimizes costs in implementing i' to one that minimizes costs in implementing i. This will

45. See Sanchirico (1998) for the more general case.

generally entail a change in the evidence plan actually employed by the agent. The resulting change in expected costs, fixing the action taken at i', is the change-in-case effect.

Proposition 5. The change-in-presenter effect $\sum_{s=1}^{S} p_s(c_{is}(e_{is}) - c_{i's}(e_{is}))$, where $i' < i$, is always strictly negative.

The intuition is as follows. In order to implement i over the lower i' we must be rewarding the agent with higher expected hearing payoffs if it takes action i instead of the less privately costly action i'. A fortiori, the agent must do at least as well if it obediently takes action i and honestly presents e_{is} in each state s, than if it *dis*obediently takes action i' and then dishonestly mimics an obedient agent at the hearing, presenting e_{is} (as opposed to $e_{i's}$) in each state. (There may be even more profitable ways for the disobedient agent to be dishonest at the hearing.) Since private costs are strictly higher for the obedient and honest agent, it must be that the obedient and honest agent's expected hearing payoffs are strictly higher than those of the disobedient and dishonest agent. Since both agents present the same evidence in each state, they obtain the same liability in each state. Thus, the obedient and honest agent's expected hearing payoffs can be higher only if his expected evidence costs are strictly lower. (Note that we cannot conclude that his evidence costs are strictly lower in any given state.)

While the change-in-presenter effect is always negative, the change-in-case effect may go in either direction. In the Appendix, I provide a simple and natural example in which the effect is negative, reinforcing the change-in-presenter effect and ensuring that the second best exceeds the first.[46]

3. Conclusion

Many forms of regulation rely in whole or in part on information supplied by the party in interest. Yet, despite simultaneous advances in both law-and-economics and information economics, the academic literature

46. The change-in-case effect will always be *non*negative when evidence costs satisfy a single-crossing property. See Sanchirico (1998).

still lacks a full account of this problem—that is to say, an account that not only integrates incentives in the primary activity and the subsequent hearing but also acknowledges that agents can and will lie when it is in their interest to do so. This paper has set out to remedy that deficiency. Though much work remains to be done, the model proposed makes several points that taken together represent a conceptual shift in the way evidence has been viewed both in law and in economics.

First, in a world in which agents can and will lie, evidence is of use in inspiring care on the street or in the factory only to the extent that the exercise of care lowers presentation cost in the hearing room. Second, this being so, enforcing higher levels of the action in the primary activity turns agents into lower-cost evidence producers and may reduce the cost of implementation—a result that calls into question recent claims that the tort system "overdeters." Third, the central role of evidence costs makes clear that the best evidence is not necessarily the most "conclusive." Presentation cost differences are necessary to implement a given action, but the absolute level of evidence costs for the implemented action is also an important factor. Thus, "perfect evidence" may be inferior to relatively forgeable evidence that costs significantly less when genuine. Lastly, the relationship between truth finding and deterrence is far more tenuous than has been supposed. The importance in effecting deterrence of truth-finding *per se* is called into question. If the central object of the hearing is to set incentives on the road or at the plant, then it is of no direct concern whether the petitioner is telling us "the truth", what matters is only whether what she tells us tends to be more difficult to say when she has failed to act as the law requires.

Appendix

It is more convenient to work with an alternative formulation of the regulator's problem whose equivalence is established below. In this alternative formulation, we proceed as if the principal chooses both the agent's action and her evidence and liability in each circumstance, subject to *two* respective incentive constraints, one for the primary activity and one for the hearing. We represent the choice of liability and evidence in each circumstance by a vector rather than a function. We refer to this vector also *as the liability-per-evidence schedule.* Thus, the principal's *direct bifurcated problem* is to choose i and $(l, e) = (l_{11}, \ldots, l_{IS}; e_{11}, \ldots, e_{IS})$ to minimize $a_i + h_i + \sum_{s=1}^{S} p_s c_{is}(e_{is})$, subject to: $\forall i' = 1, \ldots, I$,

$$a_i + \sum_{s=1}^{S} p_s(l_{is} + c_{is}(e_{is})) \leq a_{i'} + \sum_{s=1}^{S} p_s(l_{i's} + c_{i's}(e_{i's})), \tag{1}$$

and $\forall (i', s'), (i'', s'')$,

$$l_{i's'} + c_{i's'}(e_{i's'}) \leq l_{i''s''} + c_{i's'}(e_{i''s''}). \tag{2}$$

Constraints (1) and (2) constitute a bifurcation of the incentive-compatibility constraint. Constraint (2) says that if the agent were to take action i' and observe realization s', it would (weakly) prefer the liability and evidence pair $(l_{i's'}, e_{i's'})$ to that assigned to every alternative circumstance (i'', s''). We call (2) the *hearing constraint.* Constraint (1) says that the agent must (weakly) prefer to take action i over all alternative actions i', *given* that it would do what is intended for it in each circumstance at the hearing. We call Constraint (1) the *primary activity constraint.*

Proposition 6. If i and $(e_1, \ldots, e_s)$ are incentive-compatible with $l(e)$, then we can find (l, e) with $e_{is} = e_s$ for all $s = 1, \ldots, S$, and $l_{i's'} = l(e_{i's'})$ for all (i', s'), such that i and (l, e) satisfy (1) and (2). Conversely, if i and (l, e) satisfy (1) and (2), then we can find a function $l(e)$ with $l_{i's'} = l(e_{i's'})$ for all (i', s') such that i and $(e_{i1}, \ldots, e_{is})$ are incentive-compatible with $l(e)$.

Proof. If $(i; e_1, \ldots, e_S)$ is incentive-compatible with $l(e)$, then set (l, e) as follows: for i and any s set $e_{is} = e_s$ and $l_{is} = l(e_{is}) = l(e_s)$. For all $i' \neq i$ and any s, set $e_{i's}$ to any e minimizing $l(e) + c_{i's}(e)$ and set $l_{i',s} = l(e_{i's})$. Then, for all (i', s'), $l_{i's'} + c_{i's'}(e_{i's'}) = \min_e[l(e) + c_{i's'}(e)]$. From this it follows that i satisfies the hearing and primary activity constraints with the constructed $l(e)$. Conversely, if i and $(l, e) = (l_{11}, \ldots, l_{IS}; e_{11}, \ldots, e_{IS})$ satisfy the direct problem's constraints, construct $l(e)$ as follows: given K, set $l(e) = l_{i's'}$, if $e = e_{i's'}$ and K otherwise. This assignment of l to e is unique since the hearing constraint guarantees that $l_{i's'} = l_{i''s''}$ whenever $e_{i's'} = e_{i''s''}$. If K is large enough, then setting e to a value that does not equal any $e_{i's'}$ is never optimal for the agent at the hearing in any circumstance. Hence, the only relevant alternatives for the agent in circumstance (i', s') are those assigned to other circumstances. Thus $e_{i's}$ minimizes $l(e) + c_{i's}(e)$ for every i' and s. It is then clear that i satisfies incentive compatibility against $l(e)$. QED

Proof of Proposition 1. Proposition 1 is an immediate consequence of the following more general result.

Lemma 2. Action $i \geq 2$ is implementable, only if for some evidence plan $(e_1, \ldots, e_S)$ the expected evidence costs savings from choosing i over any alternative action i' exceed the additional private costs in the primary activity. Formally, i is implementable, only if

$$\exists(e_1,\ldots,e_s) \in E^S \ s.t. \ \forall i' = 1,\ldots,I, \sum_{s=1}^{S} p_s(c_{i's}(e_s) - c_{is}(e_s)) \geq a_i - a_{i'}. \quad (3)$$

Proof. Consider any alternative action i'. There must be no advantage to the agent from taking action i' and then, in every state, presenting the evidence that she would have presented had she taken action i. Formally, from the primary activity constraint

$$-a_i + \sum_s p_s(-l_{is} - c_{is}(e_{is})) \geq -a_{i'} + \sum_s p_s(-l_{i's} - c_{i's}(e_{i's})). \quad (4)$$

From the hearing constraint, $\forall s = 1, \ldots, S$:

$$-l_{i's} - c_{i's}(e_{i's}) \geq -l_{is} - c_{i's}(e_{is}). \quad (5)$$

Substituting (5) into the right hand side of (4) yields $-a_i + \sum_s p_s(-l_{is} - c_{is}(e_{is})) \geq -a_{i'} + \sum_s p_s(-l_{is} - c_{i's}(e_{is}))$. Canceling the l_{is} terms and rearranging yields (3).. QED

Proof of Proposition 2. For notational convenience, reorder actions so that the action to be implemented is now $i = 1$. Consider liability schedules of the following form: $l(e) = 0$, if $e = \hat{e}$, and $l(e) = K$ otherwise. Imagine that the agent presents $e = \hat{e}$ in all circumstances. (We consider hearing incentive compatibility below.) For such single evidence schedules, primary activity incentive compatibility reduces to the system of

$I - 1$ inequalities of the form $a_i - a_1 \leq \sum p_s(c_{1s}(\hat{e}) - c_{is}(\hat{e}))$. In matrix form this is

$$\begin{bmatrix} a_2 - a_1 \\ \vdots \\ a_I - a_1 \end{bmatrix}$$

$$\leq \begin{bmatrix} p_1, \ldots, p_S & -p_1, \ldots, -p_S & 0 & \cdots & 0 \\ p_1, \ldots, p_S & 0 & -p_1, \ldots, -p_S & \cdots & \vdots \\ \vdots & \vdots & 0 & \cdots & \vdots \\ p_1, \ldots, p_S & 0 & \cdots & \cdots & -p_1, \ldots, -p_S \end{bmatrix} \begin{bmatrix} c_{11}(\hat{e}) \\ \vdots \\ \vdots \\ c_{IS}(\hat{e}) \end{bmatrix}.$$

By inspection, this matrix of probabilities has $I - 1$ linearly independent rows. Also, the right-hand side is invariant to translation of the vector $\{c_{is}(\hat{e})\}_{is}$. Thus, if $\{c_{is}(\hat{e})\}_{is}$, viewed as a function of $\hat{e}$, is onto $\mathbb{R}_+^{I \times S}$, the system has a nonnegative solution in $\hat{e}$. To satisfy hearing incentive compatibility, we need only set K larger than $\max_{is} c_{is}(\hat{e})$.

Proof of Proposition 3. Suppose, on the contrary, that $c_{i's'}(e_{is}) - c_{is}(e_{is}) > (a_i - a_1)/p_s$, for all $(i', s') \neq (i, s)$. By divisibility there exists some other e' that has strictly lower costs for (i, s) $(c_{is}(e') < c_{is}(e_{is}))$ and still satisfies $c_{i's'}(e') - c_{is}(e') > (a_i - a_1)/p_s, \forall (i', s') \neq (i, s)$. I will show that we can implement i with a liability schedule whose costs are strictly lower than those of (l, e). Set $e_{i's'} = 0 \in E$ and $l_{i's'} = -F \in \mathbb{R}$ for all $(i's') \neq (i, s)$ (including outcomes with the same action but different states, and vice versa). Set $e_{is} = e'$ and $l_{is} = -\min_{i's' \neq is} c_{i's'}(e')$. Note that the cost of this schedule is less than for (l, e): $p_s c_{is}(e') + (1 - p_s)F < p_s c_{is}(e_{is}) + (1 - p_s)F \leq \sum_{s'} p_{s'} c_{is'}(e_{is'})$. Secondly, I claim that the schedule is incentive-compatible at the hearing. Because all circumstances besides (i, s) present the same evidence, we need to check only (i, s) vis a vis its alternatives (i', s'). Hearing payoffs for truthful (i, s) are nonnegative: $-l_{is} - c_{is}(e') = \min_{i's' \neq is} c_{i's'}(e') - c_{is}(e') > (a_i - a_1)/p_s \geq 0$. Since pretending to be any (i', s') yields (i, s) payoffs of $-(-F) - c_{is}(0) = 0$, (i, s) has no incentive to lie. Conversely, pretending to be (i, s) leaves an alternative outcome (i', s') with payoffs $-l_{is} - c_{i's'}(e') = \min_{i''s'' \neq is} c_{i''s''}(e') - c_{i's'}(e') \leq 0$, while truthtelling yields payoffs of $-(-F) - c_{i's'}(0) = 0$. I complete the proof by showing that (l, e) is incentive-compatible in the primary activity. For any i',

$$\begin{aligned}
&-a_i + \sum_{s'} p_{s'}(-l_{is'} - c_{is'}(e_{is'})) \\
&= -a_i + p_s\Big(\min_{i's' \neq is} c_{i's'}(e') - c_{is}(e')\Big) \\
&\geq -a_i + p_s\left(\frac{a_i - a_1}{p_s}\right) = -a_i + a_i - a_1 \geq -a_{i'} + 0 \\
&= -a_{i'} + \sum_{s'} p_{s'}(-l_{i's'} - c_{i's'}(e_{i's'})).
\end{aligned}$$

Proof of Lemma 1. Suppose that i^{FB} is first best. Consider any lower level $2 \leq i' < i^{FB}$ of care. We will show that i' cannot be second best. Since i^{FB} is first best implementable, the sum of precaution and accident costs is lower at i^{FB} than at i': $-a_{i^{FB}} - h_{i^{FB}} \geq -a_{i'} - h_{i'}$. Since C_i is downward sloping, implementation costs are strictly lower at i^{FB}. Thus i^{FB} has strictly lower *total* costs than i', so i' cannot be second best.

Proof of Proposition 5. Immediate from the proof of Lemma 2. QED

Example: [strictly negative change-in-case effect]. We have three actions 1, 2, and 3, with private costs 0, 4, and 10, respectively. Further, we have two pieces of evidence. The first piece of evidence $\underline{e}$ costs \$20, \$10, and \$0 for actions 1, 2, and 3, respectively. The second piece of evidence $\bar{e}$ is more expensive for all actions, costing \$25, \$20, and \$15 for actions 1, 2, and 3, respectively. Note that each piece of evidence is less expensive for actions with higher private costs. Thus evidence costs are ordered "normally." (However, evidence costs do not satisfy a single crossing property.)

Now, action 3 can be implemented with the lowest cost evidence $\underline{e}$: if the agent must present $\underline{e}$ in order to avoid some large amount of liability, then action 3's total payoffs of $-10 - 0 = -10$ are larger than both action 1's, $-0 - 20 = -20$, and action 2's, $-4 - 10 = -14$. Hence, the minimal-cost implementation of action 3 requires that action 3 present evidence $\underline{e}$. Action 2, however, *cannot* be implemented with the lower-cost evidence $\underline{e}$. For suppose that we were implementing action 2 with a liability schedule in which action 2 presents $\underline{e}$. Then action 3 can always present $\underline{e}$ also. This will give action 3 the same liability as action 2 with \$10 less in evidence costs. Thus action 3's hearing payoffs, from whatever evidence action 3 is called on to produce, must be at least \$10 more than those of action 2. Since its private costs are only \$6 more, action 2 is not implemented. On the other hand, action 2 *is* implemented if all actions present the more expensive evidence $\bar{e}$. Then action 2's total payoffs are $-4 - 20 = -24$, which exceeds both action 1's payoffs, $-0 - 25 = -25$, and action 3's payoffs, $-10 - 15 = -25$. Thus the minimal-cost implementation of action 2 requires that action 2 present evidence $\bar{e}$. Thus the evidence $\bar{e}$ used to implement action 2 at minimal cost is more costly (for all actions, specifically for action 2) than the evidence $\underline{e}$ used to implement action 3 at minimal cost. We conclude that the change-in-case effect in moving from action 2 to action 3 is strictly negative.

References

Becker, Gary. 1968. "Crime and Punishment: An Economic Approach," 76 *Journal of Political Economy* 169–217.

Calfee, John, and Richard Craswell. 1984. "Some Effects of Uncertainty on Compliance with Legal Standards," 70 *Virginia Law Review* 965–1003.

Craswell, Richard, and John Calfee. 1986. "Deterrence and Uncertain Legal Standards," 2 *Journal of Law, Economics, & Organization* 279–303.

Clean Air Act, 42 U.S.C. 7414(a).

Clean Water Act, 33 U.S.C. 1318.

Daughety, Andrew F., and Jennifer F. Reinganum. 1995. "Product Safety, Liability, R&D, and Signaling," 85 *American Economic Review* 1187–1206.

———. 2000. "On the Economics of Trials: Adversarial Process, Evidence, and Equilibrium Bias," 16 *Journal of Law, Economics, & Organization* 365–95.

Davis, Michael L. 1994. "The Value of Truth and the Optimal Standard of Proof in Legal Disputes," 10 *Journal of Law, Economics, & Organization* 343–59.

Federal Rules of Evidence 403, 404, and 801(a).

Finkelstein, Michael, and William Fairly. 1970. "A Bayesian Approach to Identification Evidence," 83 *Harvard Law Review* 489–517.

Froeb, Luke, and Bruce Kobayashi. 1996. "Naïve, Biased, yet Bayesian: Can Juries Interpret Selectively Produced Evidence?" 12 *Journal of Law, Economics, & Organization* 257–71.

Hadfield, Gillian. 1994. "Judicial Competence and the Interpretation of Incomplete Contracts," 23 *Journal of Legal Studies* 159–84.

Harris, Lisa. 1996. "Perjury Defeats Justice," 42 *Wayne Law Review* 1755–1803.

356 American Law and Economics Review V3 N2 2001 (320–357)

Hermalin, Benjamin, and Michael Katz. 1991. "Moral Hazard and Verifiability: The Effects of Renegotiation in Agency," 59 *Econometrica* 1735–53.

Holmstrom, Bengt, and Paul Milgrom. 1991. "Multitask Principal-Agent Analyses," 7 *Journal of Law, Economics, & Organization* 24–52.

Kaplow, Louis, and Steve Shavell. 1994. "Accuracy in the Determination of Liability," 37 *Journal of Law & Economics* 1–15.

———. 1996. "Accuracy in the Assessment of Damages," 39 *Journal of Law & Economics* 191–210.

Katz, Avery. 1988. "Judicial Decision Making and Litigation Expenditure," 8 *International Review of Law & Economics* 127–43.

Kessler, Daniel, and Mark McClellan. 1996. "Do Doctors Practice Defensive Medicine?" 111 *Quarterly Journal of Economics* 353–90.

Lipman, Bart, and Duane Seppi. 1995. "Robust Inference in Communication Games with Partial Provability," 66 *Journal of Economic Theory* 370–405.

Milgrom, Paul, and John Roberts. 1986. "Relying on the Information of Interested Parties," 17 *RAND Journal of Economics* 18–31.

Okuno-Fujiwara, Masahiro, Andrew Postlewaite, and Kotaro Suzumura. 1990. "Strategic Information Revelation," 57 *Review of Economic Studies* 25–47.

People v. Collins 68 Cal.2d 319 (1968).

Pfaff, Alexander S. P., and Chris William Sanchirico. 2000. "Environmental Self-Auditing: Setting the Proper Incentives for Discovery and Correction of Environmental Harm," 16 *Journal of Law, Economics, & Organization* 189–208.

Polinsky, A. Mitchell, and Steven Shavell. 1998. "On Offense History and the Theory of Deterrence," 18 *International Review of Law & Economics* 305–24.

Posner, Richard. 1999. *An Affair of State: The Investigation, Impeachment, and Trial of President Clinton*. Cambridge, MA: Harvard University Press.

Rubinfeld, Daniel, and David Sappington. 1987. "Efficient Awards and Standards of Proof in Judicial Proceedings," 18 *RAND Journal of Economics* 308–15.

Sanchirico, Chris. 1995. "Enforcement by Hearing: How the Civil Law Sets Incentives," Columbia Economics Department, Discussion Paper No. 95-9603.

———. 1998. "Enforcement by Hearing: An Integrated Model of Evidence Production," University of Southern California Law School Olin Working Paper 98-19, available at http://www.ssrn.com.

———. 2000. "Games, Information, and Evidence Production: With Application to English Legal History," 2 *American Law and Economics Review* 342–80.

———. 2001. "Character Evidence and the Object of Trial," 101 *Columbia Law Review* (forthcoming).

Schrag, Joel, and Suzanne Scotchmer. 1994. "Crime and Prejudice: The Use of Character Evidence in Criminal Trials," 10 *Journal of Law, Economics, & Organization* 319–42.

Shavell, Steven. 1989. "Sharing of Information Prior to Settlement or Litigation," 20 *RAND Journal of Economics* 183–95.

Sobel, Joel. 1985. "Disclosure of Evidence and Resolution of Disputes," in Alvin Roth, ed., *Game-Theoretic Models of Bargaining*. Cambridge: Cambridge University Press.

Spence, Michael. 1974. *Market Signaling*. Cambridge, MA: Harvard University Press.

Symposium. 1986. "Probability and Inference in the Law of Evidence," 66 *Boston University Law Review* 377–952.

Symposium. 1997–98. "Truth & Its Rivals: Evidence Reform and the Goals of Evidence Law," 49 *Hasting Law Journal* 289–463.

37 C.F.R. 1.192-6 (1994).

Tribe, Lawrence. 1970. "Trial by Mathematics: Precision and Ritual in the Legal Process," 84 *Harvard Law Review* 1329–93.

21 U.S.C. 355(d).

D
Correlated Private Information

[5]

Games, Information, and Evidence Production: With Application to English Legal History

Chris William Sanchirico, *University of Virginia School of Law*

This paper studies the problem of how the legal system regulates activity outside the courtroom based on information supplied in court by interested and potentially dishonest parties. The supply of information is analyzed along a game-theoretic dimension: the extent to which the supplier has an interest in how the information will be used. Such analysis uncovers a basic trade-off in system design between the "fixed costs" of hearings (e.g., the productive activity forsaken by participation) and the cost of the evidence produced therein. This trade-off helps to explain and connect several trends in the historical evolution of English civil process.

Recent years have witnessed great progress in extending the economic analysis of law from substantive legal rules—as in property, tort, and contract law—to the system of civil litigation that gives those rules effect. Even so, relatively little has been written about what may be the fundamental question of civil process: *How does the legal system influence*

This paper was originally circulated as the second half of Sanchirico (1995). I thank seminar participants at the George Mason Law School (1995), the Columbia Economics Department and Law School (1996), the USC Law School (1997), Cal Tech (1997), the American Law and Economics Association's Meetings (1997), and the Stanford Institute for Theoretical Economics (1997). I also thank Anne Alstott, Jennifer Arlen, Ehud Kamar, John Langbein, Kenneth Leonard, Ronald Miller, Andrew Newman, Alexander Pfaff, Mitchell Polinsky, Richard Posner, Michael Riordan, Susan Rose-Ackerman, Kathy Spier, Eric Talley, and Rakesh Vohra. Special thanks to Daniel Klerman.

Send correspondence to: Chris William Sanchirico, University of Virginia School of Law, 580 Massie Road, Charlottesville, VA 22903-1789; Fax: (804) 924-7536; E-mail: csanchirico@virginia.edu.

activity outside of the courtroom on the basis of information supplied in court by interested and potentially dishonest parties? Though the literature on "suit, settlement, and trial" offers a detailed and insightful account of suit and settlement, in most models trial figures either as an occasion for the court's omniscience, or as some formless future event that the parties bargain to avoid. Thus while it is common to say that suit and settlement proceed "in the shadow of" trial, in terms of what has been written in the field, trial seems more in the shadow.[1]

This paper sets out a new framework for answering this foundational, yet largely unexamined, problem in the study of civil process. The framework is then tested by application to the historical evolution of civil process in England, yielding a new explanation for change that connects seemingly diverse historical trends.

The paper analyzes the supply of information to the court along a game-theoretic dimension: the extent to which the supplier has an interest in how the information will be used. When the supplier has such an interest—as the defendant, for example, has an interest in whether the court finds that she has been negligent—the supplier has an incentive to shade or even fabricate that information in a way that furthers these interests. The fact-finder cannot simply rely on the bare testimony of the party; it cannot suffice that defendant *says* she has exercised due care. Other means must be employed to ensure that the information supplied to the court has meaning beyond a simple expression of the party's interest.[2]

How then does the court extract meaningful information from interested parties? I have proposed elsewhere (Sanchirico, 1995, 1998) that the

1. In many existing studies of litigation, the court is implicitly assumed to be able to instantly and automatically deduce whatever factual knowledge it needs. See, for example, Arlen (1992), Brown (1973), Calabresi (1972), Ordover (1978, 1981), Polinsky and Rubinfeld (1988), Shavell (1980, 1999), and Spier (1994b). Other models collapse trial process into an exogenous probability that the court will determine the truth. See, for example, Bebchuk (1984), Daughety and Reinganum (1994), Nalebuff (1987), Png (1983, 1987), Shavell (1982, 1999), and Spier (1994a). Even models that focus on trial error posit an *exogenous* relationship between the probability of error and either the level of public spending (see, e.g., Craswell and Calfee, 1984; Kaplow and Shavell, 1994, 1996) or the preparation effort of the parties (see Katz, 1988; Landes, 1971; Rubinfeld and Sappington 1987). For more on related literature, see notes 4 and 6 and Sanchirico (1999).

2. The risk of perjury is no pat answer to this puzzle. Perjury itself must be proved. See, for example, Zelin (1999), section 82. This point is discussed in detail in Sanchirico (1999).

law uses an extension of Spence's (1974) well-known concept of "costly signaling." A defendant's evidence of due care, for example, becomes meaningful—despite defendant's evident interest—if the court can find and rely on evidence of a form that is (or at least tends to be) less "expensive" to produce for defendants that have indeed exercised due care. Liability as a function of evidence presented can then be structured in such a way that only those defendants for whom the evidence is of lower cost—in essence, defendants who have been careful—will find the potential decrease in liability worth the effort of presentation. Such evidence will then be a reliable signal of due care.[3]

But extracting useful information from interested parties by this means is a costly endeavor: the very signaling costs that give the evidence meaning are a loss to the system. Indeed, as will be shown, the greater the party's interest in how the information will be used—the larger the stakes for that party—the greater the cost of the signal that must be used to make that information meaningful.

This raises the question: why does the system not garner information from (relatively) disinterested "parties" so as to reduce these evidence costs? Indeed, early civil process in England seems to have operated much in this manner. The jury was essentially a bank of witnesses, and the ability of the parties themselves to present their own case was circumscribed.

Perhaps the reason that our modern system does not exhibit the same reliance on third parties lies in the fact that such reliance has its *own* costs. As will be explained, the efficacy of "third-party information" is tied to the breadth of circumstances triggering suit and the number of individuals participating in each action. This means that the cost of obtaining information in this manner accrues primarily in terms of the "fixed costs" of holding hearings—as opposed to the "variable costs" of the evidence therein "produced." The more often suits are filed and the greater the number of participants per suit, the greater the imputed rent on the space used, the greater the salaries and wages of staff, and, most importantly, the greater the opportunity cost, in terms of lost production and leisure, of participation by private parties.

3. More precisely, it is sufficient that trial payoffs tend to be higher for the careful. Given production cost differences, this can occur even when careful and careless present the *same* evidence. See Sanchirico (1999) for details.

A fundamental trade-off thus arises between the "fixed costs" of holding hearings and the cost of evidence produced therein, a trade-off that operates precisely along the dimension of the intensity of interest possessed by the supplier of the information. Relying on interested parties necessitates costly evidence production. Relying instead on less-interested observers necessitates more frequent hearings, or greater attendance at each, and so results in greater fixed costs.[4]

The "comparative statics"[5] of this trade-off may help explain the transformation of English civil process alluded to above. Historical increases in the opportunity cost of process, brought on by increases in the marginal product of labor, likely had an asymmetric effect on the costs of process. The fixed cost of attendance certainly increased, but, as will be explained, there is good reason to believe that the cost of using costly evidence production to extract information from interested parties did not. These changing circumstances exerted cost pressures on the system, and these pressures encouraged the essential abolition of the English civil jury and increased the system's reliance on evidence sponsored by parties to the action.

The rest of the paper is organized as follows: section 1 presents a non-technical exposition of the framework; section 2 discusses the application

4. There is, of late, a small literature modeling evidence production as "strategic search" (Froeb and Kobayashi, 1996; Daughety and Reinganum, 1998). Parties to a suit sample from a distribution for "pieces of evidence," deciding when to stop sampling and what of their sample to show the court. This paper differs from the strategic search literature (SSL) in several ways. First, as in Milgrom and Roberts (1986), parties in the SSL may decline to report, but may not fabricate, observations. Here agents are not confined to omission, but may lie outright. Second, in the SSL, the court acts on evidence in a manner hardwired by the modeler. The issue is whether such limits on the court's capacity generate "biased" decisions. Here, the court takes into account the incentives of the parties in deciding what to believe and how to assign rewards. The issue is how it does this, and what determines the best method. Third, the SSL picks up the story at trial, after an accident has occurred and one party has filed suit. The model here accounts for behavior in the primary activity and for the choice of whether to file suit, treating them as decisions that are influenced by the endogenous structure of rewards and punishments. Fourth, in the model here, the objective of system design explicitly includes both the consequences of the induced primary behavior and the cost of inducing that behavior through the legal system. The implicit objective in the SSL is the generation of "unbiased" court decisions—presumably, a proxy for the criteria just identified.

5. "Comparative statics" is the study of how a system or the solution to a problem changes with changes in the underlying parameters.

of this framework to English legal history; and section 3 presents the model, the formal results, and a diagrammatic example. The proofs of all formal results, together with intuitive explanations, appear in the Appendix.

1. Discussion

In this section, I employ a series of numerical examples to illuminate the fundamental trade-off that arises when one views evidence according to the interest of the supplier. I first discuss the basic mechanic of costly evidence production necessitated by reliance on the information of interested parties. Then I consider the possibility of relying on information supplied by those who have less of an interest in the outcome of the suit. The discussion of each possibility is immediately followed by an explanation of the structure of the costs that it imposes on the system. I conclude the section by explaining why the trade-off "tilts" toward costly evidence production in response to across-the-board increases in the costs of process.

1.1. Relying on Information from Interested Parties

1.1.1. The Basic Mechanic. Suppose the state wishes to induce individuals to drive carefully, despite the fact that exercising care costs individuals \$10. Suppose, for the moment, that the state regulates driving by means of a simplified form of process in which each individual must periodically appear before an administrative law judge and "present evidence" of how carefully she has been driving. Based solely on this evidence, the court assesses penalties and disburses rewards.

In the classic enforcement problem, and in most models of civil procedure, punishments and rewards are meted out according to some exogenous probability of detection. Here, I put aside the fiction that the civil law regulates by random audit. Rather, in this model, the state in its capacity as judge never gets up from behind the bench, basing its determination of reward and punishment solely on what evidence the driver *chooses* to present at this periodic hearing.

Inducing the individual to drive carefully under these circumstances requires that the state identify some form of presentation or performance before the judge, some form of "evidence," whose production costs for the individual vary appropriately according to how the individual has behaved on the road. Suppose, for example, that driving carefully happens to lower the cost to the individual of a particular presentation from \$14 to \$2. (What such a presentation might look like is discussed below.) Let the state announce ahead of time that it will fine the individual \$13, unless she makes this presentation. How does the individual react? First, consider her choice at the hearing, contingent on each of the two possibilities for how she has behaved on the road. If she has driven carefully, the evidence costs her \$2 to produce, but saves her \$13 in liability; hence, her "best case" will be to present the \$2 evidence and avoid the liability. If she has not driven carefully, the evidence costs her \$14 to produce, which is more than she saves in liability by presenting it; her best case now will be to rest immediately and incur the \$13 liability. Therefore, the individual's prospective payoffs at the hearing (given that she always makes the best case she can) will be −\$2 if she drives carefully, and −\$13 otherwise. Consequently, careful driving increases the individual's prospective hearing payoff by \$11. Stepping back to the individual's choice on the road, we see that this \$11 benefit outweighs the \$10 direct cost of care, and so the individual chooses to drive carefully.[6] Thus, the evidence cost advantage produced by careful driving (\$2 versus \$14) allows the state to create an \$11 "hearing-payoff advantage" for careful driving, which in turn weighs against, and in this case overwhelms, the additional \$10 cost of care incurred on the road.

1.1.2. Costly Evidence in Actual Process. Does such a mechanism inform actual process? To the extent that a party's own evidence is used to set her incentives in the primary activity, such a mechanism *must* be at work. If the court determined the individual's liability on the basis of evidence whose production cost was independent of the individual's

6. As noted, the mechanic here is a form of differentially costly signaling, à la Spence (1974). *The model differs from Spence's, however, in that signal costs ("types") are not exogenous, but rather depend on parties' choices in the primary activity.* See Sanchirico (1999) for a discussion of how *endogenous* cost signaling compares with other formal approaches to evidence, including the pure Bayesian approach (e.g., Finkelstein and Fairly, 1970), the classic moral hazard approach (e.g., Hermalin and Katz, 1991; Schrag and Scotchmer, 1994), and pure omission models (e.g., Milgrom and Roberts, 1986; Sobel, 1985).

care level, then the individual's choice as to whether to present this evidence—and, more directly, her anticipated hearing payoffs[7]—would be unaffected by her choice of care level. She would then choose care level without regard to prospective litigation—that is, she would drive carelessly.

A fresh look at the forms of evidence used in actual process indicates that differential production costs do indeed play an important role. Consider, for example, parties' sponsorship of eyewitness testimony subject to cross-examination. Why, precisely, would the current system lend credence to the production of three competent, unimpeachable, unrelated eyewitnesses who, with sincere demeanor, tell a mutually consistent story, even under cross-examination, that comports with the party's own allegations? It is certainly not impossible to fabricate such a performance; and no doubt, this has been done. Perhaps the reason for the credibility of such witnesses lies in something so mundane as production cost differences. *True* witnesses are chosen by fate, and their stories are mutually consistent by virtue of the fact that they are organized by the physical laws of time and space. False witnesses, by contrast, need intensive coaching in consistency and demeanor, and they demand compensation for their time and for the risks they face.

Consider, as well, expert testimony. Why, precisely, is any weight placed upon a party's ability to bring together three renowned experts in support of her case? Certainly not because anyone believes that these experts' opinions represent a random sampling of available knowledge, or that a party could not possibly find renowned experts willing to mislead and lie. If the court learns anything from such an event, it can only be because the cost of gathering such experts increases with both the idiosyncrasy of their views (via search costs, or the experts' market power) and the extent to which they must be induced to contradict their professional knowledge and judgment.

Media production operates in a similar manner. Any document can be forged, any photo can be doctored, any video can be staged. Technological advance is Sisyphean in this regard: the understanding required to invent each new technology of "proof" is likely sufficient to artfully manipulate it. The court must always therefore weigh the cost of forgery against the

7. See note 3.

magnitude of the party's stake in the case, taking into account the chance that genuine media of this sort would exist as a natural byproduct of what actually happened in the primary activity.

1.1.3. The Cost of Relying on Interested Parties. The cost of relying on the evidence of interested parties lies in the very production costs that lend such evidence meaning. The individual's expenditure of time and effort in putting her case together results in the production of no valuable goods or services. And unlike fines or liability, the loss to the individual is not someone else's gain. Thus, when the individual in the example is induced to drive carefully and then present evidence costing her $2, this $2 cost is the price society pays for setting incentives for care.

What determines the magnitude of this cost? The most important factor for our purposes is the size of the difference in hearing payoffs that evidence production is meant to produce. In general, the more that an individual's hearing payoffs are meant to turn on what she knows or has done, the greater the evidence costs of creating this dependence.

The reasoning behind this principle has two steps. First, evidence capable of producing a given hearing payoff difference is also capable of producing any smaller hearing payoff difference. Recall the example: liability ($13) was placed between the two evidence costs ($2 and $14); the careful presented the evidence, and the careless did not; and hearing payoffs for the careful were evidence costs (−$2), while hearing payoffs for the careless were liability (−$13). The same general pattern would apply for *any* level of liability x between the two levels of costs, except that hearing payoffs for the careless would now be $-x$ rather than −$13. In particular, as we lower x toward $2, hearing payoffs for the careless move toward −$2, hearing payoffs for the careful remain fixed, and the difference between them falls to zero.

If it is true that *any* evidence capable of producing a larger difference in hearing payoffs is also capable of producing a smaller difference, then this must in particular be true for the evidence that produces the larger difference *at least cost*. This means that the least-cost method of producing the *smaller* difference is never greater in cost and possibly even lower. Thus, imagine that the evidence in our example were in fact the cheapest way (at $2) to produce a hearing payoff difference of $11. As shown, such evidence could also be used to produce a hearing difference of $5 (with liability, x, set to $7). Potentially, other less expensive evidence is *also* capable of producing the $5 difference, in which case the cost of producing it would actually be less than $2. In any case, since the $5 difference *can* be created for $2, the minimal cost of producing it will certainly not be any greater than $2.[8]

1.2. Relying on Information from Others

This analysis suggests that the state can reduce evidence costs by garnering information from others whose interests need not be as directly tied to what they report. To start with a limiting case, imagine that the judge in our example calls in a third-party "observer" and asks him whether *he* saw the "caretaker," the driver, exercise care. Since the judge will use this information to punish the caretaker, not the observer, it will be much less costly to ensure the observer's interest in telling the truth than it would be to ensure the caretaker's. Indeed, if the observer tells the truth when he is indifferent to doing so,[9] the court need only assure him that what he reports will have no effect upon him personally. The observer then will accurately relay what he knows to the court, and the court can use this information to set the caretaker's rewards and punishments so as to inspire careful behavior. Here the court is garnering information from an actor whose hearing payoffs are of no direct relevance to the objective of inducing careful driving.

1.2.1. The Party-Opponent as Other: Decoupled System. Use of "third party" information in lieu of costly evidence production is also possible in the more complicated setting of modern civil process—even as between the parties to the action. The simplest form of civil process is a "decoupled" system in which there is no requirement that plaintiff's recovery equal defendant's liability. Imagine now the caretaker as "defendant," the observer as "plaintiff," and the administrative law judge as civil process

8. The principle that larger differences are more costly to produce also applies in a probabilistic model with more than two primary-activity actions. A proof is available from the author.

9. The observer can be given an actual *positive* incentive to be truthful if costly evidence is fashioned for the *observer*. Consistent with the previous subsection, this would entail a less costly configuration of evidence than was necessary to induce the caretaker to take $10 care.

fact-finder (judge and perhaps jury), whose job it is to mete out punishments and rewards to *both* sides. Because the plaintiff's and defendant's payoffs are decoupled, there is much scope for playing the individuals off against one another. The state can in effect use each party as an "observer" in setting the *other's* recovery or liability. The court simply asks each party what she knows, and makes it clear that what she reports will affect only what her *opponent* wins or pays at trial. Since the information provided by each party has no effect on that party's own payoffs, each party's incentive to lie is greatly reduced—and so then is the necessity for costly evidence production.

1.2.2. The Party-Opponent as Other: Coupled System. This sort of "cross-wiring" across opponents is not possible—at least not in so pure a form—in a coupled system. With coupling, if defendant's liability depends on what plaintiff tells the court, so must plaintiff's award; and that means that plaintiff no longer is disinterested in what she says.

Yet even in a coupled system cross-wiring still can operate. Instead of making the actual liability payment from one party to the other depend on what each party tells the court, we can make each party's *evidence production costs* depend on what the other party says. Evidence costs are as much a part of a party's trial payoffs as liability or recovery, and since evidence costs are not coupled even in a coupled system, there is still room for setting them by means of "cross-wiring."

Suppose, for example, that there are two possible pieces of evidence for the defendant. The first piece of "low cost" evidence costs the defendant \$2 when her evidence costs are low and \$14 when her costs are high. The costs for the second piece of "high cost" evidence are \$13 and \$33, respectively. Focus now on a defendant whose evidence costs are "cheap" for both pieces of evidence (\$2 for low cost evidence, \$13 for high cost). If the fact-finder announces that the defendant must pay \$13.50 in liability unless she presents the *low*-cost evidence, then the cheap-cost defendant will indeed present the evidence: she pays \$2 to avoid a \$13.50 charge. The same result is obtained if the fact finder announces that \$13.50 in liability can be avoided only by presentation of the *high*-cost evidence. Whichever evidence is used, the cheap-cost defendant's liability and choice of whether to present the required evidence are the same: she chooses to present the evidence and her liability is 0.

Although her liability is the same in both cases, however, the cheap-cost defendant's *overall hearing payoffs* differ according to which evidence the court employs: when low cost evidence is used, it costs her $2 to avoid liability; when high cost is used, it costs her $13. However, because *liability* is the same, regardless of which evidence is used, *plaintiff* is indifferent toward the court's choice of evidence. Thus, by determining which evidence is employed according to plaintiff's testimony, the court can make defendant's hearing payoffs depend on what plaintiff has seen, without giving plaintiff an incentive to lie and therefore without having to incur significant evidence production costs.

This example shows how we can use an opponent's information to affect evidence cost without affecting liability. More generally, an opponent's information can be used to affect *both* liability/award and evidence costs. Of course, as soon as plaintiff's case affects his own award, he will have an incentive to lie, and his contribution to the hearing will have to be fortified with the sort of costly evidence production discussed above. This will, of course, impose costs on the system. What is gained in return for those costs, however, is that defendant's payoffs can now be more dramatically affected by plaintiff's case, since the dependence now extends beyond evidence costs to liability/award. This is a benefit because it means not having to rely so much on *defendant's* own costly evidence in setting defendant's incentives. There is, then, a trade-off between plaintiff's evidence costs and defendant's; and the degree to which this trade-off should be made will depend on the comparative structure of the parties' costs.

In sum, what is being described is an "adversarial process": a system in which both parties to the action put forward costly evidence, and liability/award is determined on the basis of the *mixture* of these two sources of information. In particular, the effect on liability/award of any given presentation by one party depends on what the other party has produced—just as, in actual process, the impact of each corroborating witness or document on the final order will depend on the array of corroborating witnesses and documents presented by the other side.

1.2.3. The Cost of Relying on Others. Although increasing reliance on third-party information reduces the need for costly evidence production, it imposes costs of its own. The structure of these costs can be explained in three steps.

(1). *The importance of informational precision.* The first step is to establish the importance of informational "precision" in setting incentives. In our example, the individual's choice in the primary activity was binary: care or no care. In reality, the legal system seeks to induce one action from many alternatives. Accomplishing this requires detailed information about what would have been seen by various others in a multitude of circumstances.

Suppose that care (which costs the individual $10) reduces the probability of an accident by ten percentage points. Assume for now that the observer sees and truthfully reports whether an accident has occurred. Then, if we fine the caretaker $110 for an accident, we induce her to take care: care reduces her expected fine by 10% of $110, or $11, which is less than the cost of care. In general, two signals (such as "accident," "no accident") suffice to implement an action over one alternative.

But now suppose that the individual may also choose to be "extremely careful," where this costs $9 more than regular caution and reduces the accident probability by an additional ten percentage points. Now fining $110 for an accident will induce the caretaker to be extremely careful, rather than cautious. As above, the fine makes care a better choice than carelessness, but according to the same reasoning it also makes extreme caution a better choice than care. Indeed, with these numbers, any fine that makes caution better than carelessness for the individual also makes extreme care better than care.

Suppose, however, that we also ask the observer about the severity of the accident (and he continues to report truthfully). Suppose, further, that extreme care has relatively little effect on accident severity: choosing caution over carelessness decreases the probability of a severe accident (given that some accident has occurred) by ten percentage points, but choosing extreme care over caution reduces this conditional probability by only five percentage points. In this world, we essentially have three signals: "no accident," "severe accident," and "non-severe accident." Three signals will almost always be enough to implement one action over two alternatives. As the reader can confirm, we implement care over both alternatives if we fine the caretaker $50 for any accident and an additional $500 if the accident is severe.

(2). *Precision as a function of the frequency of and attendance at hearings.* The second point is that the precision of the court's information

354 American Law and Economics Review V2 N2 2000 (342–380)

will depend in turn on the breadth of circumstances triggering suit and the number of individuals involved in each action. The state cannot distinguish among the various circumstances that do *not* inspire suit, but only among those that do: if no hearing is held, the state learns only that *one* of the circumstances under which hearings are not held has obtained; it does not learn *which* one. Thus, the fewer the circumstances that inspire suit, the smaller the set of potential signals, and the less the fact-finder stands to learn about the state of the world. Similarly, the state cannot glean information from those who do not attend. Consequently, the efficacy of obtaining information from others is tied to the fixed costs of hearings rather than to the costs of evidence production. The less frequently that hearings are held, or the fewer the individuals who attend each, the lower the fixed costs, but, correspondingly, the less the information obtained.

Continuing the example, suppose for the moment that we have control over the circumstances that inspire the observer to come to court and tell us what he has seen. Let us compare two possibilities: (1) he comes to court whenever there is an accident and once there reports on the accident's severity; (2) he comes to court only when accidents are severe. The first alternative is more costly, because suits are more frequent. On the other hand, the first alternative is more informative: if the observer does not come to court in (1), the court knows that there has been no accident. If the observer does come to court in (1), the court learns that there has been an accident and, by listening to the observer's report at the hearing, also learns whether that accident has been severe. In the end, the court learns precisely which of the three possible circumstances has occurred. Contrast this to case (2). Here, the observer stays home both when there has been no accident and when the accident has not been severe. Thus, the court never learns which of the two possible signals are inspiring the observer to stay home, and we are essentially back in a world with only two signals, which, as we have seen, may not be enough to induce caution over both carelessness and extreme care.[10]

(3). *The role of the private instigation of suits.* The foregoing example raises the question of how the state regulates which occurrences in the primary activity trigger hearings. Notice that in the example the state

10. This example illustrates how increasing the breadth of circumstances inspiring suit refines the information received by the court. Increasing the number of parties engaged in suits serves the same function.

based its decision whether or not to hold a hearing on what had occurred in the primary activity. Yet the state first learns about what has occurred in the primary activity only at such a hearing. This is, of course, self-contradictory. The system cannot function if the court must hold a hearing in order to discover whether the circumstances are such that it would want to hold a hearing. But this circularity may be avoided by endowing private individuals with the power to instigate hearings (i.e., file suits) and by providing a system of rewards and punishments, paid out at those hearings that are held, which influences when and against whom a given party will file. Thus, the third and final point to be made with regard to the cost structure of third-party information is that the state exercises partial, de facto control over both the circumstances that inspire suit and the individuals involved in each, by providing for and influencing the private instigation of suits.

Suppose in the foregoing example that the state wishes to implement alternative (1): hearings when there is an accident (severe or not), no hearing otherwise. Suppose further that both the observer and the caretaker see the true nature of the accident. In a decoupled system, it is a simple matter to induce careful behavior with this pattern of hearings. First, we allow the observer to file suit whenever he likes. Then at each hearing that is convened, we ask both parties to tell us whether there has been an accident and, if so, whether it was severe. We then cross-wire the two individuals' testimony, using the caretaker's report on the observer and the observer's report on the caretaker in order to avoid incentives to lie. We structure the fines for the caretaker just as we did in the discussion of the second point above: $50 if the observer reports an accident, with an additional $500 if the accident is severe. Given truth telling by the observer, this fine structure ensures that the caretaker is careful. To ensure that the observer files suit as desired, we key his payoffs at trial to the caretaker's report. If the caretaker says that there was an accident of some kind, we reward the observer enough to overcome the inevitable cost to him of bringing suit. If the caretaker says there was no accident, we reward the observer nothing, in which case bringing suit is a money-losing venture for the observer. Accordingly, the observer brings suit only when he knows that at that suit the caretaker will report that there was an accident of some kind. Knowing that the caretaker has no incentive to lie (recall that the caretaker reports on the accident once the hearing has already been called, and at that time has no interest in lying, since what she says will now have no effect on her payoffs), the observer brings suit only when there has in fact been an accident.

As discussed above, coupling defendant liability and plaintiff reward limits the efficacy of relying on the information of others and complicates the calculation of incentive-setting devices. Thus, in the example just considered, coupling may require some amount of costly evidence production by either or both parties. The formal analysis to follow takes up this possibility in detail. Nevertheless, the same general principles pertain to a coupled system: the efficacy of information obtained from others depends on its precision, which in turn depends on the breadth of circumstances inspiring suit and the number of parties attending each, which *in turn* is regulated by endowing private parties with the right to file suit and setting their incentives to do so appropriately.[11]

1.3. The Asymmetric Effect of Across-the-Board Increases in Process Costs

The model of evidence laid out above contains a counterintuitive asymmetry, one that has implications for understanding the historical evolution of legal process. Suppose that the costs of process increase across the board. One's intuition is likely to be that an increase in *both* the production costs of evidence *and* the fixed costs of hearings would have a balanced effect on both methods of fact-finding. Not so. Unlike increases in the cost of attendance, increases in the costs of producing evidence can be mitigated, in part or whole, by relying on different, less costly evidence.

Suppose the cost of the $2 versus $14 evidence doubles across the board to $4 versus $28, respectively. By setting liability at $15, the state can still create a hearing payoff difference of $11 according to whether the caretaker has driven carefully. But now this hearing payoff difference costs the state $4 rather than $2. It seems, so far, that the increase in evidence costs makes inspiration of careful behavior more expensive. This conclusion ignores that the state need not continue to use the same piece of

11. In game theory parlance, the mechanic described here is one of "correlated types," (where an agent's type includes her hidden actions) *with the important wrinkle that the rank (precision) of the opponents' signal of the agent's action is endogenous to the mechanism.* See Sanchirico (1995, 1998).

evidence, however. Suppose that all along there has been another piece of evidence whose costs were initially \$.50 versus \$8 and have since doubled to \$1 versus \$16, respectively. Initially, such evidence would have been incapable of creating the requisite \$11 difference in hearing payoffs: feasible hearing-payoff differences are bounded by evidence-cost differences, which here are only \$7.50. After the general increase in costs, however, this evidence *does* have a sufficiently wide "spread": setting liability at \$12 creates the requisite \$11 difference in hearing payoffs. Indeed, the cost of this evidence is only \$1, so evidence production costs actually decrease with the general increase in costs.

Unfortunately, the same dynamic does *not* work with respect to the *fixed* costs of the hearing. If the state tries to compensate for the increase in appearance costs by halving the frequency of trials and the number of individuals attending each, it effects a real reduction in the information content of third-party information. In the end, then, an increase in costs across the board (and *a fortiori*, of appearance costs only) generates a cost pressure on the system to rely more on costly evidence production and less on relatively disinterested parties in obtaining information about the primary activity.

1.3.1. The Choice of Which Action to Induce in the Primary Activity. This analysis so far implicitly has been restricted to the question of how the least-cost means of inducing a *given* action (careful behavior) in the primary activity shifts in response to increases in process costs. Of course, this is only part of the state's overall problem of regulating primary activities by means of legal process. The state must also decide *which* action (level of care) to induce. In principle, the state can first solve the problem we have been considering—of how to induce each action level at least cost—just as a firm might first solve the problem of how to produce each level of output most cheaply. The firm, knowing its "cost function," can compare these derived costs to revenues to decide how much to produce. Similarly, the state can use information on implementation costs as data in solving its overall problem of which action to induce, also taking into account the private and social costs of each action within the primary activity (e.g., the cost of precaution and harm).

Carrying the analysis to this next step has implications for how cost pressures affect the state's optimal regulation of the primary activity—

implications that inform the historical evolution of process. As is shown in section 3, if choice of the implemented primary activity action is included in the analysis, then increased process costs lead, again, to decreases in the use of third-party information. But now such decreases may be associated with *either* increased use of costly evidence *or* implementation of an inferior "quality" action (i.e., one with higher social costs in the primary activity), or both. Insight is gleaned by imagining a firm's optimal reaction to an increase in the cost of one of its factors of production. The firm will use less of that factor, and its cost of production will increase at all levels. This will cause some substitution into other factors and some cutbacks in production.

2. Application to English Legal History

In the traffic of parallel, overlapping developments that constitute English legal history, it is sometimes difficult to see regularity, let alone rationality. Yet, even though "evolution to the optimum" seems patently implausible, the comparative statics of rational system design may still help parse the historical record. Such an exercise is well suited to sorting out the "cost pressures" that may have been important among the set of vectors jointly steering legal change. In particular, the framework developed here helps identify and explain the gradual shift from the thirteenth century on, in the mix of fact-finding methods, away from third-party information and toward costly evidence production by the parties themselves. I propose that this shift may be due in part to increases in the opportunity costs of process, costs brought on by increases in labor productivity.

The productive activity that is forsaken by collecting and preparing evidence, or simply by appearing in court, is a major component of the cost of legal process. As is well known, this cost increased, in broad trend, over the course of English legal history following the thirteenth century, with marked acceleration during the first phase of the Industrial Revolution (1760–1840) because of productivity-enhancing technologies such as the spinning jenny and the power loom. As explained in section 1.3, this across-the-board increase in costs likely had an asymmetric effect on the elements of evidence, resulting in a shift away from reliance on information from others.

The transformation of the jury from supplier of fact to trier of fact is consistent with this analysis. From its origins in the twelfth century until perhaps the beginning of the fifteenth century, the jury operated as a bank of witness-investigators: twelve "freemen" from the neighborhood in which the case arose called upon either to employ their pre-existing knowledge of the matter at hand or to conduct their own investigation. By the sixteenth century, the jury resembled more the blank-slate panel of today (Baker, 1990, p. 89; Mitnick, 1988, section II).

While the legal historical literature is careful in documenting the existence and timing of this transformation, it fails to provide a clear explanation of its cause (Mitnick, 1988, p. 202). The view proposed here is to see the transformation as essentially a cost-saving measure, made urgent by the ever-increasing opportunity costs of process. Less productive activity is sacrificed when 12 people are chosen at large on the basis of whether they happen to be available at the moment, rather than on the basis of whether they live in a particular neighborhood or have prior knowledge of or the ability to investigate the events in question. When the opportunity costs of process are high, significant savings accrue in going from a jury composed of informed, local "freemen" to one composed of not-necessarily-informed, not-necessarily-local men, who happen to be free.[12]

Shorn of its role as a supplier of information, however, the jury now had no natural advantage over an uninformed professional judge from the center. Perhaps, then, the only surprising thing about the subsequent decline of the English jury is how long it took. In the sixteenth century, postverdict procedural devices, such as the motion for a new trial, subverted the jury's authority by essentially submitting its verdict to the veto power of the judge (Baker, 1990, pp. 97–101). Then, following the end of the first phase of the Industrial Revolution, the Common Law Procedure Act of 1854 allowed parties to waive jury process, and by 1900 juries were used in only half the cases before the High Court. During World War I, the jury was "temporarily" abolished in civil cases because of lack of juror supply. In fact, it was never really reinstated. A 1933 law allows

12. Mitnick (1988, note 22) describes the gradual erosion in the requirement that jurors be "next neighbors." Six were required on each jury in the thirteenth century, four in the fifteenth, two in the sixteenth, and finally none by an act of Parliament in 1705. The act indicates that the requirement finally was abolished as a result of "defaults" by these "next neighbors" and challenges based thereon.

jury trials only by leave of the court; in practice, leave is almost never granted (Baker, 1990, p. 109).[13]

The denouement of the jury's role as supplier of information raises the question of where Common Law courts turned for information about the case. Our analysis so far suggests an increased role for information supplied through some form of costly signaling by the parties themselves. There is some indication that this occurs. As the jury was being shorn of its informational role in the fifteenth century, witnesses (presumably sponsored by the parties, though this is not clear in the historical literature) came to play a more prominent role in trial process. Between 1555 and 1565, courts acquired the power to compel witnesses to testify, and perjury became a statutory offense (Landsman, 1983, p. 726).

In some respects, however, the Common Law hesitated for several centuries before perfecting a substitution into costly evidence production. The record indicates that at least until 1750, the parties themselves, along with other "interested" persons, were prohibited from testifying or even presenting documents of their own creation, however long ago they were drafted (Langbein, 1996). One might extrapolate that such restrictions on plain testimony indicate a general restriction on the parties' ability to present their case by more convincing (differentially costly) means.

Two possible explanations bring this hesitation in line with the model. The first explanation concerns shifts in the behavior that the legal system was meant to induce in the primary activity, as discussed in section 1.3.1. The decline of the jury as a supplier of fact, without a compensating increase in costly evidence production, is consistent with the model, if it also is true that part of the historical response to rising process costs was to use the system less overall (i.e., to induce an inferior-quality action). There is indeed some indication that this was happening. For instance, in connection with the prohibition against parties' own testimony, we read that "non-suits were constant, not because there was no cause of action,

13. In the United States, where the right to a jury trial in certain civil actions has been written into a constitution that is infrequently amended, the jury has at least been reduced in size by case law. Early cases interpreted the seventh amendment to lock in place the English common law jury of 12 members. In *Colgrove v. Battin* (1973), the U.S. Supreme Court abandoned this manner of historical interpretation (though, inexplicably, other aspects of the seventh amendment continue to be interpreted historically), ruling that six sufficed for civil actions brought in Federal District Court. Almost immediately, 17 of the 94 Federal Districts adopted the six-person jury.

but because the law refused the evidence of the only persons who could prove it" (Lord Coleridge in Baker, 1990, p. 108). Moreover, the decline of the jury roughly coincided with the ossification of common law peading rules, which, according to one interpretation, acted to constrict operation of the judicial system (Baker, 1990, pp. 90–96; Landsman, 1983, p. 729).

The second explanation for the seeming time-lag in the shift toward reliance on costly evidence production by interested parties looks to the full picture of legal process in England. The end of the jury's role as supplier of information was roughly concomitant with the ascendancy of an alternative form of process: equity operating through the office of the Chancellor. The historical record seems to indicate that the Chancellor relied no more heavily on third-party information than did the rival common law courts, but that in chancery there was much more scope and flexibility for parties to "prove" their own cases. Perhaps, then, the substitution of costly evidence production for third-party information was partly manifest in a parallel substitution of equity for (common) law (Baker, 1990, chapter 6).

In any event, at the close of the first phase of the Industrial Revolution, amid a flurry of legal reform spearheaded by Jeremy Bentham and others, restraints on interested parties' ability to testify in common law procedure were finally lifted by legislative acts of 1843 and 1851. And in the modern era, parties' own presentation of costly evidence—including sponsored eyewitnesses, expert witnesses, plain testimony at risk of perjury, and media production—clearly constitutes the major source of information for the fact-finder. As a general rule, *all* the information received by the court is sponsored by one of the parties in interest, and as a result use of third-party information operates only across parties to the action, as described in section 1.2.2.

3. Formal Analysis

I begin this section by laying out the formal model. I then consider the problem of inducing individuals to behave in a particular way in the primary activity at minimal cost to the legal system. In particular, I analyze the effect of increased process costs on the solution to this problem for both coupled and decoupled systems, explaining the basic mechanic with

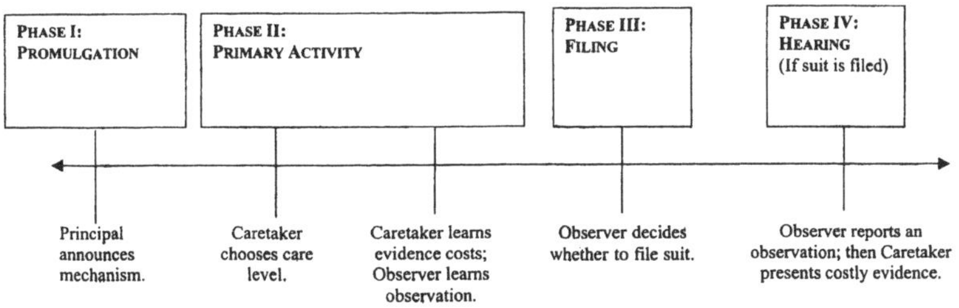

Figure 1. Timeline

reference to a diagrammatic example. Lastly, I provide the same comparative static analysis for the "overall" problem of choosing not just how best to induce a particular behavior, but what sort of behavior to induce.

3.1. Model

The formal model has four phases, as shown in Figure 1.[14] Consider first the second phase, the primary activity, a version of the classic torts model. A risk-neutral agent, the caretaker, chooses whether to be careless, cautious, or extremely careful in a hazardous activity, such as driving. Denote the caretaker's choice as $i = O, C$, or X, respectively, and her primary activity cost as $a_c(i) = a_c(O), a_c(C), a_c(X)$. This cost includes both the cost of precautionary effort and the expected harm that she herself bears. The caretaker's activities also impose expected costs on others, denoted $a_e(i) = a_e(O), a_e(C), a_e(X)$.

The caretaker's choice of care affects, probabilistically, what happens "on the road," including the physical details of any accident or near miss, as well as the character of such "evidentiary by-products" as who sees what and what physical media are generated for later presentation. The model is explicit with regard to two particular aspects of the "evidentiary state of the world": the observations of a second risk-neutral agent, the observer, and the cost to the caretaker of producing evidence of varying intensity. The observer may have one of three mutually exclusive observations: positive observations of the caretaker's care, a neutral observation, and observation of the occurrence of an accident (potentially, but not necessarily, one in which the observer is harmed). Importantly, these are

14. The model presented here is a special case of a more general model developed in earlier versions of this paper (Sanchirico 1995, 1998).

the observer's actual observations, as opposed to what he reports later at the hearing. I will refer to the observer's true observation as his "type" j_o and denote the possibilities $j_o = C, N, A$, respectively. Only the observer knows his type, though others may infer it from his behavior, depending on the reward structure in place. The caretaker's evidence costs j_c, her "type," also is probabilistically determined by her care level. She can be high or low, denoted $j_c = H, L$. Only the caretaker knows her type, though others may make deductions based on her behavior.

Given the caretaker's choice i of care level, the *joint* probability that the caretaker will be of type j_c and the observer of type j_o is denoted as $p(i)(j_c, j_o)$. Thus, for each fixed care level i, we have a probability distribution over the six possible pairs of types. Given care level i, the *marginal probability* that, for example, the observer is of type j_o is $p(i)(j_o) = p(i)(H, j_o) + p(i)(L, j_o)$. Given care level i, the *conditional probability* that, for instance, the caretaker is of type j_c, given that the observer is of type j_o, is $p(i)(j_c|j_o) = p(i)(j_c, j_o)/p(i)(j_o)$, assuming $p(i)(j_o) > \varnothing$. These probabilities are common knowledge, gleaned from past experience.

This probabilistic structure allows for two sorts of probabilistic dependence: (a) the dependence of both evidence costs and observations on care level; and (b), for any level of care, the interdependence of evidence costs and observations. For instance, the probability of the type pair "high, accident" might be decreasing in the caretaker's level of care. Then too, fixing the caretaker's level of care at "caution," the probability of an accident conditional on the caretaker's having high evidence costs might be higher than the probability of an accident conditional on caretaker's having low evidence costs. The possibility of correlation between what the observer observes and how difficult it is for the caretaker to make various presentations in court is both natural (as both phenomena derive from the same set of physical occurrences) and instrumental to the model.

Once both agents have privately learned their own types, the observer decides whether or not to file suit against the caretaker. If the observer does file suit, a hearing is held, and the attendance of both agents is mandatory. The hearing is presided over by the principal (the state/court system/fact-finder) and proceeds as follows. First, the observer publicly reports one of the three possible observations $r = C, N, A$. Next, the caretaker presents evidence. The caretaker chooses evidence e from the continuum $[0, \infty)$. Higher levels of e might, for example, correspond to the production of more corroborating media. Given the caretaker's type j_c, the cost of evidence e is the product $\varsigma j_c e$. The scalar $\varsigma > 0$ is a scaling parameter that will enable comparative statics on evidence costs.

Based solely on the caretaker's presentation and the observer's report, the court determines how much, l_c and l_o to transfer away from each agent. These transfers may be positive, as in the case of liability or fines, or negative, as in the case of recovery or award. In a coupled system, the transfer from the caretaker must equal the transfer to the observer: $l_c = -l_o$.

If there is a hearing, the caretaker's *hearing payoffs* are the negative of the sum of her liability payments, her evidence costs, and her opportunity cost of attendance, F: $-l_c - \varsigma j_c e - F$. If the observer does not file, the caretaker's hearing payoffs are zero. The caretaker's *overall payoffs* also include primary activity costs, and are written: $-a_c(i) - l_c - \varsigma j_c e - F$. The observer's hearing payoffs are $-l_o - F$, and his overall payoffs are $-a_o(i) - l_o - F$.

Before all this begins, the principal specifies the hearing-phase liability of each agent as a joint function of the caretaker's evidence and the observer's report. This is the first, promulgation phase. Promulgation might occur by means of either explicit announcement or accumulated experience. Let $l_c(e, r)$ be the caretaker's transfer and $l_o(e, r)$ be the observer's. The pair of these functions taken together forms the liability schedule.

Let us now fix a liability schedule $(l_c(e, r), l_o(e, r))$ and examine its incentive effects at each phase of the model. We will do so by working backwards from the hearing, to the filing phase, to the primary activity. In order to analyze incentives at the hearing, we also work backwards therein, beginning with the caretaker's presentation of evidence. Given that the observer has reported r and the caretaker is of type j_c, the caretaker will present the evidence e that maximizes her prospective payoffs: $-l_c(e, r) - \varsigma j_c e - F$. One may view the caretaker's choice of evidence in each contingency as a function $e(j_c, r)$ of j_c and r: that is, as an evidence plan. The observer wants to maximize payoffs in making his report, as well, and he realizes that his payoffs depend not only on his own report but also on the evidence subsequently produced by the caretaker. Because the observer knows the liability schedule and understands that the caretaker maximizes payoffs, he knows how a caretaker of any given type will respond to his report.[15] In other words, the observer can infer the caretaker's evidence plan $e(j_c, r)$. The observer, does not know the caretaker's type, however, and so does not know which evidence she will actually present following each possible report. Thus, the observer presents the report r that maximizes his *expected* hearing payoffs $E[-l_o(e(\tilde{j}_c, r), r) - F]$, where the expectation is taken with respect to random element $\tilde{j}_c$. The observer's beliefs regarding the caretaker's type are based on both the observer's own type and his subjective prior beliefs $q(i)$ about the caretaker's care level.

A reporting plan $r(j_o)$ indicates the observer's report contingent on his type. Given hearing plans $e(j_c, r)$ and $r(j_o)$, the caretaker's (type-pair-contingent) hearing payoffs are $h_c(j_c, j_o) = -l_c(e(j_c, r(j_o)), r(j_o)) - \varsigma j_c e(j_c, r(j_o)) - F$, and the observer's are $h_o(j_c, j_o) = -l_o(e(j_c, r(j_o)), r(j_o)) - F$.

At the filing stage, the observer chooses whether to file suit, knowing his own type and looking forward to what he expects his payoffs will be at the hearing. Thus he files if and only if $E[h_o(\tilde{j}_c, j_o)] \geq 0$. Write $f(j_o)$ for observer's filing plan, where $f(j_o) = 1$ if the observer files and 0 otherwise. The agents' (type-pair-contingent) litigation payoffs, calculated prospectively from the start of the filing stage are then $f(j_o)h_c(j_c, j_o)$ and $f(j_o)h_o(j_c, j_o)$.

In the primary activity, the caretaker chooses her care level, looking forward to the chance that she will be sued and to her expected hearing payoffs in court should that happen. Thus, given hearing payoffs $h_c(j_c, j_o)$ and filing plan $f(j_o)$, the caretaker chooses care level i to maximize $-a_c(i) + E_i[f(\tilde{j}_o)h_c(\tilde{j}_c, \tilde{j}_o)]$, where the subscript i on the expectation operator indicates that the probability distribution on j_c and j_o depends on choice of i.

The principal chooses the liability schedule with knowledge of both the probability structure $p(i)(j_c, j_o)$ and the fact that agents maximize payoffs in the manner just described. This prescience is embodied in the notion of "implementation." The liability schedule $(l_c(e, r), l_o(e, r))$ simultaneously *implements* the evidence plan $e_c(j_c, r)$, the reporting plan $r(j_o)$,

15. As is standard, when more than one plan maximizes an agent's payoffs, I assume that the principal specifies which the agent will use and that the choice is common knowledge.

the filing plan $f(j_o)$, and the care level i, if the following conditions obtain: (1) For every type j_c and observer report r, presenting evidence $e(j_c, r)$ would maximize the caretaker's hearing payoffs (as described above); (2) given that the caretaker would employ evidence plan $e(j_c, r)$, the report $r(j_o)$ would maximize the observer's hearing payoffs for every type j_o, regardless of the observer's prior $q(i)$ on the caretaker's care level;[16] (3) given that the caretaker and the observer would behave at the hearing according to $r(j_o)$ and $e(j_c, r)$, the filing plan $f(j_o)$ would maximize the observer's litigation payoffs for every type j_o, again regardless of $q(i)$; (4) given that the agents would behave according to $f(j_o), r(j_o)$, and $e(j_c, r)$ in litigation, care level i maximizes the caretaker's payoffs in the primary activity. Apropos of the focus on care level, let us refer to $(l_c(e, r), l_o(e, r))$, $e(j_c, r)$, $r(j_o)$, $f(j_o)$ as an implementation of care level i, if $(l_c(e, r), l_o(e, r))$ implements i, $e(j_c, r), r(j_o)$, and $f(j_o)$.

In specifying how the principal chooses among liability schedules, we may break the problem into two pieces. First, there is the minimal cost implementation of each given care level. Here, the principal seeks the particular implementation of this care level that imposes the lowest cost on the system. There are two types of costs: the caretaker's evidence costs and both agents' opportunity costs of hearing attendance. Both costs are affected by agents' filing and hearing plans. Specifically, if care level i is implemented with $(l_c(e, r), l_o(e, r))$, $e(j_c, r)$, $r(j_o)$, and $f(j_o)$, the cost is

$$E_i\left[f(\tilde{j}_o)\left(\underbrace{s\tilde{j}_c e(\tilde{j}_c, r(\tilde{j}_o))}_{\text{evidence costs}} + \underbrace{2F}_{\substack{\text{attendence}\\\text{costs}}}\right)\right]$$

$$= \underbrace{Pr_i[f(\tilde{j}_o) = 1]}_{\text{probability suit is filed}}\left(\underbrace{E_i[s\tilde{j}_c e(\tilde{j}_c, r(\tilde{j}_o)) \mid f(\tilde{j}_o) = 1]}_{\text{expected evidence costs, if suits is filed}} + \underbrace{2F}_{\substack{\text{attend.}\\\text{costs}}}\right), \quad (1)$$

where $Pr_i[X]$ is the probability of event X given caretaker's choice of care.

The principal minimizes this expression (1) among all implementations of i. This yields for i a (minimal) implementation cost C_i. Having

16. This is implementation by iterated dominance. See Sanchirico (1995, 1998) for details.

calculated C_i for each care level i, the principal solves its overall problem of deciding which care level to implement: it chooses i to minimize the sum $a_c(i) + a_e(i) + C_i$ of primary activity costs and implementation costs.

In choosing a liability schedule, the principal may be subject to a coupling constraint $l_c(e, r) = -l_o(e, r)$. The addition of the coupling constraint makes court fees relevant (see proposition 2 and its proof). Court fees, denoted C_c and C_o, are charges assessed to the agents in the event of a hearing. These charges may differ across agents, but not across evidence and reports; in other words, they are not contingent on the outcome of the suit.[17]

3.2. Minimal Cost Implementation and Increasing Process Costs

The next two propositions show that when the opportunity cost of attending hearings increases, then—whatever may be the accompanying trend in evidence costs—the principal will rely more on costly evidence production and less on third-party information in efficiently implementing any given level of care. This substitution will manifest itself in the observer's filing suit subsequent to fewer observations and in the caretaker's presenting more costly evidence whenever hearings do occur.

Proposition 1. Suppose that the cost of hearing attendance increases from F to $F' > F$ and evidence costs change from $\varsigma j_c e$ to $\varsigma' j_c e$. Let $(l_c(e, r), l_o(e, r))$, $f(j_o)$, $r(j_o)$, $e(j_c, r)$ and $(l'_c(e, r), l'_o(e, r))$, $f'(j_o)$, $r'(j_o)$, $e'(j_c, r)$ be minimal cost implementations of i for old and new process costs, respectively. Under the new implementation, suit is filed less often, and evidence costs are higher: $\Pr_i[f'(j_o) = 1] \leq \Pr_i[f(j_o) = 1]$ and $E_i[\varsigma' \tilde{j}_c e'(\tilde{j}_c, r'(\tilde{j}_0)) | f'(\tilde{j}_o) = 1] \geq E_i[\varsigma \tilde{j}_c e(\tilde{j}_c, r(\tilde{j}_0)) | f(\tilde{j}_o) = 1]$.

Proposition 2. If court fees are feasible, proposition 1 also holds when the coupling constraint is imposed.

3.2.1. Diagrammatic Example. The following example illustrates the basic trade-off between costly evidence production and third-party information. The example describes two liability schedules that implement

17. The notational adjustments necessary when court fees are imposed are obvious.

caution—one having more frequent filings and less evidence production than the other. In order to keep the example manageable, I assume that suits are decoupled, and I examine only increases in fixed costs. Primary activity costs for the caretaker are \$60, \$100, and \$120 for carelessness, caution, and extreme care, respectively. Evidence costs are \$$e$ if the caretaker is a low type and \$2e if the caretaker is a high type. Table 1 shows the joint and marginal probability distributions over agents' types.

I begin by showing how caution may be implemented with a liability schedule under which the observer files suit for all observations except care, and under which the caretaker presents no evidence, liability being determined solely on the basis of the observer's report. Let us begin with the caretaker's incentives, as depicted in Figure 2.

To understand the diagram, suppose that the principal charges the caretaker \$100 if the observer files suit and then reports an accident, and charges nothing otherwise. Assume for the moment that the observer files only when there is an accident and then truthfully reports the observation at the hearing. Then, based on the italicized marginal probabilities shown in Table 1, the caretaker's expected hearing payoffs from carelessness, caution, and extreme care would be −\$70, −\$35, and −\$10, respectively. Important for implementing caution is its *relative* advantage over carelessness and extreme care: here this is \$35 (= −\$35 – (−\$70)) and −\$25, respectively. I represent (\$35, −\$25) in Figure 2 as the darkest solid vector (pointing southeast from the origin) and refer to this vector as the *hearing advantage* of caution under this "basic" liability schedule. The other two solid vectors of lighter grey-scale are the hearing advantages for the other two observations under analogous basic liability schedules. The space of all possible hearing advantages that can be created by conditioning solely on the observer's report is the set of all linear combinations of these three vectors. (For example, if the caretaker pays \$50 for neutral observations and \$200 for accidents, the resulting hearing advantage of caution would be the head-to-tail addition of the vector for neutral shrunk to half its length and the vector for accidents expanded to twice its size.)

The dashed right angle has its corner at the point (\$40, −\$20), which is the *additional primary activity* cost of caution over carelessness (\$100 – \$60 = \$40) and extreme care (\$100 – \$120 = −\$20), respectively. The set of points northeast of this dashed corner are precisely those that exceed (\$40, −\$20) in both coordinates.

Table 1. Joint and Marginal Distribution of Types

	Carelessness			**Caution**			**Extreme Care**		
	Caretaker's Type			**Caretaker's Type**			**Caretaker's Type**		
Observer's Type	**Low Cost**	**High Cost**	**Marginal**	**Low Cost**	**High Cost**	**Marginal**	**Low Cost**	**High Cost**	**Marginal**
Accident	0	.7	.7	**.15**	.2	.35	0	.1	.1
Neutral	.1	.1	.2	.15	.15	.3	.2	.2	.4
Care	.1	.0	.1	.25	.1	.35	.5	.0	.5
Marginal	.2	.8		.55	.45		.7	.3	

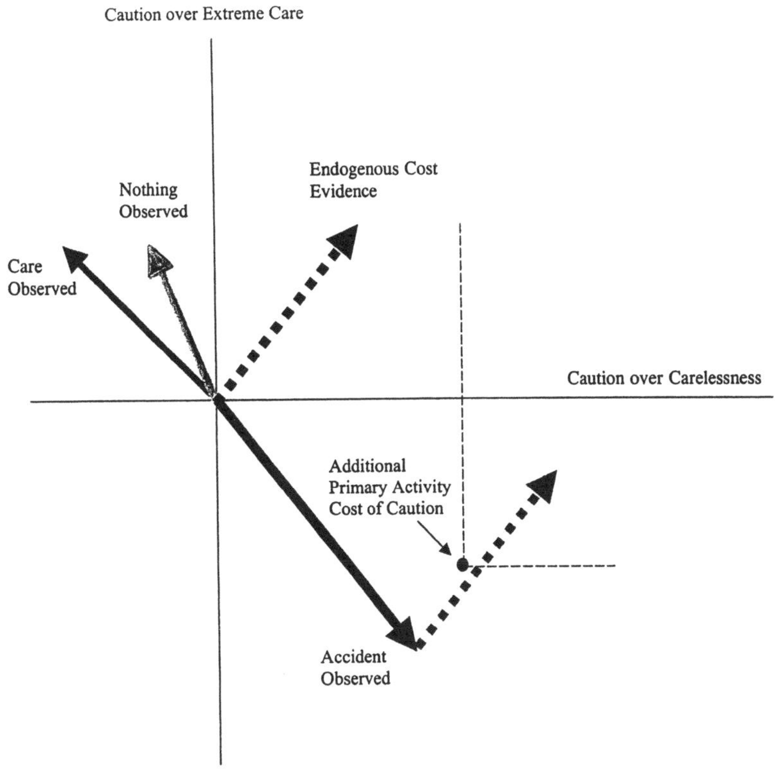

Figure 2. Implementing caution: the caretaker's incentives

Since the hearing advantage vectors for accidents and neutral span the space, we can find a linear combination vector that reaches into the region northeast of the dashed corner. This means that it is possible to set rewards (combine multiples of the accident and neutral vectors) so that the hearing advantages of caution (the coordinates of the resulting linear combination vector) jointly exceed its additional primary activity costs (the coordinates $[40, -20]$ of the dashed corner). If the principal does this—and can otherwise ensure that the observer files suit only in these two circumstances and then truthfully reports his observation—the principal will have implemented cautious behavior.

Here is how the principal may ensure the *observer's* compliance. Let the principal reward the *caretaker* \$1 for presenting evidence of $e = .90$. Since the caretaker will present e only when her evidence costs are low

(\$$e$), the presentation will serve as a signal of the caretaker's type; and since the dollar amounts are small, this collateral reward structure will not alter the primary activity incentives discussed in the previous paragraph. Let the principal then award the *observer* $F + \$1$ when the caretaker does not present the evidence (is of high type), and $F - \$.90$, otherwise. One can calculate that however careful the observer thinks the caretaker has been, he will file suit only when he sees an accident or a neutral observation. (For example, if the observer thinks the caretaker has been cautious but he still observes an accident, then his posterior belief that the caretaker is of low type is $.15/.35 = .43$. Thus, his expected payoff from the hearing will be $.57(F + 1 - F) + .43(F - \$.90 - F) = \$.183 > 0$, so he will file.)

This handles the observer's *filing* incentives. But what about his hearing incentives? Once at the hearing, the observer's payoffs do not turn on what he reports, but on what evidence the caretaker presents. Having no positive incentive to lie, he will report what he actually has seen. (He can be given a strict incentive to tell the truth if we enrich the model to allow for his presentation of slightly costly evidence.)

So far in our discussion of this example, we have been examining the implementation of care when hearings are held in two of the three circumstances that might be witnessed by the observer. Alternatively, the principal can implement caution under a liability schedule in which the observer files suit *only* when he sees an accident. This, however, will mean that the principal must also rely on the caretaker's presentation of substantially costly evidence. By inducing hearings in one rather than two circumstances, the principal stands to learn less about what the observer has seen.

This point, which was made in general terms in section 1, can be illustrated quite dramatically in Figure 2. The principal will not be able to distinguish between neutral and care, the two circumstances that do not inspire suit, since all it sees is *that* the observer has not filed, not *why*. The liability schedule for the caretaker must therefore be constant (e.g., zero) across the observations "Care" and "Neutral." As the reader can confirm, any vector that is a linear combination of care and neutral and that assigns the same coefficient to each is here (and will in fact always be) a scalar multiple of the accident vector. Clearly, the principal cannot get northeast of the dashed box solely by shrinking and expanding the accident vector.

In explaining this second implementation, I begin again with the caretaker's incentives. The explanation of these incentives has in itself two steps. First, consider the dashed vector (labeled "Endogenous Cost Evidence") emanating from the origin. The point of this vector is at ($15, $15), which represents the expected hearing advantage of caution when: (1) hearings are held only after accidents; and (2), at those hearings caretaker receives $\$200 + F - \$.10$ if she presents evidence of $e = 100$, and F otherwise. To see why, note that once at the accident hearing, only a low-evidence-cost caretaker will present $e = 100$. As a result, the low-evidence-cost caretaker ends up with hearing payoffs of roughly $(\$200 + F) - (\$100 + F) = \$100$, and the high cost with payoffs of $F - F = \$0$. Thus, it is as if the principal rewards the caretaker $100 in the *joint* event that there is an accident *and* she has low-cost evidence. Now, as indicated by the "Accidnet/Low Cost" entries in Table 1 (shown in bold), if the caretaker is cautious rather than careless, she increases the chance of this joint event by .15 (= .15 − 0). Thus, the expected hearing advantage of caution over carelessness is $15. A similar calculation reveals that the hearing advantage of caution over extreme care also is $15.

The second step in setting caretaker's incentives is to combine the costly evidence scheme just described with a baseline punishment of $100, just for the fact that the observer has filed suit. Diagrammatically, the principal is adding the vector ($15, $15) head-to-tail to the accident vector. That the summed vector enters the dashed box indicates that the hearing advantages of caution jointly exceed the accompanying additional primary activity costs. The caretaker is thereby induced to be cautious.

What remains is to ensure that the observer files only when he sees an accident and that he then reports this observation truthfully. The reader can confirm that this can be accomplished by rewarding the observer $2F + \$1$ if the caretaker fails to present evidence $e = \$100$, and $0 if the caretaker does make the presentation.

All told, this second liability structure is as follows. If the observer files suit against the caretaker and the caretaker fails to produce exonerating evidence ($e = \$100$), the observer receives $2F + \$1$ and the caretaker pays $\$100 - F$. If the caretaker does produce the evidence, the observer gets nothing, whereas the caretaker pays nothing and is reimbursed $100 and F for her evidence and attendance costs, respectively. The caretaker, anticipating the possibility of suit, including the possibility that she will find it worthwhile to present exonerating evidence, decides that it *is* worthwhile to be cautious but that there is no reason to be extremely careful.

Let us now compare the system costs of the two implementations that we have been considering. In the first, the observer files suit in two circumstances, "Accident" and "Neutral," the probabilities of which are determined by the fact that the caretaker chooses "Caution." Evidence production costs are *de minimis*. The cost of this two-hearing implementation is thus roughly $(.3 + .35)2F = 1.5F$. In the second implementation, the agents appear before the court only when there is an accident. Given the caretaker's cautious behavior, this happens with probability .35. Therefore, the opportunity costs of attendance are $.35(2)F = .7F$, substantially lower than in the first scheme. With probability .15, however, the caretaker will find herself in court (an accident having occurred) and desirous of producing $100 of evidence (i.e., of low-cost type). Expected evidence-production costs are thus $15. Total costs for this second method then are $.7F + \$15$.

Clearly, if fixed costs are low, the least costly implementation will be the first, the one with two hearings. On the other hand, if fixed costs are high, then the fact that the first implementation requires more hearings makes it less efficient. Here, the best alternative would be to suffer the evidence-production costs in exchange for a reduction in hearing frequency.

3.3. The Overall Problem and Increased Process Costs

I have already discussed in section 1.3 what happens if one accounts for the principal's choice of which level of care to implement. The formal results are contained in the following two propositions.

Proposition 3. Suppose that the cost of hearing attendance increases from F to $F' > F$ and evidence costs change from $\varsigma j_c e$ to $\varsigma' j_c e$. Let $i, (l_c(e,r), l_o(e,r)), f(j_o), r(j_o), e(j_c, r)$ and $i', (l'_c(e,r), l'_o(e,r)),$ $f'(j_o),\ r'(j_o), e'(j_c, r)$ solve the principal's overall problem for each set of process costs. Under the new implementation, suit is filed less often: $\Pr_i[f'(j_o) = 1] \leq \Pr_i[f(j_o) = 1]$. Moreover, if reliance on evidence production does not increase, then primary activity costs do: $E_i[\varsigma' \tilde{j}_c e'(\tilde{j}_c, r'(\tilde{j}_0)) | f'(\tilde{j}_o) = 1] \geq E_i[\varsigma \tilde{j}_c e(\tilde{j}_c, r(\tilde{j}_0)) | f(\tilde{j}_o) = 1]$ or $a_{i'} < a_i$.

Proposition 4. If court fees are feasible, Proposition 3 also holds when the coupling constraint is imposed.

4. Conclusion

The law and economics of litigation elected early on to put to one side the analysis of trial process in order to get directly at such pressing policy issues as how the allocation of costs affects settlement bargaining and the decision to file suit. Today's standard model of litigation packs all of trial process into an exogenous probability that the defendant will be held liable in court. Nothing specific to the information exercise of trial remains; the parties might just as well be bargaining over *any* uncertain outcome. To be sure, this approach has had many benefits, as a reading of the literature makes clear. Nonetheless, this paper has held that there are also rewards to be gained from explicitly modeling how courts garner the information necessary for their decisions. First, there is the purely explanatory benefit of gaining insight into the strategic architecture of civil process. Second, such insights help to identify, explain, and connect such puzzling historical trends as the transformation of the jury's role and the ascendancy of own-party evidence production.

Appendix

Lemma 1. Suppose the coupling constraint does not hold. Suppose further that $(l_c(e, r), l_o(e, r))$ implements $e(j_c, r)$, $r(j_o)$, $f(j_o)$, and i when process costs are (F, ς). For all alternative process costs (F', ς'), there exists a new liability schedule $(l'_c(e, r), l'_o(e, r))$ and a new evidence plan $e'(j_c, r)$ such that: (1) $(l'_c(e, r), l'_o(e, r))$ implements $e'(j_c, r)$, $r(j_o)$, $f(j_o)$, and i under new process costs (F', ς'), and (2) evidence costs for the *new* implementation under *new* process costs equal evidence costs for the *old* implementation under *old* process costs.

The general idea of the proof, which follows, is to (1) mitigate the increase in attendance costs by reducing both agents' liability; and

(2) "sterilize" the effect of evidence-cost changes by adjusting the evidence corresponding to each level of liability so that the new evidence costs the caretaker, under the new evidence costs, what the old evidence cost under the old evidence costs. If we do this, the caretaker has the same incentive to present the substituted evidence as she did to present the old evidence, the observer's incentive to report does not change, and so hearing payoffs for both do not change. Since hearing payoffs do not change, observer's filing incentives do not change; and since the prospect of litigation remains fixed so does the caretaker's incentive to take care.

Proof: Let $l'_k(e,r) = l_k((\varsigma'/\varsigma)e, r) + (F - F')$ for both $k = C, O$. Let $e'(j_c, r), (\varsigma/\varsigma')e(j_c, r)$. Given f, r, and i, e''s expected cost under ς' equals e's under ς. (To conserve notation I sometimes abbreviate functions with single letters.) To show that l'_c, l'_o implements e', f, r, and i under (F', ς'), I first claim that e' maximizes caretaker's hearing payoffs. For any j_c and r, and any alternative *piece* of evidence $\hat{e}$ (a number):

$$
\begin{aligned}
&-l(e'(j_c, r), r) - \varsigma' j_c e'(j_c, r) - F' \\
&\quad = -l(e(j_c, r), r) - \varsigma j_c e(j_c, r) - F && \text{(Definition of } l', e'\text{)} \\
&\quad \geq -l\left(\frac{\varsigma'}{\varsigma}\hat{e}, r\right) - \varsigma j_c \frac{\varsigma'}{\varsigma}\hat{e} - F && (l \text{ implements } e) \\
&\quad = -l'(\hat{e}, r) - \varsigma' j_c \hat{e} - F'. && \text{(Definition of } l', e'\text{)}
\end{aligned}
$$

A similar argument shows that r maximizes observer's hearing payoffs, given e'. Next, note that e', r generates the same hearing payoffs for both agents as e, r. This implies that f' maximizes observer's filing-phase payoffs, given e', r, and that i maximizes caretaker's primary activity payoffs given f, e', r. QED

Lemma 2. Lemma 1 holds as well with the coupling constraint, so long as the court may charge court fees. Further, even if court fees are bounded from below by $\overline{C}$ (possibly negative), then Lemma 1 holds if the aggregate increase in fixed costs does not exceed the aggregate initial slack with respect to this lower bound: in essence $(2F' - 2F) \leq (C_o + C_c) - 2\overline{C}$, where C_c, C_o in this expression are court fees used in the original mechanism.

The general idea of the proof is as follows. In Lemma 1, liability for both agents was reduced across the board by the increase in attendance costs. This is impossible with the coupling constraint, because one agent's reduction in liability must equal the other's increase. Instead, both agents' *court fees* are reduced.

The lemma goes beyond the results discussed in the text by considering the case in which court fees are bounded from below. The point is that such a constraint is less stringent than one might think. Suppose, for instance, that because of external constraints, one agent's court fees cannot be reduced far enough to compensate for increased attendance costs. An alternative is to reduce only the *other* agent's court fees and simultaneously increase this agents' liability (across the board) by an equal amount. This increases the first agent's hearing payoffs across the board in the same manner as reducing his court fees. Thus, the constraint on being able to sterilize the increase in attendance costs depends on a comparison of *aggregate* fixed costs and *aggregate* slack with respect to the lower bound on court fees.

Proof: I prove that an appropriate adjustment to court fees and liability exists if the inequality in the statement of the lemma obtains. The proof is designed to readily generalize to models with more than two agents. In terms of increases, we seek $\Delta C_c, \Delta C_o$ and $\Delta l_c, \Delta l_o$ (an "across-type" increase in court fees and liabilities) such that for both agents $k = C, O$

$$-\Delta C_k - \Delta l_k = F' - F \qquad \text{(net increase in } F \text{ is neutralized)}$$

$$-\Delta C_k \leq C_k - \overline{C} \qquad \text{(court fees don't fall below bound)}$$

$$-\Delta l_c = -\Delta l_o \qquad \text{(coupling preserved)}$$

An application of Farkas' lemma (omitted) establishes that the inequality in the statement of the lemma is sufficient for the existence of a solution. Given these adjustments to liability and court fees for all hearings, an argument similar to that in the proof of Lemma 1 may be applied. QED

Proposition 1 and 2. The general idea of the proof of these propositions is as follows. Imagine an "old" minimal-cost implementation under "old" process costs and a "new" minimal-cost implementation under "new" process costs. Let new process costs entail higher attendance costs. The lemmas above establish that the principal *could have* used the new implementation under the old process costs, when appearance costs were low. Doing so would have required the adjustments discussed, but these adjustments would not have changed the evidence costs in the implementation. But even though the principal *could have* had the evidence costs and the filing frequency of the new implementation, it *chose* the evidence costs and filing frequency of the old implementation. Conversely, with *new* process costs, which entail higher attendance costs, the principal chose the evidence costs and filing pattern of the new implementation over those of the (suitably altered) old. The first thing to conclude from these revealed preferences is that neither implementation has both lower evidence costs and less frequent filings; otherwise, the principal would have chosen that implementation in both instances. The second conclusion is that moving to the new implementation does not raise filing frequency while lowering evidence costs. If, under the *new* process costs, wherein the cost of each appearance is high, the principal were willing to take on more filings for the sake of lowering evidence costs, then it would have *also* been willing to make the same trade-off under the old process costs when the cost of each appearance was lower. It must be, then, that moving to the new implementation lowered the frequency of filings and raised evidence costs.

Proof: Let $A(F, \varsigma)$ and $V(F, \varsigma)$ be appearance and evidence costs under the old mechanism. Define $A(F', \varsigma')$ and $V(F', \varsigma')$ similarly for the new mechanism. Start with old mechanism and old process costs (F, ς) and imagine changing process costs to (F', ς'). We know from Lemmas 1 and 2 that we can find some alternative liability per evidence schedule (not necessarily (l', e')) with old evidence costs $V(F, \varsigma)$, which, when combined with the old filing plan, implements i under new process costs (F', ς'). Since this is an alternative implementation of i under new costs (F', ς'), and the new implementation is a *minimum*-cost implementation under (F', ς'), we may conclude that $V(F', \varsigma') + F'A(F', \varsigma') \leq V(F, \varsigma) + F'A(F, \varsigma)$. By the same argument, starting with the *new* mechanism and *new* process costs, we have $V(F, \varsigma) + FA(F, \varsigma) \leq V(F', \varsigma') + FA(F', \varsigma')$. Combining, $(F - F')(A(F, \varsigma) - A(F', \varsigma')) \leq 0$. Since $F < F'$, we have $A(F, \varsigma) \geq A(F', \varsigma')$. Substituting yields $V(F', \varsigma') \geq V(F, \varsigma)$, and then the rest of the proposition follows easily. QED

Proof of Proposition 3 and 4: The proof is essentially the same as for Proposition 1 and Proposition 2, with the implemented level of care also changing and the notation $V(F, \varsigma)$ now representing *both* evidence costs and primary activity costs. QED

References

Arlen, Jennifer. 1992. "Liability for Physical Injury when Injurers as well as Victims Suffer Losses," 8 *Journal of Law, Economics, & Organization* 411–26.

Baker, J. H. 1990. *An Introduction to English Legal History*, 3rd ed. London: Butterworths.

Bebchuk, Lucien. 1984. "Litigation and Settlement Under Imperfect Information," 15 *The RAND Journal of Economics* 404–15.

Brown, John Prather. 1973. "Toward an Economic Theory of Liability," 2 *Journal of Legal Studies* 323–49.

Calabresi, Guido. 1972. *The Costs of Accidents*. New Haven: Yale University Press.

Colgrove v. Battin, 413 U.S. 149 (1973).

Craswell, Richard, and John Calfee. 1984. "Some Effects of Uncertainty on Compliance with Legal Standards," 70 *Virginia Law Review* 965–1003.

Daughety, Andrew, and Jennifer Reinganum. 1994. "Settlement Negotiations with Two-Sided Asymmetric Information: Model Duality, Information Distribution, and Efficiency," 14 *International Review of Law & Economics* 283–98.

———. 1998. "On the Economics of Trials: Adversarial Process, Evidence and Equilibrium Bias," Vanderbilt Department of Economics and Business Administration Working Paper No. 98-W02.

Finkelstein, Michael, and William Fairly. 1970. "A Bayesian Approach to Identification Evidence," 83 *Harvard Law Review* 489–517.

Froeb, Luke, and Bruce Kobayashi. 1996. "Naïve, Biased, Yet Bayesian: Can Juries Interpret Selectively Produced Evidence?" 12 *Journal of Law, Economics & Organization* 257–76.

Hermalin, Benjamin, and Michael Katz. 1991. "Moral Hazard and Verifiability: The Effects of Renegotiation in Agency," 59 *Econometrica* 1735–53.

Kaplow, Louis, and Steven Shavell. 1994. "Accuracy in the Determination of Liability," 37 *Journal of Law & Economics* 1–15.

———. 1996. "Accuracy in the Assessment of Damages, 39 *Journal of Law & Economics* 191–210.

Katz, Avery. 1988. "Judicial Decision Making and Litigation Expenditure," 8 *International Review of Law & Economics* 127–43.

Landes, William. 1971. "An Economic Analysis of the Courts," 14 *Journal of Law & Economics* 61–107.

Landsman, Stephan. 1983. "A Brief Survey of the Development of the Adversary System," 44 *Ohio State Law Journal* 713–39.

Langbein, John. 1996. "Historical Foundations for the Law of Evidence: A View from the Ryder Sources," 96 *Columbia Law Review* 1168–1202.

Milgrom, Paul, and John Roberts. 1986. "Relying on the Information of Interested Parties," 17 *RAND Journal of Economics* 18–31.

Mitnick, John Marshall. 1988. "From Neighbor-Witness to Judge of Proofs: The Transformation of the English Civil Juror," 32 *American Journal of Legal History* 201–35.

Nalebuff, Barry. 1987. "Credible Pretrial Negotiation," 18 *RAND Journal of Economics* 198–210.

Ordover, Janusz. 1978. "Costly Litigation in the Model of Single Activity Accidents," 7 *Journal of Legal Studies* 243–61.

———. 1981. "On the Consequences of Costly Litigation in the Model of Single Activity Accidents: Some New Results," 10 *Journal of Legal Studies* 269–91.

Png, Ivan. 1983. "Strategic Behavior in Suit, Settlement and Trial," 14 *Bell Journal of Economics* 539–50.

———. 1987. "Litigation, Liability, and Incentives for Care," 34 *Journal of Public Economics* 61–85.

Polinsky, A. Mitchell, and Daniel Rubinfeld. 1988. "The Welfare Implications of Costly Litigation for the Level of Liability," 17 *Journal of Legal Studies* 151–64.

Rubinfeld, Daniel, and David Sappington. 1987. "Efficient Awards and Standards of Proof in Judicial Proceedings," 18 *RAND Journal of Economics* 308–15.

Sanchirico, Chris. 1995. "Enforcement by Hearing: How the Civil Law Sets Incentives," Columbia Economics Department Discussion Paper No. 9596–03.

———. 1997. "The Burden of Proof in Civil Litigation: A Simple Model of Mechanism Design," 17 *International Review of Law & Economics* 431–47.

———. 1998. "Games, Information and Evidence Production: with Application to Legal History and Decoupling," USC Law Center Working Paper No. 98–20.

———. 1999. "Relying on the Information of Interested—and Potentially Dishonest—Parties," University of Virginia School of Law, Legal Studies Working Paper No. 00–12.

Schrag, Joel, and Suzanne Scotchmer. 1994. "Crime and Prejudice: The Use of Character Evidence in Criminal Trials," 10 *Journal of Law, Economics, & Organization* 319–41.

Shavell, Steven. 1980. "Strict Liability versus Negligence," 9 *Journal of Legal Studies* 1–25.

———. 1982. "Suit, Settlement and Trial: A Theoretical Analysis Under Alternative Methods for the Allocation of Legal Costs," 11 *Journal of Legal Studies* 55–81.

380 American Law and Economics Review V2 N2 2000 (342–380)

———. 1999. "The Level of Litigation: Private versus Social Optimality," 19 *International Review of Law and Economics* 99–115.

Sobel, Joel. 1985. "Disclosure of Evidence and Resolution of Disputes," in A. E. Roth, ed. *Game Theoretic Models of Bargaining*. Cambridge: Cambridge University Press.

Spence, Michael. 1974. *Market Signaling*. Cambridge, MA: Harvard University Press.

Spier, Katherine. 1994a. "Pretrial Bargaining and the Design of Fee Shifting Rules," 25 *RAND Journal of Economics* 197–214.

———. 1994b. "Settlement Bargaining and the Design of Damage Awards," 10 *Journal of Law, Economics, & Organization* 84–95.

Zelin, Judy E. 1999. "Perjury," in 60A *American Jurisprudence*, 2nd ed. 1059–149.

Part II
Truth Finding versus Primary Activity Incentive Setting

[6]

AN ECONOMIC APPROACH TO LEGAL PROCEDURE AND JUDICIAL ADMINISTRATION

*RICHARD A. POSNER**

INTRODUCTION

It is frequently alleged that the processes of legal dispute resolution in America are dangerously overloaded, due to delay, congestion, inefficiency, and lack of resources. To appraise this allegation and formulate durable reforms requires an understanding of the operating principles of the system for resolving legal disputes. This article seeks to advance that understanding by means of the powerful tools of economic theory. Although it builds on recent articles by William M. Landes and by the present writer,[1] it is more than an extension of the previous work. That work took for granted the rules of procedure that provide the framework of the legal dispute-resolution system; the emphasis was on how plaintiffs (mainly prosecutors) and defendants maximize utility within its constraints. The present article attempts to explain the procedural rules and practices that give the system its distinctive structure and to predict the effects of changes in one part of the system on the other parts. It thus adds to the literature (as yet small) that is developing a positive economic theory of the institutions of the legal system.[2]

Part I explains the basic analytical framework of the article. The purpose of

* Professor of Law, University of Chicago; Research Associate, National Bureau of Economic Research. Gary S. Becker, Isaac Ehrlich, Richard A. Epstein, Owen M. Fiss, William H. Kruskal, William M. Landes, Melvin W. Reder, George J. Stigler, and participants in workshops at the National Bureau of Economic Research and the University of Chicago commented helpfully on earlier versions of this article. This study has been supported by a grant from the National Science Foundation to the National Bureau for research in law and economics, but it is not an official National Bureau publication since it has not yet undergone the full critical review accorded National Bureau studies, including approval by the Bureau's board of directors.

The appendix at the end of the article presents mathematical treatments of several of the topics discussed.

1 William M. Landes, An Economic Analysis of the Courts, 14 J. Law & Econ. 61 (1971); Richard A. Posner, The Behavior of Administrative Agencies, 1 J. Leg. Studies 305 (1972).

2 See Richard A. Posner, Economic Analysis of Law (forthcoming), especially pts. I, VI, for a fuller discussion of this theory. Kenneth C. Scott, Standing in the Supreme Court—A Functional Analysis, 86 Harv. L. Rev. 645, 670-83 (1973), published after this article went to press, also analyzes an aspect of legal procedure in economic terms.

legal procedure is conceived to be the minimization of the sum of two types of costs: "error costs" (the social costs generated when a judicial system fails to carry out the allocative or other social functions assigned to it), and the "direct costs" (such as lawyers', judges', and litigants' time) of operating the legal dispute-resolution machinery. Within this framework the rules and other features of the procedural system can be analyzed as efforts to maximize efficiency.[3] Part II discusses error costs in civil cases, with particular reference to accident cases, the most common type of civil action. Part III considers error costs in criminal and administrative cases. Direct costs are then taken up. Since out-of-court settlements are usually cheaper than trials, the settlement rate affects the overall cost of legal dispute resolution, and Part IV analyzes the factors influencing the decision to settle rather than litigate. Part V analyzes factors influencing litigants' behavior (including their expenditures) in cases that go to trial. Part VI discusses interactions between error and direct costs.

The article touches on a number of topics, including, among others, burden of proof, the right of the defendant before an administrative agency to a trial-type hearing, the constitutional guarantee of counsel to indigent criminal defendants, the English and Continental practice of requiring the losing litigant to reimburse the winner's attorney's and witness fees, delay in court, pretrial discovery, nuisance suits, class actions, and res judicata. Many features of the procedural system are shown to be consistent with our postulated goal of cost minimization; others should be changed if society wants to approach closer to that goal. A number of questions that a comprehensive theory of procedure would include are omitted. In particular, the article does scant justice to the role of courts as makers (as distinct from appliers or enforcers) of law; it emphasizes rather the role of courts in the resolution of factual disputes. However, a brief discussion of the role of precedent—judge-made rules—in judicial decision-making appears in Part VI.

I. A Framework of Analysis

An important purpose of substantive legal rules (such as the rules of tort and criminal law) is to increase economic efficiency.[4] It follows (as demon-

[3] "Efficiency," as used in this article, has its usual economic sense of value-maximizing. Writers on procedure often use the term differently. For example, the Columbia University Project for Effective Justice equated it with "capacity to produce settlements" and "to shorten trials." See its Field Survey of Federal Pretrial Discovery II-7 (Walter E. Meyer Research Inst. of Law, Feb. 1965). As we shall see, such usage can lead to confusion.

[4] See Richard A. Posner, *supra* note 2, at pts. I, VI. I argue there (in ch. 23) that the rules of evidence and other procedural characteristics of the litigation process have interesting parallels to the economic market and encourage the decision of cases on efficiency grounds, but this branch of the economic theory of procedure is not pursued in the present study.

strated in Parts II and III) that mistaken imposition of legal liability, or mistaken failure to impose liability, will reduce efficiency. Judicial error is therefore a source of social costs and the reduction of error is a goal of the procedural system. The reader may challenge the last proposition by citing, for example, the rule excluding from criminal trials evidence obtained by an illegal search. Such evidence is highly probative; its exclusion reduces the accuracy of the fact-finding process in criminal trials. But this type of exclusionary rule is exceptional, and is recognized—and often bitterly criticized—as such.

Even when the legal process works flawlessly, it involves costs—the time of lawyers, litigants, witnesses, jurors, judges, and other people, plus paper and ink, law office and court house maintenance, telephone service, etc. These costs are just as real as the costs resulting from error: in general we would not want to increase the direct costs of the legal process by one dollar in order to reduce error costs by 50 (or 99) cents. The economic goal is thus to minimize the sum of error and direct costs.

Despite its generality, this formulation provides a useful framework in which to analyze the problems and objectives of legal procedure. It is usable even when the purpose of the substantive law is to transfer wealth or to bring about some other noneconomic goal, rather than to improve efficiency. All that is necessary is that it be possible, in principle, to place a price tag on the consequences of failing to apply the substantive law in all cases in which it was intended to apply, so that our two variables, error cost and direct cost, remain commensurable.

To illustrate the utility of the economic approach, consider the question whether the defendant in an administrative action (such as deportation, license revocation, or the withdrawal of a security clearance) should be entitled to a trial-type hearing. The tendency in the legal discussion of this question has been to invoke either a purely visceral sense of fairness or a purely formal distinction between penal and nonpenal sanctions. The economic approach enables the question to be framed in rational and functional terms. We ask first whether error costs would be substantially increased by denial of a trial-type hearing. Error costs (discussed in detail in the next part) may here be regarded as the product of two factors, the probability of error and the cost if an error occurs. If the facts on which the outcome of the administrative proceeding turns are the kind most accurately determined in a trial-type hearing, the probability of error if such a hearing is denied is apt to be great. If, in addition, the cost of an error if one occurs would be substantial because the sanction applied by the agency, whether in formal legal terms penal or not, imposes heavy costs on a defendant, total error costs are likely to be significantly increased by the denial of a trial-type hearing. The increment in error costs must be compared with the direct costs of a hearing; but these will often be low. The cost inquiries required by the economic approach are not simple and will rarely yield better than crude approximations, but at the very least they serve to place questions of legal policy in a framework of rational inquiry.

II. The Costs of Error in Civil Actions

A. *An Analysis of Error Costs in Accident Cases*

Suppose a company inflicts occasional injuries on people with whom it cannot contract due to very high transaction costs. Victims of these injuries could prevent them only at prohibitive cost (we will initially assume), but the company can purchase various relatively inexpensive safety devices that would reduce the accident rate significantly. In the absence of legal sanctions it has no incentive to purchase such devices since, due to the costs of transacting, it cannot sell anyone the benefits of the devices in increasing safety. If the tort law makes it liable for the costs of these accidents,[5] and is enforced flawlessly, the company will purchase the optimum quantity of safety devices. If the law is not enforced flawlessly, a suboptimum quantity of safety equipment will be procured.

The goal of a system of accident liability is to minimize the total costs of accidents and of accident avoidance. If we assume that the only feasible method of accident avoidance is the purchase of a particular type of safety equipment,[6] then those total costs are minimized by purchasing the quantity of that equipment at which the marginal product of safety equipment in reducing accident costs is equal to the marginal cost of the equipment. This marginal product is the rate at which the number of accidents inflicted by the company declines as the quantity of safety equipment purchased increases, multiplied by the cost per accident. The marginal cost of safety equipment is simply the unit price of such equipment if, as we shall assume, that price does not vary with the amount of equipment that the company purchases.[7] These relationships are depicted in Figure 1. The intersection of the marginal product and marginal cost curves determines the socially optimum quantity of safety equipment for the company to buy and install (q_S).

The company, however, is not interested in minimizing the social costs of

5 Under either a strict-liability or a negligence standard. See Richard A. Posner, Strict Liability: A Comment, 2 J. Leg. Studies 205 (1973).

6 The assumption is unrealistic. In particular, the firm's output will also be an important factor in the level of accidents. We exclude it to simplify the analysis; it could be included without affecting our conclusions.

7 Presumably the firm is too small a purchaser of such equipment to affect the price by varying the quantity that it purchases. The assumption may be valid even if we are considering the behavior of the industry, rather than of a single firm, but is in any event inessential and could be abandoned without affecting our conclusions.

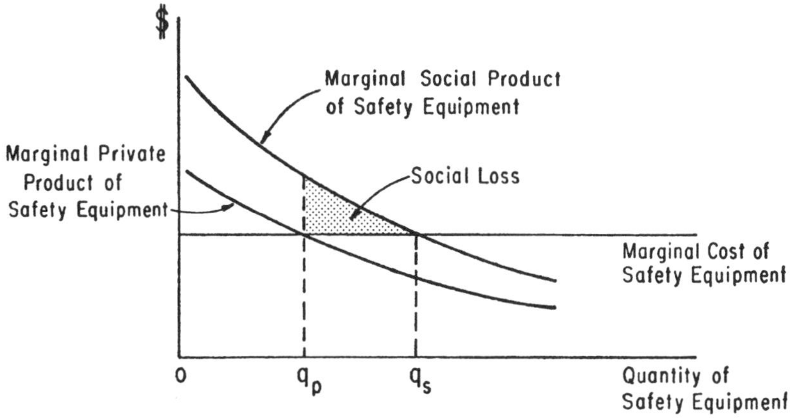

FIGURE 1

accidents and accident avoidance; it is interested only in minimizing its private accident and accident-avoidance costs. The former are the social costs of the firm's accidents multiplied by the probability that the firm will actually be held liable—forced to pay—for those costs. Since legal error presumably causes erroneous impositions as well as erroneous denials of liability, we must add a third term to the firm's cost function: the amount of money that it is forced to pay out in groundless claims. That amount is a function of the legal-error rate and disappears when that rate is zero. We ignore it for the moment.

The company minimizes its private accident and accident-avoidance costs by equating the marginal product of safety equipment in reducing its accident liability to the marginal private cost of that equipment (which we assume is the same as the marginal social cost). This marginal private product is simply the marginal social product weighted by the probability of the firm's being held liable. If that probability is one, the marginal social and private products are the same. But when the probability is less than one—that is, when the legal-error rate is positive—they diverge,[8] leading to a social loss as shown in Figure 1. The higher the error rate, the greater the reduction in the purchase of safety equipment and the greater the social loss.

The analysis is incomplete because we have ignored the possible effect of a positive error rate, operating through the third term in the company's cost function (liability resulting from groundless claims), on the firm's purchase of safety equipment. Suppose that the errors against the company took the form

[8] The effect of error on the purchase of safety equipment is identical to that of a gross-receipts tax on an industry's output. The tax shifts the demand curve (here viewed as the industry's average-revenue curve) downward by the rate of the tax and induces the industry to reduce its output. See appendix for mathematical treatment.

exclusively of accident victims' exaggerating the extent of their injuries. By increasing the company's private accident costs, these errors would increase the marginal private product of safety equipment. Thus, while errors in favor of the company would lower the company's marginal private product curve in Figure 1, errors against the company would shift it back upward. In fact, however, although all errors in favor of the company operate to lower its marginal-product curve, only some errors against the company operate to raise it. The purchase of additional safety equipment will not prevent the erroneous imposition of liability in a case in which no accident would have occurred in any event—the victim fabricated it—or in which the accident was inflicted by someone else and could not have been prevented by the defendant. Such errors do not increase the value of safety equipment to the firm and hence the marginal private product of that equipment. But even here a qualification is necessary. Additional safety equipment might strengthen the company's defense against a suit arising out of an accident actually caused by someone else. The company might be able to argue that, in view of all of the safety precautions it had taken, it could not have caused the accident.[9] Still, it seems a reasonable conclusion that a positive error rate will result in a net reduction in the company's marginal private product of safety, and hence in a net social loss.

A glance back at Figure 1 will confirm that this social loss will be greater, the more serious the accident.[10] This supports our earlier point concerning the relevance of the size of the stakes in an administrative action to the question whether the defendant should have a right to a trial-type hearing. To be sure, the stakes have another effect that is not captured in Figure 1, which treats the error rate as completely exogenous. As shown later in this article, an increase in the stakes in a case will usually induce the parties to spend more money on the litigation. This in turn will reduce the probability of an erroneous result, and so, by our previous analysis, the social loss from error. Aggregate error costs might actually be smaller in a class of big cases than in a class of small ones. But this does not invalidate our analysis of the right to a trial-type hearing, for the denial of such a hearing, in a case turning on disputed factual questions, deprives the defendant of any opportunity to reduce the probability of error by spending heavily on the factfinding process.

Thus far we have assumed that legal error will have no effect on the behavior of accident victims. In fact, by increasing expected accident costs net of

[9] Groundless claims might impose costs in another form: the company might spend heavily on lawyers, etc., to resist them. However, it might economize on these costs in the cases where, due to legal error in its favor, it was not sued at all, or where the claimant was unable to make a strong case.

[10] A higher accident cost per case raises both marginal-product curves by the same proportion. See appendix.

compensation, error encourages prospective victims to engage in self-protection. If adequate compensation were paid in every accident case, the net cost of accidents to the victims would be zero and their incentive to take precautions also zero. But if by reason of error the expected compensation is only (say) 80 per cent of the expected accident cost, the net cost of accidents to victims becomes positive and they have an incentive to adopt precautions that cost less than the uncompensated accident costs that they prevent.

The effect of error is thus to shift safety incentives from injurers to victims. If the victims can prevent the same accidents at lower cost than the injurers, such a shift will produce a net social gain rather than a social loss, but where this is possible the injurers should not be liable in the first place. If, as we assume, the substantive law places liability where it will encourage the most efficient methods of loss avoidance, the shift in safety incentives brought about by error in the legal process will produce a net social loss. But the loss may be slight.

We introduce victims' precautions into our model in Figure 2. The right-hand side of the diagram is identical to Figure 1; the left-hand side is a similar diagram depicting the purchase of safety devices by prospective victims. When legal error is zero, the marginal private product of safety equipment purchased by potential victims is also zero: since they are fully compensated, they have no incentive to invest in safety equipment. A positive error rate increases that marginal private product from zero to a level equal to the marginal social product of victim safety precautions multiplied by the error rate. Thus, if the error rate is 20 per cent, so that a victim has only an 80 per cent chance of being compensated, the value to him of taking precautions rises to 20 per cent of the value of such precautions to him if injurers were never liable. The social benefit depicted in Figure 2 that is generated when victims take precautions because the error rate is positive is larger the higher that rate is. This benefit must be subtracted from the social loss from error in order to determine the net social cost of erroneous failure to impose liability on injurers.

The analysis of legal-error costs would be very different if the purpose of the underlying substantive law were not to improve the allocation of resources but were instead to compensate victims of certain accidents. The amount of undercompensation due to legal error would be equal to the product of the error rate, the cost per accident, and the number of accidents that occur for which the injurer should be held liable. That number will be greater the higher the error rate, for we know from the previous discussion that the number of accidents rises with the error rate, and therefore undercompensation must rise with the error rate. Besides the error rate, the principal factors determining the total amount of undercompensation are the effectiveness of the law (albeit imperfectly enforced) in deterring accidents, and the scope of the law.

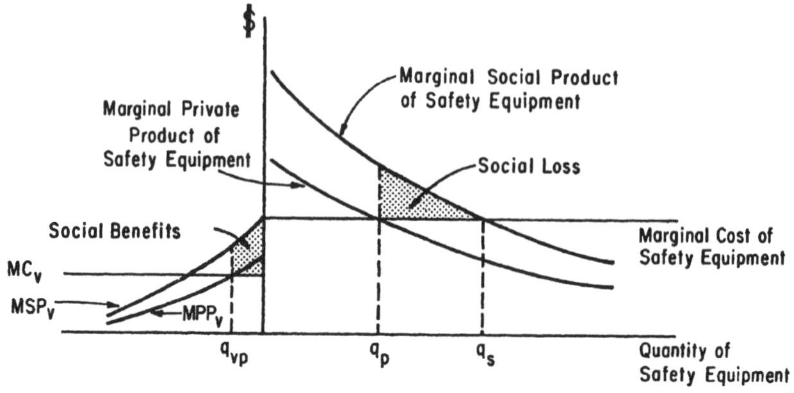

FIGURE 2

For identical error rates, the number of accidents occurring for which the injurer should be held liable will be greater if the legal standard is strict liability than if it is negligence. The costs of error are therefore likely to be higher under a strict-liability than under a negligence standard if failure to compensate where compensation is due is reckoned as a cost, and not merely as a transfer of wealth. Finally, to make undercompensation commensurable with the social loss of Figure 1, we need to know the rate at which a dollar in undercompensation is equated to a dollar in scarce resources consumed; it need not be one to one. In short the cost of legal error may differ dramatically depending on whether the purpose of the underlying substantive law is viewed as allocative or distributive.

B. *Biased and Unbiased Error*

It is useful to distinguish between "biased" and "unbiased" error. Unbiased error in our usage is any error that is as likely to operate against one party to the dispute as it is to operate against the other. Such an error gives judgment to undeserving plaintiffs in about half of the erroneously decided cases and to undeserving defendants in the other half; accepting perjured testimony is an example. A biased error is one more likely to defeat plaintiffs than defendants or vice versa. The previous analysis assumed unbiased error.

Two types of biased error may, in turn, be distinguished. The first arises from a deliberate decision to bias a source of error (as in the rule that the guilt of a criminal defendant must be proved beyond a reasonable doubt). Consider a social-loss function that consists of two terms: the social loss of Figure 1, due to failure to impose liability on injurers in all cases in which they should be held liable, and the social loss that results when the judicial system awards compensation to a victim who could have averted an accident by appropriate safety precautions at lower cost than the injurer.[11] Assume that if the parties have the same burden of proof,[12] the probability of an accurate determination of liability in both situations will be 90 per cent, meaning that in 10 per cent of the cases in which injurers should be held liable they are not held liable, while in 10 per cent of the cases in which victims should be held liable (denied compensation) for failure to take cost-justified safety precautions they receive compensation. Now let the standard of proof be changed to require that the defendant prove nonliability to a certainty. Victims will win every case. The probability of injurers' being held liable when they should be held liable will rise to one, causing the social loss from legal errors favoring injurers to fall to zero. But the probability of victims' being held liable when they fail to take proper safety precautions will fall to zero, which will cause the social loss from such failures to rise. We cannot be certain whether our total loss function will be higher or lower without knowing the specific values of the relevant parameters, but probably it will be higher. What we have done, in effect, is to impose a standard either of strict injurer liability (with no contributory negligence) or strict victim liability, depending on which probability has gone to zero. Both standards are less efficient than the alternatives.[13] The effects of moderate bias, however, cannot be appraised a priori.

A second type of biased error occurs when a source of error affects the parties' chances unequally. Consider the rule—still followed in some states—that the victim of an accident must prove his freedom from contributory negligence. In a fatal accident to which there were no witnesses, the effect of the rule, if followed to the letter, would often be to prevent recovery even though the victim was in fact free from contributory negligence; the rule would never operate in favor of victims. But courts do not apply the rule in such cases. Instead they presume in the absence of contrary evidence that the victim was exercising due care. The effect is to increase the injurer's in-

[11] There is no presumption that an injurer can avoid a costly accident more cheaply than a victim; in general an efficient allocation of responsibilities for accident prevention will require that prospective victims take some safety precautions. These optimal precautions are to be distinguished from the second-best precautions, discussed previously, that prospective victims take only because of errors in the legal process that permit injurers to escape full liability.

[12] The burdens of proof (in technical legal language, "risk of nonpersuasion") would be approximately equal if plaintiff, to prevail, had only to establish that his version of the facts was more probably true than the defendant's. Whether this is a correct characterization of the civil ("preponderance of the evidence") standard is discussed shortly.

[13] See John P. Brown, Toward an Economic Theory of Liability, 2 J. Leg. Studies 323 (1973); Richard A. Posner, *supra* note 5.

centive to take precautions and reduce the victim's. This is an improvement if we assume that the injurer is more likely to be negligent than the victim; the modified rule is better if the reverse is more likely.

C. *Burden of Proof*

Generally in civil cases, the plaintiff must persuade the factfinder that it is more likely than not that his version of the facts is true. Taken literally, this would mean that an erroneous decision was as likely to be in the plaintiff's favor as in the defendant's, since "more likely than not" implies a percentage barely greater than 50 per cent. It would not follow that half of the judgments in civil cases were erroneous; presumably most are correct.[14] But within the fraction of the erroneous, about as many judgments would be for plaintiffs as for defendants.

In cases where substantial evidence is introduced by the plaintiff, the more-likely-than-not—or "preponderance of the evidence"—standard seems to be adhered to literally, which is consistent with the economic approach. It is interesting to note that the standard implicitly equates a dollar lost by someone erroneously adjudged liable to a dollar lost by one erroneously denied compensation. Some people would say that it is worse to be forced to pay for an injury one did not actually inflict than to be erroneously denied compensation for an injury suffered. But this approach would be inconsistent with the modern economic view that interpersonal comparisons of utility are arbitrary, and it is not followed in ordinary civil cases.[15] Another question raised by the preponderance standard is why the risk of nonpersuasion should be placed on the plaintiff rather than on the defendant. The answer is that since no allocative purpose would be served by shifting a loss in a case where the defendant's liability was indeterminate, the rule economizes on litigation expenditures. This also implies, however, that the burden of persuasion as to

[14] As explained in Part V(A)3 *infra*.

[15] A fuller discussion of the distributive effects of the preponderance standard may be in order. The preponderance standard sets the same value on two types of error, assuming the same dollar amount is involved in the two types of case. One error is to transfer wealth from a deserving defendant to an undeserving plaintiff. The other is to fail to transfer wealth from an undeserving defendant to a deserving plaintiff. Assume that the parties have identical marginal-utility-of-money curves (negatively sloped) and, before the legal dispute in question, the same wealth, W. The plaintiff's claim is that $1000 was wrongfully transferred from him to the defendant. If the claim is false but the plaintiff wins, the plaintiff's wealth rises to W + $1000 and defendant's falls to W − $1000. The loss to the defendant is greater than the gain to the plaintiff because of the identity and negative slope of the parties' marginal-utility-of-money curves. If the claim is true but the plaintiff loses, this means that the dispute itself reduced plaintiff's wealth to W − $1000 and increased defendant's wealth to W + $1000; the erroneous legal decision merely confirms the redistribution. Thus the errors are symmetrical even under assumptions that permit interpersonal comparisons of utility.

defenses (grounds for nonliability that the defendant must plead) should be placed on the plaintiff rather than defendant—as used to be the general rule, in fact, with respect to contributory negligence.

In some cases, modification of the preponderance standard may be in order. Thus, suppose that a pedestrian is struck by a bus in circumstances suggesting that the bus company is liable, but his only evidence of the injurer's identity is that 80 per cent of the buses on this route are owned by the defendant, one of two bus companies that use the route. The evidence would be considered insufficient to satisfy the plaintiff's burden of proof, a result defended on the ground (among others) that otherwise the defendant would be held liable for all bus accidents occurring on the route although responsible in fact for only 80 per cent.[16] This argument is unsatisfactory. It implies that it is better that the bus company escape liability in the 80 per cent of the accidents for which it is in fact responsible than that it pay for some accidents that it did not cause, without explaining *why* this is better. The real issue is different. If the only evidence introduced in the case is that the defendant operates 80 per cent of the buses on the route in question, the probability that a judgment in favor of the plaintiff will be erroneous is at least 20 per cent, which is high. Moreover, were this the only evidence ever introduced in such cases, the other bus company on the route would have no incentive to adopt any safety precautions, so the accident rate would rise.[17] Since the error turns out to be very costly, it makes sense to eliminate the cause of the error if possible to do so at moderate cost. Now if the defendant can adduce additional evidence as cheaply as the plaintiff, no harm is done by permitting a jury to find in favor of the plaintiff when all he has presented is evidence of the bus company's market share; and even if it is more costly for the defendant to present evidence as to which bus company was really liable, so long as it is not *too* costly, the 20 per cent margin of error will be greatly reduced or eliminated. Nonetheless, if the plaintiff can adduce additional evidence more cheaply than the defendant, the pure preponderance standard should yield to a threshold approach in order to induce the plaintiff to present such evidence and thus economize on litigation costs.[18]

16 Laurence H. Tribe, Trial by Mathematics: Precision and Ritual in the Legal Process, 84 Harv. L. Rev. 1329, 1349-50 (1971).

17 Not only would the second bus company have a higher accident rate, but its liability-cost advantage might enable it to increase its market share. The result would be a further increase in the accident rate (the weighted average of the companies' individual accident rates) on the route.

18 A similar approach seems to be implied in Laurence H. Tribe, *supra* note 16, at 1341 n.37, and 1349-50. Consistently with the discussion in the text, the doctrine of *res ipsa loquitur* has been used to induce defendants to produce facts that would be more costly for the plaintiff to produce—such as what when on in defendants' operating room while plaintiff was unconscious. See Ybarra v. Spangard, 25 Cal. 2d 486, 154 P.2d 687 (1944); Louis L. Jaffe, Res Ipsa Loquitur Vindicated, 1 Buff. L. Rev. 1 (1951).

In some cases the preponderance standard may be too high. Suppose that a certain form of radiation for which the emitter is strictly liable increases the risk of developing cancer by one-tenth of one per cent. A person who is exposed to the radiation and later develops cancer will not be able to prove that it was caused by the radiation; there is only a small possibility that the radiation was a causal factor in any particular case. If the emitter is held liable for all cancers developed by people exposed to the radiation his judgment bill will be 1000 times greater than the actual harm he caused, while if the preponderance standard is applied he will escape all liability for the harm he caused. The correct solution would appear to be to permit each cancer sufferer among those exposed to the radiation to recover one tenth of one per cent of the costs of the cancer to him. If damages so computed are too small to justify his incurring the costs of suit, a class action (a device discussed later in this article) should be permitted.

III. Error Costs in Criminal and Administrative Cases

A. *The Optimum Probability of Convicting the Innocent*

The prosecution in a criminal case must prove the defendant's guilt beyond a reasonable doubt. This implies that the probability of convicting an innocent person is very low. Perhaps in no more than five per cent of all cases in which an erroneous judgment is made is an innocent person convicted. Can this biasing of error in favor of criminal defendants be reconciled with our theory of error?

We begin by dividing the total losses from crime into two parts: the social costs of criminal activity and the punishment costs imposed on both guilty and innocent people convicted of crime.[19] We want to determine the optimum probability that an innocent person who is charged with a criminal offense will be convicted, that is, the probability at which the total losses of crime are minimized. This conditional probability of convicting the innocent enters into our loss function in several ways. To begin with, the social cost of criminal activity is a function of the number of crimes committed, which in turn is a function of the rate at which people who commit crimes are apprehended and convicted for them. The rate of conviction of the guilty can be expressed as a decreasing function of the conditional probability of convicting the

[19] Consistently with the emphasis in this part of the article on error costs, we ignore for the moment the costs involved in determining guilt. The preventive (as distinct from deterrent) effects of punishment are also ignored for the moment. For reasons that will become clear in due course, we assume that punishment takes the form of imprisonment, death, flogging, etc., but not of a fine. We ignore the costs of administering the punishment. For other discussions of the optimum probability of convicting the innocent see John R. Harris, On the Economics of Law and Order, 78 J. Pol. Econ. 165 (1970); H. Laurence Tribe, *supra* note 16, at 1378-79, and studies referred to therein.

innocent. This is because a change in the standard of proof that increases the likelihood of an innocent person's being convicted also increases the likelihood that a guilty person will be convicted, and vice versa. If the standard of proof is set at so high a level that the probability of an innocent person's being convicted is zero, the conviction rate for guilty people will also be zero, since only with a zero conviction rate can all possibility of an innocent person's being convicted be eliminated. Conversely, if the standard of proof is set at so low a level that innocent people, if charged with crime, are always convicted, then presumably the rate of conviction of the guilty will also be 100 per cent. In fact conviction rates are moderately high[20] even though the conditional probability of convicting the innocent is very low, which suggests a function of the general shape depicted in Figure 3.

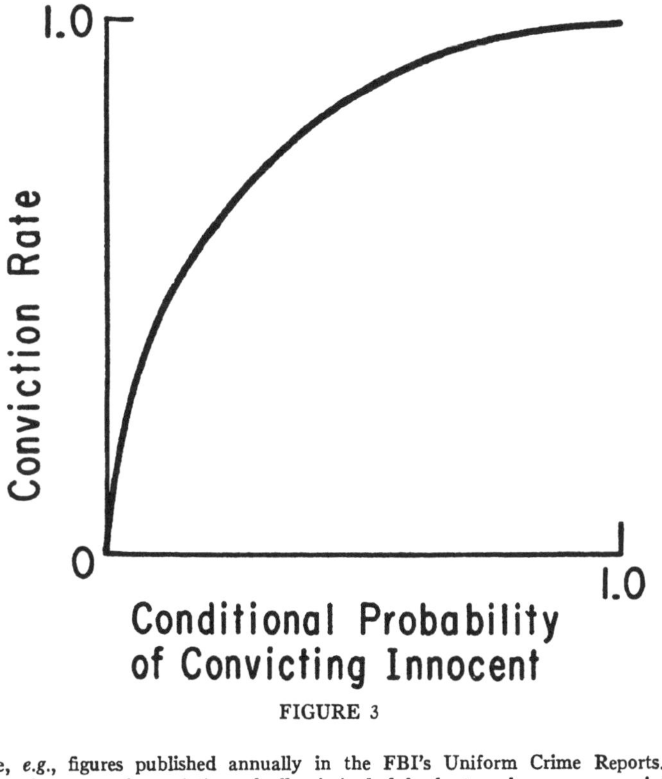

FIGURE 3

[20] See, *e.g.*, figures published annually in the FBI's Uniform Crime Reports. These rates are the rates of conviction of all criminal defendants, whereas we are interested only in the rates of conviction of the guilty. But probably the two kinds of rates do not differ substantially, since the very low probability of convicting an innocent person implies that most acquitted defendants are guilty, assuming—realistically—that only moderate resources are devoted to criminal factfinding (cf. note 22 *infra*).

The conditional probability of convicting the innocent affects the social costs of criminal activity in another way. The number of crimes committed is presumably a decreasing function of the expected punishment costs of crime, and punishing the innocent reduces those expected punishment costs and hence increases the number of crimes and the social costs of crime. To explain, if the expected punishment cost from committing some crime is X, a person who refrains from committing the crime will still have an expected punishment cost, Y, since the conditional probability of punishing the innocent is positive and people consequently face a possibility of being punished for crimes committed by others. The net punishment cost of committing the crime is thus $X - Y$; it is this figure that enters into the prospective criminal's calculations; and the figure is smaller the greater the conditional probability of being punished for someone else's crime.

A reduction in the rate at which the guilty are convicted will affect the punishment costs inflicted on the guilty, which are a social cost too (so long as we abjure interpersonal comparisons of utility). These costs are equal to the product of the number of crimes committed, the probability that someone will be arrested and charged for each crime committed and that he is actually guilty, the probability of his being convicted, and the severity of the sentence imposed. While a reduction in the conviction rate directly reduces one of these factors, it indirectly increases another: the number of crimes committed.

The conditional probability of convicting the innocent also affects, of course, the punishment costs inflicted on the innocent. Those costs are equal to the product of the number of crimes committed, the probability that someone will be arrested and charged for each crime, the probability that this person will actually be innocent, the probability that he will nonetheless be found guilty, and the severity of the sentence imposed. The effect of the conditional probability of punishing the innocent is not, however, so straightforward as this suggests, since that probability also affects the number of crimes committed and the probability of an innocent person's being accused of crime. The latter point is based on the assumption that police and prosecutors prefer to convict guilty rather than innocent people to the extent that it is easier (cheaper) to convict the guilty and therefore that they will attempt to screen out people whom they believe to be innocent so long as this condition holds. The higher the conditional probability of convicting the innocent, the less incentive the police and prosecutor have to screen out the innocent suspect in advance of trial. This suggests another way in which the conditional probability of convicting the innocent affects the social costs of crime. The more advance screening the police and prosecutor do, the less likely a guilty person is to be prosecuted since the screening will exclude some people who appear to be but are not innocent.

Actually to determine the optimum conditional probability of convicting the innocent would require data that are difficult, perhaps impossible, to obtain, but we can form some tentative impressions by considering the extreme cases. Assume first that the conditional probability of punishing the innocent were much lower than it is today, which would bring it very close to zero. A glance at Figure 3 will show that, at this level, the rate of conviction of the guilty is apt to be negligible. This means that unless criminal punishment has very little effect in deterring crime, the number of crimes committed and hence the total social costs of crime will be very high. And, perhaps surprisingly, the aggregate punishment costs imposed on innocent people may not be trivial, for although only a small fraction of innocent suspects will be charged or convicted, it will be a fraction of a larger whole (all people suspected of crime) since the number of crimes committed will be so much greater. Aggregate punishment costs imposed on the guilty may also, and for the same reason, be high. It is in any event unlikely that a reduction in the conditional probability of punishing the innocent below existing low levels would generate much savings in the punishment costs imposed on innocent people. These punishment costs must already be very small in aggregate, so a further reduction would yield only small savings. In summary, it is unlikely that a substantially lower conditional probability of punishing the innocent than we have today would be optimum, and it seems altogether untenable to suggest that the optimum probability might be zero,[21] since this would imply a zero conviction rate and hence no punishment for crime whatsoever.

Now assume that the conditional probability of convicting the innocent were raised substantially above its existing very low level. One effect would be to increase the rate of conviction of the guilty and thereby reduce the number of crimes and the total social costs of crime. The increase in the conviction rate would be very marked up to a point, but if the conditional probability of convicting the innocent rose to 30 per cent or more, Figure 3 suggests that further increases would have only slight effects on the conviction rate. Moreover, at these high levels of probability of convicting innocent people, the effect of additional convictions in reducing the expected punishment costs of criminals and hence in increasing the social cost of criminal activity would become substantial, while at the same time the punishment costs imposed on both innocent and guilty would be very great. Unfortunately, even if we assume that a conditional probability of convicting the innocent that exceeded 30 per cent could not possibly be optimum, the implications for the proper standard of proof are unclear. The conditional probability of convicting the innocent is a function not only of the standard of proof but

[21] As perhaps implied by Professor Tribe when he states that it is proper to insist "upon as close an approximation to certainty as seems humanly attainable in the circumstances." Laurence H. Tribe, *supra* note 16, at 1374. To the same effect, see his A Further Critique of Mathematical Proof, 84 Harv. L. Rev. 1810, 1818 (1971).

also of the ease of marshaling convincing evidence of innocence, which is generally greater when the defendant is in fact innocent.

Now let us relax the unrealistic assumption in the preceding discussion that the amount of resources devoted to the trial of criminal cases is fixed. Conceivably the only consequence of reducing the conditional probability of convicting the innocent would be an increase in the resources devoted to prosecution. The conviction rate of the guilty might not fall at all,[22] and the additional resources necessary to prevent its falling might be small in relation to the reduction in the punishment costs borne by innocent people. But it is a fair guess that the proportionate increase in prosecutorial resources that would be necessary to maintain existing conviction rates in the face of a conditional probability of convicting the innocent that was at or near zero would be very large; and possibly the proportionate *decrease* in those resources that would be made possible by increasing the conditional probability would be small until that probability reached a level unacceptably high because of its effect on the social loss from convicting innocent people. Moreover, it is unlikely that the effect on the conviction rate of a significant reduction in the conditional probability of convicting the innocent brought about by a change in the standard of proof could be completely offset by an increase in the resources devoted to prosecution. To anticipate later discussion, such an increase might be met by an increase in the resources devoted to defense that would largely nullify the effect of the additional prosecutorial resources in increasing the probability of convicting the guilty. Since a large fraction of criminal defense expenditures are financed by the government, the ability of defendants to match increases in prosecution resources could be curtailed, but the resulting imbalance might move the conditional probability of convicting the innocent back up to where it had been before the attempt to reduce it, for those defendants—the large majority—whose ability to pay for their defense is severely limited.

If our analysis does not establish whether proof beyond a reasonable doubt is the proper standard to apply in criminal cases, still it is helpful in explaining important aspects of criminal procedure, not least the fact that subjective certainty of guilt is ***not*** required. Another aspect is the generally shared impression that the standard of proof is in fact stricter the more serious the offense. The gravity of the offense is positively related to the severity of the

[22] An analogy may be drawn to the statistician's distinction between Type I and Type II errors. A Type I error is the erroneous rejection of the null hypothesis (here, that defendant is not guilty). A Type II error is the erroneous rejection of the alternative hypothesis (defendant is guilty). With a given sample size, a test of statistical significance that reduces the likelihood of committing a Type I error increases the likelihood of committing a Type II error, and vice versa. But both probabilities of error can be reduced by increasing the sample size, which is analogous to increasing the expenditures devoted to finding the truth in a legal proceeding.

penalty, and an increase in severity not only increases the punishment costs imposed on innocent (and guilty) people who are convicted of crime, but also, as we shall see later, induces the parties to spend more money on the litigation. Since greater expenditures should have the effect of reducing the probability of an error whether in favor of or against the defendant, a reduction in the conditional probability of convicting the innocent in grave crimes may reduce the costs imposed on the innocent without reducing substantially the rate of conviction of the guilty. If so, a reduction in the conditional probability may also reduce the social costs of criminal activity through its effect on the expected punishment costs of people who commit crimes.

The analysis also suggests why punitive remedies, when they take the form of fines or other money transfers exclusively, as in the case of antitrust treble damages, are often governed by the laxer civil, rather than the criminal, standard of proof. In such cases, the punishment costs inflicted on the innocent do not represent a net social cost because they show up on the social ledger as equal benefits to the state or other plaintiff. (Indeed, the analysis of error costs in Part II seems fully applicable in such cases.) This distinction may also explain why the burden of proof in a civil fraud case ("clear and convincing evidence") is intermediate between the preponderance and beyond-reasonable-doubt standards. A judgment of liability in such a case imposes a reputational loss on the defendant that is in addition to the money judgment received by the plaintiff but is less costly than most criminal punishments. Most important, the distinction explains why some difference in the standards of proof followed in criminal and civil cases may be entirely consistent with economic theory.

B. *Other Applications*

1. *Administrative Proceedings.* Some administrative proceedings, such as Interstate Commerce Commission reparations cases and National Labor Relations Board back-pay cases, closely resemble ordinary civil cases in that they involve a money transfer. Other administrative proceedings, where restitution is not a feature, resemble criminal prosecutions. A Federal Trade Commission false-advertising order, for example, imposes costs on the defendant that presumably have a deterrent or preventive value, but there is no transfer. However, there is an important difference between such proceedings and criminal cases: prevention, which we ignored in our discussion of criminal cases, often plays a greater role than deterrence in the administrative process. The primary significance of an FTC false-advertising order, for example, is not to impose costs for past violations but to expose the defendant to sanctions if, by repeating his unlawful conduct, he violates the terms of the order.[23]

[23] See Federal Trade Commission Act, 15 U.S.C. § 45(*l*) (1970). However, the FTC's

If we assume both that administrative sanctions are characteristically much less severe than criminal sanctions and that prevention is apt to be a more important objective of the administrative sanction than deterrence, it is easy to see why administrative agencies, even when they impose sanctions that resemble the criminal in that they do not involve a pure money transfer, are not required to follow the criminal standard of proof beyond a reasonable doubt. The less severe the sanction, the higher, by our earlier analysis, the optimum probability of convicting the innocent.[24] And if the major purpose of the sanction is prevention rather than deterrence, we need not worry that by convicting many innocent people the agency will reduce the expected punishment costs of violation and hence the deterrent effect of punishment.

The analysis also suggests, however, that the characteristic combination of prosecution and adjudication in the same agency may be a source of inefficiency. To find the socially optimum probability of punishing an innocent person accused of unlawful conduct, an adjudicator must treat a dollar in cost of punishment of the innocent as equal to a dollar in benefit from punishing the guilty. Having no prosecutorial responsibilities, courts presumably do this. But an agency that is responsible for prosecution may weight a dollar in benefits from successful prosecution more heavily than a dollar in costs of punishing the innocent. The benefits presumably accrue to the agency, however indirectly; it does not bear the costs.

If the agency does not treat the costs imposed on innocent people whom it punishes as a social loss that enters into the determination of the optimum probability of convicting the innocent, it will establish a conditional probability of convicting the innocent that is higher than the social optimum. It will not ignore completely the costs of punishing innocent people, since those costs reduce the deterrent effect of punishment. But since, as mentioned, they do not reduce its preventive effect, and since deterrence may not be an important objective of the administrative sanction, the agency may ignore those costs almost completely with the result that its (private) optimum probability of convicting the innocent accused may be very high. This provides a strong argument for affording defendants in administrative proceedings a right of judicial review of the agency's factfindings (and such other procedural protections as may be necessary to make the right effective[25]), even though the

---

recent practice of compelling firms found guilty of false advertising to print retractions ("corrective advertising") has introduced a significant penal element—unless it is assumed that corrective advertising is as valuable to the consuming public as it is costly to the advertiser.

[24] Where the administrative sanction is very severe, as in deportation, the standard followed, as we would predict, is stricter than the preponderance, and approaches the criminal, standard. See Woodby v. Immigration and Naturalization Service, 385 U.S. 276 (1966).

[25] A recent study found no evidence that one such protection—formal separation of

agency's presumed "expertise" in finding facts within the area of its special competence, and the provision of an internal agency appellate process,[26] might, but for the economic considerations advanced here, argue against any need for judicial review of agency factfindings.

2. *Right to Counsel.* A similar analysis of prosecutors' incentives suggests a possible economic justification for the constitutional guarantee of counsel to indigent criminal defendants. As between two groups of criminal defendants, one guilty but able to afford counsel, the other innocent but unable to afford counsel, we want prosecutors to prosecute only members of the first group, in order to maximize the deterrent (and preventive) effect of criminal punishment. If, however, the prosecutor's maximand is number of convictions (presumbly weighted by seriousness of offense), he will prosecute the guilty only if it is less costly to convict them than it is to convict the innocent. Ordinarily it is; but it may not be if the innocent person is not represented by counsel while the guilty person is. In that event the provision of counsel to indigents may be necessary to avoid an overinvestment in their prosecution. This conclusion would not follow if the prosecutor's maximand were assumed to be deterrence, rather than simply conviction.

[7]

ACCURACY IN THE ASSESSMENT OF DAMAGES*

LOUIS KAPLOW and STEVEN SHAVELL
Harvard Law School and National Bureau of Economic Research

ABSTRACT

Assessment of damages is a principal issue in litigation and, in light of this, we consider the social justification for, and the private benefits of, accurate measurement of harm. Greater accuracy induces injurers to exercise levels of precaution that better reflect the magnitude of the harm they are likely to generate, and, relatedly, it stimulates uninformed injurers to learn about risks before acting. However, accuracy in assessment of harm cannot influence the behavior of injurers—and is therefore of no social value—to the degree that they lack knowledge of the harm they might cause when deciding on their precautions. Regardless of the social value of accuracy, litigants generally gain by devoting resources toward proof of damages, leading often to socially excessive private incentives to establish damages.

I. INTRODUCTION

ASSESSMENT of damages is often a principal issue in litigation because the primary objective of the plaintiff usually is to collect as much as possible and that of the defendant is to pay as little as possible. Accordingly, litigants frequently devote substantial time and effort attempting to establish the level of harm. In light of this, the question naturally arises concerning the underlying social purpose of accurate determination of harm. Our object here is to address this question and to compare socially desirable effort to ascertain harm with what parties in litigation wish to expend on the task. To this end, we consider a version of the now standard model of liability for harm[1] in Section II of the article, and we develop the following four points.[2]

* We are grateful to Marcel Kahan, the Journal's editors, and participants in seminars at Harvard and New York University Law Schools for helpful comments, and for research support from the John M. Olin Center for Law, Economics, and Business at Harvard Law School. Shavell also acknowledges aid from the National Science Foundation (grant no. SES-911-1947).

[1] See, for example, John P. Brown, Toward an Economic Theory of Liability, 2 J. Legal Stud. 323 (1973); William M. Landes & Richard A. Posner, The Economic Structure of Tort Law (1987); and Steven Shavell, Economic Analysis of Accident Law (1987).

[2] As will be seen, the emphasis in this article is on the points that assessment of damages is not socially worthwhile if parties do not know the magnitude of harm when they act and that, despite this, parties may have strong incentives to spend to determine damages in court. These points have not been developed elsewhere to our knowledge, although Louis

[*Journal of Law and Economics*, vol. XXXIX (April 1996)]

First, accuracy in the assessment of harm leads potential injurers to act in a way that reflects the magnitude of the harm they might cause—to take greater precautions the greater the harm they are likely to bring about. This fundamental and familiar point is the social justification for accurate assessment of damages in the model.[3]

Second, accuracy in the assessment of harm cannot influence the behavior of injurers—and is therefore of no social value—to the degree that they lack knowledge of the level of harm they might cause when they make their decisions. Thus, if, when choosing his precautions, an injurer knows only that the average level of harm that would be caused in an accident is $500,000, there is no point in the court's measuring harm accurately. As long as the injurer's expected liability is $500,000, his behavior will be the same as if harm were measured precisely.

Third, accuracy in assessing harm may spur injurers to learn more before they act about the harm they might cause, for then they can benefit by altering their level of precautions. They will have no motive to learn about the level of harm in advance if damages will be based on average harm, for then the particular level of harm will not affect their damage payments. That injurers have an incentive to learn about harm before they act may of course be socially beneficial because it is desirable for the level of precautions to reflect the magnitude of the potential harm.

Fourth, litigants' incentives to provide information about harm to courts may be socially excessive. Defendants will want to establish the true level of harm if it is less than estimated harm, and plaintiffs will want to demonstrate the true harm if it exceeds the estimated level. But these incentives to establish harm exist independently of the social value,

---

Kaplow, A Model of the Optimal Complexity of Legal Rules, 11 J. L., Econ., & Org. 150 (1995), deals with closely related issues in analyzing which variables courts optimally ought to include in legal rules. In addition, for an informal discussion that expands on the one in the present paper, see Louis Kaplow, The Values of Accuracy in Adjudication: An Economic Analysis, 23 J. Legal Stud. 307 (1994). There are, in addition, a number of articles on the subject of accuracy concerning issues different from those addressed in this article, including Richard Craswell & John Calfee, Deterrence and Uncertain Legal Standards, 2 J. L., Econ., & Org. 279 (1986) (on mistake in assessing negligence); Louis Kaplow & Steven Shavell, Accuracy in the Determination of Liability, 37 J. Law & Econ. 1 (1994); Ivan Png, Optimal Subsidies and Damages in the Presence of Judicial Error, 6 Int'l Rev. L. & Econ. 101 (1986); A. Mitchell Polinsky & Steven Shavell, Legal Error, Litigation, and the Incentive to Obey the Law, 5 J. L., Econ., & Org. 99 (1989); and Daniel Rubinfeld & David Sappington, Efficient Awards and Standards of Proof in Judicial Proceedings, 18 Rand J. Econ. 308 (1987) (all on mistake in determining who committed a punishable act); and Richard Posner, An Economic Approach to Legal Procedure and Judicial Administration, 2 J. Legal Stud. 399 (1973) (a general discussion of accuracy).

[3] Another possible justification for accuracy is that it assures victims full compensation. We mention this issue in Section III below but note that its importance is not substantial, in part due to the presence of insurance markets. (The issue does not enter in our model because parties are assumed to be risk-neutral.)

if any, of accurate assessment of harm. For example, the incentives exist when defendants, at the time that they act, do not know the level of harm, which is to say, when accuracy in determining harm has no effect on behavior and hence no social value. It is true as well that if defendants know or may learn the level of harm when they act, incentives to demonstrate harm may be excessive.

After analyzing these points, we consider briefly in Section III the generality of our analysis and extensions to it concerning settlement, risk aversion, the effect of injurers' behavior on the magnitude of harm, and certain aspects of information. In Section IV, we discuss the implications of our analysis—including the possible utility of restricting expenditures on ascertaining damages, and also the use of tabular damages—in some typical settings of adjudication.

II. Analysis

Assume that risk-neutral injurers choose levels of precaution x to reduce the risk $p(x)$ of accidents, where $0 < p(x) < 1$, $p'(x) < 0$, and $p''(x) > 0$. A particular injurer will cause one particular level of harm h if involved in an accident, but different injurers cause different levels of harm. Let $f(h)$ be the density of h on $[0,\infty)$, where $f(h) > 0$. Injurers and courts are presumed to know the density f. (This assumption can be reinterpreted and relaxed, without affecting our results; see Sections III*e* and III*f* below.)

If an accident occurs, the injurer who caused it will be held strictly liable and will be required to pay damages d in court (on the possibility of settlement, see, as noted, Section III*b* below). Assume also that there is a cost k to an injurer of presenting information about harm to courts.[4] In addition, in one version of the model, we will assume that there is a cost c to an injurer of obtaining information about harm before he chooses his precautions.

Social costs exclusive of the expense of obtaining or presenting information about h are

$$\int_0^\infty [x(h) + p(x(h))h]f(h)\,dh,$$

where $x(h)$ denotes the precautions taken by injurers who would cause losses of h. The social goal is to minimize the sum of the foregoing expression and any relevant expenses of obtaining and presenting information about h. Let $x^*(h)$ denote the x that minimizes $x + p(x)h$.

[4] The assumption that k is borne by injurers rather than by courts is, for the most part, inessential. If k is borne by courts and damages are raised by k from the level we say below is optimal, our conclusions remain valid except, as will be obvious, in Section II*C* below.

A. *Ex Ante Information Is Exogenous*

We consider first the cases in which injurers do and do not know h ex ante. We ask whether it is desirable for h to be observed by courts, which would involve a cost k. Our conclusion (proved in the appendix) is:

PROPOSITION 1. (*a*) Suppose that injurers do not know harm h ex ante. Then it is optimal for courts not to observe h and for damages to equal $\bar{h}$, expected harm. In this case, injurers will behave socially optimally given their lack of information about h.

(*b*) Suppose that injurers know harm ex ante. Then it is optimal for courts to observe h and for damages to equal h (rather than $\bar{h}$) if and only if the cost k of observing h is sufficiently low. If damages equal h, injurers will behave socially optimally.

The reason for 1(*a*) is, of course, that if injurers do not know h ex ante, their behavior cannot be affected by the fact that their damage payments will depend on h; because social resources must be expended for damage payments to depend on h, this cannot be desirable.[5] Furthermore, if $d = \bar{h}$, injurers will correctly take into account the expected harm caused by their activity and thus be led to take proper precautions.

The explanation for 1(*b*) is that, when injurers know h ex ante and their damage payments depend on h, they will, desirably, choose their level of precautions in accord with h. Hence, if it is not too costly for h to be observed by courts, that will be socially worthwhile.

B. *Endogenous Acquisition of Information Ex Ante*

Suppose now that injurers choose whether to acquire information ex ante by making an expenditure: initially, they do not know h, but if they spend c, they learn h ex ante. In this case, the result is:

PROPOSITION 2. Suppose that injurers can learn harm h ex ante by making an expenditure c.

(*a*) If it is not socially optimal for injurers to learn h ex ante, it is optimal for courts not to observe h and for damages to equal $\bar{h}$. In this case, injurers will not learn h and will behave optimally given their lack of information about h.

(*b*) If it is socially optimal for injurers to learn h ex ante, it is optimal

[5] More precisely, taking as given an injurers' ex post litigation costs, we see that behavior is unaffected by whether or not damages depend on h. But when damages do not depend on h, injurers do not spend k in the event of an accident. Expected liability costs are thus lower, and so will be injurers' precautions. This change in behavior, however, is efficient: the social cost of accidents is lower because resources are no longer spent determining h each time there is an accident. (This is apparent in the proof in the Appendix.)

for courts to observe h and for damages to equal h. In this case, injurers will learn h and will behave optimally.[6]

The result in 2(a) follows from proposition 1(a) and the fact that injurers will clearly have no incentive to learn h ex ante when damages are $\bar{h}$. The result in 2(b) will follow from proposition 1(b) if, when damages are h and it is socially optimal for injurers to learn h, they are in fact induced to learn h. We prove this in the Appendix. Essentially, the result holds because the social benefit of injurers becoming informed is internalized by injurers when damages equal h.

C. *Endogenous Reporting of Information Ex Post*

Suppose here that, whether or not injurers know h ex ante, after accidents occur injurers (defendants) and victims (plaintiffs) know h and either type of party can elect to establish h to courts at cost k. (We assumed above that courts, not parties, decide whether or not k is spent to establish h.) Let us first reconsider the case in which injurers do not know h ex ante.

PROPOSITION 3. Suppose that injurers do not know harm h ex ante and that, after an accident, parties choose whether or not to spend k to establish h to courts.

(a) It is optimal for damages to equal expected harm $\bar{h}$ regardless of whether a party establishes h. In this case, no parties will spend to establish h.

(b) If instead damages equal h whenever a party establishes h, plaintiffs and defendants will sometimes spend k to establish h, which is inefficient.

With regard to 3(a), we know from proposition 1(a) that, when injurers do not know h ex ante, setting damages equal to $\bar{h}$ will induce them to take optimal precautions given their lack of knowledge of h. And when damages equal $\bar{h}$, parties will obviously have no incentive to spend to establish h, which could only add to social costs. Moreover, with respect to 3(b), if damages equal h whenever a party establishes h, defendants will spend k to do this when $h + k < \bar{h}$, and plaintiffs will spend k when $h - k > \bar{h}$; thus k will be spent when $|h - \bar{h}| > k$.

The excessive private incentive to spend to establish h, described in

[6] This result about the desirability of accurate assessment of h by courts may be compared to another beneficial effect of accuracy under assumptions different from ours. Suppose that, if courts do not accurately assess harm, parties will expend effort to predict the errors courts would make (even though the parties might know the true harm). Then accurate measurement of harm by courts would be beneficial because it would discourage parties from investing effort to predict courts' errors. On this general issue, see Louis Kaplow & Steven Shavell, Private versus Socially Optimal Provision of Ex Ante Legal Advice, 8 J. L., Econ., & Org. 306 (1992).

3(*b*), exists because, after an accident occurs, a party may well have a positive motive to spend to establish h so as to alter damages in his favor. But this motive is unrelated to the incentive benefit associated with establishing h—a benefit that is nonexistent when injurers do not know h ex ante.

Now let us reconsider the case in which injurers know harm ex ante. We have (see the Appendix for the proof):

PROPOSITION 4. Suppose that injurers know harm h ex ante and that, after an accident, parties choose whether or not to spend k to establish h to courts.

(*a*) The optimal damages rule is defined as follows:
 (i) if a party establishes h and h lies outside a specified interval $[h_1, h_2]$, damages equal h;
 (ii) if a party establishes h and h lies inside the interval, or if both parties are silent, damages equal $\bar{h}_c$, the conditional mean of h in $[h_1, h_2]$;
 (iii) defendants reimburse plaintiffs for the cost k of establishing h when plaintiffs establish h and h lies outside the interval.

(*b*) Under the optimal damages rule, defendants will establish h when $h < h_1$, both parties will be silent when h lies in $[h_1, h_2]$, and plaintiffs will establish h when $h > h_2$.

(*c*) If instead damages equal h whenever a party establishes h and plaintiffs are reimbursed for k whenever they establish h, then more plaintiffs and more defendants will establish h than under the optimal damages rule.

The central feature of the socially optimal rule is that parties are discouraged from demonstrating h if h lies in a midrange—the interval $[h_1, h_2]$—and otherwise they are led to establish h. The reason for this feature of the rule is in essence that the cost k of establishing h to courts is socially worthwhile to incur if and only if the resulting improvement in incentives is sufficiently large, something that will be true if and only if h is relatively high or low.

The argument establishing that the rule is optimal may be sketched as follows (the proof is in the Appendix). Consider a dictator who not only can set damages but also can order individuals to report h or to be silent. If it can be demonstrated that the rule of the proposition leads to the same outcome as the dictator can achieve, then the rule of the proposition must be optimal.

The dictator would set damages equal to h when individuals establish h because injurers will be induced to take optimal precautions if they pay the full costs of accidents, $h + k$. Note that this amount is what injurers will in fact pay if damages are h and they establish h and thus bear k, or if plaintiffs establish h and injurers reimburse them for k. The dictator would also want damages to equal $\bar{h}_c$ when parties are silent, for $\bar{h}_c$ is the expected harm due to accidents caused by those who will be silent.

Finally, the dictator must choose the interval $[h_1, h_2]$ for which parties must be silent. The optimal h_1 is less than $\bar{h}_c - k$. To explain, consider a defendant who has caused harm h equal to $\bar{h}_c - k$. His precautions will be $x^*(\bar{h}_c)$ if he will not report h, and his precautions will be the same if he will report h (for then his damages will be $\bar{h}_c - k$ and he will spend k, so that his total expenses will be $\bar{h}_c$). Because his precautions will not be altered if he reports h, it must be best for the defendant to be ordered to be silent, saving resources of k; hence, the optimal h_1 is lower than $\bar{h}_c - k$. Similar reasoning explains why the optimal h_2 exceeds $\bar{h}_c$.

Now it is evident that under the damages rule of the proposition, with $[h_1, h_2]$ being the interval that the dictator would choose, individuals will behave as asserted in 4(*b*) and report h if and only if h lies outside the interval. (Thus, the outcome under the rule will indeed be that achievable by the dictator.) In particular, a defendant will want to reveal h when it is less than h_1 even though this costs him k because, as just discussed, $h_1 < \bar{h}_c - k$. No party will want to spend k to reveal h if h is in $[h_1, h_2]$, for then damages will be $\bar{h}_c$ regardless of the particular value of h in the interval. And a plaintiff will always want to establish h if $h > h_2$, for the plaintiff does not bear k.

With regard to excessive incentives to prove h under the usual rule, as described in 4(*c*), observe that defendants would sometimes inefficiently spend to demonstrate h if doing so would always result in damages of h: because $h_1 < \bar{h}_c - k$, defendants would pay k to prove h when h is in $[h_1, \bar{h}_c - k)$. Also, plaintiffs obviously would sometimes inefficiently spend to establish h if this would always result in their receiving damages of h and being reimbursed for k, for then they would choose to establish h whenever $h > \bar{h}_c$.[7] These problems of excessive incentives to demonstrate h when doing so always affects damages are again caused by the fact that a party's motive to prove h is unrelated to the associated incentive benefit.

Last, let us consider the case in which injurers choose whether or not to spend c to learn about harm ex ante.

[7] We remark that plaintiffs might not have an excessive incentive to establish h if they have to bear k (which would not be optimal). The reason is that then defendants would be underdeterred. See the preceding version of this article: Louis Kaplow & Steven Shavell, Accuracy in the Assessment of Damages (Working Paper No. 4287, Nat'l Bureau Econ. Res. 1993).

PROPOSITION 5. Suppose that injurers decide whether or not to learn harm h ex ante and that, after an accident, parties choose whether or not to establish h to courts.

(*a*) If it is not socially optimal for injurers to learn h ex ante, then the optimal rule is that given in proposition 3, and injurers will not be induced to learn h.

(*b*) If it is socially optimal for injurers to learn h ex ante, then the optimal rule is that given in proposition 4, and injurers will be induced to learn h.

Part 5(*a*) is obvious, for when damages are unaffected by revealing h, injurers will have no incentive ex ante to obtain information about h or to spend ex post to establish it. Part 5(*b*) is clear, assuming that injurers are led to spend c to learn h when that is socially optimal, for then proposition 4 applies; the proof in the Appendix establishes that injurers will in fact be induced to spend c when that is socially optimal, by reasoning analogous to that given for proposition 2.

III. EXTENSIONS OF THE ANALYSIS

a) Generality of Conclusions. On reflection, it can be seen that our main conclusions apply more generally than to assessments of harm in accidents. Consider the conclusion that it is not socially desirable for resources to be spent informing courts of the magnitude of harm to the degree that harm was unknown to parties when they made their decisions. This conclusion is true also of any elements other than harm (such as facts about causation) unknown to parties when they made their decisions, under any legal rule in any area of law (for instance, under the negligence rule, or under a rule of contract damages). The reason, of course, is that making liability depend on elements not known to parties when they choose their actions cannot affect their behavior. Similarly, the other conclusions—about the effect of considering a factor in assessing damages on parties' incentives to learn about the factor ex ante, and about parties' excessive incentives to present information to courts about such a factor ex post—also hold more generally.

b) Settlement. We assumed in the model that all accidents resulted in trials, but if we were to allow for settlement, the qualitative nature of the conclusions would not be substantially altered. The reasons are twofold. First, the amounts paid in settlement tend to reflect the amounts that would be paid at trial, so that the incentive effects associated with amounts paid in settlement would resemble those associated with amounts paid at trial. Second, settlement, like trial, involves expense. Settlement is achieved through bargaining, voluntary exchange of information, and required disclosure of information (legal discovery). These are costly processes, and the more so when the information of relevance to the parties includes the actual magnitude of harm.[8] Thus, the assumption in the model that parties incur a cost establishing harm to courts is mirrored by the added costs parties incur in the settlement process when courts base damages on accurate assessments of harm.

c) Risk Aversion and Insurance. Defendants' risk aversion is a factor disfavoring accuracy in the determination of harm, for a risk-averse defendant would prefer damages to be based on average harm than to bear the risk of actual harm.[9] Conversely, plaintiffs' risk aversion favors accuracy in determination of harm because this assures compensation equal to losses.[10] The availability of liability and first-party insurance, however, qualifies these points, for insurance coverage protects parties against risk.

It should also be noted that ownership of liability insurance reinforces our point that accurate assessment of harm may not much affect incentives. This is because the level of damages that are imposed in the particular instance will often matter little to a covered party, as his liability insurer will pay most or all of a court award.

d) The Effect of Injurers' Precautions on the Magnitude of Harm. We assumed in the model that an injurer's precautions affected only the likelihood of harm, but they might also influence the magnitude of harm by shifting downward the probability distribution of harm, as in Kathryn Spier's article.[11] If that is so, then determining harm accurately has social value even when injurers do not have foreknowledge of a victim's type.

Specifically, suppose that courts do not determine actual harm and

[8] See Lucian Bebchuk, Litigation and Settlement under Imperfect Information, 15 Rand J. Econ. 404 (1984), for a model of settlement with asymmetric information; see Steven Shavell, Sharing of Information prior to Settlement or Litigation, 20 Rand J. Econ. 183 (1989), for a model in which information that is initially asymmetric is shared, or disclosed under discovery, and in which parties then frequently settle; and see also Bruce Hay, Civil Discovery: Its Effects and Optimal Scope, 23 J. Legal Stud. 481 (1994), on discovery. See, in addition, Kathryn Spier, Settlement Bargaining and the Design of Damage Awards, 10 J. L., Econ., & Org. 84 (1994), for a model in which settlement becomes less likely when damages are based on accurate assessment of harm because this introduces an added element about which there can be asymmetric information.

[9] Uninsured risk-averse defendants would take lower precautions if damages equalled average harm rather than actual harm because the prospect of causing an accident involves lower risk-bearing costs. Such a reduction in precautions, however, would tend to be efficient because defendants' risk-bearing costs are social costs. Compare the discussion of defendants' prospective litigation costs in note 5 above.

[10] This statement applies if harm is monetary. If a component of harm (such as pain and suffering) is not monetary and does not affect the marginal utility of wealth, then risk-averse plaintiffs as well as defendants will prefer damages for that component to be based on average harm.

[11] See Spier, *supra* note 8.

instead set damages equal to average harm. Then an injurer will know that the level of damages he will pay if an accident occurs will be a constant and will not be affected by his level of precautions—even though the distribution of harm will be lower the higher the level of precautions. Thus, injurers will have inadequate incentives to exercise precautions. (They will consider only the reduction in the probability of harm, but not the reduction in its magnitude, conditional on harm occurring.) By contrast, if courts accurately determine harm, injurers will know that the damages they pay, if accidents occur, will tend to be lower the greater the level of precautions they exercise, so injurers' incentives to take precautions will be optimal.

Note, however, that complete accuracy in the determination of harm is unnecessary: as long as courts' estimates are unbiased (given the injurers' level of precaution), incentives will be optimal. Suppose that courts' estimates of average harm are derived from a simple description of an accident (which would contain some information about the severity of injury). Then injurers who take greater precautions will expect to pay lower damages and thus will have appropriate incentives to take precautions. Greater accuracy will produce little if any additional benefit.[12]

e) Quality of Information. Although we assumed in the model that parties and the courts either possessed no information about harm—they knew only its probability density *f*—or possessed or acquired perfect information, the model can be interpreted more broadly. The "ignorant" state of knowledge can reflect real knowledge of harm: *f* can describe the distribution of losses for any class of accidents, however narrow (such as mistaken releases of a specific pollutant into the atmosphere). At the same time, the "perfectly informed" state of knowledge can be less than perfect: *h* can be reinterpreted as the mean of *h* conditional on receipt of information about *h* (such as the expected harm given the quantity of the pollutant that escaped), rather than as the true *h* (the actual losses caused by the pollutant), without any effect on our analysis.

[12] Assume, for example, that there are two types of harm—minor injury and long-term disability—and that the magnitude of each type of harm varies among victims. Assume too that precautions not only reduce the probability of accidents but also make it less likely that harm will be of the more serious type. Finally, assume that injurers do not know, ex ante, anything about a particular potential victim. Now a court's immediate observation about an accident would include the type of harm, even though substantial additional expenditure might be required to determine a particular victim's harm. Using only the courts' initial estimate of harm would be sufficient to induce injurers to take optimal care (conditional on the information they possess ex ante): the damage award for each type of harm would be an unbiased estimate of harm given that type, and injurers only know the likelihood of each type of harm ex ante and the distribution of harms for each type, not the actual harm a particular victim would suffer.

f) Courts' Information. We supposed for simplicity in the model that courts knew the probability density f of harm at the outset. Another assumption, which is often realistic, is that courts do not know f, but when harm occurs, courts costlessly observe certain characteristics z of the harm (for example, that a car of a certain type was demolished, that a person of a certain age was killed). The court then has two options. First, it may set damages equal to the mean harm, conditional on these characteristics, denoted by $\bar{h}(z)$. Second, it may hear evidence sufficient to allow it to determine the actual level of harm. This would require an expenditure of k.

Under this alternative assumption, the essential nature of our results would be unchanged. Where we had said that courts should set damages equal to $\bar{h}$, we now say that courts should set damages equal to $\bar{h}(z)$. Consider, for example, Proposition 1(a), dealing with the case where injurers do not know harm ex ante. Our claim now is that courts should not observe h and should set damages equal to $\bar{h}(z)$. When this is done, the expected liability of injurers will again be $\bar{h}$ because the mean of $\bar{h}(z)$ equals $\bar{h}$. As a result, injurers will behave just as they would if damages were $\bar{h}$.[13]

IV. Discussion

The most immediate implications of our analysis can be well illustrated by considering the assessment of damages in a familiar and important context—automobile accident cases. Typically, a person who is injured in an automobile accident will gather and present evidence from a variety of sources, notably, from medical experts and from labor market specialists on forgone earnings. The defendant in response will seek to counter the plaintiff's assertions about his losses. The parties' expenditures are likely to be substantial because either will spend a dollar whenever it is expected to alter expected damages by more than a dollar in his favor. Thus, if the stakes in an accident were in the neighborhood of, say, \$100,000, each side might well expend \$20,000 contesting damages.[14]

Yet, as our analysis suggests, the prospect of such spending on proof of damages in automobile accidents is unlikely to influence drivers' incen-

[13] Consider also proposition 1(b), dealing with the case where injurers know harm ex ante. It is clear that, again, it will be optimal for the courts to observe h if the cost k is sufficiently low because, if the courts use $\bar{h}(z)$, injurers' incentives to take precautions will be less desirable than if courts use h. (However, injurers' incentives to take precautions will be superior when courts use $\bar{h}(z)$ than when courts use $\bar{h}$. Hence, k must be lower now for it to be worthwhile for the courts to observe h than in the model we studied.)

[14] Moreover, as we noted in Section IIIb above, the parties might find it rational to spend significantly on establishing damages prior to settlement.

tives toward safety. When choosing his level of precautions—how fast to drive, whether to go home by taxi after indulging—a driver cannot predict the *particular* level of harm he would cause in an accident—whether the victim will be a bricklayer or a doctor, whether the victim's injuries will be minor, include broken bones, or result in death. Rather, a driver's prior knowledge will be only vague and approximate.

It follows that resources could be saved without compromising incentives by circumscribing the damage assessment process. Now in our analysis, we had assumed that courts know the average harm and use this as the quantum of damages. But it is unnecessary for courts to know average harm. At the outset of a case, courts will possess, essentially free of cost, a simple physical description of the plaintiff's injury—for instance, that a 35-year-old person suffered a broken leg. If damages are based on this description—if damages equal expected harm conditional on this description—then injurers' expected liability will equal average harm, so their incentives toward safety will be the same as if damages equal average harm. (This was the point that we discussed in Section III*f*.)

How can courts constrain the use of resources on damage assessment? One approach is for courts to impose restrictions on parties' litigation effort devoted to demonstrating damages. For example, the number of testifying experts could be limited. Such steps are quite plausible: judges are routinely involved in controlling the intensity of litigation, and recent procedural reforms are designed to curtail litigation efforts generally. As long as restrictions do not generate systematic biases in damage awards, they should not have any effect on drivers' incentives.

Another approach, and a radical departure from practice, is to eliminate the damage assessment process and replace it with the use of damage tables.[15] Each entry in a damage table would equal the mean loss for a specific, physically described injury (such as for a broken arm).[16] In such

[15] Although the use of damage tables would be a radical departure from practice *in the courts*, it is of course true that various statutory compensation systems, such as the workers' compensation system, employ damage tables to determine awards. For an analysis of the adequacy of workers' compensation damage payments, see Patricia M. Danzon, The Political Economy of Workers' Compensation: Lessons for Product Liability, 78 Am. Econ. Ass'n Papers & Proc. 305 (1988).

[16] If the table were biased, injurers' incentives would not be optimal. Any biases would have to be compared to those arising with jury awards that may reflect sympathies for parties and other extraneous factors. Indeed, some have advocated damage tables in large part because of a belief that the tables would be less biased than jury awards are today. See, for example, Albert W. Alschuler, Mediation with a Mugger: The Shortage of Adjudicative Services and the Need for a Two-Tier Trial System in Civil Cases, 99 Harv. L. Rev. 1808 (1986); and Frederick S. Levin, Pain and Suffering Guidelines: A Cure for Damages Measurement "Anomie," 22 Univ. Mich. J. L. Reform 303 (1989). For a discussion of methods for constructing damage schedules and of difficulties that may be encountered in so doing, see Randall R. Bovbjerg, Frank A. Sloan, & James F. Blumstein, Valuing Life and Limb in Tort: Scheduling "Pain and Suffering," 83 Nw. U. L. Rev. 908 (1989).

a system, it is apparent that, as just stated, a driver's incentives would indeed be no different from what they are in today's regime: a driver would say to himself, "I cannot forecast the kind of accident and the injuries that I may cause, but I do know that if I am found liable, damages will be based on a physical description of the injuries together with a table giving average losses for those injuries." It is plain, we think, that this driver would behave in much the same way he would if he anticipated that losses would be calculated to the last penny.[17]

The potential appeal that we see in restricting litigation effort or in using damage tables is what others have long stressed as their virtue: the achievement of cost savings. But prior discussions have largely ignored the question of whether changing the process of damage assessment might detrimentally influence injurers' behavior.[18] What we add to prior work, therefore, is the point that simplified damage assessment would not distort injurers' behavior when, as we believe to be true in the context of driving, injurers' foreknowledge of harm is ordinarily less precise than what courts would immediately observe about harm after an accident.[19]

We hasten to say, however, that in many contexts substantial regulation of parties' efforts to establish damages or the use of damage tables will be undesirable because injurers' ex ante perceptions of harm will be more accurate than courts' initial estimates. Consider a situation where a builder might cause a delay in completing a commercial building. Here the builder would often have a fair understanding of the cost of delay (or could inquire about it). Damage tables based on general averages of loss for construction delay would tend to be less accurate than the builder's prior estimate. Accordingly, the use of tables, or of only cursorily considered losses, to arrive at damages would influence contract breach behavior relative to a reasonably full consideration of losses. For example, when losses are known to be higher than in the tables, breach would be too frequent. (To be sure, such inefficient breach is often avoidable through the use of liquidated damage provisions or through bargaining before breach.)

[17] For qualifications concerning litigation costs and risk aversion, see notes 5 and 9 above.

[18] For example, the commentary to the recently implemented amendments to the Federal Rules of Civil Procedure does not discuss the effect of litigation on injurers' behavior, either in suggesting the rationale for various limits or in offering guidance to judges in exercising their discretion. The literature on damage tables is somewhat more attentive to injurers' behavior. It sometimes suggests that behavior would be improved because the tables would *more* accurately measure harm than present jury awards; see note 16 *supra*. This contrasts with our point about damage tables: we assume that damage tables will be *less* accurate than present jury awards and emphasize that, even so, injurers' behavior will not be detrimentally affected.

[19] Our analysis also adds to the literature because of its relevance to the design of damage tables: it raises questions about the social value of highly detailed tables and of permitting parties to prove that their losses are different from those in the tables.

Thus, there are circumstances where the magnitude of losses can be well anticipated by potential injurers and, consequently, where our analysis implies that accuracy in estimating damages would improve incentives. Nonetheless, the reader will recall that we showed that parties may still have an excessive incentive to spend to show damages, so that some restrictions on their efforts may be warranted.[20]

Last, we should say that constraining the ability of litigants to prove damages, whether through use of tables or through limitations on their expenditures, is likely to be met with the objection that victims will be compensated less accurately. It is true, as we noted in Section III*c*, that imprecise matching of damage payments to victims' losses represents a social cost when victims are risk-averse and are not insured.[21] But it can be demonstrated that, even if the sole function of liability were to compensate uninsured, risk-averse victims, their incentives to establish harm in adjudication would be excessive.[22] Moreover, the relevance of victims' risk aversion is attenuated by the fact that ownership of insurance is widespread.[23]

APPENDIX

Proof of Proposition 1. (*a*) If courts do not observe h, then a single level of damages d applies to all injurers, and each injurer chooses x to minimize

$$x + p(x)d, \tag{A1}$$

so all choose $x^*(d)$. Social costs are given by

$$\int_0^\infty [x^*(d) + p(x^*(d))h]f(h)dh = x^*(d) + p(x^*(d))\bar{h}. \tag{A2}$$

[20] This is always true with regard to proof beyond what injurers could have anticipated, and our analysis demonstrates that it may be true even when injurers accurately anticipate harm.

[21] We also noted that more accurate compensation of victims means that more risk is imposed on injurers, which lowers social welfare to the extent that injurers are risk-averse and do not possess liability insurance.

[22] This is because, after a victim has suffered a loss, his incentive to spend to demonstrate the level of his losses is quite strong: he will spend up to a dollar to increase his coverage by a dollar. (And defendants' incentives to reduce liability are similar.) Yet such post-loss expenditure exceeds that which can be justified on grounds of risk reduction. See, generally, Louis Kaplow, Optimal Insurance Contracts When Establishing the Amount of Losses Is Costly, 19 Geneva Papers on Risk & Ins. Theory 139 (1994), on excessive incentives of insureds to establish their losses to an insurer.

[23] An implication of the discussion in this paragraph is that accuracy in estimating loss is more important for purposes of insurance than for the liability system (when injurers lack precise ex ante information about loss). Yet the liability system employs more expensive means of assessing damages than is typical in consensual first-party insurance contracts (where simple appraisal schemes and binding arbitration are common).

As (A2) is minimized when $d = \bar{h}$, $\bar{h}$ is the optimal level of damages, and social costs are

$$x^*(\bar{h}) + p(x^*(\bar{h}))\bar{h}. \tag{A3}$$

If courts observe h and $d = h$ (which will be shown to be an optimal choice of d), then because injurers do not know what h will be, they will choose x to minimize

$$x + p(x)\int_0^\infty (h + k)f(h)\,dh = x + p(x)(\bar{h} + k), \tag{A4}$$

so they will choose $x^*(\bar{h} + k)$, and social costs will be

$$x^*(\bar{h} + k) + p(x^*(\bar{h} + k))(\bar{h} + k). \tag{A5}$$

It follows also that $d = h$ must be an optimum when h is observed, for when injurers do not know h ex ante and thus all choose the same x, (A4) gives social costs, which are minimized when x is $x^*(\bar{h} + k)$.[24] Because (A5) exceeds (A3) for any positive k, we have established 1(a).

(b) In this case, if courts do not observe h, injurers will behave as they did in the previous case, so optimal damages will again be $\bar{h}$, and (A3) will again give social costs.

If courts observe h and $d = h$ (which will be shown to be optimal), then a party of type h minimizes $x + p(x)(h + k)$ because he will pay damages of h and bear costs of k if there is an accident. Hence, he will select $x^*(h + k)$. Because this choice of x is optimal given the assumption that h is observed, it is optimal for damages to equal h. Social costs in this situation are

$$\int_0^\infty [x^*(h + k) + p(x^*(h + k))(h + k)]f(h)\,dh. \tag{A6}$$

The difference in social costs between the situations where h is not observed and when it is observed is (A3) minus (A6):

$$x^*(\bar{h}) + p(x^*(\bar{h}))\bar{h} - \int_0^\infty [x^*(h + k) + p(x^*(h + k))(h + k)]f(h)\,dh. \tag{A7}$$

When $k = 0$, (A7) equals

$$\int_0^\infty \{[x^*(\bar{h}) + p(x^*(\bar{h}))h] - [x^*(h) + p(x^*(h))h]\}f(h)\,dh, \tag{A8}$$

which is positive because for every h other than $\bar{h}$, $x^*(h)$ differs from $x^*(\bar{h})$—the optimal level of precaution exceeds (is less than) $x^*(\bar{h})$ when h exceeds (is less than) $\bar{h}$. In addition, it is clear that (A7) is decreasing in k because, as k increases, (A6) rises; also, (A7) is negative for all k that are sufficiently large.[25] It follows that there is a critical $k^* > 0$ such that $k < k^*$ implies that it is socially desirable to observe h and such that $k > k^*$ implies that it is not socially worthwhile to observe h.

Proof of Proposition 2. We need to complete the proof of part 2(b). To deter-

[24] Of course, $d = \bar{h}$ for all h is also an optimum.

[25] If $k \geq \bar{h}$, then the integrand in (A7) exceeds $x^*(\bar{h}) + p(x^*(\bar{h}))\bar{h}$ for all positive h, so (A7) must be negative for such k.

mine whether it is socially optimal for injurers to learn h, note that, if injurers do not observe h ex ante, minimum social cost is (A3) by proposition 1(a), and if injurers do observe h ex ante, minimum social cost is (A6) plus c, by proposition 1(b). Hence, it is socially optimal for injurers to learn h if and only if

$$x^*(\bar{h}) + p(x^*(\bar{h}))\bar{h} - \left\{c + \int_0^\infty [x^*(h+k) + p(x^*(h+k))(h+k)]f(h)dh\right\} > 0. \tag{A9}$$

(This will hold if c and k are sufficiently low.)

We need to show that when (A9) holds, injurers will be induced to learn h if $d = h$. If an injurer does not learn h ex ante, he will choose x to minimize

$$x + p(x)\int_0^\infty (h+k)f(h)dh = x + p(x)(\bar{h}+k), \tag{A10}$$

so that his costs will be $x^*(\bar{h}+k) + p(x^*(\bar{h}+k))(\bar{h}+k)$. If an injurer does learn h ex ante, his costs will be (A6) plus c. Hence, an injurer will be led to learn h if

$$c \le [x^*(\bar{h}+k) + p(x^*(\bar{h}+k))(\bar{h}+k)] - \int_0^\infty [x^*(h+k) + p(x^*(h+k))(h+k)]f(h)dh. \tag{A11}$$

We want to show that (A9) implies (A11). But this follows because

$$x^*(\bar{h}) + p(x^*(\bar{h}))\bar{h} < x^*(\bar{h}+k) + p(x^*(\bar{h}+k))(\bar{h}+k).$$

Proof of Proposition 3. The remarks in the text constitute a proof.

Proof of Proposition 4. To prove that the optimal rule is as claimed, consider the problem of a dictator whose goal is to minimize social costs and who can command parties whether or not to spend k to reveal h to courts (but who cannot command levels of precaution). The level of social costs achievable by the dictator will clearly be at least as low as under the optimal rule. We will determine the optimal solution to the dictator's problem and then show that this solution can be sustained under the rule described in the proposition. Thus, that rule must be optimal.

Let S be the optimal set of h where individuals are ordered by the dictator to be silent about h, and let R be the optimal set of h where individuals are made to reveal h. We assume for convenience that each set is a union of nondegenerate intervals.[26] It is evident (by the logic in proposition 1(a)) that for h in S, the optimal x for defendants to choose is $x^*(\bar{h}_c)$, where $\bar{h}_c$ is the conditional mean of h in S; this x will be chosen if $d = \bar{h}_c$. It is apparent also that for h in R, it is optimal for defendants to choose $x^*(h+k)$; this will occur if a defendant's expenses are $h + k$, that is, if $d = h$ and defendants bear k.

Let us assume provisionally that S is not empty (we will prove this below), so

[26] If we did not make this assumption, then in particular we would have to concern ourselves with the fact that the optimal R and S are not unique with respect to isolated points; any number of isolated points can be assigned to either R or S without affecting social cost, as the integral over isolated points is zero.

that $\bar{h}_c$ exists, and let us characterize the form of S. Let h_1 be the supremum of h in R that are less than $\bar{h}_c$. We claim that any $h < h_1$ is in R. Now for any h in R, we know that

$$x^*(h + k) + p(x^*(h + k))(h + k) \leq x^*(\bar{h}_c) + p(x^*(\bar{h}_c))h. \quad \text{(A12)}$$

That is, expected costs are lower (or equal) if a party reports harm than if he does not. It follows that

$$x^*(h_1 + k) + p(x^*(h_1 + k))(h_1 + k) \leq x^*(\bar{h}_c) + p(x^*(\bar{h}_c))h_1. \quad \text{(A13)}$$

Inequality (A13) implies that $h_1 + k \leq \bar{h}_c$: otherwise,

$$\begin{aligned} x^*(h_1 + k) + p(x^*(h_1 + k))(h_1 + k) &> x^*(\bar{h}_c) + p(x^*(\bar{h}_c))\bar{h}_c \\ &\geq x^*(\bar{h}_c) + p(x^*(\bar{h}_c))h_1, \end{aligned} \quad \text{(A14)}$$

which contradicts (A13). Hence, $p(x^*(h_1 + k)) \geq p(x^*(\bar{h}_c))$, so that

$$p(x^*(h_1 + k))(h_1 - h) \geq p(x^*(\bar{h}_c))(h_1 - h)$$

for $h < h_1$. The latter inequality and (A13) imply that, for $h < h_1$,

$$x^*(h_1 + k) + p(x^*(h_1 + k))(h + k) \leq x^*(\bar{h}_c) + p(x^*(\bar{h}_c))h. \quad \text{(A15)}$$

But, for $h < h_1$,

$$x^*(h + k) + p(x^*(h + k))(h + k) < x^*(h_1 + k) + p(x^*(h_1 + k))(h + k). \quad \text{(A16)}$$

This and (A15) imply

$$x^*(h + k) + p(x^*(h + k))(h + k) < x^*(\bar{h}_c) + p(x^*(\bar{h}_c))h. \quad \text{(A17)}$$

Hence, for $h < h_1$, it is better for a party to report h than not; h is in R, as claimed. A parallel argument shows that, if h_2 is defined as the infimum of h in R that are greater than $\bar{h}_c$, then all $h > h_2$ are in R. Thus, we know that S consists of the interval $[h_1, h_2]$.

Because S is optimal, h_1 and h_2 must be selected to minimize social costs. Social costs as a function of h_1 and h_2 are given by

$$\begin{aligned} &\int_0^{h_1} [x^*(h + k) + p(x^*(h + k))(h + k)]f(h)dh \\ &\quad + \int_{h_1}^{h_2} [x^*(\bar{h}_c) + p(x^*(\bar{h}_c))h]f(h)dh \\ &+ \int_{h_2}^{\infty} [x^*(h + k) + p(x^*(h + k))(h + k)]f(h)dh. \end{aligned} \quad \text{(A18)}$$

The derivative of (A18) with respect to h_1 is

$$\{[x^*(h_1 + k) + p(x^*(h_1 + k))(h_1 + k)] - [x^*(\bar{h}_c) + p(x^*(\bar{h}_c))h_1]\}f(h_1). \quad \text{(A19)}$$

For $h_1 \geq \bar{h}_c - k$, (A19) is negative, as demonstrated in (A14). Therefore, $h_1 < \bar{h}_c - k$, assuming such an h_1 is feasible (otherwise, $h_1 = 0$). The derivative of (A18) with respect to h_2 is

$$\{[x^*(\bar{h}_c) + p(x^*(\bar{h}_c))h_2] - [x^*(h_2 + k) + p(x^*(h_2 + k))(h_2 + k)]\}f(h_2). \quad \text{(A20)}$$

At $h_2 = \bar{h}_c$, this is negative, because

$$x^*(\bar{h}_c) + p(x^*(\bar{h}_c))\bar{h}_c < x^*(\bar{h}_c + k) + p(x^*(\bar{h}_c + k))(\bar{h}_c + k). \quad \text{(A21)}$$

Hence, $h_2 > \bar{h}_c$.

It remains to show that S is not empty. If this is not true—that is, if R equals the set of all positive h—select any positive h and denote it by h_1. Then social costs will be lowered if parties are silent and pay h_1 whenever h falls in some small nondegenerate interval $[h_1, h_2]$.[27] This contradicts the supposed optimality of R.

We have now proved that the optimal rule for the dictator is characterized as follows: there is an interval $[h_1, h_2]$, where $h_1 < \bar{h}_c - k$ and $h_2 > \bar{h}_c$, on which parties do not report h and pay damages of $\bar{h}_c$; outside the interval, parties report h, pay damages of h, and defendants bear k. It is clear (and was explained after the proposition) that under the rule of the proposition, with this $[h_1, h_2]$, parties behave as the dictator would want. Thus, as stated at the outset, because the rule in the proposition implements the dictator's optimal scheme, the rule in the proposition must be optimal.

Proof of Proposition 5. From the notes following the proposition, it is clear that it suffices to show that if it is optimal for injurers to spend c to learn h ex ante, they will be led to do this under the rule specified in proposition 4.

If injurers do not learn h ex ante, minimum social costs will be (A3), and if injurers do learn h, minimum social costs will be

$$\begin{aligned} &\int_0^{h_1} [x^*(h + k) + p(x^*(h + k))(h + k)]f(h)dh \\ &\quad + \int_{h_1}^{h_2} [x^*(\bar{h}_c) + p(x^*(\bar{h}_c))h]f(h)dh \qquad \text{(A22)} \\ &+ \int_{h_2}^{\infty} [x^*(h + k) + p(x^*(h + k))(h + k)]f(h)dh + c, \end{aligned}$$

where $[h_1, h_2]$ is the optimal interval. Thus, it is socially desirable for injurers to learn h if (A22) is less than (A3).

Now let us show that when (A22) is less than (A3), injurers will in fact learn h, provided that the rule in proposition 4 applies. Given that this rule applies, if injurers do not learn h, they will choose x to minimize

$$\begin{aligned} &\int_0^{h_1} [x + p(x)(h + k)]f(h)dh + \int_{h_1}^{h_2} [x + p(x)h]f(h)dh \qquad \text{(A23)} \\ &\quad + \int_{h_2}^{\infty} [x + p(x)(h + k)]f(h)dh. \end{aligned}$$

If injurers do learn h, their expected costs will be given by (A22). Thus, they will learn h if (A22) is less than (A23). But (A23) exceeds (A3) because (A3) is the minimum value of

[27] Social costs will be given by (A18), but with the integrand in the second integral $x^*(h_1) + p(x^*(h_1))h$. The derivative of this with respect to h_2 is $\{[x^*(h_1) + p(x^*(h_1))h_2] - [x^*(h_2 + k) + p(x^*(h_2 + k))(h_2 + k)]\}$. At $h_2 = h_1$, the derivative is negative, so that social costs are lower for some $h_2 > h_1$.

$$\int_0^\infty [x + p(x)h]f(h)dh. \tag{A24}$$

Hence, when (A22) is less than (A3), (A22) will also be less than (A23), and injurers will decide to learn h ex ante.

Bibliography

Alschuler, Albert W. "Mediation with a Mugger: The Shortage of Adjudicative Services and the Need for a Two-Tier Trial System in Civil Cases." *Harvard Law Review* 99 (1986): 1808–59.

Bebchuk, Lucian Arye. "Litigation and Settlement under Imperfect Information." *Rand Journal of Economics* 15 (1984): 404–15.

Bovbjerg, Randall R.; Sloan, Frank A.; and Blumstein, James F. "Valuing Life and Limb in Tort: Scheduling 'Pain and Suffering.'" *Northwestern University Law Review* 83 (1989): 908–76.

Brown, John Prather. "Toward an Economic Theory of Liability." *Journal of Legal Studies* 2 (1973): 323–49.

Craswell, Richard, and Calfee, John E. "Deterrence and Uncertain Legal Standards." *Journal of Law, Economics, and Organization* 2 (1986): 279–303.

Danzon, Patricia M. "The Political Economy of Workers' Compensation: Lessons for Product Liability." *American Economic Association Papers and Proceedings* 78 (1988): 305–10.

Hay, Bruce L. "Civil Discovery: Its Effects and Optimal Scope." *Journal of Legal Studies* 23 (1994): 481–515.

Kaplow, Louis. "The Value of Accuracy in Adjudication: An Economic Analysis." *Journal of Legal Studies* 23 (1994): 307–401.

Kaplow, Louis. "Optimal Insurance Contracts When Establishing the Amount of Losses Is Costly." *Geneva Papers on Risk and Insurance Theory* 19 (1994): 139–52.

Kaplow, Louis. "A Model of the Optimal Complexity of Legal Rules." *Journal of Law, Economics, and Organization* 11 (1995): 150–63.

Kaplow, Louis, and Shavell, Steven. "Private versus Socially Optimal Provision of Ex Ante Legal Advice." *Journal of Law, Economics, and Organization* 8 (1992): 306–20.

Kaplow, Louis, and Shavell, Steven. "Accuracy in the Assessment of Damages." Working Paper No. 4287. Cambridge, Mass.: National Bureau of Economic Research, 1993.

Kaplow, Louis, and Shavell, Steven. "Accuracy in the Determination of Liability." *Journal of Law and Economics* 37 (1994): 1–15.

Landes, William M., and Posner, Richard A. *The Economic Structure of Tort Law*. Cambridge, Mass.: Harvard University Press, 1987.

Levin, Frederick S. "Pain and Suffering Guidelines: A Cure for Damages Measurement 'Anomie.'" *University of Michigan Journal of Law Reform* 22 (1989): 303–32.

Polinsky, A. Mitchell, and Shavell, Steven. "Legal Error, Litigation, and the

Incentive to Obey the Law." *Journal of Law, Economics, and Organization* 5 (1989): 99–108.

Posner, Richard A. "An Economic Approach to Legal Procedure and Judicial Administration." *Journal of Legal Studies* 2 (1973): 399–458.

Png, I. P. L. "Optimal Subsidies and Damages in the Presence of Judicial Error." *International Review of Law and Economics* 6 (1986): 101–5.

Rubinfeld, Daniel L., and Sappington, David E. M. "Efficient Awards and Standards of Proof in Judicial Proceedings." *Rand Journal of Economics* 18 (1987): 308–15.

Shavell, Steven. *Economic Analysis of Accident Law*. Cambridge, Mass.: Harvard University Press, 1987.

Shavell, Steven. "Sharing of Information prior to Settlement or Litigation." *Rand Journal of Economics* 20 (1989): 183–95.

Spier, Kathryn. "Settlement Bargaining and the Design of Damage Awards." *Journal of Law, Economics, and Organization* 10 (1994): 84–95.

[8]

Settlement Bargaining and the Design of Damage Awards

Kathryn E. Spier
Harvard University

An injurer undertakes precautions to reduce both the probability and the severity of an accident. The damages that the victim suffers are privately observed, and will be verified at a cost if the case is litigated. While finely tuned damage awards induce the injurer to take appropriate precautions ex ante, they increase the probability that the litigants will disagree about the case, and thereby aggravate the settlement process. Flat damage awards reduce the level of costly litigation, but lead to underinvestment in precautions. We show that when the litigation costs are small the optimal award is finely tuned to the actual damages, and when litigation costs are large the optimal award is a flat penalty. Applications to scheduled damages and workers' compensation are discussed.

1. Introduction

While deterrence has been the primary focus in economic analyses of optimal damage awards, administrative and procedural issues are often at the center of the debate over legal reform. Since the court dockets are overflowing with lawsuits, all else equal, litigants should be encouraged to resolve their disputes privately through out-of-court settlement. This article explores an inherent tension between the social objectives of ex ante deterrence and ex post administrative efficiency. Although finely tuned awards may provide individuals with strong incentives to take appropriate actions ex ante, they may also increase the probability that the litigants will disagree about the case, and thereby aggravate the dispute resolution process. If the costs of litigation are large, then a simple flat award may outperform a finely tuned one.[1]

In the formal model, the injurer undertakes (unobservable) precautions to reduce both the probability and the severity of an accident. The damages that

I would like to thank James Dana, Louis Kaplow, Bruce Kobayashi, Andrew Newman, A. Mitchell Polinsky, Alan Schwartz, Steven Shavell, and the referees for helpful comments. Financial support from the Olin Foundation is gratefully acknowledged.

1. A finely tuned award is based upon the actual level of harm sustained by the victim, while a flat award is insensitive to the underlying harm. Asymmetric information between the litigants concerning the state of nature presents an obstacle in the bargaining process when awards are finely tuned.

the victim suffers from an accident (if one occurs) are privately observed by the victim prior to the trial and are verified at a cost if the case is litigated rather than settled. We show that the optimal damage award necessarily takes one of two forms: it is either "finely tuned," equal to the victim's actual damage level, or "flat," equal to the victim's expected damage level.[2] If the court's policy is to base the award upon the victim's actual damages, then in equilibrium the injurer will undertake a desirable level of precautions, but victims with high damages will reject settlement offers and go to trial. The flat damage award reduces the costs of litigation by encouraging cases to settle out of court, but generates underinvestment in precautions. The trade-off is clear: when litigation costs are small, then an award based upon the actual damages is preferred; when litigation costs are large, the flat award is preferred.

One of several applications of this trade-off is the "scheduling" of damages, or standardizing awards for injuries that fall into particular categories.[3] Although this is the typical method of assessing damages for personal injuries and death in Great Britain (Munkman, 1985), judges and juries in the United States are not typically bound by rigid schedules. An interesting exception in the United States is the separation of employer responsibility for job-related injuries from the law of torts. Under state and federal workers' compensation laws, an injured employee is entitled to prompt coverage of medical expenses and a proportion of lost wages under a fixed schedule, while waiving the right to sue the employer for full damages (Darling-Hammond and Kniesner, 1980). For example, the Longshore and Harbor Workers' Compensation Act includes very specific guidelines for determining damages for death, the loss of a limb, etc.[4] Legal scholars have suggested that scheduled damages be applied more widely, especially because the huge variability in jury awards aggravates the settlement process (Bovbjerg et al., 1989; Blumstein et al., 1991).[5]

Previous theoretical studies of legal complexity and the accuracy of damage assessment have largely ignored the settlement process. Rather, they have emphasized the cost to individuals of learning more about the harmfulness of their actions, and the cost of learning information ex post to implement the more complicated rule (Kaplow, 1991; Kaplow and Shavell, 1993, 1994).[6] In our context, the cost of complexity is endogenous: the litigants have the

2. These awards also include adjustments for litigation costs.

3. An application in the criminal context are the federal sentencing guidelines that seek to achieve uniformity in sentencing by limiting judicial discretion (United States Sentencing Commision, 1990: §1A1.2).

4. An important purpose of this act is to "minimize the need for litigation as a means of providing compensation for injured workmen" (33 U.S.C.A. §901 note 7 (1986)).

5. The primary motivation behind no-fault accident insurance is also the saving of administrative costs (Carroll et al., 1991: 2).

6. Among other things, Kaplow and Shavell (1993) consider the incentives of litigants to establish their information in court (at a cost), and show that private incentive to reveal information tends to be too large. In our framework, it is shown that when the costs of litigation are sufficiently large, the private incentive to litigate under a regime that bases the damage aware on the actual level of harm tends to be too large. The court can remedy this by making awards flat.

opportunity to completely avoid the costs of litigation through settlement bargaining.[7] However, information asymmetries when combined with legal complexity present an obstacle to efficient dispute resolution.[8]

This article is not the first to consider the impact of settlement on deterrence. P'ng (1987) explores the impact of strategic settlement negotiations on ex ante behavior under the negligence rule. Polinsky and Rubinfeld (1988) analyze the social desirability of settlement under a strict liability rule, weighing both deterrence properties and administrative costs. While Polinsky and Che (1991) derive optimal awards, they abstract from strategic settlement issues and focus instead on the plaintiff's incentive to bring suit.[9] Here, we explore the relationship between legal complexity and asymmetric information between the litigants prior to the trial, and design optimal damage awards for the court.

The following section presents the formal model and its assumptions. Section 3 characterizes the equilibrium of the pretrial negotiation game. Section 4 characterizes the penalties that maximize social welfare. Concluding remarks follow.

2. The Model

There are two players: an injurer and a victim. The injurer may take precautions (or exert effort) to reduce the probability and severity of an accident: e_1 denotes the level of precautions taken to reduce the probability of an accident, and e_2 denotes the level of precautions taken to reduce the accident's severity.[10] Both e_1 and e_2 are constrained to be nonnegative.[11] The injurer's cost of

7. Unlike in the previous literature, the litigation costs are not assumed to be larger for finely tuned awards. If settlements were impossible in our framework, then finely tuned awards would always be preferred to flat awards.

8. Similar issues are explored in a contractual framework by Spier (1992b). Incompleteness in the contractual framework is analogous to flat damage awards in the tort framework.

9. In Polinsky and Che's model, holding the plaintiff's award fixed, as the plaintiff's litigation cost rises, his incentive to bring suit falls. Although this has adverse consequences for deterrence, raising the defendant's liability can align the private and social incentives to sue. Here, when the cost of litigation is sufficiently large, tying the award to the actual level of harm induces too large an incentive to litigate. Flattening the awards structure aligns the private and social incentives to settle.

10. Anti-lock brakes in automobiles, for example, may serve to reduce the likelihood of an accident. Airbags, on the other hand, serve to reduce the severity of the harm, conditional upon an accident occurring. In a factory, workplace rules may create a safer environment where accidents are less likely to occur, while certain safety devices on the machines (off switches, for example) may reduce the average level of harm in the event of a mishap.

11. This specification is related to Hölmstrom and Milgrom's (1991) analysis of multitask principal–agent problems, and to Shavell's (1987) analysis where the injurer chooses an activity level and a level of care to reduce the damages of an accident. Similar results would be obtained in Shavell's framework.

An alternative specification would consider a single effort decision that simultaneously influences the likelihood and severity of an accident. In such a model, a flat award could induce the socially optimal level of effort. However, if the marginal impact of effort on the probability of an accident is extremely small, then the optimal flat award would have to be extremely large in order

taking these precautions is a differentiable function $C(e_1,e_2)$, and we let $C_i(e_1,e_2)$ denote the partial derivative with respect to e_i. We assume that $C_i(e_1,e_2)$ is strictly positive for all e_1 and e_2 (so the injurer incurs greater costs when he takes more precautions) and that $C_1(0,e_2)$ and $C_2(e_1,0)$ are finite. Although the levels of precautions are known to the injurer and possibly the victim, they are not verifiable in a court of law.[12] Consequently, we do not consider negligence rules where the award may be conditioned directly upon the injurer's precautions.[13] We do allow the award to be sensitive to the victim's damages, which serves as a signal of the injurer's care.

The accident may be mild, causing a low level of harm $x_L > 0$ to the victim, or severe, causing a high level of harm $x_H > x_L$. The probability of an accident, $\pi(e_1) \in (0,1]$, is differentiable and decreasing in e_1. A higher level of Type 1 precautions reduces the probability of an accident but cannot eliminate the possibility entirely. If an accident occurs, the conditional probability that the accident is mild is denoted $p_L(e_2)$ and the conditional probability that it is severe is denoted $p_H(e_2)$, where $p_L(e_2) + p_H(e_2) = 1$. These functions are differentiable and satisfy $p_L'(e_2) > 0$ and $p_H'(e_2) = -p_L'(e_2) < 0$. In other words, a higher level of Type 2 precautions corresponds to a lower conditional probability of a severe accident, and a higher conditional probability of a mild accident. Finally, for technical reasons, we assume that $\pi'(0) = p_H'(0) = -\infty$.[14] The first-best outcome cannot be obtained in this model through a flat damage award because such a rule would not induce the injurer to undertake severity-reducing precautions, e_2.[15] The "best" flat award would lead to underinvestment in e_2 while inducing a more appropriate level of e_1.

Although occurrence of an accident is assumed to be observable to both the victim and the injurer, the level of harm is not. The victim privately observes her damages, $x \in \{x_L,x_H\}$, while the injurer must rely on his prior beliefs (which are conditioned upon his effort level). The court is assumed to be able to observe and verify both the occurrence of an accident and the level of damages; however, use of the court is costly for the litigants.

---

to encourage efficient precaution taking. If the injurer has limited wealth, then efficiency would be unattainable with a flat damage award and a finely tuned damage award would be valuable. This alternative specification would yield similar results to those presented here.

12. In our context, it does not matter whether the victim observes the injurer's precautions or not. As will be apparent later, the victim's decision to accept a settlement offer depends only on his damages and not upon the injurer's precautions.

13. Cooter (1984, 1991) has argued that negligence rules are undesirable when it is costly to evaluate precautions in a court of law. It is in this spirit that we focus on strict liability rules. Nevertheless, the insights developed here are readily applicable to negligence regimes. If the injurer has private information about his level of care, then awards that are based upon his care level are more likely to lead to costly disputes.

14. This, combined with the boundedness of $C_i(e_1,e_2)$, $i = 1, 2$, is sufficient to guarantee an interior solution for e_1 and e_2.

15. The best flat award is based on the expected damages of the accident, conditioned upon the court's beliefs about the injurer's precautions. Since the injurer's actual precautions are not observed by the court, a flat damage award cannot provide incentives for reducing the severity of an accident.

After an accident has occurred, the players attempt to resolve their dispute privately through an out-of-court settlement. The negotiations are assumed to take a simple form: the injurer makes a single take-it-or-leave-it offer, s, to the victim. If the offer is accepted, then the game ends; if it is rejected, then the case proceeds to trial.[16] The court verifies the precise value of the victim's harm, and enforces a transfer or award from the injurer to the victim.[17] Since the award may be contingent upon the severity of the accident, we denote the award structure $\langle d_L, d_H \rangle$, where d_L corresponds to the award when damages are low, x_L, and d_H corresponds to the award when damages are high, x_H.[18] To simplify the exposition, we maintain the assumption throughout that $d_L \leq d_H$.[19] Finally, the injurer's private cost of litigation is denoted k_I, and the victim's cost is denoted k_V.[20] The sum of these private costs is given by k.[21]

The court's problem is to choose an award structure $\langle d_L, d_H \rangle$ to maximize social welfare, or equivalently to minimize the social cost (which includes the dangers from the accident, litigation costs, and costs of taking precautions).[22] To construct the optimal awards, we will work backwards. Taking $\langle d_L, d_H \rangle$ and the effort levels as given, Section 3 characterizes the outcome of the pretrial bargaining game. It is shown that whenever $d_L < d_H$, if the costs of litigation are sufficiently small, then there is a separating outcome: the low types settle out of court and the high types go to trial. If the costs are sufficiently large, then a pooling outcome results, in which both types settle. In Section 4 we partition the set of all award structures into two categories: those that ultimately lead to separation in the pretrial bargaining game, and those that lead

16. This timing and informational structure are similar to Bebchuk (1984). Allowing the informed player (the victim) to make a final offer introduces signaling elements (Reinganum and Wilde, 1986) and their associated multiple equilibria. A more complicated model with offers and counteroffers would lead to the same bias in the types of cases that proceed to court. See Spier (1992a) and the surveys of Cooter and Rubinfeld (1989) and Kennan and Wilson (1993).

17. We do not allow the court to dismiss cases at random while applying a multiplier to the damage award for litigated cases. Nor do we allow direct-revelation mechanisms where the litigants are punished if their announcements conflict.

18. A more general specification would allow the victim's damages to be a continuous variable. Then the court would choose a function mapping the victim's actual damage level into an award. Given the structure of the bargaining game, there will be a cutoff where victims with low damages will accept offers and those with high damages will reject offers and litigate. An optimal award structure would induce more settlement than one that fully reflects the victim's damages; in other words, the lower tail of the award distribution would be flatter.

19. This is without loss of generality, for $d_H < d_L$ would never be optimal.

20. The careful reader will notice that we have abstracted from the victim's incentive to bring suit. Assuming that $x_L - k_V \geq 0$ is sufficient to assure that the victim would never want to drop a case prior to trial.

21. The analysis abstracts from the subsidized nature of the court; in reality, there are other costs of maintaining a court system that are not borne by the litigants.

22. The court in our model represents a social planner who is interested in maximizing the welfare of society. In reality, damage schedules are often established by legislatures or government agencies rather than by courts. Nothing in the model would change if the court were interpreted more broadly to include these other bodies.

to pooling. We then characterize the most preferred award structure within each set. A comparison of the two gives the main result.

3. Pretrial Negotiation

Imagine that an accident has occurred and that the victim and injurer are negotiating a settlement in the shadow of a trial. Given the award structure, $\langle d_L, d_H \rangle$, we can represent the victim as one of two "types," d_H or d_L, corresponding to her private information about the court's award. Given a settlement offer, s, rationality dictates that the victim of type d_i will accept if and only if $s \geq d_i - k_V$—that is, if the settlement offer is greater than the amount the victim will receive in court minus her litigation costs.[23] It is easy to verify that only two settlement offers are possible in equilibrium: $d_H - k_V$ or $d_L - k_V$. To see this, imagine that $s > d_H - k_V$. Since both types of victim strictly prefer to accept the offer than go to trial, the injurer's payoff is higher when the offer is slightly reduced. If $s \in (d_L - k_V, d_H - k_V)$, the low-damage type strictly prefers to accept the offer (while the high-damage type prefers to reject the offer and go to trial), and the injurer could certainly increase his payoff by lowering his offer slightly. If $s < d_L - k_V$, neither type accepts. By choosing $s = d_L - k_V$, the injurer induces the low type of victim to accept the offer and saves his own litigation cost, k_I, with probability $p_L(e_2)$.

The injurer's choice of s depends upon d_L and d_H, as well as upon his subjective beliefs about the victim's type, which are conditional upon his own effort level: $p_H(e_2)$ and $p_L(e_2)$. If the injurer sets $s = d_H - k_V$, both types of victim accept and the injurer's payoff is simply $-d_H + k_V$. If $s = d_L - k_V$, the low type accepts and the high type opts for a trial, giving the injurer an expected payoff of $-p_L(e_2)(d_L - k_V) - p_H(e_2)(d_H + k_I)$. Comparing these payoffs, we may easily characterize the optimal strategy for the injurer. When the litigation costs, $k = k_I + k_V$, are small, the injurer prefers to offer $d_L - k_V$, and therefore litigates the case when damages are high. When the costs are small, the benefit to the injurer from discriminating between the two types of victim exceeds the cost. When the litigation costs are sufficiently large, however, the injurer prefers to offer $d_H - k_V$ and settle with both types of victim. The equilibrium of the pretrial bargaining game is summarized in the following lemma:

Lemma 1. Given an award structure $\langle d_L, d_H \rangle$ and an effort level e_2, two types of equilibria can occur following an accident:

(i) If $k_I + k_V < [p_L(e_2)/p_H(e_2)](d_H - d_L)$, then the equilibrium is separating. The injurer offers $s = d_L - k_V$, the low type of victim accepts the offer, and the high type rejects it and goes to trial.

(ii) If $k_I + k_V \geq [p_L(e_2)/p_H(e_2)](d_H - d_L)$, then the equilibrium is pooling. The injurer offers $s = d_H - k_V$ and both types of victim accept the offer.

---

23. When $s = d_i - k_V$, the victim is actually indifferent. We adopt the convention that when indifferent, the victim accepts the offer.

4. Optimal Damage Awards

The injurer's strategy may be represented by the vector (e_1,e_2,s); the injurer chooses precaution levels and a settlement offer to be made in the event of an accident.[24] The result from the previous section allows us to divide the set of all award structures, $\langle d_L,d_H\rangle$, into two categories: those that ultimately lead to separating outcomes in the pretrial bargaining game, and those that ultimately lead to pooling outcomes. Let $D_S(k)$ denote the former set (the subscript indicates "separating") and let $D_P(k)$ denote the latter set (the subscript indicates "pooling").[25]

The social cost associated with any element of $D_S(k)$ is

$$\pi(e_1)[p_L(e_2)x_L + p_H(e_2)(x_H + k_I + k_V)] + C(e_1,e_2).$$

When the accident is mild, the case settles out of court and the social cost includes the damage caused by the accident and the cost of precautions. When the accident is severe, the case is litigated and the litigation costs k_I and k_V are also included in the social cost. The effort levels that minimize the expected social cost, which we denote by $(e_1^\ddagger,e_2^\ddagger)$, must satisfy the first-order conditions:

$$\pi'(e_1^\ddagger)[p_L(e_2^\ddagger)x_L + p_H(e_2^\ddagger)(x_H + k_I + k_V)] + C_1(e_1^\ddagger,e_2^\ddagger) = 0, \tag{1}$$

$$\pi(e_1^\ddagger)[p_L'(e_2^\ddagger)x_L + p_H'(e_2^\ddagger)(x_H + k_I + k_V)] + C_2(e_1^\ddagger,e_2^\ddagger) = 0. \tag{2}$$

Generally speaking, the precautions chosen by the injurer would not correspond to those that a social planner would choose. If $\langle d_L,d_H\rangle \in D_S(k)$, then the injurer's optimal strategy must specify a low settlement offer ($s = d_L - k_V$) and precaution levels e_1 and e_2 that solve the following minimization problem:

$$\min_{e_1,e_2} \pi(e_1)[p_L(e_2)(d_L - k_V) + p_H(e_2)(d_H + k_I)] + C(e_1,e_2). \tag{3}$$

When the accident is mild, the case settles out of court for $s = d_L - k_V$ and no costs are incurred; when the accident is severe, the case fails to settle and the injurer incurs cost k_I. The first-order conditions for this program are given by[26]

$$\pi'(e_1)[p_L(e_2)(d_L - k_V) + p_H(e_2)(d_H + k_I)] + C_1(e_1,e_2) = 0, \tag{4}$$

24. Note that this strategy is time consistent. No new information is learned about the damages after the accident occurs and the injurer has no reason to change his choice of settlement offer at the pretrial bargaining stage.

25. From Lemma 1 we know that the type of equilibrium (pooling or separating) of the pretrial bargaining game depends upon the total litigation costs, $k = k_I + k_V$.

26. Since $\pi'(0) = p_H'(0) = -\infty$ and $C_1(0,e_2)$ and $C_2(e_1,0)$ are finite, this program will have an interior solution.

$$\pi(e_1)[p_L'(e_2)(d_L - k_V) + p_H'(e_2)(d_H + k_I)] + C_2(e_1,e_2) = 0. \quad (5)$$

Note that these conditions do not generally correspond with those for the social optimum given in (1) and (2). However, if the award structure specifies a simple markup over the victim's harm, $\langle d_L,d_H\rangle = \langle x_L + k_V,x_H + k_V\rangle$, and if this award structure leads to a separating outcome, $\langle x_L + k_V,x_H + k_V\rangle \in D_S(k)$, then Equations (4) and (5) are equivalent to Equations (1) and (2). With this carefully chosen award structure, the injurer's choice of e_1 and e_2 will correspond precisely with the levels that minimize the expected social cost, (e_1^*,e_2^*) (that is, for the class of structures that lead to separating outcomes). Setting the award equal to a simple markup over the victim's harm forces the injurer to fully internalize the externality generated by his actions.

Finally we can easily verify that no other award structure $\langle d_L,d_H\rangle \in D_S(k)$ will lead the injurer to choose e_1^* and e_2^*. Equations (2) and (5) imply that $x_L - d_L = x_H - d_H$ (since $p_L'(e_2^*) = -p_H'(e_2^*)$), and setting Equations (1) and (4) equal gives us that $d_H = x_H + k_V$ and $d_L = x_L + k_V$.

Lemma 2. If the award structure $\langle d_L,d_H\rangle = \langle x_L + k_V,x_H + k_V\rangle$ leads to a separating outcome—that is, $\langle x_L + k_V,x_H + k_V\rangle \in D_S(k)$—then this award structure is strictly preferred to any other structure in the set $D_S(k)$.

Within the class of damage awards that lead to separation in the pretrial bargaining game, the best structure (from a social perspective) specifies a simple markup of k_V over the victim's actual damages. Note that this is equivalent to awarding actual damages with an English rule for allocating legal costs (since the victim always "wins"). However, this result is sensitive to the assumption that the defendant has all of the bargaining power. If the victim had some bargaining power, too, then the injurer would settle out of court for a greater amount. With more equal bargaining power, the optimal awards would tend to be scaled downward.

The following lemma characterizes the (weakly) preferred award structure among those that lead to pooling outcomes in the pretrial bargaining game. Two features are apparent. First, the damage award is flat, or insensitive to the victim's actual damages. The intuition is straightforward: any penalty structure $\langle d_L,d_H\rangle \in D_P(k)$ is equivalent to a flat penalty structure that specifies d_H be paid regardless of the true damages—that is, $\langle d_H,d_H\rangle$. Second, the award will lead to underinvestment in accident severity-reducing activities: $e_2 = 0$. The reason is clear: if the injurer is determined to make an offer corresponding to high damages, then there is no incentive for him to take care to reduce the expected damages. The optimal flat award will specify an award equal to the expected harm from an accident, conditional upon an accident occurring and $e_2 = 0$, plus the victim's litigation costs.

Lemma 3. An award structure that specifies a flat damage payment, $d_H = d_L = p_L(0)x_L + p_H(0)x_H + k_V$, regardless of the accident's actual severity is weakly preferred to any other award structure that leads to pooling in the pretrial bargaining game, $\langle d_L,d_H\rangle \in D_P(k)$.[27]

Proof. First, for any $\langle d_L,d_H\rangle \in D_P(k)$, the settlement offer, s, must equal $d_H - k_V$. Second, any award structure belonging to the set $D_P(k)$ will lead the defendant to choose $e_2 = 0$. Suppose not: $e_2 > 0$; by reducing e_2 and leaving the settlement offer, $s = d_H - k_V$, unchanged, the injurer increases his payoff. Therefore, we can represent the social cost associated with any element of $D_P(k)$ as

$$\pi(e_1)[p_L(0)x_L + p_H(0)x_H] + C(e_1,0).$$

If $d_H = d_L = p_L(0)x_L + p_H(0)x_H + k_V$, then the injurer offers $s = p_L(0)x_L + p_H(0)x_H$ in settlement and will choose e_1 to minimize this social cost. ■

Under the flat award in Lemma 3, the injurer has no incentive to raise e_2. If he did, his expected payments (conditional upon an accident occurring) would be the same. Therefore the best flat award must presume that the injurer takes no precautions, a presumption that is fulfilled in equilibrium.

Given the previous lemmas, we now state our main result:

Proposition. There exists $\bar{k} > 0$ such that when the total litigation costs exceed this value, $k_I + k_V \geq \bar{k}$, the court can do no better than specify a flat award structure, $d_H = d_L = p_L(0)x_L + p_H(0)x_H + k_V$, that is insensitive to the victim's actual damages, and all cases settle out of court. When the litigation costs are below this value, $k_I + k_V < \bar{k}$, the unique optimal award structure is based upon the victim's actual damages, $\langle d_L,d_H\rangle = \langle x_L + k_V, x_H + k_V\rangle$, and the case proceeds to trial if and only if $x = x_H$.[28]

Proof. Define $\bar{k}$ by

$$\min_{e_1,e_2} \pi(e_1)[p_L(e_2)x_L + p_H(e_2)(x_H + \bar{k})] + C(e_1,e_2)$$
$$= \min_{e_1} \pi(e_1)[p_L(0)x_L + p_H(0)x_H] + C(e_1,0). \qquad (6)$$

27. This flat award is not strictly preferred in the class $D_P(k)$; on the contrary, an award structure with $d_H = p_L(0)x_L + p_H(0)x_H + k_V$ and $d_H - d_L$ sufficiently small will be observationally equivalent.

28. In order to implement the optimal flat damage award characterized in the proposition, the court needs information about the distribution of damages. This suggests that scheduled damages may be easier to implement when the court (or relevant social planner) has prior experience with the type of case (as is probably true for workers' compensation). However, even absent extensive experience, the court may be able to obtain an estimate of the harm through a brief trial or investigation, making ex ante commitment to damage awards unnecessary. For example, rather than trying to place an exact dollar value on an individual's back injury, the court might restrict attention to evaluating the harm caused to typical victims in similar circumstances. Expert witnesses who specialize in back injuries may be more likely to agree on the value of the latter than the former, reducing the degree of asymmetric information.

It is easy to verify that $\bar{k}$ is uniquely defined since the right-hand side of (6) is constant and the left-hand side is strictly increasing in $\bar{k}$. To see this, imagine a small decrease in $\bar{k}$. Holding e_1 and e_2 constant, the left-hand side clearly falls. Since the injurer optimizes over e_1 and e_2, the value of the left-hand side may fall even further. Also, $\bar{k}$ is strictly positive since we know that $e_2^* > 0$. (This follows from the assumptions that $\pi(e_1)$ is bounded away from 0 and $p_H'(0) = -\infty$.)

When $k_I + k_V \geq k$, the right-hand side (which represents the social cost of the best flat award) is smaller than the social cost of a finely tuned award (assuming that the accurate award leads to separation in the bargaining game). However, by Lemma 2, when $k_I + k_V \geq \bar{k}$, the flat award outperforms any element of $D_S(k)$. Therefore a flat award is adopted when $k_I + k_V \geq \bar{k}$.

It remains to be shown that when $k_I + k_V < \bar{k}$, the finely tuned award outperforms the flat award. It is sufficient to show that if $k_I + k_V < \bar{k}$, then $\langle x_L + k_V, x_H + k_V \rangle \in D_S(k)$. To do this, we will first show that there exists a $\hat{k}$ such that if $k_I + k_V \geq \hat{k}$, then the finely tuned award leads to a pooling outcome, and if $k_I + k_V < \hat{k}$, then the finely tuned award leads to a separating outcome. Second, we will show that $\bar{k} < \hat{k}$, which will establish the result.

Define a separating strategy to be one with $s = d_L - k_V$, and a pooling strategy to be one with $s = d_H - k_V$. Under the award structure $\langle x_L + k_V, x_H + k_V \rangle$, the best separating strategy that the defendant could adopt minimizes Expression (3). The best pooling strategy minimizes $\pi(e_1)x_H + C(e_1,e_2)$ and, as before, it is clear that $e_2 = 0$. Let $\hat{k}$ be defined as the litigation cost that makes the defendant indifferent between the best separating and the best pooling strategies:

$$\begin{aligned}&\min_{e_1,e_2} \pi(e_1)[p_L(e_2)x_L + p_H(e_2)(x_H + \hat{k})] + C(e_1,e_2)\\ &\quad = \min_{e_1} \pi(e_1)x_H + C(e_1,0). \qquad (7)\end{aligned}$$

The right-hand side of (7) exceeds the right-hand side of (6) since $x_H > p_L(0)x_L + p_H(0)x_H$. The left-hand sides of (6) and (7) are identical when $\hat{k} = \bar{k}$. Since the left-hand side of (7) is monotonically increasing in $\hat{k}$, we conclude that $\hat{k} > \bar{k}$. ■

The general intuition for this result is straightforward: although flat awards provide poor incentives for the injurer to take precautions to reduce the severity of an accident, they are desirable in that they minimize the administrative costs. While awards that are sensitive to the true level of damages lead to more disagreement during settlement negotiations (and hence to greater administrative costs), they provide better incentives for care. When the administrative and litigation costs are small, awards that are based on the true level of damages outperform flat awards, while if the costs are large then the reverse is true.

5. Conclusion

Although characterization of the optimal awards derived here may be sensitive to the particular assumptions of the model, the result that a finely tuned awards structure is preferred when the litigation costs are small is robust to generalizations on the distribution of damages and the sequence of offers in the pretrial bargaining game. It is clear that when the costs of litigation are very small, then awarding true damages will force the injurer to bear costs that are close to the actual damages suffered by the victim. In the extreme case where litigation costs are zero, the settlement outcome will be accurate and awarding true damages induces the appropriate levels of severity-reducing activities. However, when the litigation costs are large, then the costs of disagreement will outweigh these beneficial incentives. Generally speaking, finely tuned rules combined with asymmetric information present an obstacle in the settlement process, and force greater resources to be expended. Although simple flat awards reduce the level of costly litigation, they may not induce a desirable level of ex ante precaution-taking by the injurer.

References

Bebchuk, Lucian. 1984. "Litigation and Settlement Under Imperfect Information," 15 *RAND Journal of Economics* 404–15.

Blumstein, James F., Randall R. Bovbjerg, and Frank A. Sloan. 1991. "Beyond Tort Reform: Developing Better Tools for Assessing Damages in Personal Injury," *Yale Journal on Regulation* 171–212.

Bovbjerg, Randall R., Frank A. Sloan, and James F. Blumstein. 1989. "Valuing Life and Limb in Tort: Scheduling Pain and Suffering," 83 *Northwestern University Law Review* 908–90.

Carroll, Stephen J., James S. Kakalik, Nicholas M. Pace, and John L. Adams. 1991. *No-Fault Approaches to Compensating People Injured in Automobile Accidents* (Report R-4019-ICJ). Santa Monica, Calif.: RAND Institute for Civil Justice.

Cooter, Robert. 1984. "Prices and Sanctions," 84 *Columbia Law Review* 1523–60.

———. 1991. "Economic Theories of Legal Liability," 5 *Journal of Economic Perspectives* 11–30.

———, and Daniel Rubinfeld. 1989. "Economic Analysis of Legal Disputes," 23 *Journal of Economic Literature* 1067–97.

Darling-Hammond, Linda, and Thomas J. Kniesner. 1980. *The Law and Economics of Workers' Compensation* (Report R-2716-ICJ). Santa Monica, Calif.: RAND Institute for Civil Justice.

Hölmstrom, Bengt, and Paul Milgrom. 1991. "Multitask Principal–Agent Analyses: Incentive Contracts, Asset Ownership, and Job Design," 7 (SP) *Journal of Law, Economics, & Organization* S24–52.

Kaplow, Louis. 1991. "A Model of the Optimal Complexity of Legal Rules," Harvard Law School Program in Law and Economics Discussion Paper No. 97.

———, and Steven Shavell. 1993. "Accuracy in the Assessment of Damages," National Bureau of Economic Research working paper No. 4287.

———, and ———. 1994. "Accuracy in the Determination of Liability," forthcoming in *Journal of Law and Economics*.

Kennan, John, and Robert Wilson. 1993. "Bargaining with Private Information," 31 *Journal of Economic Literature* 45–104.

Munkman, John H. 1985. *Damages for Personal Injuries and Death*. 7th ed. London: Butterworth.

P'ng, Ivan P. L. 1987. "Litigation, Liability, and Incentives for Care," 34 *Journal of Public Economics* 61–85.

Polinsky, A. Mitchell, and Daniel Rubinfeld. 1988. "The Deterrent Effects of Settlements and Trials," 8 *International Review of Law and Economics* 109–16.

———, and Yeon-Koo Che. 1991. "Decoupling Liability: Optimal Incentives for Care and Litigation," 22 *RAND Journal of Economics* 562–70.

Reinganum, Jennifer, and Louis Wilde. 1986. "Settlement, Litigation and the Allocation of Litigation Costs," 17 *RAND Journal of Economics* 557–66.

Shavell, Steven. 1987. *Economic Analysis of Accident Law*. Cambridge, Mass.: Harvard University Press.

Spier, Kathryn E. 1992a. "The Dynamics of Pretrial Negotiation," 59 *Review of Economic Studies* 93–108.

———. 1992b. "Incomplete Contracts and Signaling," 23 *RAND Journal of Economics* 432–43.

United States Sentencing Commission. 1990. *Guidelines Manual*.

Part III
Adversarial Process versus Inquisitorial Process

A
Balance or Bias in Adversarial Competition

[9]

JLEO, V12 N1 257

Naive, Biased, yet Bayesian: Can Juries Interpret Selectively Produced Evidence?

Luke M. Froeb
Vanderbilt University

Bruce H. Kobayashi
George Mason University

In an idealized model of civil litigation, interested parties incur costs to produce statistical evidence. A subset of this evidence is then presented to a naive decision-maker (e.g., a jury). The jury is naive in that it views evidence as a random sample when in fact the evidence is selectively produced. In addition to being naïve, the jury is also biased by prior beliefs that it carries into the courtroom. In spite of the jury's naiveté and biasedness, a full-information decision is reached as long as both litigants choose to produce evidence. Our results suggest that criticisms of the jury process based on jury bias or the jury's use of simple or heuristic rules may be overstated, and underscore the potential importance of competitively produced evidence in legal decision-making.

1. Introduction

Jury decision-making in civil cases, especially those that involve complex or expert testimony, has been criticized by lawyers, judges, statisticians, economists, sociologists, and representatives of just about every other discipline that comes in contact with the legal system.[1] Defenders of the jury system generally focus

Froeb received research support from the Dean's fund for faculty research at the Owen Graduate School of Management. Kobayashi received research support from the Law and Economics Center at George Mason University School of Law. We wish to acknowledge advice about related work from Cynthia Frobian Williams and editorial help from Lisa Granoien. We also wish to acknowledge constructive criticism from Timothy Brennan, Stephen Fienberg, Preston McAfee, and Kathryn Spier. The usual disclaimer must be strengthened here to note that some or all of those mentioned disagree with our characterization of the adversarial process.

1. For discussion of the history of the controversy over the merits of using lay juries, see Kalven and Zeisel (1966: 4–6) and Simon (1975: 13–18). Among the more outspoken judicial critics of the jury were Chief Justice Warren Burger and Judge Jerome Frank. For example, in *Skidmore v. Baltimore and Ohio R.R.*, 116 F.2d 54 (1947), Frank wrote: "While the jury can contribute nothing of value so far as the law is concerned, it has infinite capacity for mischief, for twelve men can easily misunderstand more law in a minute than the judge can explain in an hour." Dean Griswold of Harvard Law School argued: "The jury trial at best is the apotheosis of the amateur. Why should anyone think that 12 persons brought in from the street, selected in various ways, for their lack of general ability, should have any special capacity for deciding controversies between persons?" (see Guinther, 1988: xiv).

on its use in criminal trials, where juries are seen as a line of defense against the state's ability to inappropriately deprive individuals of life and liberty.[2] However, such concerns are viewed as less compelling in civil cases, suggesting to many critics that the costs imposed by the use of juries on the adjudicative process outweigh the benefits.[3]

Much of the debate has focused on the role of scientific or statistical evidence in the courts and on the role of experts in the courtroom.[4] Critics suggest that naive and potentially biased lay juries are inadequately prepared to evaluate scientific or statistical evidence.[5] Further, critics argue that these problems are exacerbated by the adversarial presentation of evidence, a process that can yield selectively produced evidence. Such concerns have led many commentators to suggest a movement toward neutral nonadversarial proceedings[6] and to make various proposals for reform, including the elimination of the right to a jury trial in complex civil cases,[7] increasing the power of judges to prevent issues from reaching the jury,[8] the appointment of court-appointed experts or special masters,[9] the constitution of court-approved science panels,[10] fee

2. The right to a jury trial is guaranteed by the Sixth Amendment for criminal trials. The Seventh Amendment guarantees this right for civil trials where the amount in controversy exceeds $20. For a discussion of the history of jury trials, see Kalven and Zeisel (1966: 6–8).

3. See the discussion in Cecil, Hans, and Wiggins (1991: 730–31) and Guinther (1988: xiv).

4. In response to perceived problems faced by the courts in assessing scientific evidence, the Federal Judicial Center has undertaken and recently published a manual on scientific evidence (see Federal Judicial Center, 1994 1–4). The issue of admissibility of expert testimony was recently undertaken by the Supreme Court. See *Daubert v. Merrill Dow Pharmaceuticals*, 113 S. Ct. 2786 (1993), in which the Supreme Court rejected the general acceptance test of the Frye standard in favor of the "more liberal" standard under the Rules 702 and 703 of Federal Rules of Evidence. For discussion of the implications of *Daubert*, see Parker (1995) and Cecil and Willging (1994b).

5. For proposals to introduce Bayes's theorem into court proceedings to assist the trier of fact, see Finklestein and Farley (1970) and Wagenaar (1988). For alternative views on this debate, see Tribe (1971), who suggests that statistical evidence will be given too much weight, and Saks and Kidd (1981), who suggest that juries underuse such evidence. For evidence that supports the latter view, see Goodman (1992), Faigman and Baglioni (1988), and references cited therein. For experimental evidence suggesting that experimental subjects do not conform to a Bayesian rule when integrating probabilities, see Grether (1992), Nisbett and Ross (1980), Tversky and Kahneman (1974); see also the discussion in Smith (1991) and a survey by Camerer (1995).

6. See Rubinfeld (1985), Johnston (1988), and Coulam and Fienberg (1986). See also Fienberg (1989) for a discussion of this issue.

7. For arguments in support of a complexity exception to the Seventh Amendment, see Campbell (1988) and Campbell and LePoidevin (1980). For arguments that do not support the existence of such an exception, see Arnold (1980). In addition, the Supreme Court has not incorporated the Seventh Amendment as applying to the states (see Stone et al., 1991: 784) and has allowed the use of juries of less than 12 people in federal civil trials [see *Colgrove v. Battin*, 413 U.S. 149 (1973)] and in state criminal trials [see *Williams v. Florida* 399 U.S. 78 (1970)].

8. These devices include expanded use of summary judgment, summary juries, and expanded use of directed verdicts. For a discussion of these issues, see Cecil et al. (1991: 736–38).

9. Court appointment of expert witnesses is provided for under Rule 706 of the Federal Rules of Evidence. Special "reference" masters can be appointed under "exceptional conditions" under Rule 53(b) of the Federal Rules of Civil Procedure. However, use of court-appointed experts and non-pretrial special masters has been rare (see Cecil and Willging, 1994a; and Farrell, 1994).

10. See, e.g., Meier (1986).

shifting,[11] and reform of the discovery rules to include mandatory disclosure of information.[12]

On the other side of the debate are those who offer a "Hayekian" justification for the adversarial presentation of testimony to the jury. While both juries and the adversarial system are inferior to an idealized centralized decision-maker, such imperfect decentralized bodies may have inherent advantages over imperfect centralized decision-makers.[13] Thus, the relevant comparison for normative purposes is a comparison between the performance of imperfect institutions. While such a comparative analysis is beyond the scope of this article, we hope to advance the debate by explicitly modeling the incentives of the parties to produce costly information and by examining decision-making by a naive and potentially biased decision-maker faced with selectively produced evidence.

This article focuses on one aspect of the debate—the ability of juries to competently evaluate selectively produced statistical evidence.[14] Previous attempts

11. Although the Supreme Court substantially limited the recoverability of expert witness fees in fee-shifting cases in *West Virginia University Hospital v. Casey*, 111 S. Ct. 1138 (1991) (holding that a provision in 42 U.S.C. §1988 that grants statutory authority for courts to shift "reasonable attorney's fees" to the losing party does not include expert fees), Congress has recently authorized the shifting of expert fees by explicitly including such provisions in statutes. Congress chose to overrule *Casey* by explicitly authorizing judges to award expert fees in civil rights cases. See the Civil Rights Act of 1991, Pub. L. No. 102-166, §113(b), 105 Stat. 1071 (1991), 42 U.S.C. §§1988, 2000e-5(k)C. Fee shifting of expert fees is also provided in other statutes. For example, the fee-shifting provision in the Clean Air Act, which became the model for nearly identical provisions in other environmental statutes, states: "The court ... may award costs of litigation (including reasonable attorney and expert witness fees) to any party, whenever the court determines such an award is appropriate." See 42 U.S.C. §7604(d) (1982).

12. For an economic analysis of discovery, see Cooter and Rubinfeld (1994) and Schrag (1994). Dissatisfaction with discovery under the adversarial process led to the recent amendments to Rule 26 of the Federal Rules of Civil Procedure, which controls discovery in the federal courts. The most controversial part of this rule was a provision that required early disclosure of both favorable and unfavorable information. See F.R.C.P. Rule 26(a)(1). However, the rule allows local district courts to opt out of the rule. An examination of the district courts' decisions revealed that the majority of the courts have used the local opt-out provision. Thirty-seven districts required no initial disclosures, and nine districts require disclosure only of information that is favorable to the disclosing party. For a discussion of the courts' decisions and the process of procedural reform, see Kobayashi, Parker, and Ribstein (1994).

13. See, e.g., Hayek (1945, 1948) and Demsetz (1969). The fact that jurors decide verdicts in groups after deliberations provides protection against idiosyncratic views or biases (see Cecil et al., 1991: 749; Lempert, 1981). For an economic model of the effect of jury deliberations, see Klevorick and Rothschild (1979) and Klevorick, Rothschild, and Winship (1984). Further, opposing litigants can have more or better information than even a sophisticated decision-maker, and competition among the litigants forces them to reveal relevant information (see Milgrom and Roberts, 1986; Froeb and Kobayashi, 1993; Lipman and Seppi, 1995).

14. Our analysis does not directly address the ability of juries to deal with complex evidence; for a discussion of this issue, see Cecil et al. (1991). The problem of understanding overly complex issues is not limited to juries; see the discussion in note 4, *supra*. While judges are experts in the law, they are not necessarily experts with respect to evaluating statistical or factual questions. For an argument that the Supreme Court has inconsistently adopted and often misused social science research, see Bersoff and Glass (1995). For examples of "judicial missteps" in evaluating

at examining this issue have not considered one or more aspects of this problem. Gay et al. (1989) consider criminal defendants' choice of judge versus jury trials. In their model, information processing by juries is assumed to be "noisier" than information processing by judges. Sophisticated judges and/or juries draw inferences from both prior information and the defendant's choice of trial mode. Their analysis does not explicitly model competition between litigants nor the problem of evidence production.[15]

The lines of research most closely related to ours are Sobel (1985) and Milgrom and Roberts (1986). Sobel (1985) considers the ability of litigants to withhold evidence in a game in which it is costly to report preexisting evidence.[16] He finds a mixed-strategy equilibrium where a judge maximizes social surplus by "favoring" one of the litigants with a lower burden of proof. His judge is a benevolent, sophisticated decision-maker. In this respect our model is more like that of Milgrom and Roberts (1986) who consider both naive decision-making and the selective reporting of evidence. In their model, evidence not reported by one party because it is unfavorable will be reported by the opposing party, and vice versa. In equilibrium, all relevant information is reported, suggesting the following equivalence result: an unsophisticated decision-maker faced with selectively produced evidence will reach a full-information decision, as long as the litigants' interests are sufficiently opposed. In their model, it is the competing incentives of the parties, rather than the sophistication of the decision-maker, that permits a full-information decision.

However, Milgrom and Roberts' model ignores two salient features of the legal system: the cost of producing evidence[17] and the potential for biased decision-makers.[18] When evidence is costly to produce, and when parties must

statistical evidence, see Finklestein and Levin (1990). Evidence from private arbitration suggests that arbitrators possess neither the characteristics of juries nor those of public judges. That is, they are neither lay persons nor experts on the law, but rather are chosen based on their familiarity with the subject matter (see Landes and Posner, 1979). For a model of arbitrator behavior, see Ashenfelter and Bloom (1984).

15. Because judge trials are assumed to be more accurate, innocent defendants will choose judge trials, while guilty defendants will prefer juries as long as judges and juries both act naively. Sophistication on the part of juries will cause all defendants to choose judge trials, while an equilibrium where judges are sophisticated and juries are not leads to innocent defendants choosing judges and guilty ones mixing between judges and juries. Gay et al. argue that empirical evidence on trial outcomes supports the equilibrium generated by naive juries and sophisticated judges.

16. In Sobel's model of dispute resolution, the parties choose between incurring a cost to report evidence or not reporting evidence to a third-party decision-maker. Sobel also examines how shifting the burden of proof affects the incentives of the parties to disclose costly information. However, in Sobel's model, litigants cannot misrepresent their information.

17. Indeed, the perception that litigation under an adversarial system has resulted in excessive expenditures has been one of the driving forces behind recent attempts at reform, including the recent amendments to the rules governing sanctions and discovery. For a discussion of these amendments, see Kobayashi and Parker (1993) and Kobayashi et al. (1994). Other critics of the adversarial system argue that selective evidence production involves social costs, including the costly production of misleading information or the costly production of information that is not used (see Tullock, 1975, 1980).

18. For evidence that experimental jurors make decisions based on nonneutral priors, see Good-

overcome bias, not all relevant information will be reported to the decision-maker. Instead, the decision of how much evidence to produce depends on the costs, as well as the benefits, of producing evidence.

In this article, we develop a model that allows for costly evidence production and decision-maker bias. Despite the added complications, we find that a naive decision-maker can still reach a full-information decision. There are two forces at work here: the first is the tendency of the party favored by the underlying distribution to produce more favorable evidence, due to the lower costs of doing so;[19] the second is the tendency of the parties to "free ride" on the prior beliefs of the decision-maker in a way that negates decision-maker bias. In equilibrium, competition in the selective production of evidence leads to a full-information decision by a naive and biased decision-maker. We find that the original intuition of Milgrom and Roberts about the importance of competition, rather than the sophistication of the decision-maker, can be extended to situations in which evidence is costly to produce and to situations in which the decision-maker is biased.

Our results suggest that the competing incentives of litigants may work to mitigate some of the potential costs attributed to the use of juries. Consequently, criticisms of the jury process based on the observation that jurors use simplifying strategies or heuristics when assessing information may overstate the shortcomings of lay juries' decision-making abilities. Likewise, experimental research that does not subject jurors to the competing forces of adverse litigants and jury deliberations may miss the role these forces play in leading to accurate decision-making—even by lay decision-makers using simple rules.[20] This finding is similar in spirit to those drawn from experiments conducted in market settings, which find that individual biases tend to disappear in market settings.[21] It is also consistent with the large body of empirical research on jury competence, which, in contrast to the predictions of jury critics, points to the general competence of the jury.[22]

man (1992). The potential for bias is not limited to individual jurors or juries. For a critique of centralized systems of producing evidence based on bias, see Parker (1995) and McChesney (1977). Further, asymmetric stakes and asymmetric burdens of proof and other procedural rules often introduce bias into the litigation process. For an overview of these issues, see Cooter and Rubinfeld (1989).

19. Our results can be applied to other areas of adversarial litigation where parties expend resources to affect the probability of victory. Litigation expenditures by competing litigants have been examined by Tullock (1980), Katz (1988), and Kobayashi and Lott (1996). These models do not consider the ability of litigants to selectively use information. For models of one-sided litigation expenditures, see Rubinfeld and Sappington (1987) and Miceli (1990). Our results are also similar to those found in the literature on asymmetric contests or tournaments (see, e.g., Rosen, 1986; and Lazear and Rosen, 1981).

20. For examples of experimental design, see Grether (1992); Goodman (1992), who incorporates both types of designs; and Faigman and Baglioni (1988). See also Smith (1991).

21. See, e.g., Camerer (1987), Franciosi et al., (1985), and Forsythe et al. (1991). See Smith (1991) for a survey of the difference between psychology experimental literature, which focuses on the individual, and economics experimental literature, which focuses on market settings.

22. The best known empirical study of jury behavior is by Kalven and Zeisel (1966), who report

2. Naive and Biased Juries

In this section, we examine the behavior of a jury in the context of an idealized model of civil litigation where parties have failed to reach out-of-court settlement and are preparing for trial.[23] The culpability of the defendant is represented by the mean of a binomial distribution, p, and both parties present evidence to a jury drawn from this distribution. At issue in the trial is the value of p.[24] Using the analogy of a coin-flipping experiment, let heads be a piece of evidence that is favorable to the plaintiff and tails be evidence that is favorable to the defendant. The parties each report a number of heads and tails to the jury, and the jury must infer the value of p from the evidence presented in court. The total evidence reported is $\{H, T\}$, where H is the number of heads and T is the number of tails reported by the parties. We explicitly assume that evidence can be reported in arbitrarily small units so that we can treat $\{H, T\}$ as continuous.[25]

There are several ways to draw inferences about the value of p (Lindley and Phillips, 1976). Classical inference proceeds from an assumption about the sample space out of which the evidence is drawn. For example, if the jury assumed that each party took a fixed number of flips and truthfully reported the outcomes, then the probability of getting the outcome $\{H, T\}$ would be $(H : T)p^{H}(1 - p)^{T}$, where $(H : T)$ denotes the choose function. The method

on the results of the Chicago Jury Project. See also Cecil et al. (1991: 745–64), Simon (1975: 147), and Guinther (1988: 230). These studies generally find that juries are able to comprehend even complex issues and that there is a high rate of judge/jury agreement. For a recent empirical study of judge/jury agreement, see Claremont and Eisenberg (1992), who find that, contrary to popular belief, judges are more favorable to plaintiffs in medical malpractice and personal injury cases than are juries, and that these results are not attributable solely to case-selection effects. See also Vidmar and Rice (1993).

23. We do not explicitly consider the trial/settlement process in this article. Our main results are not affected if the assumption that each litigant knows p is changed so that each litigant possesses only an unbiased estimate of p at the trial/settlement decision. Trials would be generated when parties' prior estimates of the prior distribution were relatively optimistic (see, e.g., Priest and Klein, 1984). Further, trials could also be generated even if the parties agree on p—e.g., if the litigants' differential valuation of precedent causes the absence of a settlement range (see, e.g., Kobayashi, 1996; Kobayashi and Lott, 1996; and Rubin, 1977).

24. We assume that accuracy in adjudication is a relevant societal goal, so that the litigants' increased investment in information is not a social cost. For example, accurate information may improve individuals ex ante incentives to behave properly, and it may effect marginal deterrence (see, e.g., Kaplow and Shavell, 1992, 1994; Kaplow, 1994; and Rasmussen, 1992). Uncertainty can also increase the "option value" of lawsuits, and can increase the number of nonmeritorious suits (see Cornell, 1990; Landes, 1992; Kobayashi and Parker, 1993). In addition, more accurate information (i.e., lower variance information) can more effectively offset erroneous prior beliefs held by the decision-maker. For an analysis of the costs and benefits of competitively versus centrally produced information, see Froeb and Kobayashi (1993).

25. For the discrete case, in equilibrium, it must be profitable for both litigants to take the last flip (to get to the optimal stopping point), but unprofitable to flip further. These four conditions (two for each litigant) characterize the Nash equilibrium, but do not guarantee its existence. In fact, equilibrium in pure strategies does not always exist unless evidence units become arbitrarily small. As evidence is measured in smaller and smaller units, the discrete equilibrium converges to the continuous equilibrium.

of moments estimator is derived from this distribution function:

$$\hat{p} = H/(H + T). \tag{1}$$

Different assumptions about the sample space lead to different estimators, but some assumptions about the sample space must be made in order to derive an estimator.

Bayesian inference, however, proceeds from different assumptions. The jury does not need to know the sample space out of which the evidence are drawn, only that they form an "exchangeable" sequence (Heath and Sudderth, 1976). Exchangeability means that the sequence of heads and tails is generated "fairly," by some experimental process. Unlike classical inference, the exact form of the experiment need not be known. The jury uses evidence to update its prior beliefs about the value of p. The estimator of p is the mean of the posterior distribution. We assume that the jury has a Beta(a, b) prior over the unknown value of p. The Beta distribution is the conjugate prior[26] to the binomial and is a function over the interval [0, 1], with mean $a/(a+b)$, that includes the uniform distribution $\{a = 1, b = 1\}$ as a special case. The posterior distribution is a Beta$(a + H, b + T)$ distribution, with posterior mean:

$$\hat{p} = (a + H)/(a + b + H + T). \tag{2}$$

Whether it uses a classical or Bayesian approach to infer the value of p, the jury must make some assumption about the process used by the litigants to generate the evidence. In the classical case, it is an assumption about the sample space; in the Bayesian case, it is the somewhat less restrictive assumption of exchangeability. The jury in our model makes one of these two assumptions, but neither are true. Thus, the jury is "naive" in the sense that it mistakenly believes or assumes that evidence presented in court is a random or exchangeable sequence when in fact it is selectively reported by each of the interested parties.[27]

The jury's mistaken beliefs about the randomness or exchangeability of the data means that neither the classical estimator given by (1) nor the Bayesian estimator given by (2) can be justified on statistical grounds. The two estimators discussed above are neither classical nor Bayesian, because they are derived from mistaken assumptions.

In addition to being naive, the jury is "biased" by the prior beliefs that it carries into the courtroom. We have characterized the bias by a prior probability distribution over the unknown value of p. Although juries in civil case s are supposed to choose a decision rule according to a "preponderance of the evidence" standard, there are no sanctions for behaving otherwise, and jury

26. We choose a Beta distribution because it is the only distribution that allows an analytic solution for the posterior mean. Other prior distributions are possible, but the posterior mean could only be calculated numerically. The results that follow depend critically on the functional form of the posterior mean that derives from the use of the Beta prior.

27. For research suggesting that experimental jurors fail to appropriately combine evidence, see the references contained in note 20, *supra*.

bias is a well known phenomenon.[28] We explicitly allow for jury bias through the parameters $\{a, b\}$. A jury with a prior such that $a > b$ ($a < b$) favors the plaintiff (defendant). Large values of a or b mean that the jury's prior beliefs are very strong, or that it is less likely to be swayed by evidence presented in court.[29] For example, a jury with $\{a = 2, b = 2\}$ has the same prior mean as a jury with $\{a = 1, b = 1\}$ but is less easily swayed by evidence produced in court. This is seen by examining the variance of the Beta(a, b) prior distribution, $ab/((a+b)^2(1+a+b))$. Using our examples, the variance of the Beta(2, 2) is $\frac{1}{20}$ while the variance of the Beta(1, 1) is $\frac{1}{12}$. A smaller prior variance signifies stronger prior beliefs.

The jury behavior described above can be characterized completely by the single estimator given in Equation (2), $\hat{p} = (a + H)/(a + b + H + T)$. The classical estimator given in Equation (1) is a special case of the Bayesian estimator, characterized by the parameters $\{a = 0, b = 0\}$. The classical estimator can also be motivated as a "split the difference" decision rule. The classical estimator does not require that the jury use any type of formal statistical inference—it can be generated by a jury that uses a simple weighting scheme to evaluate the competing claims of the litigants.

3. Competitively Produced Evidence

In this section, we model the behavior of a defendant and plaintiff who are preparing for trial, facing a naive and biased jury. As mentioned above, we allow the parties to attempt to mislead the jury by selectively reporting favorable evidence. Continuing with the coin-flipping analogy, the plaintiff is allowed to report a favorable subset of the flips taken, as is the defendant. As it turns out, neither party has an incentive to report unfavorable flips—that is, the plaintiff reports only flips that come up heads, and the defendant reports only those that come up tails. This feature comports well with the observation that litigants rarely report unfavorable evidence (e.g., Rubinfeld, 1985). In addition, we assume that evidence is costly to produce, according to the number of flips that each party decides to take.

This assumption of costly evidence production differentiates our approach from that of Milgrom and Roberts (1986), who study litigation under the assumption that parties can costlessly and credibly produce and report evidence. In their model, evidence not reported by one party would be reported by the other, and vice versa. In equilibrium, all relevant evidence would be reported—that is, the jury would know the exact value of p. In contrast, we consider a different type of evidence: that which is costly to produce and which cannot be costlessly revealed. In our model, for any party to reveal the exact value of p would require an infinite number of flips, a prohibitively costly undertaking. While Milgrom and Roberts's assumption is probably best suited to evidence

---

28. See the discussion in note 14, *supra*.

29. Bias can also be imposed by varying the standard of proof. For discussion of this issue, see Sobel (1985), Rubinfeld and Sappington (1987), Davis (1994).

that can be costlessly reported, our assumption is better suited to more costly types of evidence, the archetypal example being that of expert testimony.[30]

Continuing with the coin-flipping analogy, the number of flips is analogous to the effort that it takes to produce favorable evidence. For example, the plaintiff produces evidence of quantity H after, on average, H/p flips. Similarly, the defendant produces evidence of quantity T after, on average, $T/(1-p)$ flips. We are implicitly assuming that the jury can verify that evidence is drawn from the distribution of interest but cannot verify the existence of unfavorable, and unreported, evidence.[31]

One can immediately see that for $p > .5$, when the plaintiff is favored by the distribution, the plaintiff will have to flip fewer times, on average, than the defendant, to produce evidence of equal strength ($H = T$). If, as we postulate, evidence is costly to produce (according to the number of flips) then for $p > .5$, it is more costly, on average, for the defendant to produce evidence of the same strength as evidence produced by the plaintiff. This difference in cost turns out to be important because it induces the party favored by the distribution to produce more favorable evidence than the opposition.

Formally, suppose we interpret p as the defendant's level of fault under a comparative negligence tort standard. The plaintiff's award equals $\hat{p}S$, where $\hat{p}$ is the jury's estimate of the true p, and S is the amount of harm, which is assumed to be uncontested. Given the jury's weighting scheme, the decision of how much evidence to produce becomes an optimal stopping problem for each of the litigants. The parties stop producing evidence when they have "enough" favorable evidence.[32] The effort that it takes to produce evidence is a random

30. A distinction between the two types of evidence can be made on the basis of Hirschleifer's classic separation of information into "foreknowledge" and "discovery." The former type of information is either preexisting or inelastically supplied, while the latter type of information can be produced only with costly effort (see Hirshleifer, 1971). For discussion of this in the context of legal issues, see Easterbrook (1981), Kaplow and Shavell (1989), and Allen et al. (1990) regarding legal privileges; Kobayashi et al. (1994) on mandatory disclosure; and Parker (1995) and Froeb and Kobayashi (1993) on expert testimony.

31. While the recent amendments to discovery practice under the Federal Rules of Civil Procedure attempted to reduce a litigant's ability to hide information, hiding unfavorable expert information generally can be accomplished by hiring multiple experts and selecting for trial those with favorable results. Under Rule 26(b)(4) of the Federal Rules of Civil Procedure, the ability of a party "to discover facts known or opinions held by an expert who has been retained or specially employed by another party in anticipation of litigation or preparation for trial and who is not expected to be called as a witness at trial" is severely limited. See Johnston (1988) for a discussion of the practice of "expert shopping." For a discussion of the amendments to the discovery rules, see the discussion in note 12, *supra*.

32. When the distribution is unknown to the litigants, flipping takes on an "option" value. Using the intuition of Roberts and Weitzman (1981), if the uncertainty is large relative to the cost of flipping, litigants will always take a few initial flips because it gives them the option of flipping more if they learn that the distribution is favorable. In our model, this would change the nature of equilibrium for cases in which one of the litigants would not flip, absent the option value of flipping. It would move the estimator further away from the true value toward the prior mean. However, when the cost of flipping is low, Rothschild (1974) finds that for the Dirichelet/multinomial conjugate distributions, which are generalizations of the beta/binomial, "not invariably, but in many instances"

variable, but we assume that the parties are risk neutral, so they care only about the mean level of effort required to produce favorable information and not about variance in the level of effort. Under these assumptions, the litigants choose stopping values, $\{H^*, T^*\}$, which satisfy

$$H^* = \text{argmax}[\hat{p}S - cH/p] \qquad \text{such that } H > 0, \tag{3a}$$

$$T^* = \text{argmax}[-\hat{p}S - cT/(1-p)] \qquad \text{such that } T > 0, \tag{3b}$$

where c is the cost of flipping and $\hat{p} = (a+H)/(a+b+H+T)$. For $H > 0$ and $T > 0$, this litigation game has a unique[33] Nash equilibrium:

$$\{H^*, T^*\} = \{-a + p^2(1-p)S/c, -b + (1-p)^2 pS/c\}$$
$$\text{if } H^* > 0 \text{ and } T^* > 0. \tag{4a}$$

The notable thing about this equilibrium is that when both plaintiff and defendant produce strictly positive amounts of evidence, the estimator used by the jury is exact—that is,

$$\hat{p}^* = H^*/(H^* + T^*) = p. \tag{5}$$

Note that there is no variance to the estimator given by Equation (5). There is variance in the number of flips required to produce the estimator, but not in the estimator itself. Thus, when evidence is produced by both sides, the adversarial process and the naive jury produce a costly but accurate (unbiased and zero variance) estimate. We say it is "costly" because the litigants throw away information (unreported flips), but the reported flips are produced in exactly the "right" proportion.

There are two forces at work here. First is the tendency of the party favored by the distribution to produce more favorable evidence, due to the lower costs of doing so. Second, is the tendency of the parties to "free ride" on the prior beliefs of the jury. When the jury has prior beliefs that favor one party, that party produces less evidence, which exactly counteracts the effects of the prior beliefs of the jury. This happens because jury bias lowers the marginal benefit of flipping, reducing by a the number of heads produced by the plaintiff and by b the number of tails produced by the defendant. Effectively, the jury's bias gives a "head start" to one side—it is as if they were endowed with some free evidence. And in equilibrium, when both parties choose to flip, jury bias disappears.

Note that this "exactness" result depends explicitly on our characterization of the unequal costs of producing evidence as a negative binomial experiment. The litigant favored by the distribution has a lower marginal cost of evidence

---

the distribution is "learned" as more draws are taken so that the stopping rule is similar to that used when the distribution is known in advance. For recent review of optimal stopping, see McMillan and Rothschild (1994).

33. The uniqueness of the equilibrium is proved in the Appendix.

production, and therefore flips more in equilibrium. The equal marginal costs of flipping, as opposed to the unequal costs of evidence production, can be justified by assuming a competitive market for expert coin-flippers. An expert charging a supracompetitive rate would not attract any clients.

To illustrate the equilibrium, we present a numerical example. Suppose that the true p equals $\frac{2}{3}$, so that the plaintiff is favored by the distribution, and the jury has a uniform prior over the unknown p, that is, $\{a = 1, b = 1\}$. Suppose further that the amount at risk is \$2,000,000, and the cost of flipping is \$100,000. In equilibrium the plaintiff reports 1.96 heads, and the defendant reports 0.48 tails. On average, the plaintiff will take 2.94 flips, costing \$294,000, and the defendant 1.44 flips, costing \$144,000. The jury's estimate of p is exact: $(1 + 1.96)/(2 + 1.96 + 0.48) = .667$.

When p is close to zero, or one, the marginal benefit of flipping is so small that the party favored by the distribution takes no flips. In this case, the Nash equilibrium takes the following form, depending upon who decides not to flip:

$$\{H^{**}, T^{**}\} = \{-a - b + (1/c)(-ac(1-p))^{1/2}, 0\} \quad \text{if } T^* < 0 \quad (4b)$$

$$= \{0, -a - b + (1/c)(bcpS)^{1/2}\} \quad \text{if } H^* < 0. (4c)$$

The stronger the beliefs of the jury—that is, the larger are $\{a, b\}$—the fewer flips the respective parties take. A party produces no evidence when the bias of the jury is strong, and when p is near zero or one. In this case the marginal benefit of flipping is so small, that it is better to not flip at all. When this happens, the opposing litigant decides to flip more because the reaction functions of the litigants are upward sloping. The net effect of these changes is to bias the estimator of the jury toward the prior mean of the jury. Note that although the estimator is biased, it represents a improvement relative to the no-evidence case, because it moves the jury's estimator from the prior mean toward the true p.

The Nash equilibrium is illustrated for all possible p values in three different cases for $S = \$2{,}000{,}000$ and $c = \$100{,}000$: in Figure 1, $\{a = 1, b = 1\}$; Figure 2, $\{a = 2, b = 1\}$; and Figure 3, $\{a = 0, b = 0\}$. In all three figures, the true value of p is on the horizontal axis; the top graph plots the number of heads and tails reported by the litigants; and the bottom graph plots the value of the jury's estimator relative to the true value of p. In Figure 1, the jury has a uniform prior over the unknown value of p. In the top graph of Figure 1, when the value of p is near zero, only the plaintiff flips, and the jury's estimator of p is biased toward the prior mean. The jury's prior is represented by a dashed horizontal line. The bias is represented in the bottom graph as a deviation from the 45 degree line. As p increases, when the defendant begins flipping, the jury's estimator becomes exact—that is, $\hat{p}^* = H^*/(H^* + T^*) = p$. As p approaches one, the plaintiff stops flipping, and the jury's estimator is again biased toward the prior mean.

The effects of jury bias are illustrated in Figure 2, where the jury's prior

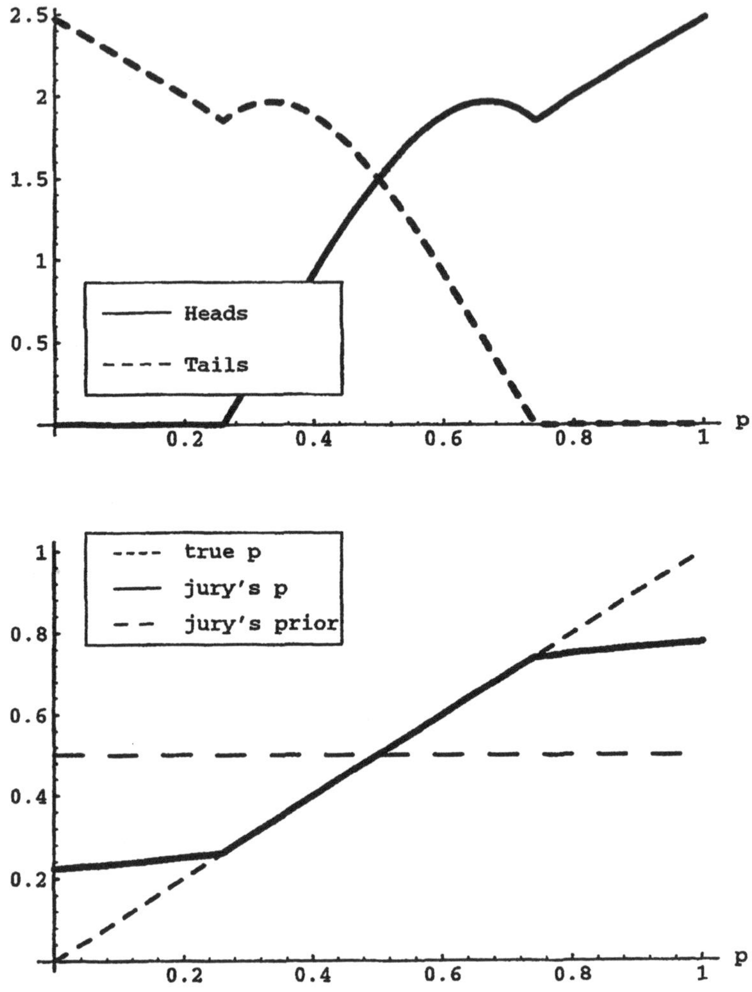

Figure 1. Effects on evidence when jury has uniform priors: $\{a = 1, b = 1\}$.

favors the plaintiff. Here the plaintiff "free rides" on the jury's stronger prior, and doesn't begin flipping until a much higher value of p. This means that there is a larger range over which the jury's estimator is biased toward the prior mean $\frac{2}{3}$, but, as above, when both parties produce evidence, bias disappears.[34]

34. Note that, in the cases illustrated in Figures 1 and 2, a corner solution is reached (i.e., one of the parties produces no evidence). When p is close to zero or one, there is bias, but not in cases where p is "close" to .5. According to the Priest and Klein (1984) model of litigation versus settlement, the selection of cases for litigation will be biased toward cases where p is close to .5.

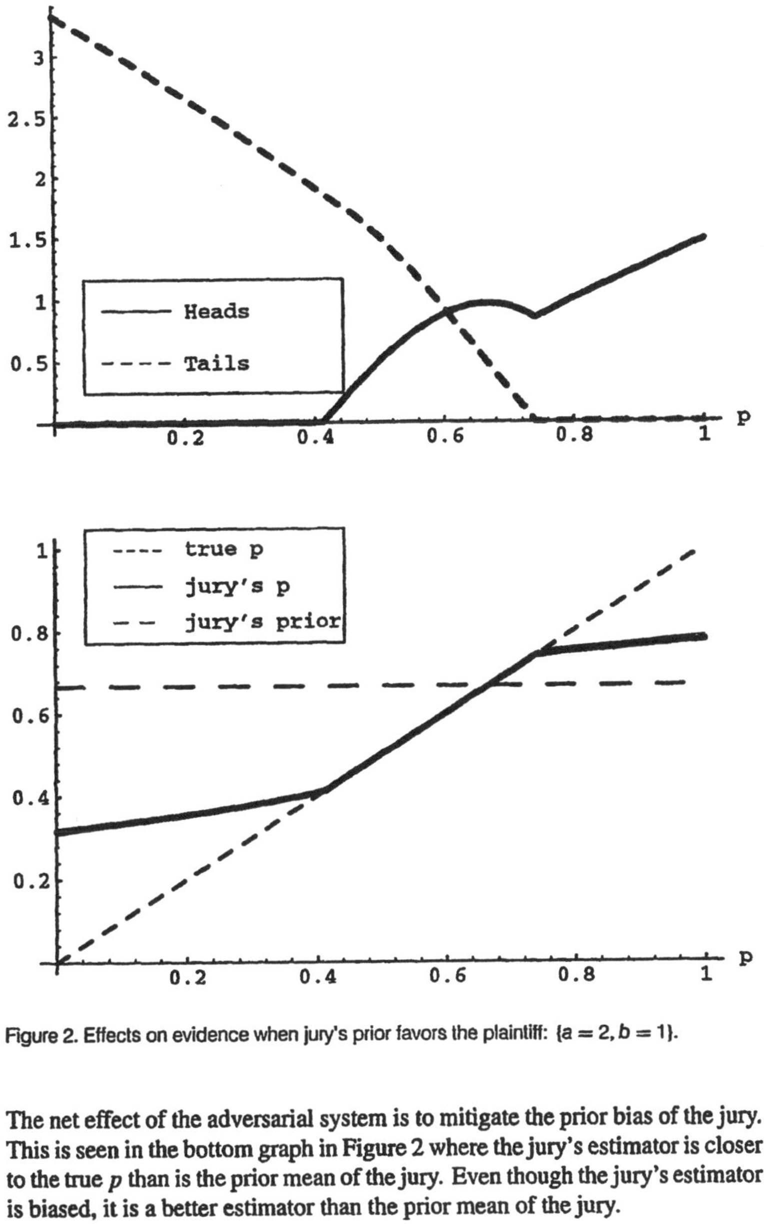

Figure 2. Effects on evidence when jury's prior favors the plaintiff: $\{a = 2, b = 1\}$.

The net effect of the adversarial system is to mitigate the prior bias of the jury. This is seen in the bottom graph in Figure 2 where the jury's estimator is closer to the true p than is the prior mean of the jury. Even though the jury's estimator is biased, it is a better estimator than the prior mean of the jury.

See the discussion in note 23, *supra*. Thus, under the Priest–Klein hypothesis, the set of litigated cases will be relatively free of bias. However, the amount paid in settled cases (those where p is close to zero or one) will reflect the jury's bias.

The "classical" jury is illustrated in Figure 3 $\{a = 0, b = 0\}$. In this case, the estimator used by the jury is exact, no matter what the value of p, because there is no region where the parties do not flip.[35]

4. Conclusions

The exactness of the jury's estimator is sensitive to a number of assumptions, implicitly associated with the functional forms used in the model. The payoff functions,[36] the way bias is modeled, the simultaneous presentation of evidence, the specific distributional assumptions used, and the assumption of constant marginal costs of flipping[37] are all critical to the results of the model. Though stylized, our model of litigation captures four salient features of the legal system: competition between the litigants, selective production of favorable evidence, costly production of evidence, and a naive and biased decision-maker. Our results suggest that, in equilibrium, the decision-maker is able to overcome these shortcomings and reach a full-information decision when both parties choose to produce evidence. This implies that competitively produced evidence in an adversarial setting may mitigate some of the costs attributed to decision-

35. Note that in the case of the classical jury (Figure 3), a tax on evidence will increase welfare, as the amount of evidence and thus the costs of producing evidence will fall. However, this is not true in the cases set out in Figures 1 and 2. In these cases, a tax on evidence will increase the range over which one party produces no evidence. Although evidence production costs are lower, the accuracy of the estimator will decrease. Further, given the assumption of the model, the additional bias will be predictable ex ante, thereby affecting both settlement and ex ante behavior.

36. Fee shifting, or "loser pays" rules, are somewhat difficult to address in the context of this model because of the discarded unfavorable evidence. If one of the litigants winds up paying the other's legal costs, the payer would presumably learn about the other's discarded evidence. In addition, the fee shifting used in England and Rule 68 of the Federal Rules of Civil Procedure apply only to marginal expenditures incurred following an offer of judgment. Since we do not model settlement, it is difficult to evaluate these rules in the context of our model. However, putting these considerations aside, with fee shifting the party disfavored by the distribution produces no evidence, because fee shifting leads to more costly evidence production for which he will likely end up paying. This leads to a bias in the jury's estimator, in favor of the litigant favored by the distribution. For discussions of similar effects of fee shifting on the rates of filings, settlement, and trial, see Shavell (1982).

37. With rising marginal costs (with the number of flips), the nature of optimal search changes for the parties. No longer are open- and closed-loop strategies equilvalent (McMillan and Rothschild, 1994; Roberts and Weitzman, 1981). If the litigants stop and reoptimize, the optimal number of flips changes because the marginal conditions are likely to change. If for example, the plaintiff started off with an unlucky streak (no heads), he would end up settling, on average, for fewer heads than he would have produced following an open-loop strategy (computed before any flips were taken). This changes the nature of the equilibrium by introducing variance into the estimator of the jury. Sometimes the plaintiff will get lucky and sometimes the defendant will get lucky. On average, the "luck" will balance out, but this is difficult to prove analytically because closed-loop equilibria are difficult to compute. Instead, we have examined open-loop equilibria as an average benchmark for the closed-loop equilibria in the rising marginal costs case. We find that the principal accuracy result for the constant-cost case is robust with respect to rising marginal costs for the "classical" estimator but not for the "Bayesian" estimator. For $a \neq 0$ or $b \neq 0$, we find that while the jury's estimator is close to the true p, it is not exact.

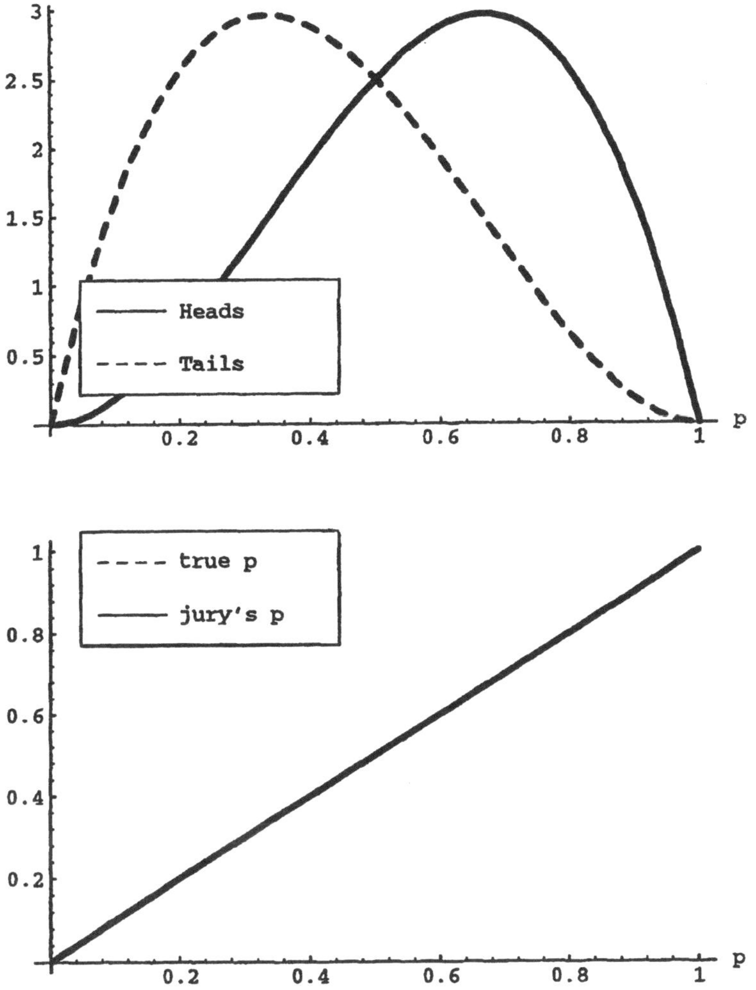

Figure 3. Effects on evidence for a "classical" jury, one that has no priors: $\{a = 0, b = 0\}$.

maker bias and to the use of simplified rules or heuristics to evaluate selectively produced information.

Appendix: Characterization of Nash Equilibrium

This section characterizes the Nash equilibrium of the litigation game in the case where evidence is continuous, or measured in small enough units to be effectively continuous. In essence, we permit litigants to present "pieces" of evidence, like 2.94 heads. In this case, the expected payoff vector to the plaintiff and defendant is

$$\{\hat{p}S - cH/p, -\hat{p}S - cT/(1-p)\}.$$

The first derivatives whose roots characterize a Nash equilibrium are

$$\{-(c/p) - ((a+H)^*S)/(a+b+H+T)^2 + S/(a+b+H+T),$$
$$c/(-1+p) + ((a+H)^*S)/(a+b+H+T)^2\}.$$

The roots of these derivatives have an explicit solution, given in Equation (4a), which we reproduce below.

$$\{H^*, T^*\} = \{-a + p^2(1-p)S/c, -b + (1-p)^2 pS/c\} \quad \text{if } H^* > 0 \text{ and } T^* > 0 \tag{4a}$$

That this solution is unique can be seen by examining the matrix of second partial derivatives of the payoff vector:

$$\{\{(-2^*S^*(b+T))/(a+b+H+T)^3,$$
$$(S^*(a-b+H-T))/(a+b+H+T)^3\},$$
$$\{(S^*(-a+b-H+T))/(a+b+H+T)^3,$$
$$(-2^*(a+H)^*S)/(a+b+H+T)^3\}\}.$$

The determinant of this matrix is equal to $S^2/(a+b+H+T)^4$. For $H > 0$, $T > 0$, it is seen that the principal minors alternate in sign, implying that the matrix is negative definite, which guarantees that the solution given in (4a) is unique.

When the constraints, $H > 0$ or $T > 0$, are binding, we compute the Nash equilibria by first computing the reaction functions implied by the derivatives of the payoff vector:

$$\{-a - b - T + (c^*p^*S^*(b+T))^{1/2}/c, -a - b - H$$
$$+ (c^*(1-p)^*S^*(a+H))^{1/2}/c\}.$$

The reaction function of the nonconstrained litigant is positively sloped in the region of interest, so for p's near zero, where the plaintiff would like to produce negative amounts of evidence (sell evidence to the experts) but must produce more evidence (zero), the defendant produces more than he would like in an unconstrained equilibrium. Substituting the constraints into the appropriate reaction functions leads to the constrained equilibrium represented by Equations (4b) and (4c), which we reproduce below:

$$\{H^{**}, T^{**}\} = \{-a - b + (1/c)(-ac(1-p))^{1/2}, 0\} \quad \text{if } T^* < 0 \tag{4b}$$
$$= \{0, -a - b + (1/c)(bcpS)^{1/2}\} \quad \text{if } H^* < 0. \tag{4c}$$

References

Allen, Ronald J., Mark F. Grady, Daniel D. Polsby, and Michael S. Yashko. 1990. "A Positive Theory of Attorney-Client Privilege and the Work Product Doctrine," 19 *Journal of Legal Studies* 359–98.

Arnold, Morris S. 1980. "A Historical Inquiry into the Right to Trial by Jury in Complex Civil Litigation," 128 *University of Pennsylvania Law Review* 829–48.

Ashenfelter, Orley, and D. E. Bloom. 1984. "Models of Arbitrator Behavior," 74 *American Economic Review* 111–24.

Bersoff, Donald N., and David J. Glass. 1995. "The Not So Weisman: The Supreme Court's Continuing Misuse of Social Science Research," 2 *University of Chicago Law School Roundtable* 279–300.

Camerer, Colin. 1987. "Do Biases in Probability Judgment Matter in Markets? Experimental Evidence," 77 *American Economic Review* 981–97.

______. 1995. "Individual Decision Making," in John Kagel and Alvin Roth, eds., *Handbook of Experimental Economics*. Princeton, N.J.: Princeton University Press.

Campbell, James S. 1988. "The Current Understanding of the Seventh Amendment," 66 *Washington University Law Quarterly* 63–70.

______, and Nicholas LePoidevin. 1980. "Complex Cases and Jury Trials: A Reply to Professor Arnold," 128 *University of Pennsylvania Law Review* 965–85.

Cecil, Joe S., Valerie P. Hans, and Elizabeth C. Wiggins. 1991. "Citizen Comprehension of Difficult Issues: Lessons from Civil Jury Trials," 40 *American University Law Review* 727–74.

______, and Thomas E. Willging. 1994a. "Court-Appointed Experts," in Federal Judicial Center, *Reference Manual on Scientific Evidence*. Colorado Springs, Col.: Shepard's McGraw Hill.

______, and ______. 1994b. "Accepting Daubert's Invitation: Defining a Role for Court-Appointed Experts in Assessing Scientific Validity," 43 *Emory Law Journal* 995–1070.

Claremont, Kevin M., and Theodore Eisenberg. 1992. "Trial by Jury or Judge: Transcending Empiricism," 77 *Cornell Law Review* 1124–77.

Cooter, Robert D., and Daniel L. Rubinfeld. 1989. "An Economic Analysis of Legal Disputes and their Resolution," 27 *Journal of Economic Literature* 1067–97.

______, and ______. 1994. "An Economic Model of Legal Discovery," 23 *Journal of Legal Studies* 435–64.

Cornell, Bradford. 1990. "The Incentive to Sue: An Option Pricing Approach," 19 *Journal of Legal Studies* 173–89.

Coulam, Robert, and Stephen Fienberg. 1986. "The Use of Court-Appointed Statistical Experts: A Case Study," in M. H. DeGroot, S. E. Fienberg, and J. B. Kadane, eds., *Statistics and the Law*. New York: Wiley.

Davis, Michael L. 1994. "The Value of Truth and Optimal Standard of Proof in Legal Disputes," 10 *Journal of Law, Economics, & Organization* 343–59.

Demsetz, Harold. 1969. "Information and Efficiency: An Alternative Viewpoint," 12 *Journal of Law & Economics* 1–22.

Easterbrook, Frank H. 1981. "Insider Trading, Secret Agents, Evidentiary Privileges, and the Production of Information," 1981 *Supreme Court Review* 309–65.

Faigman, David, and A. J. Baglioni Jr. 1988. "Bayes' Theorem and the Trial Process," 12 *Law and Human Behavior* 1–17.

Farrell, Margaret G. 1994. "Special Masters," in Federal Judicial Center, *Reference Manual on Scientific Evidence*. Colorado Springs, Col.: Shepard's McGraw Hill.

Federal Judicial Center. 1994. *Reference Manual on Scientific Evidence*. Colorado Springs, Col.: Shepard's McGraw Hill.

Fienberg, Stephen, ed. 1989. *The Evolving Role of Statistical Assessments as Evidence in the Courts*, New York: Springer.

Finkelstein and Farley. 1970. "A Bayesian Approach to Identification Evidence," 83 *Harvard Law Review* 489–517.

Finkelstein, Michael O., and Bruce Levin. 1990. *Statistics for Lawyers*. New York: Springer-Verlag.

Forsythe, Robert, Forest Nelson, George Newman, and Jack Wright. 1991. "The Iowa Presidential Stock Market: A Field Experiment," in R. M. Isaac, ed., *Research on Experimental Economics*, Vol. 4. Greenwich, Conn.: JAI Press.

Franciosi, Robert, Praveen Kujal, Roland Michelitsch, Vernon Smith, and Gang Deng. 1995. "Fairness: Effect on Temporary and Equilibrium Prices in Posted-Offer Markets," 105 *Economic Journal* 1–13.

Froeb, Luke M., and Bruce H. Kobayashi. 1993. "Competition in the Production of Costly Information: An Economic Analysis of Adversarial versus Court Appointed Presentation of Expert Testimony," Law and Economics Working Paper No. 93-005, George Mason University School of Law.

Gay, Gerald D., Martin F. Grace, Jayant R. Kale, and Thomas H. Noe. 1989. "Noisy Juries and the Choice of Trial Mode in a Sequential Signalling Game: Theory and Evidence," 20 *RAND Journal of Economics* 196–213.

Goodman, Jane. 1992. "Juror's Comprehension and Assessment of Probabilistic Evidence," 16 *American Journal of Trial Advocacy* 361–89.

Grether, David. 1992. "Testing Bayes Rule and the Representativeness Heuristic: Some Experimental Evidence," 17 *Journal of Economics Behavior and Organization* 31–57.

Guinther, John. 1988. *The Jury in America*, New York: Facts on File Publications.

Hayek, F. A. 1945. "The Use of Information in Society," 35 *American Economic Review* 519–30.

——— 1948. "Individualism, True and False," in *Individualism and Economic Order*. Chicago: University of Chicago Press.

Heath, David, and William Sudderth. 1976. "De Finetti's Theorem on Exchangeable Variables," 30 *American Statistician* 188–89.

Hirshleifer, Jack. 1971. "The Private and Social Value of Information and the Reward to Inventive Activity," 61 *American Economic Review* 561–74.

Johnston, Pamela Louise. 1988. "Court Appointed Scientific Expert Witnesses: Unfettering Expertise," 2 *High Technology Law Journal* 249–80.

Kalven, Harry, and Hans Zeisel. 1966. *The American Jury*. New York: Little, Brown.

Kaplow, Louis. 1994. "The Value of Accuracy in Adjudication: An Economic Analysis," 23 *Journal of Legal Studies* 307–402.

———, and Steven Shavell. 1989. "Legal Advice about Information to Present in Litigation: Its Effects and Social Desirability," 102 *Harvard Law Review* 567–614.

———, and ——— 1992. "Private versus Socially Optimal Provision of Ex Ante Legal Advice," 8 *Journal of Law, Economics, & Organization* 306–20.

———, and ——— 1994. "Accuracy in the Determination of Liability," 37 *Journal of Law & Economics* 1–16.

Katz, Avery. 1988. "Judicial Decision Making and Litigation Expenditure," 8 *International Review of Law & Economics* 127–43.

Klevorick, Alvin K., and Michael Rothschild. 1979. "A Model of the Jury Decision Process," 8 *Journal of Legal Studies* 141–64.

———, ———, and C. Winship. 1984. "Information Processing and Jury Decision Making," 23 *Journal of Public Economics* 245–78.

Kobayashi, Bruce H. 1996. "Case Selection, External Effects, and the Trial/Settlement Decision," in David A. Anderson, ed., *Dispute Resolution: Bridging the Settlement Gap*. Greenwich, Conn.: JAI Press (forthcoming).

———, and John R. Lott Jr., 1994. "Judicial Reputation and the Efficiency of the Common Law," mimeo, George Mason University School of Law.

———, and ——— 1996. "In Defense of Criminal Defense Expenditures and Plea Bargaining," forthcoming in *International Review of Law and Economics*.

———, and Jeffrey S. Parker. 1993. "No Armistice at 11: A Commentary on the Supreme Court's 1993 Amendment to Rule 11 of the Federal Rules of Civil Procedure," 3 *Supreme Court Economic Review* 93–152.

———, ———, and Larry E. Ribstein. 1994. "The Process of Procedural Reform: Centralized Uniformity versus Local Experimentation," mimeo, George Mason University School of Law.

Landes, William M. 1992. "Sequential versus Unitary Trials: An Economic Analysis," 22 *Journal of Legal Studies* 99–135.

———, and R. A. Posner. 1979. "Adjudication as a Private Good," 8 *Journal of Legal Studies* 235–85.

Lazear, Edward P., and Sherwin Rosen. 1981. "Rank Order Tournaments as Optimum Labor Contracts," 89 *Journal of Political Economy* 841–64.

Lempert, Richard O. 1981. "Civil Juries and Complex Cases: Let's Not Rush to Judgment," 80

Michigan Law Review 68–132.
Lindley, D. V., and L. D. Phillips. 1976. "Inference for a Bernoulli Process (A Bayesian View)," 30 *American Statistician* 112–19.
Lipman, Barton L., and Duane J. Seppi. 1995. "Robust Inference in Communication Games with Partial Probability," 66 *Journal of Economic Theory* 370–405.
McChesney, Fred S. 1977. "On the Procedural Superiority of a Civil Law System: A Comment," 30 *Kyklos* 507–10.
McMillan, John, and Michael Rothschild. 1994. "Search," in R. J. Aumann and S. Hart, eds., *Handbook of Game Theory*, Vol. 2. New York: Elsevier Science.
Meier, Paul. 1986. "Damned Liars and Expert Witnesses," 81 *Journal of the American Statistical Association* 269–76.
Miceli, Thomas, J. 1990. "Optimal Prosecution of Defendants Whose Guilt is Uncertain," 6 *Journal of Law, Economics, & Organization*" 189–201.
Milgrom, Paul, and John Roberts. 1986. "Relying on the Information of Interested Parties," 17 *RAND Journal of Economics* 18–32.
Nisbett, Richard, and Lee Ross. 1980. *Human Inference: Strategies and Shortcomings of Social Judgment*. Edgewood Cliffs, N.J.: Prentice-Hall.
Parker, Jeffrey S. 1995. "Daubert's Debut: The Supreme Court, the Economics of Scientific Evidence, and the Adversarial System," 4 *Supreme Court Economic Review* 1–56.
Priest, George L., and Benjamin Klein. 1984. "The Selection of Disputes for Litigation," 13 *Journal of Legal Studies* 1–56.
Rasmussen, Eric. 1992. "Damage Awards when Court Error is Predictable," Indiana University Working Papers in Economics No. 92-023.
Roberts, Kevin, and Martin Weitzman. 1981. "Funding Criteria for Research, Development, and Exploration Projects," 49 *Econometrica* 1261–88.
Rosen, Sherwin. 1986. "Prizes and Incentives in Elimination Tournaments," 76 *American Economic Review* 701–15.
Rothschild, Michael. 1974. "Searching for the Lowest Price When the Distribution of Prices Is Unknown," 82 *Journal of Political Economy* 689–711.
Rubin, Paul H. 1977. "Why is the Common Law Efficient?" 6 *Journal of Legal Studies* 51–64.
Rubinfeld, Daniel. 1985. "Econometrics in the Courtroom," 82 *Columbia Law Review* 689–711.
______, and David E. M. Sappington. 1987. "Efficient Awards and Standards of Proof in Judicial Proceedings," 18 *RAND Journal of Economics* 308–18.
Saks, Michael J., and R. Kidd. 1981. "Human Information Processing and Adjudication: Trial by Heuristics," 15 *Law and Society Review* 123–60.
Schrag, Joel L. 1994. "Managerial Judges: The Judicial Management of Pretrial Discovery," mimeo, Emory University.
Shavell, Steven. 1982. "Suit, Settlement, and Trial: A Theoretical Analysis under Alternative Methods for the Allocation of Legal Costs," 11 *Journal of Legal Studies* 55–82.
Simon, Rita James, ed. 1975. *The Jury System in America: A Critical Overview*. Beverly Hills, Calif.: Sage.
Smith, Vernon L. 1991. "Rational Choice: The Contrast between Economics and Psychology," 99 *Journal of Political Economy* 877–897.
Sobel, Joel. 1985. "Disclosure of Evidence and Resolution of Disputes: Who Should Bear the Burden of Proof?" in Alvin E. Roth, ed., *Game Theoretic Models of Bargaining*. Cambridge: Cambridge University Press.
Stone, Geoffrey R., Louis M. Siedman, Cass R. Sunstein, and Mark V. Tushnet. 1991. *Constitutional Law*, 2d ed. Boston: Little, Brown.
Tribe, Lawerence H. 1971. "Trial by Mathematics: Precision and Ritual in the Legal Process," 84 *Harvard Law Review* 1328–93.
Tullock, Gordon. 1975. "On the Efficient Organization of Trials," 28 *Kyklos* 745–62.
______ 1980. *Trials on Trial: The Pure Theory of Legal Procedure*. New York: Columbia University Press.
Tversky, Amos, and Daniel Kahneman. 1974. "Judgment Under Uncertainty: Heuristics and Biases," 185 *Science* 1124–31.

Vidmar, Neil R., and Jeffrey J. Rice. 1993. "Assessments of Non-Economic Damage Awards in Medical Negligence: A Comparison of Jurors with Legal Professionals," 78 *Iowa Law Review* 883–911.

Wagenaar, Willem A. 1988. "The Proper Seat: A Bayesian Discussion of the Position of the Expert Witness," 4 *Law and Human Behavior* 499–510.

[10]

On the Economics of Trials: Adversarial Process, Evidence, and Equilibrium Bias

Andrew F. Daughety
Vanderbilt University

Jennifer F. Reinganum
Vanderbilt University

The adversarial provision of evidence is modeled as a game in which two parties engage in strategic sequential search. An axiomatic approach is used to characterize a court's decision based on the evidence provided. Although this process treats the evidence submissions in an unbiased way, the equilibrium outcome may still exhibit bias. Bias arises from differences in the cost of sampling or asymmetry in the sampling distribution. In a multistage model, a prodefendant bias arises in the first stage from a divergence between the parties' stakes. Finally, the adversarial process generates additional costs that screen out some otherwise meritorious cases.

1. Introduction

Many economic analyses implicitly (or explicitly) rely upon incentives derived from the legal system; in such discussions the legal system provides an impartial threat that supports the economic activity of interest. Models with contracts anticipate enforcement or appropriate damages should breach occur; models with caretaking by potential injurers and potential victims anticipate compensation, and this feeds back to the choice of precaution by both parties. Many models of markets assume an economic environment involving truthful advertising or noncooperative behavior, implicitly relying on the imposition of appropriate penalties for misrepresentation or collusion. Moreover, it is probably a common perspective that while legal processes are costly, agents should expect that (at least on average) legal processes are fundamentally unbiased. After all, if a trial occurs, each participant can hire competent counsel, access the same quality of expert testimony, and so forth. In short, we expect the adversarial process embodied by the legal system to generate (at least, on average) unbiased estimates of liability and damages, and therefore agents in the economy should not anticipate significant relative distortions due to the legal process: a

We thank Luke Froeb, Tracy Lewis, Richard Posner, Kathryn Spier, Nick Zeppos, and two anonymous referees for helpful comments and suggestions.

deadweight loss, yes, but one that is not systematically influencing different sides of the market differently.[1]

We show that this need not be true even if the process treats the parties in an unbiased manner and they have access to the same resources. In our model, evidence is generated through strategic sequential search,[2] with both litigants sampling the *same* evidence space. Each litigant develops a case wherein they present the best evidence obtained. Evidence is costly and each party's payoff reflects any potential award for damages as well as the costs that party incurred in developing its case. Thus, in equilibrium, the evidence generated and the resource costs are both stochastic, and each party's decisions and costs are influenced by the presence (and attributes) of the other party.

We abstract from the court's (Bayesian) inference problem of assessing the credibility of evidence by restricting consideration to credible evidence. For instance, experts might be employed by both parties to assess the extent of damages and to testify about their opinions. Different expert witnesses (who are all independent and credible to the court, and use "scientific" methods) may have different opinions or use different (but equally scientific) procedures, though their estimates will be correlated because they all draw from the same distribution of evidence. This allows us to model the court's problem as one of applying rules of evidence and procedure in a systematic way to generate a judgment. This is accomplished by employing a set of axioms (stylized versions of the rules) that characterize the aggregation of credible evidence. These axioms, and our motivation for using a non-Bayesian approach to evidence aggregation, are described in Section 2; this discussion is based on Daughety and Reinganum (2000; hereafter, DR). While we are not attempting to fully characterize an ideal system (though we do briefly address this issue in Section 3), our purpose is to provide a framework that captures important relevant attributes of the existing legal system, some of which are likely to be consistent with an ideal system. We use this framework to examine the source and nature of biases that arise in an adversarial system.

We analyze trials as a two-stage game (this is partly a simplifying assumption, but there are many sequential aspects to a trial, which we discuss in more detail below). In the first stage, the plaintiff and the defendant separately develop and present evidence pertaining to liability. If the defendant is found not liable, the game ends and the payoffs reflect the costs incurred to that point; otherwise the next stage involves

1. Our interest here is in sources of bias in the adversarial process. One might want to affect different sides of the market differently if the issue is deterrence, which is not our focus in this article.

2. Strategic sequential search was first discussed by Jennifer Reinganum (1982) in the context of research and development (R & D) by firms in a duopoly.

both litigants developing and presenting evidence about damages. Thus, for instance, in a products liability case wherein the trial has been bifurcated into a liability phase, followed by a damages phase, the use of expert witnesses by each side in each phase creates the sort of credible evidence generation and presentation costs modeled in Section 2. The anticipation of this evidence being aggregated into a decision results in strategic behavior by both parties: they sample the space of experts, constructing the best case they can and suppressing inconvenient evidence when possible.

We identify four potential sources of bias that may be relevant to a particular case. First, differences in evidence sampling costs can lead to systematic bias in the liability and/or the damages stage, with the bias operating in favor of the party with the lower sampling costs. Second, asymmetry in the sampling distribution of evidence can lead to bias; which party benefits from this asymmetry may also depend on the level of sampling costs. Third, a multistage trial process causes a divergence in the parties' stakes at the liability stage (since, in the damages subgame, the defendant will lose the award plus expected trial costs, while the plaintiff will gain the award minus expected trial costs). This results in an equilibrium prodefendant bias, as it causes the defendant to search more aggressively than the plaintiff in the liability stage. Generally, this suggests that multistage legal processes, involving investments by litigants in the various stages, create incentives for relatively greater investments by defendants in the early stages. Finally, since the first move (filing suit) is the plaintiff's, anticipated equilibrium bias in the liability and damages stages, as well as the noncooperative, socially excessive investment in evidence generation, also distorts the decision to file. Returning to our products liability case, we find that most (if not all) of these biases favor the defendant. First, the defendant (typically a corporation) seems likely to have lower evidence sampling costs than the plaintiff in a products liability suit. Second, when damages estimates are exponentially distributed and there are high evidence sampling costs, the asymmetry in the sampling distribution tends to favor the defendant (because few draws will be taken and thus the plaintiff is unlikely to obtain a high damages estimate). Third, the defendant is always favored by the divergence in stakes. Finally, these accumulated biases lower the plaintiff's expected return to litigation, while the dissipative investment in evidence gathering raises the costs of litigation, leading to a greater likelihood that such cases will be screened out (i.e., never brought by the plaintiff).

Our analysis raises questions about the distortion in economic decisions due to adversarial legal processes, since systematic bias in the outcomes of such processes is likely to influence markets and bargaining that occurs in the "shadow" of the law. For example, again in the products liability context, the typical plaintiff is a consumer and the typical defendant is a manufacturer. We have shown elsewhere that if both parties anticipate undercompensation of consumers then there are reduced incentives for safety-enhancing R & D (Daughety and Reinganum, 1995) and increased incentives for intentional misrepresentation of product safety (Daughety and Reinganum, 1997, 1998a). As another example, this one in a contracts setting, anticipated undercompensation makes breach more likely, reducing the incentive to make relationship-specific investments.

We discuss some piecemeal remedies in Section 3. Examples of such remedies include taxes and subsidies on evidence gathering, fee shifting, and decoupling of monetary judgments and awards. The main problem with all of these remedies concerns the pervasive asymmetric information between the court and the parties. Employing the above remedies generally relies upon information that courts do not have and are not able to acquire in a purely adversarial system.

These biases, and the market distortions they induce, may be unavoidable and reflect a more fundamental trade-off involving the costs and benefits of decentralized evidence generation in judicial systems. The adversarial process, as a means by which a judicial system generates and evaluates evidence, is one of the two main procedures employed by democratic legal systems; the other is the inquisitorial process, used in many civil law countries, which involves considerably more centralized management of evidence generation by courts (as opposed to each litigant's counsel). We do not consider alternative processes in this article, but the concentration of power such a centralized process entails may also induce inefficiencies,[3] possibly in excess of the strategically induced bias we consider here.

In Section 2 the model of the court's evidence aggregation procedure is described. In addition, models of the liability and damages stages are developed and analyzed. Section 3 illustrates potential sources of equilibrium bias via a series of examples and discusses potential remedies and problems with their implementation. Section 4 provides a brief review of related literature. Section 5 contains a summary and conclusions. Formal statements and proofs of the propositions and related results are contained in the appendix.

2. Model and Analysis

Imagine the following setting. An incident has occurred in which someone has suffered a harm; that person is the plaintiff (P), who sues the defendant (D). We assume that the likelihood, p, that D actually caused the harm and the level of the harm, d, are common knowledge

3. See Posner (Section II.A.1, 1999) for an extensive discussion of the relative efficiencies of adversarial and inquisitorial processes. See also Shin (1998) and Dewatripont and Tirole (1999) for models in which the adversarial process is superior to the inquisitorial process.

to both P and D but are not verifiable, so they are unknown to the court.[4] Courts recognize the litigants' incentives to misrepresent the level of p and d, so courts require evidence about the likelihood of liability and about the level of damages. Our model involves the selective presentation of verifiable facts which, in aggregate, make a case. This production and presentation of the case is viewed as occurring in two stages, each of which involves strategic search in the relevant evidence space by both litigants. In the first stage, evidence on the likelihood that D is liable is presented by both sides; if D is found liable then the game proceeds to the second stage, wherein each side again engages in strategic search, now in the space of damages estimates.

Thus, formally, we study a "bifurcated" trial. Federal Rule of Civil Procedure 42(b) specifies the court's option[5] of conducting separate trials "in furtherance of convenience or to avoid prejudice." For instance, bifurcated trials[6] occur in medical malpractice cases in which the plaintiff was severely affected. Trials have been bifurcated in insurance cases if coverage of an event was disputed; the second stage considered the extent of the insurance company's liability. This procedure is also used in various tort cases and some states require it in actions involving punitive damages awards. A very important sphere of application of bifurcation is to class action suits. In cases involving, for example, a dispute over whether a particular product (or company policy) caused plaintiffs' injuries, the issue of liability may be determined jointly for all plaintiffs, with individual suits for damages following upon a finding of liability (see Federal Rule of Civil Procedure 23).

Finally, an alternative interpretation of our two-stage model is that the first stage represents trial, while the second stage represents appeal. Although we view the trial and appeals stages as being inherently about

4. Our model picks up after any settlement negotiations have failed. Typically, pretrial negotiation occurs after some preliminary evidence gathering by each side, but before all the evidence that would be used at trial has been gathered. Thus the negotiations are conducted under asymmetric information. In a revealing equilibrium for a signaling model of such negotiations (see, e.g., Reinganum and Wilde, 1986) two things happen: the asymmetric information is revealed and some cases fail to settle. Thus the parties can end up failing to settle despite having learned the true values of p and d. They then continue to gather evidence for the anticipated trial, generating asymmetric information again, now about what can be demonstrated to the court.

5. According to Landes (1993:99–100), "Rule 42(b) gives courts wide discretion to separate substantive issues. These include bifurcating liability and damages, separating claims asserted by the plaintiff, separating counterclaims raised by the defendant, deciding whether a contract exists before considering claims based on its existence, and deciding whether a product-liability defendant manufactured the allegedly defective product before considering liability and damages."

6. Usually the two stages follow in close succession, though in some cases there may be a substantial lag. When Polaroid sued Kodak for patent infringement with respect to instant photography, the liability trial occurred in 1985 and the damages trial occurred in 1990 (Landes, 1993:99, footnote 1).

different things (facts versus law; see DR), the impact of sequentiality is the same: the existence of a second stage makes the first-stage stakes diverge for the parties, inducing the type of liability-stage bias we find in Section 3.

In each stage of our model we focus on the incentives for litigants to develop and present evidence, when there is a given cost for acquiring evidence and a known process which aggregates the evidence submitted. In general, we think of each stage as having three components: 1) evidence generation; 2) determination of the credibility of the evidence submitted; 3) aggregation of both parties' evidence into the court's assessment for that stage. As suggested earlier, we collapse the first two components into a model of strategic search for credible evidence. Since both litigants must anticipate how the court will aggregate the submitted evidence, we turn to that issue first.

2.1 Modeling the Court's Evidence Aggregation Process

Any positive analysis of a court faces a basic modeling issue: how to model the outcome of the court as a function of the evidence presented (in Section 4 we briefly review how others have modeled court decision making). It is tempting to assume that the judge or jury is a sophisticated Bayesian decision maker. Certainly there are points in a trial where this seems to be an appropriate model; for example, the court can exercise its discretion in determining the credibility of witnesses, and in interpreting the law (subject to review by a superior court). In addition, there are specific uses of statistical evidence (such as DNA evidence), where the probability of misclassification can be clearly quantified, in which Bayesian inference is suitable.

More generally, in a Bayesian model of the liability stage, a court would posit a subjective prior distribution over the submitted evidence on liability (denoted π^{P*} and π^{D*}) and true liability p. Then it would try to estimate p using π^{P*} and π^{D*}. Note that π^{P*} and π^{D*} are both *statistically* related to p (since they represent the result of sequential sampling from a distribution conditioned on p) and *strategically* related to p (since they represent the parties' best observations under strategically chosen stopping rules). Thus the court is trying to "unwind" both statistical effects and strategic effects. However, the court lacks much of the usual information that would be useful in this "unwinding" process. For instance, included in the category of "missing information" are

Evidence that is relevant and available, but not presented, either because it is strategically suppressed by the parties or because it is inadmissible under the rules of evidence. For example, less favorable observations are not presented, while character evidence, settlement offers and information concerning the insurance status of the defendant are inadmissible (under, e.g., Federal Rules of Evidence 404, 408, and 411, respectively).

The extent of each party's search behavior (e.g., how much the party spent on evidence-gathering and the stopping rule employed) as well as information needed to compute equilibrium stopping rules (such as the parties' wealth and their costs of search) are also unobservable to the court.

The sampling distributions for evidence are conditional on the true values of p and d, which are unobservable to the court (but known by the parties).

Thus a Bayesian court's decision process would, of necessity, substitute a subjective prior distribution for this missing data, making the resulting estimate highly prior dependent. As Posner (1999) points out, to the extent that a court's decision relies on a (possibly strong) subjective prior, this reduces the incentives for the parties to provide evidence. It seems likely that exculpatory evidence will be easier to produce if the defendant really has been careful, so reducing the value of exculpatory evidence also reduces the defendant's incentive to take care. To support the provision of both care and evidence, it is reasonable for the legal system to try to restrict the fact-finder's reliance on subjective priors and to focus it instead on the evidence presented at trial.

Moreover, the trial court process itself is *not* purely Bayesian, since some rules of evidence and procedure are distinctly inconsistent with Bayesian decision making. This does not mean that these rules are inefficient, only that they may be designed to promote broader objectives than accurate decision making in the instant case given the instant evidence. Posner (1999) discusses efficiency-based rationales for many rules of evidence and procedure and Lewis and Poitevin (1997) and Sanchirico (1997a) provide models wherein a sophisticated Bayesian decision maker prefers to commit (ex ante of observing the evidence) to a decision rule that would not be optimal ex post.

Some policies clearly conflict with an unconstrained Bayesian treatment. In some cases (e.g., the self-incrimination privilege), no inference is to be drawn from a party's decision not to present certain evidence. On the other hand, if a plaintiff provides only statistical evidence, then the plaintiff loses. As Posner (1992:552) observes, "If, for example, the only evidence the victim of a bus accident had linking the accident to the defendant bus company was that the defendant operated 80 percent of the buses on the route where the accident occurred, the victim could not win without additional evidence of the defendant's liability." This is because the "burden of production" of evidence is (at least initially) allocated to the plaintiff, so as to discourage nuisance suits.

Alternatively, the law sometimes requires a specific inference. For example, in employment discrimination cases, the *McDonnell Douglas* rule "permits a plaintiff... to establish his prima facie case... with evidence merely that he was qualified for the job but was passed over in favor of someone of another race. But the rule does more: satisfying the just-described burden of production creates a presumption of discrimination, meaning that if the defendant puts in no evidence the plaintiff is entitled to summary judgment," even though "the probability that he lost the job opportunity *because* he was discriminated against might not seem to be very high if the only evidence is as described" (Posner, 1999).

If a judge determines that the evidence in a case is insufficient to support (that is, cannot be construed as supporting) a verdict of liable, he may dismiss the case, enter a directed verdict in favor of the defendant, or even overrule a jury finding of liability by entering a judgment notwithstanding the verdict (j.n.o.v.). Indeed, self-interest alone is not viewed as a reason to discount evidence which is not otherwise impeached by the adversary. According to James and Hazard (1985:348):

> Where the proponents, having also the persuasion burden, offer testimonial evidence that strongly supports their side of the case and the opponents fail to shake it on cross-examination and offer no countervailing evidence, the proponents may move for a directed verdict. If at this point no presumption operates in the proponents' favor the question may arise whether the jury may reasonably *disbelieve* their evidence . . . the prevailing view regards the clear, uncontradicted, self-consistent, and unimpeached testimony of even interested witnesses as sufficient basis for a directed verdict in favor of the party having the persuasion burden as well as the initial production burden.

The aforementioned rules and conventions conflict with a purely Bayesian approach, since one could certainly construct very reasonable subjective priors which would reach a decision opposite to the one implied by the rule or convention. Rather these rules and conventions seem to focus decision making on the evidence presented at trial and to discourage the substitution of the court's subjective prior. This focus on the evidence presented at trial, and restrictions on the conclusions that can be drawn from it, may also prevent the judge/jury from exercising ideological preferences that differ from the social objective (which is embodied in the restrictions). James and Hazard (1985, Section 7.4) provide a detailed discussion of devices available to judges (such as the provision of instructions, directed verdicts, j.n.o.v., and special verdicts) for the express purpose of controlling a jury with the intent of focusing them on their mission of fact finding.

Thus we model the trial court's assessment of credible evidence in non-Bayesian terms, not because we do not believe in Bayesian decision making, but because we believe that the evidence aggregation process is highly constrained. Whether one models this as "mostly Bayesian with a few constraints" or "mostly constrained with a few opportunities for Bayesian updating" is a judgment call. In this article we take the latter route, but the former is also potentially interesting. As suggested earlier, we confine the use of Bayesian updating to the assessment of credibility and the interpretation of law, and model the evidence aggregation process axiomatically; that is, we use a set of properties (axioms), representing rules of evidence and procedure, to characterize this process. Moreover, we abstract from the credibility issue by assuming that the evidence presented by the parties and evaluated by the court is credible evidence. Alternatively, one could view the trial process as having a preliminary stage that involves evaluating evidence with respect to credibility (using a Bayesian model to appropriately discount it). Thus the litigants provide credible evidence whether directly submitted or as the result of "preprocessing" for credibility by the jury/judge.

Elsewhere we have considered the problem of modeling a court's assessment process, whereby it aggregates credible evidence on D's liability into an overall assessment (see DR). In particular, let x and y denote the assessments of the likelihood of D's liability proffered at trial by P and D, respectively, where $x \in [0,1]$ and $y \in [0,1]$. In DR we require that the court's aggregation of credible evidence be (1) strictly monotonically increasing in each of the submissions, (2) bounded by the minimum and maximum of the cases presented, (3) unbiased in the sense that it is symmetric in the evidence in both an absolute and proportional sense, and (4) independent of the order in which individual elements of the submissions are compared.

We have assumed symmetry, that is, the court's assessment would be the same for the credible evidence pair (x, y) and (y, x). Since the court is unable (due to informational problems) to "unwind" both the strategic and statistical relationships between evidence and the true p and d, and in light of the assumption that the evidence is credible, it seems reasonable to examine a process for evidence aggregation that is not biased toward either party. Thus the responsibility for redressing the impact of a party's evidence on the trial outcome falls on the adversary. In DR we also examine the effect of relaxing the symmetry assumption; we maintain it here because our focus is on how bias might arise within an unbiased (symmetric) system.

In DR we show that the foregoing properties imply that the court's liability assessment function can be represented by a member of the family of continuous functions of the form $\ell(x, y; q) = \{(x^q + y^q)/2\}^{1/q}$, $q \in (-\infty, \infty)$, $q \neq 0$; and $\ell(x, y; 0) = (xy)^{1/2}$. It can be shown (see DR) that $\ell(x, y; q)$ is an increasing function of q (for $x \neq y$), so that as q increases, D is more likely to be found liable for any given evidence pair (x, y). Thus q can represent the breadth of the court's interpretation of the applicable law, with a broader interpretation working against D. In DR we model how different levels of the court system (trial versus appeals courts) determine an appropriate value of q; in Daughety and Reinganum (1999), we use this model to examine horizontal influence (via inference about q) among a collection of appeals courts. In this article we simply assume that a value of q has been determined and is common knowledge, and we examine how the parties gather evidence in anticipation of this aggregation process.

Differentiation of $\ell(x, y; q)$ shows that the cross-partial ℓ_{xy} is positive for $q < 1$, zero if $q = 1$, and negative for $q > 1$. For a given q, the sign of the cross-partial derivative is the same for all possible evidence submissions (x, y). This property will be of significant interest in discussing the slopes of the best response functions of the litigants later in this section.

In the damages stage we could employ a similar notion of a "damages assessment function," but have elected to simply use the average of the damages evidence in that stage of the game. This is for two reasons. First, since the damages stage is a subgame of a fairly complex two-stage game, tractability suggests a simple damages function. Second, simple averaging of the damages estimate is consistent with the court imposing the Nash bargaining solution for the bargaining game that would arise once all evidence has been presented; that is, the court splits the difference between the competing claims. For the sake of brevity, we provide the analysis for the liability stage only, and simply summarize the results of a similar analysis for the damages stage at the end of this section.

2.2 The Liability Stage

Let $V^{\mathrm{P}}(d)$ and $V^{\mathrm{D}}(d)$ denote the values of continuing optimally for P and D, respectively, following a finding of liability, when it is common knowledge to the parties that the true harm is d. For P, this value represents the expected award less the expected costs associated with equilibrium evidence generation in the damages stage. For D, this value represents the expected award plus the expected costs associated with equilibrium evidence generation in the damages stage. Thus these values, which represent the "stakes" for the liability stage, will not be equal. Rather, $V^{\mathrm{D}}(d) > V^{\mathrm{P}}(d)$; that is, the defendant has more to lose than the plaintiff has to gain.

In this stage, D's liability is to be determined (or, more precisely, the likelihood that D is liable for P's harm will be assessed, with determination modeled as a coin flip employing the assessed likelihood). Recall that p is the true probability that D harmed P and that we assume that p is common knowledge to P and D, but is not verifiable to a third party. Hence in the liability stage, both parties will develop and present evidence regarding p. Evidence is represented by a draw from a distribution function which is conditioned on p; since evidence is assumed to be independent of the parties' preferences (i.e., it cannot be manufactured at will), we assume that both parties draw their observations from the same distribution. However, each party's number of observations and their realizations are assumed to be private information. The best observation[7] among those taken will be presented by each party at trial. We assume that each party must take at least one draw: P must present a case based on some evidence and D must respond with some evidence.

Let π_i^{P} represent the outcome of a single observation by P; similarly, let π_j^{D} represent the outcome of a single observation by D. Both are assumed to be drawn from the interval $[\underline{\pi}, \overline{\pi}]$ according to the distribution function $G(x \mid p) = \Pr\{\pi_k \leq x \mid p\}$ with mean p and density function $g(\mathrm{x} \mid p)$, where the interval itself may also depend on p. Both parties may sample as many times as they wish from the distribution $G(\cdot \mid p)$. We assume that each draw costs k^{P} for P and k^{D} for D. There is also a fixed cost of presenting evidence at trial for each litigant; we denote these costs as K^{P} and K^{D} for P and D, respectively. We assume a large number of potential sources of credible evidence, so the sampling is with replacement; thus the draws are independent and identically distributed (given p). Each party will choose as a strategy a *stopping rule*, which specifies when that party should stop sampling as a function of the observations to date. Since each party's number of draws taken and realized observations are private information, each party's stopping rule can depend only on the outcomes of its own evidence-generation process and a conjectured stopping rule for the other party. Larger observations are preferred by P and smaller observations are preferred by D. Thus an optimal stopping rule for P can be characterized by a *minimum* stopping value, denoted r^{P}: stop the first time the evidence draw exceeds r^{P}. Thus a higher value of r^{P} corresponds to a more aggressive ("tougher") search behavior on the part of P. Similarly, an optimal stopping rule for D can be characterized by a *maximum* stopping value, denoted r^{D}: stop the first time the evidence draw falls below r^{D}. In this case, a higher value of r^{D} corresponds to a less aggressive ("softer") search behavior on the part of D. Let $\pi^{\mathrm{P}*}$ and $\pi^{\mathrm{D}*}$ denote the best evidence observed by P and D, respectively, using these stopping rules. From the perspective of the parties (who know p), the density function for P's evidence at trial is given by $g(x \mid p)/[1 - G(r^{\mathrm{P}} \mid p)]$ on the interval $[r^{\mathrm{P}}, \overline{\pi}]$. The density function for D's evidence at trial is given by $g(y \mid p)/G(r^{\mathrm{D}} \mid p)$ on the interval $[\underline{\pi}, r^{\mathrm{D}}]$.

7. An alternative (but fundamentally equivalent) approach to that used here is that a case is developed incrementally and is the sum of evidence observations rather than the maximum/minimum. In this approach, the distribution of each additional evidence draw is conditional on the current sum, with an increasingly higher mass point at zero (corresponding to the outcome "no new favorable evidence") to reflect decreasing returns to sampling.

For arbitrary evidence pairs (x, y), the court uses the function $\ell(x, y)$ to aggregate the evidence so as to assess the likelihood of D's liability (we suppress the parameter q when it is not relevant to the discussion at hand). As will become clear, the sign of ℓ_{xy} determines the sign of the slope of the best response functions for P and D [recall that, given q, this sign is the same for all (x, y) pairs]. If this cross-partial derivative is positive, then this suggests that $\ell(x, y)$ displays the property of *complementarity of evidence*, while if it is negative, $\ell(x, y)$ displays the property of *substitutability of evidence*.[8] In what follows we will assume that $\ell_{xy} > 0$ for the following theoretical and empirical reasons. Under complementarity, the resulting best response functions will have intuitively reasonable slopes (P will be positive and D will be negative) in that they predict that as P becomes more aggressive, D does too; this prediction seems particularly appropriate as it is D's wealth that is at stake should D be found liable. If we assumed $\ell_{xy} < 0$ (that is, substitutability), our technical analysis would go through, but the slopes of the best response functions (and some comparative statics results) would be reversed. We do not consider this the most plausible case: we would be predicting that D would become less aggressive in response to P being more aggressive. Moreover, it is complementarity that is consistent with empirical analysis of the slopes of the best response functions in the strategic search for evidence. Shepherd (1999) uses data from 369 federal civil suits and studies the responses of litigants to pretrial discovery effort; he finds the pattern of response implied by complementarity. For these reasons, we proceed under the assumption that $\ell(x, y)$ displays the property of complementarity; that is, $\ell_{xy} > 0$ at all points in the evidence space E.

Propositions 1 and 2 (see the appendix for formal statements and derivations) characterize the best-response functions for the parties. For any stopping rule r^{D} chosen by D, P has a unique best response $\mathrm{BR}^{\mathrm{P}}(r^{\mathrm{D}})$, and for any stopping rule r^{P} chosen by P, D has a unique best response $\mathrm{BR}^{\mathrm{D}}(r^{\mathrm{P}})$. Our maintained assumption that $\ell_{xy} > 0$ ensures that the function $\mathrm{BR}^{\mathrm{P}}(r^{\mathrm{D}})$ is increasing: as D searches less aggressively (referred to earlier as playing "softer"), P searches more aggressively (plays "tougher"). This same assumption ensures that the function $\mathrm{BR}^{\mathrm{D}}(r^{\mathrm{P}})$ is decreasing: as P searches more aggressively, D searches more aggressively. Proposition 3 (see the appendix) asserts that there is a unique Nash equilibrium in stopping rules, $(r^{\mathrm{P}*}, r^{\mathrm{D}*})$. Figure 1

8. In terms of $\ell(x, y; q)$, complementarity implies that $q < 1$, while substitutability implies that $q > 1$. This means that if $\ell(x, y; q)$ reflects complementarity, then it acts like a production function from neoclassical economics (in this case, a symmetric CES production function), while if $\ell(x, y; q)$ reflects substitutability, it acts like a norm, or distance measure.

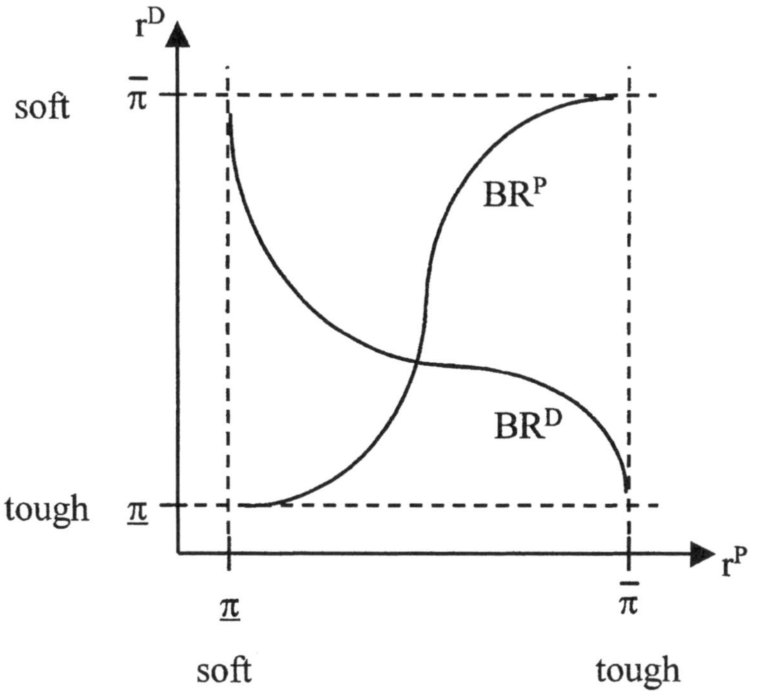

Figure 1. Best response functions and Nash equilibrium.

illustrates the best response functions and the equilibrium for a representative case.

The impact of changes in the underlying parameters on the best response functions and on the equilibrium strategies are displayed in Table 1. The signs in the table indicate the effect of an increase in the column entry on the row entry. In Table 1, a positive entry for BR^P or r^{P*} corresponds to a rightward shift of the curve in Figure 1, while a positive entry for BR^D or r^{D*} corresponds to an upward shift of the curve in Figure 1. If an increase in d leads to increases in both $V^P(d)$ and $V^D(d)$, then the new equilibrium involves D being more aggressive

Table 1. Comparative Statics

	$V^P(d)$	$V^D(d)$	k^P	k^D
BR^P	+	0	–	0
BR^D	0	–	0	+
r^{P*}	+	–	–	+
r^{D*}	–	–	+	+

but the effect on P's behavior is indeterminate. Increases in sampling costs have an impact that depends upon whose costs increased. If P alone suffers an increase in both sampling costs [k^P and P's sampling cost in the damages stage, an increase in which lowers $V^P(d)$], then r^{P*} falls and r^{D*} rises: both parties play softer by adjusting their stopping rules, so as to put less effort into evidence gathering. This is because both the direct effect (via k^P) and the indirect effect [via the negative effect of an increase in P's sampling costs in the damages stage on $V^P(d)$] reduce r^{P*} and increase r^{D*}. On the other hand, if D alone suffers an increase in both sampling costs [k^D and D's sampling cost in the damages stage, an increase in which raises $V^D(d)$], then the effect is ambiguous for both parties: the direct effect via the liability sampling cost k^D is to make P more aggressive and D less aggressive. The indirect effect [the positive effect of an increase in D's sampling costs for the damages stage on $V^D(d)$] is to make P less aggressive and D more aggressive. The net result will be case specific.

Since P stops the first time an observation occurs in the interval $[r^{P*}, \overline{\pi}]$, it follows that the expected number of draws for P is given by $1/[1 - G(r^{P*} \mid p)]$ and the expected cost of liability evidence for P is given by $k^P/[1 - G(r^{P*} \mid p)] + K^P$. Similarly, since D stops the first time an observation occurs in the interval $[\underline{\pi}, r^{D*}]$, it follows that the expected number of draws for D in the liability stage is given by $1/G(r^{D*} \mid p)$ and the expected cost of liability evidence for D is given by $k^D/G(r^{D*} \mid p) + K^D$. Note that, in equilibrium, these expressions are also conditional on d since both r^{P*} and r^{D*} depend on both d and p; we suppress this dependence unless it is of specific interest.

2.3 The Damages Stage

Finally, we briefly indicate how the same analysis can be used to derive the continuation values $V^D(d)$ and $V^P(d)$, which are the equilibrium payoffs for the damages stage (for details, see Daughety and Reinganum, 1998b). Let δ_i^P represent the outcome of a single observation by P; similarly, let δ_j^D represent the outcome of a single observation by D. Both are assumed to be drawn from the interval $[\underline{\delta}, \overline{\delta},]$ according to the distribution function $F(x \mid d) = \Pr\{\delta_k \leq x \mid d\}$ with density function $f(x \mid d)$ and mean d, where the interval $[\underline{\delta}, \overline{\delta}]$ may also depend on d. Both parties may sample as many times as they wish from the distribution $F(\cdot \mid d)$, at constant per draw costs of c^P and c^D, respectively (sampling costs may also depend on true harm d, but we suppress this dependence for notational convenience; we return to this issue in Section 3). There is also a fixed cost of trial associated with presenting the evidence for the damages stage at trial; we denote this cost for P by C^P and for D by C^D. As before, we assume that P submits only the most favorable evidence at trial, which is denoted δ^{P*}; similarly D's most favorable evidence is denoted δ^{D*}. Thus the court observes only the pair $(\delta^{P*}, \delta^{D*})$. In the damages stage, we consider the case of $q = 1$; that is, the award at trial is the simple average of the evidence: $A = (\delta^{P*} + \delta^{D*})/2$.

An equilibrium stopping rule for P is characterized by a *minimum* stopping value, denoted s^{P*}, while an equilibrium stopping rule for D is characterized by a *maximum* stopping value, denoted s^{D*}. Under these stopping rules, the expected award at trial, given true damages d, is given by $E(A \mid d) = (1/2)[E(x \mid x \geq s^{P*}; d) + E(y \mid y \leq s^{D*}; d)]$, where the expectation is with respect to the distribution $F(\cdot \mid d)$. The expected number of draws for P is given by $1/[1 - F(s^{P*} \mid d)]$ and the expected cost of damages evidence for P is given by $c^P/[1 - F(s^{P*} \mid d)] + C^P$. Similarly, the expected number of draws for D is given by $1/F(s^{D*} \mid d)$ and the expected cost of damages evidence for D is given by $c^D/F(s^{D*} \mid d) + C^D$. Thus, $V^D(d) = E(A \mid d) + c^D/F(s^{D*} \mid d) + C^D$ and $V^P(d) = E(A \mid d) - c^P/[1 - F(s^{P*} \mid d)] - C^P$.

3. Sources and Examples of Equilibrium Bias

Here we illustrate the sources of equilibrium bias via a series of examples. We employ a uniform distribution for evidence because it allows straightforward computation and because its symmetry allows us to isolate differences in sampling cost and differences in stakes as sources of bias. We also consider the exponential distribution in the particular case of damages evidence, on the basis that very high damages estimates, substantially in excess of the average estimate, are rare but possible. After presenting the examples we will discuss some potential remedies and problems with their implementation.

Example 1: Uniformly-Distributed Damages Evidence

Conditional on the true harm d, let the distribution of evidence obtained on a single draw be given by the uniform distribution $F(x \mid d) = (x - \underline{\delta})/\Delta$, where $\Delta \equiv \bar{\delta} - \underline{\delta}$. The endpoints of the interval ($\bar{\delta}$ and $\underline{\delta}$) are assumed to be increasing in d. In order to understand whether adversarial sampling leads to equilibrium bias, assume that simple random sampling would yield an unbiased estimate of the true damages: $E(x \mid d) = (\bar{\delta} + \underline{\delta})/2 = d$. In order to ensure interior solutions for s^{P*} and s^{D*}, we assume that both sampling costs are less than $\Delta/4$. The equilibrium strategies are $s^{P*} = \bar{\delta} - 2(\Delta c^P)^{1/2}$ and $s^{D*} = \underline{\delta} + 2(\Delta c^D)^{1/2}$. The expected award can be calculated to be $E(A \mid d) = d + \{[(\Delta c^D)^{1/2}] - [(\Delta c^P)^{1/2}]\}/2$, where the term in brackets is the difference between the defendant's and the plaintiff's expected sampling costs. Thus the expected value of the award penalizes the party with the higher sampling cost. If both parties have the same sampling costs

($c^P = c^D = c$), then the award will be unbiased in that the expected award will equal the true harm.[9]

Example 2: Exponentially Distributed Damages Evidence

Conditional on the true harm d, suppose that the distribution of evidence is given by $F(x \mid d) = 1 - \exp(-x/d)$ for $x \in [0, \infty)$. Thus, for this case, the support of F is unbounded on the right and $\underline{\delta} = 0$. This sampling distribution represents conditions wherein there is a higher probability that a draw comes from the portion below the mean than from the portion above. For instance, limitations on what the law allows as part of a damages estimate (Is mental anguish allowed? How are foregone profits on a new product to be computed?) suggest a higher probability of damages estimates below the mean than above it. Thus, for example, in the case of expert witnesses, this may reflect the accumulation of statutes and precedents that have influenced a sizable proportion of these experts to provide relatively "conservative" estimates of damages. On the other hand, creative accounting, varying choices of future returns and likely discount rates, as well as novel but well-supported arguments about sources of potential losses may result in very high damage estimates. Both possibilities are better represented by the exponential distribution, which concentrates much of the mass of the distribution below the mean, but has a rapidly thinning tail to the right of the mean. While it is true that, in reality, damages estimates are not unbounded, specifying an upper bound creates tractability problems, and adds nothing to the analysis. Note also that the tail of the exponential distribution converges (exponentially) to the axis, suggesting that the probability of draws even moderately higher than the mean is small.

By construction, the expected value of evidence on any one draw is equal to the true harm: $E(x \mid d) = d$. Thus, again, simple random sampling will lead to an unbiased estimate of the damages. The equilibrium strategy for P is $s^{P*} = \max\{d\ell n(d/2c^P), 0\}$ (that is, a boundary solution occurs when $d/2c^P \leq 1$). D's equilibrium strategy, s^{D*}, is defined implicitly by $(s^{D*}/d) + \exp(-s^{D*}/d) = 1 + (2c^D/d)$. Since

9. If $c \leq \Delta/16$, then $s^{P*} \geq s^{D*}$; that is, P's evidence will always suggest damages in excess of those suggested by D's evidence. If $c > \Delta/16$, then $s^{P*} < s^{D*}$; in this case, there is a chance that P's evidence will suggest lower damages than those suggested by D's evidence. This counterintuitive second possibility can occur if sampling is very costly because of the simultaneous presentation of evidence. One might think that, upon hearing the plaintiff's expert ask for lower damages than the defendant's expert, the defendant would simply stipulate to the plaintiff's estimate. However, this should lead the plaintiff to wonder why the defendant's expert is not testifying and might lead the plaintiff to call the defendant's expert to get his higher estimate into the record as well. This possibility suggests a model involving the sequential submission of evidence and the ability to cross-examine, which is beyond the scope of the present analysis.

the left-hand side is increasing in s^{D*}, there is a unique interior solution to this equation; moreover, $2c^D < s^{D*} < d + 2c^D$.

The expected award given true harm d is $E(A\,|\,d) = d + [s^{P*} + s^{D*} - ds^{D*}/(s^{D*} - 2c^D)]/2$. The term in brackets may be positive, negative, or zero; that is, the plaintiff may be over-, exactly, or undercompensated relative to the actual harm d. Comparative statics analysis indicates that an increase in sampling costs (holding d fixed) makes the respective litigant less aggressive, while an increase in harm d (holding sampling costs fixed) makes P more aggressive and D less aggressive.

Recall that the plaintiff's expected cost of gathering damages evidence is $c^P/[1 - F(s^{P*}\,|\,d)]$ and that similarly the defendant's expected cost of gathering evidence is $c^D/F(s^{D*}\,|\,d)$. For the exponential case, it is straightforward to show that the equilibrium strategies, the expected award, and these expected evidence costs, as well as the measure of bias $b^A(d) = E(A\,|\,d) - d$, are all homogeneous of degree 1 in (d, c^P, c^D). Thus equal proportional increases in the basic model parameters d, c^P, c^D result in equal proportional increases in the equilibrium levels of the stopping rules, the equilibrium expected award, and the equilibrium expected evidence costs.

Although we have heretofore suppressed any dependence of the sampling costs on the magnitude of harm, it is not unreasonable to assume that there is some relationship between these two. Assuming that $c^P = c^D = c$, Figure 2 describes combinations of c and d that yield various outcomes. The dashed line labeled "$b^A = 0$" gives (d, c) combinations for which $E(A\,|\,d) = d$. For instance, a case involving more harm may be (technically) more complex, so one would expect that sampling costs should increase with harm d. Let $c(d)$ denote the sampling costs for P and D as a function of the commonly known damages d. If $c(d)$ is proportional to d, then the equilibrium outcome is associated with a ray in Figure 2; two such rays are illustrated as solid lines from the origin. The uppermost ray corresponds to a high propor-

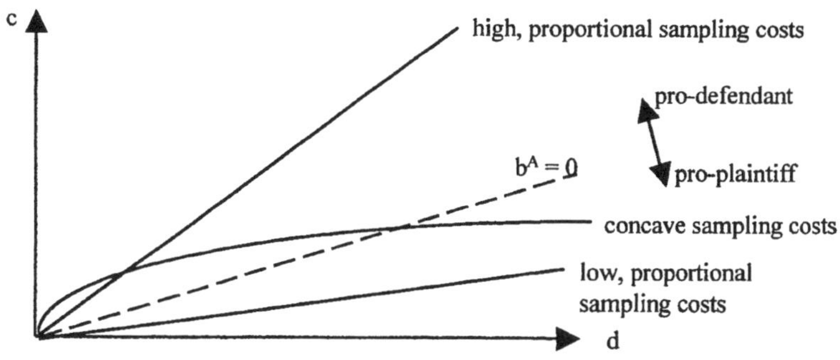

Figure 2. Combinations yielding various damages—trial outcomes and three sampling cost functions.

tional sampling cost. In this case, sampling always yields outcomes in which the resulting equilibrium is biased toward D in the sense that $b^A < 0$. The lowermost ray corresponds to a low proportional sampling cost, yielding outcomes in which the resulting equilibrium is biased toward P in the sense that $b^A > 0$. Note that this means that whatever is true for an outcome of a given level of damages, say d', is true for all levels of damages: in the case of proportional sampling costs, all outcomes are either biased toward D ($b^A < 0$), biased toward P ($b^A > 0$), or unbiased ($b^A = 0$).

The case of $c(d)$ concave is shown as the curved line in Figure 2. This is likely to be a reasonable representation in that increases in the severity of the harm may initially occasion greater reliance on specialized experts, but this specialization effect should eventually disappear: as d increases, the same general level of experts will be used. In the concave cost case, plaintiffs with low values of d will suffer prodefendant bias, while those with high levels of d will enjoy proplaintiff bias.[10] Thus the general pattern is one of systematic bias in equilibrium, but who benefits depends on the level of actual harm. Plaintiffs with low levels of harm tend to be undercompensated, while those with high levels of harm are potentially overcompensated in equilibrium.

Example 3: Equilibrium Bias in the Liability Stage

Due to the complexity of the analysis of the liability stage, we consider the simplest possible unbiased system, wherein $\ell(x,y) = (x+y)/2$, the distribution of evidence (given p) is uniform on $[\underline{\pi}, \overline{\pi}]$ with $(\underline{\pi} + \overline{\pi})/2 = p$, and $\underline{\pi}$ and $\overline{\pi}$ are also functions of p.[11] Thus the court gives equal weight to both parties' evidence and the common evidence distribution being sampled provides equal likelihood of any piece of evidence being drawn. As shown below, even if the sampling costs in both stages are symmetric (that is, $k^P = k^D$ and $c^P = c^D$), the fixed costs are symmetric ($K^P = K^D$ and $C^P = C^D$) and the damages stage is unbiased (e.g., F is the uniform distribution), the libability stage will favor the defendant.

In this example the equilibrium strategies are given by $r^{P*} = \overline{\pi} - 2(k^P\Pi/V^P(d))^{1/2}$ and $r^{D*} = \underline{\pi} + 2(k^D\Pi/V^D(d))^{1/2}$, where $\Pi \equiv \overline{\pi} - \underline{\pi}$.[12] The expected costs of liability evidence for P are

10. Note that, if $c(d)$ was a constant positive number, then the same pattern would arise. It is possible, however, that the sampling costs curve eventually becomes convex at high values of d, where congestion effects predominate (e.g., where extensive use of technology-intensive batteries of expert witnesses may be necessary).

11. Note that in this case, $\ell_{xy} = 0$; thus the litigants have dominant strategies.

12. In order to ensure that r^{P*} and r^{D*} lie in the interval $[\underline{\pi}, \overline{\pi}]$, it is necessary to assume that $k^P \leq \Pi V^P(d)/4$ and $k^D \leq \Pi V^D(d)/4$, respectively. Again, it is possible for the stopping sets $[\underline{\pi}, r^{D*}]$ and $[r^{P*}, \overline{\pi}]$ to overlap if sampling is relatively costly; for the case of symmetric costs ($k^P = k^D = k$), a sufficient condition for $r^{P*} \geq r^{D*}$ is $k \leq \Pi V^P(d)V^D(d)/4[(V^P(d))^{1/2} + (V^D(d))^{1/2}]^2$.

$[(\Pi V^{P}(d)k^{P})^{1/2}]/2$, while for D they are $[(\Pi V^{D}(d)k^{D})^{1/2}]/2$. Thus in each case, the expected costs of gathering liabiilty evidence are increasing in both the continuation payoff from the damages stage and in the per sample evidence cost of the liability stage.

The question of bias in the liability stage concerns the liability assessment that such a trial is likely to produce. In particular, the liability stage is unbiased if the expected assessment of liability produced by the trial, $E[\ell(\pi^{P*}, \pi^{D*})\,|\,p, d]$, equals the true underlying likelihood, p. To measure this, let $b^{\ell}(p, d) \equiv E[\ell(\pi^{P*}, \pi^{D*})\,|\,p, d] - p$. The equilibrium expected liability assessment is given by

$$E[\ell(\pi^{P*}, \pi^{D*})\,|\,p, d] = [E(\pi^{P*}\,|\,p, d) + E(\pi^{D*}\,|\,p, d)]/2$$
$$= ([(\overline{\pi} + r^{P*})/2] + [(\underline{\pi} + r^{D*})/2])/2.$$

Substituting the equilibrium strategies for P and D yields:

$$E[\ell(\pi^{P*}, \pi^{D*})\,|\,p, d]$$
$$= p + \left[(\Pi k^{D}/V^{D}(d))^{1/2} - (\Pi k^{P}/V^{P}(d))^{1/2}\right]/2.$$

Assuming an otherwise symmetric process in which sampling costs are the same for both parties (i.e., $k^{P} = k^{D} = k$), it is clear that the liability stage is equilibrium biased toward defendants, since $V^{D}(d) > V^{P}(d)$. In this case,

$$b^{\ell}(p, d) = (\Pi k)^{1/2}\left[(V^{D}(d))^{-1/2} - (V^{P}(d))^{-1/2}\right]/2 < 0.$$

Notice that the direction of the liability stage equilibrium bias is independent of both the extent and direction of any damages stage equilibrium bias, including the possibility that the damages stage is unbiased (as was discussed in the uniformly distributed damages evidence example presented above).[13] Moreover, if there is systematic bias

13. Landes (1993) uses an "inconsistent priors" model (i.e., parties have individual subjective assessments of the probability of their winning at trial, which are common knowledge, but do not obey any consistency condition such as being conditional probabilities derived from the same prior) to examine the impact of bifurcating trials on the aggregate cost of litigation. He notes (p. 117) that the sequential nature of a bifurcated trial affects the parties' incentives to invest (lowering the plaintiff's incentives and raising the defendant's), so that the defendant's chance of prevailing (as perceived by either party) is increased relative to a nonbifurcated trial. While he does not address the issue of bias directly, if the nonbifurcated trial were itself unbiased (which issue cannot be addressed using inconsistent priors since there is no "correct" probability), then his finding would be consistent with ours.

in the damages stage, the liability stage may simply reinforce it. If we consider exponentially distributed damages evidence with concave sampling costs, then plaintiffs with low actual damages, who expect the damages stage to be prodefendant equilibrium biased, also suffer from prodefendant equilibrium bias in the liability stage. On the other hand, plaintiffs with high actual harm, who expect the damages stage to be proplaintiff equilibrium biased, anticipate a prodefendant equilibrium bias in the liability stage. Finally, if $V^{\mathrm{P}}(d)$ and $V^{\mathrm{D}}(d)$ are linearly homogeneous in d, then the extent of bias diminishes as d increases.[14]

Example 4: Adversarial Bias

As shown above, systematic bias can readily arise in either stage and the two biases studied need not cancel each other. In each stage bias which favors one party disfavors the other. If we consider the overall game, however, the adversarial procedure as the means for generating evidence may readily work against both parties. To see this, we compare the payoffs from the game [denoted $V^{\mathrm{P}*}(p,d)$ and $V^{\mathrm{D}*}(p,d)$] with a hypothetical payoff constructed from a nonadversarial alternative [denoted $V^{\mathrm{PN}}(p,d)$ and $V^{\mathrm{DN}}(p,d)$]. For the nonadversarial alternative we consider the expected payoffs if each party drew one observation for each stage and liability and damages were based on these draws using simple averaging for both the liability assessment and the damage award assessment. Thus, $V^{\mathrm{PN}}(p,d) = p(d - c^{\mathrm{P}} - C^{\mathrm{P}}) - k^{\mathrm{P}} - K^{\mathrm{P}}$ and $V^{\mathrm{DN}}(p,d) = p(d + c^{\mathrm{D}} + C^{\mathrm{D}}) + k^{\mathrm{D}} + K^{\mathrm{D}}$, while

$$
\begin{aligned}
V^{\mathrm{P}*}(p,d) = {} & E\left[\ell(\pi^{\mathrm{P}*},\pi^{\mathrm{D}*})\,|\,p,d\right] \\
& \times\left\{E(A\,|\,d) - c^{\mathrm{P}}/\left[1 - F(s^{\mathrm{P}*}\,|\,d)\right] - C^{\mathrm{P}}\right\} \\
& - k^{\mathrm{P}}/\left[1 - \mathrm{G}(r^{\mathrm{P}*}\,|\,p)\right] - K^{\mathrm{P}}
\end{aligned}
$$

and

$$
\begin{aligned}
V^{\mathrm{D}*}(p,d) = {} & E\left[\ell(\pi^{\mathrm{P}*},\pi^{\mathrm{D}*})\,|\,p,d\right] \\
& \times\left\{E(A\,|\,d) + c^{\mathrm{D}}/F(s^{\mathrm{D}*}\,|\,d) + C^{\mathrm{D}}\right\} \\
& + k^{\mathrm{D}}/G(r^{\mathrm{D}*}\,|\,p) + K^{\mathrm{D}}.
\end{aligned}
$$

For example, in $V^{\mathrm{P}*}(p,d)$, the expression on the right-hand side in braces is the net expected value to P from the damages stage (expected award minus the expected costs of damages evidence). Multiplying that on the left is the expected outcome from the liability stage, while to the

14. If we consider the exponential damage estimates case with symmetric sampling and trial costs which are proportional to d, then $V^{\mathrm{P}}(d)$ and $V^{\mathrm{D}}(d)$ are linearly homogeneous in d.

right of the braces we subtract the expected costs to P of liability evidence; the terms in $V^{D*}(p,d)$ can be similarly interpreted. In order to discuss *adversarial bias*, we define $B^{P}(p,d) \equiv V^{P*}(p,d) - V^{PN}(p,d)$ and $B^{D}(p,d) \equiv V^{D*}(p,d) - V^{DN}(p,d)$.

The presence of variable and fixed costs of evidence gathering and presentation, even in the nonadversarial case, screens out some otherwise meritorious cases, but this would seem to be an unavoidable friction necessary to ration use of the court system. If $B^{P}(p,d)$ is negative, however, this means that the adversarial process results in yet more meritorious cases never reaching trial. As the earlier examples suggest, $B^{P}(p,d)$ is likely to be strongly negative unless the award bias $b^{A}(d)$ is sufficiently positive. Thus if damages estimates are uniformly distributed (or exponentially distributed with high proportional sampling costs), all plaintiffs would expect to be undercompensated. In the exponential case with concave sampling costs, cases with low to moderate harm would be screened out entirely: only cases involving substantial harm are likely to actually benefit from adversarial evidence generation.

The results for the defendant are more mixed. In general, as should be clear from the biases examined earlier in this section, cases involving lower levels of harm are likely to favor the defendant, both in absolute terms and when compared with a nonadversarial process. However, in cases involving high levels of harm, the adversarial process may work against the defendant as well (when compared with nonadversarial evidence generation, since adversarial litigants will typically sample more than once). While these conclusions regarding the nature and extent of equilibrium bias are based on computational examples using simple functional forms, it seems unlikely that more complex functional forms will result in a complete "undoing" of the biases described here.

3.1 Remedies and Problems of Implementation

While a number of possible piecemeal remedies suggest themselves, all are plagued by problems of implementation due to the limited information available to the court. For example, suspicion of bias due to asymmetry of sampling costs suggests taxing the low-cost (or subsidizing the high-cost) sampler, so as to relevel the playing field. To tax or subsidize each draw necessitates knowing the number of draws. Since this is private information, there are incentives to misrepresent it. Shifting some or all of one litigant's costs to the other creates yet more problems, as it encourages overinvestment in evidence generation by the party able to shift costs. For instance, following a finding of liability, a pure loser-pays rule means that P should spare no expense in the damages stage. Thus this would both raise costs and contribute to a proplaintiff bias in the damages stage; anticipating this will lead both P and D to further overinvest in the liability stage.

As we found in the exponentially distributed damages evidence example, even when sampling costs are equal, bias arises. Here correction would require that the court know d, the true damages, because the sampling distribution is conditioned on d and the direction of the bias may change as a function of d (as in the nonlinear case illustrated in Figure 2). Of course, "knowing" d begs the question, as the point of the trial is to estimate d. Moreover, since each trial presents biased evidence, one cannot rely upon experience in "similar" cases to generate a valid estimate of the underlying damages evidence distribution: the outcome of a series of trials does not provide, for example, a simple random sample; it provides a complexly biased sample, with unknown characteristics of how the sample was generated.

A natural solution to the bias induced by the divergence of stakes is to make the stakes equal (a form of decoupling; see Polinsky and Che, 1991). Either society subsidizes at least one of the litigant's costs (with the attendant problems of misreporting and overinvestment in evidence generation) or the award P receives must be subsidized to equate the stakes. Moreover, the amount of subsidy required depends upon unobservables (e.g., d).

Finally, as discussed in our last example, adversarial litigants sample too much. A tax is the natural remedy, with all the problems raised earlier for taxes and subsidies when the underlying parameters are unknown and the number of draws is unobservable.

A possible solution lies in greater centralization, via either a properly designed mechanism for (decentralized) information gathering and revelation or centralized information gathering. The latter possibility is subject to the problems raised by Posner (1999) and others with respect to inquisitorial systems. While the former is appealing, it cannot be applied to the trial portion of the legal process in a vacuum. Rather, one needs to characterize the optimal mix of incentive constraints and opportunities for discretion throughout the entire legal process, so as to induce efficient choices of care as well as evidence generation and revelation. This does suggest, however, an intermediate remedy that may ameliorate the aforementioned informational effects. Courts in adversarial systems could independently acquire evidence, something that is commonly used in child custody disputes and has been used in a few tort cases (e.g., appointing a scientific panel to evaluate the medical evidence regarding breast implants). A careful analysis of the incentives facing litigants and the implications for bias in the aggregate decision generated by use of this option is beyond the scope of this article.

4. Related Literature

There are several different models of trial court decision making. For instance, one alternative views the trial outcome as an exogenous function of the litigants' levels of effort or expenditure (for a review of much of this literature, see Cooter and Rubinfeld, 1989; specific examples include Danzon, 1983; Braeutigam, Owen, and Panzar, 1984; Katz, 1987, 1988; Plott, 1987; Hause, 1989; Landes, 1993). Our approach differs in that the function used by the court to assess the evidence is not specified exogenously, but is derived from a set of axioms [Skaperdas (1996) has recently provided an axiomatic basis[15] for the relative effort models used in these earlier works]. A second difference is that the trial outcome is based on evidence provided by the parties rather than on effort or expenditure, both of which are unobservable in our model. Indeed, we find that trial outcomes cannot be represented by a function of expenditure (and expected trial outcomes are not a function of expected expenditure).[16] Since evidence is obtained through sequential search, trial effort and expenditures are stochastically related to the actual evidence presented in such a way that one cannot substitute effort or expenditure for evidence in the liability determination.

Another expenditure-based approach assumes multiple potential types of defendants (e.g., innocent and guilty, or negligent and nonnegligent). A defendant's type is private information; only the level of expenditure can signal (to a sophisticated Bayesian decision maker) his guilt or innocence. Assuming it is less costly for an innocent defendant to claim innocence, an innocent defendant reveals himself to be innocent by (essentially) outspending a guilty one [specific examples include Rubinfeld and Sappington (1987) and Sanchirico[17] (1997b, c)]. In these signaling-based models, the litigants are unable to present evidence that is inherently credible (i.e., "scientific"); rather it is his willingness to engage in significant expenditures that reveals his type. Sobel (1985), Shin (1994, 1998), Lewis and Poitevin (1997), and Sanchirico (1997a) provide models in which the parties have private information, but may not present it because it is costly to do so. They allow a sophisticated Bayesian arbitrator or court to reallocate the burden of proof (either ex post, based on the evidence provided, or ex ante, to influence the evidence to be provided).

Milgrom and Roberts (1986) assume that the decision-maker is uninformed and strategically naive, but that both parties know all the pieces of relevant information, which can be conveyed costlessly and credibly to the decision maker. They show that the adversarial behavior of the parties results in full revelation; thus the outcome coincides with the full information optimal decision [extensions include Lipman and Seppi (1995) and Seidmann and Winter (1997)]. In our model, the parties have

15. We thank Tracy Lewis for pointing out this related article.

16. This is because we employ sequential search with a continuous evidence space. A model employing nonsequential search, in which parties commit to a specific number of draws (or commit to a specific level of evidence), could generate such a representation.

17. In Sanchirico's principal-agent model, the cost of evidence is actually determined by the court; that is, the defendant is charged a fee which varies with the evidence presented.

common knowledge of the defendant's true liability and the plaintiff's true damages, but these are unverifiable to the court; and while the outcomes of their evidence draws are verifiable, they are also private information for each party and will therefore only be provided selectively.

Finally, Froeb and Kobayashi (1996) address the issue of trial bias by focusing on liability determination by a jury in a comparative negligence framework (with known damages). They model evidence generation as a sequence of coin flips conducted by both litigants; each litigant chooses when to stop. The jury is assumed to be strategically naive (i.e., it does not recognize the parties' strategic incentives to present or suppress evidence) and potentially biased. On the other hand, it is statistically sophisticated, updating its prior distribution on the basis of the number of heads and tails reported. Given this updating process and the specific functional form of the sampling distribution, Froeb and Kobayashi show that the jury will nevertheless make unbiased decisions (i.e., its posterior expected liability equals the defendant's true liability). However, this result is sensitive to a number of assumptions, including the form of the sampling distribution, the symmetry of the litigants and the specification of comparative negligence.[18] Farmer and Pecorino (1998) reexamine this model under an alternative specification of jury bias and find that initial bias can be exacerbated (not ameliorated) by selective evidence production. Our model differs from Froeb and Kobayashi's (as well as from the signaling-based literature described above) in that our court is constrained by the rules of evidence and procedure to obey a set of axioms in its aggregation of (credible) evidence, rather than using statistical methods.

5. Conclusions and Extensions

In this article we have examined aspects of the adversarial trial process which might lead to systematic bias in trial outcomes. Through a collection of algebraic examples we have shown that systematic bias can be imparted in several ways. First, systematic bias can arise due to differences in the cost of sampling evidence. For instance, when the damages stage involves a uniform distribution from which evidence is drawn, the party with the lower sampling costs will sample (on average)

18. Since completing this article, we have become aware of another working paper by Froeb and Kobayashi (1999) in which they model evidence generation as sequential search. Each party presents only their best evidence at trial, and the court aggregates evidence by using a simple average (leading to dominant strategies). Thus their model is similar to our treatment of the damages stage. However, they do not address the issue of bias; indeed, they eliminate bias by construction and focus on comparing the adversarial and inquisitorial processes in terms of cost and variance. Moreover, they consider a single-stage rather than the two-stage trial we consider; we also allow more general aggregation procedures, leading to equilibria that do not rely on dominant strategies.

more often and the award will be systematically biased in this party's favor. Second, asymmetry in the sampling distribution (given equal sampling costs) can result in systematic bias. When the damages stage involves an exponential distribution from which the evidence is drawn, if sampling costs are identical and proportional to true harm, then the award will exhibit a constant proportional bias which may be either positive or negative, with the direction of the bias a function of the sampling cost parameter. A high value of the cost parameter favors the defendant, since few draws will be taken and the chance of the plaintiff obtaining a draw in the upper tail is low; a low value of the cost parameter favors the plaintiff, since many draws will be taken and the chance of the plaintiff obtaining a draw in the upper tail is higher. If sampling costs are not proportional to actual harm, the award will be downward biased for some levels of harm and upward biased for others; however, there is no reason to believe that these biases "cancel out" in expectation. Third, a systematic prodefendant bias arises in the liability stage due to a divergence between the parties' respective stakes. This divergence is a consequence of sequential decision making over multiple stages: at each stage, the plaintiff's continuation value is the expected award less future evidence and trial costs, whereas the defendant's continuation value is the expected award plus future evidence and trial costs. Finally, the adversarial process itself generates additional costs relative to a nonadversarial evidence generation process and acts to further screen out otherwise meritorious cases.

Such systematic bias is important because it is likely to have an impact on market processes that rely on legal enforcement. For example, the undercompensation of consumers harmed by products is likely to lead to reduced demand, which may mean fewer products developed or units produced. Products liability defendants who anticipate that consumers will be undercompensated have a further incentive to intentionally misrepresent safety and weakened incentives to improve it. Our example with exponentially distributed damages evidence and concave sampling costs suggests that R & D may be diverted to developing products with a low probability of causing high harm, but a relatively high probability of causing low to moderate harm. This pattern of bias may also encourage firms to devote resources to legal and political efforts to limit compensatory damages; such limits have been implemented in a number of states. Finally, in a contracts setting, anticipated undercompensation reduces the incentive to make relationship-specific investments, as breach becomes more likely.

The point of this article is that there is reason to expect that adversarial processes are not unbiased and may create inefficiencies in the economic relationships that depend on them for enforcement or compensation. The source of such inefficiencies is the now familiar combination of incomplete information and sequential choice by self-interested agents. If agents in economic relationships anticipate a systematic bias in enforcement or compensation, then prediction of the outcome of those relationships (prices charged, units sold, investments made, bargains struck) must also account for this bias.

Appendix

Proposition 1. P's optimal strategy is to stop after m draws with most favorable evidence of $\tilde{\pi}_m^{\mathrm{P}}$, given that D uses the stopping rule r^{D} and the true probability of liability is p, if and only if the expected contribution of the incremental evidence, net of the cost of another draw, is nonpositive:

$$\mathscr{W}^{\mathrm{P}}(\tilde{\pi}_m^{\mathrm{P}}, r^{\mathrm{D}}; p) \equiv [V^{\mathrm{P}}(d)/G(r^{\mathrm{D}} \mid p)] \times \int\int [\ell(x,y) - \ell(\tilde{\pi}_m^{\mathrm{P}}, y)] \times g(y \mid p) g(x \mid p)\, dy\, dx - k^{\mathrm{P}} \leq 0,$$

where the first integral is over $x \in [\tilde{\pi}_m^{\mathrm{P}}, \overline{\pi}]$ and the second is over $y \in [\underline{\pi}, r^{\mathrm{D}}]$.

Proof. Since the sampling cost is constant, a myopic stopping rule is optimal. Let $W^{\mathrm{P}}(\tilde{\pi}_m^{\mathrm{P}}, r^{\mathrm{D}}; p)$ denote the payoff to the plaintiff from stopping now with best observation $\tilde{\pi}_m^{\mathrm{P}}$, given that the defendant uses the strategy r^{D} and that the true probability that D harmed P is p; then

$$W^{\mathrm{P}}(\tilde{\pi}_m^{\mathrm{P}}, r^{\mathrm{D}}; p) = [V^{\mathrm{P}}(d)/G(r^{\mathrm{D}} \mid p)] \int \ell(\tilde{\pi}_m^{\mathrm{P}}, y) g(y \mid p)\, dy,$$

where the integral is over $y \in [\underline{\pi}, r^{\mathrm{D}}]$. If, rather than stopping with evidence $\tilde{\pi}_m^{\mathrm{P}}$, P samples once more and then stops, P's payoff (gross of sampling costs) is given by

$$EW^{\mathrm{P}}(\tilde{\pi}_{m+1}^{\mathrm{P}}, r^{\mathrm{D}}; p) = W^{\mathrm{P}}(\tilde{\pi}_m^{\mathrm{P}}, r^{\mathrm{D}}; p) G(\tilde{\pi}_m^{\mathrm{P}} \mid p) + \int W^{\mathrm{P}}(x, r^{\mathrm{D}}; p) g(x \mid p)\, dx,$$

where the integral is over $x \in [\tilde{\pi}_m^{\mathrm{P}}, \overline{\pi}]$. Thus it is optimal for P to stop at $\tilde{\pi}_m^{\mathrm{P}}$ if and only if the benefits of one more draw do not exceed the costs of one more draw. Let the benefit of one more draw net of the cost of one more draw be denoted

$$\mathscr{W}^{\mathrm{P}}(\tilde{\pi}_m^{\mathrm{P}}, r^{\mathrm{D}}; p) \equiv \int [W^{\mathrm{P}}(x, r^{\mathrm{D}}; p) - W^{\mathrm{P}}(\tilde{\pi}_m^{\mathrm{P}}, r^{\mathrm{D}}; p)] g(x \mid p)\, dx - k^{\mathrm{P}},$$

where the integral is over $x \in [\tilde{\pi}_m^{\mathrm{P}}, \overline{\pi}]$. Substituting and simplifying yields $\mathscr{W}^{\mathrm{P}}(\tilde{\pi}_m^{\mathrm{P}}, r^{\mathrm{D}}; p) \equiv [V^{\mathrm{P}}(d)/G(r^{\mathrm{D}} \mid p)] \int \int [\ell(x, y) - \ell(\tilde{\pi}_m^{\mathrm{P}}, y)]$

$g(y\,|\,p)g(x\,|\,p)\,dy\,dx - k^{\mathrm{P}}$, where the first integral is taken over $x \in [\tilde{\pi}_m^{\mathrm{P}}, \overline{\pi}]$ and the second is taken over $y \in [\underline{\pi}, r^{\mathrm{D}}]$. Q.E.D.

Note 1. Notice that $\mathscr{W}^{\mathrm{P}}(\overline{\pi}, r^{\mathrm{D}}; p) < 0$ and that $\mathscr{W}(^{\mathrm{P}}(\tilde{\pi}_m^{\mathrm{P}}, r^{\mathrm{D}}; p)$ is a decreasing funciton of $\tilde{\pi}_m^{\mathrm{P}}$. The limiting value of $\mathscr{W}^{\mathrm{P}}(\tilde{\pi}_m^{\mathrm{P}}, r^{\mathrm{D}}; p)$ as $r^{\mathrm{D}} \to \underline{\pi}$ is $\mathscr{W}^{\mathrm{P}}(\tilde{\pi}_m^{\mathrm{P}}, \underline{\pi}; p) = V^{\mathrm{P}}(d)\int[\ell(x, \underline{\pi}) - \ell(\tilde{\pi}_m^{\mathrm{P}}, \underline{\pi})]g(x\,|\,p)\,dx$, where the integral is taken over $x \in [\tilde{\pi}_m^{\mathrm{P}}, \overline{\pi}]$. Under the additional assumption that $\mathscr{W}^{\mathrm{P}}(\underline{\pi}, \underline{\pi}; p) > 0$, it follows for all r^{D}, P has a unique best response $\mathrm{BR}^{\mathrm{P}}(r^{\mathrm{D}}) \in (\underline{\pi}, \overline{\pi})$ that is defined implicitly by $\mathscr{W}^{\mathrm{P}}(\mathrm{BR}^{\mathrm{P}}(r^{\mathrm{D}}), r^{\mathrm{D}}; p) = 0$. The sign of $\mathrm{dBR}^{\mathrm{P}}(r^{\mathrm{D}})/dr^{\mathrm{D}}$ is the same as the sign of

$$\begin{aligned}\partial\mathscr{W}^{\mathrm{P}}/\partial r^{\mathrm{D}} = {} & \left[V^{\mathrm{P}}(d)g(r^{\mathrm{D}}\,|p)/(G(r^{\mathrm{D}}\,|p))^2\right] \\ & \times \int\!\!\int [\ell(x, r^{\mathrm{D}}) - \ell(\tilde{\pi}_m^{\mathrm{P}}, r^{\mathrm{D}}) - (\ell(x,y)) - \ell(\tilde{\pi}_m^{\mathrm{P}}, y))] \\ & \times g(y\,|p)g(x\,|p)\,dy\,dx,\end{aligned}$$

where the first integral is taken over $x \in [\tilde{\pi}_m^{\mathrm{P}}, \overline{\pi}]$ and the second is taken over $y \in [\underline{\pi}, r^{\mathrm{D}}]$. Our previous assumption that $\ell_{xy} > 0$ ensures that $\partial\mathscr{W}^{\mathrm{P}}/\partial r^{\mathrm{D}} > 0$.

Proposition 2. D's optimal strategy is to stop after m draws with most favorable evidence of $\tilde{\pi}_m^{\mathrm{D}}$, given P uses the stopping rule r^{P} and the true probability of liability is p, if and only if

$$\begin{aligned}\mathscr{W}^{\mathrm{D}}(\tilde{\pi}_m^{\mathrm{D}}, r^{\mathrm{P}}; p) = {} & [V^{\mathrm{D}}(d)/(1 - G(r^{\mathrm{P}}\,|p))]\int\!\!\int[\ell(x, \tilde{\pi}_m^{\mathrm{D}}) - \ell(x,y)] \\ & \times g(x\,|p)g(y\,|p)\,dx\,dy - k^{\mathrm{D}} \le 0,\end{aligned}$$

where the first integral is over $y \in [\underline{\pi}, \tilde{\pi}_m^{\mathrm{D}}]$ and the second is over $x \in [r^{\mathrm{P}}, \overline{\pi}]$.

Proof. Again, since the sampling cost is constant, a myopic stopping rule is optimal. Let $W^{\mathrm{D}}(\tilde{\pi}_m^{\mathrm{D}}, r^{\mathrm{P}}; p)$ denote the payoff to the defendant from stopping now with best observation $\tilde{\pi}_m^{\mathrm{D}}$, given that the plaintiff uses the strategy r^{P} and that the true probability that D harmed P is p. Then

$$W^{\mathrm{D}}(\tilde{\pi}_m^{\mathrm{D}}, r^{\mathrm{P}}; p) = [V^{\mathrm{D}}(d)/(1 - G(r^{\mathrm{P}}\,|p))]\int\ell(x, \tilde{\pi}_m^{\mathrm{D}})g(x\,|p)\,dx,$$

where the integral is taken over $x \in [r^{\mathrm{P}}, \overline{\pi}]$. If, rather than stopping with evidence $\tilde{\pi}_m^{\mathrm{D}}$, D samples once more and then stops, D's payoff (gross of sampling costs) is given by

$$EW^{\mathrm{D}}(\tilde{\pi}^{\mathrm{D}}_{m+1}, r^{\mathrm{P}}; p) = W^{\mathrm{D}}(\tilde{\pi}^{\mathrm{D}}_{m}, r^{\mathrm{P}}; p)[1 - G(\tilde{\pi}^{\mathrm{D}}_{m} | p)] + \int W^{\mathrm{D}}(y, r^{\mathrm{P}}; p) g(y | p)\, dy,$$

where the integral is over $y \in [\underline{\pi}, \tilde{\pi}^{\mathrm{D}}_{m}]$. Thus it is optimal for D to stop at $\tilde{\pi}^{\mathrm{D}}_{m}$ if and only if the benefits of one more draw do not exceed the costs of one more draw. Since D wants to minimize loss, the benefit of one more draw net of the cost of one more draw is given by

$$\mathscr{W}^{\mathrm{D}}(\tilde{\pi}^{\mathrm{D}}_{m}, r^{\mathrm{P}}; p) \equiv \int [W^{\mathrm{D}}(\tilde{\pi}^{\mathrm{D}}_{m}, r^{\mathrm{P}}; p) - W^{\mathrm{D}}(y, r^{\mathrm{P}}; p)] \times g(y | p)\, dy - k^{\mathrm{D}},$$

where the integral is over $y \in [\underline{\pi}, \tilde{\pi}^{\mathrm{D}}_{m}]$. Substituting and simplifying yields $\mathscr{W}^{\mathrm{D}}(\tilde{\pi}^{\mathrm{D}}_{m}, r^{\mathrm{P}}; p) = [V^{\mathrm{D}}(d)/(1 - G(r^{\mathrm{P}} | p))] \int\int [\ell(x, \tilde{\pi}^{\mathrm{D}}_{m}) - \ell(x, y)]\, g(x | p) g(y | p)\, dx\, dy - k^{\mathrm{D}}$, where the first integral is over $y \in [\underline{\pi}, \tilde{\pi}^{\mathrm{D}}_{m}]$ and the second is over $x \in [r^{\mathrm{P}}, \overline{\pi}]$. Q.E.D.

Note 2. Notice that $\mathscr{W}^{\mathrm{D}}(\underline{\pi}, r^{\mathrm{P}}; p) < 0$ for all r^{P} and that $\mathscr{W}^{\mathrm{D}}(\tilde{\pi}^{\mathrm{D}}_{m}, r^{\mathrm{P}}; p)$ is an increasing function of $\tilde{\pi}^{\mathrm{D}}_{m}$. The limiting value of $\mathscr{W}^{\mathrm{D}}(\tilde{\pi}^{\mathrm{D}}_{m}, r^{\mathrm{P}}; p)$ as $r^{\mathrm{P}} \to \overline{\pi}$ is $\mathscr{W}^{\mathrm{P}}(\tilde{\pi}^{\mathrm{D}}_{m}, \bar{\pi}; p) = V^{\mathrm{D}}(d) \int [\ell(\overline{\pi}, \tilde{\pi}^{\mathrm{D}}_{m}) - \ell(\overline{\pi}, y)]\, g(y | p)\, dy$, where the integral is over $y \in [\underline{\pi}, \tilde{\pi}^{\mathrm{D}}_{m}]$. Under the additional assumption that $\mathscr{W}^{\mathrm{D}}(\overline{\pi}, \overline{\pi}; p) > 0$, it follows that for all r^{P}, D has a unique best response $\mathrm{BR}^{\mathrm{D}}(r^{\mathrm{P}}) \in (\underline{\pi}, \overline{\pi})$ which is defined implicitly by $\mathscr{W}^{\mathrm{D}}(BR^{\mathrm{D}}(r^{\mathrm{P}}), r^{\mathrm{P}}; p) = 0$. The sign of $d\mathrm{BR}^{\mathrm{D}}(r^{\mathrm{P}})/dr^{\mathrm{P}}$ is the opposite of the sign of

$$\partial \mathscr{W}^{\mathrm{D}} / \partial r^{\mathrm{P}} = [V^{\mathrm{D}}(d) g(r^{\mathrm{P}} | p)/(1 - G(r^{\mathrm{P}} | p))^2] \times \int\int [\ell(x, \tilde{\pi}^{\mathrm{D}}_{m}) - \ell(x, y) - (\ell(r^{\mathrm{P}}, \tilde{\pi}^{\mathrm{D}}_{m}) - \ell(r^{\mathrm{P}}, y))] \times g(x | p) g(y | p)\, dx\, dy,$$

where the first integral is over $y \in [\underline{\pi}, \tilde{\pi}^{\mathrm{D}}_{m}]$ and the second is over $x \in [r^{\mathrm{P}}, \overline{\pi}]$. Our previous assumption that $\ell_{xy} > 0$ ensures that $\partial \mathscr{W}^{\mathrm{D}} / \partial r^{\mathrm{P}} > 0$.

Proposition 3. There exists a unique Nash equilibrium for the liability stage $(r^{\mathrm{P}*}, r^{\mathrm{D}*})$.

Proof. The composition of the two continuous monotonic best response functions is a continuous, decreasing function from $[\underline{\pi}, \overline{\pi}]$ to itself. Therefore a fixed point exists and, since the composition function intersects the 45° line only once, the fixed point is unique. Q.E.D.

References

Braeutigam, Ronald, Bruce M. Owen, and John Panzar. 1984. "An Economic Analysis of Alternative Fee-Shifting Systems," 47 *Law and Contemporary Problems* 173–185.

Cooter, Robert, and Daniel Rubinfeld. 1989. "Economic Analyses of Legal Disputes and Their Resolution," 27 *Journal of Economic Literature* 1067–1097.

Danzon, Patricia Munch. 1983. "Contingent Fees for Personal Injury Litigation," 14 *Bell Journal of Economics* 213–224.

Daughety, Andrew F., and Jennifer F. Reinganum. 1995. "Product Safety: Liability, R & D, and Signaling," 85 *American Economic Review* 1187–1206.

______. 1997a. "Everybody Out of the Pool: Products Liability, Punitive Damages, and Competition," 13 *Journal of Law, Economics, & Organization* 410–432.

______. 1998a. "A Note on Multiple Equilibria and Punitive Damages Rules in 'Everybody Out of the Pool'," 14 *Journal of Law, Economics, & Organization* 379–387.

______. 1998b. "On the Economics of Trials: Adversarial Process, Evidence and Equilibrium Bias," Working Paper no. 98-W02, Department of Economics, Vanderbilt University, April 1998 (revised June 1999).

______. 1999. "Stampede to Judgment: Persuasive Influence and Herding Behavior by Courts," 1 *American Law and Economics Review* 158–189.

______. 2000. "Appealing Judgments," 31 *Rand Journal of Economics* forthcoming.

Dewatripont, Mathias, and Jean Tirole. 1999. "Advocates," 107 *Journal of Political Economy* 1–39.

Farmer, Amy, and Paul Pecorino. 1998. "Does Jury Bias Matter?" working paper, Department of Economics, University of Tennessee.

Froeb, Luke M., and Bruce H. Kobayashi. 1999. "Evidence Production in Adversarial vs. Inquisitorial Regimes;" originally circulated as "Competition in the Production of Costly Information: An Economic Analysis of Adversarial versus Court-Appointed Presentation of Expert Testimony," George Mason Law and Economics Working Paper no. 93-005, 1993.

______. 1996. "Naive, Biased, yet Bayesian: Can Juries Interpret Selectively Produced Evidence?" 12 *Journal of Law, Economics, & Organization* 257–276.

Hause, John C. 1989. "Indemnity, Settlement, and Litigation, or, I'll Be Suing You," 18 *Journal of Legal Studies* 157–179.

James, Fleming, Jr., and Geoffrey C. Hazard, Jr. 1985. *Civil Procedure*, 3rd ed. Boston: Little, Brown.

Katz, Avery. 1987. "Measuring the Demand for Litigation: Is the English Rule Really Cheaper?" 3 *Journal of Law, Economics, & Organization* 143–176.

______. 1988. "Judicial Decisionmaking and Litigation Expenditure," 8 *International Review of Law and Economics* 127–143.

Landes, William M. 1993. "Sequential versus Unitary Trials: An Economic Analysis," 22 *Journal of Legal Studies* 99–134.

Lewis, Tracy, and Michel Poitevin. 1997. "Disclosure of Information in Regulatory Proceedings," 13 *Journal of Law, Economics, & Organization* 50–73.

Lipman, Barton L., and Duane J. Seppi. 1995. "Robust Inference in Communication Games with Partial Provability," 66 *Journal of Economic Theory* 370–405.

Milgrom, Paul, and John Roberts. 1986. "Relying on the Information of Interested Parties," 17 *Rand Journal of Economics* 18–32.

Plott, Charles R. 1987. "Legal Fees: A Comparison of the American and English Rules," 3 *Journal of Law, Economics, & Organization* 185–192.

Polinsky, A. Mitchell, and Yeon-Koo Che. 1991. "Decoupling Liability: Optimal Incentives for Care and Litigation," 22 *Rand Journal of Economics* 562–570.

Posner, Richard A. 1992. *Economic Analysis of Law*, 4th ed. Boston: Little, Brown.

______. 1999. "An Economic Approach to the Law of Evidence," 51 *Stanford Law Review* 1477–1546.

Reinganum, Jennifer F. 1982. "Strategic Search Theory," 23 *International Economic Review* 1–17.

______, and Louis L. Wilde. 1986. "Settlement, Litigation, and the Allocation of Litigation Costs," 17 *Rand Journal of Economics* 557–566.

Rubinfeld, Daniel L., and David E. M. Sappington. 1987. "Efficient Awards and Standards of Proof in Judicial Proceedings," 18 *Rand Journal of Economics* 308–315.

Sanchirico, Chris William. 1997a. "The Burden of Proof in Civil Litigation: A Simple Model of Mechanism Design," 17 *International Review of Law and Economics* 431–447.

______. 1997b. "Evidence Production, Adversarial Process and the Private Instigation of Suits," working paper, Department of Economics, Columbia University.

______. 1997c. "An Integrated Model of Evidence Production" working paper, Department of Economics, Columbia University.

Seidmann, Daniel J., and Eyal Winter. 1997. "Strategic Information Transmission with Verifiable Messages," 55 *Econometrica* 163–169.

Shepherd, George B. 1999. "An Empirical Study of the Economics of Pretrial Discovery," 19 *International Review of Law and Economics* 245–264.

Shin, Hyun Song. 1994. "The Burden of Proof in a Game of Persuasion," 64 *Journal of Economic Theory* 253–264.

______. 1998. "Adversarial and Inquisitorial Procedures in Arbitration," 29 *Rand Journal of Economics* 378–405.

Skaperdas, Stergios. 1996. "Contest Success Functions," 7 *Economic Theory* 283–290.

Sobel, Joel. 1985. "Disclosure of Evidence and Resolution of Disputes: Who Should Bear the Burden of Proof?" in A. Roth, ed., *Game-Theoretic Models of Bargaining*. Cambridge: Cambridge University Press.

B
Explicit Comparison

[11]

RAND Journal of Economics
Vol. 29, No. 2, Summer 1998
pp. 378–405

Adversarial and inquisitorial procedures in arbitration

Hyun Song Shin*

How should a dispute be settled between two opposing parties? The adversarial procedure invites the parties to make their cases to an impartial arbitrator, while the inquisitorial procedure requires the arbitrator to adjudicate on the basis of his own investigations. Even if it is assumed that the arbitrator is, on average, as well informed as the two opposing parties, the adversarial procedure is shown to be strictly superior. This superiority stems from the ability within the adversarial procedure to allocate the burden of proof in an effective manner, and thereby extract the maximal informational content from apparently inconclusive contests.

1. Introduction

■ What is the most effective way of settling a dispute between two parties when the underlying facts of the case are in question? This question is of interest to those concerned with the smooth functioning of the judicial system as well as a host of quasi-judicial institutions, such as industrial tribunals and disciplinary panels. More broadly, the same question arises for regulatory and antitrust authorities, whose brief is to adjudicate in cases of contested takeovers or predatory practices so as to further the public interest. This is also the question addressed in this article.[1]

When two interested parties with diametrically opposed goals are well informed about the underlying state of the world, it is possible for a disinterested arbitrator who has the task of resolving the conflict to rely on the information of the interested parties. This is so even though each party will be reluctant to reveal information that it deems to be disadvantageous. Any relevant piece of information will favor one party or the other, and for any relevant piece of information, one of the two parties will have an incentive to bring it to the attention of the arbitrator. Milgrom and Roberts (1986) discuss sufficient conditions for full revelation in this context, which are developed in Lipman and Seppi (1995) and Seidmann and Winter (1997).

But when there is uncertainty about how well informed the interested parties are, the argument above loses much of its force. When the interested parties are genuinely

* Nuffield College, Oxford University; hyun.shin@economics.ox.ac.uk.

I thank the referees and the Editor, David Scharfstein, for their comments and guidance. I have gained much from discussions with Meg Meyer at various stages of this project, and I also thank Bart Lipman and Daniel Seidmann for their comments.

[1] A referee rightly pointed out that the term "arbitration" is also commonly applied to the rather different case of the resolution of a surplus-sharing problem, as in labor disputes. This article has little to contribute to that issue.

uninformed about the true state, they will not always be able to submit the reports that will enable the arbitrator to infer the true state. More important, because this possibility exists, an interested party (say, the plaintiff) who has information unfavorable to his own case may benefit from suppressing it. This is so because the defendant may not have this piece of information (and so will not be able to submit it) and because the arbitrator cannot "assume the worst" about the plaintiff's case. In short, there will be some pooling between genuinely uninformed types and types who are informed but whose information is unfavorable to their case. Lewis and Sappington (1993), Austen-Smith (1994), Shin (1994b), and Dewatripont and Tirole (1995) discuss this sort of pooling. Glazer and Rubinstein (1997) discuss the optimal sequencing of announcements in such environments.

When the arbitrator cannot rely on the information of the interested parties to secure full revelation, it is important to ask how well the arbitrator can do by conducting investigations himself and adjudicating on the basis of the information thus uncovered. Clearly, if it is within the grasp of the arbitrator to gain full information about the circumstances, and if the costs of gaining this information are not too large, then it would be better for the arbitrator to conduct this investigation himself and not rely on the submissions of the interested parties.

However, in the more realistic case where the arbitrator cannot hope to gain full information at reasonable cost, it is an open question as to whether the arbitrator should opt for a procedure in which the opposing parties are invited to make their cases or instead adjudicate on the basis of his own investigation. I refer to the first as the *adversarial procedure* in arbitration and to the second as the *inquisitorial procedure.* This terminology is intended as a parallel to the juxtaposition of the trial procedure in countries in the tradition of the Anglo-Saxon common law, in which partisan advocates present their cases to an impartial jury, and the trial procedure in countries under the tradition of the Roman civil law, in which judges take a much more active role in investigating the circumstances of the case.

Although it would be presumptuous to attempt to reduce the complex historical and legal considerations underlying the choice of trial procedure into a simple economic setting, issues such as the informativeness of disclosures and the quality of adjudications under uncertainty are best addressed in an explicitly economic setting. In particular, I shall conduct a welfare comparison of the two alternative procedures in arbitration by constructing a game-theoretic model of decision making by an arbitrator in the face of self-interested reporting strategies by the interested parties.

Our untrained intuitions offer only limited help in assessing the relative superiority of one system over the other. The adversarial procedure has the virtue of there being *two* sources information for the arbitrator, one for each of the opposing parties. However, if it is supposed that each party will suppress information unfavorable to its own case, the arbitrator does not receive all relevant information in existence. In contrast, under the inquisitorial procedure, any information the arbitrator can unearth himself will be utilized in his decision. Thus, an important consideration in the welfare comparison is the relative merit of having one piece of unbiased information against having two pieces of partial (i.e., biased and incomplete) information.

Perhaps surprisingly, my analysis reveals a robust conclusion in support of the superiority of the adversarial procedure. This is so even though I assume that the arbitrator is, on average, as well informed as the two opposing parties. Also, this superiority persists whether I consider binary arbitration, in which the arbitrator can find in favor of only one of the two parties, or arbitration with a smooth action set, in which the arbitrator can express fine distinctions in the strength of support for one party over the other, as in the case of the award of a sum of money in damages.

The adversarial procedure draws its superior performance from its ability to allocate the burden of proof in an effective manner, thereby extracting the maximal informational content from apparently inconclusive contests where neither side has been able to submit a convincing argument for its own case. If the nature of the dispute favors one of the parties in its ability to marshal evidence, then the case put forward by this party must meet an accordingly stronger test. Thus the line of reasoning is a counterfactual one. If the facts of the case are indeed as claimed by this party, then it should be quite likely that it would come up with a strong case. In the absence of such a case, one must conclude that (on balance) the underlying facts of the dispute do *not* favor this party.

The robustness of this type of reasoning lies in the fact that the arbitrator need not acquire first-hand knowledge of the issues under debate. If the arbitrator knows that one party has spent considerable time and resources in preparing its case and the other has not, then it would be reasonable to place the burden of proof on the former. Cases of contested takeovers are just such an example. If the raider has been planning the bid for some time out of the public gaze, then it would be reasonable for the competition authorities defending the "public interest" to place a more stringent test on the arguments put forward by the raider than on those of the intended target. I shall return to this example in a later section.

In more technical terms, the source of the superiority of the adversarial procedure lies in a nonconvexity. The marginal benefit to the arbitrator of an improvement in the information of one of the interested parties is not constant. It depends on how well informed this party is relative to the other. In particular, the marginal increase in the informativeness of disclosures is larger if the information of the *better-informed* party is improved further. If the arbitrator had the choice, he would choose to exacerbate the disparity in information between the two parties rather than to arrange a "level playing field." In contrast, the payoff of the arbitrator is increasing linearly in its own information. No such increasing returns exist under the inquisitorial procedure.

When averaged over a large number of diverse arbitration problems, the arbitrator in the adversarial procedure benefits from the increasing returns to information described above, whereas the inquisitorial arbitrator does not. For this reason, the *ex ante* payoff of an arbitrator in the adversarial system can be shown to be strictly higher than that of an inquisitorial arbitrator.

However, it would be misleading to suggest that the adversarial procedure is superior to the inquisitorial procedure in all conceivable cases of dispute. The ongoing litigation in the United States concerning the long-term health consequences of silicone breast implants provides a salutary lesson in the potential fragility of the reasoning outlined above in cases involving contested scientific evidence. As I write the final draft of this article (in August 1997), a consolidated pretrial phase for many separate litigations is taking place in Birmingham, Alabama, in which the so-called national panel of four court-appointed scientific experts is assessing the merits of the scientific evidence to be put forward in the forthcoming cases. This is reminiscent of the inquisitorial procedure in settling disputes, and the fact that such a panel has been deemed necessary points to the potential pitfalls with the adversarial procedure when the so-called verifiability condition is violated. This condition stipulates that no party can concoct false evidence. The penalties against perjury and similar sanctions in nonjudicial contexts is enough to rule out the worst cases of such a violation. However, the line is not so clear-cut when complex scientific evidence is involved. I shall return to this issue in a later section.

Subject to this qualification, the broad message to emerge from my article is that the adversarial procedure is superior to the inquisitorial procedure. It is also worth emphasizing that the result is obtained under the hypothesis that the inquisitorial arbitrator is, on average, as well informed as the two interested parties are themselves. If one is prepared to argue that the interested parties are better informed about the circumstances than the arbitrator is (as in Milgrom and Roberts (1986)), then the argument for the superiority of the adversarial procedure acquires added force.

2. The model

■ The basic problem faced by the decision maker is to adjudicate a large number of disputes, each of which has two claimants with diametrically opposed interests. I shall refer to the two claimants as the plaintiff and the defendant, and the issue at stake in each problem is whether the outcome of a Bernoulli trial is zero or one. I refer to the realization of this random variable as the true circumstance. Circumstance 0 is favorable to the defendant and circumstance 1 is favorable to the plaintiff. The decision maker is a disinterested party whose concern is to get at the truth and who has to find in favor of one of the two parties. I formalize this by defining the decision maker's action set to be $\{P, D\}$, where P is to find in favor of the plaintiff and D is to find in favor of the defendant. The payoff of the arbitrator at the two circumstances is shown in Table 1. The arbitrator's decision is binary, reflecting the judicial or quasi-judicial nature of the problem. In a later section, however, continuous action sets will also be considered, where the arbitrator can fine-tune the support for one or the other party.

At the very beginning of the game, the arbitrator can choose between two procedures to elicit information, which will then be applied uniformly to all the arbitration problems encountered. The arbitration procedure is chosen *ex ante,* and the choice of procedure cannot be conditioned on the specific arbitration problem faced by the decision maker. The premise here is that changes in procedures take much longer to implement than the specific application of these procedures.

The two procedures available to the decision maker are, first, the adversarial procedure, in which the decision maker is uninformed and relies exclusively on the submissions of the interested parties, and second, the inquisitorial procedure, in which the decision maker has access to information about the problem at hand and relies exclusively on this information.

The body of evidence pertaining to the particular case is summarized by a signal σ, which takes values in the set $\{0, 1\}$, correlated with the true circumstance. The realization of σ is interpreted as the body of available evidence that is admissible in court, where I allow the possibility that σ is a noisy signal of the true circumstance. When $\sigma = 0$, there is a preponderance of evidence that favors the defendant, so that if this evidence can be marshalled and produced in court it would constitute grounds for finding in favor of the defendant. If $\sigma = 1$, the reverse is the case, and there is a preponderance of evidence in favor of the plaintiff. The source of the noise for σ is not modelled here, and the results that follow do not rest on the existence of this noise. However, assuming its existence allows me to inject a degree of realism by driving a wedge between the truth and the body of admissible evidence.[2]

The joint density over the true circumstance and the realizations of σ is denoted by $p(s, \sigma)$, where s is the true circumstance. (See Table 2.) Thus, the off-diagonal elements give the degree of noise. However, the monotone likelihood ratio property is assumed to hold, so that $p(0, 0) \geq p(1, 0)$ and $p(1, 1) \geq p(0, 1)$. That is, conditional on $\sigma = i$, circumstance i is more likely than j, where $j \neq i$.

In choosing the procedure, the decision maker considers the relative incidence of

[2] I am grateful to the Editor and the referees for encouraging me to pursue this line.

TABLE 1

Act	Payoff at 0	Payoff at 1
D	1	0
P	0	1

different types of potential arbitration problems. First, the density p varies across problems. The incidence of p is summarized by the probability density

$$f(p), \tag{1}$$

which has full support over the appropriate set (in this case, the subset of the three-dimensional unit simplex consistent with the monotone likelihood ratio property). Furthermore, another respect in which arbitration problems will differ is the degree to which the various parties may have access to the signal σ and hence be able to marshal the available evidence for presentation to the court. Formally, let ϕ denote the probability that the plaintiff has access to σ and ψ denote the probability that the defendant has access to σ. Lastly, let θ denote the probability that the arbitrator himself has access to σ. Any arbitration problem has its characteristic triple (ϕ, ψ, θ), and I shall denote by

$$g(\phi, \psi, \theta) \tag{2}$$

the probability density over these triples in the population of arbitration problems. I assume that g has full support. Let $\bar{\phi}$ denote the average value of ϕ, and define $\bar{\psi}$ and $\bar{\theta}$ as the average values of ψ and θ respectively.

At the very beginning of the game, the decision maker's choice of the arbitration procedure will be governed by these values. If, for example, $\bar{\theta}$ is large relative to $\bar{\phi}$ and $\bar{\psi}$, then the inquisitorial procedure may be more attractive than the adversarial procedure, since the decision maker can count on having good information, on average, across the range of arbitration problems. If, however, $\bar{\phi}$ and $\bar{\psi}$ are large relative to $\bar{\theta}$, the adversarial procedure may be more attractive.

There may be good grounds for presuming that the interested parties are better informed on average than the arbitrator, given that they are "closer to the facts," and this has been one of the arguments used in favor of the adversarial procedure (Milgrom and Roberts, 1986). However, the main message of my article is that the adversarial procedure is superior to the inquisitorial procedure even if the interested parties are no better informed on average than the arbitrator. Thus, for the sake of argument I shall work under the following assumption.

Assumption. $\bar{\phi} = \bar{\psi} = \bar{\theta}$.

Needless to say, if the interested parties are better informed on average than the arbitrator, then my case for the superiority of the adversarial procedure will hold with added force.

TABLE 2

	$\sigma = 0$	$\sigma = 1$
$s = 0$	$p(0, 0)$	$p(0, 1)$
$s = 1$	$p(1, 0)$	$p(1, 1)$

Having outlined the nature of the choice facing the arbitrator, we may now define formally the extensive form of the game. There are three players in the game: the arbitrator, the plaintiff, and the defendant. The game is played out as follows.

(i) The arbitrator chooses between the adversarial and inquisitorial procedures.

(ii) Nature picks an arbitration problem (p, ϕ, ψ, θ) according to densities f and g.

(iii) If the inquisitorial procedure has been chosen, the arbitrator receives, with probability θ, the realization of σ.

(a) Based on this information alone, the arbitrator then decides whether to find in favor of the plaintiff or the defendant.
(b) The payoff to an interested party is one if the arbitrator's decision is favorable and zero if the decision is unfavorable.
(c) The arbitrator's payoffs are given in Table 1.

(iv) If the adversarial procedure has been chosen, the two opposing parties each observe σ with some probability. With probability ϕ, the plaintiff observes σ, while with probability ψ, the defendant observes σ.

(a) The two opposing parties then decide whether or not to submit the evidence they have gathered. If a party has observed σ, this may either be submitted in evidence or not. If a party has not observed σ, then no submission can be made. In this sense, any report of the interested parties is verifiable. Any submission made to the court is truthful.
(b) Based on the submissions of the two opposing parties, the arbitrator decides whether to find in favor of the plaintiff or the defendant.
(c) The payoff to an interested party is one if the arbitrator's decision is favorable and zero if the decision is unfavorable.
(d) The arbitrator's payoffs are given in Table 1.

It should be emphasized that the subgame under the adversarial procedure admits only verifiable reports from the opposing parties. Thus, neither party may concoct false evidence, although they are permitted under the rules of the game to withhold information unfavorable to their cause. In this sense, although manufacturing false evidence is forbidden, the opposing parties are permitted to be "economical with the truth." The assumption of verifiable reports has been a standard feature of disclosure games, both in the context of judicial and quasi-judicial procedures (Milgrom, 1981; Milgrom and Roberts, 1986) and in the context of accounting disclosures by firms (Dye, 1985; Shin, 1994a). This assumption is motivated by the existence of large sanctions against perjury or fraudulent behavior that may be subsequently uncovered. This is an assumption that deserves some scrutiny, however, and I shall return to this issue later in the article. The result in favor of the adversarial procedure is robust to many variations of the model, but it may not be robust to the relaxation of the verifiability assumption.

To close the model and to compute the payoffs under the two subgames, an equilibrium must be specified in each subgame. Doing so for the inquisitorial subgame is straightforward, since the inquisitorial system is a single-person decision problem.

For the adversarial subgame, I focus on the equilibrium in which both of the opposing sides engage in the maximum permissible management of news, in which any unfavourable information is suppressed. In intuitive terms, this equilibrium may be described as follows. By virtue of the verifiability of submissions and the monotone likelihood ratio property, any realization of σ will favor one party or the other, and if it emerges in court, it will constitute good grounds for finding in favor of one of the parties. Knowing this, the two opposing parties will be reluctant to submit evidence they know will be disadvantageous to their case. If the plaintiff observes that $\sigma = 0$, no submission will be made, thereby suppressing this evidence. Similarly, if the defendant learns that $\sigma = 1$, this information is suppressed by submitting no evidence. Whenever the realization of σ is submitted by one of the parties, the arbitrator has a straightforward decision and acts according to the submitted evidence. But when neither party submits conclusive evidence for its case, the arbitrator must decide in a sophisticated manner, exercising due skepticism.

We may describe the equilibrium more precisely as follows. The submission of an interested party consists of either the realization of σ (so that a preponderance of evidence for one party is produced in court) or the empty set. Hence, subject to the rule on verifiability, the action set of both the plaintiff and the defendant consists of $\{\sigma = 0\}$, $\{\sigma = 1\}$, and $\emptyset$.

The information set of the arbitrator consists of the submissions of the two disputants. Since the verifiability condition rules out the manufacture of false evidence, we may represent the arbitrator's possible information as consisting of either the realization of σ (when one of the two parties produces a preponderance of the evidence) or the inconclusive case (when neither party submits the realization of σ). I denote these possible information sets of the arbitrator respectively as $\{\sigma = 0\}$, $\{\sigma = 1\}$, and $\emptyset$.

I claim that the following strategies then constitute an equilibrium of the adversarial subgame. The plaintiff's strategy is

$$\begin{cases} \{\sigma = 0\} \mapsto \emptyset \\ \{\sigma = 1\} \mapsto \{\sigma = 1\} \\ \qquad \emptyset \mapsto \emptyset, \end{cases} \tag{3}$$

the defendant's strategy is

$$\begin{cases} \{\sigma = 0\} \mapsto \{\sigma = 0\} \\ \{\sigma = 1\} \mapsto \emptyset \\ \qquad \emptyset \mapsto \emptyset, \end{cases} \tag{4}$$

and the arbitrator's strategy is

$$\begin{cases} \{\sigma = 0\} \mapsto D \\ \{\sigma = 1\} \mapsto P \\ \qquad \emptyset \mapsto \begin{cases} D & \text{if } \pi(0) \geq \pi(1) \\ P & \text{otherwise,} \end{cases} \end{cases} \tag{5}$$

where

$$\begin{aligned} \pi(0) &= p(0, 0)(1 - \psi) + p(0, 1)(1 - \phi), \\ \pi(1) &= p(1, 0)(1 - \psi) + p(1, 1)(1 - \phi). \end{aligned} \tag{6}$$

To see that these strategies do, indeed, constitute an equilibrium, let us first show that (5) is the arbitrator's best reply to the reporting strategies (3) and (4).

The arbitrator faces three possible information sets, corresponding to the announcements of the two realizations of σ and the third possibility of no announcements. Denoting by I the information set of the arbitrator, the joint density over the triples (s, σ, I) generated by the reporting strategies (3) and (4) can be represented by the cells of Table 3. The matrix on the left gives the probability weights when $\{\sigma = 1\}$ is announced by the plaintiff,

TABLE 3

	$\sigma = 0$	$\sigma = 1$	$\sigma = 0$	$\sigma = 1$	$\sigma = 0$	$\sigma = 1$
$s = 0$	0	$p(0, 1)\phi$	$p(0, 0)\psi$	0	$p(0, 0)(1 - \psi)$	$p(0, 1)(1 - \phi)$
$s = 1$	0	$p(1, 1)\phi$	$p(1, 0)\psi$	0	$p(1, 0)(1 - \psi)$	$p(1, 1)(1 - \phi)$
	$\{\sigma = 1\}$		$\{\sigma = 0\}$		$\emptyset$	

the matrix in the middle gives the weights when $\{\sigma = 0\}$ is announced by the defendant, and the matrix on the right gives the weights when no announcement is made. The probability weights across all the matrices clearly sum to one.

Conditional on the announcement of $\{\sigma = 1\}$ by the plaintiff, the posterior probability of $s = 1$ can be obtained from the matrix on the left and is given by $p(1, 1)/(p(0, 1) + p(1, 1))$. This exceeds ½ (by the monotone likelihood ratio property), hence it is optimal for the arbitrator to find in favor of the plaintiff. Similarly, conditional on the announcement of $\{\sigma = 0\}$ by the defendant, the posterior of $s = 0$ exceeds ½, so the optimal action of the arbitrator is to find in favor of the defendant. This shows that the first two clauses of (5) are best replies.

When no announcements are made, the posteriors are calculated from the matrix on the right. The posterior of $s = 0$ is higher than that of $s = 1$ if and only if the sum of the top two elements is greater than the sum of the bottom two elements, i.e., when

$$p(0, 0)(1 - \psi) + p(0, 1)(1 - \phi) \geq p(1, 0)(1 - \psi) + p(1, 1)(1 - \phi). \tag{7}$$

The arbitrator's optimal action is to find in favor of the defendant whenever this inequality holds and in favor of the plaintiff otherwise. This is what the last clause of (5) states, so the arbitrator's strategy is a best reply to the reporting strategies of the two interested parties.

It now remains to demonstrate that the reporting strategies of the plaintiff and defendant are best replies to the arbitrator's adjudication strategy. When (7) holds, the arbitrator's default action is to find in favor of the defendant, in the sense that when neither party submits σ, the arbitrator finds in favor of the defendant. In these circumstances, the plaintiff aims to announce the realization $\sigma = 1$ whenever possible and suppress the realization $\sigma = 0$ whenever the plaintiff learns of this. The strategy (3) accomplishes this. For the defendant, he is indifferent between announcing $\{\sigma = 0\}$ and not announcing it, since the arbitrator's action is the same. However, the strategy (4) is clearly a best reply. When the inequality (7) holds in the opposite direction, a symmetric argument shows that the reporting strategies of the plaintiff and defendant are best replies. We can conclude, therefore, that (3), (4), and (5) constitute an equilibrium.

Uniqueness of equilibrium can be obtained if a tie-breaking rule is imposed asserting that an interested party prefers to submit a report when indifferent between submitting and not submitting. In any case, for the purpose of calculating the payoffs (which is our primary concern), there is no loss of generality from confining our attention to the equilibrium identified above.

Having outlined the basic problem, we may now turn our attention to calculating the payoffs in the two subgames, representing the two arbitration procedures. Denote by $u(p, \theta)$ the arbitrator's payoff under the inquisitorial procedure from arbitration problem (p, ϕ, ψ, θ). The notation reflects the fact that the arbitrator's payoff does not depend on ϕ or ψ under the inquisitorial system. Denote by $v(p, \phi, \psi)$ the arbitrator's payoff under the adversarial procedure when confronted with the same arbitration problem. The notation reflects the irrelevance of θ under the adversarial system.

By taking averages of u and v over the set of arbitration problems, we will be able to compare the expected payoffs in the two subgames and thus rank the *ex ante* payoffs from the choice of arbitration procedure at the very beginning of the game. We first calculate the *ex ante* payoff from adopting the inquisitorial procedure.

□ **Payoff under inquisitorial procedure.** Under the inquisitorial procedure, the arbitrator either observes the realization of σ (with probability θ) or not (with probability $1 - \theta$). The possible information of the arbitrator, its probability, and the payoff conditional on this information are summarized in Table 4, where I have used the notation p_i for the probability that $s = i$. That is, $p_0 = p(0, 0) + p(0, 1)$ and $p_1 = p(1, 0) + p(1, 1)$. When the realization $\sigma = 0$ is observed, the arbitrator finds in favor of the defendant. This gives a payoff of one when $s = 0$ but entails a payoff of zero when $s = 1$. Hence, conditional on the information $\{\sigma = 0\}$, the payoff is the posterior of $s = 0$. The second row can be explained in an analogous manner. The final row pertains to the case when the arbitrator receives no signal. In this case, the arbitrator relies on the prior probabilities p_0 and p_1 and finds in favor of the defendant if and only if $p_0 \geq p_1$. If the decision is to find in favor of the defendant, the expected payoff is p_0. Similarly, the expected payoff to finding in favor of the plaintiff is p_1. Thus, the payoff in this case is

$$\begin{cases} p_0 & \text{if } p_0 \geq p_1 \\ p_1 & \text{if } p_0 < p_1, \end{cases}$$

which is $\max\{p_0, p_1\}$, as given in the last line of the matrix.

By weighting these payoffs by the respective probabilities, we arrive at the following expression for $u(p, \theta)$, the payoff under the inquisitorial procedure for the particular arbitration problem.

$$u(p, \theta) = \theta p(0, 0) + \theta p(1, 1) + (1 - \theta)\max\{p_0, p_1\}. \tag{8}$$

We now turn to the payoff under the adversarial procedure.

□ **Payoff under adversarial procedure.** There are three conditioning events under the adversarial procedure. Either the defendant reveals $\{\sigma = 0\}$, the plaintiff reveals $\{\sigma = 1\}$, or there is no conclusive submission.

TABLE 4

Information	Probability	Conditional Payoff
$\{\sigma = 0\}$	$\theta[p(0, 0) + p(1, 0)]$	$\dfrac{p(0, 0)}{p(0, 0) + p(1, 0)}$
$\{\sigma = 1\}$	$\theta[p(0, 1) + p(1, 1)]$	$\dfrac{p(1, 1)}{p(0, 1) + p(1, 1)}$
$\varnothing$	$1 - \theta$	$\max\{p_0, p_1\}$

Table 5 is derived from Table 3 and summarizes the probabilities and conditional payoffs for these three events, where I have used the following shorthand notation:

$$A = (1 - \psi)[p(0, 0) + p(1, 0)] + (1 - \phi)[p(0, 1) + p(1, 1)]$$

$$B = \max \{p(0, 0)(1 - \psi) + p(0, 1)(1 - \phi), p(1, 0)(1 - \psi) + p(1, 1)(1 - \phi)\}.$$

The first two rows of Table 5 are analogous to the corresponding rows in Table 4 for the inquisitorial procedure. The arbitrator receives the submission $\{\sigma = 0\}$ from the defendant with probability $\psi[p(0, 0) + p(1, 0)]$, in which case the optimal decision is to find in favor of the defendant, and the expected payoff is the posterior of circumstance 0. The second row is explained similarly.

To confirm the correctness of the last row of Table 5, consider the case when neither party submits the realization of σ. Then, the posteriors over the true circumstances can be calculated from Table 3 (the matrix on the right). Thus, the posterior of $s = 0$ is

$$\frac{1}{A}[p(0, 0)(1 - \psi) + p(0, 1)(1 - \phi)], \tag{9}$$

while the posterior of $s = 1$ is

$$\frac{1}{A}[p(1, 0)(1 - \psi) + p(1, 1)(1 - \phi)]. \tag{10}$$

It is optimal to find in favor of the defendant if and only if (9) is larger than (10). The expected payoff to finding in favor of the defendant is the posterior of $s = 0$, and the expected payoff to finding in favor of the plaintiff is the posterior of $s = 1$. Thus, the optimal decision implies the payoff

$$\begin{cases} \frac{1}{A}[p(0, 0)(1 - \psi) + p(0, 1)(1 - \phi)] & \text{if } (9) \geq (10) \\ \frac{1}{A}[p(1, 0)(1 - \psi) + p(1, 1)(1 - \phi)] & \text{if } (9) < (10), \end{cases} \tag{11}$$

which boils down to B/A. Finally, the probability that neither party submits a report is given by the sum of entries in the rightmost matrix in Table 3, which yields A.

By weighting each conditional payoff by the corresponding probability, we arrive

TABLE 5

Information	Probability	Conditional Payoff
$\{\sigma = 0\}$	$\psi[p(0, 0) + p(1, 0)]$	$\frac{p(0, 0)}{p(0, 0) + p(1, 0)}$
$\{\sigma = 1\}$	$\phi[p(0, 1) + p(1, 1)]$	$\frac{p(1, 1)}{p(0, 1) + p(1, 1)}$
$\emptyset$	A	B/A

at the following expression for $v(p, \phi, \psi)$, the payoff to the arbitrator under the inquisitorial procedure:

$$v(p, \phi, \psi) = \phi p(1, 1) + \psi p(0, 0) + \max\begin{Bmatrix} p(0, 0)(1 - \psi) + p(0, 1)(1 - \phi), \\ p(1, 0)(1 - \psi) + p(1, 1)(1 - \phi) \end{Bmatrix}. \quad (12)$$

□ **Superiority of the adversarial procedure.** The main result can be stated as follows.

Theorem 1. The *ex ante* payoff under the adversarial procedure is strictly higher than that under the inquisitorial procedure.

In other words, the claim is that the expected value of (12) is strictly larger than the expected value of (8), where the expectation is taken over the set of possible arbitration problems. Since different random variables make their appearance in the two expressions, a direct comparison of these payoffs would not yield much insight into the problem. Instead, we will take a more indirect route in proving this result, which is also designed to illuminate the main mechanism behind the result.

When plotted in (ϕ, ψ)-space, the arbitrator's indifference curves generated by v are concave to the origin. To see this more clearly, rearrange (12) to give

$$v(p, \phi, \psi) = \max\{p_0 + \phi(p(0, 0) - p(1, 0)), p_1 + \psi(p(1, 1) - p(0, 1))\}. \quad (13)$$

The set of points (ϕ, ψ) at which the two terms in the curly brackets are equal define a straight line that passes through (1, 1) and whose intercept is positive if and only if $p_0 > p_1$. Above this line the indifference curves are horizontal; below it they are vertical. Figure 1 illustrates these indifference curves.

FIGURE 1

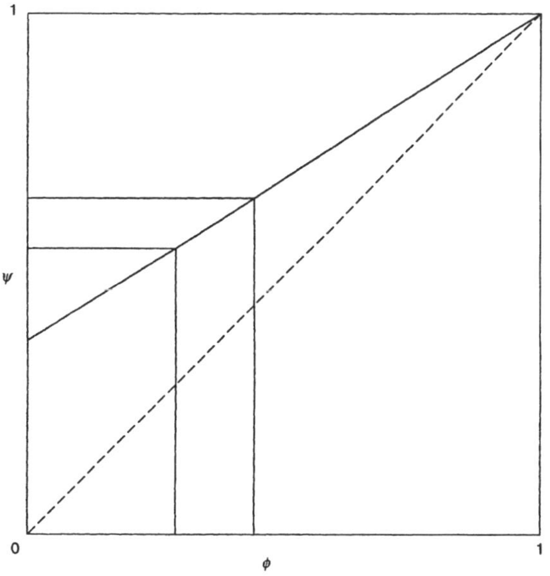

When ϕ is sufficiently high relative to ψ, we are in the region below the line of kinks. In this region there is no change in the arbitrator's payoff to an improvement in the defendant's information. Only an improvement in the plaintiff's information increases the arbitrator's payoff. Roughly speaking, the arbitrator's payoff increases only if the information of the better-informed party improves. The arbitrator's payoff improves by exacerbating the disparity in the information of the two opposing parties, rather than by reducing this disparity.

To understand where this feature originates, it is instructive to refer to expression (12). When the information of one of the interested parties improves, there are two effects on the arbitrator's payoff. First, the probability of a conclusive submission increases. This raises the arbitrator's payoff unambiguously. This effect is captured in the first two terms of (12), which are increasing in ϕ and ψ, respectively. However, the third term may present a countervailing effect. It is large when there is a large disparity in the posterior weights given to $s = 0$ and $s = 1$ in the absence of a conclusive announcement. Thus, if the improvement in the information of one of the parties closes the gap between these posteriors, then this second effect cancels out the increase in the arbitrator's payoff through the first effect. But, if the disparity between the posteriors is not reduced, then there is an unambiguous effect, serving to increase the arbitrator's payoff.

In intuitive terms, the absence of a conclusive report is more informative if one of the interested parties is well informed but the other is not. Since each party reveals favorable news only, the absence of a report from the well-informed party makes it likely that the well-informed party knows the true circumstances but that the news is unfavorable to him. The greater the disparity of information, the more informative is the absence of any announcement.

The concavity of the indifference curves generated by v is the key to Theorem 1, and the proof of this theorem will bring this out explicitly. The strategy behind the proof is to define a function $z(p, \phi, \psi)$ that is linear in (ϕ, ψ) and has two features. First, it is bounded by the payoff function v, so that

$$z(p, \phi, \psi) \leq v(p, \phi, \psi),$$

strictly so for a nonnegligible proportion of arbitration problems. Second, $z(p, \phi, \psi)$ has the same *ex ante* expectation as the payoff function u for the inquisitorial procedure. From these two features, we are able to conclude that

$$E(v) > E(z) = E(u),$$

thereby proving Theorem 1. The function $z(p, \phi, \psi)$ that performs this role is defined as

$$z(p, \phi, \psi) = \begin{cases} p_0 + \phi(p(1, 1) - p(0, 1)) & \text{if } p_0 \geq p_1 \\ p_1 + \psi(p(0, 0) - p(1, 0)) & \text{if } p_0 < p_1. \end{cases} \tag{14}$$

The iso-value contours of z in (ϕ, ψ)-space are either horizontal or vertical, depending on p_0 and p_1. Moreover, since the value of v is the maximum of the two clauses defining z, we have $v \geq z$ everywhere, strictly so over a nonnegligible set of arbitration problems. Figure 2 illustrates iso-value contours for z and v for the case when $p_0 > p_1$.

The next step in the argument for Theorem 1 is to show that $E(z) = E(u)$.

Lemma 1. $E(z) = E(u)$.

To prove this lemma, rearrange (14) to give

FIGURE 2

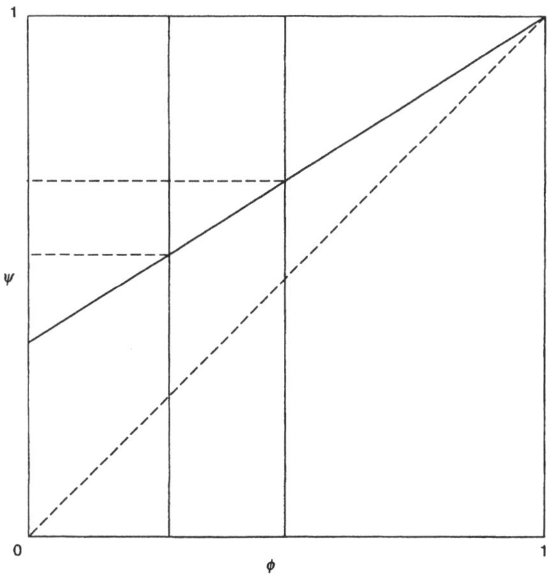

$$z(p, \phi, \psi) = \begin{cases} \phi(p(0, 0) + p(1, 1)) + (1 - \phi)p_0 & \text{if } p_0 \geq p_1 \\ \psi(p(0, 0) + p(1, 1)) + (1 - \psi)p_1 & \text{if } p_0 < p_1. \end{cases} \tag{15}$$

Taking the expectation of this expression with respect to the density $g(\phi, \psi, \theta)$, we have

$$\begin{aligned} E(z(p)) &= \begin{cases} \bar{\phi}(p(0, 0) + p(1, 1)) + (1 - \bar{\phi})p_0 & \text{if } p_0 \geq p_1 \\ \bar{\psi}(p(0, 0) + p(1, 1)) + (1 - \bar{\psi})p_1 & \text{if } p_0 < p_1 \end{cases} \\ &= \bar{\theta}(p(0, 0) + p(1, 1)) + (1 - \bar{\theta})\max\{p_0, p_1\} \\ &= E(u(p)), \end{aligned}$$

where the equality of the first two lines follows from our hypothesis that $\bar{\phi} = \bar{\psi} = \bar{\theta}$, and the equality of the last two lines follows by taking the expectation of $u(p, \theta)$ (given by (8)) with respect to the density g. Finally, by taking expectations with respect to the density $f(p)$, we obtain the statement in Lemma 1.

This lemma gives an insight into the role of the increasing returns to information. The inquisitorial procedure does equally well as a function that is linear in ϕ and ψ. Thus, the superiority of the adversarial procedure must come from the nonlinearity of the payoff v. This nonlinearity is reflected in the concavity of the indifference curves generated by v.

With the above lemma, the proof of Theorem 1 is immediate. By hypothesis, the densities g and f have full support, so that $E(v) > E(z)$. Together with the lemma, we have

$$E(v) > E(z) = E(u),$$

which proves Theorem 1.

3. Noise

■ Since the two arbitration procedures are alternative devices for generating information for the arbitrator, a natural way to paraphrase Theorem 1 is to say that the adversarial procedure "generates more information" than the inquisitorial procedure. This idea can be made more precise.

A joint distribution p over (s, σ) pairs is said to be a noisier version of p', if there is a 2×2 stochastic[3] matrix M such that

$$\begin{bmatrix} p(0,0) & p(0,1) \\ p(1,0) & p(1,1) \end{bmatrix} = M \begin{bmatrix} p'(0,0) & p'(0,1) \\ p'(1,0) & p'(1,1) \end{bmatrix}.$$

Then p is less informative than p', in the sense of Blackwell (1951). Under p, the realization of the signal σ gives a more diffuse posterior distribution over s.

It is possible to make precise the notion that the adversarial procedure generates more information by showing how the inquisitorial procedure can be seen as a noisier information-generating mechanism as compared to the adversarial procedure. In this argument, the following function plays a key role.

$$w(p, \phi, \psi) \equiv \max\begin{Bmatrix} p(0,0)(1-\psi) + p(0,1)(1-\phi), \\ p(1,0)(1-\psi) + p(1,1)(1-\phi) \end{Bmatrix}. \tag{16}$$

w is the last term in the expression for the payoff under the adversarial procedure, as given by (12). It has the feature that if p is a noisier version of p', then

$$w(p, \phi, \psi) \leq w(p', \phi, \psi). \tag{17}$$

To see this, suppose p is a noisier version of p'. Then, $w(p, \phi, \psi)$ is given by the largest element of the vector

$$\begin{bmatrix} \pi(0) \\ \pi(1) \end{bmatrix} \equiv \begin{bmatrix} p(0,0)(1-\psi) + p(0,1)(1-\phi) \\ p(1,0)(1-\psi) + p(1,1)(1-\phi) \end{bmatrix}$$
$$= M \begin{bmatrix} p'(0,0)(1-\psi) + p'(0,1)(1-\phi) \\ p'(1,0)(1-\psi) + p'(1,1)(1-\phi) \end{bmatrix}$$
$$= M \begin{bmatrix} \pi'(0) \\ \pi'(1) \end{bmatrix},$$

where M is a stochastic matrix. Thus, $\pi(0)$ and $\pi(1)$ are convex combinations of $\pi'(0)$ and $\pi'(1)$, and

$$w(p, \phi, \psi) = \max\{\pi(0), \pi(1)\} \leq \max\{\pi'(0), \pi'(1)\} = w(p', \phi, \psi). \tag{18}$$

Inequality (17) follows.

[3] That is, a matrix of probabilities whose rows sum to one.

Also, there is a "noisiest" p, which can be seen as a noisy version of any p' that satisfies the monotone likelihood ratio property. It is given by

$$\mathring{p} = \frac{1}{2}\begin{bmatrix} p_0 & p_0 \\ p_1 & p_1 \end{bmatrix}. \tag{19}$$

Its rows consist of identical entries, so that the signal σ is completely uninformative concerning s. Any p that satisfies the monotone likelihood ratio property can be transformed into $\mathring{p}$ by adding noise.[4]

Now, for a fixed p, consider the gap between the adversarial payoff v and the inquisitorial payoff u averaged over the triples (ϕ, ψ, θ). In other words, consider

$$\int_0^1 \int_0^1 \int_0^1 [v(p, \phi, \psi) - u(p, \theta)]g(\phi, \psi, \theta)\, d\theta\, d\psi\, d\phi. \tag{20}$$

Denote this difference as $E(v(p) - u(p))$. Then we can show the following:

Theorem 2. $E(v(p) - u(p)) = E(w(p) - w(\mathring{p}))$.

In other words, the payoff difference between the adversarial procedure and the inquisitorial procedure for a given p is equivalent to the loss in the expected value of w resulting from a switch from p to the completely uninformative distribution $\mathring{p}$.

To prove this result, consider the difference $v(p, \phi, \psi) - u(p, \theta)$. From (12) and (8),

$$\begin{aligned} v(p, \phi, \psi) - u(p, \theta) &= (p(0, 0) + p(1, 1))(\phi + \psi - 2\theta) + w(p, \phi, \psi) \\ &\quad - (1 - \theta)\max\{p_0, p_1\}. \end{aligned}$$

Taking expectations with respect to the density $g(\phi, \psi, \theta)$, the first term disappears due to our hypothesis that $\bar{\phi} = \bar{\psi} = \bar{\theta}$, leaving

$$E(v(p) - u(p)) = E(w(p)) - (1 - \bar{\theta})\max\{p_0, p_1\}.$$

However,

$$\begin{aligned} E(w(\mathring{p})) &= \frac{1}{2}((1 - \bar{\psi}) + (1 - \bar{\phi}))\max\{p_0, p_1\} \\ &= (1 - \bar{\theta})\max\{p_0, p_1\}, \end{aligned} \tag{21}$$

which proves Theorem 2.

□ **Numerical example.** To get a feel for the numerical magnitudes involved, for both the actual payoff differences between the two arbitration procedures and the illustration of the noise effect, let us consider some numerical examples. First I illustrate

[4] The appropriate stochastic matrix is

$$\frac{1}{2\Delta}\begin{bmatrix} p_0(p(1, 1) - p(1, 0)) & p_0(p(0, 0) - p(0, 1)) \\ p_1(p(1, 1) - p(1, 0)) & p_1(p(0, 0) - p(0, 1)) \end{bmatrix},$$

where

$$\Delta = p(0, 0)p(1, 1) - p(0, 1)p(1, 0).$$

the contours generated by the function $w(p, \phi, \psi)$ for a variety of cases, each of which is a noisier version of the previous case. In these diagrams (Figures 3 through 6), the horizontal axis measures ϕ, and the vertical, ψ. The four cases to be considered are as follows.

$$\text{Case 1:} \quad p = \begin{bmatrix} \frac{1}{2} & 0 \\ 0 & \frac{1}{2} \end{bmatrix}$$

$$\text{Case 2:} \quad p = \frac{1}{10}\begin{bmatrix} 4 & 1 \\ 1 & 4 \end{bmatrix}$$

$$\text{Case 3:} \quad p = \frac{1}{10}\begin{bmatrix} 3 & 2 \\ 2 & 3 \end{bmatrix}$$

$$\text{Case 4:} \quad p = \frac{1}{4}\begin{bmatrix} 1 & 1 \\ 1 & 1 \end{bmatrix}.$$

The above sequence illustrates the fall in the value of w as noise increases, culminating with the "noisiest" case, which we have referred to as $\mathring{p}$. Furthermore, by imposing a simple density $g(\phi, \psi, \theta)$ over the set of arbitration problems, it is possible to derive numerical values for the expected payoffs under the two arbitration procedures by simple geometric arguments. For this purpose, assume that the density $g(\phi, \psi, \theta)$ is uniform over the unit cube $[0, 1]^3$.

Recall the expressions for the payoffs under the two arbitration procedures (given by (8) and (12)):

$$v(p, \phi, \psi) = \psi(p(0, 0)) + \phi(p(1, 1)) + w(p, \phi, \psi)$$
$$u(p, \theta) = \theta(p(0, 0) + p(1, 1)) + \max\{p_0, p_1\}(1 - \theta).$$

By taking expectations with respect to the (assumed uniform) density $g(\phi, \psi, \theta)$, and from (21), we have the following expressions for the expected values of v and u:

$$E(v(p)) = \frac{1}{2}(p(0, 0) + p(1, 1)) + E(w(p))$$
$$E(u(p)) = \frac{1}{2}(p(0, 0) + p(1, 1)) + E(w(\mathring{p})). \tag{22}$$

Thus, it remains to find numerical values for the second term in each expression. $w(\mathring{p})$ is linear, as illustrated in case 4 above, and

$$E(w(\mathring{p})) = \frac{1}{4}((1 - \bar{\phi}) + (1 - \bar{\psi})) = \frac{1}{4}. \tag{23}$$

To calculate $E(w(p))$ for general p without recourse to computers, split the range of integration into the two triangles separated by the main diagonal, and exploit the symmetry of the example and the linearity of w when restricted to each triangle. So,

FIGURE 3

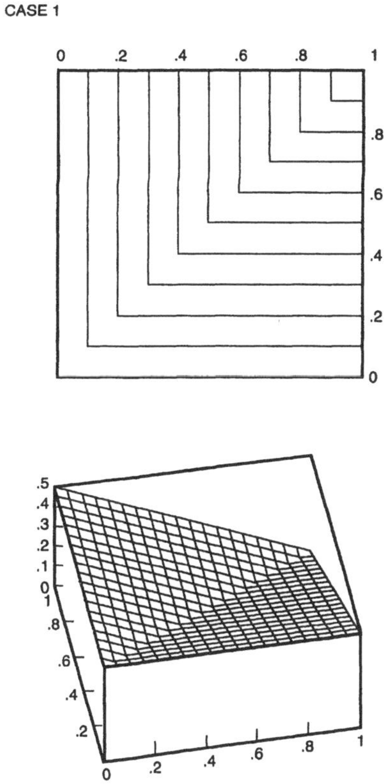

$$E(w(p)) = 2\int_0^1 \int_0^{\psi} w(p, \phi, \psi)\, d\phi\, d\psi$$

$$= 2w\left(p, \frac{1}{3}, \frac{2}{3}\right)$$

$$= \frac{1}{3}(2p(0, 0) + p(0, 1)).$$

Thus, we obtain the following simple expressions for the expected payoffs under the two arbitration procedures:

$$E(u(p)) = \frac{1}{2}(p(0, 0) + p(1, 1)) + \frac{1}{4},$$
$$E(v(p)) = \frac{1}{2}(p(0, 0) + p(1, 1)) + \frac{1}{3}(2p(0, 0) + p(0, 1)). \qquad (24)$$

FIGURE 4

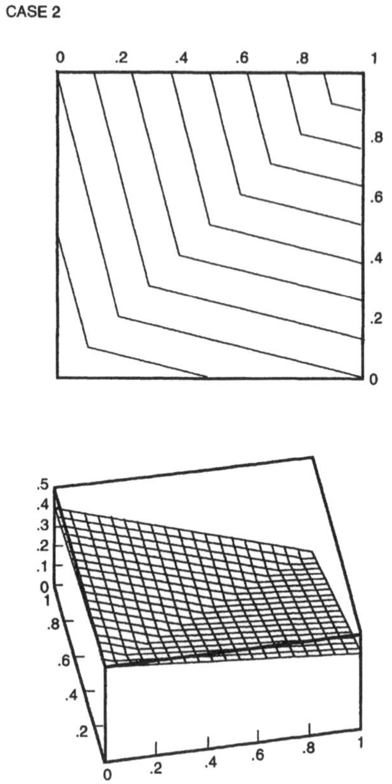

For the four cases of p examined above, the tabulated values of these payoffs, together with the proportional gain in payoff by moving to the adversarial procedure (shown in the last column), are shown in Table 6. As predicted by Theorem 2, the superiority of the adversarial procedure disappears when p is completely uninformative but can be as high as 11%, when there is no noise. For the intermediate cases, the relative superiority levels are 8% and just over 3%, which might be regarded as being rather small. However, alternative parameterizations of the density may yield substantially larger differences.

4. Assessment

■ The superiority of the adversarial procedure has its source in the discretion of the arbitrator to exercise the appropriate degree of skepticism and to react in a sophisticated way to the self-interested reporting strategies of the two opposing parties. In practice, the exercise of the appropriate degree of skepticism translates into a decision about the appropriate allocation of the burden of proof. This is particularly clear in the binary arbitration problem we have been examining, in which the arbitrator's decision is to

FIGURE 5

CASE 3

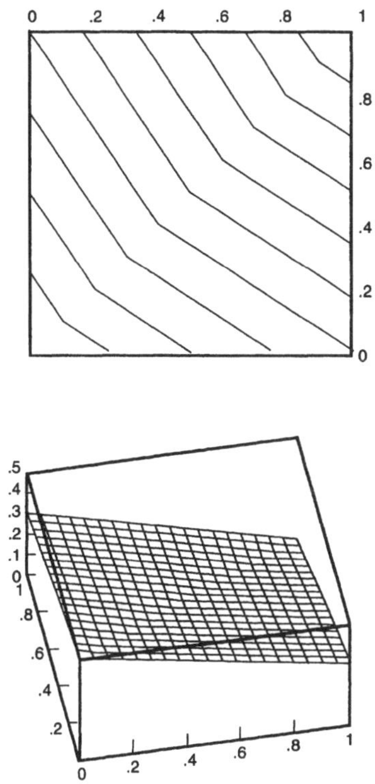

find in favor of one of the parties unless the opposing party can submit a convincing argument in favor of its own case.

There are at least three questions we may ask at this stage:

(1) How realistic is it to suppose that the arbitrator has the discretion to set the burden of proof?

(2) What if the arbitrator has access to a continuous action set, so that the support for one party or the other can be fine-tuned? Does the superiority of the adversarial procedure survive this generalization?

(3) How robust are the results to more general relaxations of the assumptions? Is it not conceivable that the inquisitorial procedure may outperform the adversarial system in some cases?

Let us tackle each of these points in turn.

□ **Burden of proof.** In many cases of interest, it is possible for the arbitrator to come across evidence of how well informed some party is without needing to acquire first-hand knowledge of the issues concerned. For example, if the arbitrator knows that the defendant has expertise in a field related to the current arbitration problem, while

FIGURE 6

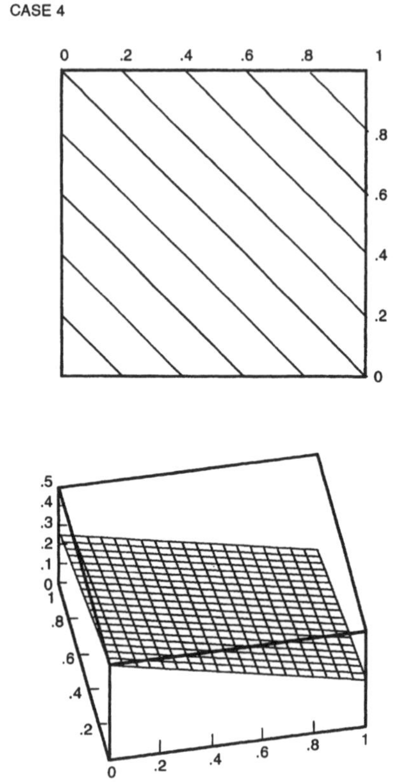

TABLE 6

p	$E(u(p))$	$E(v(p))$	$\frac{[E(v(p)) - E(u(p))]}{E(u(p))}$
$\frac{1}{2}\begin{bmatrix}1 & 0\\0 & 1\end{bmatrix}$	$\frac{3}{4}$	$\frac{5}{6}$	$\frac{1}{9}$
$\frac{1}{10}\begin{bmatrix}4 & 1\\1 & 4\end{bmatrix}$	$\frac{13}{20}$	$\frac{14}{20}$	$\frac{1}{13}$
$\frac{1}{10}\begin{bmatrix}3 & 2\\2 & 3\end{bmatrix}$	$\frac{33}{60}$	$\frac{34}{60}$	$\frac{1}{33}$
$\frac{1}{4}\begin{bmatrix}1 & 1\\1 & 1\end{bmatrix}$	$\frac{1}{2}$	$\frac{1}{2}$	0

the plaintiff does not, then it would be reasonable for the arbitrator to surmise that the defendant is more likely to have access to evidence of the true circumstance. This is so even though the arbitrator has no first-hand knowledge of what such evidence might be. In short, it is easier to ascertain *that* someone knows something than to know *what* this person knows. Thus, the appropriate allocation of the burden of proof does not presuppose expert knowledge of the circumstances of the dispute.

Submissions to competition authorities would be a prime example of such a situation. When a contested takeover is under consideration by the competition authority, and it has the submissions of both the raider and the intended target as to the effect on the "public interest" of the proposed takeover, the authority is in the appropriate position to allocate the burden of proof. If the raider has been planning the bid for some time, there may be grounds for concluding that the raider's information is likely to be better than that of the target firm (which may have been forced to hurry its submission). In such a case, it would be appropriate for the competition authority to allocate the burden of proof to the raider.

In the United Kingdom, the 1978 Green Paper[5] provides an interesting instance of this debate. At the time, there had been a presumption against intervention in the market for corporate control, and the Monopolies and Mergers Commission had acted only when there were clear signs that the merger would be against the public interest. The Green Paper recommended that the permissive bias in mergers be replaced by a more neutral burden of proof, although this recommendation was not taken up at the time (Hay and Vickers, 1988). Currently, after the election of 1997, the wheels may have turned full circle, with the incoming Labour administration taking a much more interventionist and skeptical posture towards mergers. Such a stance could be argued to be consistent with the findings of my article, if it is supposed that the raiders are likely to be better informed, and hence that the burden of proof rightly lies with them.

However, there are limits to how much discretion the arbitrator has in allocating the burden of proof. If the loss function is not symmetric but instead heavily skewed in one direction, the burden of proof is unlikely to be changed from one problem to the next. The "presumption of innocence" in criminal trials should not be viewed in terms of the relative information of the prosecution and defense, but rather should be seen as the greater loss resulting from convicting an innocent party as compared to acquitting a guilty one. This would suggest that our results have limited applicability to criminal proceedings.

□ **Continuous action set.** Instead of the binary decision of finding in favor of one or the other party, what if the arbitrator has access to a continuous action set in which the burden of proof embodied in the default settlement can be fine-tuned by choosing from a continuous action set? Is the superiority of the adversarial procedure robust to this change?

To examine this issue, consider a variation of my model in which the action set of the arbitrator is given by the unit interval [0, 1]. The interpretation is that the arbitrator chooses a sum of damages to be awarded to the plaintiff by the defendant, and where the arbitrator faces the squared loss function

$$-(s - t)^2, \tag{25}$$

where t is the transfer imposed by the arbitrator and s is the true circumstance.

[5] 1978 Green Paper, "A Review of Monopolies and Mergers Policy," Command 7198, Her Majesty's Stationery Office, London.

To minimize duplication of discussion with the early sections, I shall illustrate the argument for the case when the signal σ has no noise, so that exhibiting σ is equivalent to presenting conclusive evidence on the true circumstance. The equilibrium for the adversarial subgame for the continuous case has a very similar structure to that examined for the binary problem. The strategies of the plaintiff and defendant remain the same (given by (3) and (4)), while the arbitrator's strategy is

$$\begin{cases} \{\sigma = 0\} \mapsto 0 \\ \{\sigma = 1\} \mapsto 1 \\ \quad\;\; \emptyset \mapsto \dfrac{p_1(1-\phi)}{p_0(1-\psi) + p_1(1-\phi)}. \end{cases} \tag{26}$$

To see that these strategies do, indeed, constitute an equilibrium, note from (26) that the transfer in the absence of any news is between zero and one, so that (3) and (4) are best replies against the arbitrator's strategy. Now, check that (26) is the best reply for the arbitrator. If the information of the arbitrator is either $\{\sigma = 0\}$ or $\{\sigma = 1\}$, then the arbitrator can choose with full information. When neither party is able to submit a conclusive report, there are two possibilities. Either the true circumstance is zero but the defendant does not have information of this, or the true circumstance is one but the plaintiff does not have information. The former has probability $p_0(1 - \psi)$, while the latter has probability $p_1(1 - \phi)$. Hence, the posterior weights in the absence of conclusive submissions are

$$\left(\frac{p_0(1-\psi)}{p_0(1-\psi) + p_1(1-\phi)}, \frac{p_1(1-\phi)}{p_0(1-\psi) + p_1(1-\phi)}\right). \tag{27}$$

The transfer t is chosem to maximize

$$-\frac{p_0(1-\psi)(0-t)^2 + p_1(1-\phi)(1-t)^2}{p_0(1-\psi) + p_1(1-\phi)}, \tag{28}$$

so that optimal $t = p_1(1 - \phi)/(p_0(1 - \psi) + p_1(1 - \phi))$, as stated in (26).

As before, denote by $u(p, \theta)$ the arbitrator's payoff under the inquisitorial procedure from the arbitration problem and denote by $v(p, \phi, \psi)$ the arbitrator's payoff under the adversarial procedure when confronted with the same arbitration problem.

Under the inquisitorial procedure, when the arbitrator receives conclusive evidence on the true circumstance, the decision can be taken with full information and a zero loss can be guaranteed. The arbitrator receives conclusive evidence on the true circumstance with probability θ. When no such evidence is forthcoming, the arbitrator's beliefs over the two circumstances are governed by the prior distribution (p_0, p_1), so that the expected payoff from transfer t is

$$-p_0(0-t)^2 - p_1(1-t)^2,$$

which is maximized when $t = p_1$. Thus, the payoff under the inquisitorial system is

$$\begin{aligned} u(p, \theta) &= \theta * 0 + (1-\theta) * (-p_0 p_1) \\ &= -p_0 p_1 (1-\theta). \end{aligned} \tag{29}$$

Under the adversarial procedure, when one of the opposing parties submits a conclusive report on the true circumstance, the arbitration takes place with full information and a zero loss can be guaranteed. The arbitrator receives conclusive evidence from the defendant with probability $p_0\psi$ and from the plaintiff with probability $p_1\phi$. When neither party submits a conclusive report, the payoff is the expression obtained by substituting the optimal action t into (28). Since the probability that neither party submits a conclusive report is $p_0(1 - \psi) + p_1(1 - \phi)$, the arbitrator's expected payoff from the arbitration problem (p, ϕ, ψ, θ) is given by

$$\begin{aligned} v(p, \phi, \psi) &= -(p_0(1 - \psi)(0 - t)^2 + p_1(1 - \phi)(1 - t)^2) \\ &= -\frac{p_0 p_1(1 - \psi)(1 - \phi)}{p_0(1 - \psi) + p_1(1 - \phi)}. \end{aligned} \tag{30}$$

The *ex ante* payoff under the adversarial system is thus the expectation of this expression. Then, for the model sketched in this subsection, the superiority of the adversarial procedure can now be proved.

Theorem 3. Even with a smooth action set, the *ex ante* payoff under the adversarial procedure is strictly higher than that under the inquisitorial procedure.

In other words, the claim is that the expected value of (30) is strictly larger than that of (29). The argument is analogous to that given in the proof of Theorem 1. When plotted on (ϕ, ψ)-space, the arbitrator's indifference curves generated by v have the slope

$$\frac{d\psi}{d\phi} = -\frac{\partial v/\partial\phi}{\partial v/\partial\psi} = -\frac{p_0(1 - \psi)^2}{p_1(1 - \phi)^2}.$$

The slope of an indifference curve is increasing in the ratio $(1 - \psi)/(1 - \phi)$, so that the indifference curves are concave to the origin.[6] Figure 7 illustrates the indifference curves generated by v.

The increasing returns to information are clear here, as evidenced by the concavity of the indifference curves. Given this analogy with the earlier sections, we can employ the same strategy behind the proof. I define a function $z(p, \phi, \psi)$ which is linear in (ϕ, ψ), bounded above by v, and has the same *ex ante* expectation as the payoff function u for the inquisitorial procedure. From these two features, we will be able to conclude that $E(v) > E(z) = E(u)$, thereby proving Theorem 3. The function $z(p, \phi, \psi)$ that performs this role is defined as

$$z(p, \phi, \psi) \equiv -p_0 p_1\{p_0(1 - \phi) + p_1(1 - \psi)\}. \tag{31}$$

z is linear in (ϕ, ψ), and it takes the same value as v along the 45-degree line, since

$$z(p, k, k) = -p_0 p_1(1 - k) = v(p, k, k).$$

Also, any iso-value contour of z has slope $-p_0 p_1$. Thus, for the indifference curve

[6] Alternatively, since $d\psi/d\phi < 0$,

$$d^2\psi/d\phi^2 = -[-2p(1 - p)(1 - \phi)^2(1 - \psi)\, d\psi/d\phi + 2p(1 - p)(1 - \phi)(1 - \psi)^2]/(1 - p)^2(1 - \phi)^4 < 0,$$

so that the indifference curves are concave.

FIGURE 7

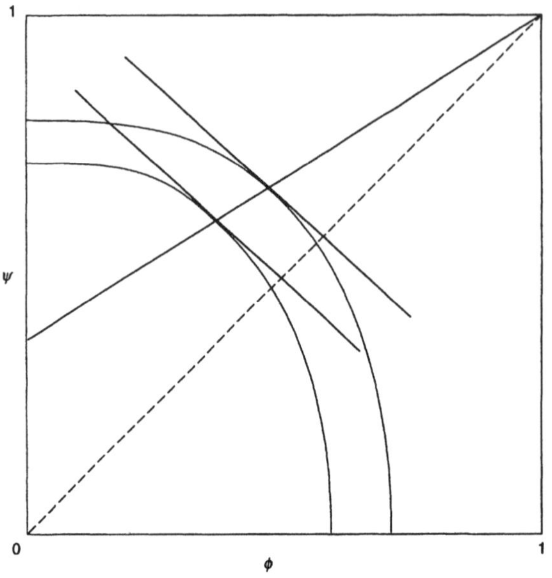

$v(p, \phi, \psi) = K$ passing through the point (k, k), the straight line given by $z(p, \phi, \psi) = K$ is the tangent to this indifference curve at (k, k). See Figure 8.

Since the indifference curves generated by v are strictly concave, we expect to have $z(p, \phi, \psi) < v(p, \phi, \psi)$ unless $\phi = \psi$, in which case they are equal. Indeed, some manipulation of (30) and (31) yields

$$v(p, \phi, \psi) - z(p, \phi, \psi) = \frac{(p_0 p_1(\phi - \psi))^2}{p_0(1 - \psi) + p_1(1 - \phi)}, \tag{32}$$

which is positive for $\phi \neq \psi$. Finally, taking expectations with respect to the density $g(\phi, \psi, \theta)$,

$$\begin{aligned} E(z(p)) &= -p_0 p_1\{p_0(1 - \bar{\phi}) + p_1(1 - \bar{\psi})\} \\ &= -p_0 p_1(1 - \bar{\theta}) \\ &= E(u(p)), \end{aligned}$$

where the equality of the first two lines follows from our assumption that $\bar{\phi} = \bar{\psi} = \bar{\theta}$. With this, the proof of Theorem 3 is immediate, since the density functions over the set of arbitration problems have full support.

□ **How robust are the results?** So far, the tenor of the discussion has been to bolster the superiority of the adversarial procedure. There are reasons to believe that the allocation of the burden of proof may be subject to discretion, and the results are not sensitive to whether the action set is binary or smooth.

FIGURE 8

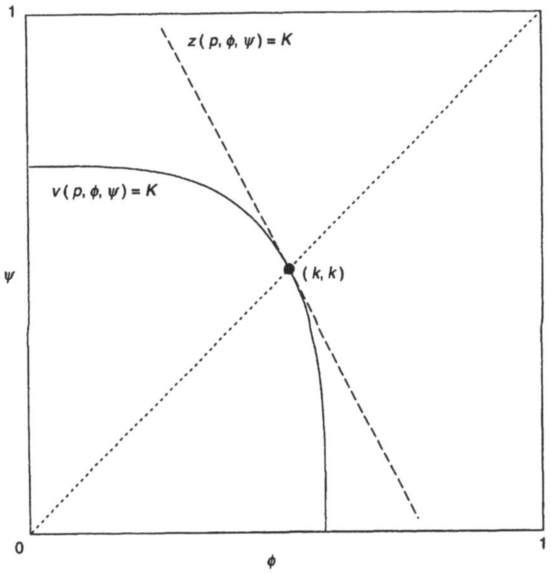

However, I conclude with an important proviso. Throughout this article, the assumption that reports are verifiable has played a key role. This assumption (shared by the other articles in the literature) rests on the premise that the interested parties are forbidden to fabricate evidence and that any such fabrication can be dealt with severely enough so that the disputants will not do it. The penalties for committing perjury, and analogous sanctions in quasi-judicial contexts, make this assumption reasonable. In some instances, however, the assumption of verifiability ought to be reconsidered.

One such instance is when specialist or scientific evidence is involved. When a dispute hinges on disputed scientific facts, the submissions rely on the current scientific understanding, including the possible controversies and uncertainties in existence at the time. Even when dealing with well-established methods and techniques, it would be rare that any single piece of scientific work is faultless. Understanding whether this flaw is significant takes training and experience. Under the adversarial system, each side can appoint its own expert witnesses (often highly paid), and the consequent potential for the perversion of research and the confusion of the jury may be seen as important considerations. Although judges may be given some limited training to help them, educating juries poses greater problems.

Under such circumstances, there may be a case for restricting expert witnesses to those appointed by the court, who in turn would advise the judge. Such a procedure is closer to the inquisitorial procedure than it is to the adversarial procedure. The current litigation on the health consequences of silicone breast implants in the United States[7] provides important insights into the limitations of the adversarial procedure. In Oregon at the end of 1996, a federal judge excluded a number of the plantiff's expert witnesses after an independent panel of scientists advised on the acceptability of the science. At

[7] *The Economist*, April 26 (p. 65), July 26 (pp. 95–96), and August 23 (p. 58), 1997.

the time of this writing, a "national panel" of four scientists is evaluating the cogency of the scientific evidence in the consolidated pretrial phase in Alabama of many separate litigations throughout the United States. The conclusions reached by the panel are expected to be influential in determining the conduct of these litigations. The fact that such a panel has been deemed necessary provides important lessons on the fragility of the verifiability assumption.

In such instances, the verifiability assumption does not have much bite in blocking potentially misleading submissions. When submissions rely on a body of underlying theories or hypotheses, the credibility of the underlying body of knowledge must also be assessed. The line between truth and falsehood is not so clear-cut. The criterion involved is the altogether fuzzier one of whether an argument meets the conventional standards of scientific plausibility as judged by the mainstream opinion of the day. Even if we accept the fact that we have little choice but to rely on current mainstream science to be the appropriate criterion, assessing the cogency of a body of scientific evidence is difficult and time-consuming for a lay jury. Thus, potential violations of the verifiability assumption will be an important limiting factor in qualifying our findings in favor of the adversarial procedure. Future research is clearly called for.

5. Concluding remarks and related literature

■ I conclude by discussing the relationship between the results reported here and those in Meyer (1991) and Dewatripont and Tirole (1995), both of which explore lines of argument that may guide further research in this area.

One way in which I have paraphrased the superiority of the adversarial procedure has been to say that if the arbitrator had the choice of improving the information of one of the two interested parties, he would improve the information of the better-informed party. Meyer (1991) shows that something quite analogous holds in the context of sequential sampling by a decision maker.

For illustration, consider a binary decision problem in which the decision maker observes a signal σ in inferring the relative likelihood of two circumstances, $s = 0$ and $s = 1$, which are equally likely (see Table 7). For simplicity, suppose that $p(1, 0)/p(0, 0) = p(0, 1)/p(1, 1)$, so that the extent of the "noise" is the same for both realizations of the signal.

Then, observing two draws from this distribution is no more valuable to the decision maker than observing just one draw. This is so since two draws that agree will only reinforce the decision with a single draw, whereas two conflicting draws will nullify each other, so that the decision maker has to rely on just the prior probabilities of the circumstances. In either case, the decision maker's *ex ante* payoff is no higher with two draws than with one.

But if the draws are made sequentially and the decision maker is able to affect the underlying probabilities between the two rounds of experiments, then he can do strictly better with two signals than with one. This is accomplished by introducing bias in the second experiment conditional on the outcome of the first, so that the realization observed in the first round is more likely to be observed in the second round. In other words, the bias is toward the candidate optimal action (the "default action") after the

TABLE 7

	$\sigma = 0$	$\sigma = 1$
$s = 0$	$p(0, 0)$	$p(0, 1)$
$s = 1$	$p(1, 0)$	$p(1, 1)$

first round. In this way, if the second draw recommends the opposite action, this draw now becomes a very informative signal indeed. The analogy with my model is that the absence of a conclusive submission by either the plaintiff or defendant can be treated as a signal in itself, and this signal is more informative if the disparity in the information of the two opposing parties is greater. Two conflicting pieces of information may be viewed as the absence of a knock-down argument, and a bias toward the default action improves the informativeness of the signal.

Dewatripont and Tirole (1995) conduct a wide-ranging discussion of the role of advocacy in decision making inside the firm and in other similar contexts, such as the rivalry between government departments, in which a principal aims to set the right incentives for information generation and for the revelation of such information. The principal may either employ two competing agents, each with a brief to argue in favor of one of two conflicting cases, or employ a single agent with a brief to act as an impartial inquisitor. All agents face costs of information gathering, so the focus is on the correct incentives to generate information.

Dewatripont and Tirole show that the principal's choice rests on the relative magnitudes of two types of inefficiencies. The first is excessive inertia, in which the decision maker chooses the status quo too often. The second is excessive "extremism," in which the decision maker rejects the status quo too often. The single inquisitor is likely to generate excessive extremism, since the agency problem poses difficulties for the agent to demonstrate that he is "actively being passive." In other words, the inquisitor faces disincentives in recommending the status quo. (A very similar effect occurs in Dow and Gorton (1997) in the context of delegated portfolio management, which leads to excessively active trading by the portfolio manager.) Such an inefficiency must be weighed against the tendency toward excessive inertia when two advocates are employed.

One important point made in Dewatripont and Tirole (1995) that has been neglected in my article is the possibility of second-order manipulation. To be more specific, I have taken for granted that the arbitrator is a seeker of truth and is not motivated by his own agenda. I have not addressed issues such as possible biases of the arbitrator or questions of political influence and competence. Dewatripont and Tirole have argued that the adversarial system has a robustness of the second order in which the existence of an appeal procedure ensures against possible incompetence or corruption on the part of the arbitrator.

The discussion in my article has a "welfarist" flavor in that the arbitrator's payoff is given a status higher than that of the interested parties. In effect, I have been identifying the arbitrator's payoff with the social welfare function. Relaxing this assumption would pose interesting challenges both in modelling and in terms of the analysis. Since I have been careful to conduct the discussion in terms of a fully fledged game, alternative views of the arbitrator can be accommodated by selecting a suitable payoff function. Indeed, issues of political competition and rivalry among special interest groups are amenable to the treatment given in this article. Developments of the arguments employed here may prove useful in such research.

References

Austen-Smith, D. "Strategic Transmission of Costly Information." *Econometrica*, Vol. 62 (1994), pp. 955–963.

Blackwell, D. "The Comparison of Experiments." *Proceedings of the Second Berkeley Symposium on Mathematical Statistics and Probability*. Berkeley: University of California Press, 1951.

Dewatripont, M. and Tirole, J. "Advocates." Unpublished paper, ECARE, Université Libre de Bruxelles, and IDEI, University of Toulouse, 1995.

DOW, J. AND GORTON, G. "Noise Trading, Delegated Portfolio Management, and Economic Welfare." *Journal of Political Economy,* Vol. 105 (1997), pp. 1024–1050.

DYE, R.A. "Strategic Accounting Choice and the Effect of Alternative Financial Reporting Requirements." *Journal of Accounting Research,* Vol. 23 (1985), pp. 544–574.

GLAZER, J. AND RUBINSTEIN, A. "Debates and Decisions: On a Rationale of Argumentation Rules." Unpublished paper, School of Economics, Tel Aviv University, 1997.

HAY, D. AND VICKERS, J. "The Reform of UK Competition Policy." *National Institute Economic Review,* Vol. 125 (1988), pp. 56–68.

LEWIS, T.R. AND SAPPINGTON, D.E.M. "Ignorance in Agency Problems." *Journal of Economic Theory,* Vol. 61 (1993), pp. 169–183.

LIPMAN, B.L. AND SEPPI, D.J. "Robust Inference in Communication Games with Partial Provability." *Journal of Economic Theory,* Vol. 66 (1995), pp. 370–405.

MEYER, M.A. "Learning from Coarse Information: Biased Contests and Career Profiles." *Review of Economic Studies,* Vol. 58 (1991), pp. 15–42.

MILGROM, P.R. "Good News and Bad News: Representation Theorems and Applications." *Bell Journal of Economics,* Vol. 12 (1981), pp. 350–391.

——— AND ROBERTS, J. "Relying on the Information of Interested Parties." *RAND Journal of Economics,* Vol. 17 (1986), pp. 18–32.

SEIDMANN, D.J. AND WINTER, E. "Strategic Information Transmission with Verifiable Messages." *Econometrica,* Vol. 65 (1997), pp. 163–169.

SHIN, H.S. "News Management and the Value of Firms." *RAND Journal of Economics,* Vol. 25 (1994a), pp. 58–71.

———. "The Burden of Proof in a Game of Persuasion." *Journal of Economic Theory,* Vol. 64 (1994b), pp. 253–264.

ELSEVIER

Economics Letters 70 (2001) 267–272

economics letters

www.elsevier.com/locate/econbase

Evidence production in adversarial vs. inquisitorial regimes

Luke M. Froeb[a,*], Bruce H. Kobayashi[b]

[a]Vanderbilt University, Owen Graduate School of Management, Nashville, TN 37203, USA
[b]School of Law, George Mason University, Arlington, VA, USA

Received 21 January 2000; accepted 15 July 2000

Abstract

The advantage of the adversarial regime of judicial decision-making is the superior information of the parties, while the advantage of an idealized inquisitorial regime is its neutrality. We model the tradeoff by characterizing the properties of costly estimators used by each regime. The adversarial regime uses an 'extremal' estimator that is based on the difference between the most favorable pieces of evidence produced by each party. The inquisitorial regime uses the sample mean. We find that neither regime dominates the other. © 2001 Elsevier Science B.V. All rights reserved.

Keywords: Litigation; Evidence; Procedure; Information production

JEL classification: K41; D83

1. Introduction

The trade-off between an inquisitorial and adversarial system of justice is essentially one of centralized vs. decentralized evidence production. In an adversarial system, the decision-maker must rely on the reports of interested parties, rather than gather evidence for himself. Milgrom and Roberts (1986) find that even a naïve decision-maker can reach a full information decision provided that the interests of the parties are sufficiently opposed, and evidence is costless to produce. The same theoretical result is extended to costly access by Froeb and Kobayashi (1996) (see also McAfee and Reny (1992)), and is consistent with recent experimental findings comparing adversarial with non-adversarial presentation in terms of both revelation of hidden information and accuracy of litigated outcomes (Block et al., 1999; Parker and Lewisch, 1998).

However, these results are qualified by reference to the assumption of symmetrical access to

*Corresponding author. Tel.: 1 1-615-343-6009; fax: 1 1-615-343-7177.
E-mail addresses: luke.froeb@vanderbilt.edu (L.M. Froeb), bkobayas@gmu.edu (B.H. Kobayashi).

0165-1765/01/$ – see front matter
PII: S0165-1765(00)00356-6

information and verification of parties' reports, which highlights the potential importance of the pretrial discovery process (Cooter and Rubinfeld, 1994; Hay, 1994; Jost, 1995; Sobel, 1989) and evidentiary rules (Parker and Kobayashi, 1999; Lewis and Poitevin, 1997; Daughety and Reinganum, 1998).

In this article, we characterize the adversarial and inquisitorial regimes by the estimators they use to resolve legal disputes. This article adds to the growing literature comparing adversarial and inquisitorial procedures (Posner, 1999; Shin, 1998; Dewatripont and Tirole, 1999; Parisi, 2000). Welfare comparisons are made by comparing statistical properties of the estimators. We find that the inquisitorial regime does not strictly dominate the adversarial regime. For some distributions, the adversarial system may produce a lower variance estimator than the inquisitorial system. However, this is not always the case. Further, it may be relatively more costly to obtain a lower variance with the adversarial system.

2. Model

To motivate the model, we consider a stylized model of litigation between two parties. Evidence is produced by drawing out of a probability distribution, $F(x)$, whose mean, m, represents the issue being litigated, e.g. the amount of monetary damages that must be paid by the defendant to the plaintiff. The court's role is to estimate the mean.

In an adversarial regime, the court is a passive, unsophisticated actor, using a simple split-the-difference scheme to evaluate the evidence put before it:

$$x^* 5 (x_p 1 x_d)/2, \tag{1}$$

where x_p is evidence produced by the plaintiff and x_d is evidence produced by the defendant. We assume that the litigants report only the most favorable information to the court. If the plaintiff and defendant take N_p and N_d draws respectively, the litigants reports will equal:

$$x_p 5 \text{Maxh}x_1, x_2, x_3, \ldots, x_{N_p}\text{j} \tag{2p}$$

and

$$x_d 5 \text{Minh}x_1, x_2, x_3, \ldots, x_{N_d}\text{j} \tag{2d}$$

Evidence is costly to produce, so the decision of how much evidence to produce is an optimal stopping problem for each of the litigants. We assume that both parties know the distribution out of which they are drawing.[1] The payoff functions are:

$$p_p 5 x^* 2 cN_p \tag{3p}$$

and

$$p_d 5 \; 2 x^* 2 cN_d, \tag{3d}$$

[1]Note that Rothschild (1974) has shown that even if the litigants do not know the distribution, they learn very quickly, so that they behave almost as if they know the underlying distribution.

where '*c*' is the cost of a draw.

In a dominant strategy equilibrium, the plaintiff stops producing evidence after a draw greater than v_p; and the defendant stops after a draw lower than v_d. The stopping values are calculated by equating the marginal cost of drawing to the marginal benefit of drawing (e.g. Malliaris and Brock, 1982):

$$c\ 5\ \mathrm{E}_{v_p}(x\ 2\ v_p)dF(x)/2 \tag{4p}$$

and

$$c\ 5\ \mathrm{E}^{v_d}(v_d\ 2\ x)\ dF(x)/2. \tag{4d}$$

One can immediately see that if $F(x)$ is symmetric, then $v_p\ 2\ m\ 5\ m\ 2\ v_d$, i.e. stopping values are symmetric around the mean of the distribution. As a consequence, the court's split-the-difference estimator of the mean is unbiased because the litigants are stopping equidistant from, but on either side of the mean.[2] On average, each party takes the same number of draws, $N_d\ 5\ N_p\ 5\ 1/[1\ 2\ F(v_p)]$. The variance of the court's estimator equals:

$$[\mathrm{Var}(xu\ .\ v_p)\ 1\ \mathrm{Var}(xu\ ,\ v_d)]/4\ 5\ \mathrm{Var}(xu\ .\ v_p)/2. \tag{5}$$

An inquisitorial court would gather evidence for itself, without discarding unfavorable evidence. We presume that it would use the sample mean for its well-known optimality properties. Since both the sample mean and the adversarial estimator are unbiased, we can compare the estimators by comparing variances. The variance of the adversarial regime is smaller than the variance of the inquisitorial regime when:

$$\mathrm{Var}(xu\ .\ v_p)/2\ ,\ \mathrm{Var}(x)/N_c \tag{6}$$

where N_c is the number of draws taken by the arbiter. To compare the efficiency of each regime, we compare estimators of equal cost (equal number of draws) by making the substitution $N_c\ 5\ 2/[1\ 2\ F(v_p)]$. The adversarial estimator has lower variance when:

$$\mathrm{Var}(xu\ .\ v_p)\ ,\ \mathrm{Var}(x)[1\ 2\ F(v_p)]. \tag{7}$$

This result does not violate the Gauss–Markov theorem, proving the optimality of the sample mean, because the adversarial estimator is not in the class of linear estimators to which the theorem refers. In the adversarial regime, litigants know the distribution out of which they are drawing and use the knowledge to produce optimal stopping rules that sometimes dominate the sample mean, depending on the characteristics of the distribution out of which evidence is produced.

---

[2] If the distribution is asymmetric, then the court's split-the-difference estimator will not, in general, be unbiased. Although it is difficult to classify asymmetric distributions, it is easy to construct examples in which the party drawing on the longer tail of the distribution stops further out from the mean than the party drawing on the shorter tail of the distribution. In these examples, the court's estimator x^* is biased towards the party drawing on the longer tail of the distribution.

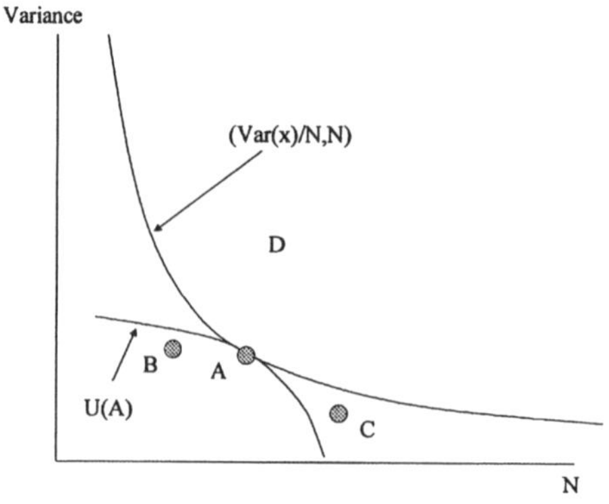

Fig. 1. The trade-off between cost and variance.

Condition (7) is a necessary, but not sufficient, condition for the adversarial estimator to be preferred to the sample mean. Fig. 1 plots the trade-off between cost and variance offered by the sample mean. On the horizontal axis is the number of draws (a proxy for the cost), and on the vertical axis is the variance of the estimator. The variance of the sample mean is plotted as $\mathrm{Var}(x)/N$. If society prefers estimators with lower costs and lower variance, then indifference curves are concave toward the origin. With the illustrated societal preferences, the inquisitor will choose the point A. Points B and C illustrate equilibrium outcomes under the adversarial system cases where condition (7) holds because each has lower variance than the sample mean with an equivalent number of draws. At point B, the adversarial system is preferred to the inquisitorial system; at point C, the inquisitorial system is preferred. If condition (7) does not hold, the adversarial estimate will lie in the inferior region labeled D in Fig. 1.

Condition (7) can be illustrated with some examples. For a uniform $[a, b]$ distribution, condition (7) becomes:

$$(b\,2\,v_p)^2/12\,,\;[(b\,2\,a)^2/12][(b\,2\,v_p)/(b\,2\,a)], \tag{8}$$

which reduces to

$$a\,,\,v_p, \tag{9}$$

which is satisfied for all v_p. Thus, holding the number of draws constant, the adversarial regime has lower variance when the distribution of x is uniform. The intuition behind this result is that the uniform distribution has a large variance and this imparts a large variance to the sample mean. In the adversarial regime, the litigants choose stopping values that move them quickly to the endpoints of the distribution, resulting in a low-variance estimator, regardless of the value of v_p.

The opposite result can be illustrated using a double exponential distribution centered on m, where the distribution functions decay exponentially at the same rate to the left and to the right. In this case, the adversarial regime does much worse. The intuition for this result comes from the 'memoryless' characteristic of an exponential distribution, i.e. when the parties move out on the tails of the distribution, the variance does not decrease. Expenditure in the adversarial system is wasted because Var(x) 5 Var(xu . v_p), and condition (7) is never satisfied.

The intermediate case can be illustrated with a Normal Distribution. If the parties stop near the middle of the distribution due to a small stopping value or equivalently, a large cost of drawing, then the adversarial regime is preferred for the same reason as in the uniform. For a larger stopping value out on the tail of the distribution, the adversarial regime throws away too much information to be efficient.

3. Discussion

The adversarial system has been criticized on the basis of its cost, and the tendency for litigants to report only favorable evidence. In contrast to the claims of the critics, we find that the adversarial process is not dominated by even an idealized inquisitorial process.

Our theoretical results suggest caution in concluding that centralized systems of evidence gathering are inherently superior. Further, under circumstances where centralized evidence gathering would dominate, incentives for the litigants to voluntarily choose such rules are created. Thus, a system where such choices are made available, but are not imposed as a mandatory system, would be best able to achieve the benefits identified by the proponents of centralization without incurring the potential costs of imposing these rules when they decrease welfare.

References

Block, M.K., Parker, J.S., Vyborna, O., Dusek, L., 1999. An experimental comparison of adversarial versus inquisitorial regimes. American Law and Economics Review, In press.

Cooter, R.D., Rubinfeld, D.L., 1994. An economic model of legal discovery. Journal of Legal Studies 23, 435–463.

Daughety, A.F., Reinganum, J.F., 1998. On the Economics of Trials: Adversarial Process, Evidence and Equilibrium Bias. Vanderbilt, Working paper [98-W02.

DeGroot, M., 1970. Optimal Statistical Decisions. McGraw-Hill, New York.

Dewatripont, M., Tirole, J., 1999. Advocates. Journal of Political Economy 107, 1–39.

Froeb, L., Kobayashi, B., 1996. Naive, biased, yet Bayesian: can juries interpret selectively-produced evidence. Journal of Law, Economics and Organization 12, 257–276.

Hay, B.L., 1994. Civil discovery: its effects and optimal scope. Journal of Legal Studies 23, 481–515.

Jost, P.J., 1995. Disclosure of information and incentive for care. International Review of Law and Economics 15, 265–85.

Lewis, T., Poitevin, M., 1997. Disclosure of information in regulatory proceedings. Journal of Law, Economics and Organization 13, 50–74.

Malliaris, A.G., Brock, W.A., 1982. Stochastic Methods in Economics and Finance. North Holland, New York.

McAfee, R.P., Reny, P., 1992. Correlated information and mechanism design. Econometrica 60, 395–421.

Milgrom, P., Roberts, J., 1986. Relying on the information of interested parties. Rand Journal of Economics 17, 18–32.

Parisi, F., 2000. Rent-seeking through litigation: adversarial and inquisitoral systems compared. International Review of Law and Economics, In press.

Parker, J.S., Lewisch, P., 1998. Materielle Wahrheitsfindung im Zivilprozess [The revelation of truth in civil procedure. In: Lewisch, P., Rechberger, W.H. (Eds.), 100 Jahre ZPO: Okonomische Analyse des Civilprozesses [Civil Procedure Code Centennial: Economic Analysis of Civil Procedure. Manz, Wien, pp. 203–223.

Parker, J.S., Kobayashi, B.H., 1999. Evidence. In: Bouckaert, B., De Geest, G. (Eds.). The Encyclopedia of Law and Economics, Vol. 5. Edward Elgar, Cheltenham, UK, pp. 290–306.

Posner, R., 1999. The law and economics of economics expert witnesses. Journal of Economic Perspectives 13, 91–99.
Rothschild, M., 1974. Searching for the lowest price with the distribution of prices is unknown. Journal of Political Economy 16, 689–711.
Shin, H.S., 1998. Adversarial and inquisitorial procedures in arbitration. RAND Journal of Economics 29, 378–405.
Sabel, J., 1989. An analysis of discovery rules. Law and Contemporary Problems 52, 133–159.

ELSEVIER International Review of Law and Economics 22 (2002) 193–216

International Review of Law and Economics

Rent-seeking through litigation: adversarial and inquisitorial systems compared

Francesco Parisi*

School of Law, George Mason University, 3401 North Fairfax Drive, Arlington, VA 22201, USA

Accepted 24 May 2001

Abstract

This paper compares the adversarial system of adjudication, dominant in the common law tradition, with the inquisitorial system, dominant in the civil law tradition, using a rent-seeking, Nash equilibrium, model of litigation expenditure in which the litigants simultaneously choose their levels of effort with the goal of maximizing their returns from the case. The choice between the two systems is modeled as a continuous variable showing the equilibrium solutions of the game and their implications for procedural economy. The results are then utilized to characterize the optimal levels of adversarial and inquisitorial discovery with respect to the social benefits of truth-finding and correct adjudication, and the private and administrative costs of litigation.

[A] common law trial is and always should be an adversary proceeding.

Hickman v. Taylor (1947), 329 U.S. 495, 516 (Jackson, J., concurring)

Scholars of comparative civil procedure often contrast American and continental European legal systems by reference to the distinctive functions fulfilled by judges and lawyers in the two legal traditions. A distinction is often drawn between "adversarial" and "inquisitorial" procedural systems. The two opposing paradigms refer to the different roles played by the judge in the conduct of a civil case.

In a typical inquisitorial proceeding, the trial is dominated by a presiding judge, who determines the order in which evidence is taken and who evaluates the content of the gathered evidence. In those proceedings, the court determines the credibility and relative weight of each

* Tel.: +1-703-993-8036.
E-mail address: parisi@gmu.edu (F. Parisi).

0144-8188/02/$ – see front matter © 2002 Elsevier Science Inc. All rights reserved.
PII: S0144-8188(02)00089-3

piece of evidence without being constrained by strict rules in that respect. By contrast, in a typical adversarial system, the case is organized and the facts are developed by the sole initiative of the parties. The process develops through the efforts of the litigants before a passive decision maker who reaches a decision on the sole basis of the evidence and motions presented by the litigants.

Law and economics scholars have occasionally examined the various methods of discovery in a comparative perspective. The discussion has often invoked alternative ideological paradigms. Most notably, in a well-known debate, Posner (1988) and Tullock (1988) have taken opposite sides on this issue, defending respectively the adversarial and the inquisitorial systems, on a variety of grounds. Posner argues that the adversarial system is preferable because it allows the parties who bear the costs and benefits of the litigation to shape the litigation. Alternatively, the inquisitorial method shifts power to judges, and thus promotes an expansion of the public sector as well. Posner contends that it is doubtful whether such a shift would improve the performance of our judicial system.

In this paper I consider the strategic implications of these procedural alternatives, showing the impact of a change in the extent of the inquisitorial role of the judge on parties' incentives to expend in litigation. In Part I, I consider the key differences between the conduct of a case in an adversarial procedural system and an inquisitorial system. The analysis evaluates some general features of alternative modes of discovery. The results can be extended to both civil and criminal procedure, notwithstanding the different goals and concerns associated with civil and criminal adjudication. In Part II, I show the impact of the two procedural rules on the equilibrium expenditures on litigation for the two parties. The results suggest that both an increase in the weight attached to the judge-obtained evidence and an increase in judicial scrutiny of the adversary's arguments and evidence will have a negative impact on the equilibrium levels of litigation expenditures undertaken by the litigants. In Part III, I depict the optimal weight to be attached to the inquisitorial efforts of the judge as the value that maximizes the social benefits from truthful adjudication net of the private and administrative costs. The comparative statics of the model show how the optimal weights placed on the adversarial and inquisitorial components of the process vary with some key features of the cost and benefit functions. The results indicate that the optimal weight attached to the adversarial component of the process is positively related to the visibility and social relevance of the litigated case and to the judicial scrutiny applied by the court to the parties' evidence, while it is negatively related to the private cost of litigation for the parties, the relative efficiency of the court in obtaining and evaluating evidence, and the number of litigants competing for the adjudication of a fixed award. Part IV offers a few concluding remarks about the costs of the adversary system.

1. The adversarial and inquisitorial systems compared

The distinction between adversarial and inquisitorial systems finds its origin in twelfth century European law. Adversarial processes could only be initiated by the action of a private party (the so-called *processus per accusationem*), while inquisitorial proceedings could be triggered *ex officio* by the judicial system (the so-called *processus per inquisitionem*).

The meaning of the distinction evolved in later medieval times to include other features generally associated with the two procedures.[1] Most notably, the distinction came to refer to the general role of the judge in the fact-finding phase of the trial. In medieval times, the judge was generally conceived as an official truth seeker. In a well-known *dictum*, fourteenth century jurist Bartolus from Sassoferrato argued that, with or without a proposal by a party, courts could produce and examine witnesses for the purpose of truthful discovery.[2] Along similar lines, Baldus de Ubaldis, a jurist who wrote during the second half of the 14th century, argued that, because of their institutional role as cognitional judges, medieval courts were at liberty to hear those witnesses whose depositions they considered necessary for establishing the facts at issue.[3] Production and evaluation of the evidence were the sole prerogatives of the judge who could summon witnesses to assist the court's fact-finding efforts. In this context, Baldus further argued that it was not part of the prerogatives of the individual litigants to examine the witnesses or to produce them.[4]

Historically, the procedural systems of the common law tradition developed away from the inquisitorial models, adopting the adversarial paradigm of adjudication in both criminal and civil legal proceedings. In common law proceedings the presentation of evidence became the exclusive task of the parties. As pointed out by Damaska (1997) this is not surprising, given the absence from England of an official apparatus capable of routine judicial investigations. In spite of much legal evolution, the ancient roots of the adversarial trial are still evident in the current rules of procedure.[5] The role of the victim in the trials against the accused is replicated in modern times through the adversarial process, with a public accuser carrying out the victim's task in the accusation of the wrongdoer.

Nineteenth century classical liberal ideas allowed the adversarial model to outlive its historical origins. Adversarial procedure was defended for its closer proximity to "dialectical" models, with emphasis on assertion and refutation, and yet attacked by enlightened rationalists, generally skeptical of information provided by biased and self-interested actors.[6] In the evolved conception of the adversarial procedure, the parties' attorneys became responsible for discovering and presenting evidence for their clients and for challenging the evidence presented by their opposition.[7] Similarly, the parties bore the full responsibility for presenting the law: legal theories were formulated by the parties' attorneys and expressed in oral and written arguments. In this setting the judge played the role of a neutral and passive arbiter, ruling, often without explanation, on objections and contentions moved by the parties. Even relatively active judges were limited in the scope of their action, compared with the role played by the typical judge serving in a civil law jurisdiction.[8]

In the current legal usage, the distinction between inquisitorial and adversarial proceedings continues to refer to the general differences in approach between the civil law and common law procedural systems.[9]

In a typical common law trial, the process is party-controlled. The case is organized and the facts are developed by the sole initiative of the parties.[10] The process develops through the efforts of the litigants before a passive decision maker who reaches a decision on the sole basis of the evidence and motions presented by the parties. In an adversarial system of legal procedure, the judge thus enjoys limited initiative in the process. While the judge has some discretion over the nature and extent of his or her participation, in no case may he or she contribute to the fact-elucidation efforts of the parties. The truth of the case cannot be searched directly by the judge, but shall instead emerge out of the adversarial dynamic of the process, with a partisan presentation of the facts.[11]

In a typical civil law trial, judicial officials perform a more active role which is not limited to the examination of the evidence presented by the parties or to the execution of the parties' motions. The control over the process is shifted from the parties to the court, which enjoys greater discretion in the evaluation of the evidence and may guide the discovery process with bench requests. In these systems, the presiding judge determines the order in which evidence is taken and is free to weigh up the relative value of conflicting evidence, acting independently of the proposals and motions of the parties (Ullmann, 1946). The inquisitorial character of the procedure generally implies that judges are generally not bound by any formal rule in the evaluation of the facts but are to decide on the basis of their "internal conviction" (*intime conviction*).[12] Accordingly, in several civil law jurisdictions, the court determines the credibility and relative weight of each piece of information without being guided by formal rules of evidence.[13] In this respect, the court is vested with a large degree of initiative to shape the course of the litigation. Concepts such as "plaintiff's case" or "defendant's case" are unknown to the procedural systems of the civil law tradition.[14] In a typical civil law court, the judge contributes to ascertaining the facts and identifying potentially relevant evidence, and actively screens and evaluates the evidence presented by the parties.[15] The civil law judge has authority to investigate the facts on his own initiative, exercising the power by asking supplemental questions when the advocates have concluded their questioning, and often conducting the primary examination of witnesses.[16]

In an inquisitorial proceeding, the direct involvement of the judge in the gathering of evidence often avoids the consolidation of two contrary point of views resulting from an independent partisan search and presentation of the facts. In contrast, an adversarial process often leads to two clashing positions. As pointed out by Damaska (1997) this format is often conducive to an exacerbation of the differences and a neglect of the common grounds: "Neutral information tends to be short-changed. ... the world presented to the triers of fact is illuminated by two narrow beams of light."[17] Froeb and Kobayashi (2000) have further analogized the fact-finding process in an adversarial system to an "extremal" estimator based on the difference between the most favorable pieces of evidence produced by each party.[18] This, in turn, yields an important testable proposition: with the judge's involvement vanishing, the litigants' differences will surface more noticeably, and greater overall expenditures in litigation will obtain.

In a typical civil law case, the active participation of the judge in the gathering and evaluation of evidence further creates a blurring of the distinction between pretrial and trial. As pointed out by Adams (1998), this implies that in civil law jurisdictions, trial is not a single continuous event. Rather there are several hearings in which the court meets with the litigants to gather and evaluate the evidence of the case. The ongoing involvement of the judge in the discovery process has important implications for procedural economy.

In a two-stage process, the parties tend to gather and disclose all the evidence that may in some way relate to the litigated case. Evidence that is not gathered and disclosed in the pretrial phase often becomes inadmissible at trial. Given the likely uncertainty over the usefulness and relevance of each piece of information in the later trial phase, the litigants tend to introduce much more evidence than is actually utilized in the trial phase. The litigants compete in the adversarial supply of information, in order to dominate the opponent in the subsequent presentation of their case. Such advantage may indeed prove very valuable in jury trials, where a lay jury decides, in the absence of a professional judge, which facts have been proved.

In a one-stage process, instead, the judge guides and actively participates in the discovery process, indicating the issues and factual questions that he would like to investigate. In doing so, the court confines the scope of the adversarial supply of information by the parties to those issues that appear more obscure to him. The judge will discourage the litigants from dissipating their efforts and resources to prove a factual circumstance that has been rendered irrelevant by other findings of the court. The parties have an opportunity to get some preliminary feedback from the judge as to the likely relevance of costly information, thus avoiding expenditures in discovery that may later prove unnecessary or irrelevant.

2. Rents, rent-dissipation, and rational litigation

The dichotomous distinction between adversarial and inquisitorial proceedings obviously embraces several dimensions of the legal process, summarizing them within two discrete categories. This approach has been criticized by scholars of comparative law who observe that there are too many elements that these legal terms attempt to consider.[19] The legal systems of the world, although historically interrelated, have assumed different forms and procedural connotations that render the dichotomous distinction inapt.[20] The following analysis considers the adversarial nature of the process as a continuous variable.[21] This enables us to consider the range of real world alternatives without artificial and arbitrary dichotomies.

In the model developed in the present section, I follow the conventional wisdom (Posner, 1973; Damaska, 1983), which models the dispute resolution process as a simulation of, and substitute for, the private conflict between two parties. This leads to the central image of proceedings as a contest of two sides before a judge or arbiter. According to this line of thinking, the task is then to consider alternative procedural arrangements as instrumental to the most efficient resolution of the parties' conflict. For example, if the judge were permitted to conduct independent inquiries into the facts of the case, the discovery process would logically cease to be a mere party contest and the return to private litigation efforts would be reduced accordingly.

In this setting, I classify procedural systems according to the allocation of control over the process and the relative dominance of inquisitorial and adversarial formats. The variable I captures the weight attached to the inquisitorial (i.e., non-adversarial) findings in determining the size of the award. Greater values of I indicate that the judge, as opposed to the litigants, has greater control over the process, or that the evidence obtained directly by the judge is, *ceteris paribus*, given greater weight than the evidence provided by the parties. I use the subscripts A and I to identify the returns from the adversarial and inquisitorial components of the litigation.

In this model, legal expenditure at trial is endogenous.[22] In this section, I consider how the equilibrium expenditures in litigation vary with the institutional choice of I. E_J is the judicial effort exerted by the court in independent investigation and examination of independently obtained evidence. This level of effort will depend positively on the level of I. S

denotes the level of scrutiny to which the evidence provided by the parties is subjected. S is considered a parameter for our analysis, and is not chosen by the judge. The level of S may denote procedural safeguards against the admission of certain types of evidence, like hearsay. As S increases, the likelihood than any piece of evidence submitted by the parties will be discarded increases, and so the equilibrium level of expenditures by the parties will decrease.

Following Posner (1973, 1999), I set the probability of prevailing in litigation as a function of relative party expenditures. Equilibrium is achieved via independent spending decisions by the litigants. In this model, a relative increase in litigation spending reduces the opponent's expected return from the case.[23] More specifically, the parties' total expected return R^e depends upon the following two components: (i) the merits of the disputed case, R_I, as ascertained through the inquisitorial discovery; (ii) the disputed case, R_A, captured through the adversarial efforts of the parties $E_{\mathrm{p,d}}$. A shift in the weight attached to the inquisitorial and adversarial components of the process may change the expected return from the parties' case. The total marginal effect of a procedural change for all parties is zero-sum.[24] Note that R_I and R_A represent plaintiff awards. The former represents the award level that would be given if no adversarial effort is exerted, and the judge's decision is made only on the basis of independently gathered evidence. The latter is the award amount that results from the parties' evidence. The plaintiff's adversarial award amount will depend on R_A and on the relative amount of effort he spends in litigation.

The return from the non-adversarial component is a function of the underlying merits of the plaintiff's case as well as the judicial discovery efforts, E_J. The returns from the adversarial component, instead, are a proportional share function of the parties' respective efforts, and the residual value of the case which depends on the adversarial evidence and the level of scrutiny that evidence is subjected to by the court. An adversary's expected return from the case is a weighted average of the inquisitorial and adversarial components, with the institutional choice variable I determining the weights. The same functional form could be used to characterize a winner-takes-all system where the parties' respective probabilities of success are proportional to their shares of effort.

For two litigants (plaintiff, defendant), the respective objective is to maximize their expected return from litigation. For the typical case of a zero-sum judgment, the plaintiff will try to maximize the net judicial award, while the defendant will try to minimize the total loss from litigation. The plaintiff's objective could thus be to maximize:

$$R_{\mathrm{p}}^{\mathrm{e}} = IR_I(E_J) + (1 - I)R_A(S)\frac{E_{\mathrm{p}}}{E_{\mathrm{p}} + E_{\mathrm{d}}} - CE_{\mathrm{p}} \tag{2.1}$$

Symmetrically, the defendant wishes to minimize the sum of the expected judgment and his litigation costs. This objective can be represented as maximizing:

$$R_{\mathrm{d}}^{\mathrm{e}} = -IR_I(E_J) - (1 - I)R_A(S)\frac{E_{\mathrm{p}}}{E_{\mathrm{p}} + E_{\mathrm{d}}} - CE_{\mathrm{d}} \tag{2.2}$$

Given the zero-sum constraint, the effect of a change in procedure, I, on the parties' expected payoffs will have opposite signs for the two litigants.[25]

The first-order conditions for the optimal levels of efforts, E_p^* and E_d^*, for each party will be respectively:

$$H_p = \frac{\partial R_p^e}{\partial E_p} = (1 - I)R_A(S)\frac{E_d}{(E_p + E_d)^2} - C = 0 \tag{2.3}$$

$$H_d = \frac{\partial R_d^e}{\partial E_d} = (1 - I)R_A(S)\frac{E_p}{(E_p + E_d)^2} - C = 0 \tag{2.4}$$

We can verify that $\partial H_1/\partial E_1$ and $\partial H_2/\partial E_2$ are non-zero by explicitly solving for the optimal values of E_1^* and E_2^*. This, in turn, allows us to characterize the litigants' respective reaction functions as:

$$E_p^* = \sqrt{\frac{(1 - I)E_d R_A(S)}{C}} - E_d \tag{2.5}$$

$$E_d^* = \sqrt{\frac{(1 - I)E_p R_A(S)}{C}} - E_p \tag{2.6}$$

In equilibrium, $E_p^* = E_d^*$, such that

$$E_p^{**} = E_d^{**} = \frac{(1 - I)R_A(S)}{4C} \tag{2.7}$$

For the special, yet most common, case of two litigants, the total expenditure in litigation, at cost C, for the adjudication of the adversarial portion of the award will be given by:

$$L = C(E_p^{**} + E_d^{**}) = \frac{(1 - I)R_A(S)}{2} \tag{2.8}$$

This implies that in a symmetric two-litigant case, parties will exert litigation effort in proportion to the value of the adversarial component of the case and the weight assigned to adversarial evidence in the decision-making process. In a purely adversarial system ($I = 0$) the parties will spend a full half of the value of the case in litigation.

For the more general case of N litigants, it is necessary to distinguish two main cases: (a) N litigants competing for the adjudication of a mutually exclusive award, where the returns from the adversarial efforts are a proportional share function of the parties' respective efforts;[26] and (b) N litigants litigating as joint actors in a joint or class action claim. In the first case, the individual maximization problem of (2.1) can be recast as:

$$R_i^e = IR_{I(i)}(E_J) + (1 - I)R_A(S)\frac{E_i}{\sum_{i=1,\ldots,N} E_i} - CE_i \tag{2.9}$$

We can replicate the steps (2.3) through (2.7) to obtain the Nash expenditures in discovery for the general case of N litigants. The individual expenditure in discovery, E_i^{**}, and the total private cost of discovery for the N litigants at unitary cost, C, become respectively:

$$E_i = \frac{(1 - I)R_A(S)(N - 1)}{CN^2} \quad \text{and} \quad L = \frac{(1 - I)R_A(S)(N - 1)}{N} \tag{2.10}$$

This implies that in the more general case of N litigants with competing claims over a fixed award, a share equal to $(N - 1)/N$ of the value of the adversarial case from the perspective of the parties (i.e., an amount ranging from at least one half and up to the full value of the disputed case) will be dissipated through litigation.

Different results obtain in the case of joint or class actions, where more joint plaintiffs or joint defendants litigate, as a group, for the adjudication of R_A. If the two groups have successfully corrected the collective action problems in pursuing their common cause, then the plaintiffs' and defendants' teams will behave as two individual agents, facing an optimization problem similar to (2.1). Conversely, if the collective action of the various actors is affected by free-riding, the private incentives to litigate may be undermined. Thus, the total private expenditures in adversarial discovery may decrease with an increase in the number of joint claimants.

For the general case of multiple litigants with competing claims, we can further study the behavior of the Nash values of aggregate private expenditure L, characterizing it more compactly as:

$$L \equiv C \sum_{i=1,\dots,N} E_i^{**} = \ell(I, E_J, R_A, N) \tag{2.11}$$

Having verified that (2.2) and (2.3) are non-zero,[27] we can use the Implicit Function Theorem to study how the equilibrium value of L varies with (i) the institutional weight attached to the inquisitorial findings and (ii) the judicial scrutiny applied to the evidence submitted by the parties; (iii) the value of the disputed case which rests on the findings from the adversarial discovery; (iv) the number of litigants competing for the adjudication of a mutually exclusive award. These calculations, which have been omitted for the sake of brevity,[28] respectively yield:

$$\frac{\partial L}{\partial I} = \frac{-H_I}{H_E} < 0 \tag{2.12}$$

$$\frac{\partial L}{\partial S} = \frac{-H_S}{H_E} < 0 \tag{2.13}$$

$$\frac{\partial L}{\partial R_A} = \frac{-H_A}{H_E} > 0 \tag{2.14}$$

$$\frac{\partial L}{\partial N} = \frac{-H_N}{H_E} > 0 \tag{2.15}$$

where H_E, H_I, H_S, H_A and H_N are the partial derivatives of (2.2) with respect to E_p, I, S, R_A, and N, respectively.

The comparative statics of this problem yield interesting and unambiguous results. The result of (2.12) suggests that the total amount of litigation expenditure rises with an increase in weight accorded to adversarially produced evidence. This should not be surprising, since the evidence that is privately produced in an adversarial system is given more decisional weight and therefore is likely to generate higher returns for the litigants.

Likewise, (2.13) indicates that the parties' total expenditure in discovery is reduced with an increase in the scrutiny used by the judge in the fact-finding process. With an increase in judicial scrutiny, the evidence that is privately produced by the parties is more likely to be discarded and thus yields lower returns. Notice that this result depends on the same level of scrutiny being used with both parties' evidence. A different definition of judicial activism which is not result-neutral may alter our results.

In (2.14) we learn that the expenditure in discovery and litigation is exacerbated by an increase in the value of the case which rests on the findings from adversarial evidence. For pure wealth-maximizers, there will be a straightforward relationship between the value of the case, R_A, and the equilibrium expenditure in litigation. Risk aversion would add a concave curvature to such a relationship. Finally, (2.15) indicates that the total expenditure in discovery increases with the number of litigants competing for the adjudication of a mutually exclusive award. This result is a mere restatement of the explicit relationship between number of litigants and total expenditure, identified in Eq. (2.10). The total share of the judicial award that is expended in litigation increases monotonically with the number of litigants at a rate $(N-1)/N$. Thus, under conditions of symmetry and linear production functions for the litigants, total expenditures would range from a minimum of one half to the full value of the litigated case from the perspective of the parties.[29]

3. Truth-finding, litigation costs and optimal procedures

In the previous discussion, we considered the different costs associated with the inquisitorial and adversarial procedures.

Duplication of costs is not the only effect of adversarial procedures. In an adversarial system, the strategic interaction of the parties creates additional costs (and potential benefits) that are not the mere consequence of the uncoordinated efforts of the litigants. In this respect, the claim that the inquisitorial system is more efficient merely because it involves only one searcher of truth (the judge) instead of two or more searchers (the parties and their counsels) overlooks an important dimension of the problem.

The strategic nature of the parties' choices produces a systematic discrepancy between the private and social incentives to gather evidence. The parties' (privately) optimal level of discovery and adversarial activity may be inconsistent with the judge's optimal choice of inquisitorial efforts.[30] Since the damage award the parties gain is a zero-sum result, the efforts of the litigants yield offsetting benefits from a private standpoint but may yield positive net benefits from a social standpoint if adversarial evidence contributes to a correct decision. Furthermore, the efforts of the litigants often shed light on the weaknesses and flaws of the evidence presented by their opponents.[31]

The above considerations should be further examined in light of the concerns that public choice theory may raise regarding the judges' ability to identify the optimal level of inquisitorial efforts (i.e., the formidable weighing of costs and benefits of judicial action). We shall proceed assuming that judges attempt to optimize social benefit from correct decisions, and have a varying degree of efficiency, ϕ, in acquiring and processing information.

In this section, I explore the implications of the divergence between private incentives and social incentives in the discovery of a case, extending the previous analysis to additional variables. I treat the choice of the inquisitorial share of the process as endogenous and characterize the optimal level of inquisitorial effort as that which maximizes the net social benefits from litigation. The relevant welfare function, W, includes the social benefits from accurate discovery and adjudication, B,[32] and the social cost of litigation, given by the sum of the private cost and public cost of the discovery process.

In what follows, I set up the social net benefit function which depends on I, the institutional weight placed on inquisitorial findings, the parties' and judge's levels of effort, and model parameters. I derive I^*, the optimal "mix" of adversarial and inquisitorial systems. The stylized representation of the cost and benefit functions allows us to perform comparative statics exercises to study how the optimizing value I^* varies with a change in the exogenous variables, such as the level of judicial scrutiny, S, the cost of private production of evidence, C, the efficiency of the judicial system, ϕ, and the social relevance and visibility of the litigated case, V.

I assume that social benefit results from accurate decisions, such as correct interpretations of legislation or proper application of precedent or general principles of law. Social cost is simply the sum of private and judicial costs, so that the problem faced by society in setting the value of I is

$$\max W = B[E_p, E_d, E_J, S, V] - C(E_p + E_d) - C_J(E_J, \phi) \tag{3.1}$$

where the effort levels of the parties to the litigation are the Nash equilibrium levels of effort obtained above, and judicial effort is chosen to maximize social welfare.

The benefits from accurate decision making increase directly with the social relevance and visibility of the case. To keep things simple, I have assumed that the administrative and private cost functions do not depend on the social relevance and visibility of the case.

In order to find the optimal level of inquisitorial procedure for our welfare function, we can study the first-order conditions of (3.1) with respect to I. Assuming complete symmetry between the two parties to the litigation, we can define:

$$\frac{\partial B}{\partial E_{adv}} \equiv \frac{\partial B}{\partial E_p} = \frac{\partial B}{\partial E_d} \quad \text{and} \quad \frac{\partial E^*_{adv}}{\partial I} \equiv \frac{\partial E^*_p}{\partial I} = \frac{\partial E^*_d}{\partial I}$$

This yields the first-order condition:

$$F = 2\left(\frac{\partial B}{\partial E_{adv}} - C\right)\frac{\partial E_{adv}}{\partial I} + \left(\frac{\partial B}{\partial E_J} - \frac{\partial C_J}{\partial E_J}\right)\frac{\partial E_J}{\partial I} = 0 \tag{3.2}$$

Notice that since adversarial effort decreases and judicial effort increases as I rises, the two terms in parentheses in (3.2) must have the same sign. In other words, at the socially optimal value of I, either the adversaries and the judge are inputting too much effort from the social perspective, or they are inputting too little effort, or both the parties and the judge are exerting the socially optimal level of effort. To see why this is the case, consider the possibility that the parties are inputting too much effort from the social perspective, while the judge exerts too little effort. The socially optimal level of I could then be increased, resulting in less adversarial and more judicial effort, and thus social welfare would increase.

Under our assumption that the judge exerts effort to maximize social welfare, both terms in parentheses above must equal 0, so that the adversarial parties and the judge input the correct levels of effort from the social perspective. Essentially, our assumption about the behavior of the judge is equivalent to giving the social decision-maker two instruments, I and E_J, instead of just one. Under different assumptions about how judicial effort is set, such as self-serving behavior by the judge or incomplete information about the relevance or underlying truth-value of the case, it is possible that no level of I would achieve optimal effort exertion by the parties and the judge. The level of I would then be set to achieve a second-best solution, in which net marginal social costs from the distortions in the parties' and the judiciary's effort are equalized.

After verifying that $\partial F/\partial I$ is strictly negative, we can assume the existence of the welfare-maximizing value I^*. I further assume that when one party's level of effort increases, the effect of this change on the marginal social benefit from that party's effort is (negative and) greater in magnitude than the effect of this change on the marginal social benefit of its opponent's effort.[33] This assumption is quite innocuous and insures that social benefit cannot increase indefinitely as any party's level of effort continues to increase. This interior solution indicates that neither the pure inquisitorial system nor the pure adversarial system are likely to represent the social optimum. This may explain the gradual convergence of both procedural traditions towards mixed solutions. In common law jurisdictions, for example, the creation of very rigorous rules of evidence constrains the adversarial efforts of the parties and limits the wealth dissipation occasioned by adversarial litigation.[34] In civil law jurisdictions an increasing number of procedural choices are left, as a matter of judicial practice, to the motions of the litigants.

Having determined the existence of a maximum, we can proceed to study the comparative statics of the model. I will invoke the usual assumptions regarding the curvature of the cost functions (increasing marginal costs), and the curvature of the benefit function (decreasing marginal benefits).[35] I assume that all second partials are non-positive, so that the benefit function is concave. Regarding cross partials, I assume that increases in E_p raise the marginal benefit of E_d, increases in E_J raise the marginal benefit of E_p and E_d, and so on. This is because the efforts exerted by the judge and the parties are complementary in the sense that they shed light on the same truth. As the judge expends more effort in fact-finding, he is more likely to find evidence that confirms correct evidence presented by the parties, or negates bad evidence submitted by the parties. Thus, additional judicial effort increases the truth-finding benefit of the parties' effort. Similarly, increases in S cause the marginal truth-finding benefit of the parties' effort to increase. Recall that parties will exert less effort in litigation when S is higher, because their evidence is more likely to be thrown out. Thus, increasing S makes the parties less willing to input effort, even as it makes their efforts more valuable to society.[36] The level of scrutiny has no effect on the marginal social benefit of additional judicial fact-finding, since scrutiny is only directed at the parties' evidence. Finally, I assume that more visibility increases the marginal benefits of the parties' and the judge's effort. This is because mistakes in the formation or application of the law are more costly if they are known to more third parties and can thus affect more future dealings between such parties.

Under these assumptions, I use the Implicit Function Theorem to study how I^* varies with the other arguments of the welfare function (3.1). We can start by studying the impact of an increase in judicial scrutiny, S, on the optimal level of inquisitorial proceedings, I^*. Given our assumptions we can derive:

$$\frac{\partial F}{\partial S}=\frac{\partial^2 B}{\partial E_p \partial S}\frac{\partial E_p}{\partial I}+\frac{\partial^2 B}{\partial E_d \partial S}\frac{\partial E_d}{\partial I}+\left(\frac{\partial B}{\partial E_p}-C\right)\frac{\partial^2 E_p}{\partial I \partial S}+\left(\frac{\partial B}{\partial E_d}-C\right)\frac{\partial^2 E_d}{\partial I \partial S} \quad (3.3)$$

Since scrutiny increases the public marginal benefit of the parties' effort, and in equilibrium the parties will be exerting socially optimal effort levels, (3.3) is negative. Given that the second-order condition is strictly negative, we can determine that

$$\frac{\partial I^*}{\partial S} = \frac{-F_S}{F_I} < 0 \tag{3.4}$$

This indicates that with an increase in judicial scrutiny, the optimal institutional weight attached to the inquisitorial findings should diminish.[37] This result can be explained considering that, in the present context, judicial scrutiny and inquisitorial proceedings are substitutes. Litigants will consider an increase in the weight attached to inquisitorial evidence as qualitatively similar to an increased scrutiny by the court of the evidence they present. In either case, the private discovery of the parties becomes less valuable and the total private expenditures in litigation diminish.

Although this section explicitly considers only two parties to the case, the effect of changes in the number of litigants could be studied by extending (3.1) to include additional parties in both the social benefit function and the private cost function. As N increases, private incentives to engage in litigation expenditures will increase, as found in the previous section. Thus, we would find that the optimal I^* increases with the number of litigants, because the marginal social benefit of each party's expenditure falls as all parties spend more.

This suggests that greater reliance should be placed on court-obtained evidence in multiple-litigant cases, given the greater rate of dissipation of private resources in adversarial discovery. As shown in Section II, when more than two parties are competing for the appropriation of a fixed judicial award, the portion of the award that will be dissipated increases relative to the two-litigant case. Thus, an increased weight on inquisitorial evidence in multiple-party cases will minimize the social cost of litigation.

This result does not apply to the case of joint or class actions, where the multiple plaintiffs—having coordinated their collective action—should be viewed as a single entity, keeping N invariant. Likewise, this result does not apply (and the normative conclusions may indeed be reversed) for the case of multiple joint litigants with imperfect internal coordination. In this latter case, free-riding may indeed affect the private incentives to procure evidence, and a lower value of I (and consequential greater value of the "adversarial case") may be necessary to offset the diminished private incentives.

Additionally, we allowed only the private expenditure in litigation to vary with the number of litigants. If the administrative costs of adjudicating multiple-party cases were to increase at a faster rate than the total private costs of discovery, our result would no longer hold.

Proceeding in our analysis, we can study the effect of a change in the private cost of discovery and litigation on the choice of the optimal amount of inquisitorial procedures.

$$\frac{\partial F}{\partial C} = -\left(\frac{\partial E_{\mathrm{p}}}{\partial I} + \frac{\partial E_{\mathrm{d}}}{\partial I}\right) > 0 \tag{3.5}$$

Hence

$$\frac{\partial I^*}{\partial C} = \frac{-F_C}{F_I} < 0 \tag{3.6}$$

The results in (3.6) suggests that more reliance on court-obtained evidence should be placed with an increase in the private cost of discovery and litigation for the parties. In this case, higher private costs will reduce the privately optimal choice of discovery, and will also reduce the socially optimal level of litigation effort by the parties. Contrast this with a case in which private litigation costs are higher but this does not increase the social cost of litigation. For example, richer individuals have a higher value of time and thus it is more costly for them to pursue litigation. Nevertheless, the social cost of their time may not be greater than that of poorer individuals. In such a case, our results could be reversed. A lower value of I may become necessary to offset the diminished private incentives to procure evidence.

This result raises a question as to whether the judicial process is likely to become increasingly biased in favor of the rich against the poor. In general this may not be the case, once the mixed procedural system that results from Eq. (3.2) is compared to its alternatives. A pure adversary system depends to a much greater degree on effective advocacy.[38] The market for legal services ensures that those who are able to pay higher professional fees can attract more effective advocates.[39] A procedure which gives lesser weight to the adversarial efforts of the parties will, at the limit, facilitate access to the justice system for indigent individuals.

In the present model, the adversarial share of the judicial award, R_A, depends only on the procedural variable S, denoting judicial scrutiny of evidence presented by the parties. If the adversarial portion of the judgment was allowed to vary autonomously, an additional partial derivative would be necessary to study the effect of a change in R_A on the optimal choice of the institutional variable, I. The results would be quite intuitive. An increase in the value of the unsettled portion of the litigated case, R_A has an impact on the Nash levels of efforts found in (2.7). Given the presence of R_A solely in the numerator of the Nash values, a greater use of inquisitorial proceedings may be appropriate with an increase in the value of R_A. The result is consistent with the fundamental idea that the value of the rent dissipated through litigation is proportional to the value of the unsettled portion of the dispute.[40]

Analogous, unambiguous, results can be reached with respect to the other exogenous arguments of (3.1). I begin by considering the effects of notoriety, visibility and the social, political, or moral importance of the disputed issue, V. The effect of an increase in the visibility and social relevance of the case, V, on the optimal level of inquisitorial proceedings, I^*, can be studied by finding $\partial F/\partial V$. If we assume that $\partial E_{\text{adv}}/\partial I$ and $\partial E_{\text{adv}}/\partial I$ do not depend on V, we obtain:

$$\frac{\partial F}{\partial V} = 2\frac{\partial^2 B}{\partial E_{\text{adv}}\partial V}\frac{\partial E_{\text{adv}}}{\partial I} + \frac{\partial^2 B}{\partial E_J \partial V}\frac{\partial E_J}{\partial I} \tag{3.7}$$

Given our assumptions about the signs of cross partial derivatives and the effect of changes in I on the effort levels of the parties and the judge, the sign of (3.7) is theoretically ambiguous. This sign depends on whether visibility makes the parties' or the judge's effort relatively more beneficial to society. If, for example, we assume that the cross partial derivatives in (3.7) are roughly of the same size, then we would obtain:

$$\frac{\partial I^*}{\partial V} = \frac{-F_V}{F_I} < 0 \tag{3.8}$$

In other words, since visibility increases the marginal benefits from both the parties' and the judge's efforts, but lowering I increases the parties' effort more than it diminishes the judge's effort, the optimal level of I falls when visibility increases. Note that an increase in the visibility of the case affects the benefits from accurate adjudication. High profile and notorious cases have a greater impact on the general community. The accuracy of the adjudication process is thus more critical in such cases. The social sense of justice may be more seriously offended by the wrongful decision of a publicly known case. In addition, the creation of an erroneous legal rule can affect the incentives of private parties to invest or to enter into beneficial contracts. Due to the importance of precedent in many legal systems, incorrect rules formulated by the court tend to cause persistent error in the adjudication of other cases. Many of these adverse effects of wrong decisions are exacerbated by high visibility and publicity. The reader should note that the current model treats visibility, V, as analytically independent of R_A, which represents only the portion of the case the adjudication of which rests on the adversarial evidence provided by the parties. By relaxing this simplifying assumption, and creating some interaction between the visibility of the case, V, and the value of the unsettled share of the judgement, R_A, more ambiguity in signing (3.7) would be generated.

A similar conclusion holds with respect to cases involving important moral, political or social issues. An increase in the moral or social importance of the litigated issue increases the importance of an accurate adjudication. To the extent that a precise assessment of the factual circumstances is relevant for the outcome of such issues, the accuracy of the discovery and adjudication process becomes more critical in the resolution of this group of disputes. Put differently, the forward-looking function of judicial decision making may be more seriously compromised by the wrongful decision of a politically or socially important issue.

An alternative interpretation of (3.8) would consider the different benefits associated with accurate adjudication in criminal and civil cases. Higher competition in providing evidence and greater adversarial scrutiny of the evidence offered by the other party lessen the possibility of convicting an innocent person and increase the possibility that the guilty may escape conviction. By keeping the barriers to conviction high, as mandated by the adversary system, the costs associated with wrongful convictions are minimized. As observed by Damaska (1983), where this is recognized, proponents of the adversary system accord decisive weight to liberal values. Type I and Type II errors in adjudication are regarded as having socially different costs, thus making it preferable to let a larger number of the guilty go free than to convict a smaller number of innocent persons.[41]

The above argument explains the stronger emphasis on adversarial proceedings in criminal rather than civil cases. Unlike the criminal law scenario, Type I and Type II judicial errors have symmetric social costs in most civil law disputes. Assuming non-systematic bias, errors of either type only bring about a transfer of wealth between the litigants and the incentives of the parties remain unaltered. If litigants are risk averse, some social loss is occasioned due to the parties' uncertainty, and such loss would have to be balanced against the additional litigation costs that would be induced by a greater use of adversarial proceedings.

Finally, I consider the effect of a change in ϕ, the parameter measuring judicial efficiency in fact-finding, on the optimal level of inquisitorial proceedings, I^*. In this case the result is straightforward. The variable ϕ captures the direct and indirect changes in the administrative cost of non-adversarial discovery. Actually ϕ denotes the level of administrative inefficiency: higher levels of ϕ imply higher marginal social cost of judicial discovery. The effect of a change in ϕ on the choice of optimal level of non-adversarial discovery, I^*, can be studied by deriving:

$$\frac{\partial F}{\partial \phi} = -\frac{\partial^2 C_J}{\partial E_J \partial \phi}\frac{\partial E_J}{\partial I} < 0 \tag{3.9}$$

This means that

$$\frac{\partial I^*}{\partial \phi} = \frac{-F_\phi}{F_I} < 0 \tag{3.10}$$

This indicates that more non-adversarial discovery may be appropriate with an increase in the efficiency of the courts in the procurement and evaluation of evidence, other things being equal. The last result is self-explanatory. If the court system has a comparative advantage in the use of specialized technology or information, greater court involvement in the discovery process may be desirable.[42] Conversely, if the specialized or trade-specific nature of the evidence renders the judicial involvement too costly or inefficacious, greater reliance on the adversarial efforts of the litigants may be appropriate.

4. Costs of the adversarial system

While practitioners from both civil and common law jurisdictions appear to be content with their procedural system, legal scholars continue their debate on the theoretical and policy implications of alternative discovery systems. Comparative scholars suggest that inquisitorial and adversarial systems have gradually converged towards mixed solutions, but procedural differences still remain marked. In the intellectual debate, different rationales have been invoked in support of one or the other procedural systems, including private autonomy of the litigants and historical tradition (for the case of adversarial procedure), and neutral truth-finding and economy in adjudication (for the case of inquisitorial procedure).

Adversarial civil procedure is viewed as consistent with the principles of personal liberty and equality that so strongly permeate the American ideal of justice,[43] and is often lauded as vital to the protection of American democracy and freedom.[44] According to Damaska (1983), the adversary system is lauded because of its competitive style of presenting evidence and argument, which is thought to produce a more accurate result than its inquisitorial alternative, with the judge monopolizing the discovery process. Along similar lines, Hazard (1978) observed that a judge who is involved in the discovery process can hardly keep an open mind and lacks sufficient incentives to do a proper job in the finding of facts.[45] In this setting, firm adherence to the adversarial approach is viewed as the best antidote against possible invasions of the personal autonomy of the parties by the constituted judicial authority.[46]

In this setting, it is often believed that the contrast between the adversarial and the inquisitorial procedural systems stems from two antithetic views about the role of government in society, contemplating, respectively, a "reactive" and a "proactive" system of government.[47] According to this view of the adversarial proceeding, the judge should come into action only to resolve disputes between the contending parties.

This paper has examined some of the features associated with adversarial judicial process, contrasting it with the results obtained under the non-adversarial procedure adopted in the civil law tradition. The results obtained in Parts II and III of this paper challenge the common idealization of adversary procedure.[48] The arguments in favor of the adversary procedure analogize the efforts of the litigants to the competition that takes place in the market for goods. The analogy between the adversary procedure and a competitive market, however, underestimates the rent-seeking dynamic of the litigation process.

For the most part, litigants compete over the division of a fixed resource (represented by the value R_A in our model). Unlike the efforts of two competitors in the marketplace, the efforts of two litigants are not capable of increasing the value of the litigated asset, R_A, and often cause a dissipation of a good portion of its net value. Indeed, the analogy between the adversary procedure and a competitive auction fails to consider the fact that, unlike an auction (in which only the highest bidder is bound to pay), litigation creates positive rent-seeking costs for each litigant. In litigation, each party has to bear the full private cost of his or her rent-seeking activity, even though only the prevailing party captures the residual value of the litigated asset, R_A. In this respect, the analogy should be revisited in light of the rent-seeking element of real world litigation. A more appropriate analogy could be drawn between litigation efforts and the advertising efforts of two competitors. Most advertising expenditures, presumably, are mutually offsetting, just like most litigation expenditures in an adversary system. Indeed, we could argue that litigation expenditures are to judicial decisions as advertising expenditures are to consumer decisions.

As illustrated earlier, the rent-seeking analysis unveils an important characteristic of the adversarial system, namely the exacerbation of the incentives for rent dissipation through litigation. The paper suggests that the adversary system conduces rent-seeking because the expenditures of each party are determined by the private rather than the social cost of winning. The comparative statics of the problem reveal that the rent dissipation problem is exacerbated with an increase in the value of the unsettled component of the disputed case, and an increase in the number of litigants with competing claims on a fixed award. Conversely, the dissipation is reduced with an increase in the involvement of the judge in the fact-finding process. The judge who gathers the facts soon comes to know the case as well as the involved parties, and will be able to concentrate its subsequent fact-finding efforts toward more important and still unresolved factual issues. As shown in this paper, the weight attached to the adversarial discovery affects the degree to which parties' efforts can influence the outcome of the case. Thus, the judge's direct involvement in the fact-finding has obvious implications for procedural economy, reducing the marginal incentives for the parties' adversarial efforts, and possibly facilitating the settlement of the case.

In this context, several arguments can be formulated to complement the classical hands-off approach to adjudication. Just as legal systems play an important role in correcting economic market failures, so a judge may play a valuable institutional role in redressing the rent-dissipating competition of the parties during a trial.[49] This conclusion poses the difficult question as to how far the judge can go in his intervention without negatively affecting the incentives of the litigants and the successful functioning of the adversary system.[50]

Undoubtedly, in a world characterized by contentious litigation and discovery, the minimization of the rent-seeking component represents only one argument in a more complex social welfare function. The normative analysis of this paper has examined some trade-offs between the costs and benefits of adversarial discovery and litigation. Most importantly, adversarial efforts may have a direct social value, insofar as they make the tribunal better informed about the case and therefore increase the likelihood of a correct decision. The social benefits from accurate decision making may further vary with the degree of visibility of the case and the social or political relevance of the litigated issue. Likewise, the private and social costs of litigation may be affected by a change in the relative costs of discovery for courts and private litigants.

The analysis could usefully be enriched by other important institutional considerations in order to yield a valid assessment of the respective merits of each procedure. For example, rent-seeking expenditures will be factored in the parties' decision to pursue litigation. The more costly litigation is, the less of it there will be. If there are negative externalities, from high levels of litigation, rent-seeking expenditures would generate a social benefit, given the reduction in the number of litigated cases. Furthermore, it is conceivable that the parties' acceptance of the judgment is facilitated where the parties are permitted to exercise greater control over discovery and procedure.

These theoretical results should be further examined in light of empirical data. Most of the empirical studies compare the efficiency of the adversary system with the inquisitorial alternative by testing the relative efficacy of those procedures in overcoming the decision-maker's bias and inducing reliable truth-finding.[51] Additional empirical evidence will be necessary to test the predictions of this paper regarding the different levels of litigation expenditure under the two procedural regimes.

One final consideration, which has been only briefly sketched in the preceding analysis, should examine the conditions under which an adversarial procedure guarantees an equal and effective representation to the parties. The conclusions of this paper should not be read to endorse *ad hoc* balancing between the inquisitorial and adversarial components of the process as a way to compensate for parties' differential wealth or access to legal representation. In cases involving indigent individuals, it may be better to pursue equal access to justice through counterbalancing procedures other than an increased role for judges in discovery. Given the availability of more neutral and cost-effective means for promoting equal representation, the determination of the optimal level of inquisitorial efforts should be based on the objective values indicated above and should not be influenced by the need to provide legal aid to unrepresented parties.

Notes

1. In a recent paper, Glaser and Shleifer (2001) have suggested that the inquisitorial system developed in France as an instrument for the protection of law enforcers from coercion by litigants through either violence or bribes. The higher the risk of coercion, the greater the need for protection and control of law enforcers by the state. According to the authors, this explains why, in the twelfth and thirteenth centuries, the relatively more peaceful England developed trials by jury, while the less peaceful France relied on state-employed judges for both collecting evidence and making decisions. Despite considerable legal evolution, these initial design choices have persisted for centuries, explaining many differences between common and civil law procedural traditions.
2. Bartolus a Saxoferrato (1313–1357), Comment to C. 9.42.2, no. 2, fol. 124: "Judex tamen potest ex officio suo testes producere ad inquirendam veritatem."

3. Baldus de Ubaldis (1327–1400), most notably, in Comment to C. 4.20.19, no. 3, fol. 53: "In examinandis testibus officium judicis debbe esse curiosum, id est, judex debet esse solicitus et ad curam judicis pertinet hoc scil. examinare, unde hoc non est in potestate parties."
4. Baldus de Ubaldis (1327–1400), Comment to C. 1.3.8, no. 8, fol. 37: "Pone, quod testes non sunt producti, sed judex ex mero officio recipit eos."
5. Damaska (1997) observes: "The interaction with the accused constantly injected disputational, 'altercating' notes into proceedings—long before the admission of lawyers to felony trials gave rise to the adversary criminal trial as we now know it." (p. 118).
6. On the theoretical underpinning of this debate, see, more extensively, Damaska (1997, p. 101).
7. Hazard and Taruffo (1993) observe that: "The advocate conducts the pretrial discovery against the opposing party. This involves taking the depositions of potential witnesses, including the opposing party, and identifying and inspecting relevant documents in the opposing party's possession. In complicated business litigation, thousands of such documents must be reviewed and analyzed. Discovery may require weeks or months of the advocate's effort, sometimes over the course of years before the anticipated trial date." (p. 88).
8. This paper considers the adversary common law process as it relates to civil proceedings. The dogma of adversarial discovery is equally applicable to the criminal proceedings in common law jurisdictions: "The principles announced today deal with the protection which must be given to the privilege against self-incrimination. ... It is at this point that our adversary system of criminal proceedings commences, distinguishing itself at the outset from the inquisitorial system recognized in some countries." (Miranda v. Arizona, 1966, 384 U.S. 436, 477).
9. More generally, see Pound (1906), Cappelletti and Perillo (1965), Damaska (1986), Gerber (1986), Herzog (1967), Kaplan (1960), Kaplan et al. (1958), Taruffo (1979) for a comparative analysis of the different approaches to the administration of justice in the civil law and common law traditions.
10. See Chayes (1976) for a stylized description of the role of the judge in U.S. litigation.
11. See Landsman (1983) for a more detailed description of the adversarial system and a discussion of its development in the United States.
12. See, e.g., Article 427 of the French Code of Criminal Procedure.
13. According to Weigend (1983), comparative legal scholars usually consider the French criminal procedure as the prototype of the inquisitorial model, where judges enjoy full discretionary power in the examination of the evidence. The same principles apply in the Japanese and Spanish systems, even though evidence is presented by the parties. Japanese criminal procedure law originally followed the model of the French and German codes, but after Word War II, American procedural principles were superimposed on its inquisitorial structure.
14. Langbein (1985) describes the concepts of "defendant's case" and "plaintiff's case" as traffic rules for the for the partisan presentation of evidence to an ignorant and passive trier of facts.
15. For a description of the German inquisitorial approach, see Langbein (1985).

16. The civil law judge often takes initiative for gathering additional evidence, and reviews the evidence presented by the parties in detail—recapitulating it prior to reaching a decision. In most jurisdictions this authority is conservatively exercised. Hazard and Taruffo (1993) observe that, in practice, neither system fully corresponds to its theoretical model: "In the civil law system the judge has dominant authority to determine the legal theory to be applied, but the judge is highly dependent on the parties for presentation of the evidence. Common law judges have authority to initiate inquiry into the evidence but rarely exercise it. In this sense, both systems depend on adversary presentations so far as the facts are concerned, notwithstanding the theoretical differences between their conceptions of the judge's role." (p. 86).
17. See Damaska (1997, p. 100).
18. Froeb and Kobayashi (2000) suggest that the advantage of the adversarial regime of judicial decision-making is the superior information of the parties while the advantage of an idealized inquisitorial regime is its neutrality. The authors characterize the properties of the estimators utilized under the two evidence regimes, analogizing the decision making process under an adversarial system to an "extremal" estimator based on the difference between the most favorable pieces of evidence produced by each party; conversely, the inquisitorial system is analogized to an unbiased sample mean. The authors find that neither regime dominates the other. In a previous paper, Froeb and Kobayashi (1996) consider an additional critique often moved to the adversarial process, namely the use of juries and lay fact finders. The authors suggest that the criticisms of the jury process based on jury bias is often overstated, and stress the importance of competitively produced evidence in legal decision-making.
19. See, for example, Damaska (1986, pp. 3–6).
20. Until recent years, comparative legal scholars have refused to theorize on the respective merits of the two systems. The analysis involved too many legal dogmas and intellectual beliefs and any comparative evaluation would have appeared, on the whole, quite suspect. Even on purely methodological grounds, differences of opinion dominate. Jorg, Field, and Brants (1995). While agreeing that real world adversarial and inquisitorial systems of (criminal) procedure are converging and do not follow their ideal types, Jorg et al. observe that the systems' basic ideologies about truth seeking are different enough that they could never converge entirely, nor present an entirely continuous set of systems.
21. In a recent paper, Posner (1999, p. 16) argues that the use of amateur judges (the jurors) in the typical adversarial proceeding makes it difficult to situate the adversarial system on a continuum with the inquisitorial. For the purpose of this paper, I will consider the features of the adversary system as independent of the use of a jury. This will allow us to use a single continuous variable to characterize the adversarial or inquisitorial nature of the process.
22. Braeutigam, Owen, and Panzar (1984) have utilized a similar approach to study the different equilibrium expenditures at trial under the English and American rules, for the recovery of legal fees. Hause (1989) followed the same approach considering asymmetric beliefs and probabilities. Most recently, Farmer and Pecorino (1997) have modeled

endogenous legal expenditures utilizing a rent-seeking framework for the study of the institution of fee shifting.

23. With similar consequences, in Posner (1973), a relative increase in litigation spending merely reduced the opponents' probability of winning. For further examples of rent-seeking functions, see Tullock (1996), Congleton (1980), Tollison and Congleton (1995).
24. The zero-sum constraint implies that, setting aside costs of litigation, $\partial R_p/\partial I + \partial R_d/\partial I = 0$. The implicit relationship between R_I, R_A, and I, allows for a fixed share coefficient of the type $J = IR_I + (1 - I)R_A$, but is not limited to it. Indeed, there may be a correlation between the judgment level J and the degree of adversary litigation. The variability of total J with respect to I may indeed be necessary to account for the (fragmentary) evidence offered by comparative legal scholars regarding the different measures of pecuniary judicial awards in the American and European legal traditions.
25. In this section, the choice of procedure is treated as an institutional variable and not as a choice variable for the litigants. In the following section, the normative analysis will consider the optimal procedural choice, treating I as an institutional choice variable.
26. Again, the same results hold in a winner-takes-all system where the parties' respective probabilities of success are proportional to their shares of effort.
27. Similar results are obtained studying the sign of the second derivative of (2.8) which represents the multiple-agent version of (2.2) and (2.3).
28. These results could be obtained with equal simplicity by inspection of (2.9).
29. The result of (2.14) holds only if the N litigants compete for the adjudication of a mutually exclusive benefit. If the various actors litigate a joint claim with a common award, free-riding may undermine their private incentives to litigate. Thus, the opposite result $\partial L/\partial N = -H_N/H_E < 0$ may hold if the N actors are litigating a common cause in the presence of free-riding.
30. Most recently, Posner (1999) recognizes this point observing that: "privatizing the search (as in the adversarial system) may result in too much or too little evidence from a social standpoint ... whereas in principle ... the inquisitorial judge can continue his search for evidence until he reaches the point at which marginal cost and marginal benefit intersect and he can stop right there."
31. On this point, see also Palumbo (1998) and Posner (1999).
32. The present model contemplates civil disputes. In extending it to other categories, one should keep in mind that the objective benefit function, B, is likely to differ between civil and criminal cases, in that inaccurate decisions may be socially more costly for criminal cases than civil cases. Thus, *ceteris paribus*, adversarial proceedings may be more appropriate in criminal cases. This conclusion is at odds with the comparative findings of Damaska (1997) who notes that, in spite of its inquisitorial tradition, Continental civil law systems tend to give a relatively greater control to the parties in civil cases, preserving the original inquisitorial approach in criminal proceedings. The author (Damaska, 1997, p. 112) explains this paradox on the basis of the greater need for expeditious adjudication of criminal cases.

33. In addition to our assumption about how judicial effort is chosen, we need to assume that
$$\left|\frac{\partial^2 B}{\partial E_{\mathrm{p}}^2}\right| = \left|\frac{\partial^2 B}{\partial E_{\mathrm{d}}^2}\right| > \left|\frac{\partial^2 B}{\partial E_{\mathrm{p}} \partial E_{\mathrm{d}}}\right|.$$
34. Posner (1999, p. 17) considers Rule 403 of the Federal Rules of Evidence and hearsay rules as examples of evidence law limiting the cost of discovery in an adversary system. The author further observes that the more limited weight given to party obtained evidence by inquisitorial systems allows greater flexibility in the continental European rules of evidence.
35. This ensures that the existence of a positive term in the second-order condition does not undermine its overall negative sign in the neighborhood of I^*, so that the first-order condition identifies a maximum in the welfare function (3.1).
36. In the previous section, we assumed that the parties choose their effort levels independently of the level of judicial effort. In other words, both the parties' and the judge's effort levels depend on I, with opposite signs, but they do not depend directly upon each other. Practically, this is equivalent to assuming that private and judicial expenditures in discovery are strategic substitutes. This assumption is plausible if an increase in judicial inquisition decreases the private returns on the parties' evidence. If we were to assume that judicial and private efforts were strategic complements, lesser weight to adversarial evidence would be necessary to confine the excessive expenditures in litigation. Furthermore, in an adversarial system, sufficiently high coefficients of complementarity may generate total expenditures that exceed the value of the case. In those situations, the participation constraint of the parties would be violated and, given an exit option for the parties, litigation would not be undertaken in equilibrium.
37. This result is complementary to the common concern that judicial activism risks compromising the outcome-neutrality of the judicial process (see Wechsler, 1959). But see Hasnas (1995, p. 201), stating that: "[T]he frequent condemnation of the judiciary for 'undemocratic judicial activism' ... is merely a reflection of the public's belief that the law consists of a set of definite and consistent 'neutral principles' which the judge is obligated to apply in an objective manner ... [even] in the face of overwhelming evidence to the contrary." Hasnas calls this a fiction and labels it "the myth of the rule of law." Other scholars share this concern, suggesting that when a judge becomes too enamored with the merits of a case, he may be induced to evaluate the evidence or the legal basis of the case through colored lenses, extending procedural advantages to one party or giving lesser weight to the evidence provided by the opposing party: "the deference accorded admissibility determinations and the existence of inconsistent rules regarding the admissibility of certain [social science] theories allows judges leeway to engage in judicial activism." Because "many social science theories generally favor one side," a judge with a personal bias can make results-oriented admissibility decisions (Etlinger, 1995, p. 1278).
38. "In our adversary system the strength with which each side is able to present its case depends in large part on the freedom to ascertain and present to the trier of fact all relevant evidence." (van Kessel, 1992, p. 420).

39. The market for legal services can also provide "litigation-biased expert witnesses that American lawyers recruit and pay to bolster preordained results." (Langbein, 1988, p. 764).
40. An increase in the value of R_A, however, may be correlated to the general visibility of the case, V. This may create some indeterminacy in our results. High stake cases, being more visible by the general public, could benefit from a more adversarial procedure, insofar as such procedure makes the tribunal better informed about the case and therefore increases the likelihood of a correct decision. Thus, high stake cases may justify greater litigation expenditures given the greater social benefits of a correct decision. The point was noted by Judge Richard Posner whose comments on an earlier draft have been very valuable for the development of this section.
41. For further analysis, see Damaska (1983, p. 26).
42. Consistent with this predicament, Erichson (1999) examines recent developments in mass tort litigation, suggesting that there has been an evolutionary shift in the direction of inquisitorial justice systems such as those of certain civil law countries. Court-appointed experts and judicial inquiry into settlement class actions resemble inquisitorial tools.
43. See Hazard and Taruffo (1993, p. 101).
44. For a more extensive discussion of the merits of the adversary system, see Hazard and Taruffo (1993, pp. 101–104).
45. See Hazard (1978, p. 121).
46. See the Jackson opinion in Hickman v. Taylor (1947), 329 U.S. 495, 516.
47. See, e.g., Goldstein (1974).
48. See also Sward's (1988) "demystifying" of the adversarial ideology, in which she endorses a more inquisitorial approach as a means of increasing the efficiency of American adjudication.
49. For further discussion, see Fuller (1961, p. 41).
50. For a more extensive discussion, see Damaska (1983, pp. 25–26).
51. Those studies often suggest that, since the adversary model requires the judge to listen passively to both sides of the case before making a decision, he would be less likely to become prematurely biased and draw a conclusion too early (see Damaska, 1983; Thibaut & Walker, 1975; Sheppard & Vidmar, 1980).

Acknowledgments

I am indebted to Richard Posner, Ugo Mattei, Roger Congleton, Joyce Sadka, and an anonymous referee for extensive comments on earlier drafts. This article is dedicated to my third child, Elvira Caterina.

References

Adams, M. A. (1998). Civil procedure in the USA and civil law countries. In P. Newman (Ed.), *The new Palgrave dictionary of economics and the law*. London, UK: Macmillan Reference Ltd.

Braeutigam, R. B., Owen, B., & Panzar, J. (1984). An economic analysis of alternative fee shifting systems. *Law and Contemporary Problems, 47*, 173–185.

Cappelletti, M., & Perillo, J. (1965). *Civil procedure in Italy*. The Hague: Martinus Nijhoff Publisher.

Chayes, A. (1976). The role of the judge in public litigation. *Harvard Law Review, 89*, 1281.

Congleton, R. D. (1980). Competitive process, competitive waste, and institutions. In J. M. Buchanan, R. D. Tollison, & G. Tullock (Eds.), *Toward a theory of the rent-seeking society*. College Station, TX: Texas A&M University Press.

Damaska, M. (1983). *Adversary system. Encyclopedia of crime and justice*. New York, NY: Macmillan Publishing.

Damaska, M. R. (1986). *The faces of justice and state authority. A comparative approach to the legal process*. New Haven, CT: Yale University Press.

Damaska, M. R. (1997). *Evidence law adrift*. New Haven, CT: Yale University Press.

Erichson, H. M. (1999) Mass tort litigation and inquisitorial justice. *Georgetown Law Journal* 87.

Etlinger, L. (1995). Note: Social science research in domestic violence law: A proposal to focus on evidentiary use. *Albany Law Review, 58*, 1259.

Farmer, A., & Pecorino, P. (1997, July). *Legal expenditures as a rent-seeking game*. Unpublished manuscript.

Froeb, L., & Kobayashi, B. H. (1996). Naive, biased, yet Bayesian: Can juries interpret selectively produced evidence? *Journal of Law, Economics and Organization, 12*, 257–277.

Froeb, L., & Kobayashi, B. H. (2000). *Evidence production in adversarial vs. inquisitorial regimes*. Vanderbilt Law School, Joe C. Davis Working Paper No. 99-13.

Fuller, L. L. (1961). In H. J. Berman (Ed.), *The adversary system: Talks on American law*. New York: Random House, Vintage Books.

Gerber, D. J. (1986). Extraterritorial discovery and the conflict of procedural systems: Germany and the United States. *American Journal of Comparative Law, 34*, 745–766.

Glaser, E. L., & Shleifer, A. (2001). *Legal origins*. Harvard Institute of Economic Research Paper No. 1920.

Goldstein, A. (1974). Reflections on two models: Inquisitorial themes in American criminal procedure. *Stanford Law Review, 26*, 1009–1025.

Hasnas, J. (1995). The myth of the rule of law. *Wisconsin Law Review, 1995*, 199.

Hause, J. C. (1989). Indemnity settlement, and litigation, and litigation, or I'll be suing you. *Journal of Legal Studies, 18*, 157–179.

Hazard, G. C., Jr., & Taruffo, M. (1993). *American civil procedure: An introduction*. New Haven, CT: Yale University Press.

Herzog, P. E. (1967). *Civil procedure in France*. The Hague: Martinus Nijhoff Publisher.

Hickman v. Taylor (1947), 329 U.S. 495.

Jorg, F., & Brants (1995). Are inquisitorial and adversarial systems converging? In Harding, Fennell, Jorg, & Swart (Eds.), *Criminal justice in Europe. A comparative study*. Oxford, Clarendon Press.

Kaplan, B. (1960). Civil procedure—Reflections on the comparison of systems. *Buffalo Law Review, 9*, 409.

Kaplan, B., von Mehren, A. T., & Schaefer, R. (1958). Phases of German civil procedure, Parts I and II. *Harvard Law Review, 71*, 1193 and 1443.

Landsman, S. A. (1983). A brief survey of the development of the adversary system. *Ohio State Law Journal, 44*, 713.

Langbein, J. H. (1985). The German advantage in civil procedure. *University of Chicago Law Review, 52*, 823.

Langbein, J. H. (1988). Trashing the German advantage. *Northwestern University Law Review, 82*, 763.

Miranda v. Arizona (1996), 384 U.S. 436.

Palumbo, G. (1998, June). *Optimal "excessive" litigation in adversarial systems*. ECARE, Université Libre de Bruxelles, Working Paper No. 98-01.

Pound, R. (1906). *The causes of popular dissatisfaction with the administration of justice* (pp. 395–408). Report of the 29th Annual Meeting of the American Bar Association. Philadelphia: Dando.

Posner, R. A. (1973). An economic approach to legal procedure and judicial administration. *Journal of Legal Studies, 2*, 399.

Posner, R. A. (1988). Comment: Responding to Gordon Tullock. *Research in Law and Policy Studies, 2*, 29.

Posner, R. A. (1999, February). *An economic approach to the law of evidence*. Chicago Working Papers in Law & Economics No. 66 (2nd Series).

Sheppard, B. H., & Vidmar, N. (1980). Adversary pretrial procedures and testimonial evidence: Effect of lawyer's role and Machiavellianism. *Journal of Personality and Social Psychology, 39*, 320–332.
Sward, E. E. (1988). Values, ideology and the evolution of the adversary system. *Indiana Law Journal, 64*, 301.
Taruffo, M. (1979). *Il processo civile "adversary" nell'Esperienza Americana*. Padua, Italy: Cedam Publishing.
Thibaut, J. W., & Walker, L. (1975). *Procedural justice: A psychological analysis*. Hillsdale, NJ: Laurence Erlbaum Associates.
Tollison, R. D., & Congleton, R. D. (1995). *The economic analysis of rent-seeking*. Aldershot, UK: Edward Elgar Publishing Ltd.
Tullock, G. (1988). Defending the Napoleonic code over the common law. *Research in Law and Policy Studies, 2*, 3–27.
Tullock, G. (1996). *The case against the common law* (1 Blackstone Commentaries Series). Durham, NC: Carolina Academic Press.
Walter, U. (1946). Medieval principles of evidence. *Law Quarterly Review, 62*, 78. Reprinted in Walter Ulmann, Law and Jurisdiction in the Middle Ages, (London: Variorum Reprints, 1988).
van Kessel, G. (1992). Adversary excesses in the American criminal trial. *Notre Dame Law Review, 67*, 403.
Wechsler, H. (1959). Toward neutral principles of constitutional law. *Harvard Law Review, 73*, 1.
Weigend, T. (1983). *Criminal procedure. Encyclopedia of crime and justice*. New York, NY: Macmillan Publishing.

Part IV
Specific Rules of Evidence and Procedure

A
Proof Burdens

[14]

The Limits of the Preponderance of the Evidence Standard: Justifiably Naked Statistical Evidence and Multiple Causation

David Kaye

The preponderance-of-the-evidence standard usually is understood to mean that the plaintiff must show that the probability that the defendant is in fact liable exceeds 1/2. Several commentators and at least one court have suggested that in some situations it may be preferable to make each defendant pay plaintiff's damages discounted by the probability that the defendant in question is in fact liable. This article analyzes these and other decision rules from the standpoint of statistical decision theory. It argues that in most cases involving only one potential defendant, the conventional interpretation of the preponderance standard is appropriate, but it notes an important exception. The article also considers cases involving many defendants, only one of whom could have caused the injury to plaintiff. It argues that ordinarily the single defendant most likely to have been responsible should be liable for all the damages, even when the probability associated with this defendant is less than 1/2. At the same time, it identifies certain multiple-defendant cases in which the rule that weights each defendant's damages by the probability of that defendant's liability should apply.

I. Introduction

Quantitative or mathematical evidence typically has been a source of bewilderment to the legal profession.[1] Consider, for example, the following hypothetical case posed by Richard Lempert:

> [T]here are two taxicab companies in town who have identical cabs except that one has red cabs and the other green cabs. [S]ixty percent of all cabs in town are red. Plaintiff has been knocked down on a deserted street by a cab. He is color blind and cannot distinguish red from green. Shortly after the accident a taxicab driver said over the air, "I just hit someone at (the

David Kaye is Professor of Law, Arizona State University. S.B., 1968, M.I.T.; A.M., 1969, Harvard; J.D., 1972, Yale.

Preparation of this article was aided by the Faculty Grant-in-Aid Program of Arizona State University. I am also grateful to Richard Lempert for prodding me into thinking about some of the issues addressed here and to Richard Epstein, Dennis Karjala, Spencer Kimball, Glen Robinson, and Dennis Young for commenting on a draft of this article.

1. See, e.g., Ira M. Ellman & David Kaye, Probabilities and Proof: Can HLA and Blood Group Testing Prove Paternity? 54 N.Y.U. L. Rev. 1131 (1979); David Kaye, The Laws of Probability and the Law of the Land, 47 U. Chi. L. Rev. 34 n.1 (1979).

> accident location). I should have seen him, but I was drinking and going too fast." The static was such that no identification of the voice was possible, but the frequency is used only by cabs from that town. Neither company keeps dispatch records, so [neither knows] what drivers were in what parts of town. And to make things complete, the garage in which all the cabs of the two companies [were] housed was burned down the night of the accident.[2]

If plaintiff could conclusively establish all these facts, should he be permitted to collect from the Red Company?

Lempert's illustration is but one of several cases, some hypothetical and some real, involving proof by what has been termed "naked statistical evidence."[3] In response to such cases courts have issued seemingly conflicting opinions often disapproving of this mode of proof.[4] Commentators, in their turn, have propounded a bewildering collection of explanations for this judicial reticence. Thus, it has been suggested that the cardinal structure of mathematical probability theory is incompatible with the law of evidence,[5] that courts seek to equalize the incidence of errors favoring plaintiffs and defendants even though this policy increases the number of mistaken verdicts,[6] and that the law governing the situation is essentially anomalous.[7] As I have argued elsewhere,[8] however, the legal issue created by naked statistical evidence can be resolved satisfactorily if it is granted that in most cases probative, nonquantitative evidence should also be readily available. In these circumstances, a rule requiring that at least some such evidence be brought to bear on the case is not so mysterious. It is merely a device calculated to enhance the accuracy of the fact-finding process in a manner that is fair to both parties and that is not overly burdensome to the proponent of the statistical evidence.[9]

2. Letter from Richard Lempert to David Kaye, Apr. 2, 1980, p. 1.

3. David Kaye, Naked Statistical Evidence (Book Review), 89 Yale L.J. 601 (1980) (*reviewing* Finkelstein), *infra* note 6.

4. E.g., Kaminsky v. Hertz Corp., 94 Mich. App. 356 (1979); David Kaye, Paradoxes, Gedanken Experiments and the Burden of Proof: A Response to Dr. Cohen's Reply, 1981 Ariz. St. L.J. 635.

5. L. Jonathan Cohen, The Probable and the Provable (London: Oxford University Press, Clarendon Press, 1977); Lea Brilmayer & Lewis Kornhauser, Review: Quantitative Methods and Legal Decisions, 46 U. Chi. L. Rev. 116, 135–48 (1978); L. Jonathan Cohen, Subjective Probability and the Paradox of the Gatecrasher, 1981 Ariz. St. L.J. 627.

6. Michael O. Finkelstein, Quantitative Methods in Law: Studies in the Application of Mathematical Probability and Statistics to Legal Problems 69 (New York: Free Press, 1978).

7. Michael J. Saks & Robert F. Kidd, Human Information Processing and Adjudication: Trial by Heuristics, 15 Law & Soc'y Rev. 123, 151 (1980–81) (decrying "the myth of particularistic proof"); Glanville Williams, The Mathematics of Proof I, 1979 Crim. L. Rev. 297, 305.

8. See Kaye, *supra* note 4, at 635 n.1.

9. A less procrustean rule might serve this same function. Where a party inexplicably fails to produce evidence under circumstances in which he would be expected to have favorable evidence, an inference that the evidence is in fact unfavorable could be drawn. See authorities cited, David Kaye, Probability Theory Meets Res Ipsa Loquitur, 77 Mich. L. Rev. 1456, 1475 n.59 (1979).

In a few situations a rule disfavoring naked statistical evidence can be defended on another

Still, this simple explanation does not supply a sufficient rationale for resolving all cases of naked statistical evidence. There may be instances in which useful, nonquantitative evidence is all but impossible to obtain. Lempert's taxicab case is one. The hypothetical facts are carefully crafted to ensure that the plaintiff could not be expected to adduce much more than the background statistics about red and green taxicabs. Nor, alas, can that case be dismissed as another manifestation of the well-known perversity of law professors. Although instances of "justifiably" naked statistical evidence may be rare, a few do find their way into the law-books. Thus, in *Sindell v. Abbott Laboratories,*[10] plaintiff brought a class action against 11 named drug companies that manufactured and marketed diethylstilbestrol. For a time, this compound, commonly referred to by its initials DES, had been prescribed to prevent miscarriage. Plaintiff alleged that the defendant companies knew or should have known that DES was ineffective in preventing miscarriage and that it would cause carcinomas in the daughters of the mothers who took it. The trial court dismissed the action because the plaintiff could not identify which company had manufactured the dosage responsible for her injuries. Plaintiff's difficulty in making this identification was not hard to explain. DES was often sold under a generic rather than a brand name, and in the two or three decades since the drug was prescribed, memories have faded and prescriptions have been lost or destroyed. Noting that DES victims can hardly be faulted for being unable to point to anything more individualized than statistics describing how much DES each company marketed for use in the prevention of miscarriages, the California Supreme Court reversed. It held that if plaintiff could prove her allegations of negligence and damages, then she should be entitled to recover from each defendant in proportion to that defendant's DES sales.[11] These figures, the court reasoned, could serve as an acceptable "measure of the

---

ground as well. Cohen's "paradox of the gatecrasher" (see note 5 *supra*) is a good illustration of a case in which the plaintiff has no evidence with which to distinguish any specific defendant from many other possible defendants who are equally likely to be liable. It can be argued that notwithstanding whatever probability theory may teach us, assuring the appearance of fairness precludes imposing liability in the absence of some evidence singling out particular defendants.

10. 26 Cal. 3d 588, 163 Cal. Rptr. 132, 607 P.2d 924 (1980).

11. The Supreme Court left open the possibility that a defendant could somehow demonstrate at trial that it did not market the quantity of DES that had caused plaintiff's cancer. 26 Cal. 3d at 612. It also indicated that plaintiff must join the manufacturers of a "substantial share" of the DES marketed for the prevention of miscarriages. *Id.* Commentary on these and other aspects of *Sindell* includes Glen O. Robinson, Multiple Causation in Tort Law: Reflections on the DES Cases, 68 Va. L. Rev. 713 (1982); Note, *Sindell v. Abbott Laboratories:* A Market Share Approach to DES Causation, 69 Calif. L. Rev. 1179 (1981) [hereinafter cited as A Market Share Approach]; Note, Market Share Liability: An Answer to the DES Causation Problem, 94 Harv. L. Rev. 668 (1981) [hereinafter cited as Market Share Liability]; Case Comment, Refining Market Share Liability: *Sindell v. Abbott Laboratories,* 33 Stan. L. Rev. 937 (1981) [hereinafter cited as Refining Market Share Liability].

likelihood that . . . the defendants supplied the product which allegedly injured plaintiff."[12] The dissent tartly observed that under this rule "a particular defendant may be held proportionately liable *even though mathematically it is much more likely than not that it played no role whatever in causing plaintiffs' injuries.*"[13]

Although *Sindell,* like the hypothetical taxicab case, involves naked statistical evidence as to the identity of a wrongdoer, the same type of evidence can arise in connection with very different factual questions. *Sindell* focuses on which defendant produced certain pills. No less important is the question of whether DES caused plaintiff's ailments. Presumably, the evidence that supports this allegation consists of a comparison of the incidence of adenosis and adenocarcinoma among "DES daughters" as opposed to otherwise similarly situated women.[14] If these conditions are sufficiently concentrated among the former group, the inference that DES is to blame in these cases seems warranted.[15] If we take the trouble to quantify the numbers involved, it becomes clear that we have another instance of proof by justifiably naked statistical evidence.[16]

Cases like *Sindell,* involving many defendants each of whom might have caused or contributed to a legally cognizable injury, also lead us into the tangled thicket of doctrines concerning multiple causation, joint tortfeasors, contribution, and apportionment of damages.[17] Did each of the *Sindell* defendants, for example, produce a share of the DES that affected the plaintiff, or did only one pharmaceutical house cause the individual plaintiff's injury? The answer to this question may determine which of several distinct legal doctrines comes into play.[18] Yet the *Sindell* court shifts unthinkingly from one perspective to the other.[19]

12. 26 Cal. 3d at 611, 163 Cal. Rptr. at 145, 607 P.2d at 937.

13. *Id.* at 616, 163 Cal. Rptr. at 147, 607 P.2d at 939.

14. It has been said that the particular form of cancer linked with DES, clear-cell adenocarcinoma, used to be rare. Comment, DES and a Proposed Theory of Enterprise Liability, 46 Fordham L. Rev. 963, 965 n.8 (1978) (*citing* Ulfelder, The Stilbestrol-Adenosis-Carcinoma Syndrome, 38 Cancer 426, 428 (1976)) [hereinafter cited as Comment, DES and a Proposed Theory].

15. It might be argued that DES is but one of several contributing causes. If such joint causation were present, the epidemiological data might be used to assess the relative magnitude of the contribution from DES. Whether it would then be appropriate to apportion damages in light of this figure is an interesting question. See, e.g., text and accompanying notes 70–73 *infra.* The apportionment issue, however, is distinct from the naked statistical evidence problem. It would arise even if the extent of relative contributions were quantified on the basis of "individualized" evidence.

16. See text accompanying notes 22–25 *infra.*

17. See generally, e.g., Frank H. Easterbrook, William M. Landes, & Richard A. Posner, Contribution Among Antitrust Defendants: A Legal and Economic Analysis, 23 J.L. & Econ. 331 (1980); William M. Landes & Richard A. Posner, Joint and Multiple Tortfeasors: An Economic Analysis, 9 J. Legal Stud. 517 (1980); A. Mitchell Polinsky & Steven Shavell, Contribution and Claim Reduction Among Antitrust Defendants: An Economic Analysis, 33 Stan. L. Rev. 447 (1981); Mario J. Rizzo & Frank S. Arnold, Causal Apportionment in the Law of Torts: An Economic Theory, 80 Colum. L. Rev. 1399 (1980); Robinson, *supra* note 11.

18. See note 15 *supra* and text accompanying notes 70–73 *infra.*

19. Compare 26 Cal. 3d at 612, 163 Cal. Rptr. at 145, 607 P.2d at 937 ("If plaintiff joins in the

In the hope of clarifying the issues arising in cases of naked statistical evidence and multiple causation, this article focuses on two recurring problems. The first is what to do when the only obstacle to recovery is plaintiff's justifiable inability to come forward with anything more than background statistics pointing to a single defendant (as opposed to natural forces or other factors that could not give rise to liability) as the cause of his injury. Part II treats this problem with the tools of statistical decision theory. It argues that ordinarily the traditional more-probable-than-not interpretation of the preponderance-of-the-evidence standard should be applied to the quantitifed probability. It contrasts this "maximum likelihood" rule with an "expected value" rule that would discount the damages by the probability involved, and it concludes that in one category of cases the maximum likelihood rule should yield to the expected value rule.

Part III enlarges the mathematical analysis to cope with the second problem—what to do when the only obstacle to recovery is plaintiff's justifiable inability to single out one of many possible causes to which liability might attach. Either the plaintiff must rely on background statistics to arrive at a probability figure greater than one-half, or, however the figure pertaining to the most probably liable defendant may be arrived at, it simply does not exceed one-half. It is shown that in these situations, the conventional understanding of the preponderance-of-the-evidence standard is in error. The maximum likelihood principle underlying this standard then demands only that liability be assigned to the single defendant who the evidence reveals was the most likely cause of the injury. Again, however, I argue that there are limited circumstances under which an expected value approach should substitute for the preponderance requirement.

Part IV illustrates how the framework constructed in parts II and III can be applied to some representative cases involving uncertainty in the identification of the one defendant who caused an injury. The now classic case of *Summers v. Tice,*[20] among others, is discussed. The distinct problem of allocating damages among concurrent causes is also mentioned but shown to be left unresolved by the analysis developed here. Finally, part V summarizes the argument, with particular attention to its assumptions and limitations.

---

action the manufacturers of a substantial share of the DES which her mother might have taken, the injustice of shifting the burden of proof to defendants . . . is significantly diminished") with *id.* at 612 n.28, 163 Cal. Rptr. at 145 n.28, 607 P.2d at 937 n.28 ("[i]f X [m]anufacturer sold one-fifth of all the DES prescribed for pregnancy and identification could be made in all cases, X would be the sole defendant in approximately one-fifth of all cases and liable for damages in those cases" (*quoting* Comment, DES and a Proposed Theory, *supra* note 14)).

20. 33 Cal. 2d 80, 199 P.2d 1 (1948).

II. Single Defendant Cases

A. Some Plausible Decision Rules

Analytically, the simplest cases of naked statistical evidence occur when only one person would be liable under plaintiff's allegations. Imagine, by way of illustration, that a worker in a chemical factory that produces phenoxy acids for herbicides develops stomach cancer. At issue is whether this is a work-related injury covered by a workers' compensation statute. Epidemiological studies, let us suppose, reveal that the incidence of stomach cancer among workers exposed to phenoxy acids is higher than the rate in the rest of the population.[21] Nevertheless, there is a nonzero rate (call it b, for base rate) outside the industry. Hence, when a particular worker develops stomach cancer, it is difficult to know whether it is the result of his working near the apparent carcinogens or whether he would have contracted the disease had he been otherwise employed. The evidence on this point is necessarily overtly statistical.[22] Assuming that the rest of the population constitutes an appropriate control group, the probability λ that the cancer was "caused" by working can be expressed in terms of the base rate b and the rate for workers (which we shall denote as a).[23] The increment in the probability of contracting liver cancer due to working is simply $a-b$. Roughly speaking, out of every a workers who develop stomach cancer, $a-b$ would not have been afflicted had they stayed away from employment near phenoxy acids. This is to say that $\lambda=(a-b)/a$.

For concreteness, suppose that the stomach cancer rate is three times higher among workers than among the rest of the population. Substituting $a=3b$ into the equation for λ indicates that $\lambda=2/3$. Should a court or agency conclude that the cancer in the case it is considering is work related? If all naked statistical evidence were disfavored, the answer would be no and recovery would be barred. Yet this "no recovery" rule seems inapt since this is a case of *justifiably* naked statistical evidence. The worker has stomach cancer, and there is no known way to tell a phenoxy acid-induced stomach cancer from other stomach cancers. Ex-

21. Although the probability figures that will be used here are merely illustrative, the possibility of some measurable discrepancy is real. See Defoliant, Cancer: Studies Show Link, 117 Sci. News 230 (1980).

22. In an important sense all empirical reasoning is statistical. The distinguishing feature of the naked statistical evidence cases is that reliance on a quantified probability is invited, to the exclusion of all nonquantified evidence. In justifiably naked statistical evidence cases this invitation seems appealing because the latter sort of evidence is impossible or impractical to obtain.

23. For simplicity, I am ignoring any latency period in carcinogenesis. The timing of disease onset in evaluating causation can be very important. See, e.g., Reyes v. Wyeth Laboratories, 498 F.2d 1264 (5th Cir.), *cert. denied,* 419 U.S. 1096 (1974).

cluding stomach cancers from coverage because there is a 1/3 chance that they would have occurred anyway would not serve the purposes of industrial accident insurance.

On the other hand, if we treat justifiably naked statistical evidence like any other form of evidence, we end up extending coverage to all workers with stomach cancers, including the ⅓ whose conditions are not work related. Under the preponderance-of-the-evidence standard, all that is required is that the probability in question exceed ½.[24] Since $\lambda = 2/3$, this "$p > 1/2$" standard is satisfied.[25]

However, there is a third solution that mediates between these two extremes. It is to give to the injured worker not the full amount of the damages but that sum multiplied by the probability that the costs are attributable to his employment. Let us denote the costs of the stomach cancer by *D*. Then this "expected value" rule would permit the injured worker to collect not *D*, as under the $p > 1/2$ rule, but only $(2/3)D$.[26] In this way we can avoid imposing "crushing liability"[27] on the enterprise. Conversely, in cases where $\lambda < 1/2$, firms do not escape liability altogether, as they would under the $p > 1/2$ rule. Instead, they are charged an amount λD, further promoting the goal of economic efficiency.[28]

Although the expected value rule may look attractive at first blush, to

24. See, e.g., Kaye, *supra* note 3; Richard Eggleston, The Probability Debate, 1980 Crim. L. Rev. 678, 680.

25. A little algebra shows that $\lambda > 1/2$ if and only if $a/b < 2$. In other words, the "balance of the probabilities" (where λ completely captures the relevant probability) favors causation as long as the industry cancer rate is twice as large as the base rate.

26. Alternatively, one could allow the worker to recover *D* with a probability $\lambda = 2/3$. The expected value of this gamble is simply $(2/3)D$. A risk-averse employee would prefer the fixed sum $(2/3)D$ to a ⅔ chance of *D* and a ⅓ chance of 0. A firm with the same degree of risk aversion would not be as concerned, however, because over a large number of cases it can be confident of paying an average figure very close to $(2/3)D$.

27. The phrase is taken from Steven Shavell, An Analysis of Causation and the Scope of Liability in the Law of Torts, 9 J. Legal Stud. 463, 465 (1980). Shavell's explanation of the term may be instructive:

> Under strict liability it is not hard to imagine circumstances where a party decides against engaging in an activity when it would have been socially worthwhile for him to have gone ahead. Consider a firm that uses a carcinogenic substance in producing a good that we agree ought to be produced because the benefits to consumers of the good exceed the costs of production plus the costs of an increased incidence of cancer among the firm's employees. Were the firm liable for *all* cases of cancer among its employees, then it might well be forced out of business, for it would be paying not only for the increased incidence of cancer due to its activities, but also for the general incidence of cancer due to such factors as pollution from other sources and medical x-radiation. By appropriately restricting the scope of liability, this type of disadvantageous outcome, to be described as the result of *crushing* liability, can sometimes be avoided. [footnote omitted; emphasis in original].

28. Assume, for simplicity, that every case of employee stomach cancer has the same cost *D* and that *N* such cases arise in an appropriate time period. On efficiency grounds, it can be aruged that the firm should pay λDN, since λ represents the increment in the stomach cancer rate due to the firm's activity. See *id*. The picture with regard to efficiency, however, is not as clear as Shavell seems to suggest. Whereas he treats the costs of production as fixed, it could be contended that even when the employer need not pay an explicit sum for the increment in stomach cancer due to employment, he pays this cost implicitly in the form of higher wages. If wage rates are subject to renegotiation in

suggest that it be used to cope with justifiably naked statistical evidence raises an intriguing question: why not use it all the time? Nothing precludes us from asking jurors to evaluate the strength of every plaintiff's case on a scale of, say, 0 to 100. The resulting figures can be taken as indicating subjective probabilities of liability given all the evidence.[29] If the damages are known, the calculation of the expected value is trivial.

Perhaps this proposal will seem fantastic. Still, some commentators have come close to endorsing it,[30] and identifying its defects is not so simple. This task, however, is worth performing because it helps expose the logical foundations of the traditional $p > \frac{1}{2}$ rule and thereby to indicate when that rule should—and should not—be applied.

B. The Expected Value Rule Versus the $p > \frac{1}{2}$ Rule

1. Some Unconvincing Arguments Against the Expected Value Rule

To begin with, one might oppose widespread application of the expected value rule on the ground that jurors are not used to thinking in numerical terms and are therefore unable to arrive at accurate or reliable estimates of the probability of liability.[31] If so, it is only in cases of justifiably naked statistical evidence, where the probability is already calculated "objectively," that the expected value rule can be confidently applied.

Yet, it is far from obvious that jurors and judges are so inept at characterizing the strength of evidence in a quantitative fashion. It is not unusual to hear people express their opinions about one thing or another "on a scale of 1 to 10." Numerical odds are quoted frequently in connection with sporting events. Nor has the inability-to-quantify argument stopped a strong movement toward comparative negligence and contribution[32]—with jury verdicts listing percentage figures[33] that are factored in-

---

an efficient labor market, then they will drop once the accident costs are imposed on the employer. E.g., Harold Demsetz, When Does the Rule of Liability Matter? 1 J. Legal Stud. 13 (1972).

Another complication arises if employer contributions are not tailored to the accident costs experienced by each employer. For the purpose of this article, I shall assume that each firm pays premiums calculated to provide the proper incentive to take cost-effective precautions.

29. See, e.g., Kaye, *supra* note 1; Anne Martin & David A. Schum, Quantifying Burdens of Proof: A Likelihood Ratio Approach, Rice University Report No. 78-02 (Dec. 15, 1978).

30. E.g., Joseph H. King, Jr., Causation, Valuation, and Chance in Personal Injury Torts Involving Preexisting Conditions and Future Consequences, 90 Yale L.J. 1353, 1396 (1981).

31. Cf. Laurence H. Tribe, Trial by Mathematics: Precision and Ritual in the Legal Process, 84 Harv. L. Rev. 1329 (1971) (arguing that most jurors cannot make reasonable quantitative estimates of the probability that a defendant is guilty).

32. See, e.g., Alvis v. Ribar, 85 Ill. 2d 1, 421 N.E.2d 886 (1981); Carroll R. Heft & C. James Heft, Comparative Negligence Manual (Mundelein, Ill.: Callaghan & Co., 1978, 1981 Cum. Supp.); Landes & Posner, *supra* note 17, at 551.

33. See, e.g., Garrison v. Funderburk, 262 Ark. 711, 561 S.W.2d 73 (1978); Downum v. Muskogee Stockyards & Livestock Auction, Inc., 565 P.2d 368 (Okla. 1977). Some fact-finders proffer such quantitative estimates even when not obliged to do so. See The Times (London) 60,948 (June 8, 1981, at 2, col. 8) (industrial tribunal finds employee 60 percent to blame for his dismissal).

to damage awards. One wonders whether there are not more compelling reasons to prefer the $p>1/2$ rule to the expected value approach.

An alternative (or perhaps supplemental) explanation emphasizes the costs that would arise in administering the latter rule. The expected value rule allows plaintiffs some recovery even when the factual case for liability is tenuous.[34] It might be thought that this feature would result in more suits being filed and tried. Naturally, this administrative cost argument also applies to justifiably naked statistical evidence cases, but such cases are, after all, infrequent. If they are easily identified and the application of the expected value rule is restricted to this class of cases, then the administrative costs should not be unduly high.

Concern with administrative costs is surely proper, but the problem is easily exaggerated. It is more difficult than it might first appear to assess the likely impact of an across-the-board expected value rule on the volume of litigation, threatened or actual. Indeed, if plaintiffs and defendants are all risk neutral, the rate at which suits are filed and settled should not change. Giving damages of pD with probability 1 instead of D with probability p does not affect the ex ante value of a case. Many suits are now instituted with full recognition that a favorable verdict is most unlikely. These cases have settlement value precisely because the defendant has a nonzero risk of losing a large sum.[35] And to the extent that the weakness in these cases is evidentiary, they are not now vulnerable to pretrial attack.

Of course, I am not suggesting that adopting the expected value rule could not conceivably increase administrative costs or affect settlements. If defendants are risk averse,[36] they would feel less pressure to settle before trial since the expected value rule exposes them to less risk. If the court could not keep a case from reaching a jury because plaintiff's evidence is very thin, plaintiffs might gain. Considering these and a number of other factors,[37] it seems fair to say that, on balance, the situation with respect to relative administrative costs is complex if not downright

34. To preclude this possibility, one might modify the expected value rule by insisting on some threshold level of p before permitting any recovery. The formal analysis of the expected value rule (to be developed shortly) applies, with obvious variations, to this modified expected value rule.

35. Plaintiffs may also be able to induce settlements by imposing heavy discovery and other trial preparation costs on defendants. A change in the evidentiary standard of the sort contemplated here should have no long-run effect on such matters.

36. For a discussion of the attitude of firms toward risk, see, e.g., Easterbrook, Landes, & Posner, *supra* note 17, at 351–53 n.50 (concluding that "the extent and intensity of risk aversion among firms is an unsettled empirical question").

37. See, e.g., Polinsky & Shavell, *supra* note 17, at 457–62; authorities cited, *id.* at 460 n.43 (considering the additional factors of litigation costs and differences of opinion about winning). See generally W. Craig Riddell, Bargaining Under Uncertainty, 71 Am. Econ. Rev. 579 (1981); Steven Shavell, Suit, Settlement, and Trial: A Theoretical Analysis Under Alternative Methods for the Allocation of Legal Costs, 11 J. Legal Stud. 55 (1982).

murky. It is hardly obvious that concern over these administrative costs adequately explains or defends the refusal to employ a generally applicable expected value rule.[38]

2. *The Expected Value Rule as the Error Equalizing Rule and the* $p>½$ *Rule as the Error Minimizing Rule*

A more satisfactory justification for the traditional $p>½$ rule does exist. It focuses on the costs of errors, and it starts from the premise that the best decision rule is one that, as far as is practical, imposes liability entirely on the party who would indeed be liable under the governing substantive law if only all the facts could be known with certainty. This premise leads to the following notion of errors in damage awards: (1) every dollar paid by a defendant who would not be found liable if the true state of affairs were known is a dollar erroneously paid, and (2) every one of D dollars not paid to a plaintiff who would be entitled to collect this sum if the true state of the world were known is a dollar erroneously "paid" by plaintiff. Plainly, these definitions do not correspond to the usual notion of *legal* error. A trial can be conducted flawlessly, but the jury's deductions and inferences as to the true state of affairs can still be mistaken. The two types of mistakes identified here, however, are real enough. They pertain to "factual" errors, and they are known in statistical theory as type I errors (or false positives) and type II errors (false negatives).

The $p>½$ rule emerges as optimal if two assumptions about these types of errors are granted. The first is that one type is neither more nor less costly than the other. A dollar mistakenly paid by defendant (a false positive) is just as onerous as a dollar erroneously paid by a plaintiff (a false negative).[39] The second assumption is that the best decision rule keeps the

38. One can say that to the extent that the expected value rule reduces the "risk premium" paid by parties who settle, it lowers social costs, enhancing the attractiveness of the rule from the standpoint of economic efficiency.

39. This equality is not intended to reflect the values held by jurors or judges in particular cases or to describe the costs to or utility functions of particular plaintiffs and defendants. It is a statement about institutional values, about the relative importance of these types of mistakes in the eyes of "the law."

This conception of "blindfolded" justice is, I believe, widely shared. Whether it can be motivated solely by an efficiency argument is a nice question. One such argument goes something like this: It would be best to look to the opportunity costs (willingness to pay to avoid errors) to each party in each case if these costs could be cheaply measured. Because this administrative cost is very high, however, it is more efficient to use average figures, and on average the cost of each type of error is the same.

This efficiency argument would not hold to the extent that there are easily identified classes of cases in which the costs of errors to each side diverge. If large businesses are risk neutral and individuals with small assets are risk averse, for example, the cost of a dollar erroneously "paid" by the latter exceeds that for the former. One suspects, however, that an instruction to consider the depth of a litigant's pocket would be superfluous. In cases where moral censure or other collateral effects would result from an award of damages, costs to plaintiffs and defendants clearly are not proportional to the dollars wrongfully paid, and the law requires plaintiffs to do more than adduce a preponderance of the evidence. See, e.g., John Kaplan, Decision Theory and the Factfinding Process, 20 Stan. L. Rev. 1065, 1072 (1968).

sum of the expected costs of each type of error to a minimum. In other words, the claim on behalf of the $p > \frac{1}{2}$ rule is that it does better than the expected value rule in minimizing the total expected number of dollars coming from the wrong pockets. In fact, I propose to prove an even stronger proposition—that the $p > \frac{1}{2}$ rule is optimal (in the sense defined above) with regard to all conceivable decision rules for cases involving a single defendant and a single plaintiff.[40]

To analyze the $p > \frac{1}{2}$ rule with the tools of decision theory, we begin by enumerating the possible outcomes under the various decision rules, given all the possible "states of nature." In our workers' compensation case, for instance, there are two relevant possibilities: s_1, that the cancer was caused by exposure to the work environment, and s_2, that it was not. Of course, we do not know which state of nature actually pertains, but the evidence (in this case the cancer rates a and b) enables us to estimate the probabilities of s_1 and s_2. The probability of s_1 is $p_1 = \lambda = \frac{2}{3}$. The probability of s_2 is $p_2 = 1 - \lambda = \frac{1}{3}$.

Now consider three decisions:

d_1: claimant or plaintiff pays D; defendant pays 0
d_2: plaintiff pays 0; defendant pays D
d_3: plaintiff pays p_2D; defendant pays p_1D

In the hypothetical phenoxy acids case, we might decide that the worker should not recover at all; he or she must absorb all the damages D without compensation. This decision is symbolized by d_1. In contrast, d_2 imposes full liability on the firm, and d_3 is the expected value rule.

If s_1 is true, then the claimant should pay nothing, but d_1 forces him to bear all the costs D. A total of D dollars is "wrongfully" paid. If s_2 is true, the substantive law says that the plaintiff deserves compensation, so that under d_1 zero dollars are paid by the wrong party. Pursuing this reasoning, we construct the following table or matrix of "losses" (money wrongfully paid) for the three decisions under each possible state of nature:

	s_1 (probability $= p_1$)	s_2 (probability $= p_2$)
d_1 (plaintiff pays all)	D	0
d_2 (defendant pays all)	0	D
d_3 (expected value rule)	p_2D	p_1D

Fig. 1. Matrix of losses for decisions d_1, d_2, and d_3

40. An essentially identical proposition was proved from a slightly different perspective in Kaye, *supra* note 3, at 605 n.19. The present development provides additional insights.

We now are in a position to state the "expected loss function" (f) for each decision. The expected value of a discrete random variable is the value of that variable multiplied by the probability that the variable will take on that value, calculated for each possible value and summed over all these values. Under d_1 there is a probability p_1 that D dollars will be wrongfully paid and a probability $p_2 = 1 - p_1$ that zero dollars will be wrongfully paid. Hence, the expected loss for d_1 is given by

$$f_1 = p_1 D + p_2 0 = p_1 D$$

In other words, making workers in the phenoxy acids illustration pay the costs of the illnesses means that on average a fraction p_1 of the costs will be borne by persons who would not have to pay in a world of perfect information. Likewise, the expected loss under d_2 is

$$f_2 = p_1 0 + p_2 D = p_2 D = (1 - p_1)D$$

Under d_3 the plaintiff recovers only a proportion of the damages D. There is a probability p_1 that $p_2 D$ dollars will be wrongfully paid and a probability p_2 that $p_1 D$ dollars will be wrongfully paid. The expected loss under d_3 is therefore

$$f_3 = p_1 p_2 D + p_2 p_1 D = 2p_1 p_2 D = 2p_1(1 - p_1)D$$

To see the implications of these algebraic expressions, let us view the probability p_1 as varying from case to case. In other words, in some instances the justifiably naked statistical evidence will suggest a low value (near 0) for p_1 (e.g., hardly any stomach cancers are work related, relatively few taxicabs belong to the Green Company, etc.). In other situations, p_1 will be close to 1 (nearly all stomach cancers are work related, almost 100 percent of the taxicabs are red, etc.). Treating p_1 as a variable, we can draw a picture of the expected losses f_1, f_2, and f_3 as functions of p_1. The loss function f_1 increases in direct proportion to p_1, while f_2 decreases linearly as p_1 increases. The loss function f_3 is a curved line that rises to $D/2$, then falls back to 0. All this is depicted in figure 2.

Which way of deciding minimizes the expected losses? Over the interval $0 < p_1 < ½$, figure 2 shows that $f_1 < f_3 < f_2$. Thus, as long as $p_1 < ½$, d_1 is best. On the other hand, over the interval $½ < p_1 < 1$, $f_2 < f_3 < f_1$; that is, for $p_1 > ½$, d_2 works best. But the prescription to have the claimant pay all the damages (d_1) if $p_1 < ½$ and to make the defendant pay (d_2) if $p_1 > ½$ is essentially the $p > ½$ rule.[41] The ordinary more-probable-than-not standard thus appears superior to the expected value rule.

Of course, d_1, d_2, and d_3 are not the only possible decisions. In fact,

41. Figure 2 shows that when $p_1 = p_2 = ½$, all the decisions are equally effective in minimizing expected losses. To break these ties the $p > ½$ rule awards the verdict to the defendant in those cases.

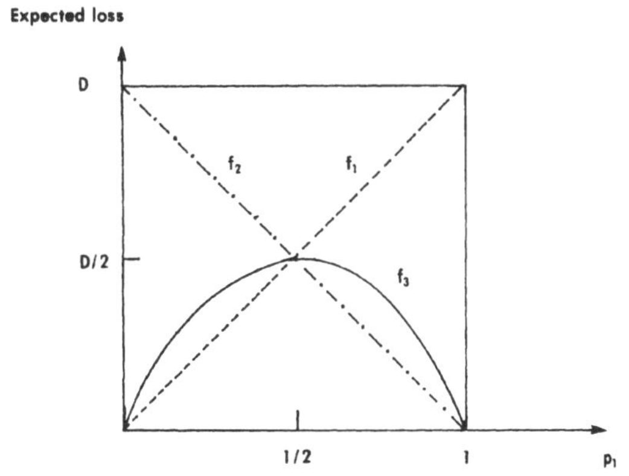

Fig. 2. Expected loss functions for decisions d_1, d_2, and d_3

each is a special case of the following, more general rule d: have defendant give the claimant xD dollars (or, D dollars with probability x). If $x=0$, plaintiff recovers nothing, and d reduces to d_1. If $x=1$, defendant pays all, and we have d_2. If $x=p_1$, damages are split according to the expected value rule d_3.

By selecting x to minimize the expected loss function f associated with this general decision rule, we specify the particular rule that is optimal with regard to all the possible decision rules—not merely d_1, d_2, and d_3. It should come as no surprise by now that this optimal rule is the $p>½$ rule.[42]

However, minimizing f has an interesting impact on the incidence of

42. The proof is straightforward, but worth stating, paying attention to the way the choice of the function $x(p_1)$ affects the rate of type I versus type II errors. The loss matrix is now given by figure A.

	s_1 (defendant liable; probability $=p_1$)	s_2 (defendant not liable; probability $=p_2$)
d (plaintiff pays $(1-x)D$; defendant pays xD)	$(1-x)D$ type II error (false negative)	xD type I error (false positive)

Fig. A. Matrix of losses for general decision rule d

If the costs of each type of error are the same, the expected loss function is just the sum of the expected number of false positive and false negative dollars:

$$f=n_I+n_{II}=p_2xD+p_1(1-x)D=p_1D+(p_2-p_1)xD$$

false positives and false negatives. Figure 3 shows the expected number of each type of error when $p_1 > \frac{1}{2}$. It reveals two very important things. First, while the $p > \frac{1}{2}$ rule keeps expected losses to a minimum (of $(1-p_1)D$), it does so in an extremely lopsided way. All the expected losses

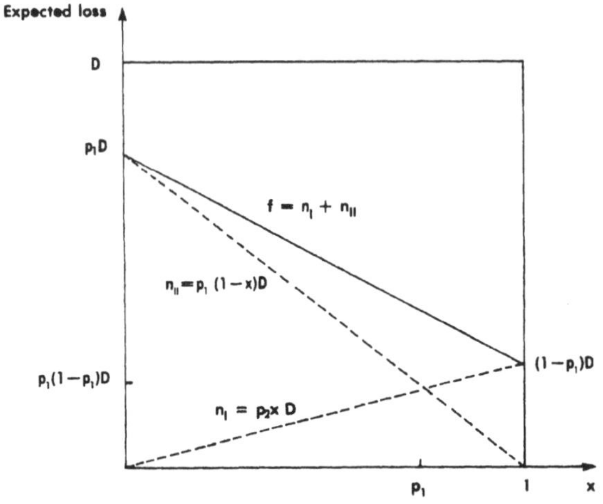

Fig. 3. Expected type I and type II losses for rule *d* (drawn for $p_1 > p_2$)

are false positives when $p_1 > p_2$. (When the $p > \frac{1}{2}$ rule is used where $p_1 < p_2$, all the losses are false negatives.) Second, the expected value rule $x = p_1$ entails larger expected losses (totaling $2p_1(1-p_1)D$), but these expected losses are equally divided among false positives and false negatives. In short, the $p > \frac{1}{2}$ rule is the error minimizing rule for each case, but the expected value rule is the error equalizing rule.[43]

3. *Minimizing Total Expected Losses Versus Equalizing Expected False Positives and False Negatives*

The criterion of minimizing the total expected losses, it will be recalled,

---

In a given case p_1, p_2, and D are fixed, and f is therefore minimized by choosing

$$x(p_1) = \begin{cases} 0 & \text{if } p_2 > p_1 \\ 1 & \text{if } p_1 > p_2 \end{cases}$$

Since $p_1 > p_2$ is the same as $p_1 > \frac{1}{2}$, we have again arrived at the more-probable-than-not rule.

43. Finkelstein has spoken of raising the threshold of the $p > \frac{1}{2}$ rule to some figure larger than $\frac{1}{2}$ to make it an error equalizing rule. See Finkelstein, *supra* note 6. The expected value rule equalizes expected errors in the same sense as Finkelstein's modified $p > \frac{1}{2}$ rule, but it operates in a distinctive way.

incorporates the assumption that it is equally objectionable for either party to absorb or pay damages that the law would require the other side to bear if all the material facts were known with certainty. Yet, we have just seen that when the $p>\frac{1}{2}$ decision rule—which best meets this appealing criterion—is applied to a case in which p_1 exceeds ½, the expected number of dollars that defendant must wrongly pay is p_2D, while the number that plaintiff must wrongly pay is 0. And we have seen that the expected value rule avoids this result.

Upon reflection, however, this feature of the $p>\frac{1}{2}$ rule should not prove paradoxical or troublesome; nor, as we shall see, does the error equalizing characteristic of the expected value rule provide a rationale for its unrestricted use. To borrow again from statistical terminology, the $p>\frac{1}{2}$ rule is a "maximum likelihood" rule. It tells us to act as if s_1 is true as long as s_1 is the most likely state of the world. In other words, if it is more probable that the defendant should pay D dollars ($p_1>p_2$), we decide that plaintiff is entitled to collect these dollars. We than have a relatively small chance (of probability p_2) of making a mistake with all these D dollars; but we have a better chance (of probability p_1) of having *no* dollars wrongly paid. On average, we err with only p_2D dollars. In contrast, the expected value rule guarantees that we will make a mistake in every case. On average, in the proportion p_1 of the cases, p_2D dollars will be wrongly borne by the plaintiff, and in the remaining proportion p_2 of the cases, p_1D dollars will be wrongly paid by defendant. So the expected value rule equates the two expected dollar error rates (at p_1p_2D apiece) but only at the cost of making more errors ($2p_1p_2D$ instead of p_2D).[44]

An analogy may clarify the mathematical characteristics of the expected value rule and the $p>\frac{1}{2}$ rule. Returning to the stomach cancer case, let us visualize an urn filled with 300 marbles. Two-thirds of these marbles are red and one-third green. We pick a marble at random and must decide whether it is red or green. The red marbles correspond to the work-related stomach cancers and the green ones to the other stomach cancers among the workers. Ordinarily, we could tell green from red at a glance, so to make the analogy complete we must imagine that we are blindfolded or colorblind. As such, we must rely on probability theory to make the most accurate guess.

The maximum likelihood approach is to announce that the marble is red. It gives the right answer two-thirds of the time. Of course, this approach is "biased" in the statistical sense.[45] It leads us to announce that

44. Since $p_1>p_2$ and $p_1+p_2=1$, it follows that $2p_1p_2D>p_2D$.

45. Statistical inference consists of using sample data to reach conclusions about the population being sampled. Suppose we wish to estimate some numerical characteristic of a large group on the basis of a limited number of randomly drawn observations. For any particular sample, the estimate

every marble so selected is red, even though we know that in the long run one-third are green. The expected value approach is not "biased" toward red. It would have us say that each marble is two-thirds red.[46] We will be wrong in every instance, but *on average,* we will be exactly right. That is, we will correctly state what percentage of the color in the urn is red.

Similarly, the expected value rule gives each worker with stomach cancer $(2/3)D$. But in $2/3$ of the 300 cases it gives $(1/3)D$ too little, and in the other $1/3$ of the 300 cases, it gives $(2/3)D$ too much. The total wrongly given is therefore $2(1/3)(2/3)D(300) = 133.33D$. The maximum likelihood $p > 1/2$ rule gives full recovery D in all cases. In $1/3$ of the 300 cases, it gives D too much, making the total wrongly given $(1/3)D(300) = 100D$, a distinctly smaller number. To summarize, the maximum likelihood rule makes a few expensive mistakes, but it does not err at all in most cases. The expected value rule errs in every case—a small amount in most and a larger amount in the rest, producing a larger weighted sum of errors.

In the example here, the "unbiased" nature of the expected value rule is appealing. It avoids overcharging the firm,[47] and the increment in the error rate does not seem extravagant at most values of p_1 and p_2. Where a single defendant faces the possibility of numerous suits from similarly situated plaintiffs and the probability that this defendant is liable is the same in each of these cases, the expected value rule seems superior to the $p > 1/2$ rule. In general, however, we need not concern ourselves with equalizing error rates at a particular probability level because the values of p_1 and p_2 are not fixed in case after case. Most activities involve a group of potential plaintiffs and defendants for whom $p_1 > p_2$ sometimes and $p_1 < p_2$ at other times. In these situations, the maximum likelihood rule would also seem to be "unbiased." As long as the probabilities are distributed across cases and parties in a symmetric way, any discrepancies in the error rates tend to average out, and the enterprise as a whole is charged the appropriate gross amount for the injuries it causes. The expected value rule therefore rarely will emerge as the better evidentiary standard.[48] For example, in automobile accident cases the maximum like-

---

will not necessarily correspond precisely to the population value. Sometimes it may be on the high side, sometimes on the low side. If the errors systematically fall in one direction, the estimator is said to be "biased." If the errors are balanced, so that on average (in the limit) the estimator is accurate, it is said to be "unbiased."

"Unbiased" estimators can be a mixed blessing, however. For any sample, an unbiased estimator could be very inaccurate. In some applications a more accurate, albeit biased, estimator may be preferred. Selecting the "best" estimator is often a subtle matter, not amenable to rigid rules.

46. One could also randomize the guesses in such a way as to announce that a marble is red in two-thirds of the selections. See note 25 *supra*.

47. See note 27 *supra*.

48. It should be clear that the analysis is confined to the expected value rule that weights damages by the probability of liability. Another expected value rule is appropriate for measuring damages themselves in situations involving future contingencies and losses of valuable chances. See, e.g., King, *supra* note 30.

lihood rule falsely absolves some defendant drivers (when $p_1<p_2$), while it falsely charges others (when $p_1>p_2$) with the accident costs. On balance, no systematic unfairness is apparent despite the apparent "bias" for fixed values of p_1 and p_2. Since the rule promotes factually accurate decision making, it is superior to the expected value rule.

III. Multiple Defendant Cases

At this point, we have seen that in cases involving undisputed damages *D* caused by a single defendant with some quantifiable probability p_1, the traditional $p>\frac{1}{2}$ rule ordinarily is superior to the expected value rule. Except in special circumstances (which are sometimes present in cases of justifiably naked statistical evidence) it involves no systematic unfairness, and it is always superior in keeping the expected sum of the costs assigned to the wrong parties to a minimum. This provides a useful explanation of why the preponderance-of-the-evidence ($p>\frac{1}{2}$) standard is suitable for most cases but why it should nevertheless be replaced by an expected value rule in some instances of justifiably naked statistical evidence.

Strictly speaking, however, the formal analysis does not extend to cases like *Sindell* and the taxicab hypothetical, which involve more than one person who may have caused the injury. This section therefore extends the mathematical analysis to multiple defendant cases.[49] It generalizes the result of part II, initially to two-defendant cases like the taxicab problem, and then to cases involving any finite number of defendants. It proves what may at first seem an unlikely result—that the error minimizing rule calls for decisions assigning total liability to the single person most likely to have caused the injury, even if the probability pertaining to this person does not exceed one-half.

A. The Two-Defendant Case

We begin with the two-defendant case[50] because it illustrates the principles of the more general problem without requiring any complicated mathematics. For simplicity, we assume that the only disputed issue is the identity of the liable defendant. As in the taxicab hypothetical, one defendant, but not both, caused an injury of *D* dollars and would be fully liable under the prevailing law if the identity of this injurer could be spec-

49. It does this by solving the most elementary sort of problem in the branch of operations research known as linear programming. For a nontechnical introduction to the field, see Robert G. Bland, The Allocation of Resources by Linear Programming, 244 Sci. Am., June 1981, at 126.

50. I use the term "two-defendant" (and "*n*-defendant") rather loosely to indicate that more than one person might have independently caused the legally cognizable injury. Factual ambiguity prevents us from knowing which such person did so. Whether all such potential defendants are actually joined or impleaded is not crucial. Independence—that either defendant one *or* defendant two *or* defendant three, etc., caused the single injury—is critical. Persons acting in concert, concurrent causes producing indivisible injuries, and indemnity defendants all present "one-defendant" cases. See text accompanying notes 69–70 *infra*.

ified.[51] The most general decision rule in this situation has one defendant Δ_1 paying x_1 dollars, the second defendant Δ_2 paying x_2 dollars, and the plaintiff absorbing the remainder, $D - x_1 - x_2$. As with the quantity x that we considered in the single-defendant case, the quantities x_1 and x_2 may depend explicitly on the probabilities p_1 and p_2 that Δ_1 and Δ_2, respectively, are indeed liable. If $x_1 = D$ and $x_2 = 0$, for instance, Δ_1 is liable for the entirety of the damages. If $x_1 = p_1 D$ and $x_2 = p_2 D$, then each defendant is liable for an expected quantity, as in the expected value approach discussed in part II. Note also that although $x_1 + x_2$ may equal D (in which case the plaintiff is fully compensated), they need not. Of course, $x_1 + x_2$ cannot exceed D, for D represents the full damages. More succinctly, the constraints on x_1 and x_2 can be expressed as follows:

$$x_1 + x_2 \leq D \quad (1)$$

$$x_1 \geq 0 \quad (2)$$

$$x_2 \geq 0 \quad (3)$$

Also, we should remember that $p_1 + p_2 = 1$.

The expected loss function f for this general decision rule is easily obtained. If the true state of the world is s_1, meaning that Δ_1 should be paying D to the plaintiff, then the amount paid by the wrong parties is everything that Δ_1 does not pay—namely, $D - x_1$. Likewise, under s_2, the loss as we have defined it is $D - x_2$. Hence, the expected loss function for the general division of damages is

$$f = p_1(D - x_1) + p_2(D - x_2) = D - p_1 x_1 - p_2 x_2 \quad (4)$$

Once again, our objective is to choose x_1 and x_2 so as to keep the expected loss f to a minimum. Attention to the geometry of the situation reveals that this is accomplished by letting $x_1 = 0$ and $x_2 = D$ (in other words by having Δ_2 pay for the full damages D) when $p_1 > p_2$, and by letting $x_1 = D$ and $x_2 = 0$ (i.e., having Δ_1 pay D) when $p_2 > p_1$. When both defendants are equally likely to have injured the plaintiff, any division of the damages D as between the two defendants ($x_1 + x_2 = D$) minimizes the expected losses.[52] Thus, the maximum likelihood $p > \frac{1}{2}$ rule is optimal with respect to all possible decision rules in cases involving two possible defendants. Again, it is optimal in the sense that this rule minimizes the expected sum of money paid by parties who should not be liable under the substantive law if the identity of the single wrongdoer were known.

Consequently, in the taxicab hypothetical the Red Company should be liable. Under the unusual circumstances of the case, the plaintiff's exclu-

51. Including the possibility that neither defendant is truly liable is straightforward. One need merely introduce an additional probabilty p_0 for the additional state s_0 (that plaintiff is liable). As far as the mathematics go, we have a three-defendant problem with the plaintiff playing the role of the third defendant.

sive reliance on background statistics is justifiable, so that the values for p_1 and p_2 may be taken from these background statistics. Letting Δ_1 stand for the Red Company, it follows that $p_1 > p_2$. The traditional preponderance-of-the-evidence standard thus selects the Red Company as

52. The inequalities (1)-(3) constrain x_1 and x_2 to the triangular region depicted in figure B.

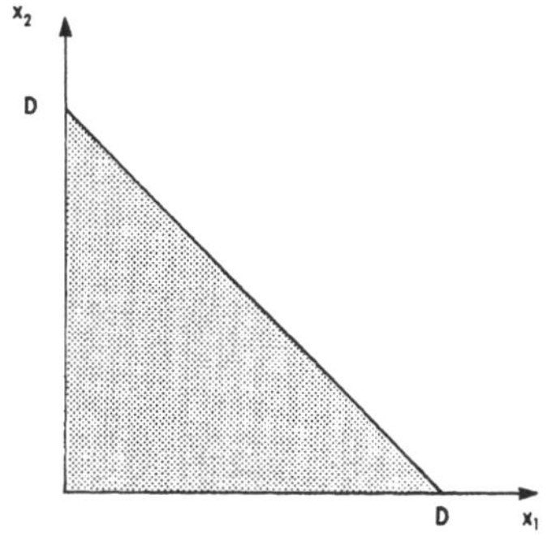

Fig. B. Feasible region for x_1 and x_2 (values for (x_1, x_2) outside the shaded area violate the constraints on x_1 and x_2)

The function f, being a linear combination of x_1 and x_2, is a portion of a plane lying above this feasible region. To sketch this plane, we need a third axis perpendicular to the x_1 and x_2 axes. From equation 4, we can readily find the height of f at the vertices of the feasible region. When $x_1 = D$ and $x_2 = 0$, then $f = p_2 D$. When $x_1 = 0$ and $x_2 = D$, then $f = p_1 D$. When $x_1 = x_2 = 0$, then $f = D$. Since three points determine a plane, we can now graph f. Suppose that $p_1 = 1/2$. Then $p_1 D = p_2 D = D/2$, and the bottom edge of the portion of the plane projecting above the feasible region parallels the hypotenuse of that region, as shown in figure C.

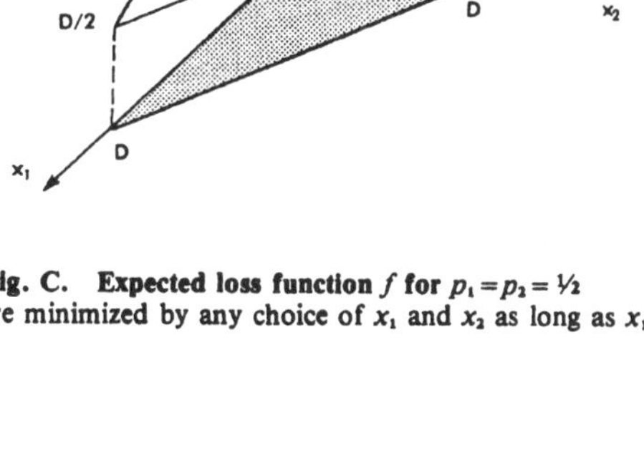

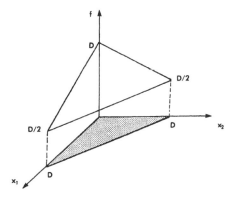

Fig. C. Expected loss function f for $p_1 = p_2 = 1/2$
(expected losses are minimized by any choice of x_1 and x_2 as long as $x_1 + x_2 = D$)

the culprit. Furthermore, no good reason for departing from this maximum likelihood choice is apparent. The type of bias described in part II is not present. Unlike the workers' compensation case, it is difficult to

---

We can see that f is at its lowest as long as plaintiff is fully compensated, regardless of how much each defendant contributes. In other words, when each defendant is equally likely to be the liable party, the minimization criterion gives no guidance as to how Δ_1 and Δ_2 should share in the payment of D to the plaintiff. The criterion is met as long as the plaintiff recovers. Either Δ_1 and Δ_2 may be treated as jointly and severally liable, or equitable principles of contribution may be applied. For discussion of the merits of these alternatives, see, e.g., Landes & Posner, *supra* note 17; Robinson, *supra* note 11. Of greater interest are the more prevalent situations in which p_1 does not equal p_2. If $p_1 > p_2$, f drops to its lowest point when $x_1 = D$ and $x_2 = 0$. This is shown in figure D.

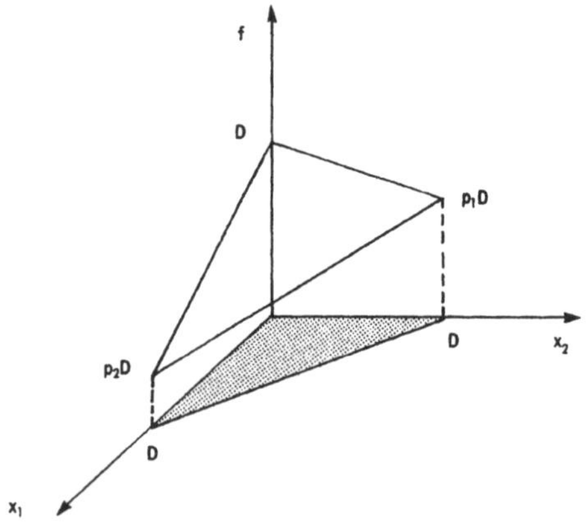

Fig. D. Expected loss function for $p_1 > p_2$
(expected losses are minimized when $x_1 = D$ and $x_2 = 0$)

Finally, if $p_1 < p_2$, the lowest value of f lies above the point $x = 0$ and $x = D$, as revealed in figure E.

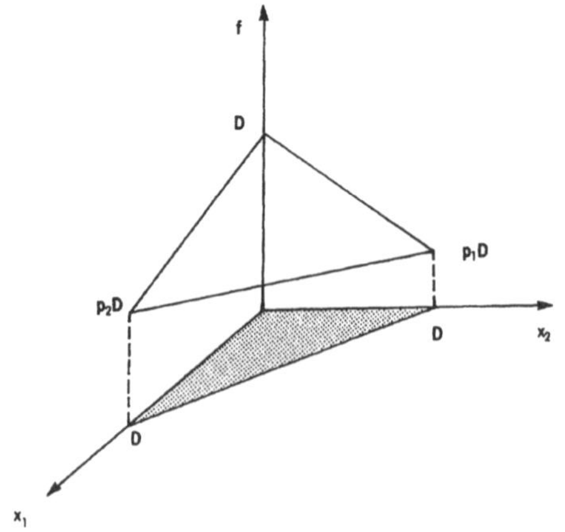

Fig. E. Expected loss function for $p_2 > p_1$
(expected losses are minimized when $x_1 = 0$ and $x_2 = D$)

envision many repeated instances of litigation in which justifiably naked statistical evidence points to the Red Company. The concern that this company will be overcharged or suffer crushing liability seems far-fetched.

B. The *n*-defendant Case

To generalize the proof of the previous section to the *n*-defendant case, we follow the same procedure. We construct an expected loss function and examine its behavior over the feasible region. We discover that f is minimized by having the single defendant for whom the probability of liability is greatest pay all the damages D.[53]

It might be misleading to continue to call this a $p>½$ rule, however, for it may select a single defendant as fully liable even if the probability associated with that defendant's liability is less than ½.[54] Nevertheless, this difference is largely superficial, since the $p>½$ rule is but a special case of the general maximum likelihood rule. When one must decide whether a disputed proposition of fact is true or false, the preponderance-of-the-evidence standard is adequately expressed by the more-probable-than-not ($p>½$) rule. This is nothing more than the maximum likelihood rule expressed for $n=2$. When the decision involves more than two possible outcomes, as it does when a court or jury considers which one of several persons caused a result for which liability attaches, the maximum likelihood approach of selecting the single most likely outcome continues to minimize expected errors.[55] Instead of the more-probable-than-not

53. The expected loss function is now a portion of a plane extending over a feasible region in an n-dimensional space. Let x be a vector whose n components x_1 through x_n represent the money paid by Δ_1 through Δ_n, respectively. Similarly, let p be a vector whose ith component p_i stands for the probability that Δ_i caused the damage. Then the expected loss is just

$$f(p,x) = D - x \cdot p$$

where

$$\Sigma x_i \leq D,\ x_i \geq 0,\ \Sigma p_i = 1, \text{ and } 0 \leq p_i \leq 1.$$

The function f is minimized by making $x \cdot p$ as large as possible for each p. Suppose that $\max(p_i) = p_j$. In light of the constraints on the components of x and the meaning of the scalar product, $x \cdot p$ is then maximized by letting $x_j = D$ and $x_i = 0$ (where $i \neq j$)—by having the single most probably liable defendant pay all the damages. In the event that no single component of p is larger than all the others, several defendants emerge as the equally likely and most probably liable parties, and the minimization principle does not enable us to choose among them.

54. Where there are only two defendants, one of whom must be liable (or one plaintiff and one defendant), this cannot happen because the larger of the probabilities associated with the parties must exceed ½. That is, the n-defendant solution reduces to the $p>½$ rule when $n=2$, as indeed it must.

55. In deriving this result, we assumed that the only issue in dispute is the identity of the single, fully culpable party, so that the justifiably naked statistical evidence supplied the probabilities that each potential defendant is in fact liable. The same result also applies if the probablities p_0, p_1, . . . , p_n are subjective estimates of liability based on all the evidence in the case. How the prob-

test, perhaps we should speak of a "balance-of-the-probabilities" test (where the single largest probability tips the balance) or more succinctly, a "most probable" evidentiary standard in civil litigation.

IV. Applying the Maximum Likelihood Rule: Some Illustrations, Caveats, and Connections

Part III showed that the maximum likelihood rule is the expected error minimizing rule, even in cases involving many defendants. Nonetheless, as we saw in part II, there are circumstances in which an expected value approach may be more suitable. This section considers how the maximum likelihood standard might be used to resolve three perplexing cases. In the process, I shall comment on the connection between the maximum likelihood rule's most serious competitor—the expected value rule—and some recently proposed schemes for "causal apportionment."[56] Again, the emphasis is on the presence of factors that might make the use of the standard misleading or undesirable.

A. *Sindell v. Abbott Laboratories*

Initially, the maximum likelihood approach appears well suited to *Sindell.* Only one pharmaceutical company manufactured the quantity of the compound that injured Judith Sindell. Because of the time between the administration of the DES and the injury, her failure to adduce more than the background statistics seems justified. Taking market shares as a reasonable measure of the probabilities p_i, the maximum likelihood rule would make the dominant firm liable for all the damages.

The California Supreme Court did not consider this approach, perhaps because it conceived of the evidentiary standard in more traditional terms. It reasoned that as to each firm, the $p>½$ test was not met, and it thought it unfair to impose liability on a group of defendants for whom the aggregate probability was under ½. Hence, it demanded the joinder of companies holding "a substantial share" of the relevant market in order to "significantly diminish" the "injustice."[57] Furthermore, it regarded the prospect of joint and several liability, which could result in the firm *least* likely to have caused the injury paying all the damages, as potentially being very unfair. At the same time, it perceived that holding none of the DES manufacturers liable had its drawbacks. Thus, it adopted an expected value approach on top of a "substantial share" requirement as, in effect, a compromise.

abilities pertaining to each element of the cause of action should be combined to obtain the overall probability of liability is beyond the scope of this article. This "problem of conjunction" is discussed in Cohen, The Probable and the Provable, *supra* note 5; Carl G. Wagner, Book Review, 1979 Duke L.J. 1071 (*reviewing* Cohen, The Probable and the Provable).

56. See Rizzo & Arnold, *supra* note 17; Robinson, *supra* note 11.

57. 26 Cal. 3d at 612, 163 Cal. Rptr. at 145, 607 P.2d at 937.

Although the court overlooked the maximum likelihood solution, its use of the expected value rule is defensible for the reasons stated in the simpler workers' compensation example. Both the evidentiary standard presupposed by the court—the $p>½$ rule—and its generalization—the maximum likelihood rule—produce biased results in this situation. In the long run, a minimum of errors occurs under the maximum likelihood approach, but these errors invariably are to the disadvantage of the "most probable" defendant. The $p>½$ rule fits even more awkwardly. If no defendant has more than half the market, it produces the maximum number of errors (100 percent assuming plaintiff would prevail on all other issues), all to the detriment of the DES victims. The probabilities, being market shares within the same geographic region and historical period, do not shift from case to case, reordering the manufacturers; hence, the bias inherent in the use of the maximum likelihood rule with a fixed set of probabilities persists throughout all DES cases. It is not as if the rule sometimes errs to the advantage of one company and sometimes to the benefit of another. Although this type of equalizing effect is typically present, as in automobile accident cases,[58] it does not occur here. As such, the expected value rule has the most merit. It increases the expected error rate relative to the maximum likelihood rule but not to the extent of the $p>½$ rule. It equalizes the expected incidence of errors affecting each firm and imposes, to the extent that we can measure it, the cost of the harm produced by each company on that firm.[59] From this perspective, *Sindell* is correctly decided.[60]

58. See text accompanying note 48 *supra*.

59. All this is a straightforward application of what was said in part II about the workers' compensation problem to the DES context. Yet, there is an intriguing distinction between the two cases. The point can be elucidated by recasting the DES situation slightly. Imagine that every DES victim joins in a class action against every DES producer. Although no single victim can prove which producer distributed the quantity that harmed her, such individualized proof would seem unnecessary and wasteful. If the probabilities used in dividing the damages among the producers are accurate, then the expected value approach quickly accomplishes what the individualized method of proof laboriously strives for: compensating each DES victim and charging each injurer for the cost of the injuries it caused. The fact that company A may pay part of company B's victim's costs while company B does the same for company A's victim is hardly a cause for alarm.

Seen in this light, the DES problem is better suited to the expected value rule than the phenoxy acids illustration. In the latter, only a fraction of the workers "deserve" compensation, but there is no way to match the employer only to these deserving workers, and we end up awarding every afflicted worker a reduced sum. In the DES situation, the causation problem amounts to matching the right firm with the right victim. See Refining Market Share Liability, *supra* note 11. There is no way to do this, but here the expected value approach does not reward any "undeserving" victims, and it awards the proper sum to each victim. For this reason, its use in *Sindell* is even more defensible than in the hypothesized phenoxy acids case. But see A Market Share Approach, *supra* note 11, at 1187–88 (administrative costs imposed on defendants may be excessive in cases involving many potential defendants).

60. If the expected value rule is used, however, it would seem that the "substantial share" requirement serves no meaningful function. See Robinson, *supra* note 11. But see A Market Share Approach, *supra* note 11, at 1197–99 (suggesting, among other things, that "[h]aving the major producers in court will facilitate the determination of the dimensions of the relevant market"). In addition, a more exacting measure of the probability than overall market share may be available. See Re-

B. *Summers v. Tice*

In essence, *Sindell* is but the mildly mutated and as yet poorly articulated offspring of the textbook case of *Summers v. Tice,*[61] decided by the California Supreme Court about 30 years earlier. Like *Sindell, Summers* involved a deficiency in the proof of causation. A shotgun blast from a fellow hunter struck the plaintiff in the eye and lip. The pellet in the eye was the major element of damages. It could have come only from a single gun. Plaintiff's two companions each negligently fired in plaintiff's direction at the same time. They were equidistant from plaintiff and used the same type of shotgun and birdshot. Each had an unobscured line of fire. Although plaintiff did not rely on any generalized background statistics to quantify the probability that each hunter was responsible for the injury, the case resembles the justifiably naked statistical evidence cases. Quantified probabilities leap to mind. A symmetry argument suggests that $p_1 = p_2 = \frac{1}{2}$, and the plaintiff's inability to single out either defendant seems understandable.

Proceeding with our usual analysis, then, we first consider what the generally applicable maximum likelihood rule dictates. If the probabilities are indeed equal, the expected loss function is the one pictured in figure C, and the maximum likelihood solution is "degenerate." It cannot distinguish between Δ_1 and Δ_2. Any division of damages between the two careless hunters minimizes the expected sum of dollars coming from persons who would not be held liable in a world of perfect information. Our analysis therefore merely requires that one defendant or the other, or both, compensate the victim.[62]

The court in *Summers v. Tice* reached this very result. Expressing discomfort with the reasoning of decisions holding defendants from the same hunting party jointly liable on a "concerted action" theory, the California court emphasized that the innocent plaintiff certainly should

---

fining Market Share Liability, *supra* note 11. It should also be clear that the expected value rule is tantamount to what some commentators have called "pro rata" liability. E.g., A Market Share Approach, *supra* note 11, at 1196. It does not permit 100 percent of the liability to be apportioned among defendants who collectively marketed less than 100 percent of the relevant DES—a point that troubled the sole dissenter in *Sindell.* See 26 Cal. 3d at 617, 163 Cal. Rptr. at 148, 607 P.2d at 940.

61. 33 Cal. 2d 80, 119 P.2d 1 (1948). For a perceptive comparison of the two cases developing this theme, see Robinson, *supra* note 11.

62. This much is required by the assumption that $p(s_o) = 0$, i.e., that the plaintiff would not be required to bear the cost of the accident if all the material facts were known with certainty. See note 51 *supra*. One might ask why the substantive law requires an injurer to compensate his innocent victims. See, e.g., George P. Fletcher, Fairness and Utility in Tort Theory, 85 Harv. L. Rev. 537 (1972); Richard A. Posner, The Concept of Corrective Justice in Recent Theories of Tort Law, 10 J. Legal Stud. 187 (1981); Robinson, *supra* note 11. The analytical tools constructed here can shed no light on such questions.

not bear any of the accident costs.[63] Hence, it upheld imposing joint and several liability on the two defendants unless one could somehow demonstrate that he was not responsible for the injury. This reasoning is often denominated an "alternative liability" theory,[64] presumably to distinguish it from the usual basis for joint liability.

The mathematical analysis presented here incorporates the operative premise of this alternative liability theory. We have assumed that $p_o = 0$—that there is no chance that the facts are such that plaintiff should absorb any of the accident cost.[65] To fail to compensate the plaintiff under this condition is to ensure that the expected loss function will not be held to a minimum. Consequently, under both our analysis and the alternative liability theory of *Summers*, what matters is that only one person caused the injury and that this person was one of the defendants. Had the two defendant hunters come from unrelated hunting parties, the analysis would be identical. That our knowledge of the event is frustratingly incomplete means that we must make our best guess. As we have seen, the maximum likelihood guess—the one that satisfies the preponderance-of-the-evidence requirement, properly understood—is to hold at least one negligent hunter liable.

One might go one step further and suggest that the cost be apportioned between the careless hunters in accordance with the expected value rule. This refinement is exactly the innovation introduced in *Sindell*, which is why I have characterized *Sindell* as a mutated progeny of *Summers*. Our analysis neither requires nor precludes this. The maximum likelihood solution entails no bias in this type of case. There are no comprehensive class actions or repeated suits against the same defendants with the same recurring probabilities. Those who are plaintiffs and defendants as well as the probabilities pertaining to each defendant will vary across a spectrum of hunting accident cases. At the same time, the mathematical degeneracy resulting from the fact that $p_1 = p_2$ means that in *Summers* itself apportionment according to expected value fulfills the objective of reducing expected losses as well as (but no better than) any other method of contribution or apportionment. One may favor dividing damages according to the probabilties p_1 and p_2, but not on the basis of the logic presented here.

63. The court also relied on the more dubious proposition "[o]rdinarily defendants are in a far better position to offer evidence to determine which one caused the injury." 33 Cal. 2d 80, 86 (1948). As the California court recognized in *Sindell*, however, the principal concern of *Summers* is that "if one [defendant] can escape the other may also and plaintiff is remediless." 199 P.2d 1 (1948) at 4.

64. See, e.g., Market Share Liability, *supra* note 11, at 672.

65. See text accompanying note 51 *supra*.

C. *Michie v. Great Lakes Steel Division*

For a final illustration of the limitations on the usefulness of the maximum likelihood interpretation of the preponderance-of-the-evidence standard, we turn to a noted air pollution case, *Michie v. Great Lakes Steel Division.*[66] Thirty-seven persons living in Canada filed a federal diversity action, complaining that discharges from seven nearby plants in the United States operated by three corporations created a nuisance that damaged them and their property. They did not allege concerted action. The district court, construing Michigan law, denied the corporations' motion to dismiss. On interlocutory appeal, the Court of Appeals for the Sixth Circuit affirmed. It reasoned that under the developing law in Michigan, either the alleged injury is not theoretically divisible, or it is divisible but there is no feasible way to determine how much of the injury each defendant produced. Either way, the court surmised, Michigan courts would impose joint and several liability to avoid the "manifest unfairness in 'putting on the injured party the impossible burden of proving the specific shares of harm done by each.'"[67]

What does our analysis reveal about how this aspect of the case should be handled? The answer depends on whether the injury resulted from the conduct of exactly one defendant. We could say this about the injuries in each of the cases examined thus far.[68] If one company actually caused all the damages here, then employing certain meteorological and physical assumptions we would use the maximum likelihood rule to pick out the major polluter as the liable party, and we would pause only to see whether an expected value rule would be appropriate to avoid serious bias.

In *Michie,* however, it seems more likely that the quantum of damage resulted from the sum of the emissions of the seven factories. For example, had the total pollution from the factories been less, the market value of plaintiffs' properties might have been higher.[69] If so, the maximum

66. 495 F.2d 213 (6th Cir. 1974).

67. *Id.* at 216, *quoting* Maddux v. Donaldson, 362 Mich. 425, 108 N.W.2d 33 (1961).

68. See text accompanying notes 76–77 *infra.*

69. This is not to say that the damage from pollution is necessarily a continuous function of the quantity of the pollutants. On the contrary, if a certain threshold amount is required before a type of injury occurs, the cost function will be discontinuous. See, e.g., Bruce A. Ackerman, Susan Rose Ackerman, & Dale W. Henderson, The Uncertain Search for Environmental Quality: The Costs and Benefits of Controlling Pollution Along the Delaware River, 121 U. Pa. L. Rev. 1225 (1973). Where discontinuities exist, it may be possible to find that some defendants are "but for" causes. Had they not contributed, the threshold would not have been reached and the damage would not have occurred. There is a problem, of course, in deciding which defendants come within this category. If some of the defendants begin polluting earlier and have a prior right to pollute so that their conduct is not tortious, then the polluter whose emissions pushed the total above the threshold could be held liable (in the amount the cost curve jumps). This attention to marginal costs in apportioning damages in some concurrent cause cases seems promising, but the concept plainly needs more development. See Donald Wittman, Optimal Pricing of Sequential Inputs: Last Clear Chance, Mitigation of Damages, and Related Doctrines in the Law, 10 J. Legal Stud. 65 (1981).

likelihood rule does not apply as among the defendants. It is inapposite because all three defendants caused damages. It is therefore pointless to ask which *one* of the three defendants caused the total damages; yet that is the question that our appeal to statistical decision theory was intended to help answer.[70]

Of course, probabilistic reasoning is not irrelevant to the issues in *Michie*. The maximum likelihood rule still applies (in the form of the $p > \frac{1}{2}$ rule) as between each plaintiff and the defendants as a group. A finder of fact must evaluate the evidence at trial under this form of the preponderance-of-the-evidence standard to decide whether the aggregate emissions damaged each plaintiff. Moreover, a court or jury could try to disentangle each company's contribution to the fallout by treating diffusion and convective mixing as sufficient to randomize all the plants' emissions before they reached the plaintiffs, by examining the locations of each plant vis-à-vis each plaintiff, and by estimating the cost imposed by each plant's discharge. Suggestions for "causal apportionment,"[71] "culpability shares,"[72] and the like[73] are not lacking. There are many subtleties here,[74] but the key point is that these matters are beyond the ken of the mathematical analysis I have expounded. That analysis is essentially parasitic. It attaches itself to the governing substantive liability rule, which is exactly what one would expect of an evidentiary rule designed to guide decisions as to whether a plaintiff has proved the existence of circumstances that, if present, would generate liability.

V. Conclusion

This article has touched upon a potpourri of issues—the logical underpinnings of the preponderance-of-the-evidence standard, the treatment of justifiably naked statistical evidence, and multiple causation in tort cases. The analysis has been single-minded but rich enough to produce a lengthy

70. See note 50 *supra*.
71. Rizzo & Arnold, *supra* note 17.
72. Refining Market Share Liability, *supra* note 11.
73. Robinson, *supra* note 11.
74. Consider, e.g., Rizzo and Arnold's proposal to apportion damages among "simultaneous causes" according to a particular function of certain probabilities. Rizzo & Arnold, *supra* note 17, at 1410–11, 1415. When the causes act "simultaneously," they advocate dividing the aggregate damages in proportion to the probability that each defendant's conduct, acting alone, would have caused this amount of damage. When the causes interact, they offer a formula for measuring the "synergistic" contribution and dividing it equally among the defendants. There are serious difficulties with their formula (see David Kaye & Mikel Aickin, A Comment on a Proposed "Economic Method" of "Causal Apportionment" (1982) (unpublished article manuscript)), and there is reason to question the ability of "economic theory" to allocate jointly caused damages without resort to what are basically accounting conventions. See Armen Alchain & William R. Allen, Exchange and Production: Competition, Coordination, and Control 256 (2d ed. Belmont, Cal.: Wadsworth Publishing Co., 1977) (impossibility of apportioning the cost of a common input to two products).

argument. It may be well to recapitulate its essential points. Some elementary concepts of statistical decision theory were used to cope with some cases that seemed problematical under the preponderance-of-the-evidence standard. These cases all involved justifiably naked statistical evidence (or something quite close to it) and a variety of candidates for the role of the single culpable cause. From the standpoint of decision theory—and the law—the problem is to come to the "best" decision as to which actor or natural force was responsible. Because of limitations in the evidence at trial, we were obliged to speak of the probability p_o that the plaintiff was responsible and the probabilities p_i associated with the other possible causes. Using these probabilities, we introduced the concept of an expected loss function, and we used one such function to discern the "best" decision rule in this situation. Specifically, we proved that the optimal decision rule is the "maximum likelihood" rule that selects the "most probable" cause (or causes). If this cause is such that liability does not attach, as with a "naturally occurring" cancer, a plaintiff who assumed the risk, or a legally immune defendant, then we argued that plaintiff should bear the costs of his injury. On the other hand, if the most likely cause is a legally responsible defendant, then we insisted that the defendant be fully liable.[75] This, we suggested, best implemented the function of the preponderance-of-the-evidence standard, and we criticized the *Sindell* court for assuming, in a case involving more than two possible causes, that this standard demanded a showing that an individual defendant was more probably than not responsible for the plaintiff's condition.

There was, however, a major qualification to these conclusions. We indicated that in situations where the probabilities never changed from case to case, the maximum likelihood approach would err systematically to the disadvantage of one person or group.[76] To avoid such bias, we advo-

75. If there are several equally likely causes, as in *Summers v. Tice*, the maximum likelihood rule leaves us indifferent as to how to allocate the damages among these causes.

76. The cases that seemed suitable candidates for the expected value rule involved the real possibility of repeated recovery from the same defendant. For example, under the maximum likelihood rule the pharmaceutical house that marketed the largest quantity of DES in California could be held liable for every DES-caused injury in California. The argument for the expected value approach also can apply when distinct defendants are implicated in different cases, yet certain probabilities remain fixed from one case to the next. Consider the scenario suggested by Glen Robinson: "Suppose [plaintiff] is exposed to carcinogen A that . . . creates a 20% probability of cancer. Carcinogen B enhances the risk of cancer by 10% (given a state of the world, which now includes A, the probability of cancer is now 30%). . . . Is it not possible that carcinogen B might *never* (or hardly ever) be the 'most likely' cause of cancer, albeit still a 'culpable' (unreasonable) contribution to the risk of cancer? Should we not therefore be concerned about the lost deterrence?" Letter from Glen O. Robinson to David Kaye, Feb. 25, 1982. The analysis developed in this article will apply if either A or B, but not both, caused the plaintiff's cancer. (If a single tumor could have resulted from the simultaneous action of the two carcinogens, the mathematical proofs are inapposite, and substantive doctrines of contribution must be considered.) If the risk due to A is independent of the risk due to

cated assigning expected damages to each potentially liable party. On this basis, we defended the most important facet of the *Sindell* case.

Finally, we turned to cases of true multiple causation primarily to make it clear that any use of probabilities to apportion damages had to rest on other principles. In every case to which we applied our analysis, only one defendant caused plaintiff's injury. In *Summers,* only one hunter fired the shot that wounded the plaintiff's eye. In *Sindell,* it is plausible to think that only one firm produced the particular DES that injured each individual plaintiff. In the taxicab hypothetical only one driver was at fault. And in the phenoxy acids hypothetical, we assumed that only those stomach cancers linked in the "but for" sense to the workplace were within the scope of workers' compensation. In all these cases, we saw that the maximum likelihood, or "most probable defendant" rule provided the best method for matching the injury with the true cause, but we also realized that in *Sindell* and the phenoxy acids case, the guess least likely to err would result in biased errors even in the long run.[77]

In sum, the recommended approach to the class of cases studied here can be cast as a two-fold injury. The court should ascertain whether the case at bar is of the type for which the maximum likelihood rule would achieve probable accuracy only at the cost of virtually certain bias. If so, it should apply rules of contribution or apportionment framed to assign expected damages to the liable parties. If, on the other hand, the case does not raise any serious, long-run bias problem, the preponderance-of-the-evidence standard should apply. The judge or jury should hold the single most likely defendant fully liable.[78]

Instances of naked statistical evidence represent hard cases for the preponderance-of-the-evidence standard, but I have attempted to show that even these cases are not inevitably beyond its reach and that the mathematical theory of probability can guide us in implementing this eviden-

---

B, then the maximum likelihood rule does make A liable (since A had a greater chance than the next most likely contender, B, of producing the cancer). If this is a recurring situation—if reasonable victims never confront the risk from B in the absence of that created by A—so that producers of B never would be found liable, then the maximum likelihood rule would yield biased results and "lost deterrence." This much follows from the fact that the probabilities associated with A and B are presumed to be fixed across a wide range of cases.

At the same time, we might hesitate before moving to an expected value rule in cases like these. In light of the vast number of carcinogens, manufacturers, and activities in which people engage, the cost of trying to apply expected value liability through the system of private tort litigation could well be prohibitive. Further discussion of the broad-based use of expected value liability can be found in Robinson, *supra* note 11.

77. As to *Sindell,* we also questioned the need for individualized matching in the first place.

78. Again, in cases of "ties" among defendants, other doctrines or theories about contribution and joint and several liability must be consulted.

tiary standard. I must confess that my treatment of these cases rests on certain assumptions, and I would not wish these to be obscured or buried. One such assumption is that the substantive law seeks to tailor the damages a culpable party must pay to the magnitude of the injury he has in fact caused and that the evidentiary standard should implement the substantive liability rules with a minimum of error or bias.[79] Another is that in the absence of any long-run bias, the law should be insensitive to the direction of errors. It is neither better nor worse for one defendant to pay damages that he would not be assessed if perfect knowledge of the facts were available than it is for a plaintiff or any other defendant to incur these costs. These sorts of value judgments are implicit in the mathematics. Although I have suggested that these assumptions are plausible, it should be plain that the mathematical aspects of this article do not guarantee the correctness or wisdom of its recommendations. Nevertheless, the formal reasoning does permit us to trace the implications of the assumptions in a careful and revealing way. To the extent this process enables us to appreciate the nature of the preponderance-of-the-evidence standard and to recognize its limitations in certain cases involving naked statistical evidence and multiple causes, the exercise will have been worth the effort.

79. In the situations of potential "bias," as I have defined them, one can say that the expected value approach reduces one sort of "error," since it imposes correctly estimated aggregate costs on the culpable parties. In addition, in a few such situations, the expected value approach is error minimizing, even as that term is used here. See text accompanying notes 53 and 59 *supra*.

[15]

ELSEVIER

The Burden of Proof in Civil Litigation: A Simple Model of Mechanism Design

CHRIS WILLIAM SANCHIRICO

Columbia University, Economics Department and School of Law
E-mail: cs282@columbia.edu

The existing literature on the burden of proof has sought the rule's reason for existence solely within the court's problem of decision making under uncertainty. Although this search has yielded many insights, it has been less successful in providing a compelling explanation for why uncertainty in the court's final assessment should act to the detriment of one party rather than the other. By viewing the problem as one of mechanism design, this paper provides one explanation for the asymmetry. A rule resembling the burden of proof emerges from the optimal design of a system of fact-finding tribunals in the presence of: (i) limited resources for the resolution of private disputes; and (ii) asymmetric information—as between the parties and the court—about the strength of cases, before the court expends the resources necessary for a hearing. The paper shows that if the objective in designing a trial court system is the accuracy of recovery granted, the "value" of having heard a case will depend in part on the certainty with which the court makes its final award. An optimally designed court system will then effectively filter out "less valuable" cases by precommitting to a recovery *policy* in which plaintiffs recover nothing unless they prove their cases with a threshold degree of certainty.

I. Introduction

Few principles of law are as well settled as that which says that the plaintiff, more generally the moving party, shall have the burden of proving her claim with a "preponderance of the evidence."[1] Yet few principles have inspired as many differing explanations and interpretations by legal and legal-economic commentators alike.

I would like to thank the Center for the Study of Law, Economics, and Public Policy at Yale Law School as well as Yale Law School's Career Options Assistance Program for financial assistance. I have benefited from helpful conversations with Chung Tae Yeong, David Pearce, Daniel Rubinfeld, and Andrew Weiss. Special thanks go to Susan Rose-Ackerman for her advice and encouragement.

[1]It is traditional to distinguish two types of burdens of proof in civil litigation: a burden of production and a burden of persuasion. In this paper, I consider only the latter concept, which is often referred to simply as the "burden of proof." [See Hay and Spier (1997) for an analysis of the burden of production as a coordinating device.] It is also worth emphasizing that the plaintiff does not *always* have this burden, as when the defendant must prove the plaintiff's

International Review of Law and Economics 17:431–447, 1997

655 Avenue of the Americas, New York, NY 10010

0144-8188/97/$17.00
PII S0144-8188(97)00020-3

To date, most of the economic analysis of the burden of proof has attempted to make sense of the rule in the context of the theory of decision making under uncertainty—in particular, within a Bayesian framework in which the court begins with prior beliefs about the veracity of relevant factual assertions and then updates these beliefs in Bayesian fashion upon hearing the evidence placed before it.[2] But the burden of proof is difficult to find within this framework. If we assert that it instructs the court to rule against the burdened party when the court is in "equipoise"—when its updated beliefs put exactly probability 0.5 on the truth of the assertion—then we have relegated the rule to a rare coincidence. If, on the other hand, we assert that the rule requires the court to accept the factual assertion only when its updated beliefs exceed some threshold *above* 0.5, then we save the rule from irrelevance, but beg even more ardently the question of why we should so favor one party over the other—why, for instance, we should feel less comfortable overcompensating plaintiffs than leaving legal wrongs "unrighted."

The premise of this paper is that the theory of decision making under uncertainty, by itself, does not and cannot provide a satisfactory explanation of what the burden of proof is or is supposed to be; instead the burden of proof must be understood in the context of mechanism design and asymmetric information. Under the present system of civil litigation, potential plaintiffs are vested with the power to set in motion a costly process of litigation, all of whose costs are not in the first instance their own. If this were the entire system, society would continually find itself spending more to resolve disputes than is warranted by the disputes themselves. One could internalize the full social cost to plaintiff by simply charging her for all expended resources. But this would conflict with the immediate object of the system: To award "proper" recovery to the plaintiff, which, however defined, must be net of her costs. On the other hand, if the court system knew beforehand which cases would be worth the resources necessary to resolve them, it could simply refuse to take those that were not. The problem is that the court does not find out the worth of a case until after society has paid to hear it. The solution, I will argue, is to announce to all potential plaintiffs that only those cases that *turn out to have been* worth hearing will receive any recovery. Then potential plaintiffs, who have superior information about the stakes and solidity of their claims, will self-select, and, on average, only those cases worth hearing will make their way to court.

The link between this rule and a burden rule based on uncertainty in the court's final assessment comes through the determination of which cases are worth hearing. For a trial court, concerned primarily with the accurate application of existing law, the value of having adjudicated a case will turn in part, I will argue, on the court's confidence that its ruling was the right one. The court's announced recovery policy will then be to award nothing to the plaintiff unless she proves her case with a threshold "degree of certainty" (defined within). Thus, as with the actual burden of proof, recovery under this rule will depend not only on the court's best estimate of the amount that the plaintiff should be

contributory negligence in a tort. There seems, however, to be general agreement among legal scholars that the plaintiff *usually* bears the burden and that, whoever bears the burden, so bearing means having to prove one's case with a "preponderance of the evidence." Finally, note that the burden (on the prosecution) in criminal cases—the "reasonable doubt standard"—is universally regarded as more difficult to bear. In this paper, I consider only civil litigation. [Rubinfeld and Sappington (1987) consider optimal adjustment of the criminal burden.] Finally, I ignore the fact that rebuttable presumptions may change the placement of the burden. For a general review, see James, Hazard, and Leubsdorf (1992), pp. 337 *et. seq.* and Lempert and Saltzburg (1983), pp. 792 *et seq.*

[2]See Jenkins and Rehnquist (1986) for examples of the Bayesian approach to litigation.

awarded, but also on the certainty with which the court makes that estimation. Moreover, the optimal recovery policy will have the same threshold structure evident in the actual rule: Roughly, if we fix the expected value of proper recovery (a random variable whose distribution is induced by the court's posterior beliefs) and progressively decrease its variance, the optimal recovery policy jumps from zero up to that expected value as the variance crosses the specified threshold. Thereafter, recovery remains fixed at that expected value regardless of the degree to which the threshold exceeds variance. On the other hand, unlike the manner in which the actual burden of proof seems to be applied in practice, the optimal threshold for any given class of cases increases with the cost of litigation and/or settlement and decreases with the expected value of proper recovery.

In Section II, I catalogue and analyze existing attempts to make sense of the burden of proof solely in the context of decision making under uncertainty. Readers familiar with this literature will want to skip first to Section III, which contains the basic model. In Section IV, I add the possibility that parties may bargain before trial. Concluding remarks appear in Section V.

II. Attempts to Find the Burden of Proof in The Theory of Decision Making Under Uncertainty

Ties Go to the Defendant

The most common interpretation of the burden of proof portrays it as a tie-breaker rule. This is, for example, the interpretation adopted in James, Hazard, and Leubsdorf (1992) and Lempert and Saltzburg (1983). In contrast to its near ubiquitous acceptance, however, the tie-breaker interpretation has a curious and unsettling property: As soon as one tries to formalize it, it disappears. As noted, the odds that the court's updated probability will land exactly on the knife edge of 0.5 are effectively nil. And because this point concerns how priors are updated on the basis of evidence, it will hold even if there are legal reasons to set the *unconditional* prior probability at 0.5.

The Raised Threshold

One way to save the burden of proof from the irrelevance of coincidence—and perhaps what those who propose the tie-breaker rule really have in mind—is to interpret the rule to mean that the court must be convinced that an assertion is true with some probability greater than a threshold $\bar{P}$, where $\bar{P} > 0.5$. But whereas increasing $\bar{P}$ above 0.5 may give some operational bite to the preponderance standard, it leaves unanswered the question of why we should favor the defendant in civil cases. As Posner (1973) remarks, there seems to be no *a priori* reason for favoring erroneous exoneration over erroneous liability.

Biased Prior

Cooter and Ulen (1988) suggest that the burden of proof means that the court should bias its *prior* in favor of the defendant. The analysis of this interpretation depends on what it means to bias a prior. One possibility is that *any* shift in probability weight that causes the unconditional (i.e., prior) probability of the truth of the factual assertion to decrease is a proper bias. But biasing the prior in this manner seems somewhat arbitrary, for it implies nothing about even the direction of change in the *posterior* for any given presentation of evidence. It is, for example, possible to decrease the uncon-

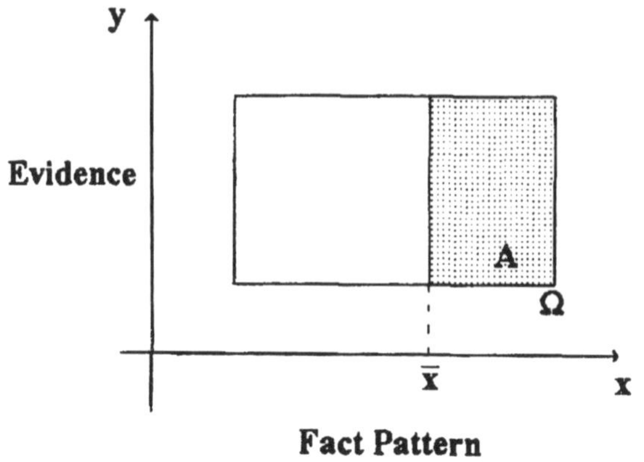

FIG. 1. The fact finder's problem.

ditional probability of the factual assertion while *increasing* the posterior after all but one possible presentation of evidence.

An alternative view is that the prior should be biased in such a way that affects all conditional probabilities "uniformly." But in this case, the biased prior rule is effectively equivalent to the raised threshold rule discussed above. More precisely, for any threshold level $\bar{P}$, we can find a "biased prior" such that for all evidence, the decision made under the new prior with the threshold level set at $P = \frac{1}{2}$ is the same as the decision made under the unbiased prior with threshold level $\bar{P}$.

Confidence Levels

Cohen (1985) views the burden of proof in terms of confidence intervals, mainstays in the tool kit of classical statistics. But though Cohen takes pains to explain the confidence interval in the context of classical statistics, he is less clear about how one would apply the notion to the generic problem of legal fact-finding.[3] One attempt to do so is illustrated in Figure 1, which identifies the set of conceivable pairs of fact patterns x and bodies of evidence y with a closed (two-dimensional) interval in the Cartesian plane. In this graph the factual assertion A—a subset of the state space—is true only at those states (x, y) for which x lies above a particular value[4] $\bar{x}$.

[3]In his general discussion Cohen seems to indicate that the fact-finder's goal is to learn about the true *probability* that the factual assertion is correct, rather than *whether* the assertion is correct. This is a direct—perhaps too direct—analogy to the canonical statistical problem of estimating the underlying probability of success (e.g., the probability of heads) in a Bernoulli distribution (e.g., a possibly biased coin toss) through repeated random sampling. To be sure, Cohen does include a hypothetical contract dispute. But rather than illustrating how confidence intervals fit into the typical fact-finding problem, the example merely embeds a typical *statistical* problem—estimation of the Bernoulli success probability—into a somewhat uncommon legal setting. In Cohen's example, the defendant retailer avers some probability that a product shipped to the plaintiff—though never received—was merchantable under the U.C.C. The mail-order contract was F.O.B., and the plaintiff, not challenging this fact, does not sue for breach. The defendant makes her case based on the random sample she obtained when testing the shipment from her wholesaler in which the plaintiff's particular product was contained.

[4]The correspondence between this problem and the canonical statistical problem of determining confidence intervals in estimating the mean of normal distribution with known variance are as follows: x, the fact pattern in the fact-finder's problem, corresponds to the mean of the normal distribution; y, the evidence in the fact-finder's problem,

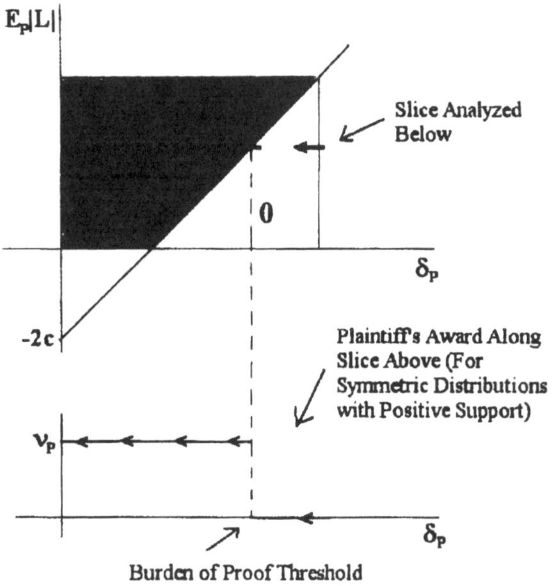

FIG. 2. The structure of the optimal policy. Note: For symmetric distributions with positive support, $E_P|L| = v_P$.

The fact finder begins with prior beliefs over the state space that induce a conditional probability measure on fact patterns x for every value of evidence presented y. Just as fixing y induces a distribution on x, fixing x induces a distribution on y. Moreover, any distribution on y induces a distribution on any function of y. A 95% (for example) *confidence interval* is any pair of functions of y, $U(y)$ and $L(y)$, with the property that for all x, the probability that both $U(y) > x$ and $L(y) < x$ is 95%.

One particular type of confidence interval, the one used by Cohen, fixes $U(y)$ at the maximal value for x, for all y. Placed in this context, Cohen's burden of proof stipulates that we accept the fact A as *legally* true if and only if the observed value l of the lower bound $L(y)$ exceeds $\bar{x}$.[5]

The first problem with applying *any* sort of confidence intervals to the legal fact-finder's problem is that none may exist. Whether we can find functions $U(y)$ and $L(y)$ with the property that the probability of $L(y) < x < U(y)$ is 95% (or any fixed percentage) *across all* x, is by no means clear. The difficulty is that these functions of y must be chosen uniformly over all x. In contrast, the problems in statistics to which confidence intervals are applied have very special structures that guarantee the existence of such intervals.

But even if we impose additional structure on the problem sufficient to guarantee the

---

corresponds to the random sample generated from the normal distribution y; the probability of y conditional on any given x corresponds to the sample distribution for a fixed mean; and finally, the fact-finder's prior beliefs over pairs (x, y) and the probability of x for any given y correspond to the nothing in the classical statistical framework, but to the prior and posterior (on x), respectively, in the Bayesian statistical framework.

[5] Cohen (1985), p. 403.

existence of the confidence interval, a larger, more significant problem of interpretation remains. The problem goes to the heart of the often heard criticism that the common mechanical techniques of classical statistics lack any theoretical justification. Classical statisticians will say that after learning a particular y and calculating the corresponding values $u = U(y)$ and $l = L(y)$, we know that the true fact pattern x lies in the interval (l, u) "with 95% confidence." Whatever "confidence" means here, it does *not* mean "probability"—it is *not* correct to say that there is a 95% chance that the true fact pattern x lies in the interval (l, u). To talk about the *probability* that x lies in any particular range, we have to view x probabilistically, an outlook that classical statistics does not admit. And even if we shift to what is referred to as the "Bayesian" viewpoint and posit prior beliefs on (x, y) updated after revelation of y, it is still not generally true that, according to our posterior belief on x, x will lie in the interval (l, u) with probability 0.95. Our posterior on x, and thus our posterior belief that x lies in (l, u) depends on both the structure of the fact-finder's prior and the particular y that has been observed. All we *can* say is that, *ex ante* revelation of y, there was a 95% chance that the true value of x would lie between whatever values of $U(y)$ and $L(y)$ were revealed. *Ex post* revelation of the evidence, y, the confidence interval has no particular interpretation.[6]

Let us take yet another step and suppose hypothetically that the fact-finder's problem has a structure sufficiently specialized to guarantee both that 95% confidence intervals exist and that they can be interpreted as one is tempted to interpret them: with the word "probability" substituted for the word "confidence."[7] Indeed, let us make the even stronger assumption that it is possible to construct such "interpretable" confidence intervals with the restriction that $U(y)$ be set constant at the maximal value taken by x. We would then know, on observing y and subsequently calculating $l = L(y)$, that x was greater than l with probability 0.95. Cohen's burden of proof stipulates that we find A to be true if and only if l falls above the threshold $\bar{x}$. With our hypothetically existent, hypothetically interpretable confidence interval, this reduces to nothing more than the rule that we find A true only in the case that its posterior probability is at least 0.95. And this is precisely the same as raising (or lowering) the threshold probability to the confidence coefficient.

Summary

Reflecting back on the four existing interpretations of the burden of proof, we see that each attempts to find the burden of proof solely within the theory of decision making under uncertainty; that each at its best reduces to the second, "raised threshold" interpretation; and that none provides an explanation for *why* the threshold should be so raised to favor one party over the other.

III. The Basic Model

In the model presented in this section, the burden of proof is derived from the court's optimization problem. The interpretation of the burden presented here, then, comes part and parcel with its justification. Furthermore, the structure that emerges does not

[6]See, e.g., Degroot, p. 398, *et seq.*

[7]There *are* results in statistics that give sufficient conditions on the structure of the problem for when confidence intervals, presuming they exist, *may* be interpreted in the probabilistic sense. See, e.g., Degroot, p. 398, *et seq.*

resemble a raised threshold, but instead is keyed to dispersion in the court's beliefs after hearing the evidence, a statistic that rarely appears in straight Bayesian analysis, but seems more in line with casual empiricism about the burden's true operation.

Our task is to design a *trial* court system, that is to say a system of fact-finding tribunals. We have already set "the law" according to principles such as fairness and efficiency. This law tells us how much a plaintiff should recover from a defendant as a function of all the relevant factual information surrounding the case.[8] The problem we face in designing our trial court system is that we will not know, in any particular dispute, what these facts are.[9] As a result, we want to design a system whereby we can learn more about the fact pattern before deciding how much, if anything, the plaintiff should recover.

In designing this system we must be cognizant of its opportunity cost. Resources used for the trial court system are resources that are not used for schools, national defense, or even the legislative process, whereby better law might be designed. We therefore face a fundamental trade-off in designing our trial court system: We must choose between, on the one hand, effectively rewarding no recovery to the plaintiff and using the unspent resources elsewhere and, on the other hand, spending the resources necessary to hear the case in the hope that the more informed decision we make by virtue of the hearing will be sufficiently "better" than awarding nothing.

Though it is difficult to make precise statements about the benefit to society of awarding any particular level of recovery, it is easy to construct examples where *not* hearing the case at all seems in retrospect like the best alternative. For example, suppose that a $100,000 hearing determines that with Probability 1, the defendant should pay the plaintiff $1. In retrospect, we probably would have been better off not hearing the case in the first place: We would have saved $100,000 at the cost of a $1 error in recovery. Whatever we take to be the societal value of the case—the $1 in damages itself or the slightly more precise alignment of defendants' incentives —it hardly seems worth the expense.

An Objective Function for the Court System and the Induced Value of Hearing Cases

To make more interesting statements about this trade-off, we must commit to some measure of the benefits of awarding a given level of recovery. I start with the much simpler case in which the court knows the true fact pattern. Then I extend the analysis to the situation where it is unsure.

Suppose we knew for certain that the fact pattern in a given dispute was $\omega \in \Omega$, where Ω, the sample space of our uncertainty, is the set of all possible fact patterns. It seems natural in this case that we would want our *trial* court to award the *proper recovery* specified by law for that particular fact pattern. Call this amount $L(\omega)$ and view L as a random variable on Ω. By convention, proper recovery here is the gross payment that should be made to plaintiff. If the payment net of the plaintiff's costs is our real concern, this number can be translated upward to account for such costs.

Saying that we prefer to award proper recovery is the same as saying that awarding any amount greater than or less than $L(\omega)$ is worse than awarding $L(\omega)$ itself. In an important sense, then, we treat the two types of legal error symmetrically.

[8] I will proceed as if money damages were the only remedy.

[9] In reality trial courts do not always know what the law is either and thus face both legal and factual uncertainty. I am abstracting from legal uncertainty faced at the trial level.

One functional form that captures this symmetry, and turns out to be relatively easy to work with, is the negative absolute difference between proper and actual recovery, $-|L(\omega) - r|$, where r stands for actual recovery awarded, which is our choice variable. For consistency, r is the actual gross award, before plaintiff's costs are subtracted. Note that the absolute difference between gross proper recovery and gross actual recovery is the same as the difference between net proper recovery and net actual recovery.

The functional form we have chosen obviously attains a maximum at $r = L(\omega)$ and is monotonically increasing to the left of this value and monotonically decreasing to the right. In the remainder of this paper, I will take this function to be the court's payoff function over certain outcomes. An appendix shows that similar results hold for more general loss functions.[10] When the court is always certain of the true fact pattern, $\omega \in \Omega$, this function is its objective function in the (quite simple) mathematical programming problem in which it chooses optimal recovery. As usual, the *value* of the problem itself is the value of the objective function at its maximum, namely, 0.

More realistically, even after the court hears the case, it is still unsure of the true fact pattern. As in Bayesian decision theory, let us say that the court began the hearing with prior beliefs, P_0, about the true fact pattern and then updated these beliefs on hearing the evidence.[11] Now it wishes to maximize expected payoffs based on these updated beliefs. If its updated beliefs over the true $\omega \in \Omega$ are denoted by P, then it will choose r to maximize $-E_P|L(\omega) - r|$.

Letting F_P denote the cumulative distribution of L under P, let us make the following assumption.

ASSUMPTION 1: *F_P is continuous.*

Then by the intermediate value theorem, the distribution of L has a median, and this is the optimal amount of recovery[12]:

LEMMA 1: *r^* solves $\max_r - E_P|L(\omega) - r|$, if and only if $F_P(r^*) = \frac{1}{2}$.*

PROOF: *A standard result.*

To understand why the median is optimal for the absolute difference, consider increasing actual recovery by one unit from some starting point below the median. We move one unit away from all values of proper recovery below our starting point, and we move one unit toward all values above. Because we start below the median, more than half the probability weight is above our starting point, and so we increase expected accuracy on net. A symmetric argument applies to reducing actual recovery when we start above the median.

Therefore, the *value* of the problem, $\max_r - E_P|L(\omega) - r|$, is precisely $-E_P|L(\omega) -$

[10]Using squared rather than absolute error would lead to the same results as below with expected value substituted for the median and variance for "dispersion," δ. As illustrated in the Appendix, the essential results of the model obtain with more general objectives. The crucial, and generalizable, characteristic of the objective used in the body of the paper is that it is decreasing on either side of its global maximum. This creates a crude concavity in the court's value function, which, in turn, produces what is essentially risk aversion. This risk aversion is the reason that the court prefers cases with lower dispersion.

[11]Such a prior belief is a probability measure on Ω (with sigma algebra understood). This probability measure induces a distribution for the random variable L.

[12]The number x is *median* of the random variable X if $\Pr(X \geq x) = \Pr(X \leq x) = \frac{1}{2}$. A random variable may have no median or many media. A random variable has a median if its cumulative is continuous. If L has many media, all yield the same payoff. If L had no media, optimal recovery in this problem is the minimum value of l such that $\Pr(L \leq l) \geq \frac{1}{2}$.

$v_p|$. (This value is invariant to which median we choose, should there be more than one.) On the other hand, if the court had *not* taken the case, recovery would have been in effect zero, and the corresponding value would be $-E_P|L(\omega)|$. The difference between these two expressions, namely, $E_P|L(\omega)| - E_p|L(\omega) - v_p|$ is one measure of the *ex post benefit of having heard the case.*

With a little manipulation we can express this expected benefit in a more informative manner. Let $\bar{\mu}$ represent the *upper mean* of the random variable L; that is, the expected value of L conditional on its exceeding its median, v_P. In the usual notation, this is $E_P[L|L \geq v_p]$. Define the *lower mean* $\underline{\mu}$ in a similar manner, $E_P[L|L \leq v_p]$. The difference $\bar{\mu} - \underline{\mu}$ between the lower and upper mean is a measure of the "dispersion" of the random variable L. If the random variable is degenerate and takes only one value, then this difference is zero. If the random variable takes only two values with equal probability, this difference reduces to the difference between these two values. This difference is, as well, a measure of dispersion for more complex distributions. One can show, for example, that if the random variable is distributed normally, uniformly, or exponentially, then this difference is proportional to the standard deviation. For convenience, I will dub this statistic, $\bar{\mu} - \underline{\mu}$, the *dispersion* of the random variable L and denote it as δ. We may then write:

LEMMA 2: $E_P|L(\omega)| - E_p|L(\omega) - v_p| = E_P|L(\omega)| - \frac{1}{2}\delta.$

PROOF: *See Appendix.*

For the intuition behind this lemma, note that the second term in the *ex post* value of having heard the case is the expected difference between L and our best estimate of L, namely v_P. Our best estimate lies at the center of L's distribution. Thus this second term is the expected difference between L and its distribution's center, and this is the common form of a measure of dispersion. The lemma shows that this difference is in fact proportional to δ.

The implication of the lemma is that the value of having heard the case increases in the *ex post* expected absolute value L and decreases in the dispersion of the court's updated beliefs. Holding expected absolute value constant, then, the court prefers cases that leave it with "concentrated" beliefs to those that leave it with "diffuse" beliefs.

In determining whether the case was worth hearing, we would want to compare this measure $E_P|L(\omega)| - \frac{1}{2}\delta$ of expected benefit with the opportunity cost of the hearing. Of course, this measure of benefit need not be immediately comparable with our most natural measure of opportunity costs. But for simplicity let us suppose that opportunity cost, c, of the hearing is stated in units that do make it comparable.[13] Then, after having heard the case, we can make the following *ex post* judgment about whether doing so was a good idea: The case was worth hearing if and only if $E_P|L(\omega)| - \frac{1}{2}\delta$ turns out to exceed c.

Optimal Choice of Recovery Policy

If the court somehow knew what its updated beliefs, P, would be after the hearing, it could determine ahead of time which cases to hear and which to dismiss according to

[13]In what follows, I proceed as if the opportunity cost of the hearing were fixed and constant across all suits. This is merely a simplifying assumption. All that is necessary for the results is that the cost of the hearing is known beforehand to the plaintiff and revealed to the court sometime before recovery is granted. In the more general case, the court's recovery policy (see below) would vary with both P and c.

this comparison of costs and benefits. The problem, however, is that the court does not learn whether a case is worth "paying" to hear until after it has paid to hear it. The parties, however, do have much information about the value of their case even before the case is played out in court. The court's problem is, thus, characterized by an asymmetry of information.

Nevertheless, the court can get around this disadvantage, at least to some degree. The court *does* learn the value of the case before awarding recovery. It can, therefore, announce to all potential plaintiffs that if they bring a case to court that, in the end, was not worth hearing, according to the criterion we have laid out, then the plaintiff will receive little or no recovery. If the court sets this level below what it costs plaintiffs to bring their cases, and plaintiffs have a good idea of what the court will think after hearing all the evidence, then this policy will filter out plaintiffs whose cases are not worth hearing. From the court's perspective, the result will resemble the hypothetical just discussed, wherein the court knows beforehand the value of each case and accepts only those that meet its criterion (subject to the constraint that the plaintiff must be induced to file). The important point for our purposes is that the court's announcement to plaintiffs will bear a stark resemblance to the current burden of proof in civil cases.

Formally, suppose that the court faces a population of potential cases, each identified by the posterior belief, P, regarding legal recovery, L, that it will inspire in the court after the hearing. Let the probability measure Q on the set of all P represent the population composition of cases.

For simplicity suppose that before bringing their cases, plaintiffs know exactly what the court's posterior beliefs, P, will be. The court chooses not just recovery in each individual case, but a *recovery policy*, $r(P)$, for implementation by the trial court, mapping posterior beliefs onto a prescribed amount of recovery for the plaintiff. Plaintiffs also know this recovery policy and believe that it will be carried out by the court system. (The credibility of the policy is an important issue and is discussed below.) We also suppose that it costs plaintiffs $\pi > 0$ to bring suit. Why brackets, rather than parentheses [In its natural state, this cost lies with plaintiff; it can always be shifted via the recovery policy, $r(P)$.] Then a plaintiff who knows her case will inspire beliefs of P will file suit, if and only if $r(P) \geqslant \pi$.

The court, like a Stackelberg leader, knows this "reaction function" and takes it into account in setting its policy. The court's problem is therefore:

Choose $r(P)$ to maximize

$$\int_{r(P)\geqslant\pi} (-E_P|L(\omega) - r(P)| - c)\,dQ + \int_{r(P)<\pi} - E_P|L(\omega)|\,dQ \tag{1}$$

The first addend here accounts for all plaintiffs who would bring their cases to court under $r(P)$. The court's payoffs in such cases are the accuracy of its award less the costs of trial. The second addend accounts for plaintiffs who would not bring their case to court under $r(P)$. Here there are no court costs, and the award to the plaintiff is effectively zero. The payoff in this case, therefore, is solely the expected accuracy of awarding nothing.

Assuming that plaintiff's trial costs are less than the opportunity cost of the hearing to society (which presumably contain plaintiff's costs), we assume the following.

ASSUMPTION 2: $0 < \pi \leqslant c$.

We obtain

PROPOSITION 1: *The recovery policy*

$$r(P) = \begin{cases} v_p, & \text{if } \delta \leq 2E_p|L(\omega)| - 2c \\ 0, & \text{otherwise} \end{cases}$$

solves the court's problem (1).

PROOF: *See the Appendix for a formal proof. See the discussion below for intuition.*

Under this recovery policy, the court announces that it will decide all cases in two steps. First it will test whether, after hearing all the evidence, the dispersion in its beliefs falls below a threshold level. This threshold level of dispersion will not be uniform across all cases but will depend on the expected level of proper recovery. If this threshold is exceeded, no recovery (or at least some amount less than π) will be awarded. If, on the other hand, dispersion falls below this threshold, the plaintiff will receive recovery equal to the court's best estimate of what the law prescribes, namely, the median of L.

This recovery policy bears a strong resemblance to, and thus helps make sense of, the burden of proof in civil litigation. Under this optimal rule, it is *not* enough for the plaintiff to prove that expected proper recovery is positive. The plaintiff must also do so in such manner as to inspire in the court a level of confidence in its estimation, as measured by the dispersion in the court's posterior belief. Should the court have sufficient confidence, the plaintiff is awarded the median, regardless of whether the plaintiff exceeds that level of confidence by a wide margin or not.

To understand the intuition behind Proposition 1, consider three cases. Suppose first that the case is not worth hearing *ex post*. Then by Lemma 2, $\delta > 2E_p|L(\omega)| - 2c$. And so by the court's recovery policy, $r(P) = 0$. Because $\pi > 0$, no such plaintiffs file, which is just what the court would want. Now consider the set of cases that are worth hearing *ex post* and divide these into two potential groups: those with $v_P \geq \pi$ and those with $v_P < \pi$. The first subgroup comes to court and receives v_P, which is just as the court would want it. What about the second? These are cases that the court would want to hear, but plaintiffs would not want to bring. The best the court can do in these cases, conditional on inducing the plaintiff to file, is to offer the plaintiff precisely π. As shown in the proof of the proposition, the assumption on the relative sizes of π and c guarantees that the expected loss from doing so always exceeds that from awarding the plaintiff nothing. Given positive trial costs, the latter is the better choice, and this is precisely what the court's recovery policy produces. Putting these three cases together, we see that our proposed recovery policy maximizes the court's objective taking into account the reaction function of the plaintiff.

Note that the last case considered in the previous paragraph establishes that the plaintiff's incentives do bind in the court's problem. The court does not achieve the first best outcome: If it knew P it could ignore plaintiff's incentives and award recovery irrespective of whether it could induce plaintiff to arrive in court.

It is important to note that this optimal policy is not subgame perfect—and it is equally important to note that subgame perfection is not an appropriate restriction in this model. The court's policy is supported by the threat that the court will in certain circumstances take actions that are not, at the time they are made, in its own best interest. That is, after hearing a case, whatever the case's *ex post* value, the best policy for the court *from that point onward* is still to award median recovery. The cost of hearing the case is already sunken and thus not relevant to the court's current decision. The recovery rule described above will only work if the court can make a credible commitment not to give in and award median recovery in cases that turn out to be, in retrospect, not worth hearing. In the typical game theoretic model of individual or firm behavior, lack of subgame perfection is a fatal flaw. However, in a model of a court system governed by rules of procedure and precedent, threats by the court *system* to follow rules that *ex post* seem senseless for all parties *are* plausible. Indeed, constructing models wherein the parties' beliefs about the court are not shaped by subgame perfection seems the *more* realistic alternative.

IV. Incorporating Pre-Trial Bargaining

Although precise figures differ across studies, it is well accepted that a supermajority of civil suits never reach trial. How does this affect the foregoing analysis of the burden of proof? In this section I show that the optimal recovery policy with pretrial settlement still resembles the burden of proof. With settlement, however, the award for those cases that meet the burden is not median legal recovery, but rather, median recovery *plus* some function of the parties prospective trial costs. Moreover, the threshold level of dispersion is tied not to these trial costs, as in the previous section, but to the cost to society of the process of litigation, including filings, discovery, and settlement negotiations, up to but not including trial.

The simple litigation "game" in this model with pretrial negotiation has several steps. First, the court announces a (gross) recovery policy, $r(P)$, to all potential parties. Second, the plaintiff, knowing P and $r(P)$, decides whether to file suit. Third, the case enters settlement negotiations, which imposes costs of $\sigma_\pi > 0$ and $\sigma_\delta > 0$ on the plaintiff and the defendant, respectively. The cost to society of this settlement phase is $\sigma > 0$. (This may be as simple as the sum of the plaintiff's and the defendant's costs, or it may include additional non-private costs.) In this settlement phase, the defendant, who also knows P, $r(P)$, and π, makes a settlement offer s to the plaintiff. Fourth, the plaintiff decides whether to accept this offer. If so, the game is over and the defendant pays s to the plaintiff. If not, the plaintiff decides whether to take his case to trial. If so, the case enters the trial phase at a cost of $\pi > 0$, $\Delta > 0$, and $c > 0$ to the plaintiff, the defendant and society, respectively. In this phase, as before, the court hears the evidence in the case, updates its prior belief about the fact pattern from P_0 to P, and then orders the defendant to pay $r(P)$ to the plaintiff.

If we fix a recovery policy, $r(P)$, we can solve the resulting game of perfect information between the plaintiff and the defendant by backwards induction. Having filed a case and rejected a settlement offer, the plaintiff continues with the case if and only if $r(P) \geqslant \pi$. Therefore, the plaintiff accepts the defendant's settlement offer if and only if $s \geqslant \max(r(P) - \pi, 0)$.

It is then optimal for the defendant to offer $\max(r(P) - \pi, 0)$. For if, on the one hand, $r(P) - \pi < 0$, then the plaintiff will not bring the case to court anyway, even if $r(P) + \Delta > 0$, and so the defendant should offer $s = 0 = \max(r(P) - \pi, 0)$. If, on the other hand, $r(P) - \pi \geqslant 0$, then the plaintiff will bring the case to court and so the defendant stands to lose $r(P) + \Delta > 0$. The plaintiff will accept any offer above $r(P) - \pi < r(P) + \Delta$, and so the defendant should offer the smallest acceptable offer: $r(P) - \pi = \max(r(P) - \pi, 0)$.

Because the plaintiff knows that this is how settlement negotiations will proceed, she files suit, if and only if $s = \max(r(P) - \pi, 0) \geq \sigma_\pi$, or equivalently, if and only if $r(P) \geq \pi + \sigma_\pi$.

In sum, only cases that meet the condition $r(P) \geq \pi + \sigma_\pi$ are filed, and of these, the defendant ends up paying the plaintiff $r(P) - \pi$. The court's problem is then: Choose $r(P)$ to maximize

$$\int_{r(P)-\pi \geq \sigma_\pi} (-E_P|L(\omega) - (r(P) - \pi)| - \sigma)\,dQ + \int_{r(P)-\pi < \sigma_\pi} - E_P|L(\omega)|\,dQ \qquad (2)$$

We can view this problem as one of choosing $(r(P) - \pi)$ to maximize equation (2) and then adding π to the answer to get the optimal $r(P)$. (We need not add π for those cases where we have set recovery low enough to induce the plaintiff not to file suit). It is clear then that the problem (2) is of the same form as the problem in the previous section, with σ_π playing the role of π and σ playing the role of c. If we similarly assume

ASSUMPTION 3: $0 < \sigma_\pi \leq \sigma$.

Then we have already proven:

PROPOSITION 2: *The recovery policy*

$$r(P) = \begin{cases} v_P + \pi, & \text{if } \delta \leq 2E_p|L(\omega)| - 2\sigma \\ 0, & \text{otherwise} \end{cases}$$

solves the court's problem (2), with pretrial negotiation.

In this optimal policy, the court is still using its recovery policy to affect the plaintiff's incentive to file suit. But, because pretrial negotiation lowers the cost of "adjudication" broadly defined, the universe of cases that are worth adjudicating is larger. Accordingly, the threshold level of dispersion is lower—it is now keyed on settlement costs, σ, rather than the costs of the entire process from filing to judgment, c. On the other hand, the court is also still using its recovery policy to make awards to plaintiffs whose cases are worth adjudicating. But this less costly method of adjudication—settlement in the shadow of trial—has a biased outcome relative to what the court would award if it heard the case, namely, the median, v_P. This is because the plaintiff's trial costs mean that defendants need not offer full expected recovery to obtain acceptance. In particular, the *gross* payment by the defendant to the plaintiff will be $r(P) - \pi$, meaning that the net payment is $r(P) - \pi - \pi$. Therefore, the court must correct for this bias by awarding the plaintiff the median plus plaintiff's trial costs in gross. (Note also that grossing net proper recovery up to gross proper recovery L in this model means adding some function of plaintiff's and/or defendant's *settlement costs*, not trial costs.)

The model is robust to the structure of pretrial negotiations. If, for example, the plaintiff made the offer and the defendant decided whether to accept or reject, recovery, when granted at all, would correct for the resulting bias in favor of the plaintiff. We can also allow for a more fluid negotiation scheme and merely assume an independent probability distribution over the plaintiff's share of the surplus (which encompasses the case wherein the surplus is always split in some fixed proportion). Then the optimal recovery policy would correct for the expected bias of settlement outcomes. For example, if the plaintiff's share were uniformly distributed between 0 and 1, and the plaintiff's and the defendant's trial costs were equal, there would be no bias and no need for correction.

The model is also robust to allowing the court to condition recovery on the defendant's settlement offer, as in Rule 68. (Note again that the recovery can include fee shifting.) In this case, the defendant will offer $\min_s s{:}s \geqslant \max(r(P, s) - \pi, 0)$. If we assume that $r(P, s)$ is lower semi-continuous in s, then for every P we can find a solution $s(P)$ to $\min_s s{:}s \geqslant \max(r(P, s) - \pi, 0)$ and at that solution $s(P) = \max(r(P, s(P)) - \pi, 0)$. Defining $r(P) = r(P, s(P))$ we may proceed as above to find the optimal $r(P)$ and then set $r(P, s) = r(P, s(P))$ for all s. Hence, the court can not improve its objective by conditioning on defendant's settlement offer.

V. Conclusion

This paper has shown how a form of burden of proof—in particular, a rule by which no recovery is granted to plaintiffs unless dispersion in the court's posterior falls below a threshold level—is the optimal solution to the court's basic problem of balancing its desire to (1) award its best estimate of proper recovery and (2) create the proper incentives for plaintiffs in their decision of whether to sue. In the simple model presented here, such a policy allowed the court to achieve its (*ex ante*) first best outcome.

The model might be extended in several directions. First, a more general objective function for the court could be used—one that allowed for: (a) the asymmetric weighting of overcompensation versus undercompensation of plaintiffs and (b) non-linear (e.g., squared or square-rooted) error costs. Generalizing the model in this manner would allow it to encompass situations wherein efficient incentives for precaution or activity level (in the activity generating the legal claim) dictate the asymmetric and/or nonlinear treatment of litigation error. Second, a more general model would allow for the possibility that plaintiffs themselves are unsure of what the court's posterior will be (but are still more certain than the court itself before the hearing). Third, a more general model would incorporate a more realistic account of settlement negotiations, one that incorporates asymmetric information, for example, and thus allows for the possibility of some cases coming to court. Finally, a more general model would incorporate the endogenous choice of trial preparation effort.

Appendix 1: Proofs

Proof of Lemma 2:

$$E_p|L(\omega) - v_p| = \int_{-\infty}^{v_P} (v_P - L(\omega))\,dF_P + \int_{v_P}^{\infty} (L(\omega) - v_P)\,dF_P$$

$$= \int_{-\infty}^{v_P} v_p\,dF_P - \int_{v_P}^{\infty} v_p\,dF_P - \int_{-\infty}^{v_P} L(\omega)\,dF_P + \int_{v_P}^{\infty} L(\omega)\,dF_P$$

$$= v_p \int_{-\infty}^{v_P} dF_P - v_p \int_{v_P}^{\infty} dF_P - F_P(v_P)\,\frac{\int_{-\infty}^{v_P} L(\omega)\,dF_P}{F_P(v_P)} + F_P(v_P)\,\frac{\int_{v_P}^{\infty} L(\omega)\,dF_P}{F_P(v_P)}$$

$$= \frac{1}{2}\,v_p - \frac{1}{2}\,v_p - \frac{1}{2}\,\underline{\mu} + \frac{1}{2}\,\bar{\mu}$$

$$= \frac{1}{2}(\bar{\mu} - \underline{\mu}).$$

Proof of Proposition 1:

Define the function

$$\Phi(r, P) = \begin{cases} -E_P|L(\omega) - r| - c, & r \geq \pi \\ -E_p|L(\omega)|, & r < \pi \end{cases}.$$

The objective in problem (1) can be rewritten as:

$$\int \Phi(r(P), P)dQ.$$

Hence, it suffices to show that for all P, $r(P)$ maximizes $\Phi(r, P)$. To this end, first consider any P such that $\delta > 2E_p|L(\omega)| - 2c \Leftrightarrow E_P|L(\omega)| - \frac{1}{2}\delta < c$, so that $r(P) = 0$. By Lemma 2, then, $-E_P|L(\omega)| > -E_p|L(\omega) - v_p| - c$, and so, by Lemma 1, for all r, $-E_P|L(\omega)| > -E_p|L(\omega) - r| - c$. Therefore, $\Phi(r, P)$ achieves a maximum of $-E_p|L(\omega)|$ at any r with $r < \pi$; in particular, at $r(P) = 0$.

Now suppose that $\delta \leq 2E_p|L(\omega)| - 2c \Leftrightarrow E_P|L(\omega)| - \frac{1}{2}\delta \geq c$ and $v_P \geq \pi$. Then by Lemma 2, $-E_P|L(\omega)| \leq -E_p|L(\omega) - v_p| - c$ and because $v_P \geq \pi$, $\Phi(r, P)$ must attain its maximum, where $r \geq \pi$. By Lemma 1, this is at $v_P = r(P)$.

Finally suppose that $\delta \leq 2E_p|L(\omega)| - 2c \Leftrightarrow E_P|L(\omega)| - \frac{1}{2}\delta \geq c$ and $v_P < \pi$. Then the largest value attained by $\Phi(r, P)$, given $r \geq \pi$, is $-E_P|L(\omega) - \pi| - c$. The largest value attained by $\Phi(r, P)$, given $r < \pi$, is trivially $-E_P|L(\omega)|$. We see that:

$$\begin{aligned} -E_P|L(\omega)| - (-E_P|L(\omega) - \pi| - c) &= E_P|L(\omega) - \pi| - (E_P|L(\omega)| - c) \\ &\geq E_P|L(\omega) - \pi| - (E_P|L(\omega)| - \pi) \\ &\geq E_P|L(\omega) - \pi| - (E_P|L(\omega)| - |\pi|) \\ &\geq 0, \end{aligned}$$

where the last inequality is the "triangle inequality." Therefore, $\Phi(r, P)$ attains its maximum at any r with $r < \pi$, in particular, at $r(P) = 0$.

Appendix 2: More General Loss Functions and More Specific Probability Measures

The model presented in the main body of the paper assumes a specific loss function, but allows general probability measures P on actual loss. In Appendix 2 I simplify the probability measures on proper recovery L and consider more general loss functions. The object is to illustrate that the paper's characterization of the burden of proof is not dependent on the particular shape of the loss function I employ. In particular, I show that, for the simple case in which proper recovery may take one of two values, the *ex post* benefit of having heard the case (as defined above) decreases when we spread these two possible values in such a way that preserves the expected stake in the case. Thus, cases with more dispersion, in this sense, have less value, and again it is not enough to convince the court that the loss from doing nothing is significant in expectation. One must also inspire in the court a sufficiently tight estimate of proper recovery.

Suppose that proper recovery is either $\underline{L} \geq 0$ or $\bar{L} > \underline{L}$ with probability α and $1 - \alpha$, respectively. Let $\lambda(x)$ be the *loss function*, where $x = L - r$ is the difference between proper and actual recovery. [In the main text $\lambda(x) = |x|$.] For convenience, I assume that λ is continuously differentiable. Aside from this, I assume only that $\lambda'(x) < 0$ for $x < 0$ and $\lambda'(x) > 0$, for $x > 0$. Thus λ is minimized at $x = 0$, i.e., $L = r$. Even more, the farther L is from r, in either direction, the larger is λ.

The expected loss from awarding any given r is now $\alpha\lambda(\underline{L} - r) + (1 - \alpha)\lambda(\bar{L} - r)$. In particular, the expected loss from awarding nothing is $\alpha\lambda(\underline{L}) + (1 - \alpha)\lambda(\bar{L})$. As in the main model $\alpha\lambda(\underline{L}) + (1 - \alpha)\lambda(\bar{L})$ may be thought of as an estimate of the "stakes" in the case—these are now affected by our attitudes toward losses, as captured in λ.

The basic idea of the formal analysis is straightforward. The expected loss minimizing r^* is between $\underline{L}$ and $\bar{L}$. Thus, when we bring $\underline{L}$ and $\bar{L}$ closer together we decrease the distance from r^* to each.[14] Hence, we decrease the *expected* distance, and so the expected *loss* at our best estimate r^*, $\alpha\lambda(\underline{L} - r^*) + (1 - \alpha)\lambda(\bar{L} - r^*)$. In particular, if we bring $\underline{L}$ and $\bar{L}$ closer together in a manner that keeps the stakes $\alpha\lambda(\underline{L}) + (1 - \alpha)\lambda(\bar{L})$ constant, then we *increase* the *ex post* benefit of having heard the case, because—as in the main text—this is

$$[\alpha\lambda(\underline{L}) + (1 - \alpha)\lambda(\bar{L})] - [\alpha\lambda(\underline{L} - r^*) + (1 - \alpha)\lambda(\bar{L} - r^*)]. \tag{A1}$$

Formally, totally differentiating equation (A1) with respect to $\underline{L}$ and $\bar{L}$, subject to the constraint that $\alpha\lambda(\underline{L}) + (1 - \alpha)\lambda(\bar{L})$ remains constant, yields

$$-\underbrace{(1 - \alpha)\lambda'(\underline{L} - r^*)}_{-}d\underline{L} - \underbrace{\alpha\lambda'(\bar{L} - r^*}_{+}\left(-\frac{\alpha\lambda'(\underline{L})}{\underbrace{(1 - \alpha)\lambda'(\bar{L})}_{-}}\right)d\underline{L} > 0, \tag{A2}$$

where we have applied the implicit function theorem to substitute for $d\bar{L}$ and the envelope theorem to eliminate the derivatives of r^*. The sign on $-\alpha\lambda'(\underline{L})/(1 - \alpha)\lambda'(\bar{L})$ follows from our assumptions on λ and the fact that $\underline{L} \geq 0$, $\bar{L} > 0$.[15] The signs on $\lambda'(\underline{L} - r^*)$ and $\lambda'(\bar{L} - r^*)$ are obtained as follows. The first-order condition for the minimization of $\alpha\lambda(\underline{L} - r) + (1 - \alpha)\lambda(\bar{L} - r)$, choosing r, is $\alpha\lambda'(\underline{L} - r^*) = -(1 - \alpha)\lambda'(\bar{L} - r^*)$. Thus, the derivatives $\lambda'(\bar{L} - r^*)$ and $\lambda'(\underline{L} - r^*)$ have different signs. Given $\underline{L} - r^* < \bar{L} - r^*$ and our assumption about λ, it must be that $\lambda'(\underline{L} - r^*) \leq 0$ and $\lambda'(\bar{L} - r^*) \geq 0$.

Noting the overall sign of equation (A2), we see that the best we can do if we take the case increases as we increase $\underline{L}$ and simultaneously decrease $\bar{L}$ so as to preserve the stake in the case. All else the same, then, cases with tighter estimates of proper recovery have a higher *ex post* benefit of having been heard.

References

COHEN, N.B. (1985). Confidence in probability: Burdens of persuasion in a world of imperfect knowledge. *New York University Law Review* **60**:385.

---

[14] Of course, we may also change r. But this has a negligible effect on expected loss because we have chosen r to satisfy first-order conditions that imply that small changes from r^* have no effect on expected losses. This is the so-called "envelope theorem."

[15] If $\underline{L} < 0$ and $\bar{L} > 0$, no spreads preserve $\alpha\lambda(\underline{L}) + (1 - \alpha)\lambda(\bar{L})$. If both $\underline{L} \leq 0$, $\bar{L} \leq 0$, the sign is the same and all results continue to hold.

COOTER, R., AND ULEN, T. (1988). *Law and Economics*, Scott, Foresman and Company, Chicago. pp/ 499-501.

DE GROOT, M. (1986), *Probability and Statistics*, Addison-Wesley Publishing Company, Reading, Massachusetts, 2nd edition, pp. 398-401.

HAY, B.L., AND SPIER, K.E. (forthcoming Summer 1997). Burdens of proof in civil litigation: An economic perspective. 26 *Journal of Legal Studies*.

JAMES, F., HAZARD, G.C. AND LEUBSDORF, J. (1992). *Civil Procedure*, Little, Brown and Company, Boston, 4th edition), pp. 337-340.

JENKINS, M.C., AND REHNQUIST J.C. (Eds.) (1986). *Symposium: Probability and Inference in the Law of Evidence. Boston University Law Review* **66**(3, 4).

LEMPERT, R.O. AND SALZBURG, S.F. (1983). *A Modern Approach to Evidence*, 2nd edition, West Publishing, St. Paul, MN, Ch. 9.

POSNER, R.R. (1973). An economic approach to legal procedure and judicial administration. *Journal of Legal Studies* **2**:399.

RUBINFELD, D.L., AND SAPPINGTON, D.E.M. (1987). Efficient awards and standards of proof in judicial proceedings. *RAND Journal of Economics* **18**(2):308-315.

[16]

BURDENS OF PROOF IN CIVIL LITIGATION: AN ECONOMIC PERSPECTIVE

*BRUCE L. HAY and KATHRYN E. SPIER**

ABSTRACT

Burden of proof rules, which require a specified party to produce evidence on a contested issue, are central to the adversary system. In this article, we model burden of proof rules as a device for minimizing the costs of litigation. The central point to emerge from the model is that, properly assigned, a burden of proof rule economizes on the transmission of information to the court. We use the model to explain characteristic practices of courts in assigning the burden of proof.

I. INTRODUCTION

ADVERSARY systems of justice typically give the parties (not the judge) the task of adducing evidence on contested issues in litigation.[1] Such a policy immediately raises the problem of dividing that task between the parties. Who, as between plaintiff and defendant, should be given the job of producing evidence on a contested issue? *Burden of proof* rules are the device courts employ to address this problem. By giving a specified party the burden of proof on a given issue, the court tells that party that he must either come up with evidence supporting his position or suffer an adverse judgment on that issue.

In this article we develop an economic analysis of the assignment of burdens of proof in civil litigation. Our principal claim is that courts can use the burden of proof to limit the costs of resolving a dispute. More precisely, we argue that the burden of proof, by giving one party the task of producing evidence, *relieves* his opponent to some extent of that task—thereby saving expenditures that might otherwise be incurred by the opponent. Optimally used, the burden of proof may minimize the expenditures devoted to gather-

* Bruce L. Hay is Assistant Professor at Harvard Law School. Kathryn E. Spier is Associate Professor, Kellogg School of Management, Northwestern University. Earlier versions of this article were presented at workshops at Harvard, Chicago, Michigan, and Stanford. We thank Louis Kaplow, Steven Shavell, Bernard Wolfman, and the workshop participants for their comments.

[1] This is, as Wigmore observed, a characteristic feature of Anglo-American legal systems. See John H. Wigmore, 9 *Wigmore on Evidence* 276 (Chadbourn rev 1970).

[*Journal of Legal Studies*, vol. XXVI (June 1997)]
 0047-2530/97/2602-0005$01.50

ing, presenting and processing information in litigation. This rationale, we suggest, is consistent with the observed practices of court in making the burden of proof assignment.

To make these points, we use a simple model of litigation in which the parties decide strategically whether to present evidence, given the burden of proof rule selected by the court. The court's problem in the model is to choose the burden of proof that minimizes the costs of litigation. Section II of this article introduces the model and specifies the court's problem. Section III examines how, in the model, the parties will behave under alternative burden of proof assignments. Building on these results, Section IV identifies the optimal burden of proof assignment and the factors on which it turns. Section V considers the extent to which the model holds up as a positive theory of how courts assign the burden of proof in practice. Section VI concludes.

II. The Problem

A. *Two Types of Decision Rule*

Consider a lawsuit in which a contested issue is whether some event X occurred; the plaintiff says X occurred, the defendant says it did not (X might be, for example, an act of negligence by the defendant). The governing substantive law, we may assume, holds that the defendant's liability to the plaintiff depends on whether X in fact occurred.

Taken alone, that substantive rule is not enough to decide cases such as this, in which the parties make conflicting assertions. The court also needs a rule instructing it on what to do when it is uncertain whether X occurred. Two possible components of such a rule are worth distinguishing.

Level of Confidence. A level of confidence rule (or "standard of proof") is a principle specifying how certain the court must be of a fact to accept it. In abstract terms, such a rule would specify a threshold of T percent: if the court believes the probability that X occurred exceeds T, it finds for the plaintiff on the issue and otherwise finds for the defendant. Standards of proof such as "beyond a reasonable doubt," "clear and convincing evidence," and "preponderance of the evidence" represent different possible choices of a value for T.[2]

Burden of Proof. In an adversary system, the court generally cannot

[2] As we have formulated it, the rule specifying T incorporates the so-called burden of persuasion—a principle for decision in cases where the trier of fact is in equipoise—in civil cases. If, for example, $T > 50$ percent, then the plaintiff has the burden of persuasion, in the sense that the defendant wins if the court thinks X is equally likely to have happened or not to have happened.

conduct its own search for information concerning *X*'s occurrence; it must wait to see what evidence the parties present. The function of a burden of proof rule is to apportion the task of presenting evidence. In effect, a burden of proof rule requires one party to produce evidence sufficient to convince the court (to the required level of confidence) of his position. Thus, if the plaintiff has the burden of proof, he loses if no evidence is introduced that *X* occurred; if the defendant has the burden of proof, he loses unless evidence is introduced that *X* did not occur.

Now, the distinction between a rule indicating the required level of confidence and a rule indicating a burden of proof is of course blurry.[3] (As we use the term, "burden of proof" corresponds to the so-called burden of production commonly encountered in textbooks.)[4] For our purposes, the important line of demarcation is that *a burden of proof rule*—as we use the term here—*specifies who must present evidence to the court.*[5] It is important to see that this question is not the same as asking how certain the court must be of *X* before concluding it occurred.

This may not be obvious. It might be thought that a rule indicating the required level of confidence *necessarily implies a corresponding burden of proof.* The line of reasoning would go as follows: if the threshold T for imposing liability is greater than 50 percent, then this must mean the court must rule in the defendant's favor if no evidence is introduced (in other words, the plaintiff has the burden of proof). That is because, if no evidence is introduced, the court must conclude the parties' positions are equally likely to be true, in which case (since $T > .5$) the defendant must win.[6]

To see the error in this reasoning, consider the follow example. Suppose that both parties have access to evidence giving a perfectly accurate signal of whether *X* occurred;[7] suppose both parties know what the evidence contains; and suppose that both parties believe (for whatever reason) that if no evidence is introduced, the court will rule for the *plaintiff.* Suppose, finally,

[3] Deciding how much evidence is necessary to discharge a party's burden of proof is similar, if not identical, to deciding what level of confidence the court should have before imposing sanctions.

[4] In contrast, the burden of persuasion is included in the rule specifying the required level of confidence. See note 2 above. For a discussion of the burdens of persuasion and production, see Fleming James, Jr., Geoffrey C. Hazard, Jr., and John Leubsdorf, *Civil Procedure* 337-43 (4th ed 1992).

[5] An inquisitorial system in its pure theoretical form—which gives the court the task of gathering evidence—would not have a burden of proof as we have described it. An inquisitorial system would, however, need to specify the required level of confidence necessary to conclude that *X* occurred.

[6] Similarly, if T is less than 50 percent, then this must mean the court must rule in the plaintiff's favor if no evidence is introduced (so the defendant bears the burden of proof).

[7] Say, a videotape whose authenticity is undisputed.

that the court knows all this (but does not know what the contents of the evidence is). Then, if the court sees no evidence introduced, it should conclude that *X* occurred: for if the evidence showed otherwise, the defendant would have introduced it.

The important thing to see in this example is that it makes no difference what level of confidence is required: *T* can be 1 percent or 99 percent; the analysis is the same no matter what its value. So long as the court knows the defendant could have introduced perfectly reliable evidence of his care but chose not to, it can conclude the defendant was negligent. In short, the value of *T* does *not* imply who should lose in the event no evidence is introduced.

This example is obviously stylized, but its point holds more broadly: the choice of a burden of proof is logically independent of the choice of a rule specifying the required level of confidence. The simple reason for this is that the parties decide strategically whether to introduce evidence, *based on what they expect the court to do if no evidence is introduced.* Given the parties' beliefs in the above example, it is perfectly coherent for the court to put the burden of proof on the defendant even though *T* may be very large; similarly, it would (if the parties had other beliefs) be coherent for the court to put the burden of proof on the plaintiff even if *T* were very small.

B. The Court's Task

Our interest will be in the problem of choosing a burden of proof on some issue in litigation, given some rule specifying the required level of confidence. To examine the court's problem, we use a simple model of litigation in which each party decides whether to gather, and present to the court, evidence on the issue of negligence; the court then rules in one or the other's favor on that issue. (We put aside the possibility of settling out of court.)

For clarity of exposition, we make the following set of assumptions about the litigation: (1) Both parties have access to a body of evidence that indicates (to the required level of certainty) whether the defendant acted negligently, and both parties know what the evidence contains. (2) This body of evidence is unitary in nature, so that the court sees either all of it or none of it. (This latter assumption might be justified on the hypothesis that if one party tries to mislead the court by a selective presentation of the evidence, the other party furnishes the rest of the evidence.)[8] (3) A party's cost of

[8] We make this assumption because (1) it enables us to put aside level-of-confidence issues (how much evidence should be required?) and (2) it enables us to put aside strategic problems associated with partial presentation of the evidence.

presenting the evidence is sufficiently low that he will present evidence on the issue of negligence, if presenting it is necessary to secure a favorable ruling on the issue.

III. Parties' Behavior under Alternative Burden Assignments

As a predicate to examining the court's problem, we begin by identifying how the parties will act in litigation under one or the other burden of proof assignment. Suppose the plaintiff has the burden of proof on whether *X* occurred. Then the parties, assuming they are informed of the burden assignment, will behave as follows in equilibrium:

The *plaintiff* presents the evidence if and only if it indicates *X* occurred.

The *defendant* presents no evidence on the question.

To see that this behavior holds (uniquely) in equilibrium, observe first that the defendant has a dominant strategy of introducing no evidence. If the evidence shows that *X* occurred, there is no point in presenting it; doing so would either cause him to lose (if the plaintiff does not present the evidence) or have no effect on the outcome (if the plaintiff does present it)—and force him to incur presentation costs. Better, in either event, to save the costs of presenting the evidence. If, instead, the evidence shows *X* did not occur, there is also no point in introducing it: he will win on the issue whether or not the evidence is introduced (since the plaintiff has the burden of proof), so again he may as well save the costs of presenting it. No matter what strategy the plaintiff follows, then, the defendant will present no evidence.

Now consider what the plaintiff will do, given this strategy of the defendant's. If the evidence shows *X* occurred, the plaintiff will present the evidence: she cannot rely on the defendant to present the evidence, and if no one presents it she will lose on the issue. If, instead, the evidence shows *X* did not occur, there is no point in presenting the evidence—doing so would bring defeat on herself and saddle her with presentation costs to boot. Thus, the above strategy profile constitutes the unique equilibrium when the plaintiff has the burden of proof.

A similar analysis shows that, if the defendant has the burden of proof, the parties will pursue the following strategies in equilibrium:

The *plaintiff* presents no evidence on whether *X* occurred.

The *defendant* presents the evidence if and only if it indicates *X* did not occur.

The intuition here is the same as in the previous case, except that the parties' roles are reversed. The plaintiff has no reason to incur the cost of presenting the evidence, whether or not it shows X occurred—since in either event presenting it will have no effect on the outcome of the case. The defendant will accordingly want to present the evidence if it supports his position, but not otherwise.

In summary, then, under either burden of proof assignment, *the party with the burden will present the evidence if and only if the evidence supports his position,* while *the other party will refrain from presenting evidence regardless of whether the evidence supports his position.*[9]

IV. Optimal Burden Assignments

A. *The Basic Model*

We turn now to the optimal assignment of the burden of proof. Our objective is to examine how the court may use the burden of proof to economize on the transmission of information in litigation. Let us suppose that the court wants to assign the burden of proof to minimize the expected costs of presenting evidence on whether X occurred. Then the court should give the plaintiff the burden if the following expression holds:

probability that X occurred	$\times$	plaintiff's costs of showing X occurred	$<$	probability that X did not occur	$\times$	defendant's costs of showing X did not occur	(1)

This follows from our analysis of the parties' equilibrium behavior. As we have seen, the plaintiff will present the evidence (given the burden of proof) if and only if it establishes that X occurred. Thus, the left-hand box indicates the expected costs of giving the burden to the plaintiff. Similarly, the

[9] In this model the court has committed itself in advance to a given burden of proof assignment. One might ask what would happen if, alternatively, the court were a player in this game and decided cases according to its posterior beliefs (given the parties' actions in the litigation) about whether X occurred. Interestingly, the strategies just described are equilibrium outcomes in this game as well. For example, if the parties believe that the court will rule for the plaintiff in the event no evidence is introduced, then the defendant will present evidence if and only if the evidence favors him. Accordingly, if no evidence were introduced, the court would infer that the evidence favored the plaintiff and would rationally rule for the plaintiff. In this way, the strategies described in the text may arise endogenously in a three-player version of the game. One way of viewing burden of proof rules, therefore, is as a mechanism for selecting between different Nash equilibria. We explore this point in more detail in a previous version of this paper. See Bruce L. Hay and Kathryn E. Spier, "The Economics of the Burden of Proof" (unpublished manuscript, April 1994).

right-hand box indicates the expected costs of assigning the burden to the defendant.

As (1) shows, two basic factors determine the optimal assignment in this setting.[10] Let us consider them in turn.

1. Parties' Costs

The first factor is the parties' relative costs of gathering and presenting evidence on the contested issue. One party may have easier access to evidence than his opponent, meaning he can assemble the appropriate evidence at lower cost than his opponent. Other things being equal, the lower one party's relative costs, the stronger the argument for giving him the burden of proof.

This question is complicated by the existence of discovery rules, which enable each party to demand the evidence in the other's possession. But discovery does not render irrelevant the question of relative presentation costs because the costs of discovery should be counted as presentation costs. Suppose, for example, that the defendant has exclusive possession of relevant evidence. Giving the plaintiff the burden of proof may lead her to demand, and sift through, piles of information that may or may not contain useful evidence—generating costs that might be avoided if the defendant were given the burden of proof.[11] Determining the parties' relative costs thus requires the court to decide who initially possesses what evidence and how costly and effective the discovery process is.

2. Probabilities

The court begins with some information Y about the case; we will call Y the "signal" the court has received about whether X occurred. Given Y, the probability that X occurred is as follows:

$$\frac{\text{prob}(X|Y) \times \text{prob}(X)}{\text{prob}(Y)}; \qquad (2)$$

[10] These factors are widely recognized as the essential ones in assigning the burden of proof on an issue. See, for example, James, Hazard, and Leubsdorf, at 344-49 (cited in note 4).

[11] Here we have in mind a setting in which the defendant, but not the plaintiff, knows which files (or which witnesses' memories) contain useful evidence. Since the plaintiff will not believe a defendant's claim that a certain file is a dry well, she may rationally demand it and search through it—though it may indeed turn out to be a dry well.

similarly, the probability that X did *not* occur is

$$\frac{\text{prob}(Y|\sim X) \times \text{prob}(\sim X)}{\text{prob}(Y)}. \tag{3}$$

In these expressions, which are derived from Bayes' Rule, prob(X) represents the unconditional likelihood that X will occur;[12] prob($\sim X$) represents the unconditional likelihood that X will not occur; prob($Y|X$) is the likelihood the court would observe Y if X were to occur; prob($Y|\sim X$) is the likelihood the court would observe Y if X were not to occur; and prob(Y) is the unconditional likelihood of observing Y. For purposes of deciding whether (1) holds, what matters is the two terms in the numerators of these expressions.

Begin with the term prob(X) in expressions (2) and (3). This term in effect represents how frequently X occurs. The less frequently X occurs, the less likely that it occurred *in this case.* For example, suppose the case is a medical malpractice suit arising out of an unsuccessful surgical operation. Assume that

$X \equiv$ surgeon's failure to exercise due care.

If surgeon carelessness is a highly infrequent event, then—all else being equal—the court should believe that it probably did not occur in this case. (We will see below how all other things may not be equal.) Conversely, if surgeons are frequently careless, then—again, all else being equal—the court should conclude that the surgeon was probably careless in this case.

Now consider the terms prob($Y|X$) and prob($Y|\sim X$). Their relative magnitude tells us, in effect, how much information can be gleaned from knowing that Y occurred. On the one hand, if prob($Y|X$) is a lot greater than prob($Y|\sim X$), then observing Y is a good indication that X occurred. For example, suppose that, in our malpractice example,

$Y \equiv$ a surgical implement is left inside the patient.

For purposes of this example let us assume that a careful surgeon would virtually never leave a surgical implement inside a patient, while a careless surgeon might well do so. Observing that an implement was left in the patient *in this particular case* is then a strong indication that the surgeon was negligent.

On the other hand, if prob($Y|X$) is not much greater than prob($Y|\sim X$),

[12] For example, if X refers to negligent driving, prob(X) is the likelihood that motorists drive negligently.

then not much information can be gleaned from Y's occurrence. In our example, suppose only that

$Y \equiv$ unsuccessful operation.

Let us assume that the operation in question often fails even when the doctor performs it carefully (though failure is more likely if the doctor is careless). Observing that the operation was unsuccessful *in this case* is not a strong indication that the doctor was negligent since the operation might well have failed even if the doctor had been careful.

B. Refinements to the Basic Model

1. The Possibility of Settlement

Suppose the parties can settle out of court without gathering or presenting any evidence to the court. This is what we would expect in cases where the parties are (as we have assumed) symmetrically informed about the evidence. Does the burden of proof assignment matter (in the sense of affecting the costs of litigation) in such instances? If so, do the prescriptions of the basic model apply to these cases?

The main effect of the burden assignment in such cases is to determine the size of the surplus from settling the case. Anytime there is a range of possible settlement amounts, there is the possibility of a costly bargaining process, in which each party attempts to capture as large a share of the surplus as possible; from a social standpoint, such bargaining investments represent a deadweight loss. In a world where cases settle, the burden assignment may (by establishing the size of the settlement surplus) influence the amount expended on bargaining.[13]

While we do not model this matter formally, the intuition can be expressed quite simply. Take a case in which X has in fact occurred. As our analysis of the parties' equilibrium litigation strategies showed, evidence will be presented (in the event of trial) if the *plaintiff,* but not if the *defendant,* has the burden. Thus, putting the burden on the plaintiff in this case has the effect of creating a settlement surplus—namely, the plaintiff's presentation costs; to settle, the parties must agree on a division of that surplus, which may consume bargaining resources. This deadweight loss would be avoided, in this example, if the defendant had the burden of proof. (By anal-

[13] For elaboration of this point, see Bruce L. Hay, *Allocating the Burden of Proof,* 72 Ind L J (1997, in press).

ogy, if X has in fact *not* occurred, giving the defendant the burden creates a deadweight loss that could be avoided by giving the plaintiff the burden.)

What is the best assignment, given that the court does not know whether X occurred? The court wants to assign the burden in a way that minimizes expected bargaining costs. We have the following result: if the resources consumed in settlement bargaining in a given case increase (in a linear fashion) as the settlement surplus increases, then the court's problem is the same as in the basic model; it achieves its objective by *choosing the assignment that minimizes expected presentation costs* (the costs that would be expended if the case failed to settle). If, however, bargaining costs do not vary in a linear fashion with the size of the surplus, the court's optimal assignment in a world of settlement will not necessarily be the same as in the basic model.

2. Drawing Inferences from Parties' Litigation Decisions

The court's information set at the time it assigns the burden, Y, includes the fact that the plaintiff has chosen to sue the defendant. But the plaintiff would not waste her time bringing a suit she expected to lose, and if X did not occur, the verdict will be against her no matter how the burden is assigned.[14] One might argue, therefore, that Y (the fact that suit was brought) is a strong indication that X occurred. Should not the court then conclude, from the fact suit was brought, that $\text{prob}(X|Y)$ is large?

This reasoning overlooks that the plaintiff might sometimes bring a nonmeritorious claim *in the hopes of extracting a settlement from the defendant.* In particular, if the defendant bears the burden of proof, he will be willing to pay a positive amount to settle the case, in order to avoid the costs of proving that X did not occur. The plaintiff, knowing this, may rationally choose to sue regardless of the merit of her claim. Accordingly, the plaintiff's decision to sue is not necessarily a strong indication that X occurred.[15]

3. Assignment's Effect on Primary Behavior

If X is an action by one of the parties, then it might be asked whether its occurrence is affected by how the burden is assigned. Suppose, to return to

[14] This is clear from our analysis of the parties' equilibrium litigation strategies. Assume X did not occur. If the plaintiff has the burden, she will present no evidence and lose the case. If the defendant has the burden, he will present the evidence and win the case.

[15] A similar argument shows that the defendant's decision to *deny* that X occurred is not necessarily a good signal of whether X occurred.

Steven Shavell has recently investigated an analogous problem in the context of appeals—namely, whether a court, in deciding whether an appeal is meritorious, should draw inferences from the fact that it was brought. See his article, *The Appeals Process as a Means of Error Correction,* 24 J Legal Stud 379, 412 (1995).

our example, that X = negligent behavior. Might not the defendant's decision whether to comply with the standard of care depend on who has the burden of proof?

Interestingly, if our simplifying assumptions about the litigation hold,[16] we get the following result. *If the standard of care is efficient, then the burden of proof assignment will not affect the defendant's decision to take care.* (By "efficient" we mean that, at the margin, the costs of precautions are less than the reduction in expected harm to the plaintiff.) We leave a demonstration of this point to the Appendix; the basic intuition is simple. From our analysis of the parties' strategies in equilibrium, we know that the defendant will (no matter who has the burden) be held liable if negligent, and not otherwise. But if the standard of care is efficient, the threat of liability will be enough to induce him to take care. In equilibrium, then, we would normally expect the defendant to (have an incentive to) take care regardless of how the burden is assigned.

Now, this result depends on the assumption that the standard of care is efficient (as well as on the other simplifying assumptions of the model). If these assumptions do not hold, there is no way of showing a priori that the burden of proof has no effect on the defendant's decision to take care. We make no claim about the extent to which, in reality, the assignment of the burden of proof affects actors' primary behavior. To the extent it does *not* have any such effect, however, two consequences follow. First, in searching for the optimal burden of proof, the court can focus on the burden's effect on litigation costs; it need not worry that the assignment will affect other social costs, such as the accident rate. Second, in evaluating (2) and (3), the court can treat prob(X) as being an independent variable, not influenced by the burden assignment.

V. The Burden of Proof in Practice

How well does the basic model comport with burden of proof assignments actually made by courts? We can restate the prescription of the basic model as follows. Plugging (2) and (3) into (1) and simplifying, we see that (1) is satisfied if and only if

$$\begin{gathered}\text{prob}(Y|X) \times \text{prob}(X) \times \text{plaintiff's costs} \\ < \text{prob}(Y|{\sim}X) \times \text{prob}({\sim}X) \times \text{defendant's costs.}\end{gathered} \tag{4}$$

The basic model states that the court should give the plaintiff the burden of proof if (4) holds, but not otherwise.

[16] That the parties are symmetrically informed and the cost of presenting evidence is low in relation to the stakes.

We want to know how well this holds up as a description of what courts do in practice. In rough terms, the following seems a fair characterization of existing practices. (*a*) As a general rule, the plaintiff bears the burden of proof on most contested issues. There is, in a manner of speaking, a "presumption" that the plaintiff has the burden of proof on most factual issues in the litigation. (*b*) There are, however, a number of instances in which the defendant is given the burden of proof on a given issue. Though we do not examine this matter exhaustively, we think the model is consistent with both the general rule and some major exceptions.

A. *The General Rule*

A striking feature of judicial practice is that, in cases that go to court, the burden of proof is seldom put in question. On most contested issues in most cases, the plaintiff does not even bother disputing that she bears the burden of proof. This is presumably because courts only reluctantly entertain arguments for giving the defendant the burden of proof. To what extent is expression (4) consistent with a general rule that the plaintiff gets the burden of proof?

Let us suppose the court wanted to establish a presumption (or default rule) that the burden of proof rests on one party on all issues in all cases. That is, suppose it wanted to say the burden always rests on one party, unless the circumstances clearly warranted giving it to the other party. (The rationale for such a presumption, of course, would be to limit the resources expended on litigating the question of *who should bear the burden of proof* in a given case.) Who would get the burden under this default rule?

Expression (4) suggests that the following conditions, if satisfied, would justify giving the burden to the plaintiff:

i) in general, the plaintiff's costs of gathering and presenting evidence on a contested issue are not substantially greater than the defendant's; and
ii) actors generally comply with the law, regardless of how the burden of proof is assigned; thus, if X refers to some sort of "wrongdoing" (commission of a tort, breach of contract, and so on), prob(X) is relatively low; and
iii) prob($Y|{\sim}X$) is not too low, that is, the signal received by the court (before assigning the burden) has a possible "innocent" explanation, in the following sense: the signal might have been received even if the defendant had complied with the law.

We conjecture that these conditions are often met in practice—or more precisely, that courts might plausibly believe they are met in practice. Regarding i, it is reasonable to assume that, given the availability of discovery, parties' costs will often be roughly identical, though of course they will not always be so. Regarding ii, it seems safe to assume that much of the time, the threat of liability (along with other forces) induces actors to comply with applicable standards of tort law, contract law, and so forth.

If we grant those two assumptions, then condition iii is relatively easy to satisfy. A numerical illustration may help make the point. Let us suppose that the plaintiff's costs of gathering and presenting evidence are 50 percent higher than the defendant's, and let us suppose that actors comply with the applicable standard of care 90 percent of the time.[17] Plugging this information into (4), we see that the plaintiff should have the burden of proof if

$$\text{prob}(Y|X) \times .1 \times 1.5 < \text{prob}(Y|{\sim}X) \times .9,$$

that is,

$$\text{prob}(Y|X) < 6 \times \text{prob}(Y|{\sim}X).$$

Thus, the court should give the plaintiff the burden *unless noncompliance with the law is six times more likely (than compliance is) to send the "signal" received by the court.* The upshot is that, unless Y is a fairly reliable signal of whether X occurred, conditions i and ii are enough to warrant giving the burden to the plaintiff.

B. *Exceptions*

Where exceptions to the general rule are made, we would expect to see them in situations where the plaintiff's costs are a lot greater than the defendant's, where prob($Y|X$) is a lot greater than prob($Y|{\sim}X$), or where the frequency of X is very large. Let us consider some of the major exceptions.

1. Res Ipsa Loquitur

Courts invoke this principle to give the defendant the burden of proof on the issue of his own negligence, in cases involving accidents that generally result from negligence.[18] (Our earlier malpractice example, involving a surgical implement left inside a patient, is a characteristic occasion for invoking the doctrine.)[19] Similarly, in product liability suits, the doctrine is used to give the defendant the burden of proving that the product causing injury was not defective, when the accident in question generally results from de-

[17] Thus, prob(X) = .1.

[18] Numerous instances of the doctrine's application are collected in Fowler V. Harper, Fleming James, and Oscar Gray, 4 *The Law of Torts* 21-84 (2d ed 1986); and Wigmore, at 487-511 (cited in note 1).

[19] See, for example, *Hestbeck v Hennepin County*, 297 Minn 419, 212 NW2d 361 (1973).

fective products.[20] Consider, for example, in such cases, prob($Y|X$) is much higher than prob($Y|\sim X$). In deciding whether to apply the rule, some courts also ask whether the defendant had "exclusive" control over the instrumentality that the caused the injury; this might be justified on the grounds that exclusive control implies the defendant has greater access to evidence of what happened.[21] Res ipsa is, then, quite easy to square with expression (4).

2. Presumptions

Courts often presume the truth of a factual statement that is almost always true.[22] Consider, for example, the presumption that a letter or telegram reaches its designated addressee; that a person inexplicably absent from home for 7 years is deceased; that the presumption (in insurance coverage cases) that a sudden death is the product of accident rather than suicide; that the maker of a will is sane.[23] Or consider the presumption that the price an investor pays for a security is influenced by accountants' opinion letters and the like.[24] In these instances prob(X) is high, so the defendant is given the burden of producing supporting evidence that it did not occur.[25]

Other presumptions are justified by differentials in the parties' costs of gathering and producing evidence. Consider, for example, the presumption that damage to goods in a bailee's possession was caused by the bailee's negligence, or the presumption that the driver of another person's auto is acting as the owner's agent.[26] Evidence about what happened to the damaged goods, or about the relation between the driver and the owner, is more

[20] Consider the famous line of cases involving exploding soft drink bottles (for example, *Escola v Coca-Cola Bottling Co of Fresno,* 24 Cal2d 453, 150 P2d 436 (1944)). Other examples are collected in the works cited in note 18 above.

[21] See Harper, James, and Gray, at 45-47 (cited in note 18), for examples. Exclusive control also increases the value of prob($X|Y$) since it makes less likely the hypothesis that *someone else's* negligence injured the plaintiff.

[22] "A presumption upon a matter of fact, when it is not merely a disguise for some other principle, means that common experience shows the fact to be so generally true that courts may notice the truth." *Greer v United States,* 245 US 559, 561 (1918) (Holmes, J).

[23] These examples are drawn from Christopher B. Mueller and Laird C. Kirkpatrick, *Evidence under the Rules* 754-55 (2d ed 1993); and James, Hazard, and Leubsdorf, at 348 (cited in note 4).

[24] See, for example, *Sharp v Coopers & Lybrand,* 649 F2d 175 (3d Cir 1981).

[25] An interesting example in this regard is the court's ruling in *Johnson v Austin,* 406 Mich 420, 280 NW2d 9 (Mich 1979), creating a presumption that hit-and-run drivers have behaved negligently in causing the accident. The court's rationale that only a driver who had been negligent (and feared being held liable) would expose himself to a prison term on a hit-and-run charge.

[26] These examples are drawn from James, Hazard, and Leubsdorf, at 349 (cited in note 4).

accessible to the defendant, rendering his costs lower. Another example is the general rule that the taxpayer bears the burden of proof in income tax deficiency actions brought in the tax court by the Internal Revenue Service. Though the IRS is the plaintiff, the taxpayer is given the burden of proof because he has greater access to evidence concerning his financial affairs.[27]

3. Prima Facie Cases

Courts sometimes shift the burden of proof to the defendant on a "prima facie" showing by the plaintiff that X occurred. A well-known instance is found in Title VII antidiscrimination litigation. Suppose the court wants to know whether a group of female employees was discharged for discriminatory reasons. Roughly speaking, if the plaintiffs can show they were treated differently from a group of similarly situated male employees, the defendant must come forward with evidence that the plaintiff was not fired for discriminatory reasons.[28] In such a setting, prob($Y|X$) is relatively high compared to prob($Y|{\sim}X$); in addition, the employer has lower costs of producing evidence on the motive for the discharge.

Similar considerations are at work in the doctrine of "negligence per se," which (in one version) holds that the violator of a safety ordinance is presumed to have acted negligently; once the defendant is shown to have violated the ordinance, he must come forward with evidence he exercised due care.[29] Here again, prob($Y|X$) is relatively high compared to prob($Y|{\sim}X$), making it sensible to require the defendant to show that Y (violation of the ordinance) was not in fact produced by X (negligence).

4. Affirmative Defenses

Courts sometimes shift the burden of proof on a given issue to the defendant by labeling his position on the issue an "affirmative defense." Certain major examples seem consonant with the basic model. For instance, courts typically require the defendant to produce evidence to support his position that the plaintiff assumed the risk in a negligence case;[30] one rationale may

[27] See, for example, *Portillo v. Commissioner of Internal Revenue,* 932 F2d 1128, 1133 (5th Cir 1991).

[28] See, for example, *Texas Dept of Community Affairs v Burdine,* 450 US 248 (1981).

[29] See, for example, *Delfino v Sloan,* 20 Cal App 4th 1429, 25 Cal Rptr 2d 265 (1994); *Bowen v Baumgardner,* 6 Wash App 18, 491 P2d 1301 (Wash App 1971). Another version of the doctrine holds that violation of the statute itself constitutes negligence, rather than just shifting the burden of proof on the question of negligence.

[30] See, for example, William L. Prosser and W. Page Keeton, *Prosser and Keeton on the Law of Torts* 494 (5th ed 1984).

be that prob(X) is very high (X = victims not assuming risk) since individuals rarely willingly expose themselves to negligently created risks.

Other examples seem explicable by the parties' relative costs. In a tort suit, the defendant generally has the burden of proving his position that he was released from liability by a previous settlement of the dispute. It is presumably far easier for the defendant to prove the fact that a case was settled (by producing a written release) than for the plaintiff to prove it was not. Similar considerations explain why, in a suit to collect payment on a debt, the defendant has the burden of proving he has already paid the debt (it is easy to produce a receipt).

A more interesting example is the issue of contributory negligence in tort suits. The issue arises frequently, yet courts are divided on who should bear the burden on the issue.[31] Why might this be?

One reason, we conjecture, is that whether (4) is satisfied depends in part on *the order in which issues are adjudicated in a case* (more precisely, the order in which evidence is presented). Consider two possibilities: in one scenario, the court adjudicates simultaneously the issues of the defendant's care and the plaintiff's care; in the other scenario, it first considers the defendant's care and then (if evidence of defendant negligence is presented) considers the plaintiff's care. In the latter scenario, the court—at the time it adjudicates the issue of the plaintiff's care—*has greater reason to believe the plaintiff was careful* (see Figure 1).[32] Thus, when the issues are litigated sequentially, the argument for giving the defendant the burden of proof is stronger.

The division in the courts may reflect disagreement over whether the parties' respective care is generally litigated simultaneously or sequentially. In some instances it makes little sense to examine the issues sequentially—when, for example, the same witnesses observed both parties' levels of care, it may be most economical to have them testify on both issues at once. In other instances, the evidentiary materials on each issue may be quite separate, so that it makes most sense to examine the issues sequentially.[33] The appropriate burden of proof rule (assuming a single rule is to govern both situations)[34] might then depend on which occurred more frequently.[35]

[31] See, for example, the cases collected in Wigmore, at 479-83 (cited in note 1).

[32] At the beginning of the litigation, the case (for all the court knows) may lie anywhere in the two circles in Figure 1. Once the court knows the defendant has been negligent, it can rule out all nonoverlapping portions of the left-hand circle—meaning it is less probable (than before) that the case in fact lies in the left-hand circle.

[33] For an analysis of related problems, see William M. Landes, *Sequential vs. Unitary Trials: An Economic Analysis,* 22 J Legal Stud 99 (1993).

[34] Courts could, of course, make the assignment on a case-by-case basis, depending on how the issues would be litigated. As noted above, though, case-by-case determination of the burden of proof has costs of its own.

[35] The orthodox rule in the nineteenth century was to put the burden on the plaintiff; the modern trend is increasingly to put the burden on the defendant. See, for example, Harper,

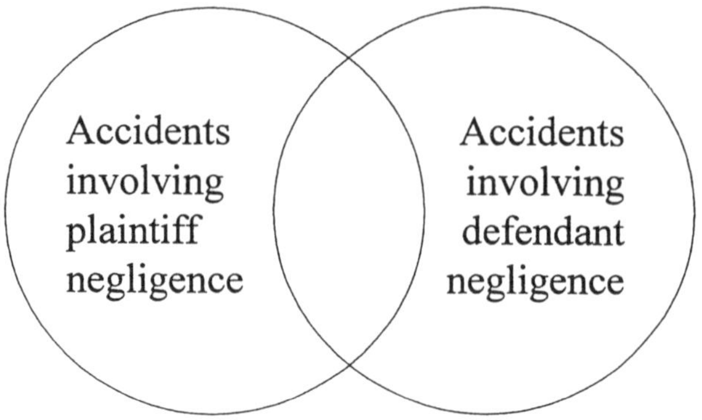

FIGURE 1.—Distribution of negligence cases. Once it is established that the case falls in one circle, the likelihood that it is in the other circle drops.

VI. CONCLUDING REMARK: THE CHOICE BETWEEN ADVERSARIAL AND INQUISITORIAL SYSTEMS

We have tried to show how, properly employed, the burden of proof assignment may minimize the expected costs of resolving a lawsuit. In our analysis, we have assumed that the court operates within the confines of the adversary system, meaning that it relies on the parties to gather and present evidence. Our analysis also gives some insight on the advantages of an adversary system in comparison to an inquisitorial system, in which the court (or an agency with adjudicative responsibilities) must gather the relevant evidence itself.

Let us suppose that expression (4) holds, so that giving the burden of proof to the plaintiff is preferable to giving it to the defendant on the question whether X occurred in a given case. Assume now that the court can choose between either (i) conducting its own investigation of the matter by gathering evidence on X's occurrence, or (ii) giving the plaintiff the burden of proof. The latter alternative generates lower litigation costs if the following holds:

James, and Gray, at 347-51 (cited in note 18). Perhaps one explanation is that, in contemporary accident cases, the defendant's conduct is frequently separate (in temporal and spatial terms) from the plaintiff's, so that the evidence on each is also separate. Consider, for example, a product liability case, in which manufacture and use of a product are quite distinct events; evidence about one does not say much about the other. (Other explanations for the modern trend of course include the unpopularity of denying compensation to victims of negligent defendants simply because they themselves have acted negligently—a sentiment reflected, for example, in the widespread adoption of comparative negligence rules.)

$$\boxed{\text{probability that } X \text{ occurred} \times \text{plaintiff's costs of showing } X \text{ occurred}} < \boxed{\text{court's costs of gathering evidence of whether } X \text{ occurred}} \qquad (5)$$

The difference in the two boxes arises because we have assumed that the plaintiff, but not the court, knows what the evidence contains. As a result, if the plaintiff is given the burden of proof, evidence is presented only if (the evidence shows that) X occurred; in contrast, if the court takes the task on itself, it gathers evidence whether or not X occurred.

Expression (5) suggests that the adversary system is likely to produce lower litigation costs unless the court's costs of gathering evidence are considerably lower than the plaintiff's costs of doing so.[36] (This might be the case if the court has superior access to the evidence, or if the contentiousness of litigation in an adversary system has the effect of generating high costs for the party with the burden of proof.)[37] An interesting question is whether (5) explains patterns actually encountered in practice. We leave this issue for future research.

APPENDIX

The Burden of Proof and Primary Behavior

Here we develop the claim advanced in Section IV*B*3 of the text. Define the following notation:

k = cost of taking care;
p_{H} = probability of accident if the defendant takes care;
p_{L} = probability of accident if the defendant does not take care;
j = plaintiff's losses from an accident;
c = a party's cost of presenting evidence (assumed the same for each party).

[36] Shavell's study of appeals makes a similar point about court review of lower court decisions. Rather than automatically reviewing all judgments, it is preferable for the appellate court to force disappointed litigants to come forward (at some cost to themselves) when an error has occurred. In this fashion, the court (assuming its objective is to correct errors) avoids wasting error resources by reviewing decisions that are correct. See Shavell, cited at note 14.

[37] Points commonly raised against the adversarial system are that (1) it invites foot dragging and abusive tactics by the adversaries, and (2) it encourages the manipulation or misleading use of evidence. See, for example, John H. Langbein, *The German Advantage in Civil Procedure*, 52 U Chi L Rev 823 (1985). Both of these features might have the effect of raising the costs of the party with the burden of proof. (Suppose, for example, that the other party attempts to cloud the litigation with the introduction of unreliable evidence, which the party with the burden of proof must expend effort to refute.)

We assume that taking care is efficient, meaning

$$k < (p_L - p_H)j, \tag{A1}$$

and also that

$$c < j. \tag{A2}$$

Suppose the plaintiff has the burden of proof. Then she will present evidence if injured by the defendant's negligent conduct. The defendant's cost of acting negligently is thus $p_L j$. The defendant, accordingly, will take care if

$$k < p_L j, \tag{A3}$$

which is true anytime (A1) holds.

Suppose, instead, that the defendant has the burden of proof. If he is negligent, he will be held liable in the event of injury; if he is careful, he will not be held liable (though he may bear the costs of proving he was not negligent). He will act carefully if

$$k + p_H c < p_L j; \tag{A4}$$

it is easily verified that this too holds anytime (A1) and (A2) both hold.

B
Character Evidence

[17]

ARTICLES

CHARACTER EVIDENCE AND THE OBJECT OF TRIAL

*Chris William Sanchirico**

Evidence of an individual's character may not in general be offered to prove that she acted in conformity with that character on a particular occasion. Most analyses of this general rule—and its many exceptions—start from the premise that trial is at heart an exercise in finding facts. Yet a clear and robust rationale for the rules governing character evidence has yet to be found on this basis. This Article views trial and character evidence in a different light. Trial is regarded as but one part of the overall mechanism by which the state regulates behavior in the larger world outside the courtroom. The Article focuses specifically on trial's role in the provision of incentives that induce individuals to account for the welfare of others in their daily activities. It is shown that the rules governing character evidence are much easier to explain—and so more fruitfully evaluated—when trial is explicitly placed in this broader context. From this finding the Article draws the larger lesson that the real object of trial lies more in shaping events than in sorting them out after the fact.

TABLE OF CONTENTS

---

* Associate Professor, the University of Virginia School of Law, 580 Massie Road, Charlottesville, Virginia 22903, csanchirico@virginia.edu, www.cstone.net/~csanchir. I have benefited from the helpful comments of Kenneth Abraham, Hilary Alger, Ronald Allen, Vincent Blasi, Craig Callen, Edward Imwinkelried, George Fisher, Kim Forde-Mazrui, Henry Hansmann, Jody Kraus, Richard Lempert, Daryl Levinson, Thomas Merrill, Jennifer Mnookin, John Monahan, Caleb Nelson, Daniel Richman, Susan Rose-Ackerman, James Ryan, Robert Scott, Alex Stein and Paul Stephan. Thanks also to workshop participants at the University of Virginia School of Law and the University of California Berkeley School of Law. Rachel Brewster, John McNutt, Kena Njoya, and Diana Phong Tu provided valuable research assistance.

Introduction

Most evidence scholarship takes as given that trial is at its core a search for truth, a sorting out of past events. Although commentators emphasize that truth seeking competes with other considerations, such as the sanctity of certain privileged relationships, the dignity of the parties, and the opportunity costs of process, few would consider these rival claims part of the purpose of trial. They are rather constraints, to be accommodated or compromised. The reason to encroach at all upon these competing principles lies, by most accounts, in the value—inherent or instrumental—of discovering what really happened.[1]

---

1. See, e.g., William Twining, Evidence and Legal Theory, 47 Mod. L. Rev. 261, 272 (1984). Twining wrote:

> The most striking feature of the [specialized literature on judicial evidence in the Anglo American tradition] is how homogeneous it is. Nearly all of the Anglo American writers from Gilbert to Cross have shared essentially the same basic assumptions about the nature and ends of adjudication and about what is involved in proving facts in this context. There is undoubtedly a dominant underlying theory of evidence in adjudication, in which the central notions are truth, reason, and justice under the law. It can be re-stated simply in some such terms as these: the primary end of adjudication is rectitude of decision, that is the correct application of rules of substantive law to facts that have been proved to an agreed standard of truth or probability. The pursuit of truth in adjudication must at times give way to other values and purposes, such as the preservation of state security or of family confidences; disagreements may arise as to what priority to give to rectitude of decision as a social value and to the nature and scope of certain competing values. . . . But the end of the enterprise is clear: the establishment of truth.

Id.; see also H. Richard Uviller, Evidence of Character to Prove Conduct: Illusion, Illogic, and Injustice in the Courtroom, 130 U. Pa. L. Rev. 845, 845 (1982) [hereinafter Uviller, Illusion] ("The process of litigation is designed for the reconstruction of an event that occurred in the recent past. And for the most part, the rules by which a trial is conducted are supposed to enhance the accuracy of the synthetic fact."); Dale A. Nance, The Best Evidence Principle, 73 Iowa L. Rev. 227, 232–33 (1988) ("The reasonably accurate determination of disputed factual issues is . . . the pivotal task to be performed at trial [and allocated to] the 'trier of fact'. . . . The best evidence principle . . . expresses the obligation of litigants to provide evidence that will best facilitate this central task of accurately resolving disputed issues of fact."); David P. Leonard, The Use of Character to Prove Conduct: Rationality and Catharsis in the Law of Evidence, 58 U. Colo. L. Rev. 1, 2–3 (Winter 1986–87) (stating that "clearly dominant" and "properly dominant" paradigm underlying modern trial is "rational truth-seeking" (emphasis omitted)); Roger C. Park, Character at the Crossroads, 49 Hastings L.J. 717, 749–54 (1998) [hereinafter Park, Character at the Crossroads] (arguing that truth seeking is the primary goal of trial). This orientation toward truth seeking is apparent in self reflective portions of the Federal Rules of Evidence. (What the rules actually call for is another issue.) Fed. R. Evid. 102 (entitled "Purpose and Construction") reads: "These rules shall be construed to secure fairness in administration, elimination of unjustifiable expense and delay, and promotion of growth and development of the law of evidence *to the end that the truth may be ascertained and proceedings justly determined*" (emphasis added). A majority of the states have adopted this rule verbatim. See, e.g., Conn. Code Evid. 1-2; Mich. R. Evid. 102; Pa. R. Evid. 102; Tex. R. Evid. 102.

Important portions of evidence scholarship would not regard truth seeking as the object of trial. These scholars go beyond arguing that truth seeking is subject to important constraints, denying that it is, or is even coincident with, the real underlying objective to be maximized. Professor Nesson, for example, argues that the purpose of judicial process is to induce individuals to internalize the instruction of the law in their primary activities. Charles Nesson, The Evidence or the Event? On Judicial Proof and the Acceptability of Verdicts, 98 Harv. L. Rev. 1357, 1359 (1985). To this end, the object of process is to produce "acceptable verdicts," which are not necessarily "probable verdicts." Id. at 1373,

This Article examines the implications of an apparently similar, but importantly distinct, view about the purpose of trial. This view rests on the methodological premise that rules governing what happens *inside* the courtroom can be understood adequately only in the context of the state's central project of regulating behavior *outside* the courtroom—on the road, in the home, at the office, in the marketplace—where most of life takes place.

More specifically, the Article focuses on trial's role in the provision of incentives—perhaps the most important means by which the state regulates such "primary" activities.[2] The incentive setting approach begins

---

1378. The former are verdicts that the public will regard as "statements about what happened," as opposed to statements about what evidence was presented at trial. Id. at 1358. These concepts diverge, argues Nesson, in several important areas of evidence law, including use of statistical evidence and hearsay. Id. at 1373, 1378. For critiques of Nesson's position, see Ronald J. Allen, Comment, Rationality, Mythology, and the 'Acceptability of Verdicts' Thesis, 66 B.U. L. Rev. 541 *passim* (1986); Roger Park, The Hearsay Rule and the Stability of Verdicts: A Response to Professor Nesson, 70 Minn. L. Rev. 1057, 1057 (1986) [hereinafter Park, Hearsay Rule]; Park, Character at the Crossroads, supra, at 51–54.

For an idea that is related to Nesson's, see Leonard, supra, at 3, 39–43 (pointing to trial's role in producing social and individual "catharsis," which is achieved partly through a visceral satisfaction with legal process that may contradict the implications of rational truth seeking). For other non truth seeking approaches, see Stephan Landsman, The Adversary System: A Description and Defense 3 (1984) (emphasizing importance of dispute resolution, as separate from truth seeking) and Mirjan Damaška, Truth in Adjudication, 49 Hastings L.J. 289, 303–04 (1998) (discussing both the lawmaking role of legal process and the dispute resolution function in civil actions, in which too much "truth" may backfire).

Those who adhere to one or more of these alternative paradigms may find of interest the proposition put forward in this Article that incentive setting—which is usually thought to be an ally of, rather than a rival for, truth—is yet another social goal that diverges significantly from truth seeking. In any event, as will be clear from the discussion in Part I of this Article, the existing explanations for the rules governing character evidence are firmly cast within the truth seeking paradigm.

2. See, e.g., Gary T. Schwartz, Reality in the Economic Analysis of Tort Law: Does Tort Law Really Deter?, 42 UCLA L. Rev. 377, 378–79, 422–23 (1994) (citing deterrence as primary rationale for tort law among mainstream legal scholars, finding sustainable the view that current tort law does significantly deter in light of institutional detail and empirical studies, but discounting the possibility of fine tuning); Isaac Ehrlich, Crime, Punishment, and the Market for Offenses, 10 J. Econ. Persp. 43, 55 (1996) ("Taken as a whole, . . . studies offer a mountain of evidence consistent with the hypothesis that both negative and positive incentives have a deterrent effect on crime."); Steven D. Levitt, Why Do Increased Arrest Rates Appear to Reduce Crime: Deterrence, Incapacitation, or Measurement Error?, 36 Econ. Inquiry 353, 353–55 (1998) (presenting empirical evidence that the association between arrest rates and reported crime rates is due in large part to deterrence effects); Daniel Kessler & Steven D. Levitt, Using Sentence Enhancements to Distinguish Between Deterrence and Incapacitation, 42 J.L. & Econ. 343, 352–59 (1999) (presenting empirical evidence that sentencing enhancements have a significant deterrent effect, as distinguished from their incremental incapacitative effect); Hashem Dezhbakhsh, Paul Rubin and Joanna Mehlhop Shephard, Does Capital Punishment Have a Deterrent Effect?: New Evidence from Post-moratorium Panel Data 25 (Emory Univ. Dep't Econ. 2001) (on file with the *Columbia Law Review*) (presenting empirical evidence that "[a]n

with the premise that, left to her own devices, the individual may fail to adequately account for the welfare of others—may in fact use violence and aggression as a means of achieving her own selfish ends. In order to prevent this sort of behavior, society sets before the individual an additional type of consequence—a legal sanction or reward—to counterbalance pure self interest in the rough calculus of choice. To work properly, these sanctions and rewards must be connected appropriately to the individual's actual behavior, and the individual must anticipate this association. An individual who is never punished or is punished regardless of her actions has no incentive to refrain; an individual who is never rewarded or is rewarded regardless of how she acts has no incentive to engage. Creating the necessary association between actions and legal consequences is the role of evidence in the overall mechanism by which the state sets primary activity incentives.

At first glance, linking consequence to conduct seems perfectly aligned with uncovering truth. If the object is to punish the individual if and only if she commits the crime, wouldn't trial have to be an exercise in determining whether she did in fact commit the crime? If the object is to hold individuals accountable for accidents when they are careless but not when they have exercised reasonable precaution, shouldn't trial be structured in a way that best determines the truth about the defendant's degree of care? In fact, the implications for trial of primary incentive setting often do correspond to those of truth seeking. But not always.

Character evidence—at once the most derogated,[3] legislated,[4] and

---

increase in any of the three probabilities of arrest, sentencing, or execution tends to reduce the crime rate," with the caveat that "deterrence reflects social benefits associated with the death penalty, but one should also weigh in the corresponding social costs . . . includ[ing] the regret associated with the irreversible decision to execute an innocent person"); Joanna Mehlhop Shephard, Fear of the First Strike: The Full Deterrent Effect of California's Two- and Three-Strikes Legislation 3 (Emory Univ. Dep't Econ. Apr. 2001) (on file with the *Columbia Law Review*) (measuring the full deterrent effect from California's three strike legislation on all offenders, not just "last strike offenders," and finding a significant deterrent effect).

3. See Michelson v. United States, 335 U.S. 469, 486 (1948) ("We concur in the general opinion of courts, textwriters and the profession that much of this law [of character evidence] is archaic, paradoxical and full of compromises and compensations by which an irrational advantage to one side is offset by a poorly reasoned counterprivilege to the other."). This sense of dissatisfaction persists in modern scholarship. See, e.g., Park, Character at the Crossroads, supra note 1, at 754 (noting "the horrifying complexity of the character evidence rules"); Uviller, Illusion, supra note 1, at 848 (same).

4. Congress has significantly amended the provisions of the Federal Rules of Evidence that govern character evidence several times since their passage in 1975. Pub. L. No. 93-595, 88 Stat. 1926 (1975). The first major change was the addition of the "rape shield" provision, Fed. R. Evid. 412, in 1978. Privacy Protection for Rape Victims Act of 1978, Pub. L. No. 95-450, 92 Stat. 2046, 2046–47 (1978). See infra Part V.B.4.b for a discussion of the current rape shield provision. In 1990, Fed. R. Evid. 609(a) was amended to allow for more liberal use of past convictions for the purpose of attacking the credibility of a witness. Amendments to Federal Rules of Evidence—Rule 609, 129 F.R.D. 347, 347–55 (1990). See infra Part V.A for a discussion of the use of character evidence for impeachment. In 1991,

litigated[5] aspect of evidence law—is one area in which the truth seeking approach and the primary incentives approach to trial point in very different directions. This Article makes use of that divergence to advance our understanding of both character evidence and trial. It demonstrates that many of the rules governing character evidence—so difficult to rationalize when trial is regarded as an isolated exercise in sorting out past events—fall easily into place when trial is viewed as but one component of the larger system by which the state regulates everyday out of court behavior. The Article draws from this stark disparity in explanatory power the important lesson that, despite most of what is said about the object of trial, our desire to find the truth is subordinate to our desire, in effect, to shape it through the provision of incentives. Finally, the Article employs this revised understanding of trial and evidence to shed new light on several prominent controversies in the modern character evidence debate.

McCormick defines "character" as "a generalized description of one's disposition, or of one's disposition in respect to a general trait, such as honesty, temperance, or peacefulness."[6] The baseline rule, which has broad application despite its many exceptions, is that evidence of an individual's character may not be offered to prove that she acted in conformity with that character on a particular occasion.[7] Thus, evidence that the

---

Fed. R. Evid. 404(b) was amended to add a pretrial notice requirement in criminal cases when the prosecutor intends to use the accused's other acts to prove state of mind, connected acts, identity or opportunity—as opposed to the actus reus. Amendment to Federal Rules of Evidence, 134 F.R.D. 717, 717–23 (1991). These "other uses" are discussed in Parts V.B–D and VI.A. The year 1994 saw much legislative activity regarding the use of character evidence in sex offense cases. The rape shield provision was significantly amended. Violent Crime Control and Law Enforcement Act of 1994, Pub. L. No. 103-322, tit. IV, § 40141(b), 108 Stat. 1918, 1919 (1994). And special rules regarding defendant's prior offenses of sexual assault and child molestation, Fed. R. Evid. 413–415, were also added by the same act. Pub. L. No. 103-322, tit. XXXII, § 320935(a), 108 Stat. 2135, 2136–37 (1994). See infra Part VI.A for a discussion of these special sexual offense provisions. Most recently, Fed. R. Evid. 404(a)(1), the so called "mercy rule," was amended so that an accused's offering evidence of a given trait of the victim opens the door to the prosecutor's offering evidence that the *accused* possesses the same trait. Amendments to the Federal Rules of Evidence, 192 F.R.D. 398, 399–400, 405 (2000). See infra Part VI.B for a discussion of the "mercy rule." Other provisions of the Federal Rules of Evidence have also been amended, but none as extensively. See, e.g., 5 Jack B. Weinstein & Margaret A. Berger, Weinstein's Federal Evidence §§ 801 App.01–04; 802 App.01–100; 803 App.01–05; 804 App.01–05; 805 App.01; 806 App.01–02; 807 App.01–03 (Joseph M. McLaughlin ed., 2d ed. 2001) (listing the less significant set of amendments to Article VIII of the Federal Rules of Evidence, which governs the admissibility of hearsay).

5. See Fed. R. Evid. 404 advisory committee's note to 1991 amendment ("Rule 404(b), ['Other crimes, wrongs, or acts,'] has emerged as one of the most cited Rules in the Rules of Evidence.").

6. Charles T. McCormick, Handbook of the Law of Evidence 340–41 (1st ed. 1954) [hereinafter McCormick, Handbook], quoted in Fed. R. Evid. 406 advisory committee's note.

7. Fed. R. Evid. 404(a). Many states have similar rules. Unless state rules differ substantially, only the federal rule will be cited in this Article. See generally Graham C.

defendant was negligent on prior occasions is not admissible to prove carelessness in general and, therefore, in the case at hand.

The rules restricting character evidence pose serious difficulties for any analysis, but especially for the conventional truth seeking approach to trial. Personality psychologists are now in general agreement that individuals do have identifiable cross situational attributes that, along with situation specific factors, help to determine individual behavior.[8] Moreover, if character is determinative of conduct, it follows that it is also informative of whether conduct has occurred. But then, how can one rationalize prohibiting character evidence for proof of conduct, if gleaning information about past conduct is an important purpose of trial?

The fact that the prohibition is categorical and a priori is what makes the question difficult. One can understand the need to balance the probative value of any given piece of character evidence against the risk of prejudice, confusion, and waste—the usual list of competing considerations.[9] And one can imagine deciding that a given piece of character evidence fails the balancing test just as any piece of evidence might fail the test. The question is: What is so different about character evidence that justifies bypassing the usual case by case balancing and rejecting en masse this large and diverse collection of potentially probative evidence?

As if answering this question were not difficult enough, it is only the first of many obstacles. In steering clear of the fact that character is indeed probative of conduct in explaining the general prohibition, one must not turn so sharply as to be incapable of also explaining the several circumstances in which character evidence *is* allowed. Consider two of the most important and perplexing examples.

Although rarely mentioned and almost never analyzed in character evidence scholarship,[10] evidence of a defendant's other acts[11] is routinely admitted for sentencing and the determination of punitive damages.[12] Thus, the same other acts that may not be used to determine conduct—

Lilly, An Introduction to the Law of Evidence §§ 5.2, 5.4–5.6 (3d ed. 1996) (reviewing the baseline rule in state and federal courts). Exceptions to Rule 404(a) are discussed throughout, especially in Parts V and VI. Many are listed in summary fashion infra note 14.

8. See infra Part I.A.

9. Fed. R. Evid. 403.

10. It appears that only one previous article in evidence scholarship compares the use of character for conduct with the use of other acts evidence for sentencing. James Landon, Note, Character Evidence: Getting to the Root of the Problem Through Comparison, 24 Am. J. Crim. L. 581, 607 (1997) (ruling out "efficiency concerns and the increased burden on the defendant to place his entire life history in issue" as rationale for character evidence ban, based on liberal use of other acts evidence in sentencing).

11. Arguably, all character evidence is ultimately other acts evidence. In particular, opinion and reputation testimony, generally favored over explicit testimony regarding specific instances of conduct, see Fed. R. Evid. 405, are summary forms of evidence about the specific instances of the subject's behavior that produced the opinion or the reputation.

12. See infra Part III.C.1 for more discussion of sentencing and Part III.C.2 for more on the determination of punitive damages.

that is, to determine whether there will be no punishment or some punishment—may be used to determine whether punishment for that conduct will be modest or severe.

Almost as puzzling is the fact that character evidence is rather liberally allowed for the purpose of impeaching witnesses.[13] Thus, while character evidence may not in general be used to prove conduct outside the courtroom, it may be used to prove conduct inside the courtroom when that conduct happens to be the act of lying on the stand. Consequently, a witness's past perjury conviction may be introduced for the inference that she is now lying under oath, and yet may not be introduced against that same individual, as a defendant, in a subsequent perjury action based on that lie.[14]

Most evidence scholars would agree that the conventional truth based approach to evidence has had serious difficulty completing the explanatory slalom posed by the rules governing character evidence; some might even say it misses all the gates from start to finish.[15] In contrast, the primary activity incentives approach to evidence weaves through the rules with relative facility. Consider the use of character evidence for the three purposes just mentioned: proof of conduct, sentencing, and impeachment.

From a primary incentives perspective, the key to understanding the general prohibition on using character to prove conduct is to recognize that evidence can be informative of conduct and yet not be affected by such conduct. "Trace" evidence such as fingerprints and eyewitness recollections are *both* informative of the act and are byproducts of the act. In contrast, character evidence, though it may rationally change our assessment of the likelihood that defendant acted in a particular way, is the

13. See Fed. R. Evid. 404(a)(3), 608, 609; infra Part V.A.

14. The list of perplexing "exceptions" continues. "Habit," as somehow distinguished from "character," is admitted to prove conduct. Fed. R. Evid. 406; see infra Part V.C.2. Evidence of other crimes, wrongs, or acts, is admissible for purposes other than proving conduct, including knowledge, intent, plan, preparation, opportunity, (absence of) mistake, identity, or (absence of) accident. Fed. R. Evid. 404(b); see infra Parts V.B, V.C.1, and V.D. (Character evidence may of course be offered when character is an element of a claim or defense, as when the defendant raises the defense of truth in a libel case. Fed. R. Evid. 405(b).) The accused may offer evidence of her own good character in order to disprove that she committed the charged crime; but if she does, she opens the door to the prosecutor's character based rebuttal. Fed. R. Evid. 404(a)(1); see infra Part VI.B. The accused may also prove a pertinent trait of the *victim*, such as a violent disposition when the accused claims self defense. Fed. R. Evid. 404(a)(2); see infra Part V.B.4. But see the "rape shield" provision, Fed. R. Evid. 412 (restricting admissibility of evidence on victim's sexual predisposition or other sexual behavior in sexual misconduct cases). And by recent amendment to the Federal Rules, evidence of the defendant's commission of other sex offenses is admissible for any purpose in sex offense cases. Fed. R. Evid. 413–415; see infra Part VI.A; see generally Lilly, supra note 7, §§ 5.3, 5.7–5.19 and accompanying chapter notes (reviewing exceptions to the general ban on character evidence).

15. See Uviller, Illusion, supra note 1, at 864.

same whether or not defendant actually did act in that way.[16] If the object were to *guess* whether the defendant engaged in the conduct, then both types of evidence would be appropriate. But because the object is to *affect* whether defendant engages in the conduct, only trace evidence of that conduct is appropriate. Only trace evidence changes with conduct. Thus, keying penalties and rewards to the production of trace evidence is the only way to make penalties and rewards change with conduct. And making penalties and rewards change with conduct is the only way to create incentives.[17]

16. Professor Uviller may have been the first to pose this distinction. But consistent with his view that truth seeking is the object of trial, he argues that the distinction is irrelevant. Id. at 847–48.

17. Most of the economics literature on evidence also assumes that truth seeking is the object of trial—this despite the fact that applications of economics to the *substantive* law are often focused directly on incentive setting. See, e.g., Paul Milgrom & John Roberts, Relying on the Information of Interested Parties, 17 RAND J. Econ. 18, 30 (1986) ("We have used game theory to examine the logic of the argument that when all interested parties have access to complete and verifiable information, competition among them in attempting to influence a decision leads to the emergence of 'truth.'"); Masahiro Okuno-Fujiwara, Andrew Postelwaite & Kotaro Suzumura, Strategic Information Revelation, 57 Rev. Econ. Stud. 25, 25–27, 30–37 (1990) (analyzing augmented asymmetric information model in which agents can announce their private information beforehand, and providing conditions for the full revelation of agents' private information when some of agents' announcements are exogenously "certifiable"); Barton L. Lipman & Duane J. Seppi, Robust Inference in Communication Games with Partial Provability, 66 J. Econ. Theory 370, 394 (1995) (finding that "with more than one speaker, conflicting preferences can lead to the revelation of a surprising amount of information—even with only very limited provability and with limited information on the part of the decision maker about the speaker's preferences or strategies"); Luke M. Froeb & Bruce H. Kobayashi, Naïve, Biased, yet Bayesian: Can Juries Interpret Selectively Produced Evidence?, 12 J.L. Econ. & Org. 257, 257 (1996) (arguing that the legal system is likely to generate unbiased estimates of liability and damages despite the jury's naiveté and initial biasedness); Andrew F. Daughety & Jennifer F. Reinganum, On the Economics of Trials: Adversarial Process, Evidence, and Equilibrium Bias, 16 J.L. Econ. & Org. 365, 365–66 (2000) (arguing, in contrast to Froeb & Kobayashi, infra, that the legal system is unlikely to generate unbiased estimates of liability and damages); Joel Sobel, Disclosure of Evidence and Resolution of Disputes, *in* Game-Theoretic Models of Bargaining 341, 351–59 (Alvin Roth ed., 1985) (analyzing a model with no element of moral hazard in the primary activity, in which, as a result, maximizing social welfare is equivalent to minimization of loss weighted trial error plus evidence costs); Daniel L. Rubinfeld & David E.M. Sappington, Efficient Awards and Standards of Proof in Judicial Proceedings, 18 RAND J. Econ. 308, 309 (1987) (positing as the social objective the minimization of the sum of loss-weighted false convictions, loss-weighted false acquittals, and litigation effort of defendants); Stephen McG. Bundy & Einer Richard Elhauge, Do Lawyers Improve the Adversary System? A General Theory of Litigation Advice and Its Regulation, 79 Cal. L. Rev. 313, 381 (1991) ("Under a theory of adjudication that emphasizes deterrence, [an] unskewed increase in favorable and unfavorable information presented ought to improve the tribunal's ability to distinguish desirable from undesirable conduct. This in turn increases expected sanctions for those who act undesirably at the same time that it decreases sanctions for those who act desirably."); Richard A. Posner, An Economic Approach to the Law of Evidence, 51 Stan. L. Rev. 1477, 1480–84 (1999). Posner says:

> If we were . . . trying to design a system for the resolution of factual disputes in litigation that would be economically efficient in the broadest sense, how would

> we frame our inquiry? I propose . . . to model factfinding as a problem in search. . . . The search process, which in the litigation setting is the process of obtaining, sifting, marshaling, presenting, and (for the trier of fact) weighing evidence, confers benefits and incurs costs. Benefits are a positive function of the probability (*p*) that if the evidence is considered by the trier of fact the case will be decided correctly, and of the stakes (*S*) in the case.

Id.

Several exceptions are worth mentioning. For a game theoretic analysis of evidence production that explicitly places evidence production in the context of regulating out of court behavior (and also explicitly considers parties' incentives to omit and to prevaricate), see Chris Sanchirico, Relying on the Information of Interested—and Potentially Dishonest—Parties, 3 Am. L. & Econ. Rev. 320, 321–22 (2001) [hereinafter Sanchirico, Relying], and its extension, Chris Sanchirico, Games, Information and Evidence Production: With Application to English Legal History, 2 Am. L. & Econ. Rev. 342, 343–44 (2000) [hereinafter Sanchirico, Games]. Both of these papers spring from an earlier working paper first circulated and presented in 1995: Chris Sanchirico, Enforcement by Hearing: How the Civil Law Sets Incentives (1995) (Columbia Economics Dep't, Discussion Paper No. 95-9603). See also A. Mitchell Polinsky & Steven Shavell, Legal Error, and the Incentive to Obey the Law, 5 J.L. Econ. & Org. 99, 100 (1989) (demonstrating in a civil law setting that chance of legal error generally reduces incentive to obey the law, but that this effect is complicated by the possibility that legal error will affect plaintiffs' incentives to file suit); Joel Schrag & Suzanne Scotchmer, Crime and Prejudice: The Use of Character Evidence in Criminal Trials, 10 J.L. Econ. & Org. 319, 329 (1994). Schrag and Scotchmer find in the context of their model that the optimal threshold quantum of evidence for guilt is systematically lower when the object is taken to be error minimization, rather than maximal deterrence. Id. at 329–32 (Propositions 1 and 2). This distinction between error minimization and maximal deterrence is orthogonal to the distinction between truth seeking and incentive setting put forth in the present Article. The conflict identified by Schrag and Scotchmer pertains even in a system that admits only trace evidence of conduct. For further discussion of Scrag and Scotchmer, see infra note 120.

See also Louis Kaplow, The Value of Accuracy in Adjudication: An Economic Analysis, 23 J. Legal Stud. 307, 312–14 (1994), and Louis Kaplow & Steven Shavell, Accuracy in the Assessment of Damages, 39 J.L. & Econ. 191, 192, 194, 201–02 (1996), for articles asserting that accuracy in the assessment of damages has zero impact (as opposed to the potentially negative impact identified in this Article) on incentives. The specific claim is that in a world in which injurers are risk neutral, there is perfect information about whether or not an accident has occurred, and precautionary choice is binary (reasonable care or not), there is no incentive difference between charging the injurer with the harm that she expected to cause or the harm that she actually did cause, even though the later assessment of damages is in a sense "more accurate." Aside from this argument, these two papers and their third companion by Kaplow & Shavell adopt and expand upon the conventional view of the relationship between accuracy and incentives. Louis Kaplow & Steven Shavell, Accuracy in the Determination of Liability, 37 J.L. & Econ. 1, 1–3 (1994). None of the three papers discusses the differing incentive effects of trace and predictive evidence of conduct.

It is also worth noting that a fair portion of the economics analysis of *procedure* does ground itself in primary activity incentives. However, this literature does not consider how claims are proven. Instead it assumes exogenous probabilities for various trial outcomes and focuses instead on filing, settlement, and fee shifting provisions. See, e.g., Janusz A. Ordover, On the Consequences of Costly Litigation in the Model of Single Activity Accidents: Some New Results, 10 J. Legal Stud. 269, 269–71 (1981) (considering the effect of litigation costs on the optimal due care standard); A. Mitchell Polinsky & Daniel L. Rubinfeld, The Welfare Implications of Costly Litigation for the Level of Liability, 17 J.

Trace evidence of conduct is, therefore, the sine qua non of incentives.[18] Arguably, however, there are circumstances—mostly in the criminal and quasi criminal realm—in which character evidence has an ancillary role to play in "tailoring" the incentives (created in the first instance by hanging legal consequences on trace evidence) to the intensity of individual propensities.[19] Perhaps those with poor "self-control"[20] are deterred from committing robbery only by a particularly swift, likely, and steep reduction in their personal welfare following commission—a prospect which for various reasons we might prefer to apply only selectively.

It is true that tailoring incentives in this way requires that the court hear evidence on propensity (and that parties anticipate this fact). But this does not detract from the incentives argument against admitting character for conduct. Rather, it allows the incentives approach to explain the seeming inconsistency of admitting other act evidence for sentencing and punitive damages and not for proving conduct. As we shall see, fine tuning incentives to propensity is a tricky business. Attempting to do so by admitting character for conduct turns out to be particularly prone to backfire, dampening rather than intensifying incentives for those who need them most. In contrast, admitting other act evidence for sentencing and punitive damages—and not for proof of conduct—turns out to be a simple and almost foolproof way of providing higher powered incentives for higher propensity offenders.[21]

The admission of character evidence for impeachment is also much easier to rationalize within the primary activity incentives approach. Under this approach, conduct on the stand *is* fundamentally different from the primary conduct that is the target of the substantive law. In order to set incentives for primary conduct successfully, the law must be sufficiently capable of discerning whether what is offered as trace evi-

Legal Stud. 151, 151–53 (1988) (examining how litigation costs affect the optimal level of damages); A. Mitchell Polinsky & Daniel L. Rubinfeld, The Deterrent Effects of Settlements and Trials, 8 Int'l Rev. L. & Econ. 109, 109–10 (1988) (arguing that trials may be more effective than settlements in inducing injurers to take socially appropriate levels of care); Kathryn E. Spier, Settlement Bargaining and the Design of Damage Awards, 10 J.L. Econ. & Org. 84, 84–86 (1994) (analyzing the effect of fine tuning damage awards on the likelihood of settlement and the injurer's level of care).

18. The issue here is proving conduct. In terms of proving other issues, like the circumstances of conduct, trace and predictive evidence are indeed on equal footing. See infra Parts V.A, V.B, V.B.3 & V.B.4.

19. See infra Part V.A. for a discussion of those circumstances.

20. See infra note 31 for theories of crime based on self control.

21. See infra Part V.B. The extent to which individuals anticipate that their sentence will be tailored to their propensity is open to question. This may be precisely the kind of fine tuning that Schwartz, supra note 2, at 378–79, 444, warns against. But if the tailoring goal is indeed too much to ask of a practical system, then this is all the more reason not to admit propensity evidence for conduct. How then can we explain sentencing enhancements based on other acts evidence? Two possibilities are incapacitation and the dynamic effects of propensity evidence. Both are considered in Part IV.

dence of primary conduct is really that.[22] In particular, the law must be proficient at distinguishing actual recollections from fabricated accounts. Thus, the central object of affecting—not necessarily guessing—primary conduct implies a subsidiary interest in both affecting *and* guessing the secondary conduct of witnesses on the stand. The law does not just want to prevent lying on the stand, it also wants to know whether the witness has in fact lied.

In addition to shedding light on why character evidence should be permitted for impeachment and sentencing and yet not for proof of conduct, the incentives approach also helps to elucidate several other puzzling aspects of the rules governing character evidence.[23] And it is safe to say that its account of the rules governing character evidence is more plausible—often much more so—than that offered by the conventional truth seeking approach to trial. But not every aspect of the rules governing character evidence is consistent with the primary incentives approach. With respect to some areas of current law, the incentives approach provides the basis for criticism rather than explanation. Some of these areas—notably, the new federal exceptions for prior sex offenses[24]—have also been roundly criticized within the conventional truth seeking analysis of character evidence.[25] But unlike the conventional approach, the incentives approach is grounded by its ability to accommodate comfortably the bulk of extant law. And this may lend additional authority to its criticism of the areas that it regards as anomalous.

Part I of the Article adds this author's voice to the chorus of criticism directed at existing explanations for the rules governing character evidence—explanations grounded in the view that trial is an exercise in truth seeking. Part II lays out the basic argument for the general prohibition on using character to prove conduct in terms of the primary incentive setting approach to trial. Parts III and IV explain why various ancillary considerations—including tailoring, incapacitation, and dynamic effects—do not upset the conclusion of the basic story laid out in Part II. Along the way, these Parts also examine the liberal use of character evidence in sentencing, the determination of punitive damages, and police investigation. The primary incentives framework is employed in Part V to explain—or perhaps recast and refine—several of the other "exceptions" and apparent inconsistencies regarding the admission of character evidence under the rules. Lastly, Part VI argues against aspects of the law that remain at odds with the incentive setting framework—in particular, the disguised admission of character for conduct under the rubric of

22. This argument also applies to elements of the claim other than primary conduct.

23. See the internal references at supra note 14.

24. Fed. R. Evid. 413–15.

25. See, e.g., Katharine K. Baker, Once a Rapist? Motivational Evidence and Relevancy in Rape Law, 110 Harv. L. Rev. 563, 565 (1997) (arguing against exceptions for prior sex offenses from a truth seeking perspective); David P. Bryden & Roger C. Park, "Other Crimes" Evidence in Sex Offense Cases, 78 Minn. L. Rev. 529, 572 (1994) (same).

"other uses," the recent amendment to the Federal Rules of Evidence for prior sex offenses, and the ancient "mercy rule" for criminal defendants.

II. The Basic Point: Trace Evidence v. Predictive Evidence

The truth seeking approach to trial has had serious difficulty explaining the rules restricting the admission of character evidence for conduct. The previous Part reviewed the list of conventional rationales in light of their shared premise that the purpose of trial is to uncover the truth about past events. Even taken as whole, these arguments fall far short of justifying a categorical ex ante restriction on a source of evidence that is potentially quite useful in sorting out what actually happened on the occasion in question—if that is the aim.

If, however, we focus on the objective of influencing what happens in the future rather than discovering what happened in the past, the rules restricting character evidence make more sense. This Part of the Article sets out the basic incentives based argument for disallowing character evidence to prove conduct. Subsequent Parts explain why adding realistic complications to this basic story does not change its basic conclusions. Following this, the Article shows how the various "exceptions" to the rules restricting character for conduct also fit well within the primary incentives setting approach to trial.

A. *Punchline*

To focus the analysis let us imagine that sometime acquaintances P and D find themselves sitting on adjacent stools at a local bar. P lights a cigarette and begins blowing smoke in D's face. D asks him, not so politely, to desist. P continues purposefully, now staring mockingly at D through the smoke. D gets up off his stool, sets his feet, clenches his fist . . . and there we stop action: in the split second during which D decides whether to throw the punch.[82]

At the beginning of his classic and scathing critique of the rules governing character evidence, Professor Uviller makes a crucial and natural distinction—one which, nonetheless, has never taken root in evidence scholarship.[83] This is the distinction between "trace" and "predictive" evidence. To recite Uviller's analogy, on the question of whether a particular individual hammered a nail, the scratch left on the head is trace evidence—evidence produced as a byproduct of hammering. That the individual is a carpenter or owns a hammer, and so is more likely to have hammered a nail, is predictive evidence.

More generally, predictive evidence of conduct describes the setting—broadly defined to include characters, props, and scenery—in which the conduct may or may not have occurred. Certain circumstances, including not only the actual physical situation but also the character or disposition of the parties involved, may be "fertile ground" for conduct; other settings may be particularly infertile. Evidence of the defendant's propensity to be violent, for example, is predictive evidence for

82. For a similar real world example, see Peter Savodnik, Man Files Assault Charge against Scottsville Mayor, The Daily Progress, Sept. 26, 2000, at B1. The story reported:

> Local businessman Steven Meeks has charged [Scottsville] Mayor Christopher J. Long with assault and battery, contending that the mayor shoved him after a dispute Friday about a table outside Long's restaurant, Caffe Bocce.
>
> Long countered Monday that "there's no credibility to this story" and insisted that he had not, in fact, touched Meeks.
>
> Meeks said Monday that . . . Long had set up a table outside Caffe Bocce, despite town regulations curbing that kind of activity. . . .
>
> "I consider him a threat to me," said Meeks, who ran unsuccessfully for the Town Council. . . .
>
> Meeks was previously charged with election fraud. Those charges were dropped . . . .

Id.

83. Uviller, Illusion, supra note 1, at 847.

his alleged act of assault. Thus, for predictive evidence the direction of causation runs from the evidenced phenomena to the act in question.

For trace evidence, on the other hand, the causal relationship runs in the opposite direction, from the act to the evidenced phenomena. Trace evidence is evidence that is generated (or, more realistically, *tends* to be generated) by the conduct in question. Such evidence includes the consistent and "cross-resistant" testimony of multiple eyewitnesses of commission or its likely aftermath, authenticated documentation, fingerprints, changes in bank account balances, DNA evidence, etc. The evidentiary byproducts of assault and battery, for instance, might include eyewitnesses' testimony. Trace evidence also would include evidence that is generated by the performance of alternative actions that tend to preclude the act in question. Eyewitness reports supporting a defendant's alibi that he was in Berkeley on the evening of the murder in Brooklyn are the byproducts of defendant's choosing *not* to commit the act.[84]

Part of the reason this simple classification scheme never became standard may be that Uviller himself argues so convincingly that the distinction lacks a difference. He invites us to consider that *both* trace and predictive evidence have probative value: Both are useful in determining whether the individual did indeed hammer the nail on the occasion in question. In particular, predictive evidence is probative because information that the setting was conducive (or not) to the act is indeed evidence about whether the act actually did occur. If one learns that conditions were ripe for an event, one thinks the event more likely to have occurred.

In arguing for the irrelevance of this distinction, Uviller—like almost all evidence scholars—rests his analysis on the premise that trial is at its core a truth probing exercise. He is clear about this from his first sentence: "The process of litigation is designed for the reconstruction of an event that occurred in the recent past. And for the most part, the rules by which a trial is conducted are supposed to enhance the accuracy of the synthetic fact."[85] In contrast, when the evidentiary rules governing character evidence are explicitly analyzed within the context of the overall system of state regulation—and in particular, the state's provision of legal incentives for primary activities—the distinction between trace and predictive evidence goes to the heart of the matter.

The law provides incentives to forego committing an act, only if committing the act tends to make the actor worse off under the law than she would be had she not committed the act. If the individual is just as likely to be punished whether or not she engages in the conduct she has no incentive to refrain. This is true regardless of how likely it is that this unconditional punishment is imposed. Thus, legal incentive setting requires *changes* in an individual's anticipated "legal payoffs," driven (per-

84. More precisely, the evidentiary byproduct of the act is the fact that mustering these forms of evidence (for either side) is less expensive as a result of the act. See Sanchirico, Relying, supra note 17, at 327–29; Sanchirico, Games, supra note 17, at 347–48.

85. Uviller, Illusion, supra note 1, at 845.

haps probabilistically) by the individual's choice of whether to commit the act. In setting such legal payoffs, the law relies on the evidentiary performance of the parties. Therefore, any change in payoffs triggered by whether the act is committed ultimately must derive from parallel changes in the sort of evidence that parties can muster for their side. Trace evidence of conduct is precisely this sort of act dependent evidence. Such evidence is a byproduct of the act and so by definition its existence depends (albeit probabilistically) on whether such conduct actually occurred. Predictive evidence, on the other hand, exists whether or not the act is actually committed. Though it is information about whether the act was committed, its existence is not altered by actual commission. Therefore, on its own it cannot be used to alter the legal consequences that the individual faces based on whether she commits the act. While predictive evidence has probative value, it has no "incentive value."

Back to the barroom. Imagine first the extreme case in which P is permitted to prove D's conduct *only* by establishing that D has a propensity for violence, trace evidence of the punch being inadmissible.[86] Trial here would be to some extent probative of whether assault and battery had occurred that night;[87] D's propensity for violence would be probative of his conduct in the barroom. But the system would to no extent provide incentives for D to refrain from assaulting P. If, on the one hand, D has no evincible propensity for violence, he can punch away without legal consequence. Given the hypothesized rules of evidence, P could never sustain his burden of proof. On the other hand, if D enters the current situation with a demonstrable propensity for violence that can be established in court, he might as well swing away, because P can recover against him the same whether or not he actually punches.

Now imagine the same scene in a regime in which conduct in assault and battery cases may *also* be proved by offering trace evidence of the act. If D punches P, there is a fair chance that traces of this incident will be left in the memories of multiple eyewitnesses, whose stories—for the fact that they are woven together by the physical laws of time and space—will tend to be mutually consistent under cross examination. To the extent that the law hangs penalties on this trace evidence, D will indeed face different legal consequences depending on whether he actually punches P. As a result, an incentive to refrain from assault and battery will be created.

These examples demonstrate that conditioning penalties on trace evidence is a necessary and sufficient condition for incentive setting. In particular, without such conditioning, there are no incentives. The implication for predictive evidence is that if it is to play any role whatsoever in

86. The effect on current incentives of admitting propensity evidence in *future* actions is discussed infra Part IV.A.

87. Plaintiff's incentive to file suit and both parties' incentives to settle can be easily accommodated in this analysis, since both proceed in the shadow of what would happen if the case reached trial.

incentive setting, this role must be secondary and derivative of the primary role played by trace evidence. At best, predictive evidence of conduct might be employed to modulate the intensity of the incentive created in the first instance by conditioning on trace evidence—a possibility to which we turn in Part III.

B. *Knowledge of the Rules*

But first it is worth considering a potential objection to the foregoing analysis. Is it really reasonable to suppose that individuals account for, or even have knowledge of, evidentiary rules in making out-of-court decisions? Professor Schwartz asks a similar question for *substantive* legal rules and finds that while fine tuning is likely ineffective, broad brush effects are well confirmed.[88] Safe to say, most students of the law would now agree that incentive setting, in various forms, is an important and real purpose of substantive legal rules—that tort law inspires precaution, that contract law induces performance, that criminal law prevents crime.

The incentives impact of evidentiary law is in turn an implication of the proposition that the substantive law has behavioral effects. The incentive effects of the substantive law rely on the population's belief that there is a connection between choosing to break the law and suffering the legal penalty for doing so. Evidence law is a critical link in this connection. When we say that an individual is sanctioned for negligence, for breach, or for criminal conduct, what we really mean is that the individual is sanctioned for the existence of what is deemed evidence of negligence, breach or crime. And the choice of what is considered evidence is far from inconsequential for the incentive effects of substantive doctrine—as the foregoing analysis of character evidence makes clear. Admitting character evidence for conduct—while it might increase the accuracy of trials—attenuates the connection between actions and consequences. The population may not understand how the connection between actions and consequences is maintained in the current system, nor the particular role played by prohibiting evidence of character. Yet it is easy to imagine that were character evidence freely admitted, the resulting disjunction between actions and assigned penalties would eventually become apparent. And this would seriously impair the effectiveness of substantive doctrine.

III. Tailoring Incentives to Propensity

If character evidence, as well as trace evidence, is admissible against D in the barroom example, won't D be especially deterred from throwing the punch if he has an evincible propensity to violence—and isn't this appropriate? In general, if those with criminal or tortious dispositions know that evidence of their disposition can be used against them in court, won't they have a greater incentive to avoid producing byproduct

88. See Schwartz, supra note 2, at 422–23.

evidence of prohibited conduct? And wouldn't the resulting additional deterrent be desirable, even necessary, in deterring those who are prone to misfeasance by nature?

The more general notion behind these intuitions is that character evidence may be of use in *tailoring* incentives to individual characteristics. If people are not all alike, the argument would run, then presumably some must be more forcefully deterred than others. Perhaps the law should attempt to fit the intensity of the disincentive to the intensity of the desire it must counter. Character evidence would be of use in determining defendants' propensity so that punishments could be appropriately adjusted.[89]

This Part of the Article explains why the desire to tailor incentives does not justify the admission of propensity evidence in the determination of guilt or liability. In the first place, tailoring incentives is desirable only in certain circumstances, which tend to revolve around the criminal law. Moreover, even when tailoring is desirable, admitting character evidence to prove conduct is not the right way to accomplish the task. Attempting to tailor incentives by allowing character to prove conduct, though theoretically possible, is especially prone to error. As likely as not, the result will be the opposite of that intended, dampening rather than amplifying incentives for high propensity individuals. Moreover, a more robust means of tailoring is readily available. Admitting past act evidence only for sentencing and punitive damages is a natural and almost failsafe means of accomplishing the same end. Moreover, police investigative techniques also serve a tailoring function.

A. *When to Tailor: Criminal versus Civil*

It is not as obvious as it may seem that a higher propensity should be met with a stiffer deterrent. Abundant propensity evidence—in the form of, for instance, many prior acts—may be a sign that the defendant enjoys large private benefits from the conduct. For many activities regulated by legal process, especially in the civil arena, such private benefits from the act are a legitimate positive input into the social choice problem that the law is meant to solve.

This helps to justify the fact that in much of the civil law, the legal consequences of the act are not keyed to the size of the *benefits* that it affords the individual, but to the size of the *costs* that it imposes on others. Doing so delegates to the individual the decision of how to trade off private gain with these (now internalized) social costs. The idea is that if an

89. For the economic analysis of past act tailoring in a setting in which commission may be by accident, see George J. Stigler, The Optimum Enforcement of Laws, 78 J. Pol. Econ. 526, 528–29; Ariel Rubinstein, An Optimal Conviction Policy for Offenses That May Have Been Committed by Accident, Applied Game Theory 406, 406–09 (S.J. Brams et al. eds., 1979); Roy Radner, Repeated Principal-Agent Games with Discounting, 53 Econometrica 1173, 1173–74 (1985). Compare this literature to that cited infra note 124, which describes the economic analysis of dynamic incentive effects.

individual's private benefits exceed social costs, she will find it worthwhile to commit the act and suffer the legal consequences—and this is precisely what we would want her to do in this case. To impose a greater disincentive on higher propensity individuals would more intensely deter precisely the group whose commission of the act we would be willing to tolerate.[90]

Nevertheless, in many circumstances, especially in the criminal arena, there is at least a colorable argument for tailoring incentives. Such an argument has two steps. First, for serious felonies such as homicide or rape, for instance, the private benefits of the act—if they even deserve the label "benefits"—are not socially cognizable, and inducing universal deterrence is the essential aim of the law.[91] Second, imposing a punishment for the act that is large enough to deter all (or almost all) individuals, however large their desire, is far from ideal. Criminal punishment, especially when it comes in the form of incarceration, often entails deadweight social loss. Moreover, as the cost of keeping a prisoner increases with the length of his incarceration, this social loss generally increases with the severity of the punishment imposed. Thus, significant cost saving may accrue if the law is at least roughly tuned to provide greater punishments only when necessary.[92]

B. *The Importance of Complementarity*

Assuming that tailoring punishments to propensities is a worthwhile objective, let us be clear about what we would be asking propensity evidence to do—and the possible pitfalls of making that request.

Consider the overall association between evidence and penalties, encompassing both the determination of guilt or liability and the determination of sentence or damages. If propensity evidence is to be used to intensify the disincentive faced by high propensity offenders, the system must be designed so that propensity evidence is a *complement to*, not a *substitute for*, trace evidence in this association.[93] Propensity evidence must magnify the effect of trace evidence on penalties, not be another means of creating the same effect.

90. More precisely, the socially optimal amount of deterrence depends not just on the balancing of its public and private net benefits, but also on system costs. The cost of the legal system is the "third pan" in the balance.

91. Even in this case, however, there may be other related, but innocent, acts that are deterred due to their complementarity in the individual's decision problem with the criminal act. For a formal analysis of this kind of side effect, see Bengt Holmstrom & Paul Milgrom, Multitask Principal-Agent Analyses: Incentive Contracts, Asset Ownership, and Job Design, 7 J.L. Econ. & Org. 24, 25–28 (1991) (Special Issue).

92. Note that if the reader does not accept the argument that punishments should be tailored to propensities, then the argument against using character evidence at the guilt/liability phase of trial for this purpose is even stronger.

93. For a basic analysis of complementarity and substitutability, see Hal R. Varian, Intermediate Microeconomics 111–12 (5th ed. 1999).

Propensity evidence complements trace evidence only when, in the presence of more propensity evidence, a given increase in trace evidence is likely to result in a greater increase in penalty.[94] Only then do higher propensity individuals anticipate a greater negative change in their well being for having committed the act compared to the negative change anticipated by low propensity individuals. Only then is the disincentive more intense for high propensity individuals.

Conversely, if the system is designed so that propensity evidence may be used *in lieu of* trace evidence—that is, as a substitute for, rather than a complement to, trace evidence—the effect reverses direction. Suppose, for example, that the rules of evidence are written so that propensity evidence is a perfect substitute for trace evidence in the link from evidence to penalty. Then low propensity individuals who generate no propensity evidence face penalties only when they commit the act—substitution of propensity evidence is not an option in their case. High propensity individuals, on the other hand, find themselves in the classic position of being "damned if they do, damned if they don't." Propensity evidence sufficient to support a finding against them is available whether or not they commit the act. This limiting case illustrates a more general proposition: The *more* propensity evidence acts as a substitute for, rather than a complement to, byproduct evidence, the more it dampens, rather than amplifies, incentives for high propensity offenders.

94. The issue is even more complex than this, because the precise probabilistic relationship between conduct and trace evidence is also material. It is sufficient to note, then, that it is even more difficult for a practical system to navigate tailoring than the main text of this Article makes it seem. The remainder of this note reviews some of the relevant considerations in mathematical language.

Consider the special case in which both forms of evidence are isomorphic to the real line. Let $F(T,P)$ be the penalty stated as a continuously differentiable function of trace evidence T and propensity evidence P. Trace evidence is a random variable whose distribution depends on whether the defendant engaged in the subject conduct. For risk neutral individuals the intensity of the incentive is the change in expected penalty due to conduct: $I = E[F(T,P)|C] - E[F(T,P)|NC]$, where C stands for conduct and NC, for no conduct, and where T is the random variable over which expectations are taken. We are interested in conditions under which I increases in P. Thus, applying Fubini's theorem, we are interested in conditions under which $E[\delta F(T,P)/\delta P|C]>E[\delta F(T,P)/\delta P|NC]$. A well known result states that the stochastically dominant distribution of a pair of distributions over a given random variable assigns a larger expected value to all increasing functions of that random variable. Conversely, even if two distributions are known to be ordered by stochastic dominance, we can only be sure that the stochastically dominant one will assign a larger value to a function of the random variable, if we also know that the function is increasing in the random variable. The function of interest here is $\delta F(T,P)/\delta P$, and the random variable argument is T. Plausibly, the distribution of T given C stochastically dominates the distribution of T given NC. In this case, to be sure that we are intensifying the incentive for higher propensity offenders, we need $\delta F(T,P)/\delta P$ to increase in T, which is to say (by Young's theorem) that we need propensity evidence to complement trace evidence in the map from evidence to penalties.

C. *Other Acts in Other Places*

To be sure, complementarity, like Lempert and Saltzburg's trial selection bias,[95] is a subtle concept, residing in the high altitude realm of "second order differences." Complementarity concerns not just differences (in anticipated penalties caused by commission), but differences *in those differences* (across individuals, keyed to their varying propensities). The management of second order differences is a lot to ask of any practical system. Throw onto the pile the risk of mistakenly producing substitutability when complementarity is intended—and thus having the opposite effect from what is desired—and the strain seems even greater.

Fortunately, there is a simple and elegant way of creating the requisite complementarities between propensity evidence and byproduct evidence. This method is to bifurcate trial into two phases, the first for the determination of guilt (liability), and the second, contingent phase for the determination of sentence (damages). Complementarity is ensured as long as propensity evidence is used only in the later proceeding to increase penalties. Given the same quantum of trace evidence (that necessary for conviction or liability), the negative impact of this trace evidence on defendant's well being (via the imposition of sentence or punitive damages) is more severe for higher propensity offenders than for low.

The manner in which this system produces the requisite complementarity between trace and propensity evidence may be illustrated by analogy to the operation of a dining room dimmer switch. If there is sufficient trace evidence in the guilt/liability phase, we push the knob in to turn on the light (we find guilt or liability). At the sentencing or damages phase, we turn the dial for brightness in proportion to the quantum of past act evidence. The end result: The effect of turning on the light (the effect of the existence of trace evidence, hence of commission) as measured by the difference between the initial darkness and the light now filling the room (this difference being the strength of the incentive), increases with how far the dimmer is turned up (the quantum of propensity evidence) after it is turned on. In particular, high propensity offenders produce a greater increase in candle power whenever they generate sufficient trace evidence to trip the light.

This method of allowing propensity evidence for determination of penalty and not guilt or liability is, as a matter of mathematical logic, the very simplest way of producing the sort of complementarity between trace and propensity evidence required to set stronger incentives for higher propensity offenders. Whether by conscious design or trial and error, this also happens to be the method that the system employs. Though many other considerations are at play,[96] one can see in the existing system for both sentencing and the award of punitive damages a reflection

95. See supra Part I.F.

96. See infra Part IV for a discussion of incapacitation and dynamic effects.

of the desire to tailor penalty to propensity. Police techniques are also fruitfully evaluated in this light.

1. *Sentencing.* — In most jurisdictions the criminal law separates determination of guilt from determination of sentence. Indeed, in most cases, sentencing is determined by the judge at a subsequent hearing, even though a jury has made the determination of guilt.[97] In setting the sentence, the judge exercises varying amounts of discretion within the bounds of legislative authority. But regardless of the degree of judicial discretion, evidence of a defendant's character, in particular evidence of his other crimes, wrongs, or acts, plays an important role. In the federal system, 18 U.S.C. § 3661 (1994) states that "[n]o limitation shall be placed on the information concerning the background, character, and conduct of a person convicted of an offense" for the purpose of determining sentence. Federal Rule of Evidence § 1101(d) makes clear that none of the Federal Rules of Evidence, including those that prohibit character evidence, apply to sentencing. And the Federal Sentencing Guidelines lay out an elaborate system under which the "guideline range" for a sentence (from which the judge may deviate) is based on two dimensions: offense characteristics[98] and a defendant's "criminal history category."[99] Further, unadjudicated prior bad acts may also be taken into account in the judge's exercise of discretion.[100] Many states have similar rules and procedures.[101] The reasons given for allowing use of a defendant's characteristics and criminal history are many and varied. But they do occasionally approximate the desire to tailor deterrence to propensity.[102]

97. There is no Sixth Amendment right to sentencing by jury. McMillan v. Pennsylvania, 477 U.S. 79, 93 (1986). However, some states allow jury sentencing (or at least jury recommendation) in capital cases. E.g., Fla. Stat. Ann. § 921.141(1) (West 2001) (requiring sentencing proceeding before jury in capital cases). Others even provide for jury sentencing for all felonies. E.g., Va. Code Ann. § 19.2-295.1 (Michie 2000) ("upon a finding that the defendant is guilty of a felony, a separate proceeding limited to the ascertainment of punishment shall be held . . . before the same jury"). When the jury handles sentencing, this part of the proceeding may or may not be separated from the determination of guilt. If it is not, jury sentencing tends to be based more on aggravating factors relating to the crime itself, as opposed to the convict's other crimes, wrongs, or acts.

98. U.S. Sentencing Guidelines Manual §§ 2–3 (1999).

99. Id. § 4.

100. Id. § 4A1.3.

101. Wayne R. LaFave & Jerold H. Israel, Criminal Procedure § 26.5 (2d ed. 1992).

102. For example, the source point for much of the current system of sentencing is the case of *Williams v. New York*. 337 U.S. 241 (1949). The convicted defendant in that capital case was sentenced to death by the judge based in part on his involvement in thirty other unconvicted, unrelated burglaries in the area, as well as other, not necessarily criminal, activities that indicated to the judge that defendant was a "menace to society" and in possession of a "morbid sexuality." Id. at 244. In ruling that the judge's use of this evidence did not violate due process, the Supreme Court gave assent to the "modern philosophy of penology that the punishment should fit the offender and not merely the crime." Id. at 247.

2. *Punitive Damages.* — Punitive damages are not generally awarded in civil cases, and compensatory damages are set without regard to a defendant's other acts. Consequently, incentives tailoring is the exception rather than the rule in the civil arena. This is consistent with the point made above that tailoring itself is often unwarranted in civil actions. Tailoring becomes a valid ancillary objective only when the act to be deterred is of the sort that society would fully prohibit (and punishment is costly). For the most part, the set of such actions is contained within the criminal arena. Nonetheless, some of these criminal-like acts—such as willful disregard, assault and battery, and fraud—have over time made their way into the civil law, as if the civil law were a backstop for gaps in the criminal law.[103]

When they are awarded, punitive damages are often determined in a manner parallel to the determination of sentence—both substantively and procedurally. Substantively, most jurisdictions stipulate that the level of punitive damages should reflect, among other things, the "reprehensibility" or "culpability" of defendant's act.[104] Most often, these concepts go to the defendant's state of mind. But courts also determine "reprehensibility" according to "the existence and frequency of similar past conduct,"[105] where such past conduct is used in a manner that implicates not so much state of mind as a desire to tailor penalty to propensity.[106]

---

103. 1 James D. Ghiardi & John J. Kircher, Punitive Damages Law and Practice § 2.02 (1999) ("[T]hose who favor the concept of punitive damages in civil law are arguing that the doctrine serves to fill gaps in the criminal law by punishing conduct which, although it deserves punishment, is not being punished through the criminal law [due, for instance, to prosecutorial discretion].").

104. For examples of states that require bad conduct for punitive damage awards, see Id. § 5.01 (noting Alabama requires that defendant's conduct must be marked by "malice, willfulness or wanton and reckless disregard for the rights of others"); Id. (noting Colorado requires "fraud, malice or willful and wanton conduct"); Id. (noting Minnesota requires that defendant must show "deliberate disregard for the rights or safety of others"); Id. (noting Mississippi requires that defendant's act be "a willful and intentional wrong").

105. Green Oil Co. v. Hornsby, 539 So. 2d 218, 223 (Ala. 1989), cited with approval in Pac. Mut. Life Ins. Co. v. Haslip, 499 U.S. 1, 21 (1991). The Alabama Supreme Court instructs that in making the determination of whether the verdict is excessive (or inadequate), a trial court is authorized to consider, among other factors "the existence and frequency of similar past conduct," which is cast as a component of reprehensibility. Id. The U.S. Supreme Court has explicitly noted the analogy between punitive damages and sentencing in this regard. BMW of N. Am., Inc. v. Gore, 517 U.S. 559, 577 (1996) ("Our holdings that a recidivist may be punished more severely than a first offender recognize that repeated misconduct is more reprehensible than an individual instance of malfeasance.").

106. In *Swans v. City of Lansing*, Swans's estate sought punitive damages against the defendant Detention Officer Moore, among others, for use of excessive force and denial of medical care. 65 F. Supp. 2d 625, 631 (W.D. Mich. 1998). Moore and his fellow officers had used the "kick-stop restraint" system on the violently schizophrenic Swans at the city jail, whereby Swans's legs and arms were tied behind his back to a strap on his waist. Contrary to the strap manufacturer's instructions, the officers had applied the restraint while Swans was face down on the floor, which caused Swans to suffocate. Important to the case was the finding that the officers had failed to administer rescue breathing promptly or

Procedurally, in order to prevent the other acts evidence used to determine punitive damages from infecting the determination of liability, many jurisdictions now either permit or require that the trial be bifurcated when punitive damages are at issue.[107] Federal Rule of Civil Proce-

call an ambulance, instead leaving Swans alone in his cell for a fatal eleven minutes after applying the restraint. Plaintiff offered evidence that Moore had on a previous occasion left another inmate to die unobserved in his cell despite the inmate's announcement that he had ingested methyl alcohol. Apparently, Moore had been punished under the law for this conduct. Id. at 633–36. The court allowed evidence of the previous incident. But this was not for the purpose of showing conduct, which was essentially out of contention given that the episode had occurred under video surveillance. Swans v. City of Lansing, No. 5:96 CV 56, 1997 U.S. Dist. LEXIS 17264, at *2, *6 (W.D. Mich. Aug. 21, 1997). Rather, the evidence was admissible "in order to assess the appropriate amount of punitive damages against [Moore] to prevent a similar occurrence in the future, considering that the past judgment against Moore had been ineffective in preventing misconduct as to Swans." *Swans*, 65 F. Supp. 2d at 646. This is precisely the sort of incentive tailoring discussed above.

The same sort of tailoring purpose appears in *Castro v. Sebesta*. 808 S.W.2d 189 (Tex. App. 1991). While under the influence of marijuana, Sebesta drove head on into Castro's car, leaving Castro permanently disabled. Given Sebesta's stipulations, the only issue was the proper size of actual and punitive damages. Id. at 191. At trial Castro was prevented from introducing evidence that "defendant, by repeatedly violating laws designed to protect the public, showed a disregard for the safety of others, and thus was responsible for punitive damages." Id. at 192. Accepting Castro's implicit theory of punitive damages, the Texas Court of Appeals held the trial court in error for not admitting evidence of Sebasta's prior drug use. Id. at 194. The Court of Appeals couched its tailoring motive in terms of culpability, but implicated a tailoring motive:

> The limitation on the evidence imposed by the court did not allow the plaintiff to show defendant's actual level of culpability. That defendant regularly smoked marihuana while driving a car was relevant to the determination of punitive damages. To determine if an award for punitive damages was appropriate, plaintiff should have been able to show the jury just how indifferent the defendant was to the danger of driving a car while smoking marihuana.

Id. at 194. Indeed, in a true approximation of criminal sentencing, the Texas Court of Appeals even ruled the trial court in error for excluding the defendant's driving record, arguing that such record showed the "context of [the defendant's] actions on the night of the accident." Id. at 195.

Similarly, in *Holt v. Grinnell* the Georgia Court of Appeals noted that:

> The extent of the defendant's willful misconduct, wantonness and entire want of care in driving under the influence cannot be gauged solely by focusing on the incident in issue. Accordingly, in such cases, evidence that the defendant pled guilty to driving under the influence prior to or even after the incident in issue would be admissible as relevant to the issue of punitive damages.

441 S.E.2d 874, 875 (Ga. Ct. App. 1994) (citation omitted).

107. See Developments in the Law: The Civil Jury, 110 Harv. L. Rev. 1408, 1529–30 (1997). This article notes that:

> The primary rationale for bifurcation is that some evidence presented for the determination of punitive damages may be irrelevant, confusing, or prejudicial to the determination of liability for compensatory damages. For example, evidence regarding a defendant's wealth or other bad acts committed by the defendant may be admissible and relevant to the issue of punitive damages, but irrelevant and highly prejudicial in the jury's determination of compensatory damages. Bifurcation allows a court to keep this sort of information away from the jury during the compensatory phase.

dure 42(b), for instance, generally allows the trial court to order a separate trial for any claim or issue. This rule has been consistently employed to separate the determination of punitive damages awards from the determination of liability.[108] The procedural rules of many states contain an analogue to Federal Rule 42(b). Furthermore, at least thirteen states go beyond the general rule for trial separation to permit or require a separate proceeding specifically for punitive damages.[109]

3. *Police Procedures: Not the Usual Usual Suspects Argument.* — At one point in his account of a year spent with New York City's Ninth Precinct, Professor Uviller reports being at first puzzled when an officer hands the picture book of mug shots to three young suspects in an open and shut street robbery. After observing their behavior, though, he suggests a rationale:

> The three . . . immediately became a group of high school chums laughing over their friends' pictures in the yearbook. Each page was turned with glee, each of the many photos they recognized got a little description: "Hey that's my aunt's old man! Ain't he the baddest?" "Look, there's Chinko. He's chilling out now." "What do you know. They got Blueboy. Wait'll Junior hears this."
>
> . . . .
>
> [Says Uviller to the officer:] "Maybe these people will convince their friends that with their photos on file here, they're sitting ducks." [The officer] agreed. Word would travel back to the streets—it always does. *Maybe some predator might think twice before pointing a blade if he knows his victim will come straight up to our office and look through a book containing a good, clear, photograph of him, front and profile.* As [the officer] knew well, while capture and conviction are the daily mission, deterrence is the object.[110]

This and other accounts of police procedures indicate that past offenses do play a role in how the police direct their efforts in investigating crime.[111] The police are more likely to ask around about an individual,

Id. at 1530.

108. Ghiardi & Kircher, supra note 103, § 12.04, at 11 & n.10 (citing, inter alia, Holben v. Midwest Emory Freight Sys., Inc., 525 F. Supp. 1224 (W.D. Pa. 1981)).

109. Different states split the action at different points; some make separation mandatory, others allow it on request of the parties. See *BMW*, 517 U.S. at 618 (Ginsburg, J., dissenting); Developments in the Law: The Civil Jury, supra note 107, at 1529–30. In Georgia, for instance, bifurcation is mandatory. The trier of fact first decides whether to award any punitive damages at all and then reconvenes to decide the amount to be awarded. Ga. Code Ann. § 51-12-5.1 (2000); Webster v. Boyett, 496 S.E.2d 459, 463 (1998); Hanie v. Barnett, 444 S.E.2d 336, 337–38 (Ga. Ct. App. 1994).

110. Uviller, Tempered Zeal, supra note 76, at 49–50 (emphasis added). Compare Uviller's statement here about the purpose of the criminal justice system—deterrence—with his previously reported statement about the purpose of trial—to find the truth. Uviller, Illusion, supra note 1, at 845. Uviller had no reason to think that these objectives were not aligned, contrary to the message of this Article.

111. See, e.g., Lempert et al., supra note 33, at 327–28 ("[T]he photographs shown to crime victims and other eyewitnesses for the purpose of identifying the criminal usually

interrogate him in person, search his person, his house and his car, call him in for a lineup and show his picture to victims, if he already has a criminal record.

Lempert and Saltzburg were perhaps the first to emphasize that police investigative techniques—including the tendency of the police to round up the usual suspects—are importantly relevant to a consideration of evidentiary rules.[112] But in the end, their analysis is limited by its attachment to the conventional premise that trial is fundamentally a truth seeking exercise. As argued in Part I.F.2.b, Lempert and Saltzburg's hypothesis that rounding up the usual suspects produces appearance at trial more often for the innocent than for the guilty is ultimately no more plausible than its logical inverse.

The analysis is quite different, however, when one views trial in the larger context of reducing crime. The question changes from whether the use of past acts in investigation produces an irreparable trial selection bias to whether the use of past acts in investigation complements or substitutes for trace evidence of the current act in the ultimate association between current conduct and sanctions—i.e., whether police techniques create stiffer or lighter disincentives for higher propensity offenders. The answer also becomes more definitive: There is good reason to think that police use of past records systematically complements trace evidence of conduct.

The conclusion that the effect is complementary rests on two almost definitional premises about the nature of investigation. The first premise is that police investigation is generally neither futile nor fraudulent: It tends to reveal new information and this new information tends to incriminate the guilty more often than the innocent and exculpate the innocent more often than the guilty. If this is not the case—if, for instance, the police investigate as zealous advocates ignoring what exonerates and overemphasizing or perhaps fabricating what incriminates—then the story will not hold. Of course, if this darker picture of police behavior is more in line with general reality, it is hard to see what if anything can be said about criminal evidence of any kind.

The second premise is that investigation's effect on the imposition of sanctions (via proof of conduct) operates through the revelation of additional trace evidence. Support for this premise starts at trial and moves upstream. First, the imposition of sanctions ultimately depends on proving conduct at trial, and trace evidence thereof is the generally permitted

come from files on people with records for similar crimes."); T. Markus Funk, A Mere Youthful Indiscretion? Reexamining the Policy of Expunging Juvenile Delinquency Records, 29 U. Mich. J.L. Reform 885, 925 (1996) ("Criminal records thus not only inform the discretion of prosecutors in handling specific cases and help correctional institutions develop effective diagnostic programs, but also directly assist the police in their most vital function—investigating criminals.").

112. Lempert & Saltzburg, supra note 64, at 217; Lempert et al., supra note 33, at 327–28.

method of doing so.[113] Second, prosecutors ultimately determine which cases go to trial, and they do so against the backdrop of the rules of evidence just described, presumably declining to waste time on cases lacking sufficient admissible evidence of conduct. Lastly, it is reasonable to suppose that the police develop some understanding of what induces prosecutors to either press or ignore a case that they have labored to investigate. Accordingly, it is also reasonable to suppose that police tend to focus their investigative efforts on uncovering admissible trace evidence of conduct.[114]

Uviller's account provides a clear example of how targeting those with a past record for investigation—when investigation is a sincere and purposeful attempt to uncover trace evidence of conduct—enhances the disincentive for repeat offenders. Uviller's compact claim is that those in the picture book face a stronger deterrent.[115] Because one gets in the picture book by having a past record, Uviller is implicitly claiming complementarity between past acts and current sanctions. Further unpacking his example, we can see how it is a special case of the general points just made. First, the book is a form of targeted investigation. The police could conceivably show victims a picture of everyone in New York City. But they do not. They target their efforts at obtaining a victim ID to those with mug shots, and so those with past records. Second, Uviller is indeed assuming that picture book identification by victims, as a form of investigation, tends to be sincere and effective. If victims were as likely to finger the innocent—whether out of encouragement from police, personal bias, or simple mistake—then those on the street would see less of a relationship between actually committing the crime and becoming a suspect. What makes the pictured subject "think twice before pointing a blade," while the rest of us are presumably thinking only once, is that having his picture in the book makes it more likely that he will be correctly identified. Lastly, in Uviller's example the targeted investigation (showing the victim the picture book) leads to trace evidence of conduct. The trace evidence consists of traces in the victim's memory of the perpetrator's facial features, evidence that will be admissible for conduct at trial in the form of the victim's testimony.

The general case, of which Uviller's account is a special example, is perhaps best illustrated by reference to the hypothetical extreme in which investigation always reveals perfectly accurate and conclusive trace

---

113. Prosecutors may use character to prove the accused's criminal conduct if the accused opens the door by introducing evidence of his own character to show that he did not commit the crime. Fed. R. Evid. 404(a)(1). Presumably, only defendants who are not vulnerable to the prosecutor's counter attack will tend to go this route. For more on this see infra Part VI.B. Prosecutors may also use evidence of past sexual offenses (inclusive of child molestation) to prove currently charged sexual offenses. Fed. R. Evid. 413–14. For more on this see infra Part VI.A.

114. See Uviller, Tempered Zeal, supra note 76, at 21–22 (discussing relationships between police and prosecutors).

115. See id. at 50.

evidence of whether the investigated suspect actually committed the crime. In this artificial world, an individual is convicted for the crime if and only if he is both guilty and investigated. (Those not investigated are, of course, not indicted. The innocent who are investigated are always exonerated; the guilty who are investigated are always indicted and convicted.) Thus, if the individual refrains from the act, he is certain not to be convicted for it; and if the individual commits the act, whether he is sanctioned depends entirely on whether he is investigated. As a result, the change in legal consequence from committing the act is more intensely negative the more likely one is to be investigated. Therefore, those with past records, because they are by hypothesis more likely to be investigated, face a stiffer disincentive.

This same basic story holds in a world in which investigation, though not perfect, tends to constitute a sincere and purposive search for trace evidence of conduct. Even if being targeted for investigation increases the chance of conviction regardless of whether one actually commits the crime, the increase is far steeper if one has in fact engaged in the investigated criminal conduct. On the one hand, investigation may well uncover exonerating trace evidence—alibis—for the innocent.[116] On the other hand, true evidentiary byproducts of the individual's criminal activity are more likely to be found if the individual is specifically investigated.

D. *Attempting Complementarity via Proof of Conduct*

We have shown that using propensity evidence to determine the intensity of the sanction or to target investigation is an effective way to tailor incentives. But this analysis does not rule out the possibility that the system would function as well or even better in this regard were propensity evidence also employed in the guilt/liability phase of trial.

In fact, it would function much worse. To be sure, it is theoretically *possible* to tailor incentives by means of manipulating the determination of guilt or liability. But in stark contrast to the simplicity and robustness of using propensity evidence in sentencing, for example, the proper employment of propensity evidence at trial is counterintuitive, epistemologically demanding, and dangerously prone to error.

Suppose, for instance, that propensity evidence becomes admissible for conduct and so counts toward meeting trial burdens on that issue. For high propensity offenders, such a policy change does increase the effect of the lesser quantum of trace evidence that is now, in conjunction with propensity evidence, sufficient for conviction. On the other hand, the policy change decreases the penalty leverage of the *additional* amounts of trace evidence that were formerly necessary for conviction. Thus, while admission of propensity evidence to show conduct amplifies the effect of the newly sufficient amount of trace evidence, it also dampens the impact of the newly excessive amount. The net effect of this trade

116. For more on "negative trace evidence" see infra Part V.D.

off on the strength of the incentive facing the high propensity individual is virtually impossible to predict in practice.

Returning to the barroom scenario, we can easily construct an example wherein allowing propensity evidence for conduct actually dampens the disincentive for violent individuals. Suppose that liability in such cases requires at least two eyewitnesses if D has no demonstrable propensity to violence, but only one eyewitness if D has a demonstrable history of physical aggression.[117] Let us suppose, as in Table 1, that the chance of at least one eyewitness is twenty percent if D punches P and ten percent if he does not, whereas the chance of at least *two* eyewitnesses is nineteen percent if D punches P and one percent if he does not. (Obviously, in some cases, these "eyewitnesses" will be mistaken or mendacious.)

Whether or not D punches P, the event "there is at least one eyewitness to D's punch" is, as it must be, more likely than the subset event "there are at least two eyewitnesses." What matters for incentives, however, is how much punching *increases* the probability of each of these two events. Importantly, D's punch increases the chance of at least two eyewitnesses by a greater amount (one percent up to nineteen percent) than it increases the chance of at least one eyewitness (ten percent up to twenty percent).[118]

TABLE 1

EYEWITNESSES	D PUNCHES	D REFRAINS
At Least 1	20%	10%
At Least 2	19%	1%

By hypothesis, if D has no demonstrable propensity for violence, then he is held liable only if at least two eyewitnesses testify that they saw him punch P. On the other hand, if he has a demonstrable propensity for violence, he is held liable if there is at least *one* eyewitness to his punch (the first row). Consequently, if D has no demonstrable propensity toward violence, then punching P increases the chance that he will be punished by eighteen percentage points (nineteen minus one). However, if D does have a demonstrable propensity toward violence, punching P increases the chance that he will be punished by only ten percentage points (twenty minus ten). Thus, allowing P to offer propensity evidence in proof of D's conduct provides weaker disincentives to D's with a higher propensity for violence.

117. For purposes of this example, hold the remedy constant.

118. This constellation of probabilities was chosen to make a point, but nonetheless reflects a natural phenomenon. The fact that the probability increase is greater for at least two witnesses means that the event "at least two eyewitnesses" is a more precise signal of commission.

This kind of reversal need not always occur.[119] But my argument does not rest on the claim that it always will. The point is that the effect on incentives of admitting character for conduct can go either way depending on magnitudes that cannot be reliably measured.[120] In contrast, increasing sentences or punitive damages for high propensity offenders, while basing guilt and liability solely on trace evidence, is almost structurally guaranteed to produce the requisite complementarities necessary to intensify, not dampen, incentives for high propensity offenders.

E. *Knowledge of the Rules—Reprise*

It is worth pausing again to consider whether the incentives stories just told ask too much of individuals' knowledge of the law.[121] Is it reasonable to suppose that individuals understand and anticipate the manner in which the legal consequences of their actions are tailored to their personal characteristics via sentencing, punitive damages, and police procedures? It is one thing to accept that evidentiary rules have broad brush incentive effects—like those identified in Part II. But perhaps this sort of fine tuning to personal characteristics is too much to ask of a practical system.[122]

For some forms of tailoring, this objection could be addressed directly. One could point to Uviller's account of the picture book described in Part III.C.3, or the pervasiveness of lineups, finger prints, and mug shots in popular culture. One might also point to the recent salience of "three strikes and you're out" laws. If more systematic evidence is

119. If the chance of at least two eyewitnesses is eleven percent with commission and nine percent without, then the high propensity will be more strongly deterred.

120. The point of this Section is inadvertently corroborated by Professors Schrag and Scotchmer. They build their analysis of character evidence on a combination of the conflict they identify—between error minimization and maximal deterrence as discussed at supra note 17—and the (questionable) assumption that the jury itself sets the evidentiary threshold (or thresholds, when the defendant's propensity is observed) in order to minimize trial error. Schrag & Scotchmer, supra note 17, at 327. Given Schrag and Scotchmer's prior findings comparing error minimization to maximal deterrence, juries who behave in this way will be lenient relative to the objective of maximizing deterrence. Id. at 329–32 (Propositions 1 and 2). Schrag and Scotchmer prove in the context of their model that admitting character evidence mitigates this leniency with respect to high propensity individuals, but exacerbates it with respect to low propensity individuals. Id. at 333–34 (Proposition 3). The net effect on crime is uncertain, as highlighted in this Section. Instead of drawing lessons from this uncertainty, as I do here, Schrag and Scotchmer choose to emphasize that if the effect on high propensity individuals is more important, admitting character evidence will increase deterrence. They give the appropriate condition within their "crime opportunities" framework for this phenomenon. Id. at 334 (Proposition 4). Schrag and Scotchmer also consider how their findings change with the introduction of jury or prosecutor prejudice. Id. at 335–40 (Propositions 5–7).

121. This Section continues the discussion begun at the end of Part II.

122. See Schwartz, supra note 2, at 379 (arguing against plausibility of fine tuning tort liability rules).

required, some recent studies show that sentencing enhancements do have real deterrent effects.[123]

But while these responses may help to shore up the tailoring explanation for sentencing, punitive damages, and police techniques, they are actually unnecessary for the more central claim of this Part of the Article—namely that tailoring does *not* justify the admission of propensity evidence in the determination of guilt or liability. For if tailoring is impractical at any level, then certainly it provides no reason to admit propensity evidence in determining guilt or liability. The hard case for my central argument against admitting character evidence for guilt or liability is the case in which individuals do clearly anticipate the manner in which legal consequences will be tailored to their personal characteristics. That is the case that I have considered and rejected in this Part of the Article.

IV. Dynamic Incentives and Incapacitation

The law creates primary activity incentives by hanging legal consequences on the production of trace evidence. If character evidence has a role to play in the regulation of conduct, that role is at best ancillary. In Part III of this Article, we examined one potential ancillary role—the tailoring of incentives to propensity—concluding that if and when tailoring is warranted, it should be accomplished by admitting other act evidence for sentencing and the determination of punitive damages, not by allowing character evidence to contribute toward meeting trial burdens in the determination of guilt or liability. This Part takes up two other potential uses for character evidence and reaches a similar conclusion with respect to each.

A. *Dynamic Incentive Effects*[124]

The prospective admission of propensity evidence in future legal actions arising from other future conduct affects the incentive to engage in

123. See, e.g., Kessler & Levitt, supra note 2, at 345 (arguing that "by looking at changes in crime immediately following the introduction of a sentence enforcement, it is possible to isolate a pure deterrent effect that is not contaminated by incapacitation").

124. For the economic analysis of dynamic incentive effects (as distinguished from tailoring, see supra note 89), see Moshe Burnovski & Zvi Safra, Deterrence Effects of Sequential Punishment Policies: Should Repeat Offenders Be More Severely Punished? 14 Int'l Rev. L. & Econ. 341, 341–43 (1994); C.Y. Cyrus Chu, Sheng-cheng Hu & Ting-yuan Huang, Punishing Repeat Offenders More Severely, 20 Int'l Rev. L. & Econ. 127, 127–28 (2000); John Nash, To Make the Punishment Fit the Crime: The Theory and Statistical Estimation of a Multi-Period Optimal Deterrence Model, 11 Int'l Rev. L. & Econ. 101, 101–02 (1991); Brendan O'Flaherty, Why Repeated Criminal Opportunities Matter: A Dynamic Stochastic Analysis of Criminal Decision Making, 14 J.L. Econ. & Org. 232, 232–34 (1998); A. Mitchell Polinsky & Daniel L. Rubinfeld, A Model of Optimal Fines for Repeat Offenders, 46 J. Pub. Econ. 291, 291–94 (1991); A. Mitchell Polinsky & Steven Shavell, On Offense History and the Theory of Deterrence, 18 Int'l Rev. L. & Econ. 305, 305–07 (1998) [hereinafter Polinsky & Shavell, Offense History].

current conduct to the extent that today's bad conduct becomes tomorrow's "prior wrong."[125] If D does punch P, for instance, this will affect the propensity history that D carries into future legal actions. D will more likely be held liable or guilty in situations perhaps similar to, but not arising from, the present circumstance in the bar. This unfavorable prospect adds an additional deterrent to anticipated penalties from suits arising directly from the punch. But the fact that admitting propensity evidence in future actions can affect current conduct does not mean that it should be employed to such effect.

As a preliminary matter, it is important to be clear about the particular purpose of admitting propensity evidence that is currently under consideration. The goal is not to learn more about the individual's propensity by watching her behavior over time. This motive for considering propensity has already been examined in this Article under the rubric of "tailoring."[126] The object now under consideration is simpler: to increase the disincentive for current conduct across the board (i.e., irrespective of individual propensity) by recourse to how guilt or liability is determined in future legal actions.

It is also worth clarifying the means by which this new goal is meant to be accomplished. The method is essentially to delay the legal effect of trace evidence of current conduct. The idea is that the witnesses who see D punch P today may, in relating the event within the community, affect D's reputation for violence, which may in turn come back to haunt D in future legal actions. Alternatively, these witnesses may themselves be called to testify in future actions to D's violent temperament on the basis of their memory of that night in the bar.[127] Essentially, then, part of the effect on penalties of the trace evidence of D's current punch is being postponed until future actions regarding different but similar conduct. Trace evidence of the original punch is still doing the work of incentive setting; the future admission of character evidence is just the means by which this trace evidence of current conduct affects future penalties.[128]

But if the object is just to increase the current deterrent, it is unclear what delay adds to the pursuit of this goal. A simpler, more direct, and thus more failsafe alternative is to simply increase penalties in actions

125. Similarly, the admission of propensity evidence in the *current* action will have affected the individual's incentives in the *past*.

126. See supra Part III.

127. In fact, testimony as to specific acts would be prohibited under Fed. R. Evid. 405.

128. If the law grounds a current conviction on the bare fact of past convictions, rather than the underlying facts, it risks creating a sort of "propensity bubble." Suppose an individual is convicted once, perhaps correctly. Suppose that the next time, however, he actually did not commit the crime, but his past record leads to a new conviction. Now he has two past convictions and is an easy mark for prosecutors, which leads to a third conviction, which makes him an even easier mark for a fourth, etc. This feedback loop is avoided if the court refers to the evidence that produced each conviction, not just the fact of conviction. The discussion in the text assumes that the law does not make this even greater mistake.

arising from the current conduct itself. Instead of fining the individual $1000 now and possibly $1000 later, fine her $1500 now (or however much she regards as equivalent to the two part, semicontingent fine).[129] Instead of sentencing the individual to six months now and possibly six more months later, sentence her to eight months now.[130]

But even if there were good reasons to lag penalties for current wrongs, the future admission of character evidence to prove conduct would not be the best way to accomplish this. When we attempt to increase current deterrence via the future admission of propensity, we are essentially asking future proceedings to influence both future and cur-

129. One might assert that wealth constraints prevent higher fines in the current action, and that therefore, some deterrence must be accomplished by admitting propensity evidence derived from the current act in future legal actions, when the individual has more cash on hand. But if we believe that the individual will have additional cash on hand in the future then we can always attach this as part of the current fine. Indeed this is to some extent accomplished in current law by means of garnishing future wages. Note in this regard that the papers listed in note 124 that advocate punishing repeat offenders more severely impose separate wealth constraints on each time period, which is to say that they do not allow this kind of "borrowing" of penalties from the future. See, e.g., Polinsky & Shavell, Offense History, supra note 124, at 308 (requiring that first period sanctions not exceed first period wealth); Chu et al., supra note 124, at 136 (same).

Of course, the state and federal statutes governing garnishment except, as they should, the portion of wages necessary for the basic support of the individual and her dependents. See, e.g., 15 U.S.C. § 1673 (1994) (exempting a portion of an individual's gross income from garnishment, which portion is adjusted upwards when the individual has dependents); N.Y. C.P.L.R. 5231(g) (McKinney 2001) (same). But the fact that not all of future wages can be currently fined is not an argument against front loading what can be. The currently untouchable portion of future wages will be just as untouchable in the future.

A secondary objection to front loading the fine might be that if we attach future resources now, there will not be anything left for the individual to lose in the future. As a result, future incentives will suffer. This is certainly a problem, but not a problem solved by linking current punishment to future legal actions. Such linkage consumes future resources in deterring current conduct in essentially the same way. If we charge the individual $100 more in the future action on account of his propensity, this is $100 of future resources that is not contingent on future conduct and so is not helping deter future conduct.

The general point is this: Either the individual has enough lifetime resources sufficient for setting fines to deter the prohibited conduct throughout her lifetime, or she does not. If the individual does not, the solution is either to give up on deterrence or resort to an alternative form of penalty, such as incarceration. The solution does not lie in some form of sophisticated intertemporal accounting.

130. In this case, diminishing marginal utility does not provide the usual argument against bunching. The object is not to allocate real punishment over time in a way that minimizes utility loss for the offender—if this were the case then we would indeed want to spread punishment over time. The object is to produce a given utility loss for the offender at the least cost to society.

Further, the fact that future punishment is only probabilistic, and so might not have to be imposed, also does not provide an argument against front loading. The fact that it is probabilistic means not only that it is of lower expected cost, but also that it has a lower effect on currently expected utility. To the extent that the punishment is probabilistic, then, it must be of greater magnitude (and so of greater expense) when actually imposed.

rent behavior. Such procedural multitasking is delicate and risky, as modifications meant to move toward one goal may detract from accomplishing the other, with indeterminate net effect. In particular, to the extent that propensity evidence grounded in past conduct crowds out trace evidence of future conduct in the determination of future penalties, the attempt to discourage current conduct via the future admission of propensity evidence will detract from the disincentive to engage in *future* conduct.

If, instead, propensity evidence deriving from past conduct is used only in future sentencing or the determination of punitive damages, this unfavorable trade off between present and future incentives is replaced by a favorable synergy. In this case, current bad conduct still produces lower future welfare: If the individual is convicted or held liable in the future, his punishment is greater for having currently engaged in bad conduct. At the same time, the individual's incentive to refrain from bad conduct in the future is also strengthened as a result of her commission of past wrongs: Trace evidence of future wrongs now triggers greater fines. Indeed, if the fact that this behavior is being repeated indicates that the individual needs a greater disincentive, then the incentives tailoring discussed in previous Sections and the lagged penalty effect of this Section are accomplished simultaneously.

B. *Incapacitation*

The premise of this Article is implicitly two tiered: First, that evidence law needs to be evaluated in the context of the regulation of primary activities; and second, that this regulation is accomplished mainly by providing individuals with incentives to think beyond their own personal interest. There is room in this conjunction to recognize that the regulation of primary activities does not and could not proceed solely by means of incentive setting. The population is vast and diverse, and there is no reason to think that everyone in it can be effectively influenced by threat of penalty or promise of reward. Some individuals may be incapable of comprehending future consequences; others may lack suitable control over their impulses. In such cases, the only option, short of abandoning the regulatory exercise, is to take the matter out of the individual's hands by rendering her incapable of such conduct.[131] Thus we commit, incar-

131. Implicit in this discussion is the premise that, among the various means of social regulation, incapacitation is a last resort. Part of the reason for this is fairly mundane. As compared to incentive setting, incapacitation is an expensive means of regulating behavior. Dismemberment, execution, and incarceration require significant resources. Further, each of these alternatives removes from circulation a potentially productive individual (or at the very least an individual capable of adding to the collective welfare through expression of her own preference to avoid incapacitation). In contrast, the expenses of regulation by incentive setting are greatly leveraged. For every hearing that must be held, for every punishment that must be meted out, there are many more cases in which an individual decides not to commit the act, thus avoiding such costs for herself and for society.

cerate, in some cases even execute, not just to deter, but also to incapacitate.[132]

At first glance, the evidentiary task of determining the identity of the "undeterrable" would seem to implicate the liberal admission of past act evidence. Whether the person has committed many prior wrongs of similar quality is certainly indicative of whether she can be effectively deterred. Importantly, propensity evidence would not in this case be admitted for the purpose of tailoring incentives; discovering the intensity of the propensity would itself be the aim.

Under the truth seeking approach to trial, the goal of incapacitation is but one more reason to allow propensity evidence to prove conduct. Proving propensity per se is in complete harmony with using propensity to prove conduct ex post. But when incapacitation is partnered instead with the goal of incentive setting, a conflict arises that calls for exercising the same sort of care required in the tailoring of incentives and the management of dynamic incentives effects.

Consider, for example, those individuals who, if they were convicted of one more "last straw" offense, would be properly regarded as targets for incapacitation rather than deterrence. Some of these individuals are presumably still responsive to incentives—otherwise one more offense is at least one too many. But if past offenses may be brought in to convict these individuals the next time they are indicted, they make an easy target for prosecutors, who may see no reason to wait for clear trace evidence of conduct. With that much less to lose, such individuals might as well engage in the prohibited conduct—which will, of course, appear to confirm that they should be incapacitated.

As with tailoring and dynamic incentives, the potentially hazardous trade off between the goals of incapacitation and incentive setting is largely avoidable by containing the evidentiary task of incapacitation to the sentencing phase of adjudication. Once the individual is found guilty of child molestation, for example, the sentencing judge could review present and past acts not for the purpose of tailoring incentives, but to determine whether incapacitation is in order. This preserves incentives for that "last straw" conviction, while at the same time using that conviction as data for determining the necessity of resorting to incapacitation.[133]

132. For two studies assessing the relative importance of deterrence and incapacitation in the current criminal law, see Levitt, supra note 2, at 353, and Kessler & Levitt, supra note 2, at 343.

133. But what if the individual's past record really does warrant incapacitating him, yet without past act evidence he cannot be convicted in the present case? By refusing to admit propensity evidence for conviction, doesn't the law miss this chance to justifiably incapacitate? If the problem here is with the reasonable doubt standard, then we should examine that directly. But if we accept the reasonable doubt standard, then the answer must be "no." For then the details of the new acquittal add no new legally cognizable information to the determination of whether the individual should be incapacitated. And if the individual's list of past convictions is on its own enough to warrant incapacitation, then he should have been incapacitated the last time he was convicted.

C
Hearsay

[18]

Toward a Partial Economic, Game-Theoretic Analysis of Hearsay

Richard D. Friedman*

[W]hen they come to model Heaven,
And calculate the stars, how they will wield
The mighty frame, how build, unbuild, contrive
To save appearances; how gird the Sphere
With Centric and Eccentric scribbl'd o'er,
Cycle and Epicycle, Orb in Orb.[1]

I. INTRODUCTION AND LIMITATIONS

Hypothetical 1: *Propco is at trial against Oppco. Through an authenticating witness, Propco offers into evidence a memorandum evidently written by one of its employees, who is not identified on the face of the memo. The memo recounts a conversation that the author of the memo says that she had with an officer of Oppco. Propco offers the memo to prove that the conversation occurred as recounted in the memo. The memo has substantial probative value for that purpose, and there is no reason to exclude it—except for the rule against hearsay. Oppco objects to the memo as hearsay.*

Thus, a typical hearsay issue is presented to the court. The memo is a statement made other than by a witness testifying at the trial, and the proponent, Propco, is offering the memo to prove the truth of a matter asserted in it. Thus, the opponent, Oppco, is correct that, as offered for this purpose, the memo is hearsay. Under the traditional doctrine, which still prevails in American jurisdictions, the statement will be excluded unless the court finds that the statement fits within an exemption from the rule against hearsay.[2] For example, Federal Rule of Evidence 801(d) lists between two and eight exclusions (de-

---

* Professor of Law, University of Michigan Law School. I am grateful for the many helpful leads, comments, suggestions, and criticisms I have received during the preparation of this Article, especially from Ron Allen, Robert Axelrod, Guido Calabresi, Mirjan Damaška, Joanna Friedman, Stephen Gardbaum, David Goodhand, Jerry Israel, Avery Katz, Lash LaRue, Roger Park, Michael Seigel and Eleanor Swift. Thanks also to John Lloyd for preparation of the diagrams and to Vivian James for her extraordinary efforts.

1. JOHN MILTON, PARADISE LOST, Book VIII, lines 79-84 (Merritt Y. Hughes ed., 1962).

2. I use the term exemption here in an all-inclusive manner, to cover

pending on how they are counted) from the definition of hearsay, and Rules 803 and 804 state twenty-seven categorical exceptions, plus two virtually identical broad-based residual exceptions.[3] The categorical exceptions are based principally on the perceived trustworthiness of statements fitting within them. The exceptions fill a role similar to that performed by the "Cycle and Epicycle, Orb in Orb" of the Ptolemaic system of astronomy scathingly described by Milton,[4] and they create a similar degree of complexity and contrivance.

In this Article, I offer a fundamentally different and nondoctrinaire way of approaching hearsay questions. In brief, I take the view that the resolution of a hearsay dispute, when the declarant is not on the stand, is essentially a matter of deciding who should bear the burden of producing the declarant, or more precisely, how courts should allocate that burden. Adopting a simple procedural improvement, concerning the examination of the declarant if she is produced as a witness, allows the court to allocate the burden optimally. If live testimony by the declarant would be more probative than prejudicial, then most often—contrary to standard doctrine—the hearsay also is more probative than prejudicial. When this is so, the court ordinarily ought to impose the burden of producing the declarant on the opponent, the party objecting to the hearsay. Sometimes, though, other considerations—such as whether the proponent has a substantial advantage in satisfying all or part of the burden of producing the declarant, or whether the proponent has given late notice of his intention to offer the hearsay—may warrant imposing part or all of the burden on the proponent.

For two reasons, I will not engage here in an extended discussion of reasons that hearsay doctrine should be fundamentally reformed. First, others have made the case before.[5] Obviously, commentators have not reached anything resembling a consensus that the law should be overhauled;[6] if they had, the change likely would have been accomplished by now.

---

both exclusions from the definition of hearsay and exceptions from the rule presumptively excluding hearsay from evidence.

3. *See* FED. R. EVID. 801, 803, 804.

4. *See supra* note 1 and accompanying text.

5. *E.g.*, Eleanor Swift, *A Foundation Fact Approach to Hearsay*, 75 CAL. L. REV. 1339, 1343-54 (1987); Jack B. Weinstein, *Probative Force of Hearsay*, 46 IOWA L. REV. 331, 340 (1961); Note, *The Theoretical Foundation of the Hearsay Rules*, 93 HARV. L. REV. 1786, 1793 (1980).

6. *See, e.g.*, RICHARD O. LEMPERT & STEPHEN A. SALTZBURG, A MODERN APPROACH TO EVIDENCE 520-25 (2d ed. 1982).

An argument that such a change should be made will not, however, surprise anybody familiar with evidentiary debate. Second, I believe the theoretical foundation of so important a doctrine is always a valid subject of inquiry, even without any prior thought that any change of doctrine might result. Such an inquiry might, in fact, reveal the extent, if any, to which a theoretically ideal doctrine differs from the doctrine actually in place. If the practical considerations in implementing the ideal doctrine are not too daunting, then the theoretical inquiry may itself be part of an argument for reform. This Article therefore tries to develop from the ground up part of the framework for an ideal law of hearsay, without any preconceptions or constraints imposed by current doctrine.[7]

As the previous sentence suggests, this Article works only toward a partial theory of hearsay. The Article is not concerned, except where otherwise noted, with the context in which a criminal prosecutor offers hearsay evidence against the accused. That, of course, is the context in which the Confrontation Clause of the Sixth Amendment to the Constitution comes into play.[8] The confrontation right raises considerations not present with other hearsay. Under current doctrine, there is a close link between the ordinary law of hearsay and the law of the Confrontation Clause.[9] I am convinced that, unless this

7. Lest there be any doubt—the system proposed here is meant to supplant, not supplement, the present hearsay system.

8. The Confrontation Clause provides: "In all criminal prosecutions, the accused shall enjoy the right . . . to be confronted with the witnesses against him." U.S. CONST. amend. VI.

9. Under the test articulated in Ohio v. Roberts, 448 U.S. 56 (1980), hearsay offered by the prosecution is not admissible unless the declarant is unavailable and the evidence demonstrates sufficient "indicia of reliability"; the second branch of this test may be satisfied "without more" if "the evidence falls within a firmly rooted hearsay exception." *Id.* at 66. I do not believe the test is a workable one, and the Supreme Court has treated it rather shabbily. *See* Lee v. Illinois, 476 U.S. 530, 544 n.5 (1986) (refusing to consider whether a confession should be considered to fit within the "firmly rooted" exception for declarations against interest, and so to satisfy the reliability test without further inquiry); United States v. Inadi, 475 U.S. 387, 394 (1986) (holding that, in *Roberts*, the Court did not intend to establish the unavailability requirement for hearsay other than prior testimony). Nevertheless, at least until recently, the Court continued to insist that it adhered to the *Roberts* test. *See* Idaho v. Wright, 110 S. Ct. 3139, 3146-47 (1990). After White v. Illinois, 112 S. Ct. 736 (1992), however, it may be that the Court will not impose the unavailability requirement as a matter of Confrontation Clause law on any statement that fits within one of the categorical exceptions of Rule 803(1)-(23) of the Federal Rules of Evidence. The ordinary exclusion of hearsay evidence under Rule 802 does not apply to statements fitting within those exceptions, irrespective of whether the declarant is available to testify at trial. The brief discussion of

link is broken, neither subject can be developed in a satisfactory manner. The need to protect criminal defendants' confrontation rights will tend to make hearsay law more restrictive than it ought to be, and the need for a practical law of hearsay will make the confrontation guarantee less protective than it ought to be. I believe the link can be broken by articulating the confrontation guarantee in terms that have nothing to do with hearsay doctrine, and under which some hearsay offered by the prosecution would not even present a confrontation issue.[10] That, however, is not the subject on which I want to concentrate. Thus, to avoid a great deal of complexity, this Article will not deal, except briefly, with prosecution evidence. When I do consider such evidence, I will assume that, for reasons extraneous to the theory presented in this Article, the Confrontation Clause presents no problem.

I will limit the discussion in other ways as well. For one thing, although I have said that I want to develop a theory unconstrained by current doctrine, the analysis here will focus on evidence that fits within the core of the standard definition of hearsay. That is, I will assume that the evidence is proof of a statement made out of court, and that it is offered to prove the truth of a matter asserted in the statement.[11] By thus assuming away the question of whether the challenged evidence is hearsay, we can concentrate instead on the issue of when hearsay should be admitted. Most of the analysis presented here, I believe, could apply equally well to evidence in the fuzzy area just outside the standard definition—for example, to evidence of a

---

the Confrontation Clause presented here is substantially similar to, but updated from, that in Richard D. Friedman, *Improving the Procedure for Resolving Hearsay Issues*, 13 CARDOZO L. REV. 883, 885-86 nn.8-9 (1991).

10. In rough terms, I believe that the Confrontation Clause should be construed to exclude evidence of an out-of-court statement offered by the prosecution, regardless of the declarant's availability, if the declarant made the statement with the anticipation that it might be used in the investigation or prosecution of a crime and the accused has not had an adequate opportunity to examine the declarant. *Cf.* Michael H. Graham, *The Confrontation Clause, the Hearsay Rule, and Child Sexual Abuse Prosecutions: The State of the Relationship*, 72 MINN. L. REV. 523, 593-95 (1988) (suggesting a test similar in nature but applicable only to available declarants). I would apply this test absolutely, though the accused might forfeit his confrontation right if he wrongfully rendered the maker of the statement unavailable—such as by intimidating, kidnapping, or killing her. Under this approach, if a hearsay statement did not fit within the confrontation protection, the accused still might assert a constitutional right to have the statement excluded unless the prosecution produced the declarant (at least if the declarant was available), but such assertions should be decided under general and flexible standards of due process.

11. *See* FED. R. EVID. 801(a)-(c) (providing the basic definition of hearsay).

person's conduct offered to prove the truth of a belief apparently reflected in the conduct—or even to evidence further removed from the usual reach of hearsay law. If that is true, it may mean that a sound approach to hearsay law would not depend on anything resembling the current definition of hearsay. It might even mean that the concept of hearsay would disappear into a doctrine of broader scope.[12] For now, however, I am not concerned with demonstrating that point, or testing the full reach of the analysis presented here. The heartland of hearsay is a large enough area for this Article to explore without having to worry about the borderland or the outland.[13]

II. THE BASIC HEARSAY MODEL

The discussion will focus on cases fitting the following pattern: One party, the *proponent*, makes known his desire to introduce evidence of a hearsay statement made by an out-of-court *declarant*. For now, we will assume that the proponent gives notice of this intention well before trial. If the declarant were to testify at trial to the substance of her out-of-court statement, the testimony would have sufficient probative value to warrant admissibility, and no other factor would result in exclusion of the evidence. Evidence from this particular declarant—that is, either her out-of-court declaration or her in-court testimony—is irreplaceable, in the sense that even if the proponent produced all the other relevant evidence that he could, the declarant's evidence would have substantial probative value.[14] The proponent's adversary, the *opponent*, raises a hearsay objection to the evidence. He points out that the evidence is defi-

12. Under such a broader doctrine, the court generally would not rule an offered item of evidence inadmissible, on the basis of the possible availability of other evidence of the proposition that might be better from the court's point of view, as long as: the procedures for presenting the better evidence are substantially the same whether the proponent or the opponent produces it; the offered evidence is more probative than prejudicial; and the opponent is not substantially less able than the proponent to produce the better evidence. The first of these conditions is simply a matter of the court's rules and generally should be maintained. If the second condition also holds but the third does not, then all or part of the burden of producing the better evidence usually ought to be imposed on the proponent. If the second condition does not hold, so that the offered evidence is more prejudicial than probative, it generally should be excluded—but not necessarily if the opponent is substantially better able than the proponent to produce the better evidence.

13. *Cf.* Charles T. McCormick, *The Borderland of Hearsay*, 39 YALE L.J. 489 (1930).

14. I address briefly the situation in which there might be a full replacement for evidence from the declarant. *See infra* note 60.

cient, as compared to live testimony, in several respects. Most importantly, the declarant did not make the prior statement under oath, the opponent cannot cross-examine her, the jury cannot observe her demeanor, and there may be doubt about whether the declarant even made the statement.

Figure 1 presents the situation, as it is ordinarily understood, once the hearsay issue is presented to the court. Under the standard doctrine, the court has two basic choices, which I will label EXCLUDE and ADMIT, in response to the hearsay objection. The court's ruling determines the presumptive evidentiary result—that is, the result that will prevail if the losing party decides to DO NOTHING in response to the ruling. If the court decides to EXCLUDE the hearsay and the proponent decides to DO NOTHING, that result is NE—no evidence from the declarant is received, either in the form of hearsay or by live testimony. If, on the other hand, the court decides to ADMIT the hearsay and the opponent decides to DO NOTHING, the evidentiary result is H—meaning that the court admits the hearsay and the declarant does not offer any live testimony.

The presumptive evidentiary result is not necessarily the final one, however. Whichever party loses on the hearsay motion may, instead of choosing to DO NOTHING, decide to PRODUCE the declarant. As is frequently recognized, if the judge decides to EXCLUDE the hearsay, the proponent may PRODUCE the declarant as a witness at trial, assuming that this is feasible, so that he will get the benefit of the declarant's evidence. Indeed, this inducement to produce "better evidence" is one possible justification for some applications of the ban on hearsay.[15] If the proponent does select PRODUCE, the evidentiary result will be live testimony by the declarant, indicated by the notation LT.

A corresponding possibility also is apparent, though it seems to be less consistently borne in mind. If the judge decides to ADMIT the hearsay, the opponent also may decide to PRODUCE the declarant as a trial witness (again assuming this is feasible). His motivation would be to eliminate the defects in the hearsay evidence about which he complained. When the opponent does produce the declarant, the prevailing procedure for examining her is, as explained in Part III, different from that used when the proponent produces her. Hence, the nota-

15. *See, e.g.*, Dale A. Nance, *The Best Evidence Principle*, 73 IOWA L. REV. 227, 282-83 (1988).

Figure 1

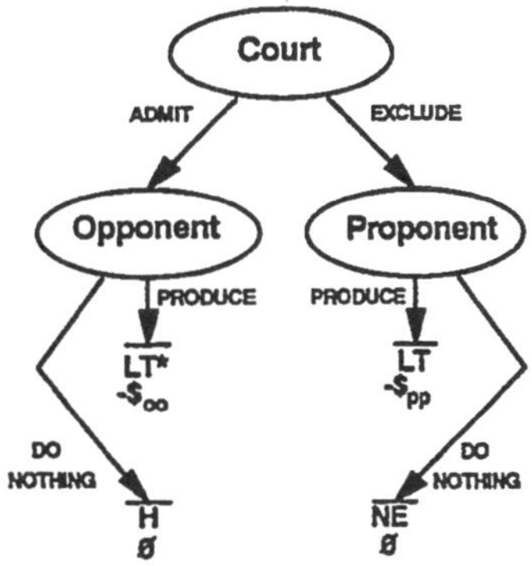

tion LT* indicates the evidentiary result of production by the opponent.

Figure 1 indicates not only the possible evidentiary results but also the costs of each. I assume that if the proponent is not produced, there is no substantial out-of-pocket cost, whether the court admits the hearsay or not.[16] Thus, 0 is marked under both H and NE. If the proponent produces the declarant, the cost is $\$_{pp}$, while if the opponent produces her it is $\$_{oo}$. The first subscript in this notation indicates who bears the cost, while the second indicates which party physically produces the declarant. The two parties do not necessarily have the same production costs. The double subscripts are necessary because, as we shall see in Part V, it may be possible for one party to bear the costs of the other producing the declarant. For now, though, we will assume that each party bears its own costs of production.

16. Although this assumption will simplify matters, it is not crucial to most of the analysis that follows; if the time or money required to produce the hearsay is significant, these costs can be considered, along with the prejudicial potential of the hearsay, as part of the total negative consequences of admitting the hearsay.

V. SELECTING A RULING

A. Introduction: The Assumed Information Base and a Summary of the Analysis

Part IV showed that the court would often have difficulty both in evaluating the payoff of an outcome and in determining how probable the outcome is given a particular ruling. In particular, the court probably will have difficulty determining whether LT is sufficiently preferable for truth-determination purposes to H and NE to warrant the cost of producing the declarant. And often it will have at least as much difficulty determining whether a party bearing all or part of the burden of producing the declarant would find LT so much more advantageous to the alternative result—H for the opponent, NE for the proponent—to warrant satisfying the burden.[51]

These considerations suggest that, as a rule, the court's best course may not be to guess and evaluate the probable outcomes of each possible ruling. Of course, when the court knows that the declarant cannot be produced, it knows what the outcome of its ruling will be—either admission or exclusion of the hear-

51. *See supra* note 49 and accompanying text (discussing the difficulties in determining the parties' preferences).

say—and it can evaluate those results. But when the court lacks this certainty, its best approach is generally to try to allocate the burden of producing the declarant in such a way that, consistent with fairness, the parties' own self-interest will lead to an efficient result.

This Part will analyze how the court should make that determination. It suggests that the court should base its decision primarily on two factors, and it assumes that the court does have adequate information on these factors. I believe that the court usually can gather this information quickly and efficiently by questioning counsel; decision making under the system I am suggesting need not entail excessive administrative costs.

The first factor is the net probativeness of the hearsay—that is, the extent to which the hearsay is more or less probative than prejudicial. Put another way, the question is whether H is preferable, from the truth-determining perspective, to NE. I will assume that the court can evaluate this factor simply by comparing the state of the proof with and without the hearsay. In other words, the court can evaluate the two alternative presumptive evidentiary results of its ruling.

The second factor is the difficulty and expense each party would have to endure to alter this presumptive evidentiary result by producing the declarant. The court needs some, but not necessarily full, information with respect to this factor. It is to each party's advantage to persuade the court that its costs of producing the declarant are high, but in most cases an inquisitive court, aided if necessary by the adversary's argument, would probably be able to detect substantial inflation in a party's statement of its costs. At least the court usually should be able to determine whether or not one party is substantially better able than the other to produce the declarant. Often that is all the court needs to know.

Thus, Section B assumes, with respect to this factor, merely that neither party has a significant advantage over the other in producing the declarant. It also assumes that the proponent has given adequate notice of his intention to offer the hearsay. Under these circumstances, the court ought to choose the presumptive evidentiary result, H or NE, that best advances truth determination. When the declarant cannot be produced, this ruling is optimal because the presumptive result is the final one as well, and it is fair as well as efficient that the result be the one that is best for determination of the truth. When production of the declarant is feasible, such a ruling offers benefits beyond the presumptive result. The party losing the ruling makes the decision whether to alter that result to LT by producing the declarant. It is efficient for this party to make the decision, because it is he who is best able to determine whether the benefits he would receive by producing her—which coincide closely with the benefits to the truth-determining process—are worthwhile given the costs. And it is fair that this party bear the costs of producing the declarant, if she is to be produced, because it is he who is dissatisfied with, and wishes to alter, the best result possible in the absence of the declarant.

Note that under this analysis, the court, having satisfied itself that neither party is substantially better able than the other to produce the declarant, need not worry how difficult producing the declarant actually would be.[52] In other words, having concluded that there is no substantial difference between the parties with respect to the second factor, the court can put that factor aside. No matter how difficult production would be—impossible, burdensome, or easy—both fairness and efficiency support admission of the hearsay if (as I have contended is usually the case) the hearsay is more probative than prejudicial.

Section C examines how this conclusion is altered when one party is in fact substantially better able than the other to produce the declarant. Here again, full information with respect to the parties' respective abilities to produce the declarant is not necessary, but it will be helpful for the court at least to have confidence that one party can feasibly produce the declarant and that the other would find production substantially more difficult or expensive. In some circumstances, it makes sense to impose at least part of the burden on the party best able to bear it, even though absent the disparity the considerations addressed in Section B would favor imposing the burden totally on the other party. The best result may involve splitting the burden between the parties, such as by imposing the finan-

52. Note the difference from standard hearsay doctrine. Under Federal Rule of Evidence 804, in some circumstances unavailability of the declarant is a decisive factor supporting admissibility of hearsay, even though there is no difference in the parties' respective abilities to produce the declarant. Put another way, under the Federal Rules, availability of the declarant may be a decisive factor supporting exclusion of the hearsay, even though the opponent is as able as the proponent to produce the declarant.

cial burden on the opponent and part or all of the physical burden on the proponent.

Finally, Section D examines the implications of late notice. Sometimes, but not always, a failure to give early notice warrants imposing all or part of the burden on the proponent.

B. Selecting a Ruling When Notice Is Adequate and Neither Party Has a Substantial Advantage in Producing the Declarant

This Section assumes that, as is usually the case, it is not substantially easier or less expensive for one party than for the other to produce the declarant. Even if the declarant is a friend of one party, for example, the other might easily secure his attendance by subpoena.

The first three subsections of this Section will examine separately three different situations that lie along a continuum—when production of the declarant is, respectively, impossible, feasible but burdensome, and easy. This breakdown is made for analytical purposes only. As suggested in Section A, a court need not be concerned about the category into which the particular case falls, because the appropriate result is the same for all three: The court should admit the hearsay if it is more probative than prejudicial.[53] The basic reason for this result may be stated briefly. Assuming that neither party is better able than the other to produce the declarant and also that (as I have proposed), if she is produced, the evidentiary result is the same whichever party produces her, then the most sensible result is to pick the best presumptive evidentiary result. This imposes on the losing party the burden of altering that result if it appears worth his while to do so.

Subsection 4 discusses the different situation presented when the declarant is actually on the stand testifying. Finally, Subsection 5 discusses the application of the approach suggested here to hearsay statements created for litigation.

1. Production of the Declarant Impossible

In some cases, it may be impossible for either party to produce the declarant. The simplest case, of course, arises when the declarant is dead. Recall Hypothetical 3, in which Paul

53. As I have already argued, this is usually the case when the only substantial hurdle to admission of the evidence is its hearsay character. *See supra* pp. 737-43.

sought to introduce the declaration of a person who observed an accident and subsequently died. Because the declarant cannot be produced and the hearsay is, by hypothesis, cost-free to produce, cost considerations do not enter into play. As a matter of both fairness and efficiency, the question comes down simply to whether H is preferable to NE for truth determination—that is, whether the evidence is more probative than prejudicial. If, as I have argued above,[54] most often hearsay as to which there is no other ground for exclusion is more probative than prejudicial, then most often the court should admit a hearsay statement by a declarant who cannot be produced.

2. Production of the Declarant Feasible but Burdensome

Consider again Hypothetical 4, in which Paul offers the hearsay statement of a declarant who lives far from the courthouse, and whom either party could produce at trial but only at considerable expense. I will analyze this situation first under the assumption that, as I believe is usually the case, the hearsay is more probative than prejudicial. At the end of this subsection, I will analyze briefly the case in which this assumption is not true.[55]

Given the truth of this assumption, it is once again better, as a matter of both efficiency and fairness, to admit the hearsay. For one thing, the presumptive evidentiary result of the decision, H, is more satisfactory than is the alternative, NE: The assumption means that H is superior for truth determination, and, under the analysis presented in the last subsection, a fairer result as well.

But, because production of the declarant is feasible, the presumptive evidentiary result may not be the final one; the party losing the court's decision might decide to produce the declarant. Accordingly, we must consider the efficiency and fairness consequences of imposing the burden on either party.

As to efficiency, the court often cannot be sure whether or not producing the declarant would be an efficient result. The court can be confident, however, that a decision to ADMIT, which will impose on the opponent the burden of producing the declarant, is likely to lead to the more efficient result. Given the assumption that H is preferable to NE for determining the truth, the key question is whether LT is enough better than H

54. *See supra* pp. 737-43.
55. *See infra* note 61 and accompanying text.

to warrant the costs of production. The opponent is clearly the party better able to make that determination, because he is the one who would benefit from the production. Indeed, given H as the alternative, the opponent's interests are similar to the court's. The court should regard as a negative factor any costs the opponent incurs in producing the declarant, and as a positive factor any probative evidence helpful to the opponent that producing the declarant yields.[56]

Thus, if the opponent perceives that the likelihood that live testimony by the declarant would benefit his case is sufficient to warrant the cost of production, he will produce the declarant. Correspondingly, if he does not think that live testimony would be sufficiently better than the hearsay to make the costs worthwhile, he will not produce her.[57] As suggested in the previous discussion of Hypothetical 4,[58] the opponent might have made the hearsay objection even though from his point of view live testimony might appear barely better, or even worse, than simple admission of the hearsay. His true objective might have been to dissuade the proponent from offering any evidence at all from the declarant. Thus, imposing the burden on the opponent makes him put his money where his mouth is.

Now compare EXCLUDE as a possible ruling. The proponent may decide that the live testimony is not worth producing and resign himself to NE. This is exactly the result the opponent wishes, but ordinarily it is one that the court should regard as unsatisfactory because, by assumption, it is worse than H. The proponent may decide to produce the declarant, but fre-

56. The opponent's interests in deciding whether or not to produce the declarant do not exactly coincide with the court's. Producing the declarant might yield probative evidence helpful to the proponent, such as vivid details and a persuasive demeanor. The court would regard this positively, but the opponent would not. Thus, in some cases, the opponent might not produce the declarant even though the court would regard production as beneficial. The court need not worry about this, however, because the fact that the proponent has offered the hearsay shows that the benefits to him of producing the declarant are ones that he is willing to forgo, given the difficulty of producing the declarant. Given that the proponent is satisfied with H and prefers it to NE, the possibility that, putting aside the difficulty of production, he might prefer LT to H cannot be the reason to decide the hearsay issue against him.

57. Sometimes the opponent may be hampered in making this judgment by uncertainty regarding the reasons for the proponent's decision to offer the hearsay rather than produce the declarant—that is, whether the proponent merely wished to save cost and effort or whether he perceived that the live testimony would be less helpful to him than the hearsay. This difficulty is not usually enough to warrant a prophylactic rule excluding the hearsay. See *infra* note 82.

58. *See supra* pp. 748-50.

quently this will be wasteful. Often it will be true (though the court will have difficulty in knowing just when) that LT is far more satisfactory, costs of production aside, to the proponent than NE, and that, from the court's point of view, LT is only moderately more helpful to the truth-determining process than H. In Hypothetical 4, for example, Paul might decide that he simply cannot do without some evidence from Deborah showing that Theresa was very upset after the run-in with Otto. It may be, though, that there is only a small chance that live testimony by Deborah, subject to cross-examination, will yield substantially more useful information than would Deborah's hearsay statement. Paul will produce the declarant as long as the costs are no greater than the large gap that he perceives between LT and NE, but the result will be inefficient, as compared to H, if the costs are greater than the smaller gap that the court would perceive between LT and H. This situation will arise often. Frequently, as discussed earlier, an opponent in Otto's position will make the hearsay objection even though, costs of production aside, he perceives H as nearly as good an evidentiary result as LT, or even better.[59]

Thus, assuming that the hearsay is more probative than prejudicial, it is efficient to impose on the opponent the burden of producing the declarant. Considerations of fairness point in the same direction. Ordinarily, when a party offers evidence that the court deems more probative than prejudicial, the court admits the evidence, leaving it up to the other side to produce rebutting evidence. Even if the court is concerned that the primary evidence, if unrebutted, may mislead the jury, it often does not exclude the evidence. Rather, the court may decide that it is up to the opponent to produce any evidence he thinks will put the primary evidence in the proper light, just as any party ordinarily has a responsibility to present whatever evidence that he hopes will support his case. The court should follow the same principle in the hearsay context. The proponent, after all, has offered the evidence—the hearsay—that he finds satisfactory, and the court has, by hypothesis, found that this evidence does more good than harm. If the opponent truly believes that another type of evidence—in particular, the live testimony of the declarant—will be more to his advantage, then it is fair and proper for him to bear the burden of producing it.[60]

59. *See supra* pp. 748-49 (discussing Hypothetical 4 and the possibility that Otto may prefer H over LT).

60. The essence of this analysis can be generalized to whatever form of

Note how much easier it is to accept imposition of that bur-

---

evidence the opponent believes would be more acceptable proof than the hearsay statement of the proposition at issue. Suppose, for example, that the opponent believes that another observer could testify to the proposition asserted by the hearsay statement and that the alternative observer could be more readily produced as a witness than the declarant could. If the proponent nevertheless decides to offer the declarant's hearsay statement, and the court concludes both that the statement is more probative than prejudicial and that the proponent is not substantially better able than the opponent to produce either the declarant or the other observer, the court probably ought to rule ADMIT. The procedural proposals offered in Part III should also be extended, however; the opponent should be given the opportunity to produce *either* the declarant or the other observer before the court finally decides the admissibility of the hearsay. It may be that, given the live testimony of the other observer, the hearsay statement has insufficient probative value to warrant admissibility. One other related caveat is appropriate: If the proponent could easily produce the other observer but nevertheless decides to produce the hearsay, the court may have reason to suspect that the proponent made his choice because of weaknesses he perceives in the potential live testimony. This suspicion is essentially the same that may arise, whether or not there is another observer in the picture, from the proponent's decision to favor the hearsay over the declarant's own testimony.

Tentatively, I believe the analysis in the text also generally applies to evidence concerning foundation facts about the circumstances surrounding a statement that allow the trier of fact to assess the reliability of the statement. *See* Swift, *supra* note 5, at 1355-61 (suggesting a reformulation of hearsay law in which the proponent's introduction of evidence bearing on foundation facts would often be critical). Sometimes, of course, the proponent may *wish* to introduce evidence bearing on foundation facts—showing, for instance, that the declarant is an honest person who would have no interest in making the statement in question if it were not true. If the opponent challenges the declarant's credibility, such evidence would presumably be permissible, to the extent that it responds to the challenge. (If the opponent makes no such challenge, the evidence might be considered needless bolstering.) But, as long as there is a sufficient basis suggesting that the declarant (or each declarant in the chain, in the case of multiple hearsay) made her statement on the basis of personal observation, I do not believe the proponent presumptively ought to be *required*, as a precondition to admission of the hearsay, to introduce evidence bearing on foundation facts. As stated in the text, the proponent has offered the evidence that he is satisfied to offer, and the court has by hypothesis determined that it does more good than harm. Therefore, it appears to me that if the opponent desires that, assuming the hearsay is admitted, evidence be introduced that bears on the foundation facts and that presumably tends to impeach the declarant, then ordinarily the burden of producing such evidence ought to be imposed on the opponent. In some cases, the opponent might be satisfied to introduce hearsay evidence bearing on the foundation facts, in accordance with standards governing ordinary hearsay.

The burden might have to be adjusted if the proponent is substantially better able than the opponent to produce the foundation fact evidence that the opponent desires. In such a case, the court might impose on the opponent the financial burden of producing the foundation fact evidence and on the proponent the physical burden. (Note that Part V.C., *infra* at pp. 775-79, discusses a similar division of the burden, and other possible divisions as well, with respect to the hearsay evidence itself.) Under such a ruling, *if* the opponent exden on the opponent given the procedural modification I have proposed, in which LT rather than LT* is the usual evidentiary result even if the opponent is the one producing the declarant. This modification means that imposing the burden on the opponent has no adverse consequences for the quality of examination he may make if the declarant does testify.

If, contrary to the assumption made in the discussion above, NE is preferable to H for truth-determination, then efficiency considerations favor choosing NE in the first instance, leaving it to the proponent to decide whether production of the declarant is worthwhile. And fairness considerations point in the same direction as efficiency, albeit perhaps less strongly than when the hearsay appears more probative than prejudicial. The proponent should bear the burden of producing the declarant, and if she is not present, the hearsay ought not be admitted.[61]

3. Production of the Declarant Feasible Without a Substantial Burden

Hypothetical 5: *Propco offers against Oppco a memorandum written five years earlier by one of its officers, Della Declarant. The memo records the terms of a fairly simple transaction that Della had just completed over the phone with an officer of Oppco. The transaction has a peripheral bearing on the litigation, and Propco is offering the memo to prove that the terms of the deal were as recorded by Della. Della's office is located one mile away from the courthouse; either*

---

pressed willingness to pay for production of the foundation fact evidence, the proponent would be obligated, subject to a sanction, to produce the evidence. A powerful sanction for the proponent's failure to produce would be exclusion of his hearsay. No more powerful sanction would ordinarily be needed, because exclusion generally gives the opponent all he could want in opposing admissibility of the hearsay. Exclusion might not be necessary, however. It may be a sufficient sanction to instruct the jury that it should draw an adverse inference from the failure to produce; this might be particularly effective if the opponent also introduces impeaching hearsay evidence bearing on the foundation facts.

61. This conclusion might be less strong because of the point made earlier that admitting rebutting evidence, rather than excluding primary evidence, is usually the preferred remedy when unrebutted primary evidence appears unduly prejudicial. At least when the superiority of NE to H for truth determination appears doubtful, the court might take the view, if it is confident that the opponent could produce the declarant, that the proponent ought to be allowed to introduce his preferred form of testimony, with the opponent retaining the ability to correct its prejudicial impact. Nevertheless, it seems to me on balance that the opponent should not have to bear a significant burden to clear up evidence that is so defective that the court regards it as more prejudicial than probative.

> *party could produce her as a witness without significant difficulty. Oppco objects to admission of the memo.*

The easier the burden is for both parties, the lower are the stakes of the hearsay decision. If the court chooses EXCLUDE and Propco is dissatisfied, it can produce Della. Similarly, if the court chooses ADMIT and Oppco is dissatisfied, it can produce her. Assuming that, as I have proposed, the court implements LT whichever party produces the declarant, the court's decision would not affect even the procedure for examining Della if, in fact, she is produced.

Though the stakes are lower, the analysis of Subsection 2 prevails. If the evidence appears to be more probative than prejudicial, it is both more efficient and fairer to select ADMIT, letting the opponent decide whether or not the value of live testimony is sufficient to warrant whatever burden production of the declarant would require. If he does not produce her, the court will admit the hearsay. If he does produce her, however, the proponent must put the declarant on the stand or forgo use of the hearsay.

The polar case of an easy-to-produce declarant is one who is already in the courtroom.

> Hypothetical 6: *Same facts as Hypothetical 5, except that Della is actually in the courtroom. Propco had not been planning to call her as a witness, however.*

In this case, producing the declarant is essentially effortless. Therefore, assuming as before that the court would implement the LT procedure even after selecting ADMIT, the court's ruling on the hearsay objection has no impact. If the court selects EXCLUDE, Propco would then be put in the position of having to decide whether to put Della on the stand or to do without evidence from her altogether. If the court selects ADMIT, Propco would be put in the exact same position: Oppco would be able to put Propco to that choice without cost to itself, because it can produce Della without effort, and clearly Oppco wants to put Propco to the choice, for if it did not it would not have made the objection in the first place. In other words, the key decisions in resolving this situation are first the opponent's, in deciding whether or not to object, and then the proponent's, in deciding whether to put the declarant on the stand or to do without evidence from her. The court really has nothing to do with the result; the stakes of the court's ruling are zero.

4. The Declarant Already Testifying

In characterizing the declarant already in the courtroom as

the polar case of a declarant who is easy to produce, I have treated separately the declarant who is already on the stand. That case, as the following hypothetical will help show, presents a different type of situation.

> Hypothetical 7: *Same facts as Hypothetical 5, except that Della is actually testifying for Propco. This might have occurred because*
>
> *(a) Propco decided on its own initiative to produce Della,*
>
> *(b) Propco offered the memo, Oppco objected, the court sustained the objection, and Propco decided to produce Della, or*
>
> *(c) Propco offered the memo, Oppco objected, the court overruled the objection, but Oppco timely produced Della, and (pursuant to the LT procedure), Propco decided to put Della on the stand rather than forgo use of any evidence from her.*
>
> *Without asking Della about the event that was the subject of the memo, Propco seeks to introduce the memo through her. Oppco objects.*

Given that Della is already on the stand and testifying, there is no remaining burden in seeking her testimony. The only burden that was, or might have been, imposed on Oppco—to produce her so that Propco could put her on the stand and examine her—has been satisfied. Demanding that Propco procure Della's live testimony only requires that Propco ask the questions.[62]

The question here, therefore, is not how to allocate the burden of producing the declarant, as it is when the proponent wishes to introduce evidence of a hearsay statement by a declarant who is absent, yet could be produced. Rather, the first issue is a procedural one. As noted in Part III, the better procedure is first to require the proponent to ask the witness for her current testimony of the underlying event or condition.[63] This procedure helps prevent the proponent from hiding behind the hearsay statement when the live testimony may not be as favorable to him. It also ensures that the ultimate ruling on admissibility of the hearsay can be made optimally, in light of the declarant's testimony. Thus, the court's best response to Oppco's hearsay objection in Hypothetical 7 would be to say something like this to Propco's counsel: "Your adversary is right. First let's find out what she can testify to from memory."

But while this procedural ruling delays, it does not avoid,

62. It is possible in some circumstances that, although Della is on the stand, the full burden of producing her has not yet been satisfied because she has a privilege that she intends to assert. I am using "on the stand" as a shorthand for "on the stand, ready, willing, and able to testify."

63. For a fuller statement of the considerations supporting this procedure, see Friedman, *supra* note 9, at 900-04.

the need to rule on the ultimate question—admissibility of the hearsay statement. Once the court is satisfied that the proponent has drawn out of the declarant the testimony she is now willing and able to give, it should then determine whether admitting the hearsay statement will, on balance, help or hinder the truth-determining process.

If the declarant claims to have no memory of the underlying event or condition, then the situation is much as if she were dead or otherwise totally unavailable, as in Subsection 1. In most cases, the hearsay will presumably be more probative than prejudicial, and so should be admitted.

At the other extreme, suppose the declarant professes to have a perfect memory of the subject, and the hearsay statement is perfectly in accord with her testimony. The court might decide, depending on the circumstances, that the statement is a virtually useless, time-wasting attempt to bolster her testimony, and so should be excluded.[64]

Of course, there are other possibilities as well. If the hearsay statement is consistent with, but more detailed than, the current testimony, the court might decide that it has enough incremental probative value to warrant admissibility. The court might reach the same result if the statement is inconsistent with the current testimony. If the statement would have been admissible had the declarant not testified, ordinarily it has no less probative value simply because the declarant testifies inconsistently with it.[65]

---

64. This would not be true if the hearsay statement was made before the time of an alleged failure in a testimonial capacity that, according to the opponent, accounts for the declarant's live testimony; for example, if the opponent contends that the declarant's testimony is explained by the fact that one year before trial the opponent fired her, this contention is undercut by proof of a statement consistent with the testimony and made two years before trial. *See* FED. R. EVID. 801(d)(1)(B) (providing that a prior statement by a witness who is subject to cross-examination at trial is not hearsay if the statement is "consistent with the declarant's testimony and is offered to rebut an express or implied charge against the declarant of recent fabrication or improper influence or motive").

65. The statement would, in any event, be admissible for impeachment; the hearsay question is whether the statement should be admitted for the truth of the matter it asserts. Under Federal Rule of Evidence 801(d)(1)(A), a prior inconsistent statement is exempted from the hearsay rule only if it "was given under oath subject to the penalty of perjury at a trial, hearing, or other proceeding, or in a deposition." Other jurisdictions, however, differ widely in their treatment of this issue.

5. Hearsay Statements Created for the Purpose of Litigation

The relatively hospitable attitude toward hearsay suggested here might encourage parties, in advance of trial, to prepare statements for adoption by cooperative declarants. The parties might then offer the statements instead of live testimony by the declarants, or in addition to the testimony when the testimony turns out not to be as favorable as the hearsay. To some extent, this seems to raise the possibility of trial by affidavit. For several reasons, though, I do not believe that this prospect is usually troublesome.[66]

First, recall again that the approach suggested here is not meant to be applied when a criminal defendant's confrontation rights are at stake.[67] In that context, the possibility of the prosecution protecting against a turncoat witness by preparing an affidavit that could be used to convict the defendant, no matter what the witness' testimony, should indeed be considered intolerable. But that is not the subject of this Article.

Second, outside the confrontation context, trial by affidavit may be a good thing to some extent. True enough, affidavits are often an inferior form of evidence, not only to live testimony but to other types of hearsay as well. Production of live evidence is often expensive, however, even where it is feasible, and the proponent does not always have the good fortune that the potential witness happens to have made a hearsay statement in provable form. Most often it is the proponent, not the opponent, who, cost considerations aside, would prefer the live testimony of the declarant to her affidavit. Much can be said for allowing the proponent to offer the type of evidence that he finds most cost-effective, so long as that evidence is more probative than prejudicial. Moreover, in some respects an affidavit, taken alone, is actually superior, even from the court's point of view, to the declarant's current testimony, taken alone. Affidavits are efficient to present in court, they may reflect a fresher memory than trial testimony, and they often reflect greater care and precision than the oral testimony of a nervous witness on the stand responding immediately to questions

66. I have addressed a related problem that might be thought to arise, *see* Friedman, *supra* note 9, at 898 n.27—the prospect that the proponent would attempt to shift costs to the opponent by declining to produce the declarant in the anticipation that the opponent will bear the costs of doing so. *See* Ronald J. Allen, *The Evolution of the Hearsay Rule to a Rule of Admission*, 76 MINN. L. REV. 797, 808-09 (1992). For reasons explained in the prior article, I do not believe that this prospect is very worrisome either.

67. *See supra* notes 8-10 and accompanying text.

posed orally. The ideal result, time and cost considerations aside, would often be presentation of the live testimony *and* the affidavit—but sometimes that result will not be efficient.

Third, to the extent that affidavits are inferior to live testimony, the opponent usually has effective remedies. At the very least, the opponent can point out the non-adversarial setting in which the affidavit was made. There seems to be no particular reason why the jury would be unable to appreciate this factor. When production of the declarant is feasible, the opponent can, as with other forms of hearsay, produce her if he really thinks the defects of the affidavit are sufficiently important to make production worthwhile. As this Section has argued, it is both efficient and fair that the opponent have the burden of producing the declarant, assuming that he is not substantially less able than the proponent to do so and that the statement is more probative than prejudicial. And if the declarant is on the stand but retreats behind the affidavit, perhaps claiming an inability to remember the underlying facts, this testimony will often provide the opponent with excellent impeachment material.

Finally, there is a short answer to the argument that the theory presented here would allow a corrosive form of evidence: If the court concludes in the particular case that the evidence is really more prejudicial than probative, the theory should *not* allow the evidence. Circumstances of the given case might, for example, arouse the court's concern that in fact the proponent's counsel prepared the statement because she could make it favorable to her side but feared the effects of live testimony in a setting not totally under her control. Sometimes, then, the court's skepticism about a statement prepared for litigation might be sufficient to exclude the evidence. This possibility does not, however, warrant a broad rule of exclusion.

C. Selecting a Ruling When One Party Has a Substantial Advantage in Producing the Declarant

Section B assumed that it is not substantially easier for one party than for the other to produce the declarant. But this is not always the case. For any of various reasons, some of which will be suggested in this discussion, one party might be better able to perform one or more of the tasks necessary to produce the declarant. Indeed, in some cases only one party could produce the declarant at all.

When the hearsay is more probative than prejudicial, as is

usually the case, and the opponent has the production advantage, the solution is easy. Under the analysis of Section B, when the parties have substantially equal ability to produce the declarant, the better ruling is ADMIT, imposing on the opponent the burden of producing the declarant. This ruling is *a fortiori* the better one if the opponent has a substantial advantage over the proponent in producing the declarant. Correspondingly, when the hearsay is more prejudicial than probative, and the proponent is better able to produce the declarant, EXCLUDE is clearly the better ruling, more strongly than when the parties are equally able to produce her.

The more difficult, and interesting, cases arise when the factors cut in opposite directions. Subsection 1 will concentrate on what I believe is the more common, and so more important, of these situations—the situation in which the hearsay is more probative than prejudicial, but the proponent has a substantial advantage in producing the declarant. Subsection 2 will briefly address the reverse situation.

1. When the Hearsay Is More Probative Than Prejudicial, and the Proponent Possesses a Substantial Production Advantage

Section B has shown that, if the hearsay is more probative than prejudicial and neither party has a substantial advantage in producing the declarant, then both efficiency and fairness call for requiring the opponent to decide whether producing the declarant is worth the cost and to bear that cost if the proponent is in fact produced. The arguments underlying this conclusion retain some force even when the proponent is substantially better able than the opponent to produce the declarant. H is still, by hypothesis, a better presumptive evidentiary result than NE, and it is still the opponent who wants to alter that result. But if the proponent's advantage in producing the declarant is sufficiently pronounced, and especially if only the proponent can produce her at all, then powerful countervailing considerations of fairness and efficiency may favor imposing the physical burden on the proponent. If the opponent would substantially prefer live testimony to hearsay, then it is both unfair and inefficient for him to have to forgo the opportunity to examine the declarant because he cannot produce her feasibly though the proponent could do so easily. And if the declarant is to be produced, putting the opponent to great trouble and expense seems clearly less fair and efficient than having the lower-cost party do the work.

How should the court resolve these competing considerations? Ideally, the court would select a ruling that achieves two aims. First, the ideal ruling minimizes costs because, if the declarant is to be produced, the proponent performs that portion of the work that he can do most easily. Second, the ideal ruling maintains the proper incentive structure (given that the evidence is net probative), because the opponent decides whether it is worthwhile to produce the declarant and bears the (minimized) cost of doing so.

Sometimes, but not always, the court might be able to achieve, or approach, this ideal result. Any of various solutions might be reasonable, depending on the circumstances of the particular case. Much of the discussion below will focus on the following hypotheticals and variations on them.

> Hypothetical 8: *Propco makes known three weeks before trial its intention to offer a hearsay statement by Dina Declarant, one of its sales representatives. Dina spends most of her time in other states, but she virtually always spends at least one night every two weeks at her apartment in Courthouse City. Oppco does not know her schedule, but it could, with some difficulty, track her down and subpoena her. Propco, on the other hand, could simply call her on her car phone at any time and tell her to come immediately to trial. The court is satisfied that the statement is more probative than prejudicial.*

> Hypothetical 9: *Propco wants to introduce a memo written five years ago by a person not identified on the face of the memo. The author is presumably no longer with Propco, because three years ago Propco closed the office from which the memo was written. By checking a coded notation on the memo against a list in its files, Propco could easily determine the name of the declarant and her address as of the time she left Propco's employ. Oppco has no feasible means of identifying the declarant. The court believes the memo is more probative than prejudicial.*

> Hypothetical 10: *In his litigation against Otto, Paul wants to introduce a statement made a year before by a casual acquaintance of his, Dorothy Declarant. Paul has lost touch with Dorothy, but they have mutual friends. Otto has no idea where Dorothy lives. The court believes that the statement is more probative than prejudicial.*

> Hypothetical 11: *Paul wants to introduce the hearsay statement of his sister, Denise. She is in Eastern Europe, beyond the subpoena power. The court believes that her statement is more probative than prejudicial. It also believes that, if it is important to Paul that Denise testify, he could persuade her to do so, so long as her expenses are paid. Otto, however, could not compel her to testify.*

Hypothetical 12: *Albert Acker is the accused in a felony case. The prosecution wants to introduce evidence of the out-of-court statement of Diana Declarant, a former collaborator of Acker's. The court is able to satisfy itself that the statement is not excluded by Acker's rights under the Confrontation Clause. The court also believes that the statement is more probative than prejudicial. Diana lives in a distant state, but either party would be able to secure her presence pursuant to the "Uniform Act to Secure the Attendance of Witnesses from Without a State in Criminal Proceedings." The problem is that Diana has made clear, through counsel, that if called to testify she would claim her Fifth Amendment privilege against self-incrimination. There is, in fact, a theoretical possibility that Diana could be prosecuted and that the prosecution would use her statement against her. It is highly unlikely, however, that she will be prosecuted, because her involvement in the criminal enterprise was tangential at best, and, in any event, the statement is at most mildly inculpatory of her.*

These hypotheticals reflect a variety of advantages that one party might have over the other in producing the declarant—an advantage in information, as in Hypotheticals 8 and 9, or in access to information, as in Hypothetical 10; an advantage in ability to persuade the declarant to appear without waiting for a subpoena, as in Hypothetical 8, or even though she is beyond the subpoena power, as in Hypothetical 11; and an advantage in extinguishing a privilege, as in Hypothetical 12. Other advantages are also possible.[68] In particular, it may be that, although the cost and effort of producing the declarant would be the same for both parties, one party is substantially more able than the other to bear those costs. I do not present any hypotheticals involving disparate ability to pay because I believe only very tentatively that it is an appropriate factor for the court to take into account.[69]

---

68. One party may, for example, have superior access to necessary means of transportation. *See* Friedman, *supra* note 9, at 919-20. The proponent may also have a significant advantage if he does not give sufficient notice of his own intention to offer the hearsay (which implies a possibility that, if the hearsay is excluded, he will produce the declarant). The problem of late notice is addressed separately. *See infra* pp. 783-91.

69. I have already addressed the question of whether ability to pay ought to be taken into account for distributional reasons. *See supra* part IV.B.3. There is a separate question of whether it ought to be taken into account for efficiency purposes. Suppose, for example, that the court is convinced of the following: H is somewhat better than NE for truth determination, but LT would be substantially better than either; if the presumptive evidentiary result were NE, the proponent would find it easily worthwhile to produce the declarant; but if the presumptive result were H, the opponent would find production too expensive. The court thus might be tempted to choose EXCLUDE rather than ADMIT, inducing the proponent to produce the declarant. The proponent is likely to object that H is really nearly as good a result as LT, and perhaps

The following pages examine in turn each of several possible rulings, suggesting circumstances in which each might be appropriate.

a. *Admitting the Hearsay*

In Hypothetical 8, Propco has an advantage, perhaps substantial, in producing the declarant. Nevertheless, the court might still select ADMIT, as it ought to do if neither party had such an advantage. True, it would cost Oppco more to produce Dina than it would cost Propco, but at least two factors still favor imposing the burden on Oppco. First, given that the evidence is more probative than prejudicial, Oppco is the party that should bear the costs of producing Dina. Second, it may be that Oppco would choose not to produce her even if its costs of doing so were as low as Propco's. If so, imposing the burden on Propco because of its advantage in producing the declarant would needlessly cause it either to produce her or to forgo evidence from her.

Beyond that, it is plausible that, even if the court selects ADMIT, Propco would agree with Oppco to produce Dina. Perhaps this seems strange at first. Propco, after all, offered the hearsay rather than Dina's live testimony, and the court's rul-

---

even better from the opponent's point of view, so that even if there were no disparity in ability to pay, the opponent would not be inclined to produce the declarant. Thus, the proponent will argue, the court has chosen an inferior presumptive result, NE, and forced him to remedy it at unnecessary expense.

A possible resolution is that the court ought to take the proponent's superior ability to pay into account only if it is confident that: first, the disparity is substantial; second, H is not substantially superior to NE for truth determination; and third, LT is so substantially superior to H for truth determination that, if the opponent had the proponent's ability to pay, the opponent would produce the declarant if the evidentiary result otherwise would be H. In addition, the court might consider splitting the financial burden—for example, by imposing on the opponent that portion of the cost that would entail the same welfare loss to the opponent as if he had the proponent's ability to pay and bore the entire cost of producing the declarant. This would be a form of the SPLIT BURDEN solution. *See infra* pp. 770-75. (Note that some other possible responses discussed in this section to a production advantage held by the proponent—selecting ADMIT and leaving it to the parties to negotiate a deal under which the opponent would compensate the proponent for producing the declarant, or imposing the physical burden of production on the proponent and the financial burden on the opponent—do not make sense when the proponent's advantage is in ability to pay.)

Thus far I have spoken of ability to pay, but it may be that, so far as efficiency is concerned, the precise question, or at least another question, is *inclination* to pay for a given benefit in litigation. That is, a party's litigation budget might be a more useful datum than his net worth, because it gives a better indication of whether he would find a given expense worthwhile.

ing of ADMIT supports its right to do so. Nevertheless, Oppco may be willing to make producing the declarant worth Propco's while. Given that Propco could produce her more cheaply than Oppco could, there is room for a deal between the parties, particularly if Propco is persuaded that, absent a deal, Oppco would produce her anyway. For example, Oppco's counsel might say to Propco's:

> Well, congratulations on beating my motion to exclude. But I can't let Dina's statement in without examining her. I'll stake out her apartment in town if I have to, but you're not really going to litigate like that, are you? Listen, if you promise to bring her in, I'll ______."

The blank might be filled in with various types of consideration—perhaps an amount of money at least as great as Propco's cost of producing the declarant, perhaps some benefit in the litigation, such as reciprocal cooperation by the opponent. The effective result of such a deal would be that Propco bears the physical burden of producing the declarant, and Oppco, in one coin or another, bears the financial burden, plus perhaps a premium to induce Propco's cooperation.

For several reasons, transaction costs may be low enough to make this sort of deal feasible. There are only two parties,[70] and they are already in contact with each other. Moreover, their counsel have recurrent dealings, perhaps from one litigation to another,[71] but, more importantly, within the same litigation. Cases last for some time, usually presenting numerous side issues subject to negotiation. Indeed, there may be many items of hearsay, offered by both sides, as to which the parties might resolve questions of admissibility and production of declarants by negotiation. Litigators learn that life is much easier if they can deal with their adversaries. Professional etiquette might also, even apart from any considerations of self-interest, encourage lawyers to be accommodating.

One advantage of this type of voluntary transaction between the parties is that they will enter into it only if it makes sense, and it will make sense only if the proponent's costs of production appear likely to be substantially lower than the opponent's. Thus, if the hearsay appears more probative than prejudicial, and transaction costs appear to be low, the court may find it best to select ADMIT, without worrying very much,

70. That is a hypothesis of this model. *See supra* p. 727. Sometimes, of course, there will be more parties, but they will always be known to each other.

71. Though rarer than in earlier times, such recurrent contact may still be important in relatively small cities and in specialized areas of practice.

at least up to a point, as to whether the proponent is substantially better able than the opponent to produce the declarant. If, in fact, it appears to the parties that the opponent can produce the declarant as or more cheaply than the proponent can, the deal will not be made. And if the parties believe that the proponent can produce the declarant much more cheaply, and the opponent would like to produce her at that cost, then the parties would likely agree between themselves to shift the physical burden. When transaction costs are low, therefore, the court can have confidence that the declarant will be produced, if at all, in the most efficient way. The court may not need to worry very much which party would produce her.

For three reasons, however, the court might sometimes hesitate to adopt this solution. First, the proponent may be unwilling to deal at all, at least at a price that the opponent would be willing to pay. This is especially possible if (as in Hypotheticals 9 through 12) it is not feasible for the opponent to produce the declarant. Under that hypothesis, a deal would not simply change the identity of the party producing the declarant. Rather, it would cause a different evidentiary result—LT instead of H. In some cases, the proponent, satisfied with H but fearful of what LT might bring, may be unwilling—at least for a price substantially less valuable than victory in the litigation—to achieve the latter result instead of the former. Thus, there may be no deal, even if the opponent would be glad to cause the declarant's production if all he had to pay was the proponent's costs and perhaps even a modest premium. The court might be inclined to select ADMIT only if it perceives that the opponent—albeit perhaps indirectly, and at a somewhat elevated cost, as the result of a deal—is essentially as able as the proponent to cause the production of the declarant. If a deal is not a practical possibility, this premise might not hold.

Second, if the parties make a deal, the proponent might extract from the opponent a large premium over the proponent's production costs. The greater the proponent's production advantage is, and the more each party thinks the declarant's live testimony would benefit the opponent of the hearsay, given that the alternative is admission of the hearsay, the larger the premium will tend to be. The court might not appreciate the proponent's use of the ADMIT ruling as the occasion for exercising a sort of monopoly power, making a profit at the expense of the opponent.[72]

72. In some cases, though, the proponent might argue with some reason

Third, in some cases, transaction costs may be quite high. The hostility between the parties may be so great that it is difficult to have efficient negotiations on the substance of the litigation, much less on side issues. Moreover, just the lawyers' time necessary to negotiate whether the proponent will bring the declarant to court, and the consideration that the proponent will receive for doing so, may not be worthwhile.

In some cases, therefore, even though the proponent is far better able than the opponent to produce the declarant, the court might decide that it should not depend on the prospect that the parties will make a deal shifting the physical burden to the proponent. In such a case, the court might conclude that the simple ADMIT ruling is not appealing (even though the hearsay is more probative than prejudicial) and therefore might impose on the proponent at least part of the burden of producing the declarant. In my earlier article, I have suggested that there are various ways the court might split that burden.[73] The best way to do this depends on the precise circumstances.

b. *Dividing the Physical Burden*

In some cases, it makes sense to give the proponent the burden of performing part of the set of tasks necessary to produce the declarant. This type of ruling may be labeled SPLIT BURDEN.

Hypothetical 9, involving a statement by an unknown for-

that any premium that the deal earned for him over his costs of production was simply the result of different perceptions of the situation by the two parties. If, excluding the possibility of a deal, the opponent's next best, or only, alternative given ADMIT is DO NOTHING, then the declarant will be produced only if the parties make a deal. In those circumstances, they will make a deal only if they perceive the situation in contradictory ways: First, the opponent must perceive that LT would be sufficiently more favorable to his litigation position than H to warrant the payment; second, the proponent must perceive either that LT is better than H for *his* litigation position, or that if it is worse the sacrifice is small enough to be worthwhile in light of the premium (i.e., the payment less his costs of producing the declarant). In this situation, the proponent arguably ought to be allowed to keep the benefit of his bargain; if, in fact, LT is far worse for him than H, he will pay the consequences of misperception.

If, on the other hand, the opponent's next best alternative was PRODUCE, then the declarant will be produced whether or not the parties make a deal. If they do make a deal, the proponent gives up nothing, and simply makes a profit by selling witness-production services more cheaply than the opponent could himself produce the declarant. The deal might be mutually advantageous, given that the burden of producing the declarant has been imposed on the opponent. Fairness and efficiency, however, weigh in favor only of imposing the actual burden on the opponent—not the burden plus a premium.

73. *See* Friedman, *supra* note 9, at 904-16.

mer employee of Propco, is an example of a case in which a rather simple SPLIT BURDEN solution seems available. The court should impose on Propco the burden of identifying the declarant and of locating her to the extent of determining her address as of the time she left Propco; the remainder of the burden should be imposed on Oppco. In other words, if Propco declines to provide Oppco with the declarant's name and last known address, the court excludes the hearsay. If Propco does provide the information to Oppco, the court admits the hearsay unless Oppco finishes the job of producing the declarant.

In Hypothetical 10, involving a statement by an acquaintance of Paul's whom Otto could not feasibly locate, a simple solution also appears available. The court probably should impose on Paul the burden of locating Dorothy, and on Otto the remaining aspects of the burden of producing her. If Paul does not provide Otto with Dorothy's current address, the court should exclude the hearsay. If he does, the court should admit the hearsay unless Otto produces Dorothy.

Note that in each of these cases, the suggested solution is to impose on the proponent only those aspects of the burden as to which it has a substantial advantage over the opponent. In Hypothetical 9, Propco can far more easily determine the declarant's identity and her past address. Given that information, Oppco appears to be in as good a position as Propco to produce the declarant. In Hypothetical 10, on the other hand, given that Paul and Dorothy have mutual friends, it is presumably much easier for him than for Otto to track her down.

In Hypotheticals 9 and 10, the proponent has an advantage in information. Sometimes the proponent might have another type of advantage that would warrant dividing the physical burden. Thus, in Hypothetical 11, Paul has an advantage in that he could persuade his sister Denise to testify, but Otto could not. The court might impose on Paul the burden of persuading Denise to testify, and on Otto the remaining aspects of the burden of producing her as a witness. For example, the court might rule that it will admit the hearsay unless Otto commits himself to arranging, and paying, for Denise's transportation, assuming she is willing to appear. Thus, Otto would have to decide whether or not it was worthwhile to go to the trouble and expense of ensuring her appearance, assuming her willingness to appear. If Otto decides in the affirmative, then Paul must decide whether or not to persuade Denise to appear. If he declines to persuade her, the hearsay would be excluded.[74]

Hypothetical 12, involving a statement by a person who could claim a Fifth Amendment privilege, presents another situation in which only the proponent, here a criminal prosecutor, could induce the declarant to testify. The prosecutor could accomplish this most simply by granting her use immunity, assuming the law of the jurisdiction will allow it. But the hearsay is more probative than prejudicial. The court therefore might impose on the prosecution the burden of nullifying the Fifth Amendment problem and on the opponent, Acker, the remaining aspects of the burden of producing the declarant, Diana. This might be done in various ways. For example, the court might rule that it will exclude the hearsay unless the prosecution commits to granting Diana use immunity (or otherwise removing the Fifth Amendment problem, as by a plea bargain) if she is brought to court; if the prosecution does make that commitment, the hearsay would be admitted unless Acker produces Diana in court.

Figure 4 represents in general terms the type of ruling discussed above, which I call SPLIT BURDEN (PROPONENT FIRST). As this diagram indicates, the declarant testifies live if and only if each party performs its designated part of the burden, indicated by PART-PRODUCE, and bears the attendant costs (indicated by the subscripts p′ and o′, read, respectively "p-prime" and "o-prime"). Under this variation of SPLIT BURDEN, the proponent is required to commit first as to whether it will perform its designated share of the burden; if it chooses DO NOTHING, the hearsay is excluded, without the opponent having to make any commitment. Other variations of SPLIT BURDEN are possible. Figure 5, for example, which in a sense is a mirror image of Figure 4, represents SPLIT BURDEN (OPPONENT FIRST). Under this version, the opponent is required to commit first, and if it chooses DO NOTHING, the hearsay is admitted without the proponent having to commit.[75] Which variation of SPLIT BURDEN is preferable depends on an assessment

74. There is actually a variety of ways in which the court might achieve the same division of the burden. *See infra* notes 75-77 and accompanying text.

75. Note that both Figures 4 and 5 indicate costs of zero if the first party chooses PART-PRODUCE but the second chooses DO NOTHING. These diagrams are drawn on the assumption that, though the first party must commit before the second party, the first party does not actually have to perform its share of the burden until after the second party commits. Thus, if the second part chooses DO NOTHING, there is no cost. *See infra* note 76.

of the precise circumstances of the case.[76]

Whichever variation of SPLIT BURDEN the court selects, by

---

76. Consider Hypothetical 12 again. In this case, either party could be called on to perform its portion of the burden (or suffer an adverse evidentiary result), before the other is called on to perform his share of the burden. That is, the prosecutor could be called on to grant use immunity to the declarant either before or after the accused brings her to court. Most often, though, where there is no doubt that if the declarant were in court she would have to testify, the respective portions of the burden have to be performed in a natural chronological order—the declarant must be identified before she can be located and must be located before she can be brought to court.

Whether or not there is flexibility as to the sequence in which the parties can be called on to *perform* their portions of the burden, there is flexibility as to the sequence in which they may be called on to *commit* as to whether they will perform. In this hypothetical, for example, it makes no sense for Acker to produce Diana in court, which might be an expensive process, unless the prosecution has at least committed to nullifying the Fifth Amendment problem. And it probably makes no sense for the prosecution to go to the trouble of nullifying that problem unless Acker has committed that, if the problem is or will be removed, he will commit to produce Diana in court. It seems, then, that to prevent wasted effort, each side should be called on to commit to whether it will perform its share of the burden before the other side is called on to perform its share.

The question then becomes the sequence in which the parties should be required to state their commitments. This question is important not only to save wasted effort but also because it might affect the ultimate evidentiary result. Whichever party is called on to commit second has an advantage: If the first party does not commit to performing its share of the burden, the second party gets the evidentiary result it desires, without ever having to commit. This asymmetry may be eliminated by effectively requiring the parties to commit simultaneously; the court might, for example, ask each party to submit a written statement of its intent. This type of ruling, which I call SPLIT BURDEN (SIMULTANEOUS MOVES), is discussed in Friedman, *supra* note 9, at 912-15. When the court wants to avoid going through this simultaneous commitment process, the following rule of thumb may be appropriate: If the hearsay is more probative than prejudicial, require the opponent to commit first (thus ensuring that if the opponent is unwilling or unable to perform his task the hearsay will be admitted), unless the task imposed on the proponent is essentially cost-free (in which case the proponent's refusal to perform is probably highly significant); correspondingly, if the hearsay is more prejudicial than probative, call on the proponent to commit first, unless the opponent's task is essentially cost-free. For a fuller discussion of this topic of sequencing, see Friedman, *supra* note 9, at 910-15.

In Hypothetical 12, the evidence is assumed to be more probative than prejudicial. Thus, a decision requiring the prosecution to commit first would reflect a judgment that eliminating the Fifth Amendment problem would be essentially cost-free for the prosecution. (This is probably so given that it is not anticipated that Diana would be prosecuted; on the other hand, granting her use immunity now might create difficult hindrances in a later prosecution, because the prosecutor would have to show that he is not relying on the immunized statement. *See* Braswell v. United States, 487 U.S. 99 (1988).). If the court is in doubt on this score, the safest thing to do might be to require simultaneous commitments.

Figure 4

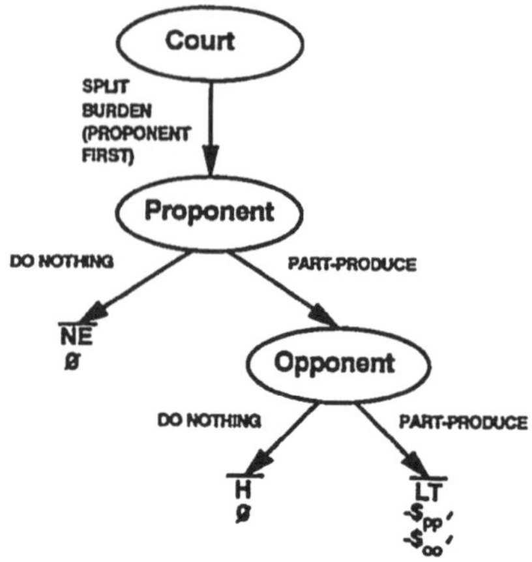

dividing the physical burden in cases such as Hypotheticals 9 through 12, the court is able to take advantage of the proponent's superior or exclusive ability to perform part of the set of

Figure 5

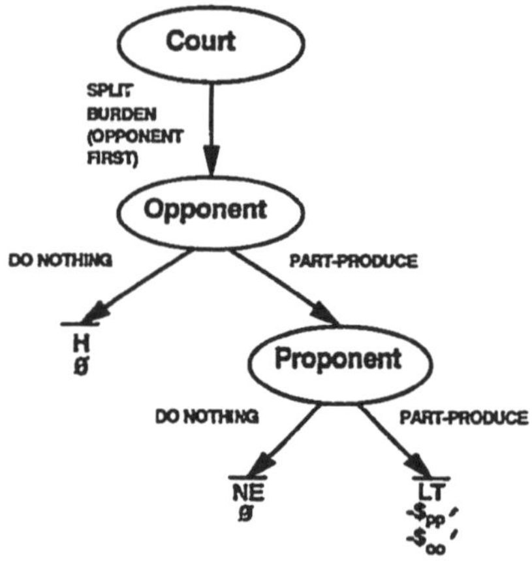

tasks necessary for producing the declarant. At the same time, because the tasks imposed on the proponent should not cost it any substantial amount of time or money, the division leaves virtually the entire financial burden where it belongs, given that the hearsay is more probative than prejudicial—on the opponent.

SPLIT BURDEN can have significant problems, however.

Sometimes it is inefficient for the burden to be broken down. In Hypothetical 8, for example, in which the proponent but not the opponent can easily locate a fast-moving declarant, it probably makes little sense to set up a procedure in which the proponent locates her and passes the information on to the opponent and the opponent then subpoenas her. Sometimes, if in the end the declarant is not produced, it might be unclear whose fault caused her absence. The court should be reluctant to have to adjudicate a squabble over who dropped this relay baton.

Furthermore, the portion of the burden imposed on the proponent might not be cost-free. Recall that for now we are assuming that the evidence is more probative than prejudicial. Thus, for goals of both fairness and efficiency, the court should impose the cost of producing the declarant on the opponent. These goals are undercut to the extent that the portion of the burden imposed on the proponent carries substantial cost, financial or otherwise. For example, if Hypothetical 12 is varied so that the prosecutor is seriously considering prosecuting Diana, he might have significant reasons not to grant her use immunity.

Finally, if the court is imposing part of the burden on the proponent simply because of the proponent's presumed advantage in carrying that portion of the burden, the court should take great care that the proponent really is able to perform that portion. In Hypothetical 11, for example, what happens if in fact Paul is not able to persuade his sister to appear? If he has tried in good faith, the court might prefer treating the case as one in which the declarant was simply unavailable, which would presumably lead to ADMIT. But the court will not wish to engage too often in adjudications of good faith.[77]

c. *Separating the Physical and Financial Burdens*

In some cases, the courts might sensibly impose the entire physical burden on the proponent and the entire financial burden on the opponent. Consider the following hypothetical.

> Hypothetical 13: *A variation on Hypothetical 9. Propco wants to introduce a memo written by an employee not identified on the face of the memo. The memo is an entry in a computerized record, and Propco can identify the author of the memo only after a search that will require a more than trivial amount of staff time and some high-priced computer time. Only Propco employees could conduct the search, at least without revealing proprietary information. Propco's*

77. This difficulty is discussed at greater length in Friedman, *supra* note 9, at 914-15.

sole office is located in Courthouse City, and the memo was written only one year before the time of the trial. Thus, once the author of the memo is identified, either party could presumably produce her as a witness without difficulty. The court is satisfied that the memo is more probative than prejudicial.

In these circumstances, ADMIT is probably not an appealing choice for the court; Oppco could not produce the declarant itself, and, given that fact, Propco might be unwilling to agree with Oppco to produce her.

Nor does it seem wise to adopt a variation of SPLIT BURDEN—for example, by imposing on Propco the burden of identifying and locating the declarant, and on Oppco the remaining

Figure 6

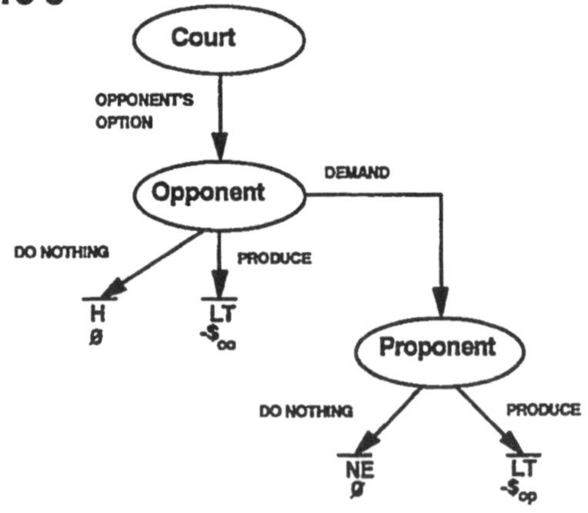

portions of producing her. Identifying the declarant may be difficult and expensive. Because the hearsay statement appears more probative than prejudicial, the expense of producing the declarant should not be incurred unless Oppco is willing to bear it. Propco should not be the one bearing that expense.

Thus, in this case, the best ruling might be to impose on Oppco the entire financial burden of producing the declarant and on Propco the entire physical burden of producing her. Figure 6 represents this allocation, which may be called OPPONENT'S OPTION, in general terms. (The reverse allocation, PROPONENT'S OPTION, is not pictured here.) OPPONENT'S OPTION would most sensibly be implemented in this case as follows:[78] The hearsay would be admitted unless Oppco de-

78. In other cases, other sequences might be preferable. *See supra* note 76

cided to DEMAND production, committing itself to paying Propco's costs of producing the declarant. If Oppco did commit itself to doing that, then the hearsay would be excluded unless Propco produced her. And if Propco did produce her, Oppco then would have to pay Propco its costs, a payment indicated by the notation $-\$_{op}$. The court would determine the amount of the payment if the parties were unable to agree.

This OPPONENT'S OPTION ruling assures that the opponent will bear the costs of producing the declarant. At the same time, the ruling gives the opponent the benefit of the proponent's production advantage—without the necessity of having to pay a premium for it and without having to negotiate for it.

This does not mean that negotiations have no role under OPPONENT'S OPTION. Because the opponent has the right to demand production by the proponent, all that must be determined is the compensation. And given that the court will set the compensation absent agreement by the parties, the parties may be able to negotiate efficiently a reasonable compensation.

Sometimes, though, negotiations will break down, and the court will have to determine the compensation. It might not be able to do this accurately. For example, if the court determines the compensation before the proponent actually produces the declarant, events might not bear out its prediction. If the court waits until after the fact to determine the compensation, the proponent will have no incentive to act efficiently, because he will in effect be spending his opponent's money. Accordingly, OPPONENT'S OPTION should not be used indiscriminately. Courts should use it only when they think that the proponent has a large enough production advantage to make the administrative costs and uncertainties worthwhile.[79]

(discussing the problem of sequencing of commitments); *infra* notes 82-83 and accompanying text (discussing a possible requirement that proponent commit first when motives are suspect). Note that, although the opponent in Hypothetical 13 cannot produce the declarant by itself, Figure 6, being drawn generally, does indicate this possibility.

79. By now, some readers might recognize a familial resemblance between the analysis here and that in Calabresi & Melamed, *supra* note 44. The decision to impose the financial burden on the opponent might be considered an initial entitlement for the proponent to have the hearsay admitted without his having to produce the declarant. The entitlement might be protected by a property rule or by a liability rule.

A property rule would mean that if the opponent wants to remove the entitlement from the proponent, he must enter into a voluntary transaction with the seller; this is ADMIT, allowing the possibility of a deal after the court issues its ruling. (I have focused in the text on a deal in which the proponent agrees to produce the declarant. There could be other deals, however, in which the

Another reason to avoid indiscriminate use of OPPONENT'S OPTION is that, as with SPLIT BURDEN, if the court is incorrect in its belief that the proponent can produce the declarant, the ruling may unintentionally amount to an exclusion of the hearsay. If the opponent realizes that the proponent cannot produce the declarant, he would exercise the option; given the proponent's failure to produce the declarant, the hearsay would then be excluded. As with SPLIT BURDEN, the court might avoid this result by providing that, if the proponent made a good faith effort to satisfy his part of the burden, he should not be held accountable for his failure. Most often, though, the court would prefer not having to resolve this issue.

---

proponent agrees to do without any evidence from the declarant, or retains the option to do one or the other. I see no reason why such agreements ought not ordinarily be honored; in other words, there is no sound reason to adopt an inalienability rule.)

A liability rule would mean that the opponent might destroy the entitlement if he is willing to pay an objectively determined price for it; this is OPPONENT'S OPTION. Removal of the entitlement would mean that the proponent must either produce the declarant or do without the benefit of any evidence from the declarant. Under OPPONENT'S OPTION, the opponent would actually have to pay the price only if the proponent chose the first alternative. One way to think of this is to say that if the proponent is unwilling to produce the declarant even though he does not have to pay the expenses of doing so, he ought to forfeit the initial entitlement. From another perspective, OPPONENT'S OPTION might be considered an order to the proponent, contingent on the opponent's making the demand, to produce the declarant in return for compensation, with the sanction for the proponent's failure to comply being the loss of the compensation for removal of the entitlement.

By a similar analysis, EXCLUDE and PROPONENT'S OPTION (imposition of the financial burden on the proponent and the physical burden on the opponent) might be considered alternative ways of protecting an initial entitlement allocated to the opponent. Whether the parties should be allowed to agree on admissibility of hearsay notwithstanding a ruling by the court tentatively excluding it is an interesting question. I believe they ordinarily should. Often, a similar result is accomplished without even presenting the issue to the court, by the parties' exercise of mutual restraint in objecting to each other's evidence.

The various forms of SPLIT BURDEN would represent a different, contingent allocation of the initial entitlement. The solution suggested for Hypothetical 9, for example, would represent an initial entitlement for Oppco unless Propco provided Oppco with the name and last known address of the declarant.

I have not used the terminology of Calabresi and Melamed in the text, in part because, although of broad applicability, it would probably seem awkward in the hearsay context. Moreover, there are substantial differences between the hearsay situation and the type of situation that is at the center of their concern; a glib attempt to apply their analysis here probably would be counterproductive. But this does not minimize the importance of their analysis in the conception and preparation of this Article.

Finally, OPPONENT'S OPTION will not effectively transfer to the opponent all the costs of producing the declarant, because not all those costs are financial. In Hypothetical 11, for example, Paul may find it distasteful to ask his sister to interrupt her travels. More significantly, in cases resembling Hypothetical 12, but in which prosecution of the declarant is a substantial prospect, nullifying the Fifth Amendment problem in the current case may pose real obstacles to the later prosecution. It probably would not make sense to try to require the accused in the first prosecution, as the price of procuring the declarant's testimony, to compensate the prosecutor for the impediment to the later case. The court will have to choose between imperfect alternatives.[80]

d. *Imposing on the Opponent All of the Financial Burden and Part of the Physical Burden*

In some instances, it might make sense to combine SPLIT BURDEN and OPPONENT'S OPTION. That is, a court might impose part of the physical burden on the proponent and the rest of the physical burden, and the entire financial burden, on the opponent.

> Hypothetical 14: *Same facts as Hypothetical 13 (involving a memo the author of which can be identified only after a substantial inquiry), except that, as in Hypothetical 9, the memo was written five years ago, and the author presumably is no longer with Propco because three years ago Propco closed the office from which the memo was written.*

Here, only Propco can feasibly identify the declarant, and it, far more efficiently than Oppco, can locate her as of the time she left its employ. Accordingly, the court should impose the physical burden of performing those tasks on Propco.

On the other hand, given that the evidence is more probative than prejudicial, the court probably should impose all the other aspects of the burden of producing the declarant Oppco. The tasks assigned to Propco are expensive, and Oppco ought to

80. If the court chooses SPLIT BURDEN, imposing on the prosecutor the burden of nullifying the Fifth Amendment problem, the prosecutor will be put to a choice of forgoing the evidence or impeding the anticipated prosecution of the declarant. (Given that the hearsay is more probative than prejudicial, this ruling is at least preferable to EXCLUDE, which denies the prosecutor this choice and simply imposes the entire burden on her.) On the other hand, if the court chooses ADMIT, the hearsay will be admitted, but the accused will not have an opportunity to cross-examine the declarant. Which ruling to choose will depend on which of these problems seems greater in the particular case.

bear the cost of performing them, if they are to be performed. Furthermore, once Propco determines the name and last known address of the declarant, Oppco is in substantially as good a position to produce her as is Propco. Thus, Oppco should bear the cost of producing her and also the risk that she cannot be produced, which, if the declarant has left Propco, may be substantial.

This best method of allocating this burden would probably be as follows: The hearsay is admitted unless Oppco demands that Propco identify the declarant and determine her address as of the latest time she was in Propco's employ. If Oppco makes the demand, and Propco does not comply with it, the hearsay is excluded. If Propco does comply, then Oppco must compensate Propco for its effort, and the hearsay is admitted, at least unless Oppco produces the declarant. If Oppco does produce her, then Propco must present her testimony or forgo use of the hearsay.

This approach isolates the tasks as to which the proponent has a production advantage, and, at the same time, does not impose on the proponent any excess burdens. The proponent avoids the financial burden of those tasks as well as the risk that any of the other tasks required to produce the declarant cannot be performed. This ruling therefore is as close to ADMIT as possible, while still taking advantage of the proponent's advantages. On the other hand, this approach may entail substantial administrative costs. As with OPPONENT'S OPTION, the court may have to determine compensation for the proponent's work. And, as with SPLIT BURDEN, the court will sometimes have to determine whose failure caused the declarant not to be produced. And, as with both OPPONENT'S OPTION and SPLIT BURDEN, the court will sometimes have to ascertain whether the proponent's failure was in good faith.

e. *Excluding the Hearsay*

To this point, we have not considered the possibility that, because of the proponent's advantage in producing the declarant, the court should decide simply to EXCLUDE the hearsay, notwithstanding the fact that it is more probative than prejudicial. But, as discussed previously, if production would have been relatively easy for the proponent and relatively difficult for the opponent, that tends to suggest that the proponent decided to offer the hearsay in the first place because he feared that the live testimony would be less advantageous to him.[81] Thus, the proponent's production advantage may be so great as to make EXCLUDE a tempting solution. Usually, though, a more parsimonious remedy would suffice. In some circumstances, the court may still find that ADMIT, accompanied by a "missing witness" argument by the opponent and a supporting instruction by the court, is an attractive ruling. Somewhat stronger medicine would be a ruling of OPPONENT'S OPTION, guaranteeing the opponent the ability to secure the declarant's production at the proponent's cost.[82] The remedy might be made stronger yet by requiring the proponent to commit before the opponent. That is, unless the proponent signifies a willingness to present the declarant's testimony, assuming the opponent demands production of the declarant, the hearsay is excluded.[83] If the proponent does express willingness, the op-

81. *See supra* pp. 741-42.

82. An argument against this remedy would be that, assuming the proponent has better access than the opponent to the declarant, the opponent may have no adequate way of assessing whether the probability that the proponent has withheld the declarant for manipulative reasons is great enough to make payment for production of the declarant worthwhile. (Conceivably, the opponent will hesitate to pay for producing the declarant because he assumes that, as in most cases, if cost and difficulty were not a factor, the proponent would have preferred live testimony to hearsay, whereas actually the proponent prefers the hearsay to live testimony because of information unknown to the opponent.) A partial response is the sequence of decisions suggested in the text, in which the court makes the proponent at least signal whether he prefers live testimony, assuming he has to pay for it, to no evidence at all from the declarant.

Beyond that, manipulation of this sort by the proponent is likely to hurt the opponent only if the hearsay is significant evidence, and manipulation is most likely to account for the proponent's decision to offer the hearsay rather than live testimony when it would be relatively easy for him to produce the declarant. In these circumstances, the opponent would have strong reason to suspect the proponent's motives and strong incentive to exercise the option, demanding production of the declarant. The option approach seems better, at least as a first resort, than a prophylactic rule excluding the hearsay. The prophylactic rule of exclusion would apply even though the hearsay appears to be net probative, and even though there is no reason, other than the disparity in ability to produce the declarant, for doubting the proponent's assertion that the desire to save costs accounts for his decision to offer the hearsay. The court might try a more finely-tuned rule, excluding the hearsay only if it has such great significance that production of the declarant at the proponent's cost clearly is worthwhile. The opponent, however, is better placed than the court to make the judgment, and if the hearsay is net probative, the opponent should bear the cost of production. (Occasionally, though, the proponent's failure to offer the live testimony might appear so suspicious that the failure contributes to making the hearsay appear net prejudicial; *see supra* pp. 741-42).

83. Thus, this sequence calls the proponent's bluff, at least in part, by making the proponent choose based on the hypothetical assumption that H is

ponent then must decide whether to demand production by the proponent. If he does not, the hearsay is admitted.

EXCLUDE does seem to be an appropriate ruling in those occasional cases in which the proponent's production advantage is absolute—that is, when the opponent has no means of producing the declarant but the proponent can do so without cost. At this limit, though, EXCLUDE merges with OPPONENT'S OPTION.[84]

> Hypothetical 15: *Acker, the accused in a felony prosecution, does not wish to take the stand in his own defense. He does, however, offer proof of a hearsay statement that he has made. The prosecution objects.*

The prosecution (the opponent here) has no way to force Acker, the declarant, to testify. Acker, on the other hand, can easily take the stand in his own defense without any out-of-pocket costs. The court might therefore rule that it will exclude the hearsay unless Acker takes the stand and testifies to his memory of the underlying event or condition that was the subject of the statement. If Acker does testify, he must, at least to some extent, waive his privilege against self-incrimination. That prospect, however, does not appear especially troubling; it seems unacceptable to allow the accused to present his version of events through his hearsay statement and then prevent cross-examination by retreating behind the privilege.

2. When the Hearsay Is More Prejudicial Than Probative and the Opponent Possesses a Substantial Production Advantage

Subsection 1 dealt with the situation in which the balance of probative value versus prejudicial potential favored admission but the proponent's advantage in some aspect of producing the declarant favored exclusion. The reverse situation might also arise: The hearsay may be more prejudicial than probative, but the opponent might have an advantage in producing the declarant. This situation will not be analyzed at great length here, because in large part the analysis is a mirror image of

---

not an available possibility. If the proponent believes that, from his point of view, LT would be worse than NE, or not sufficiently better to warrant the costs of production, he will not commit himself to producing the declarant if the opponent exercises the DEMAND option. Note how this sequence differs from that suggested in connection with Hypothetical 13.

84. Because the proponent's out-of-pocket costs are zero, the opponent who prefers that the declarant testify live, rather than that the hearsay be admitted, would have no reason not to exercise the option. The proponent therefore must produce the declarant or forgo use of the hearsay.

that of the first situation.[85] As an example, consider the following hypothetical:

> Hypothetical 16: *Paul wishes to introduce for a hearsay purpose a statement made by a friend of Otto's in a conversation with Paul and Otto. Paul, however, does not know the name or identity of the declarant. If Paul had known well enough before trial that he would want to present the statement, he could have, by means of either interrogatories or deposition questions, required Otto to provide the name and address of the friend. But the relevance of the statement became apparent only during trial, as a result of evidence introduced by Otto. The court regards the hearsay as more prejudicial than probative, though it would be inclined to admit live evidence by the friend.*

It might seem that, given that the hearsay evidence is more prejudicial than probative, the best result is simply to exclude the hearsay. But, given that live testimony by the declarant would be useful evidence and that the declarant cannot be produced without participation by the opponent, simple exclusion, imposing the full burden on the proponent, may be unwise. Imposing at least part of the burden on the opponent, by virtue of a sort of reverse best evidence rule, may induce production of beneficial evidence.[86] In this case, the best solution may be to adopt a form of SPLIT BURDEN. Because only Otto can provide the name and address of the declarant, the court ought to place the burden on him to do that. Because the hearsay is more prejudicial than probative, however, the court should place all the remaining aspects of the burden on Paul: If Otto suitably identifies the declarant, the hearsay is excluded unless Paul produces her.

D. The Implications of Late Notice

Section B argued that, under certain assumptions, it is usually appropriate to admit hearsay. Section C examined the im-

85. In at least one sense, however, the situations may not be symmetrical: If a criminal prosecutor offers evidence of a hearsay statement made by the accused, and the court believes that the statement is more prejudicial than probative, the court probably should not (attempting to reflect the logic of the solution suggested for Hypothetical 15) admit the hearsay on the ground that the accused can take the stand if he wishes. Given that the statement is net prejudicial, it seems that such a ruling would put intolerable pressure on the accused's right not to testify.

86. The so-called best evidence rule, exemplified by Article X of the Federal Rules of Evidence, excludes certain evidence, although net probative, thus imposing a burden on the proponent and giving him an incentive to produce evidence that is more net probative. A reverse best evidence rule threatens to admit evidence that is net prejudicial, thereby imposing a burden on the opponent and giving him an incentive to play a role in producing evidence that is net probative.

pact of relaxing the assumption that the parties were substantially equally able to produce the declarant. This Section relaxes another of the assumptions, that the proponent has given sufficient notice of his intention to offer the hearsay. This is important because proponents sometimes give extremely late notice. Indeed, under current practice, often the first notice the proponent gives of his intention to introduce the hearsay is his attempt to do so.[87] In some cases, the lateness of notice means that the ability of the opponent, or of both parties, to produce the declarant is prejudiced, and this may alter the optimal hearsay ruling.

Most of the discussion below assumes that, if notice had been adequate, the court would have chosen ADMIT. At the end, I will add a few comments on the consequences of late notice when another ruling would be optimal given adequate notice.

Lateness of notice will not always have much significance. For late notice to prejudice the opponent in producing the declarant, it must be true both that producing her would have been relatively easy given fuller notice, and that producing her is relatively difficult given the later notice. Thus, if the declarant died before the litigation began, lateness of notice would not be prejudicial because, even given early notice, the opponent could not have produced the declarant. And at least ordinarily, the lateness of the notice in such a case should not alter the court's determination on the hearsay motion. At the other extreme, if the declarant is easily and instantly available even during trial, the lateness of notice should have little bearing on the hearsay issue.[88]

Now suppose, however, that it appears that late notice may have prejudiced the opponent's ability to produce the declarant. It could be, for example, that it takes a significant amount of time to identify and locate the declarant and to bring her to court. Or perhaps at an earlier stage the declarant was readily available, but in the interim she has died, disappeared, or traveled a substantial distance further away from the courthouse.

If the declarant can still be produced at trial, but not in time for presentation of her testimony during the proponent's case, usually the solution would be reasonably simple.

87. Thus, the sardonic trial lawyer's observation that the chief exception to the hearsay rule is the quick answer.

88. This is true at least if the court would not, given similarly late notice, bar the proponent from calling the declarant to testify live.

Hypothetical 17: *Without giving prior notice, Propco, on the last afternoon of presenting its case-in-chief, offers the hearsay statement of Dora Declarant. If Propco had given fuller notice, the court would have ruled* ADMIT, *because it regards the statement as more probative than prejudicial. It is concerned, however, that Oppco might not be able to produce Dora immediately, because she recently left on a short trip out of town. Oppco could, however, produce Dora before all the evidence is in, which is not expected to occur for three more days.*

In a case like this, the court might rule that, as under the usual ADMIT procedure—modified as suggested in Part III—it will admit the hearsay declaration unless Oppco timely produces Dora, in which case Propco will present Dora's live testimony (perhaps supplemented by the prior statement) or forgo use of the hearsay. If the notice had been sufficient, the court might have provided that production of Dora would be timely only if it allowed Propco to present her testimony in the sequence preferred by it as part of its case-in-chief. Because of the late notice, however, Oppco should not be required to produce the declarant during Propco's case-in-chief. Instead, the court might give Oppco until the end of Propco's rebuttal to produce her. If it does not produce her then, the hearsay will be admitted. If it does produce her by then, Propco will have to present her live testimony or forgo the hearsay. Presentation of the hearsay or of Dora's live testimony on rebuttal may not be the most effective order of evidence for Propco. It is reasonable, though, for Propco to absorb that loss so that Oppco will be able to examine the declarant on cross, rather than having to make the declarant its own witness. Unless Propco has a good excuse for the late notice (and arguably even then), it is also reasonable for Propco to absorb any incremental financial costs of the late notice.

The more difficult cases occur when, because of the late notice, the opponent is seriously prejudiced in, or altogether precluded from, producing the declarant at any time during the trial, even if the court extends the trial for a reasonable period. Assume first that the proponent has a good excuse for not giving earlier notice. I will not attempt here to define what constitutes a satisfactory excuse, but will only offer a few examples of what *might* be one. In some circumstances, through no lack of prior diligence, the proponent may learn of the hearsay only at a late date. Sometimes, surprising developments during trial—perhaps testimony elicited by the opponent in examining another witness—might lead the proponent to conclude that he needs to prove a proposition that he previously did not think he would have to prove. In some cases, the proponent may expect to produce the declarant as a witness, but the declarant, through no fault of the proponent, becomes unavailable before testifying.

Hypothetical 18: *Without giving prior notice, Paul offers at trial a hearsay statement by Delores Declarant. Paul explains to the satisfaction of the court that the statement became material only the previous day, as the result of evidence introduced by Otto. Delores left the state on vacation last week, cannot be subpoenaed, and may not be back until well after the trial ends. If Paul had given fuller notice, the court would have admitted the statement, which it regards as more probative than prejudicial.*

Given that the proponent has a good excuse, the court should not necessarily accord the lateness of the notice in itself any significance. Of course, the ability of the respective parties to produce the declarant is, as always, an important consideration. But the fact that either party or both may *have been* able to produce the declarant if the proponent had known earlier that there was a potential hearsay dispute probably is immaterial. Thus, if neither party is able to produce the declarant, the court probably ought to treat the case just as it would if she were dead, or, for some other reason, the parties would both be unable to produce her even given ample notice. The court probably should not alter the decision to ADMIT, which by hypothesis it would have made given ample notice.

Hypothetical 19: *Same basic facts as Hypothetical 18, but also these in addition: Delores is Paul's sister, and he could presumably persuade her to return to testify if it was important for him.*

In this case, the proponent has a production advantage over the opponent. Thus, the best solution may be to adopt a ruling like OPPONENT'S OPTION. Under such a ruling, the opponent can, if he is willing to pay the cost, demand production by the proponent and thereby ensure, notwithstanding the lateness of notice, that either the declarant will testify or the hearsay will not be admitted. Arguably, if the opponent does demand production, the proponent should be required to absorb any incremental costs caused by the lateness of notice. Given the assumption that the proponent had a good excuse for the delay, however, it is probably best not to try such fine-tuning.

Now assume that the proponent does not have a good excuse for the failure to give earlier notice. At least ideally, the opponent should not be prejudiced by the proponent's delay; the proponent should absorb any loss. Thus, it might be tempting to conclude that the court should exclude the hearsay in this circumstance, because the proponent's unexcused delay has made production of the declarant by the opponent more difficult or impossible. The opponent will likely counter that, if the hearsay issue had been joined earlier and resolved against him, he surely would have produced the declarant, but now he is unable to, at least without incurring substantially increased expense.

Such assertions should be taken with a grain of salt. Often the opponent does not produce the declarant in response to a ruling admitting hearsay, even when he is perfectly able to do so. There is no reason to give the opponent a windfall by accepting as certain his retrospective representations that he would have produced the declarant if he had earlier notice. There is no reason to exclude the hearsay, simply because the proponent's delay in giving notice prejudiced the opponent's ability to produce the declarant, if the delay caused no genuine prejudice because the opponent would not have produced the declarant even given ample notice.

If the court is confident on this score, therefore, the lateness of the notice probably should not dissuade it from admitting the hearsay. Determining what the opponent would have done, given ample notice, does, of course, involve retrospective second-guessing. The court should ask the opponent to show not only that production is difficult or impossible now, and also that it would have been easy if the proponent had given enough notice. The court should also ask the opponent to show that he would have had strong enough reason to produce the declarant—for example, enough hope that cross-examination would be productive. In some cases, the court can make a reasonably confident determination of what the opponent would have done.[89]

Sometimes, though, the court will be unable to conclude with sufficient confidence that the opponent would not have produced the declarant if notice had been sufficient. Even then, the court should hesitate before simply excluding the hearsay. Some form of burden splitting frequently offers a better alternative, though in the end it may result in exclusion of the hearsay. The basic principles behind such a ruling would be as follows: The opponent ought to bear the financial burden, to the extent that he would have had to do so if the proponent had given ample notice; the proponent ought to bear any incre-

89. Recall that it is sometimes difficult for the court to predict whether the opponent will find production of the declarant sufficiently important to warrant the costs. *See supra* pp. 748-50. It seems possible that ordinarily the assessment would be no easier to make retrospectively.

mental financial burden caused by the lateness of notice; and because the proponent's delay in giving notice has prejudiced the opponent's ability to produce the declarant, the proponent ought to bear the physical burden of producing her, at least the incremental burden caused by the delay and at least to the extent the opponent is not able to produce her much more efficiently.

Hypothetical 20: *Without giving prior notice, and without sufficient excuse for not giving notice, Propco offers, during its case-in-chief, the hearsay statement of Dolly Declarant, an employee of Oppco. Dolly lives in distant Remoteville, and special arrangements would have to be made to bring her to Courthouse City before the close of testimony. Arranging a deposition—which in any event would not be as satisfactory as live testimony—in Remoteville at this point would not be feasible. The court is persuaded that the statement is more probative than prejudicial, and therefore would have admitted it if Propco had given adequate notice. The court also believes, however, that given adequate notice, Oppco might have produced Dolly.*

The following fictitious transcript presents a scenario of how this issue might be resolved:

THE COURT: I don't want Oppco prejudiced at all by Propco's delay. So this is how I'll rule.

I'm going to admit the hearsay now, Ms. Oppenheimer (Oppco's counsel), unless you tell me that you're willing to pay an amount equal to the commercial airfare toward the cost of bringing in the declarant. You would have had to pay that even if you had plenty of notice, assuming you really would have brought her in. Do you want to do that?

MS. OPPENHEIMER: Yes, we do, Your Honor. We really don't want to let her hearsay statement come in without a chance to cross-examine her, because we think her testimony will be a lot clearer than the statement.

THE COURT: Maybe so. I'm doubtful, but that's your choice. Given that, Ms. Pratt [Propco's counsel], now the choice is yours. You can forget about the evidence, or you can try to bring the declarant here.

MS. PRATT: Well, Your Honor, we really need her statement or her testimony. I think we can get her here tomorrow on the company plane.

I've got one problem, though. Given that Dolly is an employee of the defendant, I'm not sure that she'll come in at our behest, and I'm not even sure I can ethically speak with her to make arrangements. And a subpoena won't run that far. Therefore, will you ask Ms. Oppenheimer to tell Dolly to cooperate with us?

THE COURT: That sounds reasonable enough, Ms. Oppenheimer. It doesn't strike me that you're prejudiced by having to do that. Any objection?

MS. OPPENHEIMER: No, Your Honor.

THE COURT: OK, so ordered. I'll assume there won't be any trouble with that. Now, Ms. Pratt, understand that this case should be ready for summations by tomorrow afternoon, and I'm not going to keep the jury another day just waiting for Dolly. So if you don't get her here by then, you're out of luck. If you get her here before all the other evidence is in, I'll let you put her on during your rebuttal, and then you can send Ms. Oppenheimer a bill for the commercial airfare. I assume you'll be grown-ups, and I won't have to arbitrate what fare Ms. Oppenheimer would have had to pay if you had given adequate notice.

And by the way, counselor, you could have saved yourself a lot of gasoline and a lot of mileage on the company plane if you had given a few days' more notice.

MS. PRATT: Understood, Your Honor.

Note that if the declarant has become absolutely unavailable, or for some other reason the opponent is confident that the proponent would be unable or unwilling to pay the extra costs of production, a procedure like this would amount to exclusion of the hearsay: Knowing that the declarant could not be produced, the opponent would have no disincentive to express willingness to pay what it would have cost to produce her if notice had been ample, and this costless bravado would result in excluding the hearsay. This may give the opponent a windfall, for he may not have been prepared to produce the declarant if notice had been ample and the court ruled in favor of admitting the hearsay.

Such a windfall would only arise, however, in a limited conjunction of circumstances. It must be that the proponent gave unexcused late notice; the court cannot say with sufficient confidence that the opponent would have been either unwilling or unable to produce the declarant if notice had been ample; in fact, the opponent would not have produced the declarant if notice had been ample; *and* the opponent has confidence that the declarant cannot feasibly be produced.

In all other circumstances, this procedure would—assuming that the court could administer it reasonably smoothly and accurately—avoid giving a windfall to the opponent, but without prejudicing him on account of the proponent's delay in giving notice. The administrative costs cannot be ignored; determinations of actual costs of production, hypothetical costs assuming timely notice, and good faith can be very tricky. The benefits of the procedure are substantial, however, and so often, probably most often, it will be worth the costs to adopt this procedure rather than simply exclude the evidence because of lateness of notice.

So far, this discussion has assumed that the court's optimal ruling, if notice had been adequate, would have been ADMIT. The essence of the analysis is that, in some circumstances, the delay in notice should cause the court to impose the physical burden of production, and any incremental costs, on the proponent.[90] The same approach might be applied if the optimal ruling, given adequate notice, would have been something other than ADMIT. For example, suppose that ruling would have been OPPONENT'S OPTION, meaning that the court would impose the physical burden of production on the proponent anyway. Given delayed notice, the court probably should make the same ruling, except that the proponent should also be responsible for any incremental costs caused by the delay. And if the best ruling given adequate notice would have been EXCLUDE, the proponent's delay in giving notice can only fortify the support for that ruling.

From this analysis, it should be apparent that the court has a better chance of reaching optimal results at low administrative cost if the proponent gives ample notice of his intention to offer a hearsay statement. If the court imposes on the proponent the risks and losses caused by his unexcused delay, that probably creates enough incentive for the proponent to give sufficient notice. Such an approach avoids overly penalizing the proponent. Trials are often complex and prepared under great time pressure. A flat requirement that the parties identify and give advance notice of all the individual hearsay statements that they intend to produce would entail administrative costs and probably put excessive demands on the organizational abilities and foresight of most lawyers. Also, failure to give notice would create a ground of objection in many cases where otherwise a successful objection would be unlikely.

Courts might, however, reasonably create some extra inducement to parties to give early notice. Many courts require parties in advance of trial to provide lists of witnesses that they intend to call.[91] It may be appropriate to advise them at the

90. The same principles, in reverse, might apply when the proponent has given advance notice but the *opponent* has been dilatory in objecting to the evidence. That is, if, given a timely objection, the court would have put the burden of producing the declarant on the proponent, the delay of the objection might induce the court to shift the physical burden and the incremental financial burden to the opponent.

91. Under proposed Federal Rule of Civil Procedure 26(a)(1)(A), each party would have to provide every other party, shortly after the commencement of the action, with "the name and, if known, the address and telephone number of each individual likely to have information that bears significantly on any claim or defense." *See* 112 S. Ct. at cxxvi-cxxvii. Under proposed Rule 26(a)(3), each party must, at least thirty days before trial unless otherwise directed, provide the other parties with the names of each witness "whom the party expects to present and those whom the party may call if the need arises," the names of witnesses whose testimony the party expects to present

same time to identify all the hearsay statements that they expect to offer. That is, the court may prescribe a time and method for the parties to give pretrial notice of intent to offer hearsay (without prejudice to earlier notice where the proponent thinks that might be helpful). Failure to list a given statement would not necessarily preclude admission of the statement at trial. The judge might make it clear, however, that if a statement were not listed, she would be reluctant to conclude that the proponent had a sufficient excuse for giving late notice. The proponent therefore would likely suffer adverse consequences, at least in allocation of the burden of producing the declarant, and perhaps in the ultimate evidentiary result as well.[92]

---

by deposition, and an identification of each exhibit that the party anticipates offering. *Id.* at cxxix.

92. Note that, unlike other arguments sometimes made for notice of intent to offer hearsay, *e.g.*, Park, *supra* note 28, at 119; Weinstein, *supra* note 5, at 340-41, the argument offered here is not based to a substantial degree on the desirability of preventing surprise; rather, it is based on the desirability of facilitating the opponent's effort to produce the declarant, if he should decide to do so. It is not usually a reason for excluding testimony of a witness that the opponent is surprised by the testimony; nor should it be, particularly when liberal discovery gives the opponent satisfactory means of minimizing the chance that he will be surprised by hearing testimony for the first time at trial. Opponents probably are no more likely, or perhaps even less likely, to be surprised by hearsay than by other forms of the witness's testimony; sometimes, in fact, the opponent might have been present when the hearsay declaration was made.

Furthermore, when the opponent is surprised, the prejudice is usually no greater with respect to hearsay than with respect to other testimony—except to the extent that the surprise hinders the opponent from producing the declarant. An opponent's cross-examination of a witness who testifies to the underlying events is likely to be impaired substantially if the opponent is surprised by the testimony, and later efforts might be transparent attempts to repair the damage. When the witness's testimony is of a hearsay statement, the opponent may face the same difficulty, to the extent he wishes to challenge the credibility of the witness on the stand. To the extent the opponent wishes to challenge the statement allegedly made by the declarant, though, there is a limited amount that the opponent can do with the witness on the stand, no matter how much advance notice he has; the challenge to the declarant's credibility must come later, so that even if the opponent is surprised, he has some time to put his response together without it being manifestly a reaction to surprising evidence. In order for surprise to prejudice the opponent significantly in challenging the declarant, there would have to be some effective response, perhaps a demonstration of some non-obvious bias on the part of the declarant, that the opponent would have been able to mount had he been given fuller notice, but is unable to mount before the end of the trial given the short notice. I do not believe this problem arises often (though, of course, it is impossible to be sure). It is probably better for the court to respond individually to cases where this danger appears to be significant than to create a broad and rigid notice requirement.

D
Privilege

[19]

Do Lawyers Improve the Adversary System? A General Theory of Litigation Advice and Its Regulation

Stephen McG. Bundy
Einer Richard Elhauge

Do Lawyers Improve the Adversary System? A General Theory of Litigation Advice and Its Regulation

Stephen McG. Bundy†
Einer Richard Elhauge‡

This Article presents a rational actor account of how litigation advice influences the information that reaches the tribunal in an adversary system. The authors conclude that although advice has some disturbing or ambiguous informational effects, on balance providing advice to one or both parties will generally improve the capacity of tribunals to determine who should be sanctioned and who should not. They also identify conditions under which advice is likely to be socially undesirable. The authors apply their account to analyze a range of policy issues, including whether to award fees to private attorneys general, whether to guarantee representation to criminal defendants under the sixth amendment, and whether the due process clause should require access to counsel for claimants in government benefits cases. They also analyze various doctrines of attorney-client confidentiality and rules restricting access to advice about responding to investigations or other questioning.

The lawyer's role in the adversary system frequently calls for conduct that appears to thwart truthful or just outcomes. Acting as an advisor, the lawyer certainly may, and arguably must, provide her clients with complete and accurate advice, even when she reasonably believes that doing so will cause them to withhold or suppress evidence.[1] In

† Acting Professor of Law, Boalt Hall School of Law, University of California, Berkeley. A.B. 1973, Harvard College; J.D. 1978, Boalt Hall School of Law, University of California, Berkeley.

‡ Acting Professor of Law, Boalt Hall School of Law, University of California, Berkeley. A.B. 1982, Harvard College; J.D. 1986, Harvard Law School.

We wish to express our gratitude for the generous support of the Boalt Hall Fund and for the helpful comments of McGeorge Bundy, Evan Caminker, James Crawford, William Fletcher, Kenneth Graham, Henry Hecht, Tom Jorde, Louis Kaplow, Lewis Kornhauser, John Leubsdorf, Paul Mishkin, Bob Mnookin, Rachel Moran, Andrea Peterson, Robert Post, Dan Rubinfeld, Steven Shavell, Jan Vetter, and participants in seminars at Boalt Hall School of Law, Harvard Law School, Stanford Law School, and the University of Virginia School of Law.

1. The initial discussion draft of the Model Rules would have forbidden lawyers from giving advice that "the lawyer can reasonably foresee will . . . be used by the client to further an illegal

litigation, the lawyer's obligations of zeal[2] and confidentiality[3] require or permit her to engage in a host of dubious activities: withholding evidence, even when the resulting record is radically incomplete;[4] presenting documents or testimony that she believes, based on information unavailable to the tribunal, to be false;[5] discrediting through cross-examination witnesses she knows to be truthful;[6] and arguing for inferences from the evidence that she knows are unwarranted.[7]

Questions about the social desirability and moral standing of this troubling role have long divided those who think and write about adjudication and lawyers. Defenders argue that lawyer-aided adversary factfinding is more likely than the alternatives to produce an accurate decision because it leads to a better evidentiary record. Delegation to the parties and their lawyers harnesses their competing interests (and the lawyers' skill) in the service of the tribunal's interest in receiving a complete account of the dispute.[8] Competition between lawyers is also said

course of conduct." MODEL RULES OF PROFESSIONAL CONDUCT Rule 2.3 (Discussion Draft, January 30, 1980). Later versions dropped this language in favor of a prohibition against offering knowing counsel or assistance in a crime or fraud in Model Rule 1.2. MODEL RULES OF PROFESSIONAL CONDUCT Rule 1.2 (1989) [hereinafter MODEL RULES]. The comment to Model Rule 1.2 states that a "lawyer is required to give an honest opinion about the actual consequences that appear likely to result from a client's conduct," and that "[t]he fact that a client uses advice in a course of action that is criminal or fraudulent does not, of itself, make a lawyer a party to the course of action." *Id.* Rule 1.2 comment. The strong, though not inevitable, inference is that a lawyer is not free to withhold advice simply on the ground that it may lead to wrongdoing.

2. *See* MODEL CODE OF PROFESSIONAL RESPONSIBILITY EC 7-1 (1980) [hereinafter MODEL CODE] ("The duty of a lawyer, both to his client and to the legal system, is to represent his client zealously within the bounds of the law, which includes Disciplinary Rules and enforceable professional regulations . . . ."); MODEL RULES, *supra* note 1, Rule 1.3 comment (a lawyer "may take whatever lawful and ethical means are required to vindicate a client's cause or endeavor" and "should act with commitment and dedication to the interests of the client and with zeal in advocacy upon the client's behalf").

3. MODEL CODE, *supra* note 2, DR 4-101; MODEL RULES, *supra* note 1, Rule 1.6.

4. *See* C. WOLFRAM, MODERN LEGAL ETHICS 639-40, 640 n.31 (1986) (citing cases).

5. *See* MODEL CODE, *supra* note 2, DR 7-102(A)(4) (attorney only barred from presenting evidence known to be false); C. WOLFRAM, *supra* note 4, at 656. The Model Rules contain a provision that allows, but does not require, a lawyer to refuse to present evidence that would be persuasive to the tribunal but that she reasonably believes is false. MODEL RULES, *supra* note 1, Rule 3.3(c). The Model Code has no comparable provision. Moreover, a criminal defense lawyer may fail to provide the effective representation constitutionally required if she refuses to present exculpatory evidence that she believes but does not "know" beyond a reasonable doubt to be false. *Cf.* Johns v. Smyth, 176 F. Supp. 949, 953 (E.D. Va. 1959) (holding that a prisoner's due process rights were violated when his attorney refused to argue for acquittal based on a client statement he believed to be false). Furthermore, where the evidence consists of the client's testimony, a rule giving criminal defense counsel discretion not to present evidence might well violate the client's fifth amendment right to testify. To our knowledge, no court has yet adjudicated the constitutionality of Model Rule 3.3 in criminal cases.

6. *See* United States v. Wade, 388 U.S. 218, 257-58 (1967) (White, J., concurring in part and dissenting in part); *see also* C. WOLFRAM, *supra* note 4, at 650-51 (quoting *Wade*).

7. *See generally* Subin, *The Criminal Defense Lawyer's "Different Mission": Reflections on the "Right" to Present a False Case,* 1 GEO. J. LEGAL ETHICS 125 (1987).

8. *See* G. HAZARD, JR., ETHICS IN THE PRACTICE OF LAW 121 (1978); Luban, *The*

to improve the quality of information presented. Because each lawyer will vigorously attack unreliable information that the opposing counsel presents, such information will either be withheld or promptly discredited. In this account, confidentiality is the handmaiden of effective fact-development: if the law instead compelled lawyers to disclose the results of their investigations, it would weaken the incentive to investigate.[9]

Critics of adversary advocacy contend that lawyers make no contribution to truth.[10] They point to the lack of hard evidence that competition between legally advised partisans improves outcomes.[11] They also sharply question the underlying logic of the defenders' position. Given the lawyer's freedom or obligation to make partial and even affirmatively misleading evidentiary presentations, critics argue, why should we believe competition has an inherent tendency to enlighten the tribunal? Competitive presentations "may simply pile up . . . confusion."[12] And when one party has superior access to advice, delegation to private initiative seems more likely to skew the quest for truth than to further it.[13]

The emerging literature that applies the methods of economics to the study of adversary adjudication echoes the traditional debate. Some economic accounts assume that improved legal efforts enhance a party's chances of victory and increase the amount of information reaching tribunals.[14] Lawyers enable parties to, among other things, investigate, organize, and present information in digestible form, and expose inaccuracies in the opponent's information.[15] The lawyer's zeal ensures that motivation is high, and competition from the opposing counsel checks potential excesses and ensures that each party's increased effort enhances

---

Adversary System Excuse, in THE GOOD LAWYER 83, 94 (D. Luban ed. 1984); Saltzburg, *Lawyers, Clients, and the Adversary System*, 37 MERCER L. REV. 647, 656 (1986); *cf.* Fuller, *The Adversary System*, in TALKS ON AMERICAN LAW 30, 31 (H. Berman ed. 1961) (discussing the importance of "partisan zeal" in achieving a fair outcome).

9. *See, e.g.*, M. FREEDMAN, LAWYERS' ETHICS IN AN ADVERSARY SYSTEM 27, 30 (1975).

10. *See* J. FRANK, COURTS ON TRIAL (1947) (adversary system retards discovery of truth); M. FRANKEL, PARTISAN JUSTICE (1980) (same); Pound, *The Causes of Popular Dissatisfaction With the Administration of Justice*, 29 ABA REPORTS 395, 404-06 (1906) (decrying "the sporting theory of justice").

11. *See* Hazard, *Rules of Ethics: The Drafting Task*, 36 REC. A.B. CITY N.Y. 77, 93 (1981); *see also* D. LUBAN, LAWYERS AND JUSTICE: AN ETHICAL STUDY 74 n.14 (1988) (citing Hazard); Rhode, *Ethical Perspectives on Legal Practice*, 37 STAN. L. REV. 589, 596 (1985) (same).

12. *See* Luban, *supra* note 8, at 94; *accord* M. FRANKEL, *supra* note 10, at 16; Simon, *Ethical Discretion in Lawyering*, 101 HARV. L. REV. 1083, 1140 (1988).

13. A classic statement of this view is contained in J. FRANK, *supra* note 10, at 93-99; *see also* M. FRANKEL, *supra* note 10, at 19 (noting economic constraints on parties' ability to litigate); Simon, *The Ideology of Advocacy: Procedural Justice and Professional Ethics*, 1978 WIS. L. REV. 29, 49-50 (discussing differential access to legal services).

14. *See generally* Cooter & Rubinfeld, *Economic Analysis of Legal Disputes and Their Resolution*, 27 J. ECON. LITERATURE 1067, 1071-75, 1087 (1989) (reviewing literature).

15. R. POSNER, ECONOMIC ANALYSIS OF LAW § 19.1, at 492 (3d ed. 1986).

rather than impairs the accuracy of adjudication.[16]

Other economic accounts of legal advice tend to support the critical perspective. One leading recent account analyzes advice on the assumption that each party has exclusive access to its own information and that the sole function of lawyers is to assist parties in selecting which information to present.[17] Based on those assumptions, the account reasons that legal advice has no tendency to increase the amount of information reaching the tribunal, and that its only effect is to skew the mix of information presented in favor of the party receiving advice.[18] Not surprisingly, the account concludes that litigation advice has an ambiguous effect both on the accuracy of adjudication[19] and on the behavior of persons who decide how to act based on adjudicated outcomes,[20] and therefore has "questionable social value."[21]

We share with prior scholars the belief that rational actor analysis can help illuminate the lawyer's role in an adversary system. But we believe that prior rational actor accounts have been partial and simplistic. Our aim is to provide a comprehensive and accurate examination, within a rational actor framework, of the considerations that determine the informational effects and social value of litigation advice. Our account suggests that defenders of litigation advice give insufficient attention to its undeniable dubious or adverse consequences. Specifically, providing advice to a previously unrepresented party may increase his capacity to withhold and suppress information, to inflict costs on his opponent, and to present false or prejudicial information. Moreover, competitive presentation does not invariably prevent or correct inaccuracy, especially where one party has more access to legal advice or can control or suppress more information. Defenders ignore or minimize these effects by stressing cases in which both parties have similar access to advice and to information.

Critics are, however, too quick to dismiss several general effects of advice that increase the amount of information reaching the tribunal. Advice enhances competition in the presentation of information available to both parties, and it enables parties to sort relevant from irrelevant information. By improving investigation, it increases the amount of information identified and presented. And it introduces into the process a second actor, the lawyer, whose personal susceptibility to sanctions for misconduct in withholding or suppressing information will sometimes

16. *See id.*

17. *See* Kaplow & Shavell, *Legal Advice About Information to Present in Litigation: Its Effects and Social Desirability*, 102 HARV. L. REV. 565, 568, 571-75 (1989).

18. *Id.* at 568, 577, 581, 595.

19. *Id.* at 569, 581, 603.

20. *Id.* at 568, 586, 596, 614.

21. *Id.* at 597, 614.

cause the tribunal to receive information that an unadvised party would have withheld or suppressed. Critics avoid these positive aspects of advice by stressing cases in which there is little commonly available information, access to advice or to information is unbalanced, or lawyers are insensitive to sanctions.

We develop our account of legal advice in several stages. Part I presents our basic account of how parties in an adversary system influence the information reaching tribunals. Part II then applies this account to reach initial conclusions about the general informational effects of legal advice. We conclude that, while advice has many disturbing or ambiguous informational effects, on balance providing litigation advice to one or both parties will generally increase the information reaching tribunals and improve the capacity of tribunals to determine who deserves to be sanctioned and who does not.

Although our basic account is more complex and comprehensive than those offered in the prior literature, it nonetheless abstracts from several important complications. We reintroduce those complications in Part III, and use them to test our initial conclusions and to identify conditions where those conclusions will not hold and where litigation advice may thus have ambiguous or harmful informational effects. Part IV then normatively evaluates the informational effects of legal advice under various conditions. We there conclude that, under the conditions most likely to describe its general effects, litigation advice is socially desirable under a variety of instrumental and noninstrumental standards.

Ultimately, conclusions about the desirability of advice turn on empirical questions. We do not purport to answer all those questions, though we offer plausible intuitions about many. We do, however, claim to have isolated the right set of empirical questions. If we are correct in that claim, our account does more than focus the general academic debate about the desirability of litigation advice on the right set of issues. It also identifies the conditions likely to make particular forms of advice sufficiently harmful to merit legal restriction or sufficiently desirable to merit legal encouragement. Our analysis is thus relevant to a variety of real-world legal issues, some of which are discussed in Part V.

Section V(A) presents our analysis of measures generally intended to encourage or discourage access to advice. These include rules wholly barring the use of lawyers, such as those that sometimes apply in small claims or alternative dispute resolution procedures. They also include measures that encourage or discourage retention of a lawyer, such as rules allowing fee awards to lawyers for parties who act as private attorneys general, subsidizing representation for criminal defendants under the sixth amendment, or restricting the sum a private citizen can pay for advice. Our analysis also has implications for narrower, special purpose rules that seek to increase the information reaching tribunals. Section V(B) illustrates the implications of our analysis for proposals to reform attorney-client confidentiality, and Section V(C) applies our analysis to rules that restrict access to legal advice about responding to investigation or other questioning.

II
The Basic Account of the Informational Effects of Litigation Advice

In this Part, we derive the informational effects of the legal advice that is *actually provided* in an adversary system in which clients and lawyers both face evidentiary sanctions and in which lawyer-client confidentiality is imperfect. We postpone to Part V consideration of how evidentiary sanctions applicable to parties and their lawyers can sometimes prevent *more* legal advice from being given. Thus we do not here measure the informational effects of restrictions on advice, which would require comparing a legal regime with advice and the legal restrictions against a regime with advice but without the restrictions. Rather, this Part measures the effects of legal advice against a baseline of parties litigating with no advice.[60]

Even within our stylized basic account, the informational effects of the legal advice provided to parties in an adversary system are diverse and complicated. To clarify our exposition, we discuss separately the effects of advice on different types of evidentiary conduct. In Section A, we trace the informational effects of advice about how to categorize (as irrelevant, favorable, or unfavorable) the information the parties have identified. We subsequently consider the effects of legal advice on investigation in Section B and the effects of legal advice on the perceived and actual sanctions for withholding or suppressing unfavorable information in Section C. In each instance, we present the effects of unilateral litigation advice first and the effects of bilateral advice second.

Several informational effects of litigation advice are unambiguously positive. First, legal advice helps parties sort the relevant information from the irrelevant. Second, whenever the same information is available to both parties (so that both can compete in presenting it to the tribunal), legal advice to either party about how to categorize information as favorable or unfavorable will normally increase the amount of favorable information that the advised party presents more than it decreases the amount of unfavorable information she presents. Third, legal advice increases investigation, and thus the presentation of information that would not have been identified without legal advice. Finally, for any legal advice provided, lawyers' personal susceptibility to evidentiary sanctions will sometimes decrease withholding and suppression of unfavorable information.

Other informational effects of advice, such as those flowing from improved categorization of party-controlled and suppressible information, are disturbingly ambiguous: they skew the mix of information in favor of the party receiving advice, but they neither increase nor decrease the total relevant information reaching the tribunal. But because the unambiguously positive effects of advice are not offset by any clearly neg-

60. The distinction is important because, as Section V(B) demonstrates, a conclusion that litigation advice is desirable, ambiguous, or undesirable does not alone dictate any conclusion about whether confidentiality intended to encourage such advice is desirable or undesirable.

ative effects, we conclude that in our stylized account litigation advice has the following general effects. It decreases the proportion (and perhaps total amount) of irrelevant information presented under both the unilateral and bilateral accounts. Unilateral litigation advice increases the presentation of information favorable to the party receiving advice more than it decreases the presentation of unfavorable information, and thus increases the total relevant information presented. Bilateral advice increases the favorable and unfavorable information presented about both sides.

A. Legal Advice That Helps Parties Categorize Information

In this Section, we assume that each party has a pool of potentially relevant information that she has identified,[61] which is either nonsuppressible or suppressible.[62] Unadvised parties may mistakenly categorize such information in four ways: (1) irrelevant as relevant; (2) relevant as irrelevant; (3) favorable as unfavorable; and (4) unfavorable as favorable. Legal advice correcting these errors helps a party decide which information to present, withhold, suppress, or save from suppression.

1. Effects of Unilateral Advice

a. Nonsuppressible Irrelevant Information

We consider nonsuppressible information first. Some nonsuppressible information that a party has identified will be irrelevant. With legal advice, a party will be less likely to categorize such information mistakenly as relevant and favorable. Correcting these errors reduces the amount of irrelevant information presented.

b. Nonsuppressible Information Unadvised Parties Would Miscategorize as Irrelevant

The remaining nonsuppressible information will either be favorable or unfavorable. When legal advice corrects a party's mistaken belief that this nonsuppressible information is irrelevant, it increases that party's presentation of relevant information. Because lawyers are more likely to present favorable information than unfavorable, the additional favorable information presented out of the set that otherwise would have been mis-

61. This analysis applies only to information that a party has identified and can present. Although normally a party should be able to present or compel the presentation of any potentially relevant information she identifies, there can be information that a party can and does identify but cannot present, such as demeanor information about a witness who is beyond the subpoena power of the court. For purposes of analyzing advice about which information to present, such information is analytically the same as information the party has not identified at all.

62. We discuss in Sections II(B) and II(C) the changes in the information identified by the party or her opponent because of the effects of advice on investigation and on sanctions for withholding and suppression.

categorized as irrelevant (and consigned to oblivion) should outweigh the additional unfavorable information mistakenly presented out of that set.

c. Correcting Mistakes About Which Side Nonsuppressible Information Favors

Unilateral legal advice also reduces party errors about which side is favored by nonsuppressible information that an unadvised party would correctly categorize as relevant. These corrections increase the presentation of favorable information and decrease the presentation of unfavorable information. The relative magnitudes of these effects depend on whether the information has been identified by the advised party alone or by both parties.

i. Separately Identified Nonsuppressible Information

Information identified by the advised party alone includes information in the party's controlled set, such as a party's recollections concerning her own mental state, as well as information in the discoverable and commonly available sets that the opponent has not requested. We will call such information "separately identified." Because the opponent cannot present separately identified information, whether it reaches the tribunal will depend solely on the party's decision whether to present it.[63] Legal advice decreases the probability that a party will either withhold favorable information or present unfavorable information. The increase in favorable information presented will be the product of the change in the probability of mistaken withholding of favorable information and the amount of favorable information being considered for presentation.[64] The decrease in unfavorable information presented will be the product of the change in the probability of mistaken presentation of unfavorable information and the amount of unfavorable information being considered for presentation.

Given our simplifying assumptions, any decrease in the probability of mistaken withholding will equal the decrease in the probability of mistaken presentation. We will see, after analyzing investigation, that there is reason to believe that the mix of separately identified information being considered for presentation tends to be more favorable than unfavorable.[65] This will further bolster our conclusion that legal advice about information categorization increases the favorable information reaching

63. In effect, advice about whether to present this class of information is the only class of advice that Kaplow and Shavell model. *See* Kaplow & Shavell, *supra* note 17, at 568-75.

64. We define the change in the probability of mistaken withholding or presentation as the difference between the probability a piece of identified information will mistakenly be withheld (or presented) without legal advice, and the probability it will mistakenly be withheld (or presented) with advice.

65. *See infra* Section II(B)(2)(b).

the tribunal more than it decreases unfavorable information. At this juncture, however, we assume only that the mix of separately identified information is equally favorable and unfavorable.[66] On this working assumption we conclude that the increase in favorable separately identified information presented because of legal advice about which side the information favors should equal the decrease in unfavorable separately identified information presented. The result is no net gain or loss of relevant information reaching the tribunal, but a mix of information skewed in favor of the advised party.

ii. Commonly Identified Nonsuppressible Information

We will call information "commonly identified" if both parties have identified and correctly categorized the information as relevant. Advice about whether commonly identified nonsuppressible information is favorable or unfavorable will increase the information reaching the tribunal. This effect is easiest to recognize in the limiting case where the opponent has perfect legal knowledge and therefore presents all commonly identified information unfavorable to the party receiving advice. Against such an opponent, providing a party with advice cannot decrease the unfavorable commonly identified information presented since the opponent presents it in any case; advice will instead tend only to increase the favorable information presented.

The effect is, however, more general: whenever the party's opponent is more than minimally competent,[67] unilateral advice will tend to increase the commonly identified information presented. A minimally competent opponent is more likely to present unfavorable information (from the advised party's perspective) than favorable information.[68] Accordingly, the commonly identified information that the opponent will not present (and whose presentation can thus be affected by the quality of the decisions made by the advised party) will tend to contain more favorable than unfavorable information.[69] In selecting from commonly

66. This assumption is reasonable given our initial assumption that each side controls or can suppress an equal amount of relevant information, and that each set of information available to either party contains equal amounts of favorable and unfavorable information. *See supra* Section I(E).

67. A minimally competent opponent is one who has knowledge sufficient to make his ability to distinguish favorable from unfavorable information better than random. We expect that almost all opponents will be minimally competent by this standard, whether or not they have retained a lawyer. Even if there are isolated exceptions, we are describing the general effects of advice, and therefore find it sufficient for that purpose to assume that in general opponents will tend to be better than random selectors.

68. Throughout this Section, we use "favorable" to refer to information that benefits the advised party, even if it actually is presented by her opponent (to whom it is unfavorable).

69. To express this mathematically, suppose that the set of commonly identified information contains F items of information favorable to the party and U of unfavorable. The opponent has a probability P of selecting information unfavorable to the party receiving advice, and a probability

identified information, the party thus must make more decisions about whether to present favorable information that otherwise would not reach the tribunal than about whether to present unfavorable information that otherwise would not reach the tribunal. Legal advice that increases the probability of correct decisions about whether to present information should therefore increase the favorable information reaching the tribunal more than it decreases the unfavorable information reaching the tribunal.[70] And as the extreme case illustrates, the more competent the oppo-

1-*P* of selecting information favorable to the party receiving advice. Thus after the opponent has selected, the amount of information remaining for the party to select is (*P*)*F* and (1-*P*)(*U*). Where *F* and *U* are equal, the amount of favorable information remaining after the opponent has selected will exceed the amount of unfavorable information remaining whenever $P > 1\text{-}P$, that is, whenever *P* is greater than .5, the condition of minimal competence.

70. We are grateful to Louis Kaplow for pointing out that this effect may be offset because an unadvised party facing a more competent opponent might deduce that her best strategy is simply to present all commonly identified information unpresented by the opponent, figuring that the inferences she can draw from her opponent's nonpresentation are better than the inferences she can draw from her independent categorization. Suppose, for example, the opponent is 80% competent in categorizing information, and the unadvised party is 60% competent. Assume also that the mix of commonly identified information unpresented by the opponent contains 100 items. Given the opponent's competence, 80 of these items should be favorable to the unadvised party, and 20 should be unfavorable. The unadvised party could thus present a mix of information that is 80% favorable by blindly presenting all 100 items. This 80% success with blind presentation might sometimes be more advantageous than a selective presentation in which she applies her own 60% competence. Where this logic would lead an unadvised party to present blindly, advice will tend to make the party's presentation more selective, thus decreasing the party's presentation of commonly identified information.

However, although a strategy of unadvised blind presentation is sometimes theoretically advantageous, often it is not. Any party who is more than minimally competent can, through selective presentation, almost always make the *mix* of commonly identified information she presents more favorable than it would be if she followed a strategy of blind presentation. (The one exception is that selective presentation cannot improve the mix when the opponent has presented 100% of the favorable information.) To continue the last example, if the unadvised party applies her 60% competence to selecting among the information unpresented by her opponent, she will present 60% of the favorable items (or 48 favorable items) and only 40% of unfavorable items (or 8 items). Selective presentation will thus make the mix of information she presents 85.7% (48/56) favorable, an improvement from blind presentation. Depending on the sanctioning function and the mix of information presented by her opponent, an 85.7% favorable mix of 56 selected items can be more advantageous than an 80% favorable mix of 100 blindly presented items. Where it is advantageous, the unadvised party will be selective and present only 56 items of information. If her attorney is 80% competent, with advice she will instead present 64 favorable items and only 4 unfavorable items. Advice will then increase the items she presents from 56 to 68.

Moreover, even when theoretically advantageous, the practical extent of the incentive for unadvised blind presentation seems small because of various obstacles. First, the unadvised party cannot use the strategy unless she has the second move, so that she can observe the opponent's selection first. Second, the strategy is so complex that it is doubtful it would occur often to an unadvised party. Third, the strategy has no potential application unless the unadvised party believes her opponent is more competent. Finally, and perhaps most important, the unadvised party may not know (and may have little way of knowing) whether the information unpresented by her opponent has been commonly identified as relevant. Without such knowledge, the unadvised party has little reason to infer from the opponent's nonpresentation that information is favorable. The opponent's nonpresentation may instead mean that the opponent categorized the information as irrelevant or never identified it all.

nent the more the increase in favorable information presented because of advice will exceed the decrease in unfavorable information presented.

d. Suppressible Information

Some portion of the information that a party identifies will be suppressible. Advice enabling parties to categorize suppressible information as irrelevant, favorable, or unfavorable has at least one positive effect. When a party mistakenly categorizes irrelevant suppressible information as relevant, advice causes the party to reclassify as irrelevant some information that she would mistakenly have categorized as favorable and saved from suppression or presented. This reduces the amount of irrelevant information reaching the tribunal.

Other effects are more ambiguous. When a party mistakenly categorizes relevant suppressible information as irrelevant, legal advice sometimes results in its recategorization as relevant and either favorable or unfavorable. A party with advice is more likely to prevent opponent suppression and to avoid her own mistaken suppression of favorable information. This increases the total amount of favorable information reaching the tribunal. The advised party is also more likely to suppress from her opponent and to avoid her own mistaken presentation of unfavorable information. This reduces the amount of unfavorable information reaching the tribunal. Assuming as we do that mistakes in categorizing favorable and unfavorable information occur with equal frequency, and that the amounts of favorable and unfavorable suppressible information are equal, such advice should have no impact on the total amount of relevant information reaching the tribunal. For similar reasons, advice correcting party errors about which side is favored by relevant suppressible information increases the favorable information reaching the tribunal and decreases the unfavorable, with no net impact on the total amount of information presented. In both cases, though, the mix of information is skewed in favor of the advised party.

e. Summary

Unilateral litigation advice about how to categorize information has several positive effects. For both nonsuppressible and suppressible information, such advice decreases the amount of irrelevant information presented. For nonsuppressible information, advice that corrects mistaken beliefs that information is irrelevant increases the presentation of both favorable and (less strongly) unfavorable information. For nonsuppressible commonly identified information, advice that corrects party errors about which side is favored by the information tends to increase the presentation of favorable information more than it decreases the presentation of unfavorable information, with a net increase in total relevant information presented. Advice about categorization also has some ambiguous effects. For relevant suppressible information and (under our working assumption) for nonsuppressible separately identified information, advice causes an increase in the amount of favorable information reaching the tribunal and an equivalent decrease in unfavorable information. The overall effect of advice about categorization is therefore a decrease in the presentation of irrelevant information and an increase in favorable information greater than the decrease in unfavorable information. This increases the total relevant information reaching the tribunal.

2. *Effects of Bilateral Advice*

In a bilateral account, some effects of advice remain ambiguous. For relevant suppressible information and nonsuppressible separately identified information, advice causes each party to present more favorable and less unfavorable information, with no net effect on the total amount of favorable information or unfavorable information reaching the tribunal about either side. Other effects remain just as positive as in the unilateral account. Providing advice to both parties decreases the amount of irrelevant information each side presents, and advice correcting mistaken judgments that relevant nonsuppressible information is irrelevant increases the amount of favorable and unfavorable information each side presents. Finally, bilateral advice actually enhances the positive effect of advice on the presentation of commonly identified nonsuppressible information. As in the unilateral account, legal advice improves each party's ability to present favorable information from this set more than it improves her ability to reduce the presentation of unfavorable information. The tendency for the increase in favorable information presented to exceed the decrease in unfavorable will, however, be greater than in the unilateral account because bilateral advice will improve the opponent's competence.[71]

In sum, when both parties receive advice about categorizing information, each party presents less irrelevant and more relevant information, because advice increases her presentation of favorable information more than it decreases her presentation of unfavorable information. Because information favorable to one party is unfavorable to the other, the result of bilateral advice is an increase in the presentation of favorable *and* unfavorable information about each party.

71. *See supra* notes 67-70 and accompanying text (discussing the relation between unilateral effects and opponent competence). There may be an offsetting effect to the extent evidence comes in aggregate lumps of favorable and unfavorable information rather than the discrete units we assume. *See supra* note 32. Increased opponent competence may decrease a party's incentive to present such "lumpy" evidence, because it increases the likelihood that the opponent will recognize and present (through advocacy) the unfavorable informational aspects of the evidence.

B. Legal Advice That Alters Investigation

1. Effects of Unilateral Advice on Investigation

Legal advice helps parties conduct more and better investigations in a variety of ways. First, advice helps parties design or conceive of a wider range of feasible investigations. Lawyers better understand the full range of potentially helpful information, the possible modes of inquiry, and the art of framing investigations to maximize the expected value of the response. Lawyers also better understand the significance for the design of investigations of whatever information is already at hand. An advised party should thus identify more useful persons to interview or depose, more documents to demand, and more questions to pose in formal or informal pretrial investigation or at trial.[72] In consequence, an advised party can effectively choose from more investigative options—having both positive and negative expected value—than an unadvised party. A skilled cross-examiner, for example, effectively expands a party's investigative options by conceiving of a broad range of follow-up questions. To the extent that the additional feasible investigations identified through legal advice appear to have positive expected values, an advised party will conduct some investigations she would not otherwise have conducted.

Second, legal advice should also increase the amount of investigation performed by helping parties make more effective use of the fruits of investigation. When an investigation is completed, an advised party will make better decisions about how to categorize the information obtained, whether to present, withhold or suppress it, and how to use that information to pursue further investigation. For example, a party delegating the conduct of a file search to her lawyer can expect to identify more relevant documents and to categorize them more accurately. In consequence, a party who expects to have advice about using the proceeds of investigation will anticipate more benefits and fewer adverse consequences from each feasible investigation of which she is aware. The prospect of advice therefore strengthens the incentive to investigate.[73] Some investigations that would have had positive expected values will look even better, and others that would have had negative expected values will now appear positive. A party with advice about using the fruits of investigation

72. To the extent that sanctions for failure to produce information in response to a formal or informal demand are sufficiently high to induce production, such demands permit investigation in the discoverable set. We defer until Section II(C) discussion of how advice influences the level of expected sanctions for failing to respond to those demands for production that are made.

73. The incentive effect will be strongest when confidentiality is absolute or when the party can obtain advice without sharing information with her lawyer, because in those cases the decision to obtain legal advice, standing alone, cannot increase the risk that unfavorable information will reach the tribunal.

should thus conduct more investigations than one who does not expect to have such advice.

Finally, legal advice improves a party's accuracy in calculating the expected value of a feasible investigation and thus improves her selection of investigations. Advice reduces the probability that a party will mistakenly forego investigations that have positive expected value or mistakenly conduct investigations that have negative expected value.[74] For example, a cross-examining lawyer improves the selection of investigations by abandoning a line of inquiry that would require her to divulge unfavorable information. This final effect alters the mix of investigations conducted, but, unlike the first two effects, may increase or decrease the total number of investigations conducted.

The effects of advice on investigation uniformly tend to increase the number and proportion of investigations conducted that have positive expected value: a party will conceive of a greater number of feasible investigations, more investigations in that expanded universe will have positive value, and the party is more likely correctly to choose to conduct those positive value investigations. Whether advice will increase the number of investigations conducted that have negative expected value is ambiguous. Legal advice about investigation selection eliminates some investigations with negative expected value that an unadvised party would mistakenly have conducted. But advice also causes a party to conceive of additional feasible investigations with negative expected value that an unadvised party would not have considered. Legal advice, not being perfect, will not wholly eliminate error in deciding whether to conduct those additional negative expected value investigations, and therefore some will be conducted in error. Thus, while legal advice will tend to reduce the proportion of negative expected value investigations conducted, it may increase or decrease the total number conducted.

In general, advice that influences investigation should provide a party with a larger pool of information to present. The additional positive expected value investigations conducted because of legal advice should lead to the identification of more favorable information, more unfavorable information that the other party has also obtained, and more irrelevant information that provides helpful investigative leads. The effects of advice on the identification of useless irrelevant information and on the amount of additional unfavorable information made available to the opponent because of investigation are less straightforward. As argued above, some of the additional investigations conducted on account of legal advice will actually have negative expected value and are therefore likely to produce such untoward consequences. Moreover,

74. *See supra* notes 41-48 and accompanying text (distinguishing negative and positive value searches).

some additional investigations with positive expected values will involve an unavoidable risk of adverse consequences.[75] For example, it may be worth conducting discovery to identify critical documents even though it is likely that the discovery will alert the opponent to unfavorable information that he would not otherwise obtain. On the other hand, advice that improves a party's selection of investigations tends to reduce the occasions on which a party identifies irrelevant information or causes additional unfavorable information to reach the tribunal. The general tendency of advice, then, is to increase the amount of favorable information identified without any predictable increase or decrease in the identification, gathering, or divulging of unfavorable information that the opponent would not otherwise obtain.[76]

2. *The Combined Effects of Unilateral Advice on Categorization and Investigation*

We are now in a position to describe the composite effects of unilateral advice on the investigation and categorization of information, on the temporary assumption that legal advice does not influence the perceived level of evidentiary sanctions for either side.[77]

a. *Information Whose Identification Is Influenced by Advice*

Information whose identification is influenced by advice will either be suppressible or nonsuppressible. For nonsuppressible information, advice influencing investigation should strongly increase the presentation of favorable information. Advice influencing investigation causes a party to identify additional favorable information, and advice about categorization increases the probability that the party will correctly present that

75. *See supra* notes 46-48 and accompanying text.

76. These effects of advice may be diminished, but not eliminated, by a feedback effect. Distinct investigations with different positive or negative expected values can sometimes produce some of the same favorable or unfavorable information. Accordingly, the expected value of one investigation may depend on whether another investigation that duplicates some of its positive or negative consequences is conducted or eliminated as a consequence of advice. An investigation whose positive consequences are duplicated by a new investigation is less likely to be conducted; an investigation whose negative consequences are duplicated by a new investigation is more likely to be conducted. Because the additional investigations caused by advice have more positive than negative consequences, the feedback effect of those investigations will be a reduction of investigative activity. Similarly, an investigation whose positive consequences duplicate a search eliminated because of advice is more likely to be conducted, while an investigation whose negative consequences duplicate those of an eliminated investigation is less likely to be conducted. Since the investigations eliminated by advice are likely to have more negative than positive consequences, the feedback effect of investigations eliminated by legal advice will also tend to reduce the level of investigation. Because these feedback effects are derived from the principal effects of advice, however, they should only offset rather than eliminate those effects.

77. We relax this temporary assumption in Section II(C).

additional information.[78]

The effect of advice on the presentation of unfavorable nonsuppressible information, in contrast, depends on the net result of conflicting influences. If the negative consequences of additional investigations conducted with legal advice outweigh the negative consequences of the investigations eliminated by improved selection of investigations, then the party may divulge, identify, or gather more unfavorable information that the opponent would not otherwise obtain. This should increase the amount of unfavorable information reaching the tribunal.[79] If the decrease in negative consequences from improved selection of investigations outweighs the increase in negative consequences due to increased investigations, the nonsuppressible unfavorable information reaching the tribunal will decrease. Any increase or decrease in unfavorable information reaching the tribunal will, however, tend to be smaller than the increase in presentation of favorable information. This is because advice tends uniformly to increase the presentation of favorable information but has offsetting effects on the presentation of unfavorable information. For similar reasons, advice should reduce the proportion of irrelevant information presented, though it may not decrease the amount of irrelevant information presented.[80] Advice thus increases the amount and proportion of relevant nonsuppressible information reaching the tribunal.

For suppressible information, the composite effect of advice about investigation and categorization is ambiguous: an increase in favorable

78. To the extent attorneys streamline the presentation of cases involving an abundance of relevant information by selecting the most forceful evidence to present, legal advice might not, strictly speaking, increase the quantity of favorable information presented. Even if streamlining does decrease the *quantity* of information, however, the replacement of marginally relevant information with information of stronger relevance should still improve the *quality* of information presented with effects on adjudication similar to those of an increase in quantity. Thus, our use of the terms "increase in information" or "more information" should be understood to encompass increases in the quality as well as quantity of information presented.

79. Negative consequences of investigation can lead to an increase in presentation of unfavorable information in several ways. First, during investigation the party may divulge unfavorable information that the opponent would not otherwise have obtained. Second, the party may identify or gather additional unfavorable information that the opponent would not obtain. The party may then divulge that information during further investigation, produce it in response to a discovery demand, or mistakenly present it to the tribunal. Third, the party may identify or gather unfavorable information that the opponent has obtained but will mistakenly fail to present. If the party then mistakenly presents it, the unfavorable information reaching the tribunal will increase.

80. The additional investigations conducted with legal advice will tend to increase identification of irrelevant information, while advice about selection of investigations will tend to reduce it. The result may be an increase or decrease in the amount of irrelevant information identified. If additional irrelevant information is identified, some of it will, even with legal advice, be mistakenly presented. The overall proportion of irrelevant information presented will certainly decrease, but the absolute amount of irrelevant information presented as a consequence of advice about investigation may increase. On the other hand, if advice reduces the amount of irrelevant information identified as a consequence of investigation, then both the proportion and the amount of irrelevant information presented will decrease.

information reaching the tribunal and an equivalent decrease in unfavorable information. Party incentives to identify favorable information in order to prevent its suppression are comparable to party incentives to identify unfavorable information in order to suppress it. Legal advice about investigation should therefore effect a comparable increase in the party's identification of both classes of information. An advised party will thus: (1) rescue from suppression and present more favorable suppressible information, and (2) suppress more unfavorable suppressible information. Because we assume equal distributions of miscategorizations and of favorable and unfavorable suppressible information, the increase in favorable suppressible information reaching the tribunal should equal the decrease in unfavorable information.

b. Information a Party Would Identify With or Without Advice

A party will identify some information whether or not she has received advice: presentation of this information will be unaffected by advice that influences investigation. For such information, the effects of advice are generally those described in Section II(A): a reduction in the amount and proportion of irrelevant information, and an increase in favorable information exceeding the decrease in unfavorable information. However, the analysis in this Section suggests that the tendency of the increase to exceed the decrease may even be stronger than described in Section II(A). That Section proceeded on the assumption that nothing could be said about the mix of separately identified information.[81] The set of information a party would have identified with or without advice, however, in part consists of information the party would have identified through investigation whether or not she had legal advice. Because these investigations will tend to have positive expected values, that information should consist predominantly of favorable information. In general, the information that would have been commonly identified with or without legal advice is just as likely to be favorable as unfavorable. Accordingly, the mix of information identified by only one party with or without legal advice should be more favorable than unfavorable, and advice about presentation should to that extent tend to increase the presentation of favorable information more than it reduces the presentation of unfavorable information.

c. Summary

Out of the set of information that would have been identified with or without legal advice, the increase in favorable information exceeds the decrease in unfavorable information. Out of the additional nonsup-

81. *See supra* note 66 and accompanying text.

pressible information identified because of legal advice, favorable information increases strongly and unfavorable information may weakly increase or decrease. Out of the additional suppressible information identified, the increase in favorable information equals the decrease in unfavorable information. The combined result is that unilateral advice about investigation and categorization increases the total favorable information reaching the tribunal more than it decreases the total unfavorable information.

3. Effects of Bilateral Advice

Providing legal advice to both parties enhances the positive effects of legal advice on investigation. Each party's own advice enables it to conduct more and better investigations. Thus, each should identify and present more relevant nonsuppressible information. Conversely, whether bilateral advice that influences investigation alters the amount of suppressible information presented is wholly uncertain. With advice, each party is better able to identify and prevent the suppression of information favorable to her position, and to identify and suppress unfavorable information. In the bilateral account, improved efforts to suppress are met by improved efforts to prevent suppression. We can discern no basis for predicting whether a battle between two advised parties leads to more or less suppression than a battle between unadvised parties. The net effect of bilateral legal advice on investigation and information selection is thus to increase the favorable and unfavorable information about each party reaching the tribunal. The proportion (and perhaps amount) of irrelevant information reaching the tribunal should also decrease.

C. The Effects of Legal Advice on Effective Evidentiary Sanctions

Successful withholding and suppression of unfavorable information reduces the information reaching the tribunal. Whether a party or her opponent will find it worthwhile to withhold or suppress information that she has categorized as unfavorable will depend on the perceived sanctions for doing so. Legal advice can affect those evidentiary sanctions in three main ways. First, advice can correct misperceptions of expected evidentiary sanctions. Second, legal advice can influence the actual level of those sanctions. Finally, because in giving advice the party's lawyer sometimes becomes personally susceptible to evidentiary sanctions, retaining a lawyer can increase the effective evidentiary sanctions the client faces.

1. Effects of Unilateral Advice on Parties' Evidentiary Sanctions

Legal advice correcting party misperceptions of expected sanctions for withholding or suppression can increase or decrease the amount of information reaching the tribunal. Unadvised parties may over- or underestimate the scope or level of expected evidentiary sanctions.[82] If a party underestimates evidentiary sanctions, advice will reduce the amount of information withheld or suppressed; if the party overestimates sanctions, advice increases withholding or suppression. Since we assume in our initial stylized account that parties are just as likely to make one kind of error as the other, advice that corrects misperceptions of sanctions has no general effect on the amount of unfavorable information reaching the tribunal.[83]

Legal advice can also influence the level of actual evidentiary sanctions by improving how a party handles information about instances of withholding and suppression that may or do become the subject of the "litigation within a litigation" described in Part I. In a unilateral account, we expect that advice influencing the level of evidentiary sanctions for the party or her opponent will systematically increase the presentation of information favorable to the advice recipient and decrease the presentation of unfavorable information.

Providing advice to a party should raise expected evidentiary sanctions for her opponent[84] because an advised party can identify and pres-

82. Of course, if expected sanctions were sufficiently high to induce the production of all information the opponent demanded, legal advice on these topics would always lead a party to produce any of that information. Obviously, evidentiary sanctions are not in fact that high; nor are they likely ever to be that high because, in a world where tribunals cannot obtain perfect information about evidentiary conduct, increasing sanctions for apparently undesirable withholding will have two adverse effects. First, it will increase expected sanctions for truthful nonproduction. *See* Shavell, *Optimal Sanctions and the Incentive to Provide Evidence to Legal Tribunals,* 9 INT'L REV. LAW & ECON. 3, 4-5 (1989). For example, increasing sanctions for witnesses who appear to be withholding information because they stare at the floor or stammer will result in higher evidentiary sanctions for truthful witnesses who exhibit those behaviors. Second, it will increase sanctions for desirable withholding and suppression that is mistaken for the undesirable variety. Withholding or suppression might be regarded as desirable despite its adverse informational effects because it protects privacy, prevents coercion, or promotes other desirable conduct in or out of court. The fourth and fifth amendments, and various evidentiary privileges, protect the right to withhold or suppress information in part for these very reasons. Thus, even if optimally chosen, evidentiary sanctions can do no more than trade off underdeterrence of undesirable withholding and suppression against overdeterrence of truthful nonproduction and desirable withholding and suppression. *Cf. id.* (modeling sanctions that would optimize underdeterrence of withholding and overdeterrence of truthful nonproduction).

83. Legal advice also affects party estimates of the benefits of withholding and suppression. We have already discussed the effects on presentation, withholding, or suppression of advice that corrects party perceptions about which side is favored by information. In theory, advice may also influence party perceptions of the benefits of withholding or suppression by correcting party misperceptions of the extent to which information is unfavorable. Without legal advice, a party may over- or underestimate how damaging unfavorable information will be: such advice accordingly could increase or decrease the unfavorable information reaching the tribunal. Because this additional marginal effect has no impact on our basic conclusions, we do not consider it further.

84. This increase in evidentiary sanctions may not be socially desirable, because sanctions will also increase for socially desirable withholding or suppression and for socially desirable conduct (such as telling the truth) that sometimes is not readily distinguishable from undesirable withholding

ent more secondary information indicating that her opponent is engaged in improper withholding or suppression. In part, this advice operates before the opponent makes a decision to withhold or suppress. An advised party can better frame demands for information that increase expected sanctions for failures to produce that information.[85] Questions framed with legal advice are, to illustrate, much more likely to expose an evasive witness.[86] In part, this advice operates after the opponent's claimed act of withholding or suppression has occurred. Should a dispute arise about whether withholding or suppression has taken place, for example, legal advice will enable a party to identify and present to the tribunal more secondary information indicating that the opponent engaged in improper withholding and less secondary information indicating that the opponent did not. Finally, some forms of advice operate before and after the act. The simplest example is perhaps the most telling: to the extent an advised party identifies more information about the disputed primary conduct, the odds of detecting an opponent's lies increase. These effects, taken together, suggest that the opponent will experience an increase in expected sanctions for both withholding and suppression and will therefore withhold or suppress less information favorable to the party receiving advice. With legal advice about investigation and presentation, the party is thus able to identify and present more favorable information that the opponent fails to withhold or suppress, increasing the overall amount of favorable information presented to the tribunal.

Providing a party with advice also decreases her own expected sanctions for withholding and suppression.[87] Legal advice given prior to an act associated with a risk of evidentiary sanctions may enable a party to commit that act in a way that minimizes the creation or disclosure of

---

or suppression. *See supra* note 82. The inquiry in this Article is limited to the informational effects of advice and does not consider when and whether withholding or suppression might be desirable despite its adverse informational effects.

85. An advised party should also be able to make more demands for production. One could regard this as advice that increases the opponent's sanctions for withholding (from nothing to something). We have, however, chosen to categorize this as advice that increases investigation, *see supra* note 72 and accompanying text, and thus, to avoid double-counting, we do not also treat it as advice that influences the level of sanctions. The choice of categorization does not change the substance of our conclusions. In either event, advice that increases the number of demands for production that are made should increase the presentation of information from the opponent's discoverable set.

86. This will not always mean that the witness actually is being evasive or withholding information. Sometimes expert questioning can make the witness appear to be withholding even when she is not. Thus, legal advice can increase the likelihood that an opponent will suffer evidentiary sanctions, whether or not she actually was withholding or suppressing information.

87. As with the increase in the opponent's expected sanctions, this decrease in the party's expected sanctions may be undesirable (where the party engages in undesirable withholding or suppression) or desirable (where the party truthfully said she did not have the information or engaged in desirable withholding). *See supra* note 82.

unfavorable secondary information about the act and maximizes the creation of favorable secondary information. For example, an advised party who lies about a relevant fact may be less likely to include in her story details that can be proven false or that are true but sound "too good to be true." A party faced with a question in discovery that calls for unfavorable information but that can be evaded may give an incomplete or nonresponsive answer. Or a party may purposefully overlook a memorandum within the scope of a demand for production but take pains to document other steps suggesting that the party's production was complete and diligent. Advice thus reduces unfavorable secondary information about the evidentiary act available to the opponent, increases the favorable secondary information available for presentation, and therefore reduces the likelihood that the act will be sanctioned. In addition, after an evidentiary act, legal advice in any proceeding where the opponent claims that improper withholding or suppression has occurred enables the party, under the foregoing analysis, to present more favorable and less unfavorable secondary information about its evidentiary conduct—with the increase in favorable secondary information exceeding the decrease in unfavorable secondary information.

Both advice about how to commit an act of withholding or suppression and advice about how to defend such an act reduce the unfavorable secondary information about the evidentiary act reaching the tribunal while increasing the favorable secondary information. Expected evidentiary sanctions for the party's withholding and suppression should therefore decrease. A party with advice is thus more likely to find it worthwhile to withhold or suppress unfavorable information about primary conduct than a party without advice. The additional unfavorable primary information withheld or suppressed will reduce the opponent's presentation of unfavorable primary information and decrease the unfavorable primary information reaching the tribunal.

The cumulative effect of unilateral advice influencing the level of evidentiary sanctions is thus ambiguous. It increases the favorable primary information presented and reduces the unfavorable primary information presented. Depending on the relative magnitudes of this increase and decrease, it may either increase or decrease the total amount of relevant information reaching the tribunal.[88]

88. This overall result does not necessarily change with differences in opponent competence. As opponent competence increases, both the increase in opponent expected evidentiary sanctions and the decrease in the party's own expected evidentiary sanctions should be smaller, with offsetting effects on the total amount of information that the parties find it in their interest to withhold or suppress.

2. Lawyers' Personal Susceptibility to Evidentiary Sanctions

Sometimes legal advice will decrease the amount of information suppressed or withheld because of evidentiary sanctions applicable to the lawyer giving advice. Lawyers are sometimes subject to sanctions for providing advice about withholding or suppressing information or for failing to disclose unfavorable information to the tribunal. In addition to criminal sanctions for subornation of perjury and obstruction of justice, disciplinary rules in almost all American jurisdictions forbid lawyers from knowingly assisting or counseling the criminal or fraudulent withholding or suppression of unfavorable information and require lawyers to withdraw when they know that their clients are using advice for those purposes.[89] A lawyer is also obligated, in circumstances that vary from jurisdiction to jurisdiction, to disclose physical evidence of crimes[90] and to disclose unfavorable information to the tribunal in order to rectify withholding or suppression that results in the presentation of evidence the lawyer knows is false.[91] Withdrawal and disclosure, the two acts required of a lawyer in order to avoid sanctions, can both severely harm the party. In addition, public prosecutors and lawyers appearing in ex parte proceedings must disclose exculpatory information to opponents in circumstances where parties to civil litigation would ordinarily have no obligation to do so.[92]

A lawyer's exposure to sanctions typically depends in substantial part on whether she is aware of information unfavorable to her client. A lawyer may become aware of unfavorable information because a client divulges it to her or because the client delegates to her the tasks of investigation and presentation. Not every party will allow her lawyer to obtain unfavorable information. Sophisticated clients can sometimes make fully informed decisions without sharing information.[93] Others may decline to share information because the advantages of better informed decisions do not seem worth the increased risk of their lawyer's disclosure or withdrawal.[94] But some parties will find that the expected

89. *See, e.g.*, MODEL RULES, *supra* note 1, Rules 3.3, 3.4; MODEL CODE, *supra* note 2, DR 7-102(A)(3)-(6).

90. In some states, a lawyer who obtains possession of physical evidence of a crime committed by his client comes under an obligation to turn that information over to the prosecutor. *See, e.g.*, People v. Meredith, 29 Cal. 3d 682, 686-87, 631 P.2d 46, 48-49, 175 Cal. Rptr. 612, 614-15 (1981); Morrell v. State, 575 P.2d 1200, 1206-11 (Alaska 1978).

91. MODEL CODE, *supra* note 2, DR 7-102(B)(2); MODEL RULES, *supra* note 1, Rule 3.3(a)(4).

92. MODEL RULES, *supra* note 1, Rule 3.8(d) (prosecutor's obligation); *id.* Rule 3.3(d) (requiring the presentation of "all material facts" in an ex parte proceeding).

93. For example, a sophisticated client's lawyer may, without learning the client's information, be able to describe in hypothetical terms what kinds of information are unfavorable, confident that the client will be able to apply that knowledge to withhold or suppress information matching that description without implicating her lawyer. *See* K. MANN, *supra* note 30, at 109-11.

94. Prudent sanction-optimizing lawyers may advise clients when to share information or

benefits of better informed decisions outweigh the expected costs of sharing unfavorable information with their lawyer.[95] Others will discover that as a practical matter they cannot obtain advice about investigation and presentation without delegating execution of those activities to a lawyer, who as a result will become aware of information unfavorable to her client.

The lawyer's awareness of unfavorable information can be significant when it would be in the party's interest, given the harmfulness of the information and the level of expected sanctions applicable to the party, to withhold or suppress the information. In such cases, the lawyer's personal susceptibility to sanctions will sometimes cause the lawyer to take actions that prevent withholding or suppression. Sometimes the lawyer will increase the client's effective expected sanctions for withholding or suppression.[96] If the decision to withhold or suppress is made in consultation with the lawyer, for example, the lawyer may insist that the party refrain from withholding or suppressing the information. The lawyer may back that insistence with a threat either to withdraw from representing the party if she commits evidentiary misconduct or to disclose the misconduct or the unfavorable information to the tribunal.[97] Sometimes the lawyer may disclose the information on her own. When the party has delegated the task of compliance to her lawyer, the lawyer's differing incentives may cause the lawyer, without consulting with the client, to comply with the client's obligations more fully than the client would have done. In either case, the lawyer's action will increase the amount of information unfavorable to the party that reaches the tribunal.

---

delegate investigation by weighing the advantages of the lawyer knowing the information or executing the investigation against the disadvantages of restricting the client's ability to withhold or suppress the shared or attorney-identified information. Where a high risk exists that the information to be shared or identified is unfavorable and that any evidentiary misconduct by the attorney will be detected, and a low probability exists that the opponent would obtain the information if the client commits evidentiary misconduct, such lawyers may advise their clients against sharing information or delegating investigation. *See infra* note 235 (describing an instance of this strategy).

95. *Cf. supra* notes 54-59 and accompanying text (assuming that to some extent parties can obtain legal knowledge only by hiring lawyers during litigation).

96. Obviously, there will be some lawyers who break the rules by actively assisting in unlawful evidentiary conduct. *See* Berentson, *Integrity Test: Five of Thirteen Lawyers Fail*, AM. LAW., May 1980, at 15. The general effect we predict, however, requires only that some lawyers be deterred from doing so and that their actions sometimes increase the unfavorable information presented by their clients.

97. *See generally* Kraakman, *Gatekeepers: The Anatomy of a Third-Party Enforcement Strategy*, 2 J.L. ECON. & ORG. 53, 53-56 & n.3, 58-60 (1986) (discussing and contrasting enforcement strategies that rely on "whistleblowers" with strategies that impose a duty on "gatekeepers" to disrupt misconduct by withholding their support to wrongdoers). Lawyers who are uncomfortable forcing the production of information that their clients would find advantageous to withhold or suppress may achieve the same results by exaggerating to their clients the adverse consequences the clients might suffer by failing to comply. *Cf.* Gordon, *The Independence of Lawyers*, 68 B.U.L. REV. 1, 35 (1988) ("exercises of independence are as likely to be covert as overt, secreted in the interstices of prudential counseling").

The conclusion that evidentiary sanctions applicable to lawyers will sometimes cause lawyers to act contrary to their clients' interests is highly plausible. Lawyers as a class are repeat players with a substantial investment of human capital in their professions.[98] They also face evidentiary sanctions that are different from and often proportionately more stringent than those faced by their clients. In most instances, a single case represents a small part of an attorney's career and livelihood, and the benefit the attorney derives from assisting her client in sanctionable withholding or suppression will seem correspondingly low.[99] The expected costs of misconduct, in contrast, may loom very large even if the risk of detection for any given instance of misconduct is low. A lawyer who becomes involved in suborning perjury, destroying evidence, or deliberately disobeying discovery requests risks her reputation, disciplinary proceedings, and in some cases her career.[100] For a client, a win or loss in a given case is likely to assume much greater importance, while the effect of sanctions is more likely to be limited to the case at hand.

On some occasions, then, attorneys will conclude that their expected evidentiary sanctions exceed their personal benefit from withholding or suppressing information unfavorable to their client and will act contrary to their clients' interests.[101] We therefore expect that when a party

98. As Professor Kraakman notes, a wrongdoer has more difficulty corrupting a gatekeeper when either (1) entry into the gatekeeping market requires a significant investment (which leaves the gatekeeper more vulnerable to legal sanctions), or (2) the gatekeeper has a diversified client base (which leaves the gatekeeper less vulnerable to client pressure). Kraakman, *supra* note 97, at 70-71.

99. To be sure, sometimes lawyers who become aware of information unfavorable to their client may not experience or act upon the divergent sensitivity to sanctions that we describe. Some lawyers work "in-house" as full-time employees. Many attorneys in larger firms do most of their work for, and are beholden to, only one or two clients. R. NELSON, PARTNERS WITH POWER 250-51 (1988). To the extent that the lawyers in these law firms collectively suffer sanctions for evidentiary misconduct that benefits a firm client, the firm's expanded client base should give the firm incentives to discourage its attorneys from engaging in evidentiary misconduct. If, however, the firm escapes collective sanctions for participation by its lawyers in wrongdoing, *see* Pavelic & LeFlore v. Marvel Entertainment, 110 S. Ct. 456 (1989) (holding that sanctions under Fed. R. Civ. P. 11 cannot be imposed on the firm of a lawyer who violated the rule), does not have a diverse client base, or has an imperfect monitoring system, large firm lawyers with few clients should, compared to other lawyers, experience less of a systemic divergence between the benefits and sanctions they perceive and those perceived by their clients. Even in such cases, though, the lawyers' benefit from assisting withholding will be less than the full benefit to the parties, since the lawyers are not fully identified with the clients' interests.

100. More subtle sanctions may also operate. For example, lawyers who do not respond diligently to discovery requests that cannot be evaded honestly may find themselves repaid in kind when they make discovery requests in this or other cases.

101. This conclusion may seem at variance with recent accounts of cases in which attorneys actively engaged in discovery abuse. *See, e.g.*, Kiechel, *supra* note 44; Rhode, *supra* note 11, at 598-99. But none of these anecdotal accounts (nor to our knowledge any systematic study) compares discovery compliance when clients lack legal advice with compliance when clients have such advice.

Some evidence suggests that clients and attorneys often have the different incentive structure we suggest. *See, e.g.*, K. MANN, *supra* note 30, at 109-12, 117-22 (discussing elite white-collar criminal defense lawyers); Landon, *Clients, Colleagues, and Community: The Shaping of Zealous Advocacy in*

receives legal advice, sanctions applicable to lawyers will sometimes cause a party to fail to withhold or suppress information that the party would have withheld or suppressed without legal advice.[102]

3. *The Cumulative Unilateral Effects on Effective Evidentiary Sanctions*

In our basic account, the cumulative effects of unilateral advice that influences the withholding and suppression of information identified as unfavorable are as follows. Given our assumption that parties do not systematically over- or underestimate the level of sanctions, advice that corrects misperceptions about the level of evidentiary sanctions will neither increase nor decrease the amount of unfavorable information reaching the tribunal.[103] Advice that influences the actual level of evidentiary sanctions has no predictable effect on the amount of relevant information reaching the tribunal. It increases expected evidentiary sanctions for the opponent of the party receiving advice, which results in an increase of uncertain magnitude in the favorable information presented; it also reduces expected evidentiary sanctions for the party receiving advice, which causes a decrease of uncertain magnitude in the

Country Law Practice, 1985 AM. B. FOUND. RES. J. 81, 105-09 (discussing lawyers in smaller cities). Such divergent incentives may be more common when there is a continuing relationship between the lawyer and opposing counsel, or the lawyer and the tribunal, that increases the importance of the lawyer's reputation, and hence the significance of potential reputational sanctions for misconduct.

102. As we spell out in greater detail in Section V(B), this increase in the presentation of information unfavorable to the party receiving advice is not without costs. For the party receiving advice, the risk that the lawyer will act contrary to her interest will deter some information sharing or investigatory delegation which would in turn facilitate advice that would increase the amount of relevant information presented by each side. Thus, while providing advice to one party in a model that takes account of lawyer sanctions will cause the presentation of unfavorable information that would not have been presented if the party had no lawyer, the amount of relevant information reaching the tribunal in a regime with legal advice and lawyer sanctions may or may not be greater than the amount of information in a regime with legal advice and no lawyer sanctions.

We leave out here the effect of providing advice for one party on the evidentiary sanctions applicable to the opposing party's lawyer, if she has one. The opponent's lawyer should anticipate an increase in evidentiary sanctions because the party is better able to detect and prosecute wrongdoing. But that increase in sanctions will also be accompanied by an increase in advice deterred. Accordingly, increased evidentiary sanctions for the opponent's lawyer may or may not result in an increase in information reaching the tribunal.

103. Similarly, in cases where a party has decided to comply with an obligation to produce or preserve information, legal advice about how to comply with the party's obligation will have no predictable effect on the amount of unfavorable information reaching the tribunal. Without advice a party might mistakenly produce more or less information than called for. For example, unadvised parties may lack the technical expertise necessary to identify every document covered by a demand for all documents relevant to an issue. This may lead them to produce only the documents they can identify as responsive—thus mistakenly withholding some unfavorable information that has been demanded—or to take an "everything-and-the-kitchen-sink" approach and produce all documents they have—thus mistakenly presenting some unfavorable information not called for. Legal advice about technical compliance thus has no systemic tendency to increase or decrease the amount of unfavorable information reaching the opponent or the tribunal.

unfavorable information reaching the tribunal. Finally, lawyers' divergent susceptibility to sanctions has a positive effect. In some cases, sanctions applicable to lawyers will cause the presentation of unfavorable information that would have been withheld or suppressed without legal advice. The net effect of unilateral advice thus appears to be an increase in favorable information presented that tends to be larger than the increase in the unfavorable information withheld or suppressed.

4. *The Effects of Bilateral Advice*

In a bilateral account, evidentiary sanctions applicable to lawyers should sometimes cause each party to produce or preserve information she would have withheld or suppressed without legal advice. This increases both the favorable and unfavorable information about each party reaching the tribunal.

The effects of bilateral advice on expected evidentiary sanctions applicable to parties have less clear implications for the amount of information about primary conduct that reaches the tribunal. In a unilateral account, the party receiving advice experiences a decrease in expected evidentiary sanctions and her opponent experiences an increase. In a bilateral account, the superior knowledge and skills of the opposing attorneys will tend to offset. But the outcome should not be a wash. The prior Sections suggest that, just as for information about primary conduct, legal advice should increase the favorable secondary information presented by each side about any claimed incident of withholding or suppression more than it decreases unfavorable secondary information. Bilateral advice should accordingly increase the presentation of favorable *and* unfavorable secondary information about both parties' evidentiary conduct.

This increase in information about *evidentiary conduct* need not lead to a uniform increase in expected sanctions for withholding or suppression by either side, and thus may not increase the information about *primary conduct* reaching the tribunal. It would tend to do so if evidentiary sanctions were set on the assumption that *all* withholding or suppression is socially undesirable. But in fact evidentiary sanctions are often set on the assumption that some withholding and suppression is socially desirable.[104] Increased presentation of secondary information should, however, generally increase expected sanctions for undesirable withholding and suppression and decrease them for desirable withholding and suppression, for reasons we spell out in Part IV.

For example, expected sanctions against the willful destruction of documents should increase, with a concomitant increase in the amount of

104. *See supra* note 82.

information reaching the tribunal. But the likelihood that the tribunal will sustain appropriate assertions of doctor-patient privilege should also increase, reducing the information reaching the tribunal. The overall effect depends on whether instances of undesirable withholding or suppression (like willful destruction of documents) that would be underdeterred without bilateral advice are more or less common than instances of desirable withholding or suppression (like appropriate claims of privilege) that would be overdeterred without bilateral advice. Because we cannot tell whether under- or overdeterrence is more common, we cannot predict whether bilateral advice that influences the party's expected sanctions for withholding or suppression will increase or decrease the total amount of relevant information about primary conduct reaching the tribunal.[105]

D. *Summary of the Basic Account*

Our basic account enables us to draw some initial conclusions about the general informational effects of legal advice. In the basic unilateral account, advice reduces the proportion of irrelevant information presented. It also increases the presentation of information favorable to the party receiving advice more than it reduces the presentation of information unfavorable to that party. This initial conclusion reflects several positive effects. Advice about how to categorize relevant commonly identified information or information unadvised parties would miscategorize as irrelevant increases the presentation of favorable information strongly but has no comparable negative effect on the presentation of unfavorable information. The same is true of advice that influences the investigation of nonsuppressible information. In addition, evidentiary sanctions applicable to lawyers sometimes cause the presentation of unfavorable information that would not have been presented without legal advice. Our initial conclusion also reflects ambiguous effects: advice about how to categorize information that can be withheld or suppressed, advice about investigations conducted to identify suppressible information, and advice about how to assess or influence sanctions for withholding and suppression each tend to increase the favorable information presented but to cause possibly equivalent decreases in unfavorable information presented. On balance, though, advice increases the amount and proportion of relevant information.

105. Another complication is that increased opponent competence increases the likelihood that the opponent will recognize and present any unfavorable information a party does not withhold or suppress. This has two conflicting effects. On the one hand, it means that a greater proportion of the information that is not withheld or suppressed will reach the tribunal. This will tend to enhance the informational increase from bilateral advice. On the other hand, it increases the benefits of withholding and suppressing unfavorable information. This will tend to offset any increase in expected evidentiary sanctions and reduce the information reaching the tribunal.

In the basic bilateral account, the positive effects of advice are preserved and enhanced and some ambiguous effects appear muted. For each party, the net increase in relevant information presented will be greater than if she had been the only party to receive advice, because the positive informational effect of advice about categorization is stronger when the opponent is more competent.[106] Moreover, in a bilateral account, there is no reason to predict that advice influencing investigations that identify suppressible information or advice influencing the level of expected evidentiary sanctions will systematically increase or decrease the presentation of favorable or unfavorable information about either side's primary conduct.[107]

This general account clarifies the serious limitations of the account of legal advice recently offered by Professors Kaplow and Shavell. Kaplow and Shavell present a model of advice about information selection and establish that within the model advice has ambiguous informational effects. They then assert, with some qualifications regarding advice about investigation, that the resulting informational "analysis applies more broadly, to virtually all the choices lawyers make on clients' behalf."[108] Their model is, however, too limited to sustain this sweeping claim or to justify any general policy implications about how litigation advice should be regulated.

First, because Kaplow and Shavell's model assumes each party has "perfect control" over its information,[109] they ignore the possibility that an opponent's ability to present information favorable to his position might limit the ability of a party with selection advice to prevent the tribunal from receiving information unfavorable to her side. Second, because their model assumes that all information is relevant,[110] they ignore advice about relevance and thus the possibility that such selection

106. *See supra* notes 67-70 and accompanying text.

107. *See supra* text following note 80; *supra* note 105 and accompanying text.

108. Kaplow & Shavell, *supra* note 17, at 593.

109. *See id.* at 576. Kaplow and Shavell believe that the assumption of perfect control alters only the "extent" and not the basic nature or direction of the effects they predict for advice about how to categorize information as favorable or unfavorable. *See id.* Our analysis of commonly identified information demonstrates that this belief is false. *See supra* Section II(A)(1)(c)(ii). Our analysis of investigation also demonstrates that, even if one assumes perfect control, Kaplow and Shavell are incorrect in believing that the nature and direction of the effects of categorization advice are not affected by their assumption that lawyers have perfect knowledge. *See* Kaplow & Shavell, *supra* note 17, at 578 & n.26. Because the effect of categorization advice on investigation can increase a party's identification of unfavorable information, *see supra* Section II(B)(2)(a), an attorney's erroneous presentation of some of this additional unfavorable information could conceivably increase the unfavorable information reaching the tribunal.

110. *See* Kaplow & Shavell, *supra* note 17, at 577 n.25 (assuming all evidence is either "definitely favorable or definitely unfavorable"). Our analysis demonstrates that accounting for advice that corrects either mistaken beliefs that information is relevant or mistaken beliefs that information is irrelevant has beneficial informational effects that Kaplow and Shavell do not predict. *See supra* Sections II(A)(1)(a), (b).

advice could improve the quality of the parties' presentations. Third, their model takes no account of the influence of advice on investigation or the possibility that such advice might increase the information from which each party selects.[111] Fourth, their assumption that parties with advice exercise perfect control over their information excludes the influence of legal advice on the perceived and actual costs of withholding information. That assumption, and the further assumption that lawyers act with the sole aim of lowering their clients' expected sanctions,[112] also eliminate any possibility that the lawyer's personal susceptibility to sanctions for improper litigation conduct might lead to the production of additional information.

Our account shows that for all four aspects of litigation excluded from Kaplow and Shavell's model, advice has a general tendency to increase the information reaching the tribunal. Kaplow and Shavell have modeled the vices of competition between skilled partisans without modeling any of its virtues: competitive selection of information, focused presentation, improved investigation, and compelled production. In the cases that best fit their model, such as those where parties have no obligation to produce information or freely conspire with their lawyers in wrongful withholding, the social value of legal advice has long been doubted, and properly so.[113] Kaplow and Shavell's demonstration that within their tightly restricted focus the informational effects of advice are formally ambiguous is an important advance. But given the incomplete

111. *See* Kaplow & Shavell, *supra* note 17, at 568 (assuming that the "sole function" of lawyers is assisting parties in "selecting which evidence to present to a tribunal"). Discovery and fact-investigation are the only areas in which Kaplow and Shavell acknowledge that their model is "incomplete" in any way that might limit its general applicability. *Id.* at 594 n.67. Our analysis demonstrates that the effects predicted under a more complete model that includes investigation do in fact differ from those predicted under the Kaplow and Shavell model. *See supra* Section II(B).

112. *See* Kaplow & Shavell, *supra* note 17, at 583, 570 n.3, 577.

113. Consider, for example, a fictional example of legal advice that has engaged the attention of many professional responsibility scholars: the "lecture" from the novel *The Anatomy of a Murder*. The client, accused of premeditated murder, tells his attorney information about his mental state during the killing that plainly indicates his guilt. R. TRAVER, THE ANATOMY OF A MURDER 30-33 (1958). The attorney responds by explaining how different testimony could establish a defense of temporary insanity, and the client then "forgets" the incriminating information previously disclosed. *Id.* at 44-49. Even Monroe Freedman, perhaps the most intemperate defender of zealous advocacy, concedes that the conduct of the attorney in the "lecture" is socially undesirable and ethically indefensible. M. FREEDMAN, *supra* note 9, at 73-74. The "lecture" fits Kaplow and Shavell's model well: only the defendant has direct access to information about his mental state, the relevance is clear, little investigation is necessary to obtain the information, defendant's sanctions for withholding are low, and the attorney is apparently indifferent to the risk of sanctions for suborning perjury. We account for such cases under the heading of advice about how to categorize separately identified information that would have been identified with or without investigation, and that an unadvised party would correctly categorize as relevant. *See supra* notes 63-66 and accompanying text. As our account makes clear, however, these effects form only a small subset of the effects of advice.

and biased character of their model, it provides a shaky basis for analyzing the overall informational effects of litigation advice or deriving policy implications.

Our bilateral account seems particularly suited for analyzing the classic account of civil litigation, which posits parties of roughly equal competence who benefit equally from legal advice and who have relatively equal access to information. An example demonstrates both how our account might play out in practice and how the partial perspectives of some critics and defenders of legal advice lead to inaccurate conclusions. Consider a suit for breach of contract in which the plaintiff and defendant can each present one eyewitness to the making of an alleged oral contract. Doubters like Professors Kaplow and Shavell might focus on the information about the disputed conversation that the parties control and would identify as relevant without advice. From this partial perspective, the lawsuit appears to be simply a "swearing contest." Bilateral provision of advice will have no beneficial impact on the tribunal's ability to render judgment. Instead it will skew each party's presentation of its controlled information, with no change in the total amount of relevant information reaching the tribunal.

A defender would point, however, to other features of the case that cast legal advice in a more favorable light. Advice should increase both parties' presentation of nonsuppressible relevant information about the transaction that would mistakenly be categorized as irrelevant. It will also increase the presentation of information that is not party-controlled or that can be obtained only through investigation. This additional information should provide a better picture of the parties' conversation, the setting and circumstances in which the conversation occurred, the parties' relative sophistication and the history of their dealings with others, and the custom or practice in the relevant market. The tribunal will thus have a better baseline for evaluating the plausibility of the parties' competing claims about the alleged agreement.

The cumulative effect of bilateral advice thus emerges as an overlay of ambiguous and positive consequences. At a contested trial, the dramatic prominence of live testimony by the two witnesses to the conversation may create the impression that ambiguous effects predominate. But in reality even the witnesses' testimony about the critical conversation ought on balance to be more informative than it would have been without advice, because each will present additional party-controlled information about their interaction that they would have miscategorized as irrelevant or missed in investigation. Moreover, because the parties' joint account of the background to the transaction will also be more informative, the tribunal will be in a better position to render judgment than if the parties had no legal advice.

Other civil litigation may be more amenable to analysis under the unilateral account. Consider a case where one party can afford advice, but the other cannot. The unilateral account allows us to consider the effects of both a decision to deny advice to the party who can afford it and a decision to subsidize advice for the party who cannot. Denying advice to the first party will increase her expected sanctions for primary conduct. But because legal advice increases the amount of favorable information presented more than it decreases the amount of unfavorable information presented, denying advice will also reduce the amount of relevant information reaching the tribunal.

Providing advice to the party who cannot afford it will, on the other hand, strongly increase the amount of relevant information reaching the tribunal. An example is the claim brought by a "private attorney general," such as an antitrust, securities, or discrimination class action, or an environmental enforcement suit. In such cases the retention of counsel is sometimes made possible by the promise of an award of attorneys' fees to successful claimants.[114] Providing legal advice to the plaintiffs will increase the defendants' expected sanctions for withholding and suppression, thus increasing the amount of information that is available to both sides and not suppressed. It will also increase the amount of information that the plaintiff will identify, gather, and present from the information available to both sides.

114. The private attorney general may otherwise be unable to raise the funds for legal advice, not only because those she represents may be too poor or because their expected financial gain from litigation may not merit the cost, *see supra* note 57, but also because large groups with low per capita stakes face greater free rider problems in collecting funds, *see* M. OLSON, THE LOGIC OF COLLECTIVE ACTION 33-36 (1965).

B. *Attorney-Client Confidentiality*

A variety of rules protect the confidentiality of the attorney-client relationship. The attorney-client privilege generally bars compelled disclosure of the contents of communications between lawyer and client made in confidence for the purpose of getting or giving legal advice.[218] The ethical obligation of confidentiality generally bars attorneys from voluntarily disclosing information harmful to their clients, no matter what its source, unless the client insists on committing or has committed fraud on the tribunal in order to withhold the information.[219] Work product immunity provides qualified protection from discovery of documents and tangible things reflecting the results of investigation ("ordinary work product") and absolute or near absolute protection for the lawyer's professional judgments ("opinion work product"), even if those judgments are not embodied in advice communicated in confidence to the client.[220]

The privilege is intended to encourage parties to communicate harmful information to lawyers by reducing the risk that lawyers will subsequently disclose that information to the tribunal.[221] The general obligations of confidentiality and work product immunity similarly

---

218. UNIF. R. EVID. § 502, 13A U.L.A. 256 (1986); MCCORMICK ON EVIDENCE § 87 (E. Cleary 3d ed. 1984).

219. MODEL RULES, *supra* note 1, Rule 3.3; ABA Standing Comm. on Ethics and Professional Responsibility, Formal Op. 87-353 (1987).

220. *See* Special Project, *The Work Product Doctrine*, 68 CORNELL L. REV. 760, 773-80 (1983) (authored by Jeff A. Anderson, Gena E. Cadieux, George E. Hays, Michael B. Hingerty & Richard J. Kaplan); Note, *The Work Product Doctrine in Subsequent Litigation*, 83 COLUM. L. REV. 412, 413-20 (1983) (authored by Caroline T. Mitchell). We discuss the work product doctrine more fully at *infra* notes 247-59 and accompanying text.

221. *E.g.*, 8 J. WIGMORE, EVIDENCE IN TRIALS AT COMMON LAW § 2291, at 545 (J. McNaughton rev. ed. 1961).

encourage parties to involve lawyers in conducting investigations and evaluating the fruits of those investigations. We will describe both decisions to communicate information directly to a lawyer and decisions tc allow the attorney to learn information from other sources as decisions to "share" information.

It is often suggested that narrowing confidentiality rules, with a concomitant expansion of the attorney's obligation to disclose information to the tribunal or the opponent, would increase the amount of information reaching the tribunal.[222] Our account assists in understanding what is at stake in this claim, because it illuminates the informational effects of the information sharing encouraged by confidentiality, the informational costs of confidentiality where it does not affect information sharing, and the factors influencing the causal connection between confidentiality rules and information sharing.[223]

For clarity, we contrast two simplified regimes. The regime of absolute confidentiality neither requires nor permits attorneys to disclose information harmful to their clients' interests and requires attorneys to provide litigation advice no matter what their clients intend to do with it. The regime of absolute disclosure requires attorneys to disclose to the tribunal all relevant information and all information that might lead to the identification and presentation of relevant information.[224] We initially assume that the attorney's obligations under either regime are perfectly enforced. Thus, under the regime of absolute confidentiality, a client's decision to share information with a lawyer never increases the likelihood that unfavorable information will reach the opponent or the tribunal. Under the regime of absolute disclosure, harmful information shared with an attorney is always disclosed. We also initially assume that decisions to share information reflect a full understanding of the applicable rule of confidentiality or disclosure. Later, we discuss the implications of imperfect enforcement of attorneys' obligations and imperfect client information concerning the risk that the attorney will disclose shared information.

A regime of attorney disclosure will deter a party from sharing information with her lawyer only[225] where the party fears such sharing

222. *See* Frankel, *The Search for Truth: An Umpireal View,* 123 U. PA. L. REV. 1031, 1055-57 (1975) (evaluating this approach).

223. We limit our discussion in this Section to the informational effects of advice. To the extent that confidentiality in litigation would also promote socially desirable withholding of information, foster advice about settlement or related primary conduct, or allow the sharing of information about party preferences that would permit more satisfactory outcomes, the case for the social desirability of confidentiality would evidently be stronger.

224. This is, in essence, Judge Frankel's proposal. *See* Frankel, *supra* note 222, at 1057-58.

225. A party may also be deterred from communicating information to her lawyer by the risk that *favorable* information will be disclosed, if disclosure would be harmful or embarrassing independent of its effect on the merits. To the extent the communication of favorable information

will cause unfavorable information to reach the tribunal that otherwise would not have.[226] Confidentiality thus encourages a party to share information that she fears may be unfavorable or may lead to unfavorable information.[227] In addition, confidentiality encourages the attorney to investigate for information that the party would dismiss as irrelevant, and thus not affirmatively share, despite the risk that such investigation may produce unfavorable information.

The information-sharing caused by confidentiality improves the attorney's ability to give advice.[228] When the party is correct that disclosing the shared information would be harmful, a lawyer operating under a regime of confidentiality will often advise her client to withhold the shared information. But this consequence cannot be considered a cost of confidentiality nor of the advice that it facilitates, because neither the attorney nor the tribunal would have received that information in the absence of confidentiality. Without confidentiality, the lawyer would not have learned the information and would thus have had nothing to disclose to the tribunal. And if a client would not allow her lawyer to learn information because she feared the lawyer would disclose it, she certainly would not herself disclose it directly to the opponent or the tribunal.[229]

The lawyer may instead advise that the information communicated is favorable, rather than unfavorable or irrelevant, and should be presented. Or she may advise that, although the shared information is unfavorable or may lead to unfavorable information, the party should produce it because either the evidentiary sanctions are higher or the degree of unfavorability is lower than the party believed. These types of advice will increase the information reaching the tribunal.[230] An

would be deterred, it strengthens the case for confidentiality, but to clarify the exposition we do not discuss it further.

226. Although our account assumes the fear of unfavorable information reaching the tribunal is necessary to deter information-sharing, we do not assume it is sufficient, even when the fear is correct. *See infra* note 231 and accompanying text.

227. If parties are truth-tellers rather than sanction-optimizers, they will present all information even if it is unfavorable. Thus, confidentiality does not result in more information being shared by truth-tellers. For law-abiders, however, confidentiality is important because, without it, sharing information with an attorney may result in the attorney disclosing information that the party was not herself legally obliged to produce.

228. It may sometimes be possible for a party to receive advice about information without actually sharing it. The party may, for example, ask her attorney hypothetical questions without revealing the actual facts. Our analysis assumes only that the attorney's ability to use or give advice about the information is at least somewhat impaired by the lack of actual sharing.

229. Indeed, unless the information is the type about which clients can testify, clients are unlikely even to have any opportunity to present the information directly to the tribunal.

230. A recent article justifies the attorney-client privilege based on one specific form of beneficial advice: advice that apprises clients of a "contingent claim" that may make apparently unfavorable or irrelevant information favorable. *See* Allen, Grady, Polsby & Yashko, *A Positive Theory of the Attorney-Client Privilege and the Work Product Doctrine*, 19 J. LEGAL STUD. 359, 363-69 (1990). It seems plain to us, however, that advice about contingent claims is but one subset of advice that

information increase should also result where confidentiality facilitates attorney investigation by causing the party either to communicate information that aids the attorney's investigation or to delegate the execution of investigations to that attorney. To be sure, sharing information may also allow the identification of additional suppressible information. But some of this suppressible information will be unfavorable (and thus suppressed) and some favorable (and thus saved from suppression by the opponent), with ambiguous effects on the amount of information reaching the tribunal. On balance, then, advice resulting from the sharing of information caused by confidentiality should increase the information reaching the tribunal.

The information lost to the tribunal because of confidentiality will be a portion of the unfavorable information the party would share with her lawyer whether or not she was guaranteed confidentiality. Even under a regime of absolute disclosure, there are several reasons why a party might share information with her attorney notwithstanding the risk that doing so will cause unfavorable information to reach the tribunal. She may believe the information being shared is more likely to be favorable than unfavorable, or that, given perceived evidentiary sanctions, she will have to produce the shared information anyway. Or she may believe that the benefits of litigation advice obtainable only by sharing information (such as the skilled execution of investigations) outweigh the risk that sharing will cause unfavorable information to reach the tribunal.[231] Once the party shares the information, advice may correct the party's misperceptions that the information is favorable, overestimations of evidentiary sanctions, or underestimations of the degree of unfavorability.[232] In any of these circumstances, a regime of confidentiality will, compared to a regime of disclosure, result in less information reaching the tribunal.[233]

The net informational effects of confidentiality thus depend on

might correct party misperceptions that information is unfavorable or irrelevant. Such advice is in turn, as our textual analysis reveals, but one subset of the types of advice that can increase the information reaching the tribunal. We thus do not share the conclusion of Allen, Grady, Polsby, and Yashko that where "legal claims are not contingent . . . there would be no reason to have the privilege." *Id.* at 367.

231. *Cf. supra* Section I(C)(1) (explaining how identifying even unfavorable information the opponent will not obtain can be helpful, and how even investigations with perceived or actual positive expected value can collect harmful unfavorable information).

232. One important determinant of the degree of unfavorability is the likelihood that the opponent will independently obtain and present the functional equivalent of the information. Where the attorney advises the party that this likelihood is low, the party should be more likely to withhold the information despite the threat of evidentiary sanctions.

233. Where the opponent would present the information independently, or where the unadvised party would correctly determine that information is favorable or should be produced despite its unfavorable nature, the information will reach the tribunal whether or not there is a confidentiality rule and does not contribute to the social value of compelled disclosure.

whether the increase in information resulting from confidentiality-induced information sharing is greater than the unfavorable information lost because it would have been shared (and thus disclosed) with or without confidentiality. That tradeoff in turn depends on the extent to which confidentiality causes information sharing. If confidentiality has no effect on information sharing, then it causes the loss of much information without offsetting informational benefits. If relatively little information sharing would occur without confidentiality, then relatively little unfavorable information is lost (because attorneys would not have much to disclose without it) but more favorable (and perhaps some unfavorable) information is gained as a result of greater information sharing.

Imperfect enforcement of attorneys' obligations under a regime of disclosure or confidentiality may alter the extent of our conclusions but not their qualitative nature. The attractiveness of imposing disclosure obligations on attorneys is not that those obligations can be perfectly enforced, but rather that attorneys are often more susceptible to sanctions than their clients.[234] As long as attorneys respond to sanctions by disclosing information more often under a regime of disclosure than a regime of confidentiality, and in some cases disclose information that the party would not, then the risk that sharing information will cause unfavorable information to reach the tribunal (and thus the disincentive to share information) will be greater under a regime of disclosure, even if enforcement is imperfect. To be sure, imperfect enforcement will decrease the extent to which disclosure obligations discourage information sharing. But it will also decrease the extent to which disclosure obligations cause disclosures. It is thus ambiguous, without empirical evidence, whether imperfect enforcement will make a rule of disclosure more or less attractive.

Imperfect knowledge about the applicable rules of disclosure or confidentiality (and thus about the extent of the risk that sharing information will cause unfavorable information to reach the tribunal) makes the informational effects of confidentiality less desirable because it weakens the causal connection between the existence of confidentiality and the level of information sharing. But though the magnitude of the effects will be influenced by imperfect knowledge, the nature of the effects we describe will still hold so long as there is not complete ignorance, that is, so long as there is some positive correlation between the level of information sharing and the degree of confidentiality.

Insofar as the causal connection depends on this awareness of the applicable rule of confidentiality, there is good reason to believe it will be stronger for attorney-client confidentiality in litigation than for attorney-

234. *See supra* Section II(C)(2).

client confidentiality in nonlitigation settings or for confidentiality rules involving other professions. A litigation lawyer under an enforceable obligation to disclose will likely recognize a larger and more immediate risk to the client from information sharing, will be able to calculate that risk more accurately (and where necessary communicate it more clearly to the client), and will be more concerned with the professional and personal consequences of having to make disclosures harmful to the client.[235]

Knowledge about the risks of disclosure is, however, only one determinant of the causal connection between confidentiality and sharing of information. Another is the private value of sharing information despite the absence of confidentiality. Thus, even if litigants' decisions to share information are more likely to reflect awareness of the applicable rules of confidentiality than the decisions of clients in other relations, the causal connection may still be weaker if the private value to litigants of sharing information is unusually high.

The private value of sharing information may vary for different kinds of litigation advice. In particular, the multiple contributions of advice to the execution of investigation or to the in-court presentation of

235. These considerations are not refuted by reports that under present confidentiality rules many clients are not advised about the details of confidentiality. *See, e.g.*, Zacharias, *Rethinking Confidentiality*, 74 IOWA L. REV. 351, 377, 379 (1989). Apart from the fact that those reports do not focus on advice in litigation, their findings do not support an inference either that present rules do not affect information sharing or that changes in those rules would not do so. Parties may often have a general awareness of the applicable rule of confidentiality without having been specifically advised about it. Indeed, Zacharias' own study suggests that most clients have a general notion of lawyer-client confidentiality, although few learned about it from their lawyers and most overestimated or underestimated its scope. *Id.* at 383.

A lawyer may also not bother to advise a client about confidentiality when correcting a client's misconceptions does not seem likely to help the client, given the benefits and risks of sharing information. Furthermore, if a client's misconceptions will cause a harmful failure to share information, advice that confidentiality is absolute, although technically inaccurate and arguably paternalistic, may be more efficient, more likely to induce helpful sharing of information, and, under present rules, substantively correct for most clients most of the time. If a client's misconceptions will cause harmful sharing, the attorney may find it more efficient and tactful simply not to inquire into a particular subject or to halt information sharing about that subject, without explaining the law of confidentiality. The imprecision of clients' understanding and of lawyers' advice about confidentiality therefore may demonstrate only that, under existing rules, few serious issues arise, or that when such issues arise lawyers are able to advance their clients' interest in sharing or not sharing information without fully explaining those rules.

In fact, the only study of which we are aware that has observed lawyer-client interaction in litigation suggests that sanctioning attorneys for withholding information has a significant impact on information sharing. Professor Mann's study of white-collar criminal defense attorneys showed that they sometimes avoided inquiry into subjects when they believed the client was likely to share unfavorable information. *See* K. MANN, *supra* note 30, at 103-11. Although these attorneys operated under the strong confidentiality rules of the New York Code of Professional Responsibility, their fear that prosecutors might detect and sanction misstatements made in plea bargaining negotiations sometimes caused them to remain intentionally ignorant of their client's information so that they could avoid disclosure of unfavorable information in those negotiations. *Id.* at 83.

information from nonparties normally cannot fully be realized unless the party delegates the conduct of those activities to her lawyer and shares with her the information required to make that delegation effective. Because this increases the likelihood that such information sharing would take place without confidentiality, reduced protection may be appropriate. This may explain why the law provides less protection for information an attorney learns from persons other than the client, which is exempt only from voluntary disclosure by the attorney, while information an attorney learns from client communications is exempt even from compelled disclosure.[236]

This analysis does not pretend to demonstrate the desirability of a rule of absolute confidentiality, let alone of the present confidentiality rules. Such a demonstration would, at a minimum, require better empirical evidence about the causal connection between confidentiality and information sharing. Our aim is rather to frame the inquiry more accurately. In particular, the analysis demonstrates the error of conflating the issue of the effects and desirability of litigation advice generally with the issue of the effects and desirability of attorney-client confidentiality in litigation. In our account, the informational effects of litigation advice are, on balance, socially desirable, but the informational effects of confidentiality are uncertain because of empirical questions about the effect of confidentiality on the willingness of parties to share information with their lawyers.

But even if it were true that, on balance, litigation advice has ambiguous informational effects, it would not follow, as Professors Kaplow and Shavell have argued, that the case for attorney-client confidentiality in litigation is a priori the "weakest" of any privilege.[237] Even in Kaplow and Shavell's simplified model of advice, which considers only the effect of advice about categorization upon the production of information that is effectively party-controlled, confidentiality should encourage the party to share with her lawyer some information the party fears is unfavorable. Where the party's fears are correct, the advised party will not present unfavorable information. But that cannot be deemed a cost of confidentiality since the party would not present information to the tribunal that she would not disclose to her attorney solely because of the risk the attorney would disclose it to the tribunal. Where, however, the shared information is actually favorable, the lawyer will advise that it should be presented. The sharing of information induced by confidentiality should, under Kaplow and Shavell's model, thus increase the presentation of favorable information without reducing that of unfavorable

236. *See supra* note 45; *supra* text accompanying notes 218-20; *infra* note 249 and accompanying text.

237. Kaplow & Shavell, *supra* note 17, at 600 n.84.

information.[238] Confidentiality should, on the other hand, prevent the lawyer from disclosing some unfavorable information that the party would have shared even without confidentiality.

Thus, as in our account, the effects and desirability of confidentiality in Kaplow and Shavell's model depend critically on the extent to which parties would share information with their lawyers in the absence of confidentiality. If the causal connection between confidentiality and information sharing is strong, then the privilege will cause a strong increase in favorable information presented, with little loss of unfavorable information. This is normally desirable under any theory of adjudication, at least if both parties have lawyers.[239] While it is true that their model—like ours—provides no a priori reason to think that the favorable information gained because of attorney-client confidentiality is worth the unfavorable information lost, that a priori ambiguity exists for all privileges: we can

---

238. Kaplow and Shavell reach their conclusion that litigation advice presents the weakest case for protected confidentiality because they argue that the social value of some advice, like medical advice, is clear, whereas the social value of litigation advice is ambiguous. *See id.* at 600. Accordingly, they seem to reason that, while other privileges at least generate some clear social benefit to offset against the information lost because of confidentiality, privileging litigation advice may generate no benefit to weigh against the information lost. *See id.* at 600 & n.84, 610 & n.116.

This is wrong on two scores. First, it erroneously conflates the effects of advice encouraged by confidentiality with the effects of advice generally. Even if the Kaplow/Shavell model accurately captured the real world, and litigation advice ambiguously increased favorable information and decreased unfavorable information, the analysis in text demonstrates that the effects of the litigation advice encouraged by confidentiality would be an increase in favorable information without any decrease in unfavorable information. Such an increase in favorable information standing alone is ordinarily desirable for the reasons articulated in Part IV. To be sure, this social gain from the communications encouraged by litigation advice must be weighed against the loss of information from the communications that would have occurred even without confidentiality. But that is no different from weighing the social gain of the doctor-patient communications encouraged by confidentiality against the loss of information from doctor-patient communications that would have occurred even without confidentiality.

Second, the social desirability of encouraging medical advice is not always so clear-cut. Medical care is often wasteful or excessively costly and can cause injury. *See* I. ILLICH, MEDICAL NEMESIS (1976) (arguing that the medical system creates more illness than it relieves). Medical care can also restore the health of bad people who go on to commit bad acts. Finally, medical advice can be abused for purposes that have nothing to do with good health: for example, fraud rings use medical advice to trump up personal injury claims. Indeed, such dubious uses of medical advice may seem particularly likely when patients would not confide in doctors without assurances that their communications would be kept from a tribunal.

239. Perhaps Kaplow and Shavell would go further, and contend that even a bilateral increase in information presented to the tribunal is socially ambiguous, based on their assumption that parties are unaware of any increases in the accuracy of adjudication resulting from legal advice at the time parties engage in primary conduct. *See* Kaplow & Shavell, *supra* note 17, at 588-90, 610. We have already argued that the assumption that parties are, at the time they act, generally ignorant of court outcomes is implausible, and that, even if the assumption were accurate, increased accuracy would still be desirable under theories of adjudication that stress corrective justice, prevention of harm, or fairness. *See supra* Part IV. More importantly here, if informational increases have ambiguous social value, then that ambiguity attaches both to the benefits *and* the costs of confidentiality. Thus, it offers no grounds for concluding that the attorney-client relation in litigation presents the weakest case for confidentiality.

never know whether the benefits resulting from facilitated communications are worth the costs of the information lost without knowing the extent to which confidentiality facilitates communications.[240]

Although our account of confidentiality cannot justify the precise contours of present doctrine, it does generate some rough predictions about those contours. First, our account predicts that there should be no confidentiality protection for information that clients will normally disclose to lawyers with or without confidentiality. This prediction is clearly consistent with the requirement that to receive protection under the privilege, client communications seeking legal advice must be made "in confidence."[241] It may also help explain why the attorney-client privilege generally does not protect a client's identity.[242] Presumably most clients would communicate their identity to the lawyer with or without a guarantee of confidentiality in order to secure representation: in such cases, the privilege would deprive the tribunal of information without increasing the flow of legal advice to the client. It is also consistent with our analysis that the general rule about client identity has an exception where the client's identity is the "last link" in proving a crime.[243] The "last link" exception appears to identify a relatively narrow set of circumstances in which it is highly likely that lack of confidentiality would deter a client from seeking advice: when her identity is all the government needs to impose criminal sanctions.

Second, our account suggests that confidentiality should be restricted when the additional advice facilitated by information sharing is highly likely to lead to the presentation of false evidence or the withholding or suppression of truthful information. Evidently this is consistent with the exception to the privilege in cases where the client sought advice in aid of conduct that he knew or reasonably should have known was criminal or fraudulent[244] and with the exceptions to some general confidentiality rules requiring lawyer disclosure of unfavorable information to prevent or remedy the use of the lawyer's services in offering known false evidence.[245] It may also help explain the otherwise anomalous rule

240. *See generally Developments in the Law—Privileged Communications*, 98 HARV. L. REV. 1450, 1471-500 (1985) (explaining why the a priori desirability of any privilege cannot be determined under a variety of utilitarian and nonutilitarian theories).

241. *See, e.g.*, 8 J. WIGMORE, *supra* note 221, § 2311.

242. *In re* Michaelson, 511 F.2d 882, 889 (9th Cir.), *cert. denied*, 421 U.S. 978 (1975); 8 J. WIGMORE, *supra* note 221, § 2313.

243. United States v. Hodge & Zweig, 548 F.2d 1347, 1353 (9th Cir. 1977).

244. *See* UNIF. R. EVID. § 502(d)(1), 13A U.L.A. 257 (1986); 8 J. WIGMORE, *supra* note 221, § 2298.

245. *See* MODEL RULES, *supra* note 1, Rule 3.3. The disclosure obligations in Rule 3.3 are express exceptions to the general confidentiality obligations established in Model Rule 1.6. *Id.* Rule 3.3(d). The Model Code of Professional Responsibility does not permit attorneys to present or assist in presenting known false evidence. MODEL CODE, *supra* note 2, DR 7-102(A)(4), (6), (7). But in

requiring criminal defense attorneys in possession of physical evidence of a crime to turn it over to the prosecutor.[246] The apparent effect of that rule is to reduce the extent to which lawyers examine, move, or analyze apparently incriminating physical evidence. This effect may be socially desirable if the attorney advice in such cases would normally result in suppression of evidence. Because the consequences flowing from the prosecution's discovery of incriminating physical evidence will often be severe, because physical evidence may often be relatively easy to suppress, and because the fifth amendment may well reduce evidentiary sanctions for client suppression, the thesis that such advice is likely to lead to suppression is relatively plausible. If, however, much physical information that appears incriminating actually proves on investigation to be exculpatory, then the rule may also deter advice that would increase the presentation of truthful information. The apparent wide acceptance of the rule may reflect "hindsight bias" resulting from the fact that challenges to the rule occurred in cases where defendants were found guilty and where the relevant physical information was clearly inculpatory.

Our account also provides a clearer understanding of the justification for work product immunity. A recent rational actor account justifies the work product immunity on the ground that it increases the production of information to the tribunal by encouraging investigations that risk uncovering both favorable and unfavorable information.[247] Without an immunity, the account argues, litigants may have an insufficient incentive to investigate in such cases of "joint production."[248] As applied to fact investigation, there appears to be a serious doctrinal objection to this theory: if work product immunity is intended to encourage parties to risk uncovering unfavorable factual information, then it should protect that information from discovery. But the Supreme Court's statement of the doctrine and later cases interpreting amended Rule 26 of the Federal Rules of Civil Procedure both expressly state that the immunity does not protect information identified in investigation from discovery.[249]

A more plausible theory of the relation between work product

---

the name of confidentiality, it sharply restricts the lawyer's ability to correct known false evidence that the client has already presented in the course of the representation. *Id.* DR 7-102(B)(1).

246. *See supra* note 90 (citing cases following this rule).

247. Allen, Grady, Polsby & Yashko, *supra* note 230, at 385-87.

248. *Id.* at 385-86.

249. The Court in Hickman v. Taylor, 329 U.S. 495 (1947), stated that interrogatories drawn with sufficient breadth can oblige a party to disclose "all pertinent information gleaned by [the party's lawyer] through his interviews with the witnesses," *id.* at 508-09, and that "searching interrogatories" serve to reveal the "facts" in the lawyer's possession, *id.* at 513. The same result apparently follows under Federal Rule of Civil Procedure 26(b)(3). *See* 8 C. WRIGHT & A. MILLER, FEDERAL PRACTICE AND PROCEDURE § 2023, at 194 & nn.16 & 17 (1970 & Supp. 1990) (citing cases); 4 MOORE'S FEDERAL PRACTICE ¶ 26.64[1], at 26-348 (3d ed. 1989) (citing cases).

immunity and the production of information would begin with a clearer understanding of what the immunity protects. Clearly the rule protects "documents and tangible things" prepared in anticipation of litigation by a party or her agents, including her lawyer.[250] It also accords absolute or near-absolute protection to documents or tangible things that reflect the "mental impressions, conclusions, opinions and legal theories" of the party's lawyer.[251] Finally, in the view of some, the rule also protects—or at least ought to protect—the mental impressions and opinions of the party's lawyer even when they are not recorded or reflected in a document or tangible thing.[252] As it applies to factual investigation, then, the central thrust of the doctrine is to lower the risks associated with recording, manipulating, and analyzing information, rather than the risks of learning that information in investigation. Moreover, the absolute or near-absolute protection afforded to the opinions and mental impressions of attorneys reflects special concern with encouraging parties to use attorneys to manipulate and evaluate information in situations where the privilege would not apply.

The general effect of the conduct encouraged by the immunity is thus to enhance party preparation, and in particular to enhance the effects of legal advice across the full range of preparatory activities that influence the information reaching the tribunal. On balance, our account predicts that the additional preparation encouraged by the immunity—whether or not performed by a lawyer[253]—ought to increase the amount of information presented, although the overall positive effect should be most pronounced where the rule causes additional lawyer involvement. In our account, however, that overall increase in information presented will reflect a mix of conflicting effects of advice, rather than a simple increase in investigation. Moreover, to the extent that the immunity increases investigation, it will do so not by protecting information discovered in investigation from disclosure, but by decreasing the costs of party efforts to identify and execute appropriate investigative strategies and to evaluate and manipulate the fruits of those investigations.

Finally, it is important to recall that the social value of work prod-

250. FED. R. CIV. P. 26(b)(3).

251. *Id.*; Upjohn Corp. v. United States, 449 U.S. 383, 400-02 (1981) (recognizing that such materials are entitled to "special protection" but declining to decide whether they are absolutely protected).

252. Shapiro, *supra* note 45, at 1071.

253. Nonlawyers often have legal knowledge that can improve the presentation of a party's case. Even when they do not, their ability to record the results of their investigations without fear that doing so will ease the opponent's task should enhance the ability of those who are legally trained to make effective use of their work. The suggestion by Allen, Grady, Polsby, and Yashko that the extension of immunity to the product of nonlawyer investigators is difficult to explain except in terms of their "joint production" theory, is thus inaccurate. Allen, Grady, Polsby & Yashko, *supra* note 230, at 391.

uct immunity is not established simply by showing that the conduct caused by granting immunity increases the information reaching the tribunal. One must also ask how much of that preparation would take place in the absence of the immunity. If the marginal effects are slight, then they may not be worth the cost of the information lost on account of the immunity. In this connection it is relevant both that parties have very strong incentives to prepare their cases even in the absence of an immunity[254] and that an ill-judged statement in an internal memorandum or draft can be capitalized upon by a competent opponent with devastating effects. In *Hickman v. Taylor*, the Supreme Court appears to have adopted the view that the latter threat was sufficiently strong that it would significantly change preparation practices.[255] To the extent that this view is correct, the work product doctrine appears to have substantial social value.

Like our general account of confidentiality, our account of work product predicts that work product protection will be denied where it will not significantly increase the net private benefits of recording, manipulating, and analyzing information. The limitation of the immunity to materials prepared "in anticipation of litigation" is consistent with this prediction. The deterrent effect of discovery requests from the opponent is evidently heightened when the recording and analysis of information take place in the shadow of a ripening controversy with a specific opponent.[256] Our account also predicts that work product protection will be denied when there is no prospect that the additional preparation facilitated by protection will increase the flow of information to the tribunal. The rule allowing for contention interrogatories[257] and court decisions allowing for discovery of trial exhibits[258] may be consistent with this prediction. A party's theory of the case and her trial exhib-

254. *See* Waits, *Work Product Protection for Witness Statements: Time for Abolition*, 1985 WIS. L. REV. 305, 331-35 (parties have sufficient incentives to prepare without work product immunity); Easterbrook, *Insider Trading, Secret Agents, Evidentiary Privileges and the Production of Information*, 1981 SUP. CT. REV. 309, 362 (same).

255. *See Hickman*, 329 U.S. at 511 (Without immunity "much of what is now put down in writing would remain unwritten" and "[i]nefficiency, unfairness and sharp practices would inevitably develop in the giving of legal advice and in the preparation of cases for trial.").

256. *Accord* Allen, Grady, Polsby & Yashko, *supra* note 230, at 392. Those authors are, however, mistaken in suggesting that the limitation to documents and things "prepared in anticipation of litigation . . . is one of the most important pieces of evidence in support of the joint production theory." *Id.* The same limitation (or something very much like it) should apply in any account of work product which assumes (1) that the activities encouraged by granting immunity generally are socially desirable, and (2) that allowing a litigation opponent to discover the results of those activities significantly reduces their private value.

257. FED. R. CIV. P. 33(b) (allowing interrogatories that call for "an opinion or contention that relates to fact or the application of law to fact"). Significantly, such interrogatories are normally disfavored if propounded too early in the trial preparation process. *In re* Convergent Tech. Sec. Litigation, 108 F.R.D. 328, 333-38 (N.D. Cal. 1985).

258. Zimmerman v. Superior Court, 402 P.2d 212 (Ariz. 1965).

its both reflect the party's preparatory efforts and the lawyer's expertise in manipulating and evaluating information. When a party has had full discovery and a fair opportunity to prepare her case, however, preparatory activity will inevitably reach a point of diminishing returns. To protect the party's case beyond that point serves only to allow the party to surprise her opponent. The working assumption of the Federal Rules of Civil Procedure appears to be that surprise normally reduces the flow of truthful information to the tribunal and increases the flow of false information.[259] On that assumption, to extend the protection of a party's contentions and trial exhibits past the point of diminishing returns to preparation would reduce rather than increase the information reaching the tribunal.

C. Restrictions on Advice About Responding to Investigation

Some advice about responding to investigation (or other questioning) reduces the information reaching the tribunal. One might therefore think that it would be desirable to ban or restrict only such advice, while allowing other litigation advice with more desirable effects.[260] It turns out, however, that it is difficult to prohibit advice about responding to investigation without encompassing or deterring other advice that has socially desirable informational or behavioral effects. We employ our account to explore these issues for both civil and criminal cases.

Advice about responding to investigation (or questioning) can reduce the unfavorable information reaching the tribunal in three ways. First, advice about whether information is favorable or unfavorable will cause the party to withhold more unfavorable information that is unrequested or party-controlled. Second, advice can lower the party's expected sanctions for withholding information, thus increasing the amount of information she controls and withholds. Third, advice about the level of expected evidentiary sanctions can reduce the amount of unfavorable information the party discloses if parties overestimate those sanctions.

One might attempt to prevent advice likely to lead to such untoward

259. *See, e.g.*, 8 C. WRIGHT & A. MILLER, *supra* note 249, § 2001, at 17 & n.16. The conclusion that reducing surprise will improve the quality or quantity of information reaching the tribunal is not obvious. Surprise reduces the amount of time available for an opponent to investigate the facts underlying the party's presentation and to prepare a response. It therefore makes it more likely that the tribunal will receive only the information favorable to the party who benefits from surprise. For the same reason, surprise reduces the party's expected sanctions for presenting favorable false information. But rules permitting surprise may also increase the information reaching the tribunal by increasing the opponent's incentive to prepare its own case or by enabling a party to catch an opponent's witness in a lie.

260. Kaplow and Shavell, for example, put forth (without advocating) the possibility of deposing parties before allowing them to consult an attorney. Kaplow & Shavell, *supra* note 17, at 613.

results by formulating restrictions on the provision of advice that can be enforced without inquiring into the content of attorney-client communications.[261] Complete restrictions on advice about responding to investigation may, however, also deter other desirable advice. Parties receive a great deal of advice about whether information is favorable or unfavorable in connection with advice about the conduct of their own investigations. This advice should increase the amount of information reaching the tribunal. Parties also receive advice about how to categorize information that is integral to desirable advice about settlement and related primary conduct. To the extent that a ban on harmful advice about responding to investigation will encompass or deter such desirable advice, restrictions may have to be limited to special situations where they can be narrowly targeted and easily enforced. This, as we will show, is what the law in fact does.

Even if restrictions can be narrowly targeted to advice about responding to investigation, they may result in several adverse informational and behavioral effects. First, denying advice to the responding party will reduce the opponent's expected sanctions for suppressing information, and thus increase the opponent's suppression of information favorable to the party denied advice. Second, the unadvised party will recognize, categorize, and present less favorable information divulged in investigation by the opponent. Third, the lack of advice will increase the party's mistaken failure to produce favorable information. Although the party may later be advised that the omitted information is favorable, subsequent presentation may be infeasible or discounted by the tribunal, particularly if the party withheld the information by lying. Fourth, if parties without advice systematically underestimate evidentiary sanctions, depriving the party of litigation advice will decrease the favorable and unfavorable information reaching the tribunal.[262]

The rules regulating the provision of litigation advice reflect an awareness of these considerations. The easiest place to enforce restrictions on advice is at trial. When a witness is actually on the stand, advice must be provided in public and in the tribunal's presence. Moreover, restrictions on advising witnesses can easily be monitored, provided that they are limited in time. Accordingly, rules governing the examination of witnesses at trial sharply restrict advice to a testifying witness. Law-

261. Such an approach is ex ante in the sense that it attempts to prevent the legal advice from ever being provided. Another approach would be ex post in that it would allow legal advice to be provided but would only punish legal advice on how to reduce the information presented. Such an ex post approach would require observing attorney-client conferences or relying on reports of what occurred in them. This would raise issues discussed in *supra* Section V(B).

262. In addition to these informational effects, the party denied advice will experience an increase in expected sanctions for desirable withholding and for desirable production that resembles undesirable withholding.

yers may not ask leading questions of a friendly witness on direct examination: this effectively forbids advice during direct examination about whether information is favorable or unfavorable. More important, when witnesses are responding to cross-examination, lawyers cannot make "leading" objections that suggest whether particular information is favorable or unfavorable. In some cases, sequestration orders may bar lawyers from speaking with a witness on any topic between the time that the witness takes the oath and the time she is excused.

Restrictions on leading questions avoid many of the adverse informational effects of more general bans on responding to investigation. Because the opponent is not conducting the investigation, denying advice will not increase opponent suppression or reduce recognition of information divulged by the opponent. Although the party or witness may mistakenly omit favorable information, that effect will be ameliorated by the attorney's ability to ask additional nonleading questions. Nor does the restriction threaten advice about investigation, settlement, or primary conduct.

Restrictions on advice about responding to cross-examination also seem likely to generate substantial additional information while avoiding most adverse effects. Once a witness has testified on direct for the party who called her, she is likely to have produced almost all the information favorable to that party. Accordingly, information she has not presented is likely to be unfavorable. Denying advice about potential testimony on cross-examination should thus increase the amount of unfavorable information reaching the tribunal. The costs of this increase are probably small. Because cross-examination takes place before the party's lawyer and the tribunal, it should be possible to detect and sanction opponent suppression, to recognize unfavorable information divulged by the opponent, and to facilitate socially desirable withholding by objecting to questions that call for privileged information or are unduly coercive. Again, the reduction will not encompass advice to a party witness about investigation, settlement, or primary conduct.

So long as rules restricting advice to witnesses apply only when the witness is on the stand, they can be closely tailored to target only advice with doubtful informational effects. When rules about advice to witnesses extend beyond the time when the witness is on the stand, however, they pose difficult problems of enforceability and scope, particularly for party witnesses.

The problem is illustrated by *Perry v. Leeke,*[263] where the Supreme Court held that a criminal defendant's sixth amendment right to counsel was not violated by a court order that barred the defendant from consult-

263. 488 U.S. 272 (1989).

ing with his lawyer during a fifteen-minute break between the end of his testimony on direct examination and the commencement of cross-examination. In upholding the order, the Court expressly rejected the notion that the validity of the order required a showing that the lawyer was likely to engage in "unethical" conduct.[264] Rather it was "simply an empirical predicate" of the adversary system that cross-examination of an uncounseled witness is more likely to lead to the discovery of truth.[265] It was therefore sufficient to justify the order that legal advice would enable the party "to regroup and regain a poise and sense of strategy that the unaided witness would not possess."[266] The Court distinguished its earlier decision in *Geders v. United States*,[267] which had invalidated an order barring all consultation during an eighteen-hour overnight recess, reasoning that consultation during a longer break would "encompass matters that go beyond the content of the defendant's own testimony . . . such as the availability of other witnesses, trial tactics, or even the possibility of negotiating a plea bargain."[268] In contrast, during a fifteen-minute break, "it is appropriate to presume that nothing but the testimony will be discussed."[269]

The reasoning in *Perry*, and its distinction between fifteen-minute and eighteen-hour recesses, is consistent with the analysis offered here. Because a party who has completed her direct examination has already presented her favorable information, the predominant effect of advice about whether information is favorable or unfavorable or advice about how to shape her testimony to lower evidentiary sanctions will be a reduction in unfavorable information reaching the tribunal. This effect occurs whether or not the advice given to her is technically "unethical" in the sense that it amounts to "knowing" assistance in perjury. Moreover, on the Court's assumption that during a fifteen-minute break between direct and cross-examination the defendant's testimony would be the only topic of conversation, the order upheld in *Perry* posed no risk of deterring desirable advice about investigation or settlement. In the case of an overnight eighteen-hour ban on advice, however, the risk of preventing desirable advice may be increased sufficiently to justify the holding of unconstitutionality, notwithstanding the risk (which the Court expressly recognized) that advice given during an overnight consultation would reduce the amount of information reaching the tribunal just as effectively as advice given during a fifteen-minute break in testimony.[270]

264. *Id.* at 282.
265. *Id.*
266. *Id.*
267. 425 U.S. 80 (1976).
268. *Perry*, 488 U.S. at 284.
269. *Id.*
270. The Court acknowledged that the socially desirable discussions during an extended recess

As *Perry* suggests, outside the courtroom it is extremely difficult to craft enforceable restrictions on advice about responding to investigations without deterring desirable advice. Again the problem is most acute for party witnesses. Once investigation moves outside the presence of the tribunal, the opponent's opportunity and incentive to suppress favorable information presented by the party increase. The informational costs of denying advice to the responding party increase accordingly. It also becomes more difficult to prevent parties from obtaining litigation advice without barring desirable consultations about related primary conduct, settlement, or the party's own investigations. This is particularly true in civil litigation, because parties normally consult lawyers about whether to abandon, settle, or litigate their claim before an action is filed. Thus each party will already have received a good deal of advice before the tribunal is involved in any way. Since many disputes in which lawyers are consulted settle before filing, the task of monitoring this advice would be enormous. Once a case has commenced, most parties receive additional advice about settlement and investigation, and many receive advice about related primary conduct.

Since narrowly targeted restrictions on out-of-court advice would likely be ineffective and unenforceable and because broader restrictions would bar too much desirable advice, it makes sense that outside the courtroom parties are normally free to obtain advice about responding to investigation—subject only to the normal prohibition against advice that amounts to knowing assistance in crime or fraud. It is also consistent with this analysis, however, that the law severely restricts giving such non-courtroom litigation advice to persons other than the client. It is often a disciplinary offense and sometimes a crime for a lawyer to provide accurate advice to a nonparty with the intention of causing the nonparty to withhold or destroy relevant evidence, even where such withholding or destruction is lawful.[271] In such cases, the fact that the advice about responding to investigation is directed to a nonparty makes it easier to determine the likelihood that it will reduce the amount of information reaching the tribunal and also ensures that prohibiting the advice will not reduce the flow of desirable advice to the lawyer's client. Moreover, in most cases the prohibition of advice to the nonparty will not prevent her from obtaining advice from another, more disinterested source.

So far as we know, the foregoing examples represent the only cases in which litigation advice is expressly prohibited due to its informational

---

"will inevitably include some consideration of the defendant's ongoing testimony," but concluded that this "does not compromise" the defendant's right to unrestricted access to her lawyer during a longer recess. *Id.*

271. *See supra* note 39.

effects. Our account, however, should also assist in evaluating numerous other legal rules that encourage or limit advice about responding to investigation. In civil cases, these include the rule that prohibits a lawyer from knowingly communicating with a represented party concerning the subject of the representation without the consent of the party's lawyer.[272] In criminal cases, they include fifth and sixth amendment rules that govern the existence, invocation, and waiver of the criminal defendant's right to counsel before and after indictment.[273]

Depending on the motivations and knowledge of the parties and the amount of information that is party-controlled or suppressible, such rules may have important informational effects. For example, if most criminal defendants routinely overestimate how favorable their information is[274] or overestimate the sanctions for keeping silent in the face of custodial interrogation,[275] rules that make it easy to waive the pre-indictment right to counsel under the fifth amendment will increase the party-controlled unfavorable information reaching the tribunal.[276] This should generally hurt the innocent less than the guilty. On the other hand, if police officials conducting a custodial investigation are willing and able to suppress information favorable to the defendant and a substantial amount of the information likely to be uncovered in a custodial investigation is suppressible,[277] a relaxed waiver rule may reduce the government's expected

272. *See* MODEL RULES, *supra* note 1, Rule 4.2; MODEL CODE, *supra* note 2, DR 7-104(A)(1).

273. Under the fifth amendment, a party in custodial interrogation must be advised of her right to counsel, Miranda v. Arizona, 384 U.S. 436, 467 (1966), and cannot be interrogated if she invokes that right, Edwards v. Arizona, 451 U.S. 477, 484 (1981). Under the sixth amendment, a defendant has a right to counsel during any post-indictment interrogation, Massiah v. United States, 377 U.S. 201, 206 (1964), or post-indictment lineup, United States v. Wade, 388 U.S. 218, 237 (1967).

274. Indeed, even if party errors are unbiased, advice given in connection with investigation that corrects the suspect's mistakes about whether information is favorable or unfavorable may reduce the unfavorable information presented. If the party under investigation mistakenly believes that her information is, on balance, unfavorable, so that she claims the privilege, advice about responding to investigation would cause her to change her decision. Unless later presentation of the information will be infeasible or discounted, however, this will affect only the timing of her decision to produce, since the lawyer appointed for her later in the case will also counsel her to disclose the information. Ill-advised decisions to present unfavorable information, however, may well be more difficult to reverse. Accordingly, unless favorable information that is withheld during an initial interview will be discounted, denying advice about whether information is favorable or unfavorable will increase the flow of information to the tribunal.

275. Under the line of cases following Griffin v. California, 380 U.S. 609 (1965), and Doyle v. Ohio, 426 U.S. 610 (1976), the government's right to make use of silence following *Miranda* warnings, even for impeachment purposes, is extremely limited. Thus silence, at least for the period required to consult a lawyer, is essentially costless. It therefore seems quite likely that overestimating the costs is more common than underestimation, and that allowing easy waivers of counsel will have the positive effects described in text.

276. *See generally* Stuntz, *Waiving Rights in Criminal Procedure*, 75 VA. L. REV. 761 (1989) (discussing the effects of waiver).

277. Concern with the government's opportunity and motive to suppress information favorable to the defendant has sometimes figured in the Court's decisions concerning the right to counsel in pretrial investigation. For example, in United States v. Ash, 413 U.S. 300 (1973), the Supreme

sanctions for suppressing that information. That effect would reduce the amount of favorable information reaching the tribunal, harming the innocent more than the guilty. While the outcome of these calculations cannot by itself determine the social desirability of the waiver rule chosen, its relevance is clear.

Conclusion

In a liberal society, it is widely believed that it is desirable, indeed essential, for citizens to know the law.[278] We have attempted to determine the conditions under which that belief might be justified for legal advice about the litigation of factual disputes in an adversary system. While the matter ultimately turns on difficult empirical questions, our overall conclusion is positive. Much litigation advice appears to have desirable informational and behavioral effects, and advice with undesirable or ambiguous effects is often difficult to regulate without deterring desirable advice. Our positive general conclusion is striking because it is derived despite the adoption of the cynical premise that litigants and lawyers recognize no duty to obey the law, and indeed suppress or withhold information whenever it furthers their own interests. If parties are generally more law-abiding or truthful than our basic account assumes, then the effects of advice may be even more desirable.

Our conclusions, however, are richer and more refined than this general statement suggests. Indeed, a principal lesson of our analysis is that one cannot make responsible judgments about the desirability of legal advice or its regulation without attention to multiple and mixed effects. The complexity of our account stands as a rebuke to both simplistic defenders and simplistic critics of advice who reach sweeping judgments about its general desirability based on partial descriptions of its effects. In many cases, our account suggests hitherto unrecognized weaknesses and complications in arguments that have classically played a central role in the debate about the adversary system.

Defenders of advice, for example, frequently point to the value of

---

Court held that the sixth amendment did not entitle defense counsel to attend post-indictment sessions where a witness sought to identify the defendant from an array of photographs. In distinguishing such sessions from post-indictment lineups (where the right to counsel does apply) the Court argued that the defense counsel's opportunity to cross-examine the persons involved in the photo session at trial could "serve as a substitute for counsel at the pretrial confrontation." *Id.* at 316; *see also id.* at 324 (Stewart, J., concurring) (arguing that improper influence from use of photographs can be "readily reconstructed at trial"). This arguably reflects the judgment either that information cannot be effectively suppressed in a photographic lineup, or that expected sanctions for suppression were already sufficiently high to deter suppression without the presence of counsel. The majority also stressed that the "ethical responsibility of the prosecutor" would tend to minimize exploitation of opportunities to suppress. *Id.* at 320.

278. *See* L. Fuller, The Morality of Law 49-51 (1964).

competition in improving the presentation of information to the tribunal.[279] Our account suggests that legally advised competition between the parties will often have that effect, especially in the case of nonsuppressible information available to both parties. But competition can sometimes result in a reduction of information reaching the tribunal. Whether advice increases or decreases the competitive presentation of information turns out to depend on empirical questions about whether information is suppressible, who has access to it, and the misconceptions entertained by unadvised parties. Defenders of advice would do well to look more closely at those questions.

Critics of the system, on the other hand, frequently stress the harmful or doubtful effects of advice that is not balanced between the parties.[280] Our account confirms that when both parties have comparable advice, the positive effects of advice are more robust.[281] It also confirms that imbalances may have harmful or doubtful effects, particularly because they increase the ability of the more knowledgeable party to present false or prejudicial information and to impose costs on her opponent. But we also show that even unbalanced advice has a strong general tendency to benefit those who have acted desirably more than it benefits those who have acted undesirably. This will most clearly be socially desirable if the tribunal can make appropriate adjustments to its rules of decision. In a substantial range of cases, imbalances of representation may therefore produce results superior to those that would be possible if both parties were denied advice.

Beyond providing a more sophisticated understanding of general claims about the effects of advice, our account also explains many of the problems that arise in regulating it. It points to some significant classes of cases where broad restrictions on advice may be socially desirable. It also identifies several narrowly limited classes of advice, including advice to testifying witnesses and advice to nonclient witnesses, which are so likely to be harmful and so easily targeted that rules barring such advice may well be socially desirable. We also provide a clear framework for assessing rules of attorney-client confidentiality, which accurately identifies the nature of the tradeoffs required by such rules and the empirical questions that determine whether those tradeoffs will be worthwhile.

279. *E.g.*, R. POSNER, *supra* note 15, at 491-93.

280. *See, e.g.*, sources cited *supra* notes 10-13.

281. *See supra* Section II(D).

E
Perjury, Obstruction of Justice and Similar Sanctions: Optimal Level

[20]

International Review of Law and Economics (1989), 9(3–11)

OPTIMAL SANCTIONS AND THE INCENTIVE TO PROVIDE EVIDENCE TO LEGAL TRIBUNALS

STEVEN SHAVELL

Harvard Law School, Cambridge, MA 02138, USA

I. INTRODUCTION AND SUMMARY

The evidence provided by individuals who have come before legal tribunals constitutes an important source of information for the judicial system. Without such evidence, facts of relevance to a tribunal may be difficult or impossible for the tribunal to obtain. (For example, it may be that unless a person who is before a tribunal supplies the identity of a witness who would not come forward on his own, his testimony would never be heard.)

This paper will examine a model in which individuals decide rationally what evidence to offer to a tribunal,[1] given the "sanctioning function" that determines how their legal treatment will be affected by the evidence the tribunal receives.[2] Furthermore, the influence of the sanctioning function on individuals' behavior prior possibly to coming before tribunals will be ascertained. This will allow the socially optimal sanctioning function—and, importantly, the optimal sanction for failure to provide evidence—to be found. The model may be summarized as follows.[3]

An individual who has come before a tribunal will be assumed to be able to provide some facts but not others; here, to be "able to provide" a fact means that an individual can demonstrate it to the satisfaction of the tribunal. Of the evidence that he is able to provide, an individual will choose to provide that which will result in the lowest sanction, given the sanctioning function; the individual will reveal the favorable evidence available to him but not the unfavorable.

What will happen when an individual comes before a tribunal will influence his

I wish to thank Louis Kaplow, A. Mitchell Polinsky, and an anonymous referee for comments and the National Science Foundation (grant SES 8420226) for financial support.

[1]I do not examine the incentives to provide evidence of an individual who has not come before a tribunal. The reason is that one of the chief elements of interest here will be the influence of sanctions for failure to provide evidence. If a person has not come before a tribunal, such sanctions can hardly be imposed.

[2]For convenience, I will speak of individuals as defendants and of legal treatment as sanctions that might be imposed on them. The reader should bear in mind, however, that what is said will apply also to plaintiffs and the awards they might receive as a function of the evidence they provide; and to non-parties to a legal dispute who have come before a tribunal. See (iii) in the Concluding Remarks.

[3]Models in the economic literature of the incentive to provide information (see, for example, Grossman (1981), Milgrom (1981), Farrell (1986), and Shavell, forthcoming) are concerned mainly with identifying an *equilibrium* function, where the equilibrium value given the revelation of information (about, say, an item offered for sale) equals the mean of some relevant variable (the quality of the item) computed over all individuals who provide that information. The present model, by contrast, emphasizes the determination of an *optimal* (sanctioning or reward) function, that is, a function of revealed information that maximizes an objective function.

decision how to act at earlier times. An individual will consider that committing an act will have particular implications for the evidence that will, or may, subsequently describe his situation and that he will be able to establish before a tribunal.[4] If he commits a very bad act, he will expect that much, or at least a part, of the evidence that he will be able to provide to a tribunal will probably be very bad; if he commits a less serious act, the set of evidence that he will be able to provide will usually be less bad, and so forth. Anticipating this, and keeping in mind that he will reveal only the evidence that will minimize the sanction he suffers, an individual can calculate which act will be best for him to commit. In other words, the behavior of individuals in the model can be deduced given the sanctioning function. Therefore, the socially optimal sanctioning function can be determined.

The principal conclusions about the socially optimal sanctioning function depend on the ability of individuals to provide evidence or, more precisely, *on what a tribunal knows about their ability to provide evidence.* If a tribunal knows that an individual *definitely* is able to provide a type of evidence (that an individual definitely is aware of the identity of a witness), then under the optimal sanctioning function, he will be induced to supply the type of evidence. He will do so because the sanction for failure to provide the type of evidence will exceed the highest sanction he can possibly face if he does provide it. The sanction for the type of evidence that he will, accordingly, be led to provide will be set equal to the sanction that would be optimal if that type of evidence were directly observable by the tribunal—that is, were there no need for the individual to supply the evidence.

Suppose, however, that a *tribunal does not know whether an individual is able to provide a type of evidence* (whether or not the individual is aware of the identity of a witness). In this case, a sanction for failure to supply the type of evidence may turn out to be imposed because the individual may be unable to supply it. If the sanction for failure to supply the type of evidence is high, then since this sanction will sometimes be imposed, socially undesirable consequences may result. For example, the fear of bearing high sanctions because of one's potential inability to supply exonerating evidence may create a chilling effect on desirable activity. More generally, imposition of such sanctions may disturb the appropriate relationship between the character of an act and the expected sanction, leading to improper channelling of activity and improper deterrence. (In addition, the actual imposition of sanctions may be socially costly, as with imprisonment.) Thus it usually will not be socially advantageous for sanctions for failure to provide the type of evidence to be severe. On the other hand, the lower the sanction for failing to provide the type of evidence, the lower the motivation of individuals who are able to provide it to do so; those with relatively unfavorable evidence will prefer to suffer the sanction for silence. In determining the optimal sanction for failure to provide the type of evidence, the disadvantage of lowered sanctions must be weighed against the problems flowing from use of high sanctions. Also, in determining optimal sanctions for individuals who provide evidence, account must be taken of the possibility that had they been unable to do so, they would have borne the sanction for being silent.[5]

[4]The choice of an act will, of course, affect not only the evidence the individual is able to reveal but also the information the tribunal will be likely to be able to observe itself. This will be taken into account implicitly in the model.

[5]For example, it may be optimal to lower somewhat the sanction a person will bear when he is able to provide helpful evidence to his case in order to "compensate" him for the chance that he may have been unable to provide such evidence. This is a feature of the optimal sanctioning system in the solution of the model of harmful externalities in the third section.

The section below presents the general model of the provision of evidence. Then the optimal sanctioning function is determined explicitly in an illustrative version of the general model, namely, the classic model of harmful externalities. The concluding section comments on the interpretation of the analysis.

II. THE MODEL

Individuals choose among alternative acts. The act chosen by an individual will determine a probability distribution over "evidence sets." One such set will be available to an individual when he comes before a legal tribunal, something that will be assumed always to occur.[6] An individual will select from the evidence set available to him the particular evidence vector that he wishes to provide to the tribunal. The evidence vector that an individual provides will determine the sanction he bears, according to the sanctioning function employed by the tribunal. Specifically, let

a = a possible act;
e = an evidence vector that an individual might provide to the tribunal;
ξ_i = the i'th possible evidence *set* (comprised of different evidence vectors e that an individual can provide) that could be available to an individual when he comes before the tribunal; $i = 1, \ldots, n$;
$p_i(a)$ = probability of ξ_i given a;
$s(e)$ = sanction given e.

Each component e_j of an evidence vector $e = (e_., \ldots, e_m)$ will be associated with some type of information (for example, the name of a witness).[7] A component will either have an appropriate *value* (a name of a witness) or will be the symbol "ϕ," the interpretation of which will be that the individual makes no statement about the value of the component or that he cannot prove a claim about its value.

An evidence set implicitly incorporates an individual's choices over verifiable information that he may supply to the tribunal. Suppose, for instance, that an embezzler is able to provide the name of his accomplice and the amount stolen and that he may remain silent about either or both. Then (abstracting from other types of evidence) the evidence set will consist of four vectors: (ϕ,ϕ), namely, complete silence; (ϕ,amount) that is, silence about the accomplice; (accomplice, ϕ), silence about the amount stolen; and (accomplice,amount), complete information.[8] On the other hand, if the embezzler is not able to provide evidence of the amount he stole, his evidence set will consist of only two vectors, (ϕ,ϕ) and (accomplice,ϕ); if he is not able to provide evidence of his accomplice, his evidence set will consist of (ϕ,ϕ) and (ϕ,amount); and if he is unable to provide any evidence, his evidence set will consist only of (ϕ,ϕ). Alternatively, if, say, the amount the embezzler stole is observable (the victim may be able to prove to the tribunal what his losses are), his evidence set will consist of (accomplice,amount)

[6]It would be easy to allow for the possibility that an individual might not come before a tribunal, but that would not alter the conclusions and would unnecessarily complicate the model.

[7]One can imagine that there is a component for each conceivable type of information (including, for instance, a component for whether each person in the population was a witness to this or that act).

[8]If providing the name of the accomplice means that the tribunal will learn from the accomplice the amount stolen, then it will in effect become impossible for the individual to be silent about the single component "amount." Thus, an individual may not have the independent option to remain silent about each component that the tribunal cannot directly observe.

and (ϕ,amount). More generally, the jth component of the evidence vector is observable when, for *all* evidence vectors in the available evidence set, e_j equals the value of the component (rather than ϕ).

An individual will choose from the evidence set ξ_i available to him the evidence vector that results in the minimum sanction (assuming as I shall that he dislikes sanctions). In other words, the vector e that he will provide is

$$e(i) = \underset{e \in \xi_i}{\text{argmin}}\ s(e).$$

Hence, if

$u(a,s)$ = an individual's utility if he chooses act a and suffers the sanction s,

his expected utility if he chooses act a will be

$$p_1(a)u(a,s(e(1))) + \ldots + p_n(a)u(a,s(e(n))).$$

For instance, assume that if a person decides to embezzle, the evidence sets that he may have available are the first four mentioned in the previous paragraph, each with probability .25; that the sanctions are $s(\phi,\phi) = 100$, $s(\phi,\text{amount}) = .25\text{amount} + 30$, $s(\text{accomplice},\phi) = 40$, $s(\text{accomplice,amount}) = .25\text{amount}$; that the amount he would embezzle is 80; and that his utility is the amount he would embezzle less the sanction. Then his expected utility if he embezzles will be $.25[80 - \min(100,50,40,20)] + .25[80 - \min(100,40)] + .25[80 - \min(100,50)] + .25[80 - 100] = 80 - .25[20 + 40 + 50 + 100] = 27.5$.

An individual will choose the act that maximizes his expected utility.

An optimal sanctioning function maximizes the relevant measure of social welfare. (It is not necessary to specify the measure for present purposes.)

The conclusions described in the introduction can now be set forth. In doing so, let z denote the components (if any) of the evidence vector that the tribunal observes (recall the discussion of the embezzler).

Proposition. *Suppose that the tribunal knows that individuals about whom z is observed definitely are able to provide the value of a component e_j of the evidence vector. Then an optimal sanctioning function will be such that (a) the individuals will be induced to reveal the value of e_j when z is observed, for if they are silent about the value a higher sanction will be imposed.*[9] *And (b) this optimal sanctioning function will be essentially identical to a sanctioning function that would be optimal were the value of e_j observable when z is observed: individuals will be led to act the same way, provide the same evidence, and suffer the same sanctions under each sanctioning function.*

The proof of this proposition is virtually immediate. Let $s^*(e)$ be an optimal sanctioning function, and let $s^{**}(e)$ be a sanctioning function that would be optimal were the value of e_j observable when z is observed. Social welfare will clearly be at least as high under s^{**} as under s^*. Hence, if one can define a sanctioning function s under which social welfare will be as high as under s^{**}, then s must be an s^*. Now let $s(e) = s^{**}(e)$ when z is not observed; and when z is observed,

[9] I say "an" optimal sanctioning function because it may not be unique. For instance, it could be that the value of e_j is irrelevant, so that a sanctioning function that does not induce individuals to reveal the value of e_j would also be optimal.

let $s(e) = s^{**}(e)$ if the value of e_j is provided, and if the value of e_j is not provided let $s(e)$ be the maximum possible sanction (or, if sanctions are unbounded, a sanction exceeding the supremum of $s^{**}(e)$ over the possible values of e_j). If z is observed, an individual will therefore prefer to provide the value of e_j under s; it is thus clear that if z is observed an individual will provide the same evidence vector and suffer the same sanction under s as under s^{**}. And since s and s^{**} are identical if z is not observed it follows that individuals will choose the same acts, provide the same evidence, and suffer the same sanctions under s as under s^{**}. Consequently, social welfare will be the same under s and s^{**}, and so s must be an s^*. This proves the proposition.

It should be noted that the proposition does not say that individuals will be led to choose an act such that z is observed. They may not just because they would then be induced to provide the value of e_j.

If the assumption of the proposition does not hold—if some individuals are not able to provide the value of e_j—then under the sanctioning function s described in the above argument, these individuals suffer the sanction for failing to provide the value of e_j. Hence the argument cannot be applied; and, in general, the optimal sanction for failing to provide e_j will not be high enough to induce all individuals who are able to provide the value of e_j to do so. This is illustrated in the solution to the version of the model considered below.

III. EXAMPLE: SOLUTION OF THE MODEL OF HARMFUL EXTERNALITIES

Suppose that individuals choose whether to engage in an activity that will cause harm and that will yield them benefits; that the amount of harm and the level of benefits associated with engaging in the activity vary among individuals (for each individual, the benefits and the harm are exogenously fixed if he engages in the activity); and that if they do not engage in the activity, they will cause no harm and obtain no benefits. Let

b = benefits obtained by an individual if he engages in the activity;
$f(b)$ = probability density of b over different individuals; f is positive on $[0,b']$;
h = harm caused by an individual if he engages in the activity;
$g(h)$ = probability density of h over different individuals; g is positive on $[0,h']$.

The variables b and h will be assumed to be independent, the sanctions s to be non-negative money payments, and social welfare to be the benefits individuals obtain less the harm they do. Individuals will be assumed to know their b and h.

The first-best outcome is that an individual engages in the activity if and only if $b > h$.[10] This outcome is, of course, achievable if an individual's choice whether to engage in the activity and h are observable: let the sanctioning function be $s^*(h) = h$ for individuals who engage in the activity and let the sanction be 0 otherwise. Suppose, however, that all that is directly observable is whether individuals engage in the activity. (For instance, all that is directly observable is whether a firm operates; how much of a pollutant it discharges—and thus h—is not directly observable.)

Consider first the situation where individuals who engage in the activity defi-

[10] It is assumed for concreteness that if $b = h$, an individual ought not engage in the activity; similar assumptions about the case when $b = h$ are made below without comment.

nitely are able to provide h. Let the sanction $s(\phi)$ for parties who fail to provide h exceed h' (the maximum possible h) and let $s(h) = s^*(h) = h$. Also, let the sanction if an individual does not engage in the activity be 0. It is obvious that if an individual engages in the activity, he will provide h to the tribunal; hence he will engage in the activity if and only if $b > h$. (This illustrates the proposition.)

Next assume that individuals are able to provide their h only with a probability. (Firms may not be able to establish to the tribunal the quantity of the pollutant they discharge.) Let

r = probability that individuals are able to provide h; $0 < r < 1$.

Observe that the expected sanction $E(h)$ faced by an individual of type h who engages in the activity will be

$$E(h) = r[\min(s(\phi),s(h))] + (1 - r)s(\phi) \tag{1}$$

and an individual will engage in the activity if his benefit b exceeds $E(h)$, assuming, as I shall, that the sanction if he does not engage in the activity continues to be 0.

Three facts that will determine the optimal sanctioning function will now be demonstrated. The first two describe the optimal $s(h)$ given $s(\phi)$, and the third then determines the optimal $s(\phi)$.

(i) If $h > s(\phi)$, the optimal $s(h)$ is any s greater than or equal to $s(\phi)$. To show this, observe first that if $s(\phi) = 0$ the claim is trivially true since sanctions are assumed to be non-negative. If $s(\phi)$ is positive, then were the claim not true, we would have $s(h) < s(\phi)$, so that $E(h) = rs(h) + (1 - r)s(\phi) < s(\phi)$. But then if $s(h)$ is raised to at least $s(\phi)$, $E(h) = s(\phi)$. This, however, would mean that social welfare would be higher; since $s(\phi) < h$, raising $E(h)$ from a level below $s(\phi)$ to $s(\phi)$ will reduce the number of individuals who cause harm of h who undesirably engage in the activity.

(ii) If $h \leq s(\phi)$, the optimal $s(h)$ is given by

$$s(h) = \begin{cases} 0 & \text{for } h \in [0,(1 - r)s(\phi)) \\ [h - (1 - r)s(\phi)]/r & \text{for } h \in [(1 - r)s(\phi),s(\phi)]. \end{cases} \tag{2}$$

In other words, $s(h)$ is at first 0 and then rises with h, but is less than h until it equals h at $s(\phi)$. To demonstrate this, note that it is clearly optimal to set $s(h)$ such that $E(h) = h$ if that is possible. This is the case for h in $[(1 - r)s(\phi),s(\phi)]$. For these h, if $s(h)$ is as in (2), then $s(h)$ is non-negative and

$$E(h) = rs(h) + (1 - r)s(\phi) = h. \tag{3}$$

If $h < (1 - r)s(\phi)$, it is clearly best to set $s(h) = 0$, since this will minimize $E(h)$, which will still exceed h.

(iii) To determine the optimal $s(\phi)$, write social welfare, making use of (i) and (ii), as a function of the s used as $s(\phi)$. Social welfare is given by

$$\int_0^{(1-r)s}\int_{(1-r)s}^{b'} (b - h)f(b)g(h)dbdh + \int_{(1-r)s}^{s}\int_h^{b'} (b - h)f(b)g(h)dbdh$$
$$+ \int_s^{h'}\int_s^{b'} (b - h)f(b)g(h)dbdh \tag{4}$$

The first term is associated with individuals for whom $h \leq (1 - r)s$; by (2), $s(h) = 0$ for these individuals, so that $E(h) = (1 - r)s$, meaning that some of them (those with b in $(h,(1 - r)s]$) are undesirably discouraged from engaging in the activity. The second term is associated with individuals for whom h is in $[(1 - r)s,s]$; as we know from (2), $s(h)$ is such that $E(h) = h$ for these individuals, so they engage in the activity if and only if that is socially optimal. The third term is associated with individuals for whom $h \geq s$; from (i), we know that for these individuals, $s(h)$ is higher than s, so that $E(h) = s$, and some of them (those with b in (s,h)) engage in the activity when that is socially undesirable. Differentiating (4) with respect to s and canceling certain terms, one obtains the first-order condition

$$(1 - r) \int_0^{(1-r)s} [(1 - r)s - h]f((1 - r)s)g(h)dh = \int_s^{h'} (h - s)f(s)g(h)dh. \quad (5)$$

The left-hand side is the marginal cost of raising s: the loss due to undesirably discouraging more individuals with h in $[0,(1 - r)s]$ from engaging in the activity. The right-hand side is the marginal benefit from raising s: the gain due to desirably discouraging more individuals for whom $h > s$ from engaging in the activity. It is clear from (5) that the optimal $s(\phi)$ must be in the interior of $[0,h']$.

The nature of the optimal sanctioning function and the behavior of individuals is illustrated in Figure 1. Individuals who commit harms of magnitude less than $s(\phi)$ are induced to reveal their h if they can provide evidence of it; individuals with higher h keep silent even if they can provide h, that is, those with favorable evidence provide it if they can, those with unfavorable evidence do not. Also, if individuals provide h, the sanction is unequal to what would be optimal were h observable (namely, h). The sanction $s(h)$ is less than h for $h < s(\phi)$ to compensate individuals implicitly for the possibility that they will be unable to provide h and thus will bear the sanction $s(\phi)$; some of the individuals are still overdeterred, however. Individuals for whom $h > s(\phi)$ are underdeterred.

IV. CONCLUDING REMARKS

(i) The two main points of the model bear brief comment. The first point, that when individuals are known to be able to provide a type of evidence, it will be optimal to threaten to impose a high sanction to induce them to provide the evidence, seems roughly consistent with reality. If a tribunal is very sure that a person possesses some kind of information, he may be sanctioned (with the general expectation being that he will supply the information): discovery sanctions such as fines may be imposed if a party fails to comply with a discovery request when it is clear that he is capable of doing so; findings adverse to a party may be made on an issue if he has failed to produce evidence about it that he is known to hold; sanctions for contempt may be employed when a person refuses to obey a court order to supply information that he possesses; and punishment for obstruction of justice may result if a person destroys evidence in his possession to prevent its use in court.

(ii) The other point, that when individuals are able to provide a type of evidence it is not optimal to impose a very high sanction, helps to resolve what may fairly be regarded as a puzzle. Namely, how can the legal system rationally tolerate what it understands to be the usual situation in which parties and their counsel carefully cull the evidence that they present to tribunals, keeping silent about some significant part of it? On reflection, I think the reader will agree that evidence often is of a type that a tribunal cannot be sure that a person before it possesses. (How would a tribunal know whether a person before it had or had not mentioned

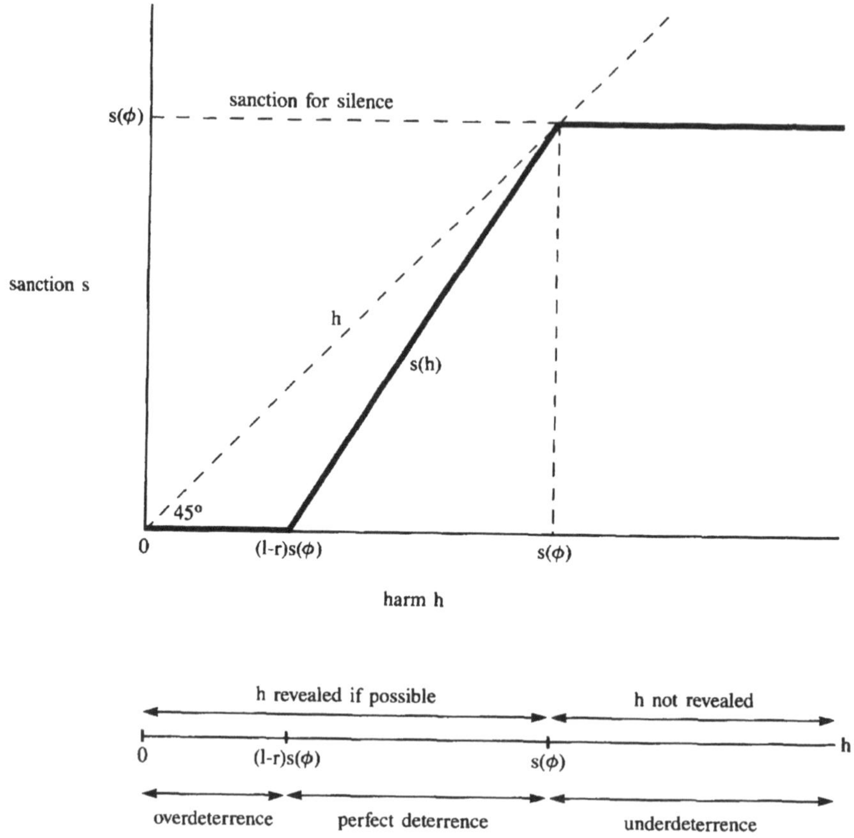

FIGURE 1. Optimal sanctions

his plans to a friend at work? Whether the person's act had or had not been witnessed by another individual whom the person knew? Whether the person had or had not established a secret bank account in which to deposit illegally obtained funds?) Were high sanctions for silence generally employed to obtain evidence, many individuals would turn out to suffer the sanctions (those who had not mentioned their plans to friends, those who did not know the identity of witnesses, and so forth), which would be undesirable. Hence, we can understand why it is that sanctions are not designed to force parties to divulge everything they know, and why, therefore, it is that they are left in a position where they reveal only what is favorable to their cases.

(iii) While this paper has examined the situation where the individuals before a tribunal are defendants, it is apparent that the principal conclusions carry over to situations where the individuals before a tribunal are plaintiffs or non-parties to a dispute. Namely, a tribunal should induce plaintiffs or nonparties to provide evidence by the threat of high sanctions if, but only if, they are known to possess the evidence. However, the socially undesirable consequences that follow from imposition of sanctions on these individuals when they truly do not have evidence are different from what was discussed above. Such imposition of sanctions discourages individuals from becoming plaintiffs, that is, from bringing suit, which may often be undesirable (it weakens deterrence and prevents injured individuals from obtaining compensation). Also, such imposition of sanctions makes individuals reluctant to appear before tribunals as non-parties, notably as witnesses, which is undesirable (it hinders acquisition of information by tribunals).

REFERENCES

Farrell, Joseph, "Voluntary Disclosure: Robustness of the Unraveling Result, and Comments on Its Importance," in Ronald Grieson (ed.), *Antitrust and Regulation*, Lexington Books, 1986, 91–103.

Grossman, Sanford, "The Informational Role of Warranties and Private Disclosure of Product Quality," 24 *Journal of Law and Economics* 461–484 (1981).

Milgrom, Paul, "Good News and Bad News: Representation Theorems and Applications," 12 *Bell Journal of Economics* 380–391 (1981).

Shavell, Steven, "A Note on the Incentive to Reveal Information," *Geneva Papers on Risk and Insurance*, forthcoming 1989.

[21]

Duke Law Journal

VOLUME 53 FEBRUARY 2004 NUMBER 4

EVIDENCE TAMPERING

CHRIS WILLIAM SANCHIRICO†

ABSTRACT

Current writing on "evidence tampering"—inclusive of the destruction, fabrication, and suppression of evidence—creates the impression that our system of litigation is in a state of fundamental disrepair. This Article suggests that this perception may merely reflect defects in the conventional view of trial's purpose. The conventional view sees trial as a stand-alone device for uncovering microhistorical truths about what has already come to pass. In contrast, this Article advocates viewing trial as but one component of the overall mechanism by which the legal system influences everyday behavior.

† Professor of Law, Business, and Public Policy, University of Pennsylvania Law School and Wharton School, Business and Public Policy Department (csanchir@law.upenn.edu). This Article has benefited from the helpful comments of workshop participants at the University of Chicago, the University of Michigan, the University of Pennsylvania, and the University of San Diego. Also beneficial were conversations and correspondence with Stephen McG. Bundy, Howard Chang, Richard D. Friedman, Edward Iacobucci, Seth Kreimer, Edward Rock, Edward Rubin, Kim Lane Scheppele, Catherine Struve, Susan Rose-Ackerman, and George Triantis. William Mulherin at the University of Pennsylvania Law Library and Barbie Selby at the University of Virginia Law Library helped to locate several elusive sources. Staff at the California Department of Justice provided generous assistance in interpreting California crime statistics. Helpful insights into the adjudication of *Lewy v. Remington* were imparted by Richard C. Miller of Monsees, Miller, Mayer, Presley & Amick, Jerry M. Kirksey of Douglas, Lynch, Haun & Kirksey, and William H. McDonald of William H. McDonald & Associates. The task of locating relevant portions of the *Lewy* docket was facilitated by kind cooperation from the Office of the Clerk of the United States District Court for the Western District of Missouri. Katherine Bierlein, Michael Diz, Adrian Guy, and John McNutt offered invaluable research assistance.

When trial is viewed less in terms of discerning past events, and more in terms of shaping future events, several apparently troublesome aspects of the existing system's treatment of evidence tampering gain substantial justification, and the way is paved for a more fruitful evaluation of current doctrine.

TABLE OF CONTENTS

INTRODUCTION

Headlines periodically remind us that the production of evidence is a game whose rules can be broken. In the 1980s, Oliver North destroyed key documents during the Justice Department's Iran-Contra investigation.[1] In the 1990s, President Clinton lied under oath about his involvement with White House intern, Monica Lewinsky.[2] In the early 2000s, Arthur Andersen shredded trunkloads of audit-related documents during an SEC inquiry into Enron's special purpose entities.[3]

In fact, according to many judges and practitioners, evidence tampering[4] is hardly confined to blockbuster events.[5] Documents that should be produced in response to a discovery request are regularly shredded, altered, or suppressed. Witnesses frequently lie to investigators, deposers, and courts. Fact finders are routinely misled by the fabrication or destruction of evidence.

Academic analysis of evidentiary foul play, however, is far from common. On the evidence scholar's bookshelf, a few lonely volumes

---

1. *See Quotations of the Day*, N.Y. TIMES, Feb. 22, 1989, at A2 ("'When the time came for Oliver North to tell the truth, he lied. When the time came for Oliver North to come clean he shredded, he erased, he altered. When the time came for Oliver North to let the light shine in, he covered up.'—John W. Keker, prosecutor.").

2. Jones v. Clinton, 36 F. Supp. 2d 1118, 1121–1125 (E.D. Ark. 1999); RONALD D. ROTUNDA, LEGAL ETHICS: THE LAWYER'S DESKBOOK ON PROFESSIONAL RESPONSIBILITY § 55-1, at 772–73 n.4 (2002).

3. Kurt Eichenwald, *Andersen Misread Depths of the Government's Anger*, N.Y. TIMES, Mar. 18, 2002, at A1; *see also* Indictment at 5–8, United States v. Arthur Andersen, LLP, No. CRH-02-121 (S.D. Tex. filed Mar. 7, 2002).

Since this Article was written, domestic icon Martha Stewart and her broker, Peter Bacanovic, were convicted of obstruction of justice, perjury, and related offenses in connection with Stewart's fortuitous sale of Imclone stock. Constance Hays & Leslie Eaton, *Stewart Found Guilty of Lying in Sale of Stock*, N.Y. TIMES, Mar. 6, 2004, at A1; *see also* Superseding Indictment, United States v. Stewart, No. 03 Cr. 717 (MGC) (S.D.N.Y. Jan. 4, 2004).

4. This Article uses the term "evidence tampering" to refer to the full range of activities by which parties alter the natural evidentiary "emissions" of the transactions and occurrences that may give rise to suit. Some of these activities add to the set of natural emissions. These include fabricating documents or things, or lying to investigators, deposers, or the court. Other activities reduce the set of natural emissions. These include destroying or preventing the creation of documents and things, or bribing witnesses not to testify. As discussed in detail in Part II, not all of these activities are subject to sanction under current law. Indeed, there is a fine line—if any line at all, in principle—between some of these activities and the legitimate "production" evidence. *See, e.g.*, Chris W. Sanchirico, *Relying on the Information of Interested——and Potentially Dishonest——Parties*, 3 AM. L. & ECON. REV. 320, 320–41 (2001) (emphasizing the importance of the probabilistic dependence of evidence presentation costs—and by extension, evidence destruction costs—to regulating out-of-court behavior). Nevertheless, for the purposes of this Article, I take as given that there is much to be said about the regulation of evidence tampering without first resolving this definitional boundary problem.

5. *See infra* Part I.

on perjury, obstruction, and spoliation[6] hide among numerous tomes on hearsay, character, privilege, experts, and the like. An uncharitable assessment might characterize the field as more concerned with whether the declarant herself testifies than with whether what she says is truthful. To be sure, rules prohibiting hearsay are often said to be designed in part to prevent foul play.[7] But notwithstanding sideways glances of this sort, evidence tampering has been something of a Medusa in evidence scholarship. Though recognizing its presence, the field has largely been reluctant to stare directly at the problem.

Among the few scholars who have investigated the web of rules that police evidence tampering, the most common reaction might be characterized as dismay. Some distillation reveals that this response is largely inspired by two perceptions regarding the current system. First, commentators perceive a dissonance between the apparent epidemic of evidence tampering, on the one hand, and the leniency of the rules prohibiting such behavior on the other.[8] Second, commentators view the practical prohibitions that do exist as myopic, given the almost exclusive focus of these prohibitions on tampering directly connected to specific ongoing or imminent litigation. Such rules, it is argued, merely encourage parties to shift their manipulative behavior "upstream" toward the underlying transaction or occurrence and away from specific litigation, with little or no impact on the problem.[9]

This Article allies itself with the small existing literature on evidence tampering in viewing the topic as worthy of far more attention than it receives. It parts company with that literature, however, in proposing that the dismay expressed in previous scholarship may well be misplaced. It contends that such dismay is more the result of a conceptual imbalance regarding the object of evidentiary process than an indication that the current system is in a state of fundamental disrepair.

6. The term "spoliation" most commonly refers to the destruction or alteration of documents, though its meaning may also encompass a broader range of activities. *See* Jay E. Rivlin, Note, *Recognizing an Independent Tort Action Will Spoil a Spoliator's Splendor*, 26 HOFSTRA L. REV. 1003, 1004 n.2 (1998).

7. *See, e.g.*, GRAHAM C. LILLY, AN INTRODUCTION TO THE LAW OF EVIDENCE 180–81 (1996) (listing exposing deception as a purpose of cross-examination and a basis for the hearsay rule).

8. *See infra* notes 52–96 and accompanying text.

9. *See infra* notes 119, 360, and accompanying text.

The imbalance concerns the ex ante versus ex post purposes of law. Regarding law's ex ante function, one need not look far for explanation or justification. When it comes to analyses of the "substantive law," the idea that legal rules set incentives for everyday behavior—incentives to perform as contracted, to disclose accurate financial information, to take reasonable precaution, to adopt a safe product design, to eschew physical violence—occupies a central position.[10] In recent decades, the importance of this ex ante approach has only increased, as law and economics has become ever more assimilated into legal scholarship.[11] In the modern teaching of torts, contracts, or criminal law, explicit reference to how such legal rules influence behavior is *de rigueur*.

At the same time, the study of the essential informational link between the substantive law and the day-to-day behavior that it supposedly regulates—namely, evidentiary process—retains a predominantly ex post perspective. Most analyses of evidence law take litigation's prime object to be the discovery of truth about past events.[12] The role that evidence law plays alongside the substantive law in shaping truths that have yet to materialize receives scant

10. *See, e.g.*, Gary T. Schwartz, *Reality in the Economic Analysis of Tort Law: Does Tort Law Really Deter?*, 42 UCLA L. REV. 377, 378–79, 422–23 (1994) (citing deterrence as the primary rationale for tort law among mainstream legal scholars).

11. *See* ROBERT COOTER & THOMAS ULEN, LAW AND ECONOMICS 1–3 (3d ed. 2000) (providing evidence of the influence of economics on legal scholarship).

12. *See, e.g.*, William Twining, *Evidence and Legal Theory*, 47 MOD. L. REV. 261, 272 (1984) (stating that according to the "dominant underlying theory of evidence . . . the primary end of adjudication is rectitude of decision"). With specific relation to evidence tampering, see JAMIE S. GORELICK ET AL., DESTRUCTION OF EVIDENCE § 1.11, at 14 (1989) ("The most obvious and perhaps the strongest justification for restricting the destruction of evidence is that destruction reduces the likelihood that the judicial process will reach accurate results."); John H. Beckstrom, *Destruction of Documents with Federal Antitrust Significance*, 61 NW. U. L. REV. 687, 689 (1966) (discussing the truth-finding benefits of a statute requiring businesses subject to federal antitrust laws to retain certain documents for a period of time to help prevent document destruction); Dale A. Nance, *Missing Evidence*, 13 CARDOZO L. REV. 831, 832, 881–82 (1991) (arguing that law's response to the "missing evidence" problem evinces its primary concern with trial accuracy); Charles R. Nesson, *Incentives to Spoliate Evidence in Civil Litigation: The Need for Vigorous Judicial Action*, 13 CARDOZO L. REV. 793, 793 (1991) ("[Spoliation] is a form of cheating which blatantly compromises the idea of the trial as a search for the truth."); Dale A. Oesterle, *A Private Litigant's Remedies for an Opponent's Inappropriate Destruction of Relevant Documents*, 61 TEX. L. REV. 1185, 1187–88 (1983) (analyzing document destruction in light of increased truth-finding and litigation costs); Lisa C. Harris, Note, *Perjury Defeats Justice*, 42 WAYNE L. REV. 1755, 1755 (1996) ("[T]he crime of perjury is the antithesis of truth that is the ultimate objective of the judicial system.").

attention.[13] Oddly, this is largely true even among the few economics-oriented scholars who study evidence.[14]

---

13. To be sure, the fact that the ex post perspective predominates the study of process does not mean that it reigns in isolation. Nearly all proceduralists are willing to admit a place for "deterrence" in the pantheon of social policy objectives by which they take the measure of doctrine. *See, e.g.*, GORELICK ET AL., *supra* note 12, § 1.11, at 15 ("[D]estruction of evidence strikes indirectly at . . . utilitarian goals served by [substantive law]."). But whereas the social objective of truth-finding has finely chiseled features following generations of careful attention, "deterrence" remains more or less a block of stone.

Several authors have challenged the dominance of ex post truth-seeking by advocating for alternatives other than primary activity incentive setting. *See, e.g.*, LEO KATZ, ILL-GOTTEN GAINS: EVASION, BLACKMAIL, FRAUD, AND KINDRED PUZZLES OF THE LAW 59–60, 67–73 (1996) (arguing that aspects of evidence law difficult to reconcile with the consequentialist goal of accurate trial outcomes are well explained by recourse to deontological concerns regarding the path taken to reach such outcomes); STEPHAN LANDSMAN, THE ADVERSARY SYSTEM: A DESCRIPTION AND DEFENSE 3 (1984) (emphasizing the importance of dispute resolution rather than truth-seeking in the adversary system); Mirjan Damaska, *Truth in Adjudication*, 49 HASTINGS L.J. 289, 303–04 (1998) (discussing how a focus on lawmaking in legal proceedings reduces the importance of fact-finding accuracy); David P. Leonard, *The Use of Character to Prove Conduct: Rationality and Catharsis in the Law of Evidence*, 58 U. COLO. L. REV. 1, 2–3 (1986–87) (pointing to trial's role in producing social and individual "catharsis," achieved through visceral satisfaction with legal process); Charles Nesson, *The Evidence or the Event? On Judicial Proof and the Acceptability of Verdicts*, 98 HARV. L. REV. 1357, 1358, 1359, 1373, 1378 (1985) (arguing that the purpose of judicial process is to induce individuals to internalize the instruction of the law and, to this end, to produce "acceptable verdicts," which are not necessarily "probable verdicts").

14. *See, e.g.*, Paul Milgrom & John Roberts, *Relying on the Information of Interested Parties*, 17 RAND J. ECON. 18, 30 (1986) (analyzing the incentive to omit evidence and positing truth revelation as the policy objective); *see also* Luke M. Froeb & Bruce H. Kobayashi, *Naive, Biased, Yet Bayesian: Can Juries Interpret Selectively Produced Evidence?*, 12 J.L. ECON. & ORG. 257, 257 (1996) (arguing that the legal system is likely to generate unbiased estimates of liability and damages despite the jury's naiveté and initial bias); Daniel L. Rubinfeld & David E.M. Sappington, *Efficient Awards and Standards of Proof in Judicial Proceedings*, 18 RAND J. ECON. 308, 309 (1987) (analyzing standards of proof and positing as the social objective the minimization of the sum of loss-weighted false convictions, loss-weighted false acquittals, and the litigation effort of defendants); Joel Sobel, *Disclosure of Evidence and Resolution of Disputes: Who Should Bear the Burden of Proof*, *in* GAME-THEORETIC MODELS OF BARGAINING 341, 351–59 (Alvin Roth ed., 1985) (analyzing a model in which maximizing social welfare is equivalent to minimization of loss-weighted trial error plus evidence costs).

In the law review literature, see, for example, Stephen McG. Bundy & Einer Richard Elhauge, *Do Lawyers Improve the Adversary System? A General Theory of Litigation Advice and Its Regulation*, 79 CAL. L. REV. 313, 381 (1991):

> Under a theory of adjudication that emphasizes deterrence, [an] unskewed increase in favorable and unfavorable information presented ought to improve the tribunal's ability to distinguish desirable from undesirable conduct. This in turn increases expected sanctions for those who act undesirably at the same time that it decreases sanctions for those who act desirably.

and Richard A. Posner, *An Economic Approach to the Law of Evidence*, 51 STAN. L. REV. 1477, 1480–84 (1999), which posits trial error minimization as the goal of evidence law.

This Article suggests that the sizable gap between how the system actually regulates evidentiary foul play and how commentators believe it should is largely the result of the fact that the literature's treatment of litigation's ex ante purpose is disproportionately cursory compared to the prominence of this purpose in actual system design. In particular, the Article shows that both sources of scholarly consternation regarding evidence tampering—the law's apparently Neronian attitude toward evidence tampering, as well as the supposedly myopic approach of the steps it does take—are more easily reconciled with an approach to evidence

---

There are exceptions. *See, e.g.*, A. Mitchell Polinsky & Steven Shavell, *Legal Error, Litigating and the Incentive to Obey the Law*, 5 J.L. ECON. & ORG. 99, 99–100 (1989) (examining the relationship between deterrence and truth-finding); *see also* Louis Kaplow, *The Value of Accuracy in Adjudication: An Economic Analysis*, 23 J. LEGAL STUD. 307, 312–14 (arguing that when there is perfect information about whether an accident has occurred, there is no incentive difference between charging the injurer with the harm that she expected to cause or the harm that she actually did cause, even though the later assessment of damages is in a sense more accurate); Louis Kaplow & Steven Shavell, *Accuracy in the Assessment of Damages*, 39 J.L. & ECON. 191, 192, 194, 201–02 (1996) (claiming that "accuracy in assessment of harm cannot influence the behavior of injurers . . . to the degree that they lack knowledge of the harm they might cause when deciding on their precautions"); Chris W. Sanchirico, *Character Evidence and the Object of Trial*, 101 COLUM. L. REV. 1227, 1259–63 (contrasting "trace evidence" and "predictive evidence" and arguing, in the context of character evidence, that the use of "predictive evidence" at trial, though helpful for truth-finding, may be harmful for primary activity incentive setting); Chris W. Sanchirico, *Games, Information and Evidence Production: With Application to English Legal History*, 2 AM. L. & ECON. REV. 342, 342–43 (2000) (extending the model in Sanchirico, *supra* note 4, to examine the trade-off between the "fixed" and "variable" evidentiary costs of litigation); Sanchirico, *supra* note 4, at 320 (modeling "the role of evidence production in the regulation of private behavior via judicial and administrative process"); Joel Schrag & Suzanne Scotchmer, *Crime and Prejudice: The Use of Character Evidence in Criminal Trials*, 10 J.L. ECON. & ORG. 319, 319–24 (1994) (finding that the optimal threshold quantum of evidence for guilt is systematically lower when the object is taken to be error minimization, rather than maximal deterrence); Chris W. Sanchirico, Enforcement by Hearing: How the Civil Law Sets Incentives (Columbia Economics Dep't, Discussion Paper No. 95-9603, 1995) (first circulated version of model in Sanchirico, *supra* note 4); Chris W. Sanchirico & George Triantis, Evidentiary Arbitrage: The Fabrication of Evidence and the Verifiability of Contractual Performance 2–4 (Sept. 2002) (unpublished manuscript, on file with the *Duke Law Journal*) (questioning the emphasis on "verifiability" in contract scholarship), *available at* http://papers.ssrn.com/sol3/Delivery.cfm/99030901.pdf?abstractid=10033.

Note that a sizable portion of the economic analysis of *procedure* does ground itself in the goal of setting incentives for everyday behavior. However, this literature is not concerned with the issue of how claims are proven; most models simply posit exogenous probabilities for possible trial outcomes. Rather, the focus of this research program is on other aspects of litigation, such as filing and settlement behavior. *See generally* ROBERT BONE, BONE'S CIVIL PROCEDURE: THE ECONOMICS OF CIVIL PROCEDURE (2003) (surveying major advances in the economics of civil procedure).

law that emphasizes setting "primary activity"[15] incentives rather than discerning past primary activity behavior.

Consider first the law's purportedly lackadaisical attitude toward tampering. Determining whether the law devotes an appropriate amount of energy to the problem of evidence tampering requires understanding the social costs and benefits of enforcing evidence-tampering law.

The social costs of anti-tampering enforcement, which are well understood by scholars in this area,[16] are roughly the same whether one takes the purpose of process to be truth-finding or primary activity incentive setting. Accordingly, such costs do not play a leading role in distinguishing these two approaches. Nor, therefore, do they play a leading role in this Article. Nonetheless, it is important to bring these costs to the fore upfront, to take off the table the notion that more enforcement is always better under any approach.

Such social costs consist essentially of the costs of running a second layer of legal process to adjudicate behavior, not in the primary activity, but in the primary layer of legal process.[17] Prosecuting a litigant for obstructing[18] her primary prosecution for narcotics trafficking, for instance, requires diverting prosecutorial resources away from other offenses, including narcotics crimes. The obstruction defendant, in addition, will divert private resources away from potentially productive activity toward her second-layer defense. And society must then pause to entertain arguments and evidence on each of the several elements of the obstruction crime. Likewise, imposing sanctions for the destruction of evidence under either specific procedural rules[19] or the court's "inherent power"[20] requires holding secondary hearings to determine whether evidence was in fact destroyed, and if so, its likely content, the destroyer's state of

15. Following common usage, I use the term "primary activity" to refer to the underlying transaction or occurrence that may give rise to litigation.

16. *See, e.g.*, Oesterle, *supra* note 12, at 1187 (analyzing the effect of evidence destruction on litigation costs); GORELICK ET AL., *supra* note 12, § 3.11, at 96 (describing the costs of hearings on evidence tampering).

17. Indeed, the costs of policing tampering accrue in a theoretically infinite regress, as was hinted at when the government recently indicted a witness for perjuring himself in Martha Stewart's trial for perjury, obstruction, and related offenses. Jonathan D. Glater, *Stewart Stock Case is Jolted by Charge That an Agent Lied*, N.Y. TIMES, May 22, 2004, at A1.

18. *See infra* Part II.A.1.

19. *See infra* Part II.B.1.

20. *See infra* Part II.B.2.

mind, and the extent to which the destruction prejudiced the other side.[21]

Unlike the social costs of policing and punishing evidence tampering, the social benefits of these activities differ markedly depending on whether one takes a truth-finding or primary activity approach. These different benefits are the subject of Part III. As explained therein, truth-finding benefits come primarily from two sources: the deterrence of tampering and the ability to rectify trial outcomes when those tamperers who are not deterred are caught in the act.[22] In contrast, and somewhat counterintuitively, the main primary activity benefit of increasing anti-tampering enforcement derives from the fact that such enforcement worsens the prospect of ending up as a litigant who still finds the tampering worthwhile.[23]

These different sources of social benefit lead to different views of the appropriate intensity of anti-tampering enforcement.[24] The truth-finding benefits of increasing anti-tampering enforcement turn out to have a self-enhancing quality: the greater the current level of enforcement, the greater the incremental benefits of additional enforcement.[25] This quality is largely inconsistent with a middling level of enforcement effort. Were the truth benefits of increasing anti-tampering enforcement up to a middling level worth the social cost, so too would be increasing enforcement from a middling level to a high level.[26] In contrast, the primary activity benefits of anti-tampering enforcement are self-*dampening*: the more we increase anti-tampering enforcement, the less reason there is to continue to increase it.[27] It follows that from a primary activity perspective, the law's seemingly halfhearted approach may well be appropriate.[28]

The Article's discussion of general enforcement effort centers on this distinction between self-enhancing truth benefits and self-dampening primary activity benefits. But, in fact, expressions of

21. *See, e.g.*, GORELICK ET AL., *supra* note 12, § 3.11, at 96 (recounting a case where the hearing to determine whether the spoliator knew that the destroyed documents were relevant "lasted 23 days and generated 3,000 pages of transcript, approximately 2,000 pages of depositions introduced into evidence, and thousands of pages of documentary exhibits").

22. *See infra* Part III.A.3.

23. *See infra* Part III.A.4.

24. *See infra* Part III.B.

25. *See infra* Part III.B.2.

26. *See infra* Part III.B.3.

27. *See infra* Part III.B.1.

28. *See infra* Part III.B.3.

dismay regarding the law's laissez-faire attitude toward evidence tampering implicate not just the general intensity of enforcement, but also the methods of enforcement employed. Here too, as explained in Part III, the implications of the primary activity approach are both distinct from those of the truth-finding approach and better aligned with current law.[29]

First, in creating a given level of legal risk for the potential tamperer, the primary activity approach provides less of a reason than the truth-finding approach to emphasize the frequency with which tampering is detected, as opposed to the size of the sanction imposed.[30] And indeed, though it may be that only a small proportion of tamperers are caught under the current regime—as is often claimed[31]—when they are caught, punishments can be severe.[32]

Second, in the event that tampering is uncovered, there is less reason under the primary activity approach than under the truth-finding approach to correct litigation outcomes that have already been skewed as a result of the tampering.[33] This may help explain the law's otherwise dismaying reluctance to make such ex post corrections under current law.[34]

The second source of scholarly dismay with evidence tampering law is commonly characterized not as a problem of lax enforcement, but as a problem of focus—myopia, to be specific. As noted, the law tends to penalize evidence tampering only when it occurs far downstream in the flow from primary activity through filing, discovery, and trial.[35] After challenging conventional explanations for this enforcement regularity, Part IV of this Article puts forward an alternative explanation founded on how the private benefits of evidence tampering change along the course of litigation.

The point of departure in Part IV is the suggestion that our system of fact-finding is remarkably inscrutable when viewed from an upstream perspective. A manufacturer of dangerous products, for example, may have little sense ex ante of precisely which evidentiary emissions will end up as damaging evidence in future lawsuits.

29. *See infra* Part III.C.

30. *See infra* Part III.C.1–2.

31. *See infra* Part III.C.3.

32. *See infra* Part II.

33. *See infra* Part III.C.1–2.

34. *See infra* Part III.C.3.

35. *See infra* Part II.

Exacerbating this uncertainty is the fact the plaintiff is in large measure free to meet her burden of persuasion however she prefers—using whatever combination of evidentiary offerings she chooses.

Whatever its drawbacks along other dimensions, the ex ante inscrutability of fact-finding lowers the private benefits of evidence tampering. When one is less able to predict whether a given piece of evidence will be decisive in future litigation, the benefits of tampering with it are reduced.[36]

Clearly, however, the evidentiary lay of the land comes into sharper focus for the parties as they head toward trial. By the time they pass through process's lower reaches, therefore, tampering is no longer as effectively discouraged by the system's erstwhile inscrutability. Consequently, other more direct devices—like spoliation inferences, discovery sanctions, or the threat of obstruction charges—become necessary to fill the growing regulatory void.[37]

These are the main substantive points of the Article. But before turning to their detailed exposition, some clarifying remarks on scope and methodology are in order.

After scarcity, the second most notable feature of scholarship on evidence tampering is fragmentation.[38] In general, the few scholars who have written in the area write on either perjury,[39] or evidence destruction,[40] or missing witnesses,[41] or some other isolated genre of manipulation. Very few treat the problem of evidence manipulation generically.[42]

But despite the inevitable sacrifice of detail and the necessity of spanning several fields of legal scholarship, there is arguably much to

36. *See infra* Part IV.A.

37. *See infra* Part IV.C.

38. *Cf.* Lawrence B. Solum & Stephen J. Marzen, *Truth and Uncertainty: Legal Control of the Destruction of Evidence*, 36 EMORY L.J. 1085, 1191–92 (1987) (criticizing "doctrinal isolationism" even within the specific rules governing evidence destruction).

39. *See, e.g.*, Rebecca Kislak & John J. Donoghue, *Perjury*, 36 AM. CRIM. L. REV. 957 (1999).

40. *See, e.g.*, GORELICK ET AL., *supra* note 12; MARGARET M. KOESEL ET AL., SPOLIATION OF EVIDENCE: SANCTIONS AND REMEDIES FOR DESTRUCTION OF EVIDENCE IN CIVIL LITIGATION (2000).

41. *See, e.g.*, Robert H. Stier, Jr., *Revisiting the Missing Witness Inference—Quieting the Loud Voice from the Empty Chair*, 44 MD. L. REV. 137 (1985).

42. Exceptions include Joseph M. Livermore, *Absent Evidence*, 26 ARIZ. L. REV. 27 (1984), who considers simultaneously missing witness instructions, use of weaker evidence when stronger evidence is available, and the failure to create or preserve evidence, and Nance, *supra* note 12, who deals with "missing evidence" generically.

be gained from an integrated treatment, if only because the potential evidence manipulator is likely also to take a holistic approach, viewing fabrication, destruction, suppression, coercion, bribery, and the like as potential substitutes and complements. This Article specifically attempts to parallel the manipulator's integrated approach.

Accordingly, the Article is forced to make the requisite sacrifices to doctrinal detail, both generally throughout, and also specifically, by focusing on the regulation of evidence tampering as it affects civil litigation in federal district court between private parties. This focus certainly does not insulate the project from administrative or criminal law, since these may be implicated by private suit behavior. But it does, nonetheless, bound the topic. Not considered herein, for example, are the special constitutional issues surrounding the destruction of evidence by police and prosecutors.[43]

Second, a remark on method. Following Professor Nesson, who in turn takes his lead from Justice Holmes,[44] this Article measures anti-tampering law by its effect on the behavior of the "bad person": the person who makes a coolly "rational" assessment of whether shredding, fibbing, or forging furthers her selfish interests, with no serious consideration of the ethical implications of her behavior. Nesson justifies designing doctrine according to its effect on the "bad" based on the risk that market evolutionary forces will otherwise drive out the "good."[45] The choice of a similar approach in this Article derives in part from Nesson's concern, but also from an additional consideration that goes more to incidence than evolution. Even if it were determined, contrary to Nesson's hypothesis, that an

43. *See, e.g.*, GORELICK ET AL., *supra* note 12, §§ 6.1–6.25, at 205–48 (discussing the problems that arise when evidence is destroyed by prosecutors or police in criminal proceedings).

44. *See* Nesson, *supra* note 12, at 795:

> Holmes tells us to consider the law from the vantage of a "bad man" who cares only for the material consequences of his actions . . . . Unlike good men and women who are influenced by conscience, the bad man is unmoved by soft considerations of ethics and morality except as they translate, through the actions of others, into bottom line effects.

(citing Oliver Wendell Holmes, *The Path of the Law*, 10 HARV. L. REV. 457, 459 (1897)).

45. *See id.* at 805:

> I do not believe that lawyers are stereotypically Holmesian bad men, or that the law should assume that they are. But neither are they saints. Many lawyers will consider these incentives and succumb to the powerful temptation to spoliate. And once some lawyers begin to serve their clientele through spoliation, the marketplace will force others to follow suit.

evolutionarily stable majority of litigants behave legally and ethically,[46] a system not specifically designed to guard against the minority who manipulate it would be a system that essentially taxes the ethical to subsidize the unethical.

A final point on methodology. Although this Article is concerned with explaining existing law, the object here is not to provide just-so stories for existing doctrine. In the first place, the justifications for existing law that are provided apply only to the broadest contours of the law in this area. A large set of interesting (though arguably secondary) issues are left aside. Secondly, as the reader will see, the analysis herein is less a justification than a suggestion to revise the justifying criteria—by shifting the focus from truth-finding to primary activity incentive setting.

That said, the Article does argue for this revision of justifying criteria specifically by making the case that the implications of the primary activity approach fit better with existing doctrine. This reflects the methodological conviction that it is in some cases legitimate to discipline legal analysis by treating as a "rebuttable presumption" the proposition that the basic outline of existing law makes sense.

Anchoring the analysis in existing law may be especially justified when it comes to evidence tampering, where the gap between what the law is and what most scholars believe it should be has been so persistent over time. Modern treatments of evidence tampering may well entice the reader with the claim that the problems of spoliation and perjury have become much more serious in recent years. But, in fact, researchers in this area have been making similar claims of urgency for at least the last five decades. In what remains one of the most thoughtful (and undervalued) treatments of document destruction, Professor Beckstrom, writing in 1966, warns of the growing prevalence of document "retention" policies (twice as many at U.S. corporations in 1961 as in 1957),[47] discusses the existence of firms specializing in the "storage" of business documents,[48] considers

46. Behavioral law and economics offers compelling evidence that some portion of the population is indeed "fair-minded." *See, e.g.*, Colin F. Camerer & Richard H. Thaler, *Ultimatums, Dictators and Manners*, 9 J. ECON. PERSP. 209, 209 (1995); Ernst Fehr & Simon Gachter, *Fairness and Retaliation: The Economics of Reciprocity*, 14 J. ECON. PERSP. 159, 159 (2000) (documenting that "many people deviate from purely self-interested behavior in a reciprocal manner").

47. Beckstrom, *supra* note 12, at 688–89.

48. *Id.* at 714.

the impact of data processing and computer science,[49] and attests to the growing prevalence of document destruction in antitrust settings.[50] Things have certainly changed since 1966. But the gap between scholarship and practice is apparently not one of them.

The rest of the Article is organized as follows. Parts I and II critically assess the two above-mentioned sources of scholarly dismay on their own terms. In particular, Part I examines the dual empirical proposition that the law is lackadaisical in policing evidence tampering and that such tampering is commonplace in actual process. Part II assesses the claim that what practical prohibitions exist are too exclusively focused on activities directly connected in time and effect to specific ongoing or imminent litigation. Because of the nature of these respective claims, Part I concerns mainly data, Part II mainly doctrine. Taken together the two parts also serve as a general review of evidence tampering in law and practice, an exercise justified, perhaps necessitated, by the dearth of attention devoted to evidence tampering in scholarship to date.[51]

Parts III and IV contrast the primary activity and truth-finding approaches to the two sources of scholarly unease. Part III concerns the law's purportedly lackadaisical attitude. Part IV addresses the law's apparently myopic approach. Concluding remarks and a technical appendix complete the Article.

---

49. *Id.* at 714–15.

50. *Id.* at 768–69.

51. Readers who wish to move quickly to the Article's main points, however, can focus on the summaries in Sections I.C. and II.E.

III. IS THE LAW TOO LAX?

According to your grandfather, a job worth doing is a job worth doing well. According to your management consultant, 20 percent of the effort yields 80 percent of the results. Neither admonishment, of course, is as universally valid as these advisors make it seem. The right amount of effort to devote to a task depends upon the relative trajectories of costs and benefits as effort is increased. Sometimes, for example, the benefits quickly level off, and 20 percent is nearly as good as 80 percent, at one quarter the cost. Sometimes, in contrast, the benefits are initially elusive, and 80 percent, though four times more expensive, is fifty times more effective.

When it comes to society's task of policing evidentiary manipulation, the trajectory of social benefits is starkly dependent on what one takes to be the object of trial. This in turn produces significant differences in what one views as the right amount of anti-tampering enforcement. As shown in this Part, under the conventional view of trial as a search for truth, there is good reason to believe that the effectiveness of anti-tampering enforcement grows, over much of its range, with each additional degree of effort devoted to the task.[339] It follows that, from a truth-finding perspective, policing evidentiary foul play is likely to be one of those jobs that is worth doing well, if it is worth doing at all.

And yet, your grandfather would probably be disappointed by the current system of anti-tampering enforcement. As demonstrated in Part I, the law apparently regards antimanipulation enforcement as a job worth doing halfheartedly. One possible response is to conclude that the litigation system is now, and has been for some time, in a state of fundamental disrepair. An alternative reaction, however, is to entertain the possibility that uncovering microhistorical truths about past transactions and occurrences is not, in fact, the primary purpose of trial—that trial's primary purpose lies not in discovering what happened, but in shaping what happens.

Shifting perspective from already filed cases to still undecided conduct does in fact raise the very real possibility that the current system is more savvy than sloppy. As this Part establishes, if trial is regarded as but one component of a larger mechanic directed at shaping everyday behavior, the effectiveness of anti-tampering enforcement declines with each additional degree of effort devoted to the task. It follows that, from a primary activity incentive perspective, anti-tampering enforcement may very well be a job worth doing "poorly"; a task for which 20 percent of the effort does indeed yield 80 percent of the benefit.

Although fleshing out the foregoing claims is a central purpose of this Part of the Article, a number of other points of independent interest lie en route, and these will also be developed.

As the preceding discussion suggests, the key to comparing optimal enforcement levels under alternative social objectives is to compare how the *incremental* social benefits of additional enforcement depend upon the current *level* of enforcement. But before understanding how incremental benefits *change*, one must first understand their source and nature. This is the object of this Part's first Section. Section A establishes that such incremental benefits are markedly different depending on whether one views truth-finding or primary activity incentive-setting as the object of trial.

339. *See infra* Part III.B.

The analysis in Section A has independent conceptual interest apart from its role in the comparison of optimal enforcement levels. It adds to our understanding of the extent to which primary activity incentive setting is not—as most would assume[340]—an ally for truth-seeking in the competition among social objectives that shapes procedural and evidentiary law.

After establishing this difference in the nature and source of incremental social benefits, the analysis moves on to examine the implications of this difference for the law of anti-tampering enforcement. Section B returns to the comparison of how the incremental benefits of additional enforcement depend on the current level of enforcement. Based on this comparison, it concludes that the law's halfhearted regulation of evidence tampering is far more easily reconciled with a primary activities approach to trial than with the conventional conception of that institution as a truth-seeking exercise.

Section C then considers the optimal *method* of enforcement, as opposed to its optimal *level*. The inclusion in this Part of some discussion of the law's chosen method of enforcement is warranted by the fact that some portion of the general claim that the law is too lax is probably best regarded as a criticism of enforcement method, rather than overall enforcement intensity. Consider, for example, the claim, examined in Part I, that too few perjurers are caught. This claim by itself is incomplete as a statement about the overall intensity of enforcement because it does not take into account how much the law invests in sanctioning those who *are* caught. The claim gains coherence, however, if it is interpreted as a criticism of the law's chosen balance between sanction level and detection frequency—in particular, that the law relies too little on detection and too much on sanction. Likewise, commentary that specifically derides the law's refusal, as discussed in Part II, to go back and correct tampered litigation outcomes is directed not at the law's overall enforcement level, but at the fact that the law has chosen to downplay a particular type of remedy. Section C of this Part concludes that both of these aspects of the law's chosen method of enforcement—its de-emphasis on both detection and correction—are also more easily reconciled with primary activity incentive setting than with truth-finding. Thus whether one measures laxity in levels or in methods, the primary activity approach is a better fit for the data of existing law.

340. *See, e.g.*, *supra* note 14.

Many of the arguments made in this Part are supplemented by discussion and formal analysis in the Appendix.[341]

A. The Purpose of Policing Evidence Tampering

1. *Thought Experiment.* To fix ideas, we will focus throughout this Part on the following thought experiment involving the law of product liability. Upstream, in the primary activity, a manufacturer decides whether to adopt a safe design for its product. Downstream, closer to, or even during litigation, the manufacturer decides whether to destroy documents relevant to product safety, including, for example, those produced by product testing.[342] The question for consideration in this Section A: what are the social benefits of marginally increasing the expected sanction for document destruction in this setting? In particular, how do the social benefits of this policy differ when the object is to provide incentives for safe product design rather than to find the truth about whether a safe design was adopted?

2. *A Taxonomy of Potential Evidence Tamperers.* The best place to begin the analysis is downstream, with the following inquiry: when would the manufacturer destroy evidence? No doubt, the moral sensitivity of managers and employees is one determinant. But, given the focus here on Holmes' "bad person,"[343] let us consider a colder calculus. Thus, imagine that the manufacturer destroys documents when it believes that the documents' expected impact on the outcome of prospective litigation would be unfavorable enough to justify bearing the expected private costs of the destruction.[344]

341. The Appendix considers several important details and caveats, including 1) the role played by the trajectory of social costs, 2) the role of the "infra-marginal *non*tamperer," as defined within, and 3) the role played by changes in the density of "marginal tamperers," also as defined within. *See infra* app.

342. This hypothetical is evocative of several prominent cases of evidence destruction. *See, e.g.*, Lewy v. Remington Arms Co., 836 F.2d 1104, 1111–13 (8th Cir. 1988); Capellupo v. FMC Corp., 126 F.R.D. 545, 549–51 (D. Minn. 1989); Carlucci v. Piper Aircraft Corp., 102 F.R.D. 472, 485–86 (S.D. Fla. 1984). See *supra* Part II.B.2 for a detailed discussion of these cases.

343. *See supra* note 44 and accompanying text.

344. This calculus is suggested in some of the practice literature. *See* GORELICK ET AL., *supra* 12, § 9.1, at 298 ("[I]f the content of certain documents is worse than the inference that would be drawn from their destruction and there is no current, pending, or imminently foreseeable request for them, they may be destroyed."). *See also* Nesson, *supra* note 12, at 794–805 (reviewing the "bad man's" decision to spoliate).

The impact of evidence destruction on the outcome of the litigation depends on the degree to which the outcome of the case hangs on the kind of evidence that the manufacturer is considering destroying. This, in turn, depends on the magnitude of the damages at issue in the suit as well as the chance that the evidence to be destroyed would be decisive in determining what, if any, damages are imposed.

The manufacturer's private cost of evidence destruction, on the other hand, includes both the expected losses from any ancillary litigation punishing the destruction—including both the expected outcome of this satellite litigation and the expected costs of lodging a defense therein—and the cost of any additional activities undertaken in an attempt to avoid such secondary litigation losses—such as would be incurred in destroying the evidence of the destruction itself.

Both in terms of perception and reality, these private costs and benefits of destroying documents will differ widely across manufacturers. But given any level of anti-tampering enforcement, it suffices for our purposes to identify three "types" of manufacturers. First, there are the marginal tamperers: those for whom tampering is just barely worthwhile given their perception of the current array of private costs and benefits.[345] Second, there are the inframarginal tamperers: those for whom the private benefits of tampering exceed the private costs by a discreet amount so that they would continue to tamper despite any marginal increase in the private cost of doing so borne from additional enforcement. Last are the inframarginal nontamperers: those who choose not to tamper and would continue to make the same choice even were anti-tampering enforcement reduced on the margin.

With this typology in place we will now review the benefits of increasing anti-tampering enforcement in terms of how it affects each of these classes of manufacturers. In particular, because truth-finding and primary activity approaches divide mainly over their effects on the first two types—the marginal and inframarginal tamperers—we will focus on these in the analysis to follow. First, we consider the benefits of increasing anti-tampering enforcement under the truth-finding approach, and then, under the primary activity incentives approach.

345. Put another way, a "marginal tamperer" is a tamperer that stops tampering in response to either a marginal decrease in the private benefits of tampering or a marginal increase in the private costs.

3. *Truth-Finding Benefits of Anti-Tampering Enforcement.* The truth-finding benefits of a marginal increase in anti-spoliation enforcement come from two sources. First, the marginal tamperer stops destroying documents. Because these documents now make it to court, the verdict imposed will tend to be closer to the ideal verdict in these cases. Second, increasing anti-tampering enforcement also has an inframarginal truth benefit. Additional enforcement effort not only prevents spoliation, it may also increase the frequency with which document destruction is detected. When such destruction is detected, case outcomes can be rectified—e.g., by means of a spoliation inference instruction.[346]

4. *Primary Activity Benefits of Anti-Tampering Enforcement.* The primary activity incentive to adopt a safe design is generated by a combination of two factors. First, there is the array of anticipated litigation payoffs contingent on ending up as each possible type of downstream tamperer. Second, there is the manner in which choosing a safe, rather than unsafe, design affects the likelihood of ending up as each kind of tamperer. A policy change increases the incentive for safe design to the extent that it worsens the payoffs of types that are more likely following unsafe design and improves the payoffs of types that are more likely following safe design. Consider, for example, what would happen to primary activity incentives if a policy change worsened the litigation position of the inframarginal tamperer, all else the same. If adopting a safe design minimizes the likelihood of ending up as an inframarginal tamperer, this policy change would increase the incentive to adopt a safe design.

a. Converting the Marginal Tamperer. As noted, increasing the private cost of evidence destruction will cause the marginal tamperer now to refrain from destroying evidence. But the fact that this marginal tamperer has markedly changed its behavior does not mean that its litigation payoff—as the manufacturer perceives this potential payoff from a primary activity perspective—has also markedly changed. In fact, its litigation payoff will remain virtually the same. While it is true that the verdict and remedy imposed in the primary litigation are now more likely to go against this manufacturer for the fact that it is no longer destroying these documents, it is also true that this manufacturer is no longer engaging in the evidence destruction

346. See Part II.B.2, *supra*, for a description of this device.

and so is no longer facing the expected private costs of this form of obstruction. Because this tamperer is marginal—i.e., because it had perceived destruction's private benefits to be roughly commensurate with its private costs—these two effects cancel each other in their effect on the tamperer's all-in litigation payoffs. Thus, increasing the private cost of evidence destruction merely transmutes the marginal tamperer's litigation loss from the private cost of evidence destruction to the private cost of worsened litigation outcomes.[347]

The crucial point here is that the primary activity incentives created by litigation are as much a matter of private litigation costs as of litigation outcomes—an aspect of the primary activity approach that distinguishes it from the verdict centrism of the truth-seeking approach. From the prospective litigant's perspective, as it is choosing its behavior in the primary activity, the principal concern is the degree to which it would be worse off in litigation if it chooses the "bad act": in the example at hand, marketing an unsafe product. Whether the litigant is worse off for having to "pay" expected private destruction costs, or worse off for having to pay in the form of a less favorable expected verdict is immaterial. Supposing, on the contrary, that the manufacturer in the example cares more about dollars in the form of damages than it does about dollars in the form of tampering costs is like imagining that the manufacturer plans its affairs with only gross income in mind, ignoring the effect of taxes.

Thus, to the extent that the potential litigant anticipates that it is either more or less likely to be a marginal tamperer as a result of "misbehaving" in the primary activity, its incentive to refrain from the bad action remains essentially the same after anti-tampering enforcement is increased.

It may well be that the most salient, dramatic and, morally uplifting aspect of heightened anti-tampering enforcement is its ability to make an honest litigant out of the spoliator. And, in fact, it *is* true, as noted, that this is one of the two important functions of anti-tampering enforcement when truth-finding is taken to be the purpose of trial. From the perspective of setting primary activity incentives, however, the social benefit of additional enforcement effort cannot derive from its ability to convert the marginal sinner

347. This analysis continues to hold when, realistically, the manufacturer's interest in the outcome of the present suit reaches beyond the current litigation to suits by future plaintiffs. Accounting for future litigation just requires a redefinition of who is marginal. By the same logic, it continues to hold under a variety of fee- and cost-shifting rules.

into the marginal saint. If there is a social benefit of additional enforcement, it must lie elsewhere.

b. Taxing the Inframarginal Tamperer. Counter to intuition, the main primary activity incentive benefits of additional enforcement come mainly through the effect on those whom the additional enforcement fails to deter. These inframarginal evidence destroyers, though they continue to destroy evidence in the face of additional enforcement, are positively worse off in litigation due to the enhanced enforcement.[348] To the extent that safe design lessens the manufacturer's chance of ending up in this worsened position, the incentive to choose a safe design increases.

In more detail, increased anti-tampering enforcement reduces the inframarginal tamperer's litigation payoffs for several reasons. First, the tamperer is more likely to be called to task for its destruction in a secondary proceeding. This means not only that it is more likely to face sanctions in satellite litigation, but also that it is more likely to have to pay the cost of defending itself against an obstruction indictment or a motion for procedural or evidentiary sanctions. Second, in the primary layer of litigation, to the extent that the probability of detection is increased, spoliation will be less often successful at improving litigation outcomes. Thus, the inframarginal spoliator will now be partially denied access to what was a relatively cheap method of minimizing litigation losses. Third, prior to the primary litigation, the inframarginal tamperer will now be inclined to expend additional effort in perpetrating her destruction in order to avoid detection and sanction.

Reducing litigation payoffs for the inframarginal tamperer improves the manufacturer's primary activity incentives to the extent that choosing an unsafe product design makes it more likely that the manufacturer will find itself in the position of the inframarginal tamperer in prospective litigation. Because it is now a worse fate to

348. Several commentators have brushed lightly against this point's outer reaches. *See, e.g.*, GORELICK ET AL., *supra* note 12, § 1.15, at 19 ("[A] strict [document destruction] regime could generate a . . . chilling of the production of useful documentary evidence . . . . Chilling the creation of documents evidencing unlawful activity, however, directly increases the cost of lawbreaking itself."); Beckstrom, *supra* note 12, at 717 (discussing author's proposed statute requiring retention of antitrust documents: "[T]he proposed statute would not completely frustrate those who would purposefully violate the substantive laws. Refuge could often be found in the simple expedient of not making records. At least this route would be inconvenient for them because it is usually better business practice . . . to make [such a] record . . . .").

end up as an inframarginal tamperer, anything that the manufacturer can do in the primary activity to avoid this fate seems more attractive. Choosing the good primary activity action rather than the bad is one of these things. The good primary activity action is less likely to emit damaging evidentiary emissions and more likely to emit favorable emissions. Thus, the manufacturer who adopts a safe design upstream predicts that it is less likely to find evidence destruction worthwhile downstream.

Drawing an analogy to tax policy may be helpful here. Increasing anti-spoliation enforcement is like taxing manufacturers who find themselves in the position of the inframarginal spoliator. Because manufacturers who adopt unsafe designs are more likely to find themselves in this position, taxing inframarginal spoliators is like taxing (albeit probabilistically) the design of unsafe products. A tax on unsafe design is, of course, an incentive to adopt a safe design. It is important to note, however, that this is a tax paid in secret. The court may never learn that the product was unsafe or that the manufacturer is paying additional costs for its evidence tampering as a result of its design choice.

Another way to see the same point is to recognize that safe design is like a substitute (in the economic sense) for document destruction in generating the manufacturer's expected payoffs in product liability litigation. Spoliation and safe design are two ways to increase expected product liability litigation payoffs. Both have a price, however. The price of spoliation includes the legal risk therefrom. The price of adopting a safe design includes the reduction in profit margins from not cutting corners. When the price of spoliation is increased—via increased anti-tampering enforcement—we can expect the manufacturer to shift toward other methods of avoiding product liability litigation outcomes. One of these is to choose a safe product design.

5. *Summary*. The *truth* benefits of marginally increasing anti-tampering enforcement are twofold: (1) the additional information that flows into the court as a result of converting the marginal tamperer to honest evidence production, and (2) the additional information that flows into court because those who still insist on tampering are more often caught in the act.

In contrast, if the object of trial is to set primary activity incentives, converting the marginal tamperer is essentially of no consequence. Under this objective, the social benefits from enhanced enforcement come primarily from worsening the downstream payoffs of those who find the higher cost of tampering still worth incurring, a situation more likely to arise following choice of an unsafe design upstream.

B. The Optimal Enforcement Level

Having established the different nature and source of incremental social benefits under the truth-seeking and primary activity approaches, we now move on to examine how these different incremental benefits *change* as the level of enforcement is increased. From this analysis we draw our main conclusion about differences in the optimal level of enforcement.

The Section begins by establishing that the social benefits of anti-tampering enforcement are self-dampening under a primary activity approach to trial. It then moves on to explain why the social benefits of anti-tampering enforcement are self-enhancing under the conventional truth-finding approach to trial. It concludes by examining the implications of these findings for the optimal level of anti-tampering enforcement under each alternative social objective.

1. *Self-Dampening Primary Activity Benefits.* Section A.4.b established that the primary activity benefits of increased anti-tampering enforcement accrue mainly through increasing the effective tax on inframarginal tamperers. The impact of increasing this tax depends on the chance that the bad action (more so than the good) puts the actor in a position wherein she chooses to pay this tax—that is, puts her in the position of the inframarginal tamperer, wherein the potentially unfavorable effect of a given piece of evidence on the case's outcome still outweighs the private costs of destroying that evidence.

The primary activity benefits of additional enforcement are self-dampening because the greater the level of anti-tampering enforcement, the lower the chance of ending up in this position following unsafe design. To take an extreme example, when anti-spoliation enforcement is particularly aggressive, the bad primary actor simply does not expect to find herself in a position where spoliation would still be worthwhile. The benefits from spoliation would have to be improbably high. Therefore, any decrease in prospective litigation payoffs in this attenuated contingency is unlikely to cause her to change her primary activity behavior. More generally, the greater the current level of anti-tampering enforcement, the smaller the chance that the bad actor will end up in a position where tampering is still worthwhile, and the smaller the effect on primary incentives of additionally raising the cost in this contingency.[349]

2. *Self-Enhancing Truth Benefits.* The self-dampening dynamic just described follows from the hypothesis that primary activity incentive setting is the main purpose of litigation. When the same analytical hardware runs the more conventional program of truth-seeking, the outputted dynamic is likely to be self-enhancing rather than self-dampening. The more the legal system is currently doing to prevent evidence tampering, the greater the incremental benefits of further increasing prevention.

As noted in Section A.3, the truth benefits of anti-tampering enforcement come mainly from two sources: conversion of the marginal tamperer and the corrective effect on trial outcomes of nabbing the inframarginal tamperer. Let us now review these in turn with an eye toward how these positive effects change in magnitude as anti-tampering enforcement increases. As we shall see, the former conversion effect is markedly self-enhancing over the relevant range, whereas the latter corrective effect is likely neutralized by a crosscurrent of conflicting forces.

a. Converting the Marginal Tamperer. Recall that when we throw an additional dollar at anti-tampering enforcement, we deter the marginal tamperer. Because the marginal tamperer is no longer misleading the fact finder, the verdict actually imposed is closer to the ideal verdict in these cases.

But how much closer? That depends on the expected impact that the marginal tamperer's spoliation was having on the outcome of the case. Importantly, this impact is likely to be larger the greater the current level of enforcement.

As we begin to increase the private cost of spoliation starting from a low level, we tend to discourage those who believe that spoliation has only a moderate impact on case outcomes. As we continue to increase the private cost of spoliation, our converts to honesty are those who believe that their evidence destruction would

349. When there is a nontrivial chance that safe product designers may also find tampering worthwhile, the primary activity benefits of additional anti-tampering enforcement need not be *monotonically* self-dampening. Yet they will still be self-dampening in general trend. *See* app.

have had a greater and greater effect on the court's findings of fact. As we drag the net farther and farther out to sea, in other words, we catch bigger and bigger fish. The conversion of each additional spoliator, thus, has a greater and greater benefit in terms of aligning actual case outcomes with ideal case outcomes. And therefore, the more we have already increased anti-tampering enforcement, the more attractive it is to increase enforcement even further.[350]

b. Nabbing More Inframarginal Tamperers. Additional enforcement effort not only prevents evidence destruction, it also leads to more frequent detection when destruction still occurs. If the authorities actually catch a greater number of inframarginal spoliators, then a greater number of case outcomes can be corrected. In determining the trajectory of the truth-finding benefits of anti-tampering enforcement, this second effect must also be considered. But unlike the effects considered thus far, this effect is fundamentally ambiguous.

In one respect, the effect is self-dampening. The greater the current level of anti-tampering enforcement, the fewer individuals are currently spoliating. Like fishing on an overfished lake, additional enforcement effort is less likely to have much corrective benefit when remaining situations in need of correction are scarce and difficult to find.

And yet, in another respect, the effect is self-enhancing. As the set of inframarginal tamperers diminishes due to increasing enforcement, authorities may be able to more effectively target their

350. Indeed, in a schematic version of this argument, the truth benefits of beefing up anti-tampering enforcement increase exponentially in the current level of enforcement. If the expected private cost of evidence destruction is $1,000, then the marginal spoliator expects that her spoliation will change the outcome of litigation by $1,000. Increasing her cost of spoliation starting from $1,000 thus results in an expected increase in trial accuracy of $1,000 for this marginal spoliator. Similarly, increasing the cost of spoliation starting from $2,000 increases expected trial accuracy by $2,000 per marginal spoliator. And increasing the cost of spoliation starting from $1,000,000 increases expected trial accuracy by $1,000,000 per marginal spoliator.

Of course, the truth benefits of additional enforcement do not accelerate *ad infinitum*. Eventually the private cost of spoliation becomes so high that marginal tamperers are few and far between. Thus, while the incremental truth benefits per marginal tamperer continue to rise, the total incremental truth benefit of increasing the cost of tampering eventually stops climbing and begins to fall. But, almost by definition, this tapering off will not become decisive until the level of enforcement effort is well beyond the middling range. Thus, it plays no role in the explanation for why a middling level of enforcement intensity is inconsistent with a truth-telling approach. Over the relevant range for the present analysis, the truth benefits of anti-tampering enforcement accelerate as anti-tampering enforcement effort is increased. *See* app.

detection and enforcement effort. Authorities can focus on the now smaller set of litigants where the apparent stakes from spoliating appear to be high enough to make the destruction of evidence still worthwhile. With enforcement resources no longer spread so thin, leads can be followed in greater depth. Thus, although a smaller infra-margin does imply that there are fewer spoliators, it also implies that a larger percentage of this smaller number can be caught.

In the end, the presence of these two countervailing effects makes it impossible to say whether the inframarginal truth benefits of additional enforcement are self-enhancing or self-dampening. The existence of opposing forces, however, does perhaps create a presumption—albeit one rebuttable by empirical investigation—that inframarginal truth benefits are not so largely self-dampening on net as to overwhelm the self-enhancing effect concerning marginal tamperers, as explained above.

3. *The Optimal Level of Anti-Tampering Enforcement.* We have seen that the primary activity incentive benefits of anti-tampering enforcement are self-dampening, while the truth-finding benefits are self-enhancing. Intuitively, this suggests that the optimal level of anti-tampering enforcement is lower under the primary activity approach than under the truth-finding approach. In fact, the logical implication is not so bold, but still quite informative. While a middling level of anti-tampering enforcement is consistent with the primary activity approach to trial, it is inconsistent with the truth-finding approach. Because the truth benefits of additional enforcement are self-enhancing, if it were worthwhile increasing anti-tampering enforcement to a middling level, it would also be worthwhile continuing to increase it. Whatever the size of the incremental benefit that convinced us to turn the enforcement dial from low to medium, an even greater incremental benefit accrues to turning the dial from medium to high.

To be precise, the claim is not that we would necessarily want to turn the dial from low to medium, but only that *if* we did so we would not want to stop there. Thus, the analysis tells what optimal enforcement cannot be (medium) and not precisely what it is (as between low or high). In other words, the conclusion is that, from a truth-finding perspective, anti-tampering enforcement is indeed a job worth doing well, if it is worth doing at all.

In contrast, if the object of trial is to set primary activity incentives, then a middling level of enforcement *is* a plausible candidate for the social optimum. Quite possibly, by the time we reach this middling level, the self-dampening primary incentive benefits of additional enforcement have fallen to such extent that additional enforcement effort would not be worthwhile. Quite plausibly, therefore, a modicum of effort yields most of the results.

C. *The Optimal Method of Enforcement*

As noted, when commentators bemoan the law's apparent laxness with regard to evidence tampering, some part of this concern goes not to general enforcement levels, but to specific enforcement methods. In particular, the infrequency with which tamperers are called to task, as well as the law's reluctance to go back and correct distorted litigation outcomes are specific sources of dismay—sources which are logically distinct from overall enforcement intensity. This Section discusses both the frequency of detection and the importance of correcting litigation outcomes. As with general enforcement intensity, it concludes that the law's current practice is far better aligned with primary activity incentive setting than with truth-finding.[351] After analyzing these issues under each approach in turn, the Section compares the results of these analyses to existing law.

1. *Truth-Finding.* As noted in the previous Section, the truth benefits of anti-tampering enforcement derive not just from deterring the tampering, but also from uncovering the tampering activity of the inframarginal tamperer and correcting the effect of this tampering on the underlying proceeding. This has implications for both the proper frequency of detection and the corrective nature of tampering remedies.

With regard to the frequency of detection, it is well known that deterrence is the product of both this frequency and the sanction imposed conditional on detection. Many considerations go into determining the proper mix of these two factors. But when the undesirable action is evidence tampering, and one takes a truth-finding approach to trial, an additional reason is added to the list of those favoring detection frequency over sanction magnitude.

351. That primary activity and truth-finding approaches have different implications for the method of enforcement justifies the implicit qualification in this Article's introduction that the social costs are only "roughly" the same across the two approaches. *See supra* note 16 and accompanying text.

To see this, consider raising the sanction on evidence tampering while lowering the frequency of detection, in such manner as to hold constant the generated level of deterrence. The proponent of truth-finding would not be indifferent to this rearrangement. Although the same number of marginal tamperers are converted to honest litigants—and, as noted, this is a boon for truth-seeking—those who still choose to tamper are less frequently caught, and the outcome of litigation is more frequently in error. Thus, all else the same, the proponent of truth-finding prefers to deter with a high rate of detection rather than a high level of sanction. For truth-finding, the former method kills two birds with one stone by both preventing tampering and more frequently allowing it to be corrected.

Part and parcel with the fact that it leans toward detection frequency, the truth-finding approach also has an additional reason to prefer that the sanctions themselves are corrective of underlying litigation outcomes. Merely fining spoliators, for instance, does nothing to correct litigation outcomes that have already been skewed by the spoliation.

2. *The Primary Activity Incentives Approach.* The primary activity approach lacks the same impetus both to emphasize detection frequency over sanction level, and specifically to correct skewed litigation outcomes. From a primary activity perspective, the best way to raise the private cost of tampering is simply that which incurs the lowest social cost. All that is important is that from an ex ante viewpoint, the primary activity actor anticipates worsened litigation outcomes for inframarginal tamperers. For the purpose of influencing the actor's primary activity choices, precisely how this tax is imposed—aside from the issue of how much its imposition costs the public—is of secondary importance.[352]

Consider how this imbues the primary incentive proponent with a different attitude toward the two enforcement-method issues considered in this Section. First, in terms of the balance between detection probabilities and sanction levels, the primary activity proponent faces a trade-off in generating the tax on inframarginal tamperers that is similar to that faced by the proponent of truth-finding. But the primary activity proponent lacks the truth-seeker's

352. This point is related to one made in Louis Kaplow & Steven Shavell, *Accuracy in the Assessment of Damages*, 39 J.L. & ECON. 191, 192–93 (1996) (finding that courts should impose ex ante expected damages on injurers, rather than actual ex post damages).

additional reason to favor detection over sanction level: namely, the desire to correct as many litigation outcomes as possible. Thus, in choosing how best to produce a given expected sanction for tampering, the primary activity approach suggests a lower optimal frequency of detection and a higher optimal sanction relative to the truth-seeking approach.[353]

Secondly, it is clear that when sanctions *are* imposed for evidence tampering, the primary activity approach also has less concern for whether those sanctions actually correct past litigation outcomes. This is not to say that the primary activity approach has no concern for correction.[354] The point is rather that the primary activity approach lacks the additional impetus to correct litigation outcomes implied by the truth-finding approach. And thus to the extent that primary activity considerations are predominant, one would expect to see less of an effort to correct outcomes.

3. *Existing Law and Practice.* Existing law and practice seem more in line with the primary activity approach on both scores. In terms of the balance between frequency of detection and size of sanction, there is some indication that perjury and obstruction are rarely punished, especially in civil actions between private parties.[355] And yet, as noted in Part I.B, when these activities are punished, the sanctions are relatively high. The sentence in the federal system for

353. It would not be correct to conclude that the primary activity approach would favor driving detection probabilities to zero and sanctions to infinity, despite how the theory of enforcement is sometimes caricatured. For example, because it raises the procedural and evidentiary effort expended by the parties, *see* Kakalik et al., *supra* note 91, at 634–50, raising sanctions is not in fact a costless alternative to raising detection probabilities. This point has recently been explored in relation to the question of whether what plaintiffs recover should equal what defendants pay in damages. *See* Marcel Kahan & Bruce Tuckman, *Special Levies on Punitive Damages: Decoupling, Agency Problems, and Litigation Expenditures*, 15 INT'L REV. L. & ECON. 175, 175–76 (1995) (questioning the effectiveness of "special levy" statutes, which "require plaintiffs to hand over portions of their punitive damage awards to the state"); A. Mitchell Polinsky & Yeon-Koo Che, *Decoupling Liability: Optimal Incentives for Care and Litigation*, 22 RAND J. ECON. 562, 562–63 (1991) (advocating "decoupled liability," whereby "the plaintiff is awarded an amount different from what the defendant is made to pay," as a method for reducing social costs); Albert Choi & Chris W. Sanchirico, *Should Plaintiffs Win What Defendants Lose?: Litigation Stakes, Litigation Effort, and the Benefits of Decoupling*, 33 J. LEGAL STUD. (forthcoming June 2004) (considering "the infra-marginal effects of both decreasing recovery and increasing damages").

354. The incentives of plaintiffs and victims must also be considered, and such incentives may be enhanced if these parties are confident that the impact of the defendant's false evidence will be nullified.

355. *See supra* Part I.B.

either obstruction or perjury is at least ten to sixteen months in prison.[356] The reputational and economic sanction—both short- and long-term—that this entails looms large for the average litigant who happens, for example, to be in court defending her firm's failure to perform on a contract, or her firm's apparent lack of care in designing a potentially hazardous product. The loss of future income from serving a prison term would pale in comparison to whatever this agent of the firm stood to gain—in terms of short-run profits or career advancement—by shorting the customer or cutting corners on product design.

Furthermore, as noted in Part II, when sanctions are imposed under current law, they rarely correct the underlying litigation result. Conceivably, on convicting litigant *X* for obstruction of justice for destroying documents during pending litigation, the law might sanction her by going back to correct the outcome in the case that she won by virtue of this destruction. Making her pay back what she won in that case would be one way to fine her. But this rarely happens. Unless there has been a "fraud upon the court"—which, as noted, means more than mere obstruction by a private litigant—or the obstruction is caught within a year after entry of judgment, that judgment will generally stand, even as the convicted obstructer is sentenced to time in prison.[357]

The spoliation inference instruction—a jury instruction "permitting" the jury to infer that nonproduced evidence would have been unfavorable to the party that had control over the missing evidence—at first appears to be a form of corrective remedy. But the effectiveness of this form of instruction is seriously open to question. First, the instruction does not prescribe a mandatory inference; it is not even a presumption, which would shift the burden of production. It is merely a suggestion to jury members, without any follow-up from the court, that they may, if they like, draw a particular inference. And this is an inference they may already be drawing, especially given that the spoliation victim is usually free to admit evidence of the spoliation and argue on its own accord for the inference.[358] Secondly, even if the jury takes important cues from the judge's instruction, the judge will issue the instruction only if there is sufficient indication that the missing evidence was indeed unfavorable to the spoliator. Evidence

356. *See supra* note 114 and accompanying text.

357. *See supra* Part II.B.3.

358. *See supra* note 297.

used to establish the content of the missing evidence will often itself be admissible directly to prove the underlying propositions for which the spoliated evidence would have been offered. Therefore, in many cases the judge will be issuing the spoliation instruction precisely when the inference encouraged by that instruction is unnecessary given available evidence on the same point. In this case, the only new information conveyed to the jury will be the judge's displeasure with the spoliator. To the extent that the instruction has any effect, therefore, the effect seems more punitive than accuracy-inducing, as other commentators have remarked.[359]

D. *Summary*

The truth-seeking approach to trial puts great weight on both deterring tampering and correcting its effects. The primary activity approach is more concerned with lowering the litigation payoffs of those who still find tampering worthwhile, and thereby raising the private cost of socially disfavored primary activity choices. This different locus of concern manifests in different prescriptions for anti-tampering policy.

Importantly for our evolving sense of trial's purpose, the prescriptions of the primary activity approach seem more in line with current law. The primary activity approach is more consistent with the middling attitude toward anti-tampering enforcement that seems to characterize the existing regime. Moreover, the primary activity approach is also better aligned with current law's reliance on high sanctions rather than frequent detection, as well as its reluctance to go back and correct litigation outcomes skewed by tampering.

359. *See, e.g.*, Maguire & Vincent, *supra* note 120, at 258 (finding that in granting a spoliation inference instruction, "courts sometimes adulterate their logic with punitive enthusiasm").

APPENDIX

This Appendix supplements the analysis in Part III. Section A contains an intuitive discussion of several issues not covered in the main text. Section B subjects the analysis in Part III to mathematical modeling in order to test its internal consistency and make explicit its underlying assumptions.

A. *Supplemental Discussion*

1. *The Trajectory of Social Costs.* As noted in the Introduction, the social costs of anti-tampering enforcement are roughly the same across truth-finding and primary activity approaches.[384] Nonetheless, the trajectory of social costs is a potentially important ingredient in distinguishing the implications of these rival approaches.

Part III.B discussed how the differing trajectories of social benefits across truth-finding and primary activity approaches had different implications for the optimal enforcement level. That discussion implicitly assumed that incremental social costs were relatively constant. How would the analysis in Part III.B change, if we included explicit consideration of the trajectory of social costs?

a. Condition on Cost and Benefit Trajectories. We start with the principle that social costs must be accelerating relative to social benefits as we increase the level of enforcement toward the socially optimum level. (This principle is sometimes referred to as the "second-order necessary condition" for an optimum.) The reasoning here has three steps. First, when we are precisely at a socially optimal level of anti-tampering enforcement—the level that balances costs and benefits to produce the largest net social benefit—the social benefits from further increasing anti-tampering enforcement must be no more than the social costs. Otherwise, capturing these additional social benefits would, impossibly, improve upon what was supposed to be the best that we could do.

Second, and by similar reasoning, starting from a level of enforcement just below the socially optimal level, the social benefits from increasing anti-tampering enforcement up to the socially

384. They are only "roughly" the same because the differing implications for enforcement methods, as discussed in Part III.C, *supra*, may produce different social cost trajectories.

optimal level must be greater than the additional costs. Otherwise, the lower level would, again, be better than the best.

Combining these first two steps, we see that marginal social benefits must be less than marginal social costs at enforcement levels just below the optimum, but greater at the optimum. In other words, the social benefits from anti-tampering enforcement must be increasing at a faster rate than the social costs at enforcement levels just below the optimum, but at a slower rate than social costs at the optimum.

This in turn has implications, in the third and final step, for the relative acceleration of social costs. If someone says that the red car was moving at a slower speed than the blue car at 11:50 A.M. and a faster speed at noon, it must be that the red car was accelerating relative to the blue car at some point between these two times. Similarly if the social benefits of anti-tampering enforcement are increasing at a faster rate than the social costs below the social optimum (i.e., at 11:50 A.M.) and a slower rate than social costs at the optimum (i.e., at noon), then social costs must be accelerating relative to social benefits as we approach the social optimum from below.

b. Implications for Truth-Finding. If we take truth-finding to be the object of trial, it is difficult to justify the middling level of anti-tampering enforcement that we seem to see in the current system. We have seen that the social costs of anti-tampering enforcement must be accelerating relative to the social benefits as we approach the social optimum from below. It is unlikely that this will happen at any middling range of anti-tampering enforcement. At a middling level of enforcement we can expect a steady (or even increasing) density of marginal tamperers. When this is the case, the social benefits of anti-tampering enforcement grow roughly exponentially,[385] which is to say that marginal social benefits increase in proportion to the level of anti-tampering enforcement—which is, in turn, to say that the social benefits accelerate.

In contrast, it is implausible that social costs of anti-tampering enforcement accelerate in their middling range, let alone that their acceleration exceeds that of the truth benefits of enforcement. In the first place, at middling levels of enforcement, economies of scale in anti-tampering enforcement are unlikely to have so exhausted themselves as to reverse into diseconomies of scale that are, in turn,

385. *See supra* note 350.

so constricting as to cause the social costs of anti-tampering enforcement to increase at an increasing rate.

Secondly, the decrease in the number of inframarginal tamperers as we increase enforcement[386] acts as a decelerating force for social costs. The cost of anti-tampering enforcement is tied in part to the number of inframarginal tamperers. The greater the number of inframarginal tamperers, the more often courts must hold evidence tampering hearings, the more frequently litigants must defend themselves at such hearings, the greater the number of litigants who spend time and effort practicing and preparing their tampering activities to avoid getting caught. Therefore, if we raise the private cost of tampering by beefing up anti-tampering enforcement, this increases social costs in part because the tampering that is still being perpetrated is more socially expensive. But, the greater the level of anti-tampering enforcement, the fewer the number of inframarginal tamperers, and so, for this effect, the lower the incremental cost of increasing anti-tampering enforcement.

Therefore, the improbability of significantly decreasing returns to scale at low and middling levels of enforcement combined with the marginal cost-reducing effects of a shrinking infra-margin make it unlikely that social costs accelerate faster than truth-oriented social benefits. This in turn makes it unlikely that a truth-oriented system would ever purposefully settle on even a middling level of anti-tampering enforcement. Thus, even allowing for a more general configuration of social costs, there is still great difficulty in reconciling the current shape of our anti-tampering enforcement efforts with the rhetoric that trial is predominantly a truth-finding exercise.

c. Implications for Primary Activity Incentive Setting. On the other hand, there is no inconsistency in explaining a middling level of anti-tampering enforcement taking primary activity incentive setting as the object of trial. We have seen that the social costs of anti-tampering enforcement must be accelerating relative to the social benefits as we approach the social optimum from below. It was further demonstrated that the social benefits of anti-tampering enforcement measured in terms of the effect on the primary activity incentives of the tamperer, rather than in terms of truth-finding, have a self-dampening character. In other words, these important social benefits of anti-tampering enforcement increase at a decreasing

386. *See supra* Part III.B.1.

rate—which is to say that they decelerate as we approach the social optimum. Therefore, the social optimum may lie anywhere that the economies of scale in anti-tampering enforcement are not so great. In particular, at any middling level of enforcement, the social costs of anti-tampering enforcement are not likely to be decelerating faster than the social benefits. Importantly, the social optimum may well be at a point where economies of scale in anti-tampering enforcement are not exhausted, as long as the increase in social costs slows less rapidly than the increase in social benefits.

2. *The Role of Inframarginal NonTamperers.* This Section considers the effect of increased anti-tampering enforcement on the inframarginal nontamperer, the third type in the taxonomy from Part III.A.2, and a type that was explicitly left out of the analysis of incremental increases in enforcement in Parts III.A.3 and III.A.4. The conclusion is this: Those who were already choosing not to destroy evidence prior to the increase in enforcement are only secondarily affected by increasing the level of anti-tampering enforcement from its current level. Further, what effect there is on these actors remains ambiguous and is unlikely to be decisive in shaping the overall effect.

In a world with no "false positives" in anti-tampering enforcement—i.e., a world in which those who do not destroy evidence are not falsely positively identified as spoliators—increasing enforcement levels has exactly no effect on the inframarginal nontamperer. First, the inframarginal nontamperer has already decided that tampering does not pay and so does not change its behavior in response to increased enforcement. Second, the inframarginal nontamperer is never mistakenly punished. Thus, whatever is done to beef up anti-tampering enforcement is, from its perspective, superfluous.

In a world with false positives in anti-tampering enforcement, the effect on the inframarginal nontamperer of increased enforcement effort is precisely as ambiguous as the effect of increased enforcement on the incidence of false positives. Some methods of enhancing anti-tampering enforcement may have as a byproduct an increase in the number or severity of erroneously imposed spoliation sanctions. This in turn will lower litigation payoffs for the nonspoliator, who now faces a heightened risk of becoming one of the system's false positives. On the other hand, additional resources devoted to anti-tampering enforcement may actually decrease the number of false indictments and convictions as investigations and satellite trials are more thoroughly conducted. This would raise the litigation payoffs for the inframarginal nontamperer.

It is thus impossible to deduce how inframarginal evidence destroyers will be affected by increased enforcement. However, it is perhaps possible to infer that the crosscurrent of countervailing effects on these still honest actors makes it likely that, whatever direction the effect points in, the net effect is unlikely to defeat the summary proposition of the foregoing analysis: the main force driving the primary activity benefits of anti-tampering enforcement is the effective taxation of those on the opposite side of the evidence tampering margin, the inframarginal tamperers.

3. *Self-Dampening Primary Activity Benefits and the Possibility that "Good" Primary Activity Actors will be Inframarginal Tamperers.* The following discussion pertains to Part III.B.1. The claim there was that decreasing the payoffs for inframarginal tamperers has less and less impact on primary activity incentives because the chance of ending up as an inframarginal tamperer declines.

However, when there is a nontrivial chance that safe product designers may also find tampering worthwhile, the primary activity benefits of additional anti-tampering enforcement need not be *monotonically* self-dampening. If anti-tampering enforcement is increased by a small amount, the probability of ending up as an inframarginal tamperer given safe product design may decrease faster than the same probability given unsafe design. For example, the probability of ending up as an inframarginal tamperer given safe design may decline by two percentage points from 5% to 3%, whereas the probability of ending up as an inframarginal tamperer given unsafe design may decline by only one percentage point from 20% to 19%. Thus, the probability difference actually increases from fifteen percentage points to sixteen. That, in turn, means that decreasing the payoffs for inframarginal tamperers has a greater impact than before.

Nevertheless, the probability difference cannot be larger than the larger of the two probabilities (i.e., the probability for unsafe design). Therefore, the primary activity benefits of additional enforcement will always exhibit self-dampening in the large, if not also in the small. If, in the above example, we continued to increase anti-tampering enforcement until the probability of ending up as an inframarginal tamperer given unsafe design was 14%, the probability difference could be no greater than 14%, implying a decrease from 15%.

In addition, for many common distributional forms, primary activity benefits will indeed be *uniformly* self-dampening over the relevant range. Imagine, for example, that the benefits of tampering given safe product design are normally distributed with mean m_s and variance one, while the benefits of tampering given unsafe product design are normally distributed with mean $m_u > m_s$ and variance one. In this case, the probability density of tampering benefits given safe design exceeds that for unsafe design at all benefits levels greater than the average of the two means. Therefore, the relevant probability difference, as identified above, is decreasing for all levels of private tampering costs greater than this average mean. That implies that as we increase the level of enforcement, primary activity benefits become once and for all self-dampening even while more than half of those who design unsafe products still find tampering worthwhile.

4. *Focus on Marginal Changes.* The thought experiment in Part III considers a marginal increase in the expected sanction for document destruction, one small enough to deter only the "marginal tamperer," as defined below. The effect of a larger increase will simply be the aggregation of the effects of many small increases.

5. *Tamperer's Opponent's Primary Activity Incentives.* In judging the primary activity incentive benefits of increased enforcement Part III focused on the impact on the tamperer's own primary activity incentives. Another thought experiment might be conducted to examine the effect on the tamperer's opponent's incentives.[387] Differences between the truth-finding approach and the primary activity incentive approach exist in either case. But they are more pronounced in the case of the tamperer's own incentives, and that is why it is highlighted in the text.

6. *Alternatively Manipulating the Stakes Attached to Evidence Production.* For the task of affecting the incidence and impact of evidence tampering, the law actually has two points of impact, corresponding to the costs and benefits that individuals weigh in deciding whether to engage in evidentiary foul play. Part III of the Article considers the law's attempts to alter the individual's perceived

387. Some of issues in this case are considered in Sanchirico, *Games, Information, and Evidence Production*, *supra* note 14 and Sanchirico & Triantis, Evidentiary Arbitrage, *supra* note 14.

private cost of engaging in evidentiary foul play. Such policy reforms include beefing up the prosecution of perjury and obstruction of justice, or more liberally meting out adverse inference instructions and discovery sanctions against the spoliator. In some contexts the law can also affect the litigants' perceived private benefits from evidence tampering, by fine-tuning how verdict and remedy hang on particular forms of evidence. This is perhaps most relevant in a contractual context.[388]

B. Mathematical Analysis

Consider the problem of choosing the level of anti-tampering enforcement to maximize social welfare.[389] The argument in Part III may be cast in terms of the *second*-order necessary conditions for an interior maximum.[390] The *first*-order necessary condition for an interior maximum is that marginal net social benefits are zero. As is well-known, this condition is not sufficient. For example, it would also be satisfied at an interior level of enforcement that *minimizes* social welfare. The *second*-order necessary condition for an interior maximum is that marginal net social benefits are decreasing in the level of anti-tampering enforcement. To say that the benefits of anti-tampering enforcement are "self-enhancing" under a truth-seeking approach is to say that marginal social benefits are everywhere *increasing*, not decreasing. Thus the second-order necessary condition for an interior maximum will be satisfied at no interior level of enforcement under the truth-seeking approach. In contrast, under a primary activity incentives approach, the second-order necessary condition for a maximum will be satisfied at all interior points. The precise optimal level of enforcement under the primary activity approach will depend on where marginal net social benefits vanish. Unlike for truth-seeking, nothing prevents that optimal level from residing in the low to middling range.

Second-order conditions fail under the truth-seeking approach because the map from anti-tampering enforcement to trial accuracy

388. *See generally* Sanchirico & Triantis, *Evidentiary Arbitrage, supra* note 14 (analyzing how fabrication of evidence is affected by altering the map from evidence to liability).

389. For purposes of the ensuing discussion, assume that social welfare is twice continuously differentiable in enforcement levels.

390. For a discussion of these conditions see, for example, ALPHA C. CHIANG, FUNDAMENTAL METHODS OF MATHEMATICAL ECONOMICS 246–47 (Patricia A. Mitchell & Gail Gavert eds., 3d ed., McGraw-Hill Inc. 1984) (1967).

exhibits a core nonconvexity.[391] Nonconvexity in this context is the technical counterpart to the self-enhancing effect described in the main text.[392] Identifying this core nonconvexity is, in turn, the core of this Article's analysis of enforcement levels (Part III). This nonconvexity may be masked by ancillary convexities in other functional components of social welfare. Yet though such masking is theoretically possible, it is empirically unlikely for reasons discussed at length below.

1. *Basic Model.* The core nonconvexity in the optimal choice of anti-tampering enforcement under a truth-seeking approach is apparent in the following simple model (which is enriched in subsequent sections). The model tracks the thought experiment laid out in Part III.A.1. In order to incorporate the complications of anti-tampering enforcement—complications that are absent in conventional models of legal process—the model simplifies other aspects of the conventional model—such as filing and settlement decisions.

a. Timeline. In period 1, a risk-neutral manufacturer chooses whether to design its product safely or unsafely. If, and only if, the product is unsafely designed, the plaintiff files suit in period 2.[393] In period 3 "nature" determines for the manufacturer its benefit from

391. *Cf.* David A. Starrett, *Fundamental Nonconvexities in the Theory of Externalities*, 4 J. ECON. THEORY 180, 189–93 (1972) (identifying a core nonconvexity in the production possibilities set in the presence of externalities and noting the troubling implications of this nonconvexity for general equilibrium theory).

392. The adjective "nonconvexity" as used in this context refers to the *set* of points that lie below the function. This set is said to be "convex" if the line segment between any two points in the set is entirely contained in the set. Unfortunately, this property is equivalent to another property of the function that is frequently termed "concavity." The function is called "concave" if the line segment between any two points on its graph lies entirely below the graph. *See generally* RALPH TYRRELL ROCKAFELLAR, CONVEX ANALYSIS (Marston Morse & A.W. Tucker eds., 1970) (reviewing the properties of convex sets and concave functions).

Whichever term is used, the important implication for our purposes is that, over a range in which an increasing function is *non*convex, the greater the function's level, the greater its current rate of increase. To relate this property to the formal definition, note that if one draws a line segment between two points on the graph of the function over this range, the line will be above the graph and so also outside the set of points that lie below that graph. Relative to a linear increase between the two points, therefore, the function starts slower, but accelerates to such extent that it reaches the same endpoint.

393. One implication of the assumption that the injurer is only sued when actually liable (a typical assumption in models of litigation) is that the primary activity benefits of additional enforcement are self-dampening everywhere, rather than just self-dampening in general trend. See the discussion *supra* note 349.

pursuing a policy of destroying evidence of product design. This benefit comes via a reduction in the probability of being held liable at trial. We denote this benefit b and assume that it has continuously differentiable density f. The probability of being held liable is then p-b, where $0 \leq p \leq 1$ is a fixed baseline probability of liability. In this subsection, we assume that b is uniformly distributed between 0 and p, and we denote the constant density:

$$\bar{f} = \tfrac{1}{p}.$$

If the manufacturer chooses to destroy evidence, it is sanctioned for that destruction with probability q. If sanctioned, it must pay a fine of s. In period 4, the manufacturer is held liable with probability p-b, and, if held liable, pays a fine of l.

b. Evidence Destruction Decision. The manufacturer chooses to destroy evidence if its expected litigation loss after destroying evidence (inclusive of the expected sanction from destruction) is less than its expected litigation loss if it refrains from destroying evidence:

$$\underbrace{\underbrace{(1-q)(\cancel{p}-b)l}_{\text{if not caught destroying}} + \underbrace{q(\cancel{pl}+s)}_{\text{if caught...}}}_{\text{expected litigation loss if destroys}} \leq \underbrace{\cancel{pl}}_{\text{...if doesn't destroy}}.$$

Equivalently, the manufacturer destroys evidence if the benefit exceeds the threshold $\hat{b}$:

$$b \geq \tfrac{qs}{(1-q)l} \equiv \hat{b}. \quad (1)$$

Personifying different states of the world, we refer to $\hat{b}$ as "the marginal tamperer." The smallest possible marginal tamperer is $\hat{b} = 0$, in which case, the manufacturer always chooses (i.e., "all manufacturers choose") to destroy evidence. The largest relevant marginal tamperer is $\hat{b} = p$, in which case—given that b is supported below p—the manufacturer never finds destruction worthwhile.

2. *The Truth-Seeking Approach.* An accurate outcome at trial means that the manufacturer is held liable for unsafe design. If the manufacturer does not destroy evidence, the chance of liability is p. If the manufacturer does destroy evidence and is not caught for doing so, the chance of liability is only p-b. And if the manufacturer

destroys evidence and *is* caught, the probability of liability returns to p. Therefore, the probability of liability conditional on trial, is:[394]

$$A(q,s) = \underbrace{\int_0^{\hat{b}} p\bar{f}\,db}_{\text{manufacturers that don't destroy evidence}} + \underbrace{\int_{\hat{b}}^{p} \left(\underbrace{(1-q)(p-\tilde{b})}_{\text{not caught destroying evidence}} + \underbrace{qp}_{\text{caught}} \right) \bar{f}\,db}_{\text{manufacturers that do destroy evidence}} . \qquad (2)$$

The policy instruments of interest here are q and s, the probability of detection for document destruction and the ex post sanction for the same. This is reflected in the notation on the left-hand side of (2).

There are social costs to creating both q and s.[395] For the moment, assume that the marginal cost of s for any given level of q is constant—i.e., social costs take the form:

$$C(s,q) = s\alpha(q) + c(q) + k , \qquad (3)$$

where k is a constant and α and c are arbitrary functions.

In order to provide an expression for social welfare, we need an expression for the value of accuracy in this kind of case. Assume that this value is some arbitrary constant multiple of accuracy itself, and recalibrate the cost function C so that this constant multiple may be taken as 1. Social welfare is then:

$$W(q,s) = A(q,s) - C(q,s) . \qquad (4)$$

In maximizing social welfare (4), q must be a probability,

$$0 \leq q \leq 1 , \qquad (5)$$

394. Throughout this Appendix, a tilde over a variable indicates that it is the variable over which integration is performed.

395. In particular, the social costs of s involve the cost of effort exerted by the parties in defending against imposition of s in ancillary process. Thus, it is not true, as is sometimes assumed, that the marginal cost of s is zero. *See generally, e.g.*, Choi & Sanchirico, *supra* note 353 (noting impact of, in effect, s on litigation effort and importance of this impact in assessing the wisdom of decoupling what plaintiffs recover from defendants pay in damages).

and s and q must place $\hat{b}$ between 0 and its upper bound, p, implying:

$$0 \leq s \leq \frac{pl(1-q)}{q}. \qquad (6)$$

Thus, the goal is to maximize (4) subject to (5) and (6). An *interior* maximum for this problem satisfies both (5) and (6) with strict inequality. Furthermore, an interior maximum satisfies the following first-order necessary conditions:

$$\frac{\partial W}{\partial q} = 0; \frac{\partial W}{\partial s} = 0 \qquad (7)$$

and the following second-order necessary conditions:

$$\frac{\partial^2 W}{\partial q^2} \leq 0; \frac{\partial^2 W}{\partial s^2} \leq 0 \qquad (8)$$

We will now show that at any pair (q^*,s^*) (not necessarily interior) that maximizes (4) subject to (5) and (6), the marginal tamperer is either $\hat{b} = 0$ or $\hat{b} = p$. In other words, either the manufacturer always chooses to tamper, there being no deterrence at all of evidence destruction, or the manufacturer never chooses to tamper, there being effectively *complete* deterrence of evidence destruction.

The method of proof is to focus on s and to show that the second-order necessary condition with respect to s can never be satisfied at any level of s that is *strictly* between 0 and what it would take to make $\hat{b} = p$. That is,

$$s = \frac{pl(1-q)}{q}.$$

These two extremes in s correspond to the two extremes in $\hat{b}$, as just discussed.

The first derivative of $W(q,s)$ with respect to s is:

$$\frac{\partial W}{\partial s} = \underbrace{p}_{\substack{\text{prob}\\\text{of}\\\text{liab.}\\\text{for}\\\text{marg.}\\\text{non-}\\\text{tamp.}}} \underbrace{\tfrac{q}{(1-q)l}\bar{f}}_{\substack{\text{"number"}\\\text{of marginal}\\\text{tamperers}}}$$

$$-\underbrace{\left((1-q)\left(p-\hat{b}\right)+qp\right)}_{\text{prob. of liab. for marg. tamperer}} \underbrace{\tfrac{q}{(1-q)l}\bar{f}}_{\substack{\text{"number" of marg.}\\\text{tamperers}}}$$

$$-\alpha(q) \tag{9}$$

$$=\left((1-q)\bar{f}\left(\tfrac{q}{(1-q)l}\right)^2\right)s-\alpha(q)\ .$$

The interpretation of the first two addends of the first statement in (9) tracks the discussion in the main text. The expression

$$\tfrac{q}{(1-q)l}\bar{f}$$

can be thought of as the number of marginal tamperers that convert from tampering to not tampering when we raise the tampering sanction s by one unit. In particular,

$$\tfrac{q}{(1-q)l}$$

is the increase in the marginal tamperer $\hat{b}$ and $\bar{f}$ is the number of manufacturers at that level. Therefore, (9) shows that the incremental benefit of raising s is the conversion of

$$\tfrac{q}{(1-q)l}\bar{f}$$

manufacturers from a lower probability of product liability, namely $(1-q)(p-\hat{b})+qp$, to a higher probability of product liability, namely p. Given this interpretation, the self-enhancing quality of anti-tampering enforcement under a truth-seeking approach can also be seen in (9). Converting marginal tamperers has a greater impact on accuracy, the greater the impact of the marginal tampering. Per marginal tamperer, the chance of rightful liability increases from $(1-q)(p-\hat{b}) + qp$ to p, an increase of $(1-q)\hat{b}$. The impact of the marginal tamperer's tampering should he not get caught, $\hat{b}$, is larger, the larger is the expected sanction s from tampering. Therefore, the larger is s, the greater is the accuracy benefit of further increasing s.

This self-enhancing effect is precisely reflected in the sign of the second-order derivative of W with respect to s, which is most easily taken from the last expression in (9):

$$\frac{\partial^2 W}{\partial s^2} = (1-q)\bar{f}\left(\tfrac{q}{(1-q)l}\right)^2 > 0. \qquad (10)$$

Expression (10) is strictly positive for all levels of q strictly between 0 and 1 and all levels of s. This means that at any interior level of $\hat{b}$ (wherein q must be strictly between 0 and 1), the marginal net social benefit of s is strictly increasing. This, in turn, means that the second-order condition with respect to s (as laid out in (8)) cannot be satisfied at an interior level of $\hat{b}$.

Expression (10) represents the core nonconvexity of truth-oriented W in the anti-tampering enforcement level. In a more complicated model, this core nonconvexity can be masked by other ancillary effects. We consider the most important of these in turn.

a. Density Effects. It is true that curvature in the density of marginal tamperers can mask the core nonconvexity exhibited in (10). But this statement is not terribly profound. To the extent that the slope of the density is up for grabs, so are the first and second derivatives of social welfare. In fact, for any desired magnitudes for these derivatives at any point, one can always find a distribution f to create these magnitudes. This fundamental ambiguity is endemic to theoretical models that posit abstract distributions—and thus all models that admit parametric uncertainty. To say anything at all one must make some commitments regarding distributional shape.

In the analysis above, we committed to a uniform distribution for b. This was, of course, much more than was necessary to enable the core nonconvexity there identified to have its effect. Indeed, the distributional assumptions required to *mask* that core nonconvexity are empirically implausible at a low to middling level of enforcement, such as is apparently seen in practice.

Intuitively, in order for distributional effects to overwhelm the effect of the core nonconvexity and enable a low to middling level of optimal anti-tampering enforcement, it would have to be the case that the density of b was falling rapidly at such a level. In other words, the fact that we catch bigger and bigger fish as we drag the net farther and farther out to sea (the core nonconvexity) would have to be offset by a declining density of fish even when we are just starting out and are still relatively close to shore. A declining density may be plausible at high levels of b. But a declining density is more difficult to reconcile with the claim that enforcement levels are low to middling and that tampering is rampant.

In formal terms, with a more general density f of b we have:

$$A(q,s)=\int_0^{\hat{b}} pf\left(\tilde{b}\right)db+\int_{\hat{b}}^{p}\left((1-q)\left(p-\tilde{b}\right)+qp\right)f\left(\tilde{b}\right)db, \tag{11}$$

$$\frac{\partial W}{\partial s}=\tfrac{q}{(1-q)l}pf\left(\hat{b}\right)-\tfrac{q}{(1-q)l}\left((1-q)\left(p-\hat{b}\right)+qp\right)f\left(\hat{b}\right)-\alpha(q)$$

$$=\tfrac{q}{(1-q)l}(1-q)\hat{b}f\left(\hat{b}\right)-\alpha(q)$$

and

$$\frac{\partial W^2}{\partial^2 s}=\left(\tfrac{q}{(1-q)l}\right)^2(1-q)\hat{b}f'\left(\hat{b}\right)+\underbrace{\left(\tfrac{q}{(1-q)l}\right)^2(1-q)f\left(\hat{b}\right)}_{\text{core nonconvexity}} \tag{12}$$

(compare the last addend in (12) with (10)). We are interested in conditions under which (12) is still positive. Dividing through by

$$\left(\tfrac{q}{(1-q)l}\right)^2(1-q)f\left(\hat{b}\right)$$

yields

$$\frac{\partial W^2}{\partial^2 s}\propto\frac{f'\left(\hat{b}\right)\hat{b}}{f\left(\hat{b}\right)}+1 \tag{13}$$

The left-hand addend in (13) is the percentage change in the density per percentage change in the marginal tamperer $\hat{b}$; thus, it is the elasticity of the density with respect to $\hat{b}$. If the density is falling, this elasticity is negative. Therefore, social welfare will be concave—that is, (12) and (13) will be nonpositive—only where the elasticity of the density is not only negative, but less than negative one. Consider how this plays out for two common families of distributions

1. *Special Case: Truncated Normal Distribution.* Suppose, for example, that *b*'s density is a symmetric, truncated normal distribution with truncation bounds 0 and *p*, mean (and mean parameter) ½ *p*, and variance parameter σ^2.[396] Some algebra shows that the elasticity of this density is:

$$\frac{f'(b)}{f(b)}b = -\frac{\left(b-\frac{1}{2}p\right)b}{\sigma^2}. \tag{14}$$

Applying the quadratic formula and ignoring the irrelevant root, this elasticity is less than negative one if, and only if,

$$b > \tfrac{1}{4}p + \tfrac{1}{2}\sqrt{\tfrac{1}{4}p^2 + 4\sigma^2}. \tag{15}$$

The right hand side of (15) is always bigger than ½ *p*, the mean of the distribution of *b*. Therefore, at any interior solution—wherein the elasticity of the density must be less than negative one, and so (15) must hold—the manufacturer will be deterred from evidence destruction *at least* half of the time. This in itself might be regarded as inconsistent with low to middling enforcement. But, in fact, quite a bit more can be said. The larger the variance parameter σ^2, the greater the point at which social welfare becomes concave, thus satisfying the second-order condition. Indeed, so long as

$$\sigma \geq \tfrac{1}{\sqrt{2}}p,$$

social welfare is concave over its *entire* range, even though the density is falling on the upper tail.[397] And this means that there is no interior solution, as in the uniform distribution case considered above.

396. The density function for this truncated normal would be

$$\tfrac{1}{\sqrt{2\pi}}\exp\left(-\tfrac{1}{2}\left(\tfrac{b-\frac{1}{2}p}{\sigma^2}\right)^2\right)\Big/\omega,$$

where ω is the integral from 0 to *p* of the corresponding normal density without truncation.

397. $\sigma \geq \frac{1}{\sqrt{2}}p$ implies $\frac{1}{4}p + \frac{1}{2}\sqrt{\frac{1}{4}p^2 + 4\sigma^2} > p$ and *p* is the upper bound on *b*.

2. *Special Case: Truncated Exponential Distribution.* Consider a truncated exponential density with truncation bounds 0 and p and with parameter λ: This density will be proportional to the exponential density without truncation: $\lambda e^{-\lambda b}$. (Note that $1/\lambda$ will not be the mean of the truncated distribution.) This density is decreasing along its entire range. Yet, its elasticity is:

$$\frac{f'(b)b}{f(b)} = -\lambda b.$$

Thus, social welfare will not be concave until $b > 1/\lambda$. So long as $1/\lambda > p$, social welfare will be nowhere concave and an interior solution will be impossible.

b. Social Cost Effects. The effect of the core nonconvexity identified above can be overwhelmed if the marginal cost of s is sufficiently increasing. Yet, this is even more implausible at low to middling levels of enforcement than a rapidly decaying density. The phenomenon of increasing marginal costs corresponds to the exhaustion of economies of scale in enforcement. In contrast, low enforcement levels most plausibly correspond to a situation in which not all economies of scale had been tapped, and in which marginal social cost is roughly constant, if not actually decreasing.

In formal terms, with a general cost function (and a general density) we have

$$W(q,s) = \int_0^{\hat{b}} pf(\tilde{b})db + \int_{\hat{b}}^{p}\left((1-q)(p-\tilde{b})+qp\right)f(\tilde{b})db - C(q,s),$$

$$\begin{aligned}\frac{\partial W}{\partial s} &= \tfrac{q}{(1-q)l}\, pf(\hat{b}) - \tfrac{q}{(1-q)l}\left((1-q)(p-\hat{b})+qp\right)f(\hat{b}) - C_s(q,s)\\ &= \tfrac{q}{(1-q)l}(1-q)\hat{b}f(\hat{b}) - C_s(q,s),\end{aligned} \tag{16}$$

and

$$\frac{\partial W^2}{\partial^2 s} = \left(\tfrac{q}{(1-q)l}\right)^2(1-q)\hat{b}f'(\hat{b}) + \underbrace{\left(\tfrac{q}{(1-q)l}\right)^2(1-q)f(\hat{b})}_{\text{core nonconvexity}} - C_{ss}(q,s). \tag{17}$$

Dividing (17) through by

$$\left(\frac{q}{(1-q)l}\right)^2 (1-q) f\left(\hat{b}\right)$$

and using the *first*-order condition (i.e., setting (16) to zero), we obtain the following restatement of the second-order condition:

$$\frac{\partial W^2}{\partial^2 s} \propto \frac{f'\left(\hat{b}\right)\hat{b}}{f\left(\hat{b}\right)} + 1 - \frac{C_{ss}(q,s)s}{C_s(q,s)}. \qquad (18)$$

Relative to (13), the new term here, on the far right, is the elasticity of marginal social costs in s. (Cf. the elasticity of *total* social costs.) We would expect this to be nonpositive at low levels of q and s. Therefore, this effect would most likely work in tandem with the core nonconvexity (represented by the "1" in (18)) to ensure that social welfare is not concave at low levels of s and therefore that the social optimum cannot there obtain. (Were it working in tandem with the core nonconvexity, the possibility that the density effects described above would be negative enough to produce convexity would be even less likely.)

Notice that in the uniform distribution, constant-marginal-cost model considered initially, the right side of (18) reduces to 1.

3. *The Primary Activity Approach.* In contrast, the social benefits of additional anti-tampering enforcement have a natural convexity under the primary activity approach.[398] Working with the general density model considered above in Section B.2.a, deterrence is:

$$\Delta = \int_0^{\hat{b}} plf\left(\tilde{b}\right)db + \int_{\hat{b}}^{p}\left(\left(1-q\right)\left(p-b\right)l + \underset{\uparrow}{q}\left(pl + \underset{\uparrow}{s}\right)\right)f\left(\tilde{b}\right)db. \qquad (19)$$

Mathematically, the important difference between (19) and the expression for accuracy (11) is not the addition of the scalar multiplier l, but rather the addition of qs to the right-hand integrand. The presence of this term signifies that, from an ex ante perspective, the manufacturer feels the expected sanction from document destruction, in those cases where destruction is worthwhile, as part of

398. As noted, this corresponds to the statement that the social welfare *function* under this approach is naturally *concave*. See *supra* note 392.

the ex ante legal cost of designing an unsafe product. The first derivative of (19) with respect to s is:

$$\begin{aligned}\frac{\partial \Delta}{\partial s} &= \cancel{\tfrac{q}{(1-q)l}\, plf\left(\hat{b}\right)} \\ &\quad - \tfrac{q}{(1-q)l}\left((1-q)\left(\cancel{p}-\hat{s}\right)l + q\left(\cancel{pl}+s\right)\right)f\left(\hat{b}\right) \\ &\quad + \int_{\hat{b}}^{p} qf\left(\tilde{b}\right)db \qquad (20) \\ &= \int_{\hat{b}}^{p} qf\left(\tilde{b}\right)db.\end{aligned}$$

Tracking the main text in Part III.A.4.b, what remains in (20) is the inframarginal effect of increasing litigation losses for manufacturers who still find it worthwhile to destroy evidence. In contrast to the effect on truth-finding, the *conversion* of marginal tamperers to marginal nontamperers has no effect on deterrence. This is because the marginal tamperer is exactly indifferent between tampering and not tampering. And so its change in behavior—from tampering to not tampering—does not change its all-in litigation losses from unsafe design, which are what matter for inducing safe design.

It is instructive to examine precisely how the first statement in (20) reduces to the second. The backslashes in the first statement in (20) represent the fact that the marginal tamperer is indifferent between tampering and not tampering taking into account the expected sanction from doing so. The cross slashes represent the fact that, given the marginal tamperer's zero net payoff from destruction, its all-in litigation losses are unaffected by changing its behavior in response to the increase in evidence destruction sanctions.

The second derivative of deterrence is:

$$\frac{\partial^2 \Delta}{\partial s} = -\tfrac{q}{(1-q)l}\, qf\left(\hat{b}\right) < 0. \qquad (21)$$

This second derivative is always negative, signifying that the positive incremental effect of increasing s on deterrence is decreasing in the level of s. As noted in the text, this is because increasing s increases deterrence by virtue of its effect on the infra-margin, and this infra-margin decreases in ex ante importance as s increases.

The convexity of social welfare when the social objective is primary activity incentives also may be masked by other effects. Such effects include the two considered above for truth-finding—density effects and cost effects—as well as complications that may follow from the possibility that safe product designers will still find tampering worthwhile, as discussed in Section A.3. In addition, this effect can be confounded by countervailing curvature in the way the level of deterrence Δ enters overall social welfare. But there is no more reason to think that any of these effects works against the convexity we have identified than to think that it works with it. And the foregoing analysis therefore justifies at least a theoretical presumption—albeit empirically rebuttable—that the primary activity approach is consistent with satisfaction of the second-order conditions at middling levels of enforcement.

F
Perjury, Obstruction of Justice and Similar Sanctions: Optimal Structure

[22]

IV. Is the Law Myopic?

According to the conventional assessment of the rules regulating evidence tampering—an assessment informed by the view that trial is primarily a truth-seeking enterprise—the law in this area is myopic. Its almost exclusive focus on tampering that occurs while litigation is pending or imminent merely encourages tamperers to shift their operations upstream, away from the time of filing, and beyond the law's limited reach.[360]

This Part of the Article suggests that what is myopic is not the law's approach to evidence tampering, but rather the analytical approach to such law that focuses solely on the direct control of tampering activities. More broadly defined, "the law" does not, in fact, focus solely on downstream tampering. Instead, the law simply employs a set of devices for the control of upstream tampering that does not include the array of criminal, procedural, and evidentiary sanctions examined in Part II.

Section A explicates those upstream devices. In the process, it provides two explanations for why anti-tampering law has always seemed shortsighted under the conventional view. In the first place, the devices used to control upstream tampering are so much a part of the accepted fabric of evidence law as to be virtually invisible. As with an optical puzzle, one must purposefully adjust one's point of focus to bring these features to the fore. Secondly, such features do not regulate upstream tampering in a way that makes sense under the dominant truth-seeking approach to trial. Their role becomes clear only when one regards evidence production as a component of the law's overall project of regulating primary activity behavior.

Sections B and C argue that these upstream devices are crucial to understanding the truncated reach of direct regulations. Section B critiques the leading alternative justification for the downstream focus of direct regulation. Section C argues that direct regulations are merely picking up where the subtler devices examined earlier in this Part leave off.

---

360. *See supra* note 119. Note that the substitution into upstream activity produced by the law's downstream focus can also come in the form of preventing the creation of documents in the first place. *See* GORELICK ET AL., *supra* note 12, § 1.15, at 19 ("[A] strict [document destruction] regime could generate a . . . chilling of the production of useful documentary evidence."). *But see* KATZ, *supra* note 13, at 52–59 (suggesting that the law may not be to blame for a "forbidden result" no longer being forbidden); Leo Katz, *Subornation of Perjury: A Definition*, WALL ST. J., Mar. 16, 1988, at A23 (arguing that the requirement that there be a pending investigation does not create a loophole in the law).

Yet, another form of substitution is upstream document creation. *See* Beckstrom, *supra* note 12, at 716 n.100 ("[A]ntitrust counselors, while urging early destruction of records in general, are agreed that one of the tenets of a good 'antitrust compliance program' is the thorough documentation of *exculpatory information* whenever companies take action in an area that is 'antitrust sensitive.'" (emphasis added)).

A. *The Ex Ante Inscrutability of Fact-Finding*

Why is evidence law so permissive regarding how parties choose to prove their claims or defenses?[361] Such a rule seems to ignore an important externality: the proponent of evidence does not pay the full cost of its consideration by the fact finder.[362] Perhaps the law should be more discriminating in this regard, admitting only evidence whose consideration is socially, as opposed to just privately, worthwhile.[363] Perhaps it should do more to insure that only the "best evidence" is considered.[364]

Some insight into this fundamental puzzle of evidence law is provided by viewing the ad hoc nature of fact-finding as one part of a kind of "decoy" strategy. Roughly stated, the clearer the parties' sense of precisely which of the evidentiary emissions of their primary activity choice will be decisive in future litigation, the more effectively they can target their destruction and fabrication efforts. And the

---

361. Alex Stein, *The Refoundation of Evidence Law*, 9 CAN. J.L. & JURISPRUDENCE 279, 279 (1996) (identifying the "core principle (albeit with exceptions) of legally unregulated fact-finding," also termed "the doctrine of 'free proof.'"). *See, e.g.*, FED. R. EVID. 401 (defining "relevant evidence" as "evidence having any tendency to make the existence of any fact that is of consequence to the determination of the action more probable or less probable than it would be without the evidence"); FED. R. EVID. 402 ("All relevant evidence is admissible, except as otherwise provided by the Constitution . . . Act of Congress, [or] by these rules . . . ."); *see also* Old Chief v. United States, 519 U.S. 172, 186–87 (1997) ("[T]he Government invokes the familiar, standard rule that the prosecution is entitled to prove its case by evidence of its own choice . . . . This is unquestionably true as a general matter.").

362. Federal Rule of Evidence 403, whose central purpose is to guard against "unfair prejudice," also permits the exclusion of relevant evidence "if its probative value is substantially outweighed by . . . considerations of undue delay, waste of time, or needless presentation of cumulative evidence." Yet, Rule 403 is hardly used as a device for internalizing evidence costs. Nor are many of the other rules by which certain forms of evidence are inadmissible. On this particular externality, see the discussion in Sanchirico, *Character*, *supra* note 14, at 1250–52 and sources cited therein.

Regarding the full set of externalities at issue here, see e.g., Steven Shavell, *The Social Versus the Private Incentive to Bring Suit in a Costly Legal System*, 11 J. LEGAL STUD. 333, 333–34 (1982) (arguing that in deciding whether to file, plaintiff ignores *both* (1) the defendant's litigation expenses, and (2) the primary activity incentives created by litigation, and proposing that the combination of these effects can result in a surplus or deficit of lawsuits).

363. Stein, *supra* note 361, at 279 (criticizing from a truth-finding perspective the "core principle (albeit with exceptions) of legally unregulated fact-finding" and "oppos[ing] the doctrine of 'free proof'").

364. Dale A. Nance, *The Best Evidence Principle*, 73 IOWA L. REV. 227, 227 (1988):

> [M]y thesis is that there exists, even today, a principle of evidence law that a party should present to the tribunal the best evidence reasonably available on a litigated factual issue. This principle is not absolute . . . . Nevertheless, it is a general principle that manifests itself in a wide variety of concrete rules governing the trial process.

more effectively parties can tamper with evidence, the lower the litigation risk from taking the bad primary activity action. These benefits of inscrutability weigh against the obvious drawbacks of a system that is not as choosy as it might be about the evidence it entertains.[365]

1. *Thought Experiment: Broadening the Range of Potentially Unfavorable Evidence.* To explore more fully the impact of fact-finding inscrutability on evidence tampering and litigation objectives, imagine the following thought experiment. First, suppose that we have identified the full set of "evidentiary emissions" that are more likely to be generated following the defendant's "bad" primary activity behavior than following her "good." Second, imagine a system—more restrictive than our own, with its lenient relevancy requirement—that admits as proof of defendant's bad behavior only those evidentiary emissions for which the probability of generation following bad behavior exceeds by some threshold the probability of generation following good.[366] If the difference in probabilities does not meet this threshold, a more stringent manifestation of Federal Rule of Evidence 403[367] prohibits admission: the evidence is judged to be insufficiently probative of bad behavior to justify the public expense of hearing it.[368]

Third, starting from this system, imagine broadening the range of evidence that counts toward liability—thus moving toward our actual system. As shown within, this broadening will magnify the defendant's incentive to choose the good primary activity action. At the same time, it will have an ambiguous effect on the court's ability to find truth.

365. Stein, *supra* note 361, at 279. The ad hoc nature of fact-finding exacerbates other sources of organic uncertainty that are already present. For instance, a manufacturer will face uncertainty regarding not just what evidence plaintiffs will use against it in court, but also which of its customers end up as plaintiffs, and which of its products lead to accidents.

366. Alternatively, and to the same effect in the following discussion, we could imagine establishing a threshold for the ratio, rather than the difference, of these conditional probabilities. This ratio corresponds to the likelihood ratio in the odds formulation of Bayes' Rule.

367. *See* FED. R. EVID. 403 (granting trial judge discretion to rule relevant evidence inadmissible when "its probative value is substantially outweighed by the danger of unfair prejudice [and] waste of time").

368. Federal Rule of Evidence 403 is rarely invoked for this kind of "efficiency" purpose. More commonly, it is employed to avoid undue prejudice.

2. *Effect on Primary Activity Incentives.* When relatively few pieces of evidence are admissible, the defendant can focus her evidence destruction efforts. Conversely, the more forms of evidence that are admissible, the more the defendant has to spend destroying evidence in order to avoid liability—or, put another way, the less effective at avoiding liability is any given level of effort devoted to evidence destruction. Thus, broadening the set of evidence that may count toward the plaintiff's burden of persuasion raises the defendant's cost of avoiding liability via tampering. This thereby decreases the defendant's litigation payoffs in states of the world where the set of natural evidentiary emissions would be sufficient for liability. These states being more likely following "bad" primary activity behavior, the end result is an increase in the defendant's incentive to eschew such bad behavior.

To take a schematic, but illustrative, example, suppose that following the defendant's choice in the primary activity, any number of twenty different "pieces" (i.e., forms) of damaging evidence are emitted into his possession. The emission of each of these pieces of evidence is more likely following the defendant's choice of the bad primary activity action than following his choice of the "good." But some of these pieces of evidence are more socially preferable than others. Their probability difference may be greater, or their probability levels lower, or they may just be less expensive to present and hear. The precise reason for the social preference is not important here.

Evidence system 1 chooses the very "best" piece of evidence from the twenty and insists that imposition of liability rests solely on the plaintiff's presentation thereof. A defendant who wants to avoid liability can, of course, always choose the good primary activity action. But in this first system, he also has the relatively viable alternative of taking the bad action—which he finds less costly in the primary activity—and focusing his efforts instead on preventing or destroying this best piece of evidence, whenever it is emitted.

Compare this with evidence system 2. This system chooses the "top ten" pieces of evidence from the full set of twenty and stipulates that only these are admissible. It then requires that the plaintiff present at least five of these to meet her burden of persuasion.[369]

369. The text stipulates that five, rather than one, out of the top ten must be presented to suggest the fact that by adjusting the number of pieces of evidence required from the admissible set, evidence system 2 may be made roughly comparable in terms of its true and false positives

Destroying or preventing evidence is now a less attractive means of avoiding liability. Formerly, the defendant could focus his destruction efforts on the single best piece of evidence. Now to avoid liability entirely the defendant must destroy the excess, if any, of the number of emitted pieces of evidence over four. For example, if five pieces are actually emitted, the defendant avoids liability by destroying one. If seven are emitted, the defendant avoids liability by destroying three. And if all ten pieces are emitted, the defendant avoids liability by destroying six.

Choosing the good primary activity is a more attractive means for the defendant of avoiding liability in system 2 than in system 1. In system 1, taking the good primary activity action competed with the relatively easy alternative of taking the bad action and (more often) precluding or destroying a single pre-specified piece of evidence. In system 2, the alternative to the good primary activity action is not as attractive. To guarantee exoneration, for example, the defendant would have to prevent or destroy the emission of up to six pieces of evidence. Alternatively, monitoring only one piece of evidence—as was completely effective in system 1—only somewhat reduces, and does not eliminate, the possibility of being held liable in system 2.

In evidence system 3, each of the twenty pieces of evidence is ruled admissible and the burden of proof may be met by the presentation of any ten. Relative to system 2, avoiding liability by evidence tampering is now even more expensive. Avoiding liability requires destroying the excess, if any, of the number of emitted pieces of evidence over nine. Thus the required amount of destruction now ranges from one to eleven, rather than from one to six. Turning these evidentiary emissions off at the source—by taking the good primary activity action—now seems all the more attractive.

The mechanism at work here is reminiscent of strategies employed in other areas. We may imagine that when the queen of a particularly troubled country traveled about, the coach that transported her was randomly and secretly selected from her fleet and then sent out as one in a sequence of departures along with other empty coaches acting as decoys. On the one hand, this procedure meant that the queen did not always travel in the fastest and most comfortable carriage. On the other hand, it helped to confound her would-be assassins. In particular, it raised the cost of producing any

to evidence system 1. Note in this regard that the existence of *any* one of the top ten would be far more likely than the existence of a *particular* one of the top ten.

given likelihood that she came to harm. An assassin had to attack all coaches to guarantee his objective. Correspondingly, attacking only one coach had less of an impact on the probability that the queen would actually come to harm. One hopeful possibility, and likely the intention of the queen's guard, was that assassins would find attacking any number of coaches not worth their while.

Similarly, as we broaden the range of admissible evidence we begin to give weight to evidence that, considered in isolation, seems of questionable merit—evidence with a scintilla of probative value, for instance. Yet admitting this evidence makes evidence destruction a less effective method of avoiding liability, and thus makes the alternative method—taking the good primary activity action—relatively more attractive.

3. *Effect on Truth-Finding.* Any policy choice that lowers litigation payoffs in evidentiary contingencies that are more likely following the bad primary activity action increases the incentive to choose the good primary activity action. The decoy effect discussed above does precisely this, and so its connection to the primary activity approach is clear.

In contrast, the connection to truth-finding is decidedly murky. Consider again the thought experiment wherein the range of potentially unfavorable evidence was extended. For the truth-finding approach, this adjustment sets in motion several contradictory forces.

First, the chance that any given bad primary activity actor will avoid liability goes down. This is because fewer bad primary activity actors find it worthwhile to destroy the now larger amount of evidence that must be eliminated to avoid liability. Naturally, this reduction in the rate of false exonerations improves truth-finding.

Second, the chance that any given good primary activity actor will be held liable goes up. This is for two reasons. First, even good actors sometimes face bad evidence. In a system with narrower admissibility, these good actors might have found it worthwhile to destroy their way out of liability. Now they may prefer to just pay the damages. Secondly, the evidence added to expand the set of admissible evidence may not be as precise a signal of the bad act. Some good actors will be held liable based solely on the additional noise. Overall, the greater rate of false liability is bad for truth-finding.

These first two effects pull in opposite directions. Nonetheless, were they the only considerations, one could perhaps argue that the news was good for truth-finding on net. Given that a larger proportion of bad actors than good are tampering in the first place, it is plausible that a larger proportion of bad actors are converted away from tampering. This suggests that the decrease in the rate of false exoneration is greater than the increase in the rate of false liability.

However, these are not the only considerations.[370] Two others are worth highlighting. First, even if the rate of false exoneration falls by more than the rate of false liability rises, the absolute number of wrongly decided cases may still increase if there are fewer bad actors than good.[371] The fewer bad actors there are to falsely exonerate, the lower the impact of a given decrease in the rate of false exonerations. Similarly, the more good actors there are to falsely hold liable, the greater the impact of a given increase in the rate of false liability.

Secondly, the policy change under consideration influences not just what happens at trial, but also what happens in the primary activity. In particular, as explained in Section 2, expanding the set of admissible evidence increases the incentive to eschew the bad primary activity act. As such, the number of bad primary activity actors will decrease and the number of good will increase. This has two central implications. In the first place, it adds to the ambiguity of the population composition effects described in the previous paragraph. These are not just uncertain, but also in flux. Second, it adds its own independent source of ambiguity. The change in primary activity behavior has a direct impact on the number of wrongly decided cases. The direction of the effect depends on whether the initial rate of false exoneration is greater or less than the initial rate of false liability. If the rate of false exoneration is greater, the population shift toward good actors will decrease the number of

370. The discussion in the following two paragraphs is guided by the following mathematics. Let b be the proportion of bad actors in the population. Let fe be the rate of false exoneration and fl, the rate of false liability. Then the number of wrongly decided "cases" (see *infra* note 371) is $bfe + (1\text{-}b)fl$. The total derivative of this expression is $b\mathrm{d}fe + (1\text{-}b)\mathrm{d}fl + \mathrm{d}b(fe\text{-}fl)$. The current paragraph considers the first two addends. The next paragraph considers the second derivative of these addends with respect to b, and the third addend.

371. Adding to the murkiness here is the fact that truth-finding is not a self-defining policy objective. In the first place, how false exoneration and false liability are combined into a single evaluative dimension must be additionally specified. The implicit assumption in this analysis is that the actual incidence of each kind of error is important in this combination. Second, one must also additionally specify how to treat cases that do not reach trial, perhaps because they are not even filed. "Cases" is used in the text in an expansive sense to mean "underlying events or conditions," including those that do not result in filed suits. A unfiled "case," therefore, is counted the same as a finding of no liability. Quite reasonably, then, when a bad actor is not even sued, this is counted as an inaccuracy.

wrongly decided cases. If the rate of false liability is greater, the number of wrongly decided cases will increase. To see this, imagine converting a single actor from bad to good. Will the chance that her case is wrongly decided increase or decrease? Clearly, it will increase if mistakes are more often made for good actors than for bad.

B. The Questionable Private-Costs Reason to Push the Tamperer Upstream

Before connecting the foregoing analysis to the downstream focus of anti-tampering enforcement, let us assess the most common alternative explanation for this apparently myopic outlook.[372]

This explanation posits that effectively blocking (i.e., preventing or destroying) a given evidentiary emission of the bad primary activity action is in effect less expensive for the potential litigant the closer the blocking is to the time of litigation. According to this view, evidentiary emissions are not just the byproducts of primary activity behavior, they also often facilitate that behavior. A document on pricing policy is not just the byproduct of anti-competitive behavior, but also facilitates the planning and implementation of business strategies, some of which may be regarded as anti-competitive under the law, and some as pro-competitive. The imperfections of the human mind and its imperfect ability to communicate make recordation a valuable business tool.[373] A business that prevents the creation of such a pricing document, or that re-collects and destroys all copies of such documents immediately after the pricing meeting, does not enjoy these benefits to as great an extent. On the other hand, a business that keeps the pricing document on file up until litigation, at which time it shreds the document or simply fails to produce the document on request, has the benefit of that recordation in devising, communicating, and implementing its business plan.[374]

372. This Article focuses on the contest between two consequentialist conceptions of trial. But there may also be deontological arguments for the law's apparently myopic focus on upstream tampering. *See, e.g.*, KATZ, *supra* note 13, at 52–59 (arguing for the moral significance of certain formal distinctions, an approach that might be applied to justifying document "retention" policies that are sufficiently nonselective); *see also* Katz, *supra* note 119 (suggesting that there is an important moral distinction between upstream and downstream obstruction).

373. This idea is explored in depth in Chris W. Sanchirico, *Evidence, Procedure, and the Upside of Cognitive Error*, 57 STAN L. REV. (forthcoming Nov. 2004) (*available at* http://papers.ssrn.com/sol3/papers.cfm?abstract_id=497882).

374. *See* Beckstrom, *supra* note 12, at 717:

> [T]he proposed statute would not completely frustrate those who would purposefully violate the substantive laws. Refuge could often be found in the simple expedient of

Because downstream blocking of a given evidentiary emission is effectively less expensive than upstream blocking, the argument continues, downstream blocking is a greater problem for legal process. Directing enforcement resources at preventing downstream tampering thus makes sense. To the extent that the literature on evidence tampering has at all considered primary activity incentive effects, this is the extent of the discussion.[375]

Although the opportunity cost of making use of one's evidentiary emissions in the time before litigation is certainly a cost of early destruction, it is not the only cost. And while opportunity costs may be lower for downstream destruction, other kinds of tampering costs are likely to be greater.

What is important to the tampering litigant, of course, is not destroying a particular piece of paper, but rather preventing the evidentiary emission represented by that piece of paper from getting into court. It profits the spoliator little to have shredded every copy of the damaging document except the one that gets admitted into evidence. Practice journals warn that damaging documents have a way of multiplying with cancerous rapidity.[376] The fact that copies can themselves be copied leads to the possibility of exponential growth. And the farther down the family tree ones goes, the less information and control there is over where the documents are. Practice guides specifically warn that copies of documents may end up in employees' personal files.[377] It may be difficult for the center to find out about

---

not making records. At least this route would be inconvenient for them because it is usually better business practice (aside from antitrust considerations) to make a record of anything so important to a business that it is willing knowingly to violate the antitrust laws to accomplish it.

375. *See* GORELICK ET AL., *supra* note 12, § 1.15, at 19 (citing Beckstrom, *supra* note 12, at 717). In fact, this precise point is only weakly made by Beckstrom. It appears in much stronger form in Hart, *supra* note 348, at 1676: "[A]n attorney [may feel] that the only way to keep certain evidence out of court is to destroy it altogether, or, in the case of documents, to recommend that they never be created."

376. *See, e.g.*, GORELICK ET AL., *supra* note 12, § 9.4, at 365–66:

> [D]uring the investigations of Ivan Boesky, Michael Milken, and Drexel Burnham Lambert, two of the keys to the prosecution where (1) the fact that, unbeknownst to Mr. Boesky, his secretary had made copies of ledgers (the originals of which Mr. Boesky ordered destroyed) that reflected a secret agreement between Mr. Boesky and Mr. Milken, and (2) the ability of Mr. Boesky's former . . . bookkeeper . . . to reconstruct the transactions from slips of paper that even those who produced them to the government could not understand.

377. *See, e.g.*, GORELICK ET AL., *supra* note 12, § 9.9, at 304 ("The 'pack-rate' [sic] phenomenon, which refers to employees who create and maintain their own personal files of documents which were to have been destroyed, drastically undermines the benefits of [document retention/destruction programs].").

these copies and even more difficult to prevent their comprehensive destruction when employees are capable of imagining that their personal interests are not always aligned with those of their current employer.[378]

The use of computers and electronic documents exacerbates the problem. No need to travel to Kinko's, no need to stuff envelopes. A few clicks and what was one pattern of electrons on one magnetized disk is nearly instantly one hundred replicas in one hundred far-flung locations, a process that is easily repeated from each of these one hundred locations.

Therefore, while the opportunity cost of early destruction may be greater than for later destruction, the actual costs of *effective* destruction are likely lower.[379] One surefire method of preventing a document from showing up on a potential plaintiff's computer screen is not to create the document in the first place. One way to be sure that the meeting agenda does not end up in the wrong hands is to completely delete it right after it is printed, and then collect and destroy all of the printed copies right after the meeting.

Another reason why downstream destruction is not necessarily less costly has to do with how the destruction itself would be proved. Throughout we have been discussing the evidentiary emissions of the primary activity action. Similarly, sanctions are imposed on document destruction on the basis of the evidentiary emissions of destructive activity. Evidentiary emissions, like environmental emissions, often dissipate and degrade over time. Witnesses' recollections become clouded. Documents do disappear. Trash is eventually burned. Important aspects of legal process—such as statutes of limitations—are designed with evidentiary half-lives in mind. Consequently, downstream destruction is a riskier activity because the destruction is still fresh at the time of litigation.

378. *See, e.g.*, *id.* § 17.4, at 373 ("Clients . . . must be made aware that their employees . . . will not be willing to go to prison for them.").

379. *See, e.g.*, *id.* § 9.4, at 300 ("As was illustrated perfectly in Oliver North's destruction and alteration of Iran-Contra memos, rarely will a document-destruction effort find all copies, computer records, or memories of the documents. In those circumstances, the document remains as evidence, accompanied by the strong negative inference arising from the attempted destruction.").

C. *The Private Benefits Reason to Focus Direct Regulation Downstream*

For the foregoing reasons it is difficult to argue that the downstream destruction or fabrication of a particular evidentiary emission is somehow more cost-effective for the litigant than the same activity upstream. It is difficult, therefore, to explain the law's preference for upstream tampering in terms of private costs.

A better explanation may reside in the differential private benefits of upstream versus downstream fabrication and destruction. This Part of the Article began with the argument that the inscrutable nature of the fact-finding process was a device for raising the cost of using evidence tampering to affect litigation outcomes. It seems clear that the effect of this characteristic of fact-finding on evidence tampering would differ systematically across upstream and downstream tampering activity. The upstream tamperer has much less of an idea of what evidentiary emissions will be decisive in future litigation. The nature of future litigation itself—let alone the evidence that will be decisive for that judge or jury—is all guesswork for the upstream tamperer.[380] For the downstream tamperer, on the other hand, many, though not all, of the uncertainties have already been resolved. More generally, the further downstream the tamperer's vantage point, the more she knows about what evidence is likely to make a difference to litigation outcomes.

Because the decoy logic described in Section A is systematically less effective the farther one travels downstream along the litigation flow, it stands to reason that some other line of defense is necessary for downstream tampering. The direct regulation of evidentiary foul play—including the criminal, procedural, and evidentiary sanctions examined in Part II—fills that role.

This argument helps to explain several specific and puzzling aspects of existing doctrine. First, it sheds some light on the law's tendency to ignore evidence tampering that predates the complaint.[381] Given all the possible lawsuits that might be filed, service of the complaint with its short plain statement of the plaintiff's claims often represents a discrete jump in the information available to parties about precisely what evidentiary emissions are likely to be decisive.

380. *See* Beckstrom, *supra* note 12, at 713 ("[I]t is easier to keep everything than spend time and effort deciding what to keep and what to throw away."); *id.* at 716 ("[O]ld documents may serve to explain, as innocent, conduct that at first glance may be suspicious.").

381. *See generally supra* Part II.

Second, the argument helps to explain the law's focus on whether the tamperer was "on notice" of the litigation in those few circumstances where the law has been willing to sanction pre-filing tampering. After the nth small airplane crashes, the nth rifle fires on safety release, or the nth train hits the car at the crossing, the plaintiff's formal statement of her complaint is nearly superfluous: the defendant already knows quite a bit about what evidence will likely be important in the evidentiary battle to ensue.

Third, the argument provides additional insight into why the system is most consistent and energetic about sanctioning the tamperer when it violates an order to produce or preserve.[382] No doubt some of the reason for this resides in the party's bold disobedience of a specific judicial dictate. But a more complete explanation might also note that a litigant's efforts to secure a court order for the preservation or production of particular evidence are a very strong indication that this evidence is important to the litigant's case. To obtain a preservation order is to tip one's hand. The order and the effort expended to obtain it provide reliable information to the other side—in the form of a costly signal with differential benefits—about the importance of such evidence to the movant's case. Thus, the order should lead the opposing side rationally to increase its assessment of the probability that this evidence will be decisive in the court's imposition of liability or awards. Accordingly, it increases the opponent's perception of the private benefits of destroying or altering this evidence. Effective sanctions summarily imposed become a necessary counterweight to this more powerful destructive impulse.

CONCLUSION

Current writing on evidence tampering creates the impression that the current system of litigation is in a state of fundamental disrepair. But determining whether the system is doing what it is supposed to be doing requires a clear conception of what the system is supposed to be doing in the first place. And, as this Article has argued, the general perception that the system is broken may have more to do with defects in the conventional view of trial's purpose.

The conventional approach to legal process focuses almost exclusively on the task of resolving the particular factual dispute that

382. *See supra* Part II.B.1.

happens to have been placed before the court. The rules of evidence, for instance, are conventionally viewed as a means of ensuring that such disputes are correctly decided. This Article suggests, in contrast, that the litigation pyramid's massive primary activity base does and should play a vital role in determining what happens at its tiny trial vertex. Most important is not the system's ability to sort out what has already come to pass in each of the ninety million transactions and occurrences that make their way into filed cases every year,[383] but rather the system's ability to influence what will happen in every transaction or occurrence engaged in by each of 275 million individuals every day.

To be sure, the implications of truth-finding and primary activity incentive setting often correspond. But, if an area of procedural law remains troubling in conventional discourse, there is a fair chance that this is a place where the generally accepted truth-finding approach is a poor proxy for the law's primary activity purpose. The law of evidence tampering confirms this tendency. It is an area that remains especially troubling to those who have studied it. And, as established in this Article, it is also an area where the goal of finding truth ex post is a poor proxy for the goal of shaping truth ex ante.

Under the truth-finding approach, anti-tampering enforcement has the dual purpose of deterring tampering and correcting litigation outcomes that are skewed by tampering that was undeterred. From a primary activity incentive perspective, anti-tampering enforcement is in the first instance a tax on those who find tampering worthwhile despite its legal risks. Because taking the socially disfavored primary activity action is more likely to place one in this position, anti-tampering enforcement is also a tax on the socially disfavored action.

From these differences it follows that the primary activity approach is more in line with the law's apparently lax attitude toward evidence tampering. Where the benefits of enhanced anti-tampering enforcement are self-enhancing under the truth-finding approach, they are self-dampening under the primary activity approach. Consequently, where reconciling the law's leniency toward evidence

383. *See* EXAMINING THE WORK OF STATE COURTS, 2001: A NATIONAL PERSPECTIVE FROM THE COURT STATISTICS PROJECT 10 (Brian J. Ostrom et al. eds., 2002) (describing the number of state transactions); LEONIDAS RALPH MECHAM, ADMIN. OFFICE OF THE U.S. COURTS, ACTIVITIES OF THE ADMINISTRATIVE OFFICE OF THE U.S. COURTS: ANNUAL REPORT OF THE DIRECTOR (2001), *available at* http://www.uscourts.gov/library/dirrpt01/2001.pdf (describing the number of federal transactions).

tampering with truth-finding requires substantial conceptual contortion, reconciling it with primary activity incentive setting merely requires hypothesizing that the self-dampening effect characterizing that approach is sufficiently prominent. Similarly, the law's preference for high sanctions rather than likely detection as a means of discouraging tampering makes less sense if a major purpose of enforcement is to rectify litigation outcomes that are skewed by tampering, as implied by a truth-finding approach. Nor is it easy to justify the law's reluctance to correct litigation outcomes when tampering is discovered after judgment is entered. Such difficulties are largely avoided, however, when anti-tampering enforcement is viewed as but one integrated component in the overall mechanism by which law affects everyday behavior.

The view that trial is primarily a truth-finding exercise also leads one away from the most natural justification for the law's apparently myopic insistence on punishing only downstream tampering. The inscrutable, ad hoc nature of fact-finding, which seems like a bad idea from a truth-finding perspective, makes sense from a primary activity perspective. The difficulty of targeting one's tampering activity raises the cost of avoiding litigation exposure for "bad" primary activity behavior. That unpredictability is greatest in the upper reaches of the litigation flow. And this helps to explain why the devices that directly sanction evidence tampering are so focused on downstream activity.

Name Index

Economic Approaches to Law

1. Law and Economic Development
   Hans-Bernd Schäfer and Angara V. Raja
2. Economics of Family Law (Volumes I and II)
   Margaret F. Brinig
3. The Evolution of Efficient Common Law
   Paul H. Rubin
4. Social Norms, Nonlegal Sanctions, and the Law
   Eric A. Posner
5. Economics of Contract Law
   Douglas G. Baird
6. Public Choice and Public Law
   Daniel A. Farber
7. Economics of Federalism
   (Volumes I and II)
   Bruce H. Kobayashi and Larry E. Ribstein
8. Economics of European Union Law
   Paul B. Stephan
9. Economics of Property Law
   Richard A. Epstein
10. Economics of Conflict of Laws
    (Volumes I and II)
    Erin A. O'Hara
11. Economics of Tort Law
    (Volumes I and II)
    Alan O. Sykes
12. Economics of Labor and Employment Law
    (Volumes I and II)
    John J. Donohue III
13. Economics of Evidence, Procedure, and Litigation
    (Volumes I and II)
    Chris W. Sanchirico

Future titles will include:

Economics of Antitrust Law
Benjamin Klein and Andres V. Lerner

Economics of Administrative Law
Susan Rose-Ackerman

Game Theory and the Law
Eric B. Rasmusen

Economics of Criminal Law
Steven D. Levitt and Thomas J. Miles

Economics of Intellectual Property Law
Robert P. Merges

Economics of Tax Law
David Weisbach

Experimental Law and Economics
Jennifer H. Arlen and Eric L. Talley

Economics of Commercial Arbitration and Dispute Resolution
Orley C. Ashenfelter and Radha K. Iyengar

Economics of Constitutional Law
Richard A. Epstein

Methodology of Law and Economics
Aristides N. Hatzis

Commons and Anticommons
Michael A. Heller

Economics of Comparative Law
Gerrit De Geest

Economics of Public International Law
Jack Landman Goldsmith

Economics of Corporate Law
Jonathan Macey

Economics of Bankruptcy
Edward R. Morrison

Behavioral Law and Economics
Jeffrey J. Rachlinsky

Austrian Law and Economics
Mario J. Rizzo

Institutional Law and Economics
Pablo T. Spiller

Economics of International Trade Law
Alan O. Sykes